Introduction to Information Technology

Introduction to Information Technology

Sanjay Sexena
Total Synergy Consulting Pvt Ltd
New Delhi

VIKAS®
VIKAS® PUBLISHING HOUSE PVT LTD

VIKAS® PUBLISHING HOUSE PRIVATE LIMITED
E-28, Sector-8, Noida-201301 (UP), India
Phone: +91-120-4078900 • Fax: +91-120-4078999
Registered Office: A-27, 2nd Floor, Mohan Co-operative Industrial Estate, New Delhi-110044
E-mail: helpline@vikaspublishing.com • Website: www.vikaspublishing.com

SALES AND MARKETING OFFICES OF VIKAS® AND S CHAND AND COMPANY LIMITED

Chennai	:	Ph: 044-2363 2120, chennai@schandpublishing.com
Guwahati	:	Ph: 0361-2738 811, 2735 640, guwahati@schandpublishing.com
Hyderabad	:	Ph: 040-4018 6018, hyderabad@schandpublishing.com
Jalandhar	:	Ph: 0181-4645 630, jalandhar@schandpublishing.com
Kolkata	:	Ph: 033-2335 7458, 2335 3914, kolkata@schandpublishing.com
Lucknow	:	Ph: 0522-4003 633, lucknow@schandpublishing.com
Mumbai	:	Ph: 022-2500 0297, mumbai@schandpublishing.com
Patna	:	Ph: 0612-2260 011, patna@schandpublishing.com

Introduction to Information Technology
ISBN: 978-81259-2857-7

Product Code: V8IIT50COMP10ENAA0X(

First Published 2009
Reprinted several times between 2009 and 2018, 2023
Reprint 2024

PRINTED IN INDIA
By Vikas Publishing House Private Limited, Plot 20/4, Site-IV, Industrial Area Sahibabad, Ghaziabad-201010 and Published by Vika
Publishing House Private Limited, E-28, Sector-8, Noida-201301

Preface

This book is designed to teach the basics of Information Technology from scratch. It is so organized so that one can learn a great deal simply by following the step-by-step instructions given in it. One does not need any previous knowledge of computers — all that is needed is access to a computer and willingness to learn.

The book is based on the syllabuses of undergraduate courses in Information Technology.

All my earlier books have been widely acclaimed and I am confident that this one will also be received well by the students and teachers alike as it completely meets the requirement of their syllabuses.

I get a lot of feedback from my readers. Though it is not possible to incorporate each and every suggestion for improvement, each one is thoroughly considered. So I would greatly appreciate your comments and suggestions. Please e-mail me at *sanjaysaxena@tscpl.com*.

Sanjay Saxena

Contents

1 Introduction to Computers

We live in an of Age Computer. Most of our day-to-day activities are being influenced by use its. Areas like science and technology depend heavily on computers for their research. It has also become necessary for each and every one of us to have a basic knowledge of computers.

WHAT IS A COMPUTER?

In simple words, a computer is an electronic device, which processes information based on the instructions provided, and generates the desired output. Like any other system, a computer system also requires an input, which is processed to get the desired output. In the case of computers, two kinds of inputs are required. One, the basic or raw data, and two, a set of instructions containing the methodology to process this data. This set of instructions is called a *program* or *software* in computer jargon. This can be schematically illustrated as in Fig. 1.

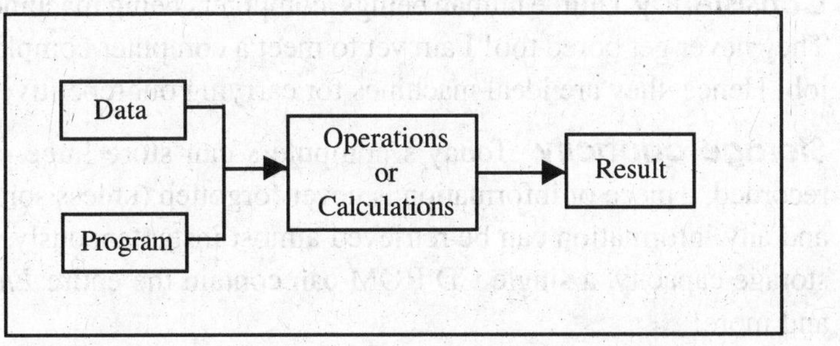

Fig. 1.1 Processing Information

Some people erroneously believe that computers can only work on arithmetic operations, or a good background in mathematics is a pre-requisite for learning computers. Nothing could be further from the truth. Although it is correct that the computer internally processes all information mathematically, the user can work on any kind of data—text, numeric, alpha-numeric, images, pictures, sound, video clippings, etc. In fact, most of the computer applications nowadays are non-numeric. After all, we can drive vehicles very well, without knowing anything about suspension, combustion, differential, etc.

WHAT IS SO SPECIAL ABOUT COMPUTERS?

The five major characteristics of computers, which have made them so powerful and useful are:

- Speed
- Accuracy
- Consistency
- Storage capacity
- Flexibility

Speed Computers work at an incredible speed. This can be gauged from the fact that the speed of the computers is measured in terms of milliseconds, microseconds, nanoseconds or picoseconds, i.e., one-thousandth, one-millionth, one-billionth and one-trillionth of a second, respectively. Chances are that the computer you are presently working on, would be processing information at the speed of a couple of million instructions per second, also called MIPS in computer jargon.

Accuracy In addition to being fast, computers are also accurate. They either give the correct answer or do not answer at all. However, it must be remembered that the computer is capable of doing only what it is instructed to do. If faulty instructions are provided for processing the data, obviously faulty answers will be given. This feature is called GIGO, i.e., Garbage In Garbage Out. Hence, the only possibility of an error occurring is due to inaccurate instructions or faulty data.

Consistency Unlike human beings, computers being machines are highly consistent. They never get bored too! I am yet to meet a computer complaining of a monotonous job! Hence, they are ideal machines for carrying out repetitive and voluminous work.

Storage capacity Today's computers can store huge amounts of data. Once recorded, a piece of information is never forgotten (unless some problem takes place) and any information can be retrieved almost instantaneously. To give you an idea of storage capacity, a single CD ROM can contain the entire *Encyclopedia Britannica*, and more!

Flexibility A computer is a versatile machine and its use is limited only by your imagination. In today's fast developing technology-world it would be very difficult, in some cases inconceivable, to find an area where computers are not being used to a great advantage. However, computers have one major limitation; they are not originally creative and perhaps will never be. They may never be able to write *An Old Man and the Sea*, and may never be able to paint a *Mona Lisa* (although they can faultlessly duplicate it), and again may never be able to compose *Beethoven's Sonata*.

REVIEW QUESTIONS

1. **What are the characteristics of a computer?**
2. **Differentiate between a computer and a typewriter.**

2 History of Computers

EVOLUTION

In order to understand today's computers; it might be worthwhile to take a quick look at the evolution of computers. Historians trace back the history of calculation with the *Abacus* (a wooden frame with balls or beads strung on parallel wires) and to its origin to around 5000 B.C. It was used for performing simple calculations. In the seventeenth century, John Napier, a Scottish mathematician, did considerable work on the aids for calculation. The most notable one was the invention of logarithms in 1614.

In 1620, just six years after the invention of logarithms, William Oughtred, an English mathematician, invented the slide rule. This is a calculating device based on the principles of logarithms. A slide rule consists of two graduated scales, one of which slides over the other. The scales are devised in such a manner that suitable alignment of one scale against the other makes it possible to compute products, additions, etc., just by inspection. In 1642, Blaise Pascal, a French mathematician, invented the first mechanical calculating machine. In this machine, numbers were entered by dialing a series of numbered wheels. Another series of toothed wheels transferred the movements to a dial, which showed the results. Gottfried von Leibnitz, a German mathematician, in 1671 invented a calculating machine, which was able to perform multiplications and divisions. Between 1802 and 1804, Joseph Marie Jacquard, a French textile manufacturer, invented a mechanical system for use in the textile industry. This machine was used to automatically control weaving looms to facilitate the production of woven cloth with complex patterns.

THE FIRST COMPUTER

In 1822, Charles Babbage, a professor of mathematics at Cambridge University, devised a machine called *"Difference Engine"* for the Royal Society. This difference engine was used to perform simple computations needed for setting up trigonometric and logarithmic tables. In short, *Babbage* had developed a prototype computer, which was 100 years ahead of its time. He is, therefore, widely considered as the *father of modern day computers.*

After World War II, there was a need for advanced calculations. By that time, many mechanical desk calculators with a high degree of reliability had been developed. Howard H. Aiken of Harvard University, while working on his doctorate in physics, in the year 1937, designed a machine that could automatically perform a sequence of arithmetic operations. Completed in 1944, it was named *Mark I.* The time taken for average multiplication and division was about four and eleven seconds, respectively. The results were printed at the rate of one result per five seconds.

NEXT GENERATIONS

ENIAC Electronic Numerical Integrator and Calculator, which was completed in 1946 was the first electronic calculator. The ENIAC performed 5000 additions per second, consumed 150 kilowatts of power, and needed to be water cooled.

EDVAC Between 1947 and 1950, the More School personnel and the Ballistics Research Laboratory of the U.S. Army built a computer named EDVAC (Electronic Discrete Variable Automatic Computer), which was based on John von Neumann's ideas. *Neumann* (frequently referred to as the *father of modern computers*) was the first to introduce the stored program concept in a computer. A comparison of generations is made in Table 2.1.

Table 2.1 *Comparison between the generations of computers*

1st Generation Computers	2nd Generation Computers	3rd Generation Computers	4th Generation Computers
▪ Use of vacuum tubes	▪ Use of transistors and diodes	▪ Use of integrated circuits	▪ Use of large scale and very large scale integrated circuits
▪ Limited storage capacity	▪ Increased storage capacity	▪ More flexibility with input/output	▪ Increased storage
▪ Slow speed	▪ Faster speed	▪ Smaller size and better performance	▪ Considerably faster and smaller
▪ Symbolic language programming; Huge size	▪ Reduction in size and heat generation	▪ Extensive use of high level programming languages	▪ Modular design, versatility and compatibility
▪ Problems of over heating	▪ High level programming language (COBOL, FORTRAN)	▪ Remote processing and time sharing	▪ Sophisticated programs and languages for special applications ▪ Increased use of microcomputers (PCs)

As you go through the history of evolution of computers, you would find that the earliest computers were very big and therefor consumed a lot of power. This resulted in their heating very quickly and they had to be frequently shut down and cooled. This made them very expensive to build and maintain. As the technology improved, computers became smaller in size, the season for the much faster and more powerful. But most importantly, from users' point of view, they became more affordable and user-friendly. This is success of computers and why they have been able to transform from 'huge monoliths' to 'personal assistants.' It right be just a matter of time before they enter the next phase of their evolution and become 'domestic appliances', as simple to operate as a refrigerator, as useful as a microwave oven and as common as a TV.

REVIEW QUESTIONS

1. **Name the devices used in each generation of computers.**
2. **What are the advantages and disadvantages of each generation of computers?**

3 Basic Anatomy of Computers

THE BASIC COMPONENTS

As explained earlier, any computer system essentially has three important parts, namely, input device, central processing device and output device. The central processing unit (CPU) itself has three parts, namely, Memory Unit, Control Unit and Arithmetic Logic Unit (ALU). These three units along with the input and output devices form the five important components of any computer system.

In addition to the five basic parts mentioned above, computers also employ secondary storage devices (also called auxiliary storage or backing storage), which are used for storing data or instructions on a long-term basis.

FUNCTIONING OF THE COMPONENTS

The input devices are used to transfer the information into the memory unit of a computer. Information from the memory can be transferred to the ALU where comparisons or calculations are done and the results are sent back to the memory unit. Thus, the memory unit is used to store the set of instructions that determines the operations to be carried out on a set of data, as well as the data on which these operations are performed. The memory unit is also called the main memory or the immediate access store (IAS). The coordination and control of the operations of a computer system is the sole responsibility of the control unit. It accepts instructions held in store, interprets these instructions and processes them for execution by appropriate parts of the system in the correct sequence. The control unit ensures that according to the stored instructions, the right operation is done on the right data at the right time. The results that are stored in the memory can be transformed into a form that can be understood by us by means of an output device.

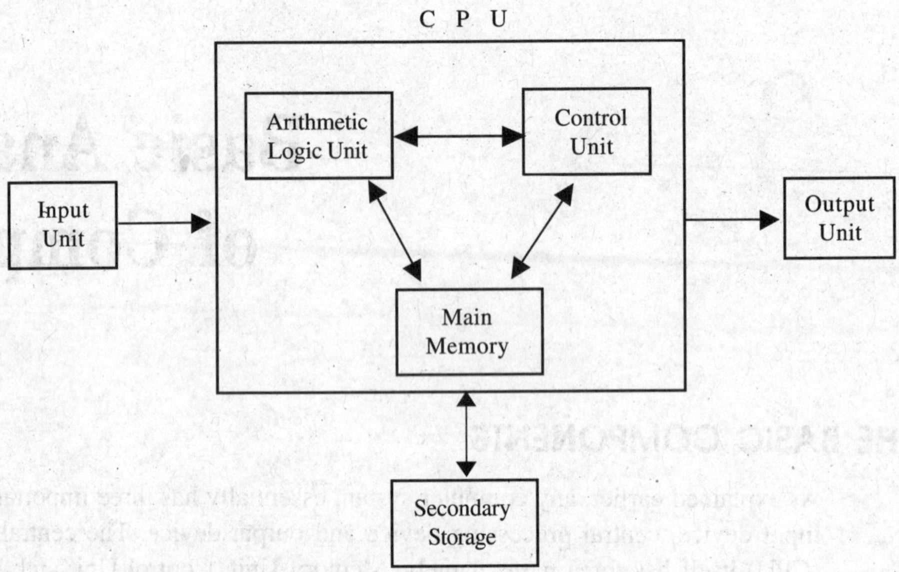

Fig. 3.1 Schematic representation of a computer system

Memory

The computer's memory is a scratch pad where information, which includes both programs and data, is kept while it is being worked on. A computer's memory consists of a large number of storage spaces known as *cells or locations*, which are organized into units of bytes, each comprising 8 bits. No matter what kind of information is being stored, it is coded in some particular form of bits, which is interpreted in a way that is appropriate to the kind of data. The same memory bytes are used to record program instruction codes, numeric or alphabetic data.

RAM Random Access Memory or RAM, as it is popularly known, is the key working area of the memory that is used for our problems and data. This area is often called user memory. When we talk of the amount of memory a computer has, we are actually talking of user memory. It varies from computer to computer and it determines the size and scope of the problems that a computer can handle. The main feature of RAM is that it can be read from or written onto any location and can be accessed randomly. In other words, reading and writing onto any location takes the same amount of time. The contents of RAM are available as long as the computer is not switched off, i.e., it loses its contents the moment the power is turned off. Hence, it is called volatile memory.

ROM Read Only Memory, as the name itself implies, holds permanent data or instructions that can only be read from, but not written onto, i.e., information is permanently recorded so that it cannot be changed by the programmers. It is non-volatile in nature, meaning that

***Table 3.1** Computer system compared with human action*

Computer element	Purpose	Human example
Input	To receive data and instructions in a form that can be understood by the computer.	The input to the system is through the eyes, ears, mouth or nose.
Output	To give out information via a suitable device, e.g., a printer. The output information is obtained from main storage.	The output is either in the form of a speech (using mouth) or some action, e.g., writing.
Storage 1. Main storage (main memory)	To hold data and instructions after input, until needed. Also to hold information awaiting output. The instructions (provided by programmers) will specify the action to be taken on the data.	In the brain, the data and instructions are stored and recalled whenever needed. (Most of us use the brain to remember some results also.)
2. Secondary storage (auxiliary or backing storage)	To supplement main storage. Used to store large amounts of data or instructions permanently. Much cheaper than main storage.	We use notebooks or some kind of aids to store data on a permanent basis. These are read or referred back whenever required.
Arithmetic & Logic Unit (ALU)	To carry out calculations and comparisons based on the instructions.	A portion of our brain is used to carry out comparisons and calculations in order to make logical judgments.
Control unit	To take stored instructions in sequence, one at a time. To interpret each instruction and prompt its execution by one of the units like input, output, storage or ALU.	Based on the calculations and comparisons, our brain controls our mental or body actions. Sometimes, before taking any action, the old results stored in our memory are also referred to. Thus, the brain acts as a CPU.

the contents of ROM are not lost when the computer is switched off. It is merely deactivated. What exactly does ROM contain? It contains instructions to get the computer started when switched on. Other uses of ROM include holding the instructions and data that control the various peripheral units of the computer, such as graphics display and disk drive etc. But, the key set of programs contained in ROM may vary from computer to computer. The contents of the ROM are built into it at the time of manufacturing itself.

Software Components

The hardware alone cannot perform any particular calculation or manipulation without being instructed exactly what to do and how to do it. These set of instructions are as important, if not more, than the hardware and are called software. The software acts as an interface between the user and the computer. A software or a program can be defined as a complete set of instructions written by the programmer, which enables the computer to obtain the solution to a problem (with or without the data). 'Software' is a general term that is used to describe any single program or a group of programs. The software used by a computer may be classified into applications software, systems software and utility software.

The applications software These are programs employed by the user to perform specific functions. For example, application software can be a program used for accounting control in business or a program used for engineering design.

The systems software They consist of all the programs, languages and documentation supplied by the manufacturer along with the computer. These programs allow the user to communicate with the computer and write or develop their own programs. This software makes the machine easier to use and makes efficient use of the hardware resources possible. Systems software programs are held permanently on a machine, which relieve the programmer from mundane tasks and improve resource utilization. Microsoft Disk Operating System MS DOS is one such widely used systems software for IBM compatible microcomputers.

The utility software These may be considered as a border line case between applications software and systems software. Such software's are either used as specific tools while developing a program or package, or to perform a limited specific task, such as scanning the hard disk for viruses.

Incidentally, viruses are also a different kind of software, created by perverts whose principal purpose is to be a nuisance to the users of computers. Viruses (depending upon the viciousness of their creators!) range from playful to fatal. Some of them can cause serious and sometimes irreparable damage to your data. It is therefore advisable to minimize the use of external storage devices (since a virus can enter you computer only through some external source) and to scan them before using them on the computer.

Before you get started, the next few pages give you a visual representation of the essential computer system.

INPUT/OUTPUT DEVICES

Input/Output devices are required for users to communicate with the computer. Input devices allow you to input data into your computer. In simplest terms they bring information **INTO** the computer. Output devices on the other hand display the results of your computer's calculations. They bring information **OUT** of a computer.

Examples of Input/Output Devices

Input Devices	*Output Devices*
Keyboard	Monitor
Mouse	Liquid Crystal Display (LCD)
Scanner	Printer
Touch Screen	Speaker
Light Pen	Plotter

Input Devices

Keyboard A text based input device that is used to type in letters, numbers and other characters.

Keyboard Keys

Enter	To execute a command or a program. Similar to the **"return"** key of a typewriter
Backspace	To remove the character directly to the left of your cursor.
Delete	To remove the character directly to the right of your cursor.
Ctrl (Control key)	Called as a helper key because it is always used in combination with other keys to perform specific actions
Alt (Alternate key)	Called as a helper key because it is always used in combination with other keys to perform specific actions.
Shift	Used to type capital letters when pressed with an alphabetic key. Also used to type the symbols located on the upper side of number keys [0-9]
Tab	Used to insert indentation into a document. Jumps from box to box when entering data in a form
Arrow keys	Used to move the cursor in top/bottom/left/right directions.
Caps Lock	Used to make the alphabetic characters to the upper case.
Esc (Escape key)	Used to cancel and abort programs.
Home	Home key is used to move the cursor to the beginning of a line.
End	End key is used to bring the cursor to the end of a line.
Page Up	Used to move the cursor up one screen length. It will not move the cursor to the 1st page if you are in the 2nd page.
Page Down	Used to move the cursor down one screen length. It will not move the cursor to the 2nd page if you are in the 1st page.
F keys	Called Function keys, which are located at the top of the keyboard. Their function depends upon the type of the program being used.

Num Lock	The numeric keypad located at the extreme right of the keyboard is activated when the **Num Lock** key is turned on.

Mouse This is used to move the cursor on your computer screen to give instructions to your computer and to run programs and applications. It can be used to select menu commands, move icons, size windows, start programs, close windows etc.

Mouse Actions

Click	Used to select an item. Click means press and release the left mouse button.
Right Click	Used to display a set of commands. Right click means press and release the right mouse button.
Double Click	Used to open a document or a program. Double means quickly press the left mouse button twice. There should not be any time gap between the two press actions.
Drag & Drop	Place the cursor over an item on the screen and then press and hold down the left mouse button. Holding down the button, move the cursor to where you want to place the item and then release the button.

Scanner It is used to input pictures and images into your computer. It converts images to digital form so that it can be fed into the computer.

Touch Screen It allows the user to operate a computer by simply touching the display screen. Example of a touch screen includes, ATM at a bank.

Light Pen It uses a light sensor device to select objects on a display screen. It is similar to a mouse except that with a light pen you can move the pointer and select any object on the screen by directly pointing to the object with the light pen.

Output Devices

Monitor It is used to display information, programs and applications in a computer. It is also called Display Screen. Like televisions, monitors come in different sizes.

LCD It is smaller, and lighter as compared to a monitor. It is mostly used with portable computers (Laptops).

Printer It is used to create a hard copy of the files stored in a computer. There are two basic qualities associated with printers: resolution and print speed. Print resolution is measured as the number of dots per inch (dpi). Print speed is typically measured in pages per minute (ppm). There are essentially four types of printers, viz. Impact Line Printers, Dot Matrix Printers, Ink Jet Printers and Laser Printers. Laser Printers are superior. They are very fast, easy to use and produce high quality output.

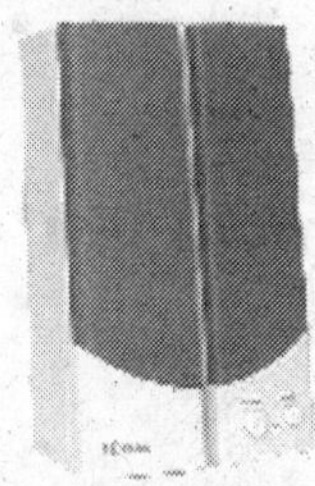

Speaker Used to produce music or speech from programs. A speaker port (a port is a connector in your computer wherein you can connect an external device) allows you to connect the speaker to the computer. Speakers can be built into the computer or can be attached separately.

Plotter A plotter interprets commands from the computer to make line drawings on a paper using multicolored automated pens. Plotters can be very useful in drawing graphs, barcharts, line drawing and maps on rolls of paper.

EXTERNAL STORAGE DEVICES

External storage is any storage other than main memory (RAM). External storage devices are peripheral devices connected to and controlled by the computer to enable permanent storage of user data and programs.

Computer uses binary system to work with data. All the data in the computer is internally stored in the form of 0's and 1's (bits). A bit can be defined as an electronic signal, which is either ON (1) or OFF (0). It is the smallest unit of information the computer uses. The capacities of storage devices or the main memory is always measured in terms of bytes. Each letter typed consumes one byte. For example, if I have typed I Love India it means I have typed 12 bytes [10 letters and 2 spaces].

1 Byte	= 8bits
1 KB [Kilo Byte]	= 1024 Bytes
1 MB [Mega Byte]	= 1024 Kilo Bytes
1 GB [Giga Byte]	= 1024 Mega Bytes
1 TB [Tera Byte]	= 1024 Giga Bytes

Examples of storage devices

Magnetic Storage	Floppy disk, Hard disk
Optical Storage	CD, DVD

Floppy Disk

- Portable storage device. It is commonly used to move files between different computers, load new programs onto the computer, or store backup of data.
- Can hold 1.44 MB of data and is usually of 3.5" size.
- It is not very reliable and can be damaged easily.
- Existing information can be erased and new information can be stored (Rewritable). It can be reused any number of times.

Hard Disk

- It is not a single flexible disk, but a stack of metal disks sealed in a box. The hard disk and hard-disk drive exist together as a unit and are usually a permanent part of the computer where most of your files are saved.
- The storage capacity of a hard disk can be several gigabytes ranging from 1GB to 100+ GB.
- Very reliable as compared to floppies.
- Rewritable
- You can access any information in a fraction of a second.

Compact Disk (CD)

- Compact Disc (CD) contains digital information, which can be read, but cannot be rewritten. It can hold vast amounts of information such as full-motion videos, animation, music, text, etc.
- CD is fairly a simple piece of plastic, about four one-hundredths (4/100) of an inch (1.2 mm) thick.
- It is portable. Its capacity usually ranges from 650-700 MB.
- Most reliable for long-term storage.
- CD drives are different for reading and writing a CD.

Digital Versatile Disc (DVD)

- DVD (Digital Versatile Disc) is primarily used to store movies or music, and can be played back on your computer as well as on your television screen.
- It is similar to a CD but has a larger capacity. Can store about 17 GB of data.
- They are not rewritable.

THE COMPUTER SYSTEM

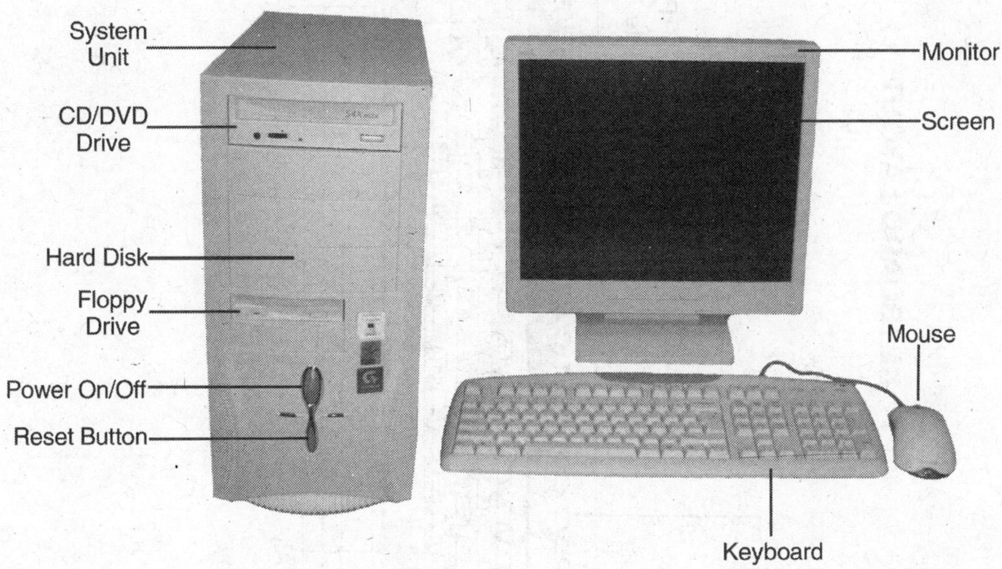

KEYBOARD LAYOUT

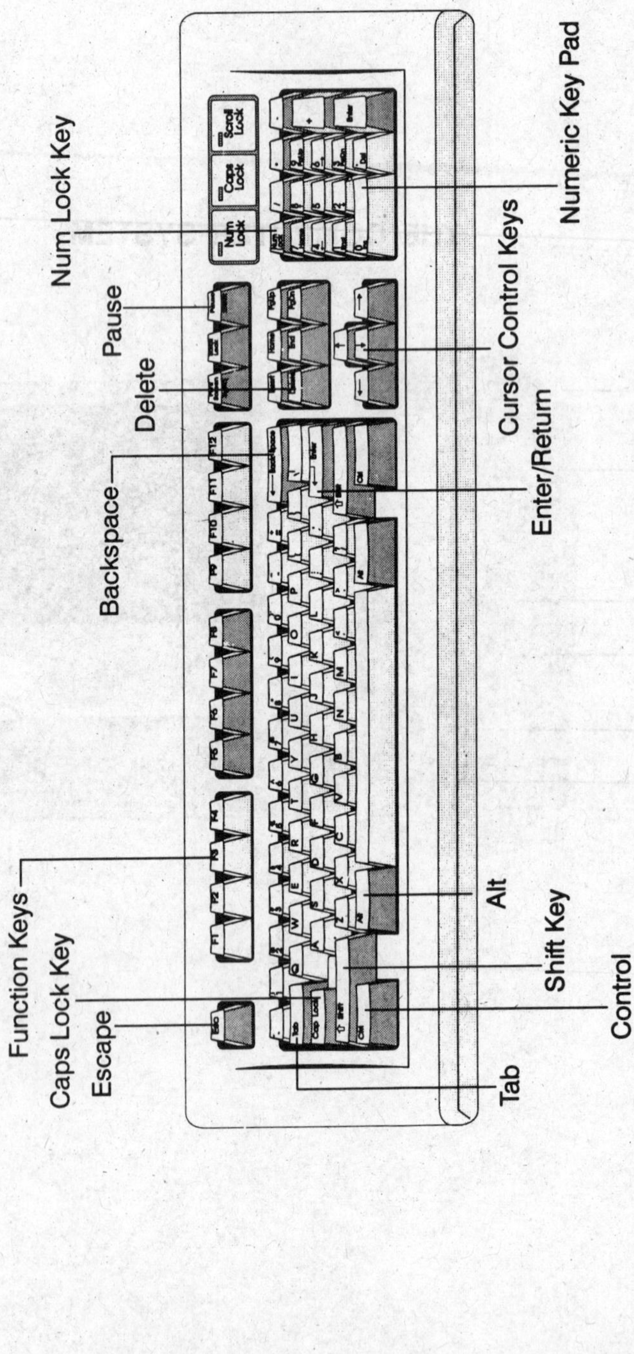

CONNECTIVITY LAYOUT

How the different parts of computer and peripherals are linked.

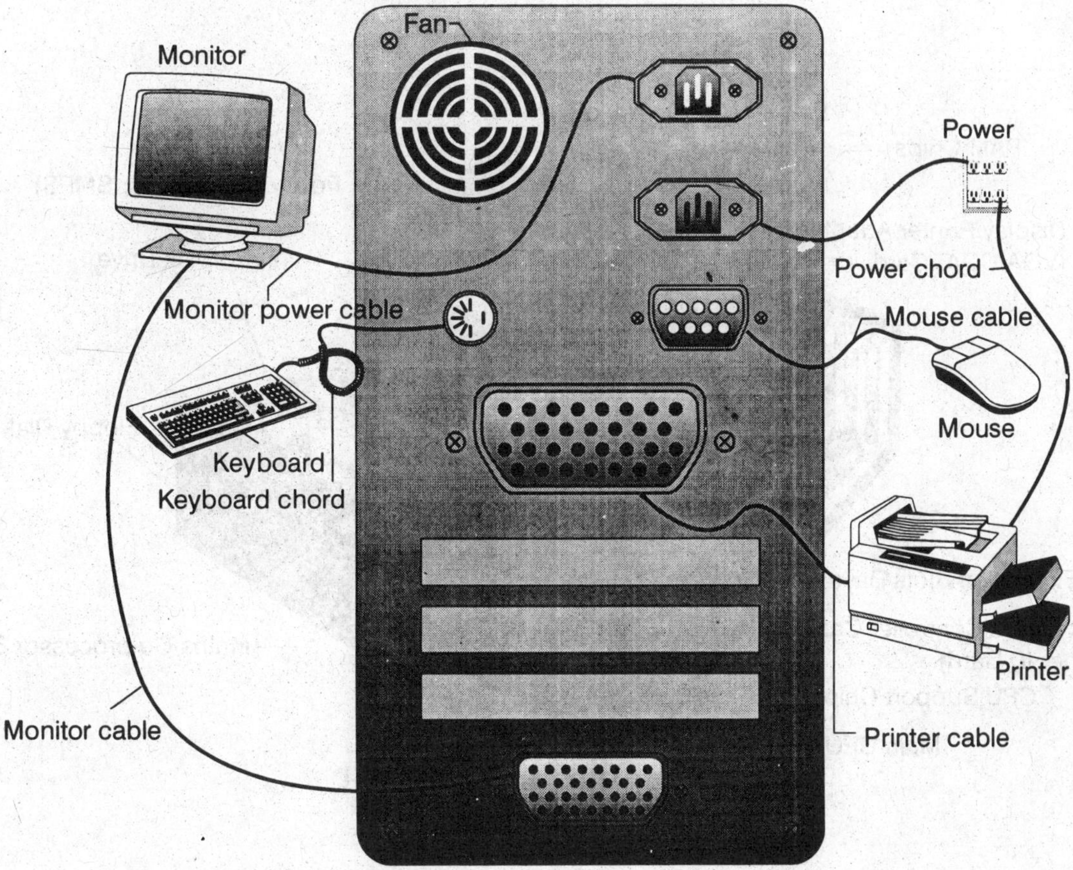

PEEPING INSIDE THE COMPUTER

(Components of a CPU)

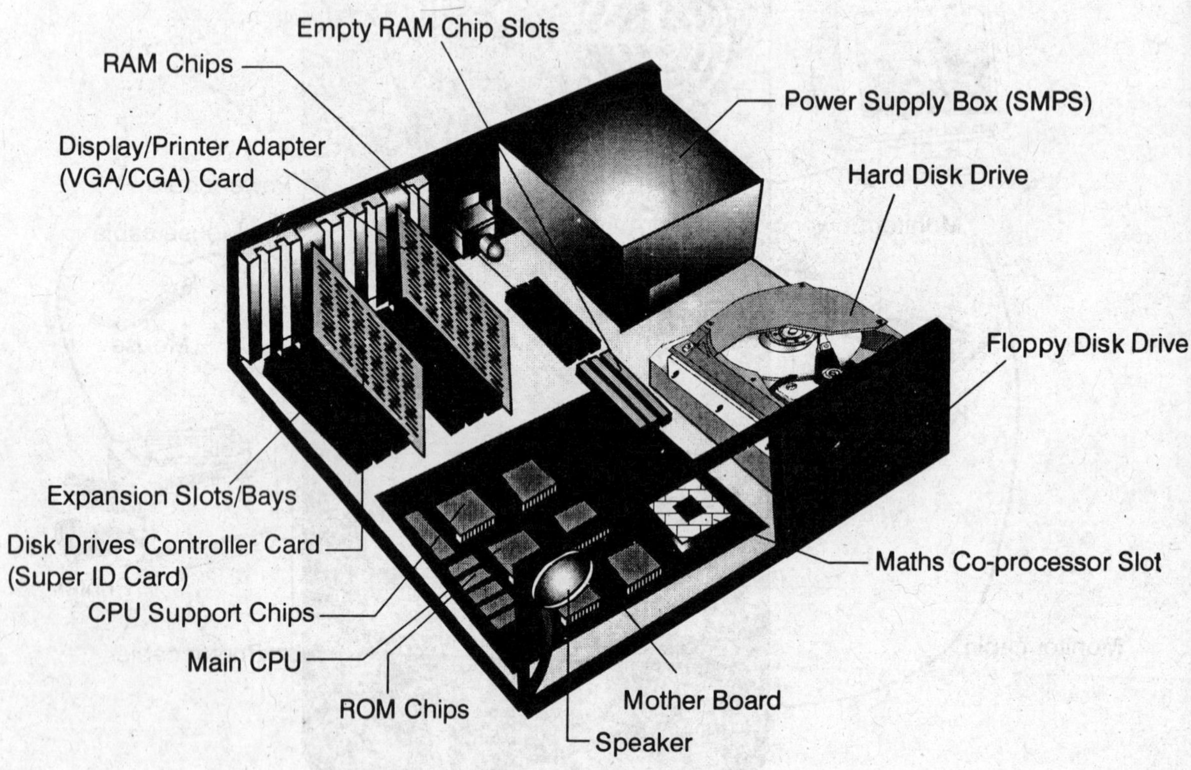

TYPES OF CABLES AND THEIR SOCKETS

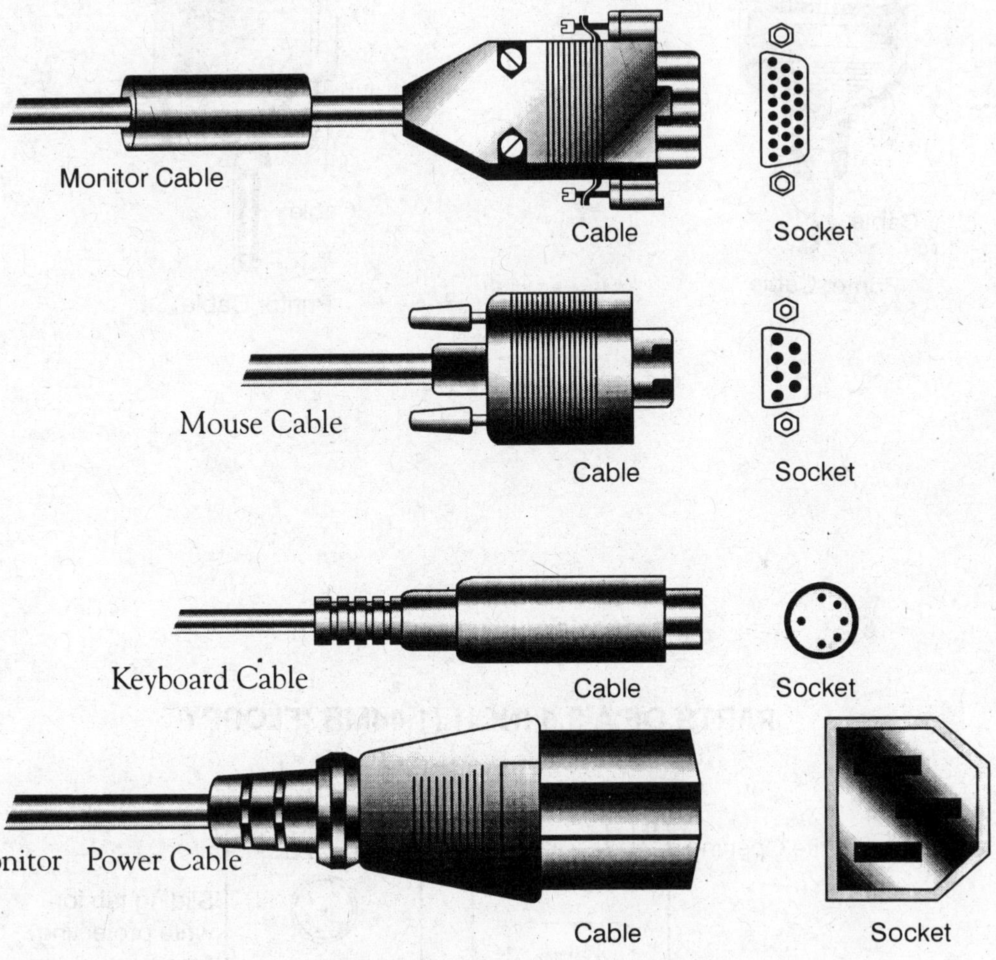

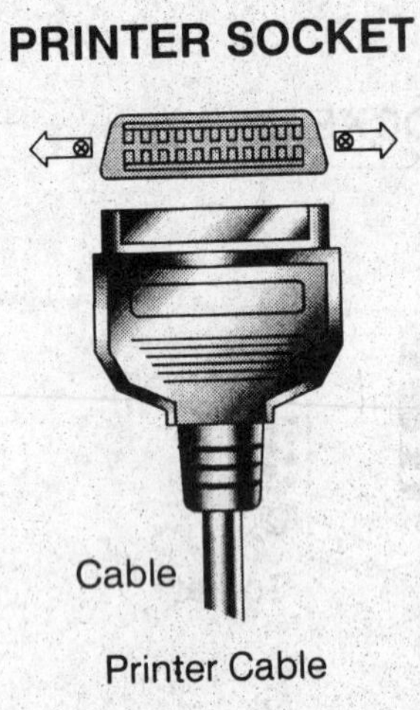
PRINTER SOCKET
Cable
Printer Cable

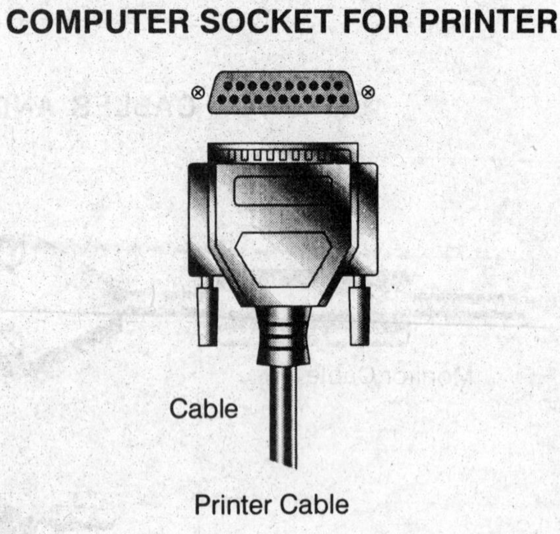
COMPUTER SOCKET FOR PRINTER
Cable
Printer Cable

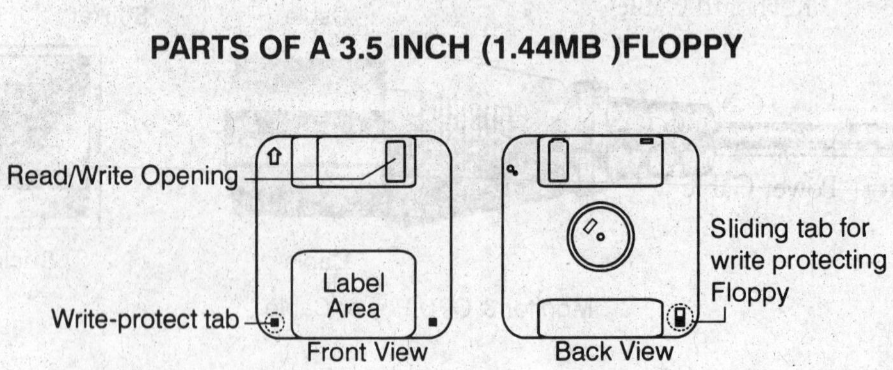
PARTS OF A 3.5 INCH (1.44MB)FLOPPY
Read/Write Opening
Label Area
Write-protect tab
Front View
Sliding tab for write protecting Floppy
Back View

TYPES OF COMPUTERS

Based on the size and complexity, computers can generally be classified under the following categories:

Personal Computer

- Personal Computer (PC) is a small, single-user computer based on a microprocessor.
- Although PC's are designed as single-user systems, it is common to link them to form a network.

Personal Computer Types

1. **Desktop:** It is not designed for portability. The expectation with desktop systems is that you will set up the computer in a permanent location.
2. **Laptop Computer:** Also called Notebook Computers. They are portable computers that can run on batteries.
3. **Palmtop:** More commonly known as **Personal Digital Assistants (PDAs)**. Palmtops are tightly integrated computers that often use flash memory instead of a hard drive for storage. They use touchscreen technology for user input. Palmtops can typically fit in your arm. A slightly larger and heavier version of the palmtop is called handheld computer.

Work Station

- A powerful, single-user computer. A workstation is like a personal computer, but it has a more powerful microprocessor.
- It is used for engineering applications (CAD/CAM), desktop publishing, software development and other applications that require a moderate amount of computing power and relatively high quality graphics capabilities.
- In networking, a workstation refers to any computer connected to a Local Area Network (LAN).

Mainframes

- Originally, mainframes were huge computers that could fill an entire room. They are expensive computers capable of supporting even thousands of users simultaneously. As the size of computers has reduced while the power has increased, mainframes have fallen out of use in favor of **enterprise server.**

Supercomputers

- Sophisticated, expensive computers, using state-of-the-art technology.
- Supercomputer is a broad term for one of the fastest computers currently available.
- They are particularly utilized in simulation and modeling of complex systems (weather, chemical processes, motion of galaxy).

REVIEW QUESTIONS

1. **Explain the function of control unit, arithmetic logic unit and memory unit.**
2. **How is software classified? Explain each of them.**
3. **What is the function of memory?**
4. **What is the use of secondary storage?**

4 Networking

INTRODUCTION

Technology today is moving very rapidly and in this age of computers and electronic revolution, more and more gadgets are being invented everyday which make our lives simpler and easier. Communication too has improved tremendously due to the advances made in communication technology such as WAP and blue-tooth technology and we are moving towards a seamless environment where all forms of communication are merging.

The idea of networking is probably as old as telecommunications itself. Consider people living in the Stone Age, when drums may have been used to transmit messages between individuals. Of course, we have come a long way from the primitive pursuits and devices of our forebears. Nowadays, we have computers talk to each other over vast assemblages of wires, fiber optics and microwaves.

The literal meaning of a computer network is, any set of computers or devices connected to each other. However, we define a ***computer network*** as a collection of hosts that are able to communicate with each other using a single technology, often by relying on the services of a number of dedicated hosts that relay data between the participants. Hosts are often computers, but one can also think of X terminals or intelligent printers as hosts. Small agglomerations of hosts are also called sites.

In short, a computer network consists of two or more linked computers in order to:

- share resources (such as printers and CD-ROMs),
- exchange files, and
- allow electronic communications

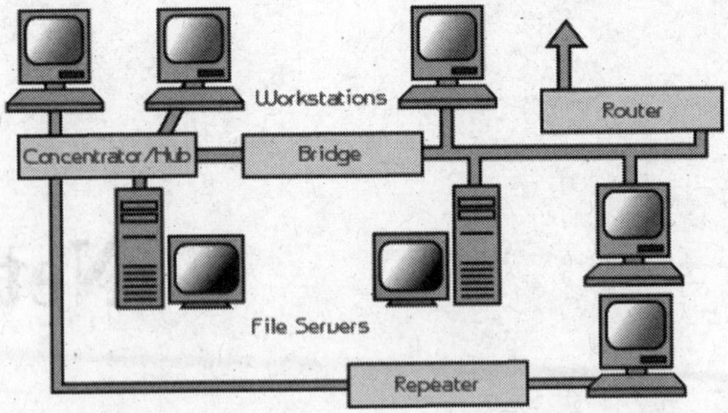

Communication is impossible without some sort of language or code. In computer networks, these languages are collectively referred to as **Protocols**. Protocols, in computer networks are nothing but very strict rules for the exchange of messages between two or more hosts.

ADVANTAGES OF NETWORKS

A network makes it easier to communicate between computers. There are 2 major ways by which networks advantage people and organisations

1. Save money by sharing resources
2. Remote services

1. Save money by sharing resources: Some examples include

- Many people can be connected using only one connection by sharing internet connection resources
- Many people are able to use one printer by sharing printing resources.
- Cost saving by sharing other resources like faxes, CD-ROM towers, network storage & directory services.
- Teacher sending notes via email instead of printing the notes, then photocopying it, collating it, stapling it and finally handing out to the students.

2. Remote services: Remote services give customers more control and reduce errors. Some examples include

- Customers ordering over the internet
- Business to business transactions such as ATMs

It can be explained in simple terms the way networks are put together, and how data packets are sent between networks and subnets along with how data is routed to the internet. This networking chapter is broken into five main sections. They are:

1. **Basics** – Explaining the different protocols and how they work together.
2. **Media** - Describing the cabling and various media used to send data between multiple points in a network.
3. **Architecture** - Explaining some of the popular network architectures. Network architecture refers to the physical layout (topology) of a network along with the physical transmission media (Type of wire, wireless, etc) and the data access method (OSI Layer). It includes Ethernet, Token Ring, ARC net, AppleTalk, and FDDI.
4. **Other Transport Protocols** - Explaining IPX/SPX, NetBEUI in brief.
5. **Functions** - Explaining the functionalities of networking like routing, firewalls and DNS.

We will start with the networking basics in order to get a good grasp of networking concepts. It would help us in understanding how each network protocol is used to perform networking, why each protocol is needed, how it is used, and what other protocols it relies upon. We would also explain the data encapsulation techniques in preparation for transport along with some of the networking protocols such as IP, TCP, UDP, ICMP, and IGMP. In functional areas, such as routers, we would get a grasp of routing, IP masquerading and firewalls and give brief explanation of how they work, how they are set up as well as how and why they are used. Application protocols such as FTP and Telnet are also briefly described.

We would also describe the setup of networking functions using Linux Red-hat version 6.1 as an operating system (OS) platform. This will apply to server functions such as routing and IP masquerading. If we know how to set up other operating servers such as Windows NT, we can apply the information to understand how to configure services on that OS platform as well.

TYPES OF NETWORKS

Local Area Network (LAN) A local area network (LAN) is the communication between different computers connected by cables, to each other in a single location, usually a single floor of a building or all the computers in a small company.

Wide Area Network (WAN) WANs are the communication between one or more LANs by telephone lines leased form the various telephone companies, satellite links, packet radio, or microwave transceivers. WANs are private and owned by the businesses that operates with them. The Internet has emerged as both the largest and the least expensive WAN in the world. Many companies take advantage of it now by forming private WANs, known as VPNs, or Virtual Private Networks, through encrypted communications over the Internet.

Benefits

Few of the benefits include:

1. **Sharing information:** A network can help you to centralize the information and maintain control over it by having one computer to store the shared information and have all other computers reference the information on that computer over the network.
2. **Sharing hardware resources:** A network allows anyone connected to the network to use printers, fax modem, scanners, tape backup units or almost any other device that can be attached to a computer.
3. **Sharing software resources:** Administrators can centrally install and configure the software and also restrict access to the software. It is easier than doing it on every one of the computers in an organization.
4. **Preserving information:** A network allows for information to be backed up on a central location. It is difficult to maintain regular backups on a number of stand-alone computers as important information can be lost easily by mistake or by accident.
5. **Protecting information:** A network provides a more secure environment for a company's important information than stand-alone computers. Networks provide an additional layer of security by way of passwords.
6. **Electronic -mail (e-mail):** Computer network also helps people to communicate through e-mail. You can attach electronic documents like photo, sound and video clip to an e-mail message.

Network Roles

The role of a computer is determined simply by its use in the network many times. There are three roles of computers in a local area network.

1. The first role is of being a client which utilizes network resources but do not provide network resources.
2. The second one is of being peers which both use and provide network resources.
3. The last one is of being servers which provide network resources.

1. **Server (domain) / Client Networks** Server-based (also called client-server) networks are defined by the presence of servers on a network that provide security and administration of the networks. It consists with many clients and one or more servers. Clients (often called the "front end") request services, such as file storage and printing, and servers (often called the "back end") deliver them. In Windows NT or Windows 2000, server-based networks are organized into domains. Domains are collection of networks and clients that share security trust information. Domain security and logon permission are controlled by special servers called domain controllers. There is one

master domain controller, called the Primary Domain Controller (PDC) and the secondary domain controllers called Backup Domain Controller (BDC) may assist PDC during busy times or when the PDC is not available for some reason.

The server-based networks have many advantages, including:

- Central file storage, which allows all users to work form the same set of data and provides
  - Easy backup of critical data and keeps data from getting lost among computers
  - Ability of servers to pool available hardware and software, lowering overall costs
  - Optimized dedicated servers, which are faster than peers at sharing network
  - Freeing of users from the task of managing network
  - Easy manageability of a large number of users
  - Ability to share expensive equipment, such as laser printers
  - Less intrusive strong central security, as only a single password need to access all shared resources on the network

Server-based networks also have some disadvantages, including:

- Expensive dedicated hardware
- Expensive network operating system software's and client licenses
- A dedicated network administrator (usually required)

2. **Peer Networks** Every computer on a peer network is equal and can communicate with any other computer on the network to which it has been granted access rights. So basically, every computer on a peer network functions both as a server and as a client. The peer network is more common in small businesses.

The advantages of peer networks are:

- No extra investment for server software and hardware are needed
- No network administrator is needed
- Easy setup
- Lower cost

The disadvantages of peer networks are:

- Additional load on computers for resource sharing
- Lack of central organization, making it difficult to find data
- Users must administer their own computers
- Weak and intrusive security

3. **Hybrid Networks** Hybrid networks consist of all three types of computers and have active domains and workgroups. This means that network users have access to any resources being shared by peers in their workgroup while most shared resources are located on servers. The advantages of hybrid networks are the same as the advantages of server-based and peer based networks. Hybrid networks shares the disadvantages of a server-based network.

Network Categories

The two main types of network categories are:

1. **Server based** In a server based network, the computers are set up to be the primary providers of services, such as file service or mail service. The computers providing the service are called servers and the computers that request and use the service are called client computers.
2. **Peer-to-peer** In a peer-to-peer network, various computers on the network can act both as clients and servers. For instance, many Microsoft Windows based computers will allow file and print sharing. These computers can act both as a client and a server and are also referred to as peers. Many networks are a combination of peer-to-peer and server based networks. The network operating system uses a network data protocol to communicate with other computers on the network. The network operating system supports the applications on that computer. A Network Operating System (NOS) includes Windows NT, Novell Netware, Linux, Unix and others.

Server Type

There are several tasks for a server in a network. All these tasks could be done by one server, or a separate server for each tasks. Server is dedicated to performing specific tasks in support of other computers on the network.

1. **File Server** File servers offer the services, which are the network applications that store, retrieve, and move data. With a file server, users can exchange, read, write, and manage shared files as well as the data contained in them. There are three ways to store a file on a network. They are:
   - **Online storage:** Online storage consists of hard drive storage. Hard drive is very fast but expensive so only the most current and frequently needed information is stored.
   - **Offline storage:** The common offline storage devices are data tapes and removable optical disks. The biggest disadvantage of offline storage is that a person must retrieve the disk or tape and mount it on the server. This type of storage is best for data that is rarely used and is generally used for data backup.

- **Near-line storage:** Near-line storage uses a machine, such as a tape carousel or jukebox and automatically retrieves and mounts the tape or disk. It is faster than offline but still only enough for infrequently used data and applications.

  File synchronization is to ensure that the changes made to a file are organized in the same chronological order in which they actually took place and that the files are properly updated. But a network operating system cannot synchronize data within files if it is not aware of the file format. So, we need an option for it usually.

2. **Print Server** Print server manages and control printing on a network and also offers fax service. The print server allows multiple and simultaneous access to print and fax services. The network operating system achieves this by using print and fax queues. The queues are special storage areas where printing and faxing jobs are stored and then sent to the printer or fax device in an organized fashion.
3. **Application Server** Application server allows a client on the network to access and use extra computing power and expensive software applications on a shared computer. Application servers are used when efficiency and security requires a program to stay close to the data, and the data stays in one place.
4. **Message Server** Message server allows a wide variety of communication methods that are much complex than a simple file server can handle. Data can take the form of graphics, digitized video, or audio, text and binary. Message servers must coordinate the complex interactions between users, documents, and applications.
5. **Database Server** A Database server is one of the application servers. Database server allows a network with powerful database capabilities. So, users of a relatively weak client can enjoy the same power of database servers.

Network Topology

The network topology describes the method used to do the physical wiring of the network. In other words, network topology is the physical layout of the network and how the cable is run between them. It is important to use the right topology. Each topology has its own strengths and weakness. The main ones include bus, star, and ring.

1. **Bus topology** – In bus topology, both ends of the network must be terminated with a terminator. A barrel connector can be used to extend it.
2. **Star topology** – In star topology, all devices revolve around a central hub, which controls the network communications, and can also communicate with other hubs. Range limits are generally about 100 meters from the hub. All Ethernet networks use the star topology.
3. **Ring topology** – In ring topology, devices are connected from one to another, as in a ring. A data token is used to grant permission for each computer to communicate.

Networking Topologies

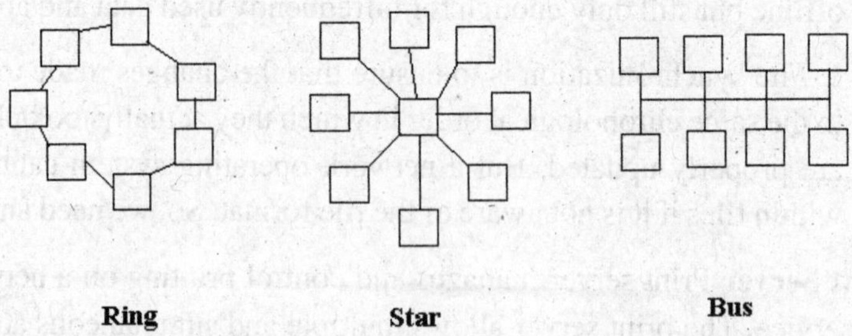

There are also hybrid networks such as a star-bus hybrid, star-ring network, and mesh networks with connections between various computers on the network. Mesh networks ideally allow each computer to have a direct connection to each of the other computers.

1. **Bus topology** A bus topology connects computers along a single or more cable to connect linearly as shown in the figure below. A network that uses bus topology is referred to as a "bus network" which was the original form of Ethernet networks. Ethernet 10Base2 (also known as thin-net) is used for bus topology. Bus topology is the cheapest way of connecting computers to form a workgroup or departmental LAN, but it has the disadvantage that a single loose connection or cable break can bring down the entire LAN. Termination is important issue in bus networks. The electrical signal from a transmitting computer is free to travel the entire length of the cable. Without termination, when the signal reaches the end of the wire, it bounces back and travels back up the wire. When a signal echoes back and forth along an un-terminated bus, it is called ringing. The terminators absorb the electrical energy and stop the reflections.

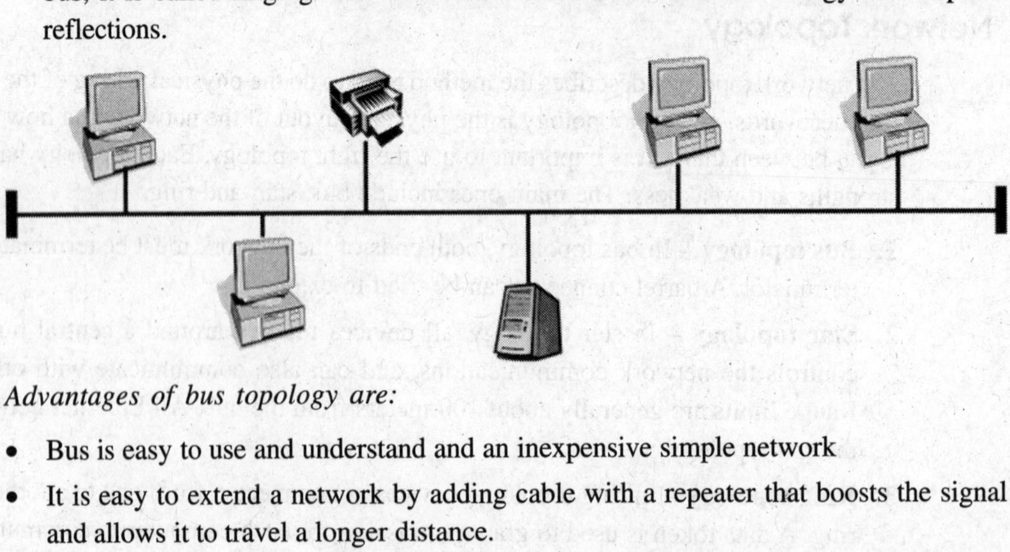

Advantages of bus topology are:

- Bus is easy to use and understand and an inexpensive simple network
- It is easy to extend a network by adding cable with a repeater that boosts the signal and allows it to travel a longer distance.

Disadvantages of bus topology are:

- A bus topology becomes slow by heavy network traffic with a lot of computer because networks do not coordinate with each other to reserve time to transmit.
- It is difficult to troubleshoot a bus because a cable break or loose connector will cause reflections and bring down the whole network.

1. **Star topology** A star topology links the computers by individual cables to a central unit, usually a hub. When a computer or other networking component transmits a signal to the network, the signal travels to the hub. Then, the hub forwards the signal simultaneously to all other components connected to the hub. Ethernet 10BaseT is a network based on the star topology. Star topology is the most popular way to connect computers in a workgroup or departmental network.

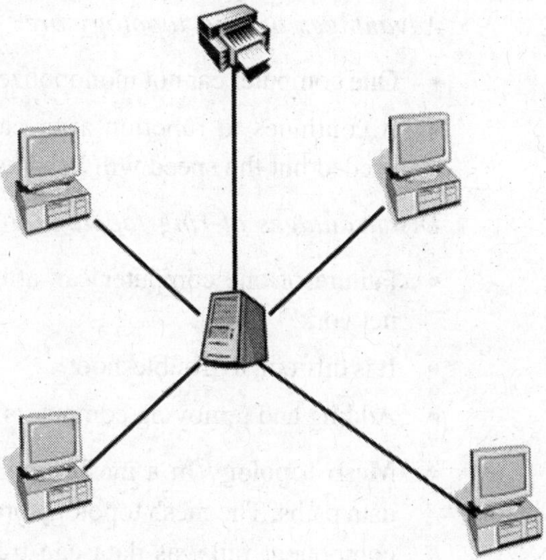

Advantages of star topology are:

- The failure of a single computer or cable doesn't bring down the entire network.
- The centralized networking equipment can reduce costs in the long run by making network management much easier.
- It allows several cable types in same network with a hub that can accommodate multiple cable types.

Disadvantages of star topology are:

- Failure of the central hub causes the whole network failure.
- It is slightly more expensive than using bus topology.

1. **Ring topology** A ring topology connects the computers along a single path whose ends are joined to form a circle or a ring. The circle might only be logical but the physical arrangement of the cabling might be similar to star topology, with a hub or concentrator at the center. The ring topology is commonly used in token ring networks and that the ring, of a token ring network is concentrated inside a device called a Multi

station Access Unit (MAU) and in fiber Distributed Data Interface (FDDI) networks, the ring is both a physical and logical ring and usually runs around a campus or collection of buildings to form a high-speed backbone network.

Advantages of ring topology are:

- One computer cannot monopolize the network.
- It continues to function after capacity is exceeded but the speed will be slow.

Disadvantages of ring topology are:

- Failure of one computer can affect the whole network.
- It is difficult to troubleshoot.
- Adding and removing computers disrupts the network.

4. **Mesh topology** In a mesh topology, each computer on the network has redundant data paths. The mesh topology provides fault tolerance -if a wire, hub, switch, or other component fails, as data can travel along an alternate path. A diagram of a mesh network looks like a fishing net. A mesh topology is most often used in large backbone networks in which failure of a single switch or router can result in a large portion of the network going down.

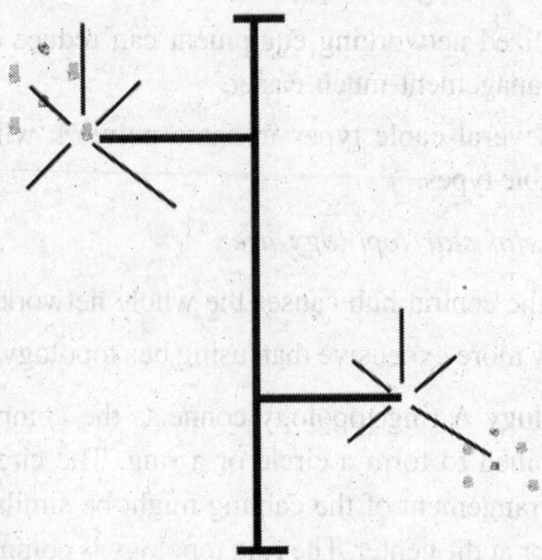

NETWORK HARDWARE CONNECTIONS

Ethernet uses star topology for the physical writing layout. A diagram of a typical ethernet network layout is shown below.

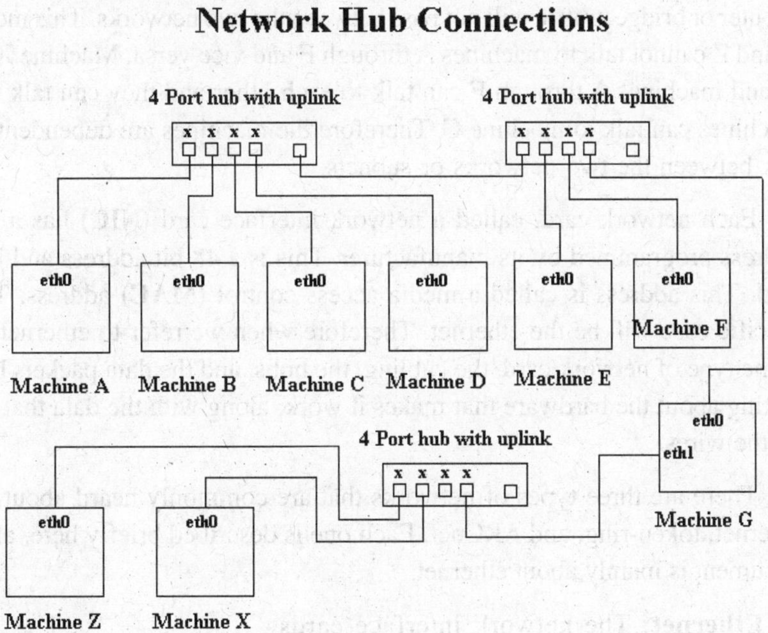

As shown in the figure of a network, a hub is basically a repeater which is used to re-time and amplify the network signals. In this diagram, please examine the hubs closely. On the left are 4 ports, close to each other with an x above or below them. This means that these ports are crossover ports. This crossover is similar to the arrangement that was used for serial cables between two computers. Each serial port has a transmitter and a receiver. Unless there was a null modem connection between two serial ports, or the cable was wired to cross transmit to receive and vice versa, the connection would not work. This is because the transmit port would be sending to the transmit port on the other side.

Therefore we can say that we cannot connect two computers together with a straight network jumper cable between their network cards. We must use a special crossover cable. Otherwise, use a hub. The hub on the upper left is full, but it has an uplink port on the right which lets it connect to another hub. The uplink does not have a crossover connection and is designed to fit into a crossover connection on the next hub. In this way we can keep linking hubs to put computers on a network. Because each hub introduces some delay onto the network signals, there is a limit to the number of hubs we can sequentially link. Also the computers that are connected to the two hubs are on the same network and can talk to each other. All network traffic including all broadcasts is passed through the hubs.

In this diagram, machine G has two network cards, eth0 and eth1. The cards eth1 and eth0 are on two different networks or sub-networks. Unless machine G is programmed as a router or bridge, traffic will not pass between the two networks. This means that machines X and Z cannot talk to machines A through F and vice versa. Machine X can talk to Z and G, and machines A through F can talk to each other and they can talk to machine G. All machines can talk to machine G. Therefore the machines are dependent on machine G to talk between the two networks or subnets.

Each network card, called a network interface card (**NIC**) has a built in hardware address programmed by its manufacturer. This is a 48 bit address and is unique for each card. This address is called a media access control (**MAC**) address. The media, in our specific case will be the ethernet. Therefore when we refer to ethernet, we are referring to the type of network card, the cabling, the hubs, and the data packets being sent. We are talking about the hardware that makes it work, along with the data that is physically sent on the wires.

There are three types of networks that are commonly heard about. They are ethernet, token-ring, and ARCnet. Each one is described briefly here, although this document is mainly about ethernet.

1. **Ethernet:** The network interface cards share a common cable. This cable structure does not need to form a structure, but must be essentially common to all cards on the network. Before a card transmits, it listens for a break in traffic. The cards have collision detection, and if the card detects a collision while trying to transmit, it will retry after some random time interval.

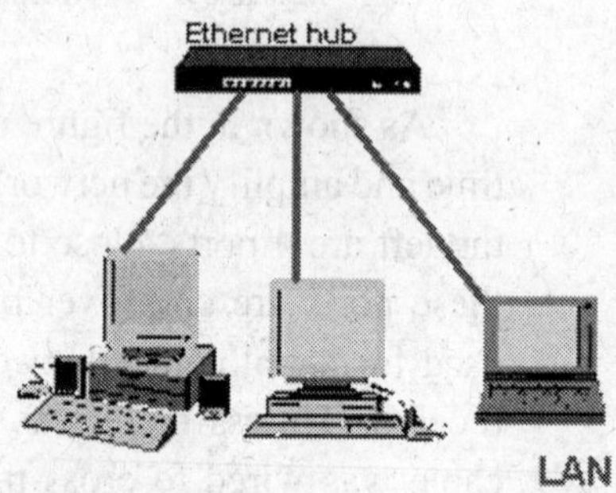

- Each computer in the network 'listens' to the cable before sending anything through the network. If the network is clear, the computer will transmit.
- If another computer is already transmitting on the cable, the computer will wait and try again when the line is clear
- Sometimes, two computers attempt to transmit at the same instance. When this happens, a collision occurs. Each computer then backs off and waits a random amount of time before attempting to retransmit. It is normal to have collisions

using this method, but the delays caused by collisions and transmissions is small, and does not effect speed of transmission on the network

- Ethernet protocol allows for data to be transmitted over:
  - twisted pair cable
  - coaxial cable
  - fiber optic cable

2. **Fast Ethernet:** Fast Ethernet allows faster transmission and has developed a new standard that supports 100 Mbps. Fast Ethernet requires the use of more expensive equipment and network cards
3. **Token Ring:** Token ring networks form a complete electrical loop, or ring. Around the ring are computers, called stations. The cards, using their built in serial numbers, negotiate to determine what card will be the master interface card. This card will create what is called a token that will allow other cards to send data. Essentially, when a card with data to send, receives a token, it sends its data to the next station up the ring to be relayed. The master interface will then create a new token and the process begins again. A single electronic 'token' moves around the ring from one computer to the next. If a computer wishes to transit and receives an empty token, it attaches data to the token which then proceeds around the ring until it comes to the computer the data is meant for.
4. **ARCnet:** ARCnet networks designate a master card. The master card keeps a table of active cards, polling each one sequentially with transmit permission.

TCP/IP PORTS AND ADDRESSES

Each machine in the network has one or more network cards. The part of the network that does the job of transporting and managing the data across the network is called TCP/IP which stands for Transmission Control Protocol (TCP) and Internet Protocol (IP). There are other alternative mechanisms for managing network traffic, but most, such as IPX/SPX for Netware, will not be described here in much detail. The IP layer requires a 4 (IPv4) or 6 (IPv6) byte address to be assigned to each network interface card on each computer. This can be done automatically using network software such as dynamic host configuration protocol (DHCP) or by manually entering static addresses into the computer.

Ports

The TCP layer requires what is called a port number to be assigned to each message. This way it can determine the type of service being provided. When we are talking about "ports" we are not talking about ports that are used for serial and parallel devices, or ports used for computer hardware control. These ports are merely reference numbers used to define a service. For instance, port 23 is used for telnet services, and HTTP uses port 80 for providing web browsing service. There is a group called the IANA (Internet Assigned Numbers Authority) that controls the assigning of ports for specific services. There are some ports that are assigned, some reserved and many unassigned which may be utilized by application programs. Port numbers are straight unsigned integer values which range up to a value of 65535.

Addresses

Addresses are used to locate computers on the network. It works almost like a house address. There is a numbering system to help the mailman locate the proper house in order to deliver the customer's mail. Without an IP numbering system, it would not be possible to determine where network data packets should go. IPv4, which means internet protocol version 4, is described here. Each IP address is denoted by what is called dotted decimal notation. This means there are four numbers, each separated by a dot. Each number represents a byte value with a possible mathematical range of 0-255. Briefly, the first one or two bytes, depending on the class of network, will generally indicate the number of the network, the third byte indicates the number of the subnet, and the fourth number indicates the host number. This numbering scheme will vary depending on the network and the numbering method used such as Classless Inter-Domain Routing (CIDR) which is described later. The host number cannot be 0 or 255. None of the numbers can be 255 and the first number cannot be 0. This is because broadcasting is done with all bits set in some bytes. Broadcasting is a form of communication that all hosts on a network can read, and is normally used for performing various network queries. An address of all 0's is not used, because when a machine is booted that does not have a hardware address assigned, it provides 0.0.0.0 as its address until it receives its assignment. This would occur for machines that are remotely booted or those that are booted using the dynamic host configuration protocol (DHCP). The part of the IP address that defines the network is referred to as the network ID, and the latter part of the IP address that defines the host address is referred to as the host ID.

IPv6 is an enhancement to the IPv4 standard due to the shortage of internet addresses. The dotted notation values are increased to 12 bit values rather than byte (8 bit) values. This increases the effective range of each possible decimal value to 4095. Of course the values of 0 and 4095 (all bits set) are generally reserved, the same as with the IPv4 standard.

An Example Network

Let us take an example to show a network without the hubs. It also shows IP addresses assigned to each interface card. As we can see there are two networks which are 192.168.1.x and 192.168.2.x. Machines A through F are on network 192.168.1.x. The machines X and Z are on network 192.168.2.x, and machine G has access to both networks.

Ethernet Network without Hubs Shown

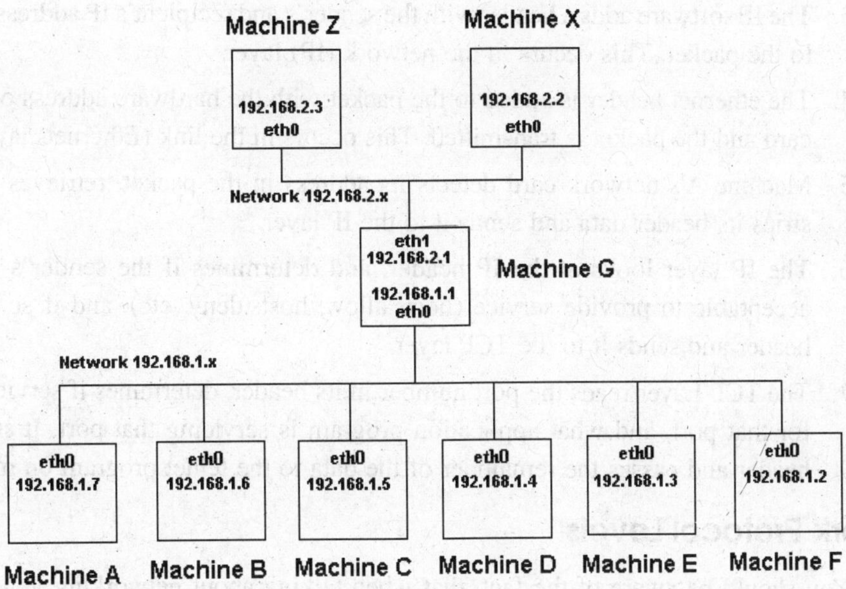

NIS	A	B	C	D	E	F	G	X	Z
eth0	192.168.1.7	192.168.1.6	192.168.1.5	192.168.1.4	192.168.1.3	192.168.1.2	192.168.1.1	192.168.2.2	192.168.2.3
eth1	-	-	-	-	-	-	192.168.2.1	-	-

Using this port and addressing scheme, the networking system can pass data, addressing information and type of service information, through the hardware, from one computer to another. There is an address for the hardware card (ethernet address, also called MAC address), and another assigned address for that same card (IP address), in order to keep parts of the network system that deal with the hardware and the software, independent of each other. It is required in order to be able to configure the IP address dynamically. Else, all computers would have a static address and this would be very difficult to manage. Also, if a modification needs to be made to the hardware addressing scheme for any reason, in ethernet, it will be transparent to the rest of the system. Conversely if a change is made to the software addressing scheme in the IP part of the system, the ethernet and TCP protocols will be unaffected. Machine F will send a telnet data packet to machine A. The following steps occur.

1. The Telnet program in machine F prepares the data packet. This occurs in the application (Telnet), presentation, and session layers of the OSI network model.

2. The TCP software adds a header with the port number, 23, to the packet. This occurs in the transport (TCP) layer.
3. The IP software adds a header with the sender's and recipient's IP address, 192.168.1.2 to the packet. This occurs in the network (IP) layer.
4. The ethernet header is added to the packet with the hardware address of the network card and the packet is transmitted. This occurs in the link (Ethernet) layer.
5. Machine A's network card detects its address in the packet, retrieves the data, and strips its header data and sends it to the IP layer.
6. The IP layer looks at the IP header, and determines if the sender's IP address is acceptable to provide service (hosts.allow, hosts.deny, etc), and if so, strips the IP header and sends it to the TCP layer.
7. The TCP Layer reads the port number in its header, determines if service is provided for that port, and what application program is servicing that port. It strips the TCP header and passes the remainder of the data to the telnet program on machine A.

Network Protocol Levels

You should be aware of the fact, that when talking about networking you will hear the word "protocol" all the time. A protocol is a set of rules that governs the communications between computers on a network. These rules include guidelines that regulate the method of access, types of cabling and speed of data transfer. In other words, a protocol is a formal description of a set of rules and conventions that govern how devices on a network exchange information. They define how various operations are to be performed. They may even define how devices outside the network can interact with the network. Protocols define everything from basic networking data structures, to higher level application programs. They define various services and utility programs. Protocols operate at many layers of the network models described below. There are protocols considered to be transport protocols such as TCP and UDP. Other protocols work at the network layer of the OSI network model shown below.

RFCs

These protocols are outlined in Request for Comments (RFCs). Although RFCs define protocols, not all RFCs define protocols and may define other requirements for the internet such as RFC 1543 which provides information about the preparation of RFCs. The following RFCs are very central to the TCP/IP protocol.

- RFC 1122 - Defines host requirements of the TCP/IP suite of protocols covering the link, network (IP), and transport (TCP, UDP) layers.

- RFC 1123 - The companion RFC to 1122 covering requirements for internet hosts at the application layer
- RFC 1812 - Defines requirements for internet gateways which are IPv4 routers

Network Models

There are several network models but the most common is the ISO network model. However there are others such as:

- The internet layered protocol
- The TCP/IP 4 layered protocol
- The Microsoft networking protocol

Network Access Methods

There are various methods of managing access to a network. If all network stations tried to talk at once, the messages would become unintelligible, and no communication could occur. Therefore a method of being sure that stations coordinate the sending of messages must be achieved. There are several methods listed below which have various advantages and disadvantages.

- Contention
  - o Carrier-Sense Multiple Access with Collision Detection (CSMA/CD) - Used by Ethernet
  - o Carrier-Sense Multiple Access with Collision Avoidance (CSMA/CA)
- Token Passing - A token is passed from one computer to another, which provides transmission permission.
- Demand Priority - Describes a method where intelligent hubs control data transmission. A computer will send a demand signal to the hub indicating that it wants to transmit. The hub will respond with an acknowledgement that will allow the computer to transmit. The hub will allow computers to transmit in turn. An example of a demand priority network is 100VG-AnyLAN (IEEE 802.12). It uses a star-bus topology.
- Polling - A central controller, also called the primary device will poll computers, called secondary devices, to find out if they have data to transmit. If so the central controller will allow them to transmit for a limited time, then the next device is polled.

Token passing performs better when the network has a lot of traffic, while ethernet which uses CSMA/CD is generally faster but loses performance when the network has a lot of traffic. CSMA/CD is basically a method that allows network stations to transmit any time they want. They, however, sense the network line and detect if another station has transmitted at the same time they did. This is called a collision. If a collision happened, the stations involved will retransmit at a later, randomly set time in hopes of avoiding another collision.

The OSI Reference Model

OSI Model Layers
7 Application
6 Presentation
5 Session
4 Transport
3 Network
2 Data Link
1 Physical

The OSI model (minus the physical medium) is based on a proposal developed by the International Standards Organization (ISO) as a first step toward international standardization of the protocols used in the various layers. It was revised in 1995. The model is called the ISO OSI (Open Systems Interconnection) Reference Model because it deals with connecting open systems—that is, systems that are open for communication with other systems.

The OSI model has seven layers. The principles that were applied to arrive at the seven layers can be briefly summarized as follows:

- A layer should be created where a different abstraction is needed.
- Each layer should perform a well-defined function.
- The function of each layer should be chosen with an eye toward defining internationally standardized protocols.
- The layer boundaries should be chosen to minimize the information flow across the interfaces.
- The number of layers should be large enough that distinct functions need not be thrown together in the same layer out of necessity and small enough that the architecture does not become unwieldy.

The Physical Layer

As per the Wikipedia encyclopedia, the physical layer defines all the electrical and physical specifications for devices. In particular, it defines the relationship between a device and a physical medium. This includes the layout of pins, voltages, cable specifications, hubs, repeaters, network adapters, Host Bus Adapters (HBAs used in Storage Area Networks) and more.

The physical layer is concerned with transmitting raw bits over a communication channel. The design issues have to do with making sure that when one side sends a 1 bit, it is received by the other side as a 1 bit, not as a 0 bit. The design issues here largely deal with mechanical, electrical, and timing interfaces, and the physical transmission medium, which lies below the physical layer.

The Data Link Layer

The data link layer provides the functional and procedural means to transfer data between network entities and to detect and possibly correct errors that may occur in the physical layer. The main task of the data link layer is to transform a raw transmission facility into a line that appears free of undetected transmission errors to the network layer. It accomplishes this task by having the sender break up the input data into data frames and transmits the frames sequentially. If the service is reliable, the receiver confirms correct receipt of each frame by sending back an acknowledgement frame.

Broadcast networks have an additional issue in the data link layer: how to control access to the shared channel. A special sub layer of the data link layer, the medium access control sub layer, deals with this problem.

The Network Layer

The network layer provides the functional and procedural means of transferring variable length data sequences from a source to a destination via one or more networks while maintaining the quality of service requested by the Transport layer. The network layer controls the operation of the subnet. A key design issue is determining how packets are routed from source to destination. Routes can be based on static tables that are ''wired into'' the network and rarely changed. They can also be determined at the start of each conversation for example, a terminal session (e.g., a login to a remote machine) or they can be highly dynamic, being determined a new for each packet, to reflect the current network load. If too many packets are present in the subnet at the same time, they will get in one another's way, forming bottlenecks. The control of such congestion also belongs to the network layer. More generally, the quality of service provided (delay, transit time, jitter, etc.) is also a network layer issue. The Network layer performs network routing functions, and might also perform fragmentation and reassembly, and report delivery errors. Routers operate at this layer—sending data throughout the extended network and making the Internet possible.

The Transport Layer

The basic function of the transport layer is to accept data from above, split it up into smaller units if need be, pass these to the network layer, and ensure that the pieces all arrive correctly at the other end. The transport layer also determines what type of service to provide to the session layer, and, ultimately, to the users of the network. The transport layer provides transparent transfer of data between end users, providing reliable data transfer services to the upper layers. The transport layer controls the reliability of a given link through flow control, segmentation/de-segmentation, and error control. Some protocols are state and connection oriented. This means that the transport layer can keep track of the segments and retransmit those that fail. The transport layer is the layer that converts messages into TCP (Transmission Control Protocol) segments or User Datagram Protocol (UDP), Stream Control Transmission Protocol (SCTP), etc. packets.

The Session Layer

The session layer allows users on different machines to establish sessions between them. It establishes, manages and terminates the connections between the local and remote application. Sessions offer various services, including dialog control (keeping track of whose turn it is to transmit), token management (preventing two parties from attempting the same critical operation at the same time), and synchronization (check-pointing long transmissions to allow them to continue from where they were after a crash). Session layers are commonly used in application environments that make use of remote procedure calls (RPCs).

The Presentation Layer

Unlike lower layers, which are mostly concerned with moving bits around, the presentation layer is concerned with the syntax and semantics of the information transmitted. In order to make it possible for computers with different data representations to communicate, the data structures to be exchanged can be defined in an abstract way, along with a standard encoding to be used "on the wire." The presentation layer manages these abstract data structures and allows higher-level data structures, to be defined and exchanged.

The Application Layer

The application layer interfaces directly to and performs application services for the application processes and also issues requests to the presentation layer. This layer provides services to user-defined application processes, and not to the end user. The application layer contains a variety of protocols that are commonly needed by users. One widely-used application protocol is HTTP (Hyper Text Transfer Protocol), which is the basis for the World Wide Web. When a browser wants a Web page, it sends the name of the page it wants to the server using HTTP. The server then sends the page back. Other application protocols are used for file transfer, electronic mail, and network news.

TCP/IP Reference Model

TCP/IP Model Layers
4 Application
3 Transport
2 Network
1 Data Link

TCP/IP includes a wide range of protocols which are used for a variety of purposes on the network. The set of protocols that are a part of TCP/IP is called the TCP/IP protocol stack or the TCP/IP suite of protocols.

Considering the many protocols, message types, levels, and services that TCP/IP networking supports, it would be very helpful to categorize the various protocols that support TCP/IP networking and define their respective contribution to the operation of networking.

There are four TCP/IP layers. They are link, network, transport, and application. The link layer is the hardware layer that provides ability to send messages between multiple locations. There are several categories some of which fit into the 4 layer protocol levels described earlier. Importance includes essential, critical, important, advanced, and useful.

1. Essential - Without this all other categories are irrelevant.
2. Critical - The network, as designed, is useless without this ability.
3. Important - The network could function, but would be difficult to use and manage.
4. Advanced - Includes enhancements that make the network easier to use and manage.
5. Useful - Functionality that you would like to be able to use as a network user.

The categories are:

Name(layer)	Importance	Names of protocols	What it does
Hardware(link)	Essential	ethernet, SLIP, PPP, Token Ring, ARCnet	Allows messages to be packaged and sent between physical locations.
Package management(network)	Essential	IP, ICMP	Manages movement of messages and reports errors. It uses message protocols and software to manage this process. (includes routing)
Inter layer communication	Essential	ARP	Communicates between layers to allow one layer to get information to support another layer. This includes broadcasting
Service control(transport)	Critical	TCP, UDP	Controls the management of service between computers. Based on values in TCP and UDP messages a server knows what service is being requested.
Application and user support	Important	DNS, RPC	DNS provides address to name translation for locations and network cards. RPC allows remote computer to perform functions on other computers.
Network Management	Advanced	RARP, BOOTP, DHCP, IGMP, SNMP, RIP, OSPF, BGP, CIDR	Enhances network management and increases functionality
Utility(Application)	Useful	FTP, TFTP, SMTP, Telnet, NFS, ping, Rlogin	Provides direct services to the user.

Ethernet, which is not really a protocol, but an IEEE standard along with PPP, SLIP, Token Ring, and Arc Net are not TCP/IP protocols but may support TCP/IP at the hardware or link layer, depending on the network topology.

The list below gives a brief description of each protocol

- Ethernet - Provides for transport of information between physical locations on ethernet cable. Data is passed in ethernet packets
- SLIP - Serial line IP (SLIP), a form of data encapsulation for serial lines.

- PPP - Point to point protocol (PPP). A form of serial line data encapsulation that is an improvement over SLIP.
- IP - Internet Protocol (IP). Except for ARP and RARP all protocols' data packets will be packaged into an IP data packet. Provides the mechanism to use software to address and manage data packets being sent to computers.
- ICMP - Internet control message protocol (ICMP) provides management and error reporting to help manage the process of sending data between computers.
- ARP - Address resolution protocol (ARP) enables the packaging of IP data into ethernet packages. It is the system and messaging protocol that is used to find the ethernet (hardware) address from a specific IP number. Without this protocol, the ethernet package could not be generated from the IP package, because the ethernet address could not be determined.
- TCP - A reliable connection oriented protocol used to control the management of application level services between computers.
- UDP - An unreliable connection less protocol used to control the management of application level services between computers.
- DNS - Domain Name Service, allows the network to determine IP addresses from names and vice versa.
- RARP - Reverse address resolution protocol (RARP) is used to allow a computer without a local permanent data storage media to determine its IP address from its ethernet address.
- BOOTP - Bootstrap protocol is used to assign an IP address to diskless computers and tell it what server and file to load which will provide it with an operating system.
- DHCP - Dynamic host configuration protocol (DHCP) is a method of assigning and controlling the IP addresses of computers on a given network. It is a server based service that automatically assigns IP numbers when a computer boots. This way the IP address of a computer does not need to be assigned manually. This makes changing networks easier to manage. DHCP can perform all the functions of BOOTP.
- IGMP - Internet Group Management Protocol is used to support multicasting.
- SNMP - Simple Network Management Protocol (SNMP) is used to manage all types of network elements based on various data sent and received.
- RIP - Routing Information Protocol (RIP) is used to dynamically update router tables on WANs or the internet.
- OSPF - Open Shortest Path First (OSPF) is a dynamic routing protocol.
- BGP - Border Gateway Protocol (BGP). A dynamic router protocol to communicate between routers on different systems.
- CIDR - Classless Inter Domain Routing (CIDR).

- FTP - File Transfer Protocol (FTP). Allows file transfer between two computers with login required.
- TFTP - Trivial File Transfer Protocol (TFTP). Allows file transfer between two computers with no login required. It is limited, and is intended for diskless stations.
- SMTP - Simple Mail Transfer Protocol (SMTP).
- NFS - Network File System (NFS). A protocol that allows UNIX and Linux systems remotely mount each other's file systems.
- Telnet - A method of opening a user session on a remote host.
- Ping - A program that uses ICMP to send diagnostic messages to other computers to tell if they are reachable over the network.
- Rlogin - Remote login between UNIX hosts. This is outdated and is replaced by Telnet.

Each protocol ultimately has its data packets wrapped in an ethernet, SLIP, or PPP packet (at the link level) in order to be sent over the ethernet cable. Some protocol data packets are wrapped sequentially multiple times before being sent. For example FTP data is wrapped in a TCP packet which is wrapped in a IP packet which is wrapped in a link packet (normally ethernet). The diagram below shows the relationship between the protocols' sequential wrapping of data packets.

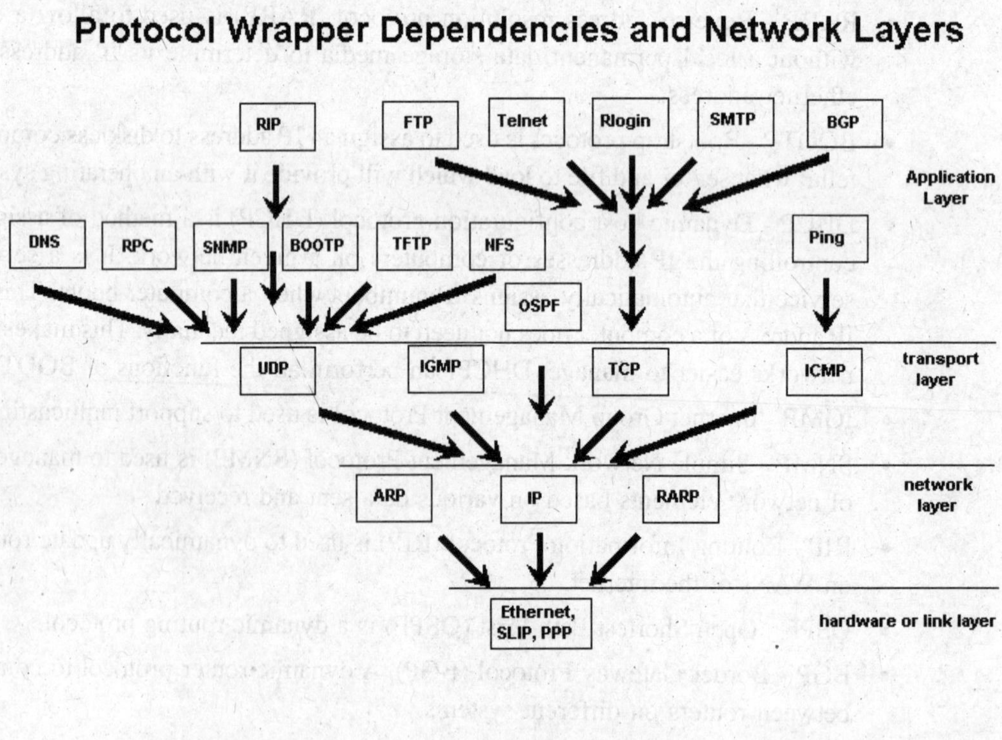

NETWORK DEVICES

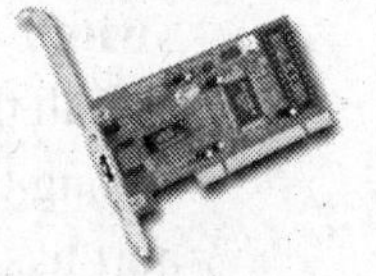

Network Interface Cards (NICs) A network interface card may be wired or wireless. It puts the data into packets and transmits packet onto the network.

Network Repeater A repeater connects two segments of the network cable. It retimes and regenerates the signals to proper amplitudes and sends them to the other segments. When talking about, ethernet topology, we are probably talking about using a hub as a repeater. Repeaters require a small amount of time to regenerate the signal. This can cause a propagation delay which can affect network communication when there are several repeaters in a row. Many network architectures limit the number of repeaters that can be used in a row. Repeaters work only at the physical layer of the OSI network model. In short, a network repeater is

- Used to boost the signal between two cable segments or wireless access points.
- Can not connect different network architecture.
- Does not simply amplify the signal, it regenerates the packets and retimes them.
- Resides on Layer 1 of the OSI model.

Concentrators / Hubs A concentrator is a device that provides a central connection point for cables from workstations, servers and peripherals. Hubs are multi-slot concentrators. A hub is a device that takes any incoming signal and re-broadcasts it down to all the outgoing wires connected to it. Hubs can have from 5 ports to 128 ports and can transmit and receive at up to 100Mbps. In short a concentrator/hub is

- An unintelligent network device that sends one signal to all of the stations connected to it.
- All computers/devices compete for attention as it takes the data that comes into a port and sends it out to all the other ports in the hub.
- Traditionally, hubs are used for star topology networks, but they are often used with other configurations to make it easy to add and remove computers without bringing down the network.
- Resides on Layer 1 of the OSI model

Switch A vital difference between a hub and a switch is that all the nodes connected to a hub share the bandwidth among themselves, while a device connected to a switch port has the full bandwidth all to itself. A switch

- Splits large networks into small segments, decreasing the number of users sharing the same network resources and bandwidth
- Understands when two devices want to talk to each other, and gives them a *switched* connection
- Helps prevent data collisions and reduces network congestion thereby increasing network performance.
- Most home users get very little, if any, advantage from switches, even when sharing a broadband connection.
- Resides on Layer 2 of the OSI model

Bridge A bridge reads the outermost section of data on the data packet, in order to tell where the messages are going. It reduces the traffic on other network segments, since it does not send all packets. Bridges can be programmed to reject packets from particular networks. Bridging occurs at the data link layer of the OSI model, which means that the bridge cannot read IP addresses, but only the outermost hardware address of the packet. In our case the bridge can read the ethernet data which gives the hardware address of the destination address, not the IP address. Bridges forward all broadcast messages. Only a special bridge called a translation bridge will allow two networks of different architectures to be connected. Bridges do not normally allow connection of networks with different architectures. The hardware address is also called the MAC (media access control) address. To determine the network segment a MAC address belongs to, bridges use one of the following:

- Transparent Bridging - They build a table of addresses (bridging table) as they receive packets. If the address is not in the bridging table, the packet is forwarded to all segments other than the one it came from. This type of bridge is used on ethernet networks.
- Source route bridging - The source computer provides the path information inside the packet. This is used on Token Ring networks.

In short, a bridge

- o Connects two LANs and forwards or filters data packets between them.
- o Creates an extended network in which any two workstations on the linked LANs can share data.

- o Transparent to protocols and to higher level devices like routers.
- o Forwards data depending on the Hardware (MAC) address, not the Network address (IP).
- o Resides on Layer 2 of the OSI model.

Network Router A router is used to route data packets between two networks. It reads the information in each packet to tell where it is going. If it is destined for an immediate network it has access to, it will strip the outer packet, re-address the packet to the proper ethernet address, and transmit it on that network. If it is destined for another network and must be sent to another router, it will re-package the outer packet to be received by the next router and send it to the next router. The section on routing explains the theory behind this and how routing tables are used to help determine packet destinations. Routing occurs at the network layer of the OSI model. They can connect networks with different architectures such as Token Ring and Ethernet. Although they can transform information at the data link level, routers cannot transform information from one data format such as TCP/IP to another such as IPX/SPX. Routers do not send broadcast packets or corrupted packets. If the routing table does not indicate the proper address of a packet, the packet is discarded. A router is

- A device that connects any number of LANs.
- Uses standardized protocols to move packets efficiently to their destination.
- More sophisticated than bridges, connecting networks of different types (for example, star and token ring)
- Forwards data depending on the Network address (IP), not the Hardware (MAC) address.
- Routers are the only one of these four devices that will allow you to share a single IP address among multiple network clients.
- Resides on Layer 3 of the OSI model.

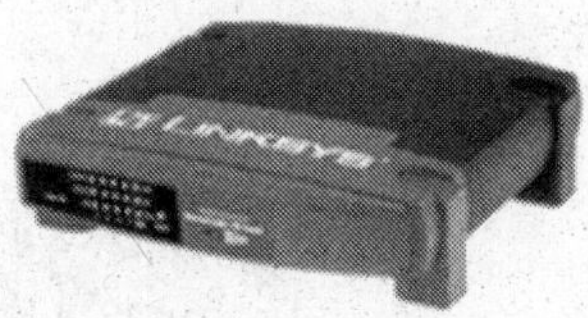

Brouter

There is a device called a Brouter which will function similar to a bridge for network transport protocols that are not routable, and will function as a router for routable protocols. It functions at the network and data link layers of the OSI network model.

Gateway A gateway can translate information between different network data formats or network architectures. It can translate TCP/IP to AppleTalk so computers supporting TCP/IP can communicate with Apple brand computers. Most gateways operate at the application layer, but can operate at the network or session layer of the OSI model as well. Gateways will start at the lower level and strip information until it gets to the required level and repackage the information and work its way back toward the hardware layer of the OSI model. To confuse issues, when talking about a router that is used to interface to another network, the word gateway is often used. This does not mean that the routing machine is a gateway as defined here, although it could be. A gateway

- Connects networks with different protocols like TCP/IP network and IPX/SPX networks.
- Routers and Gateways often refer to the same device.

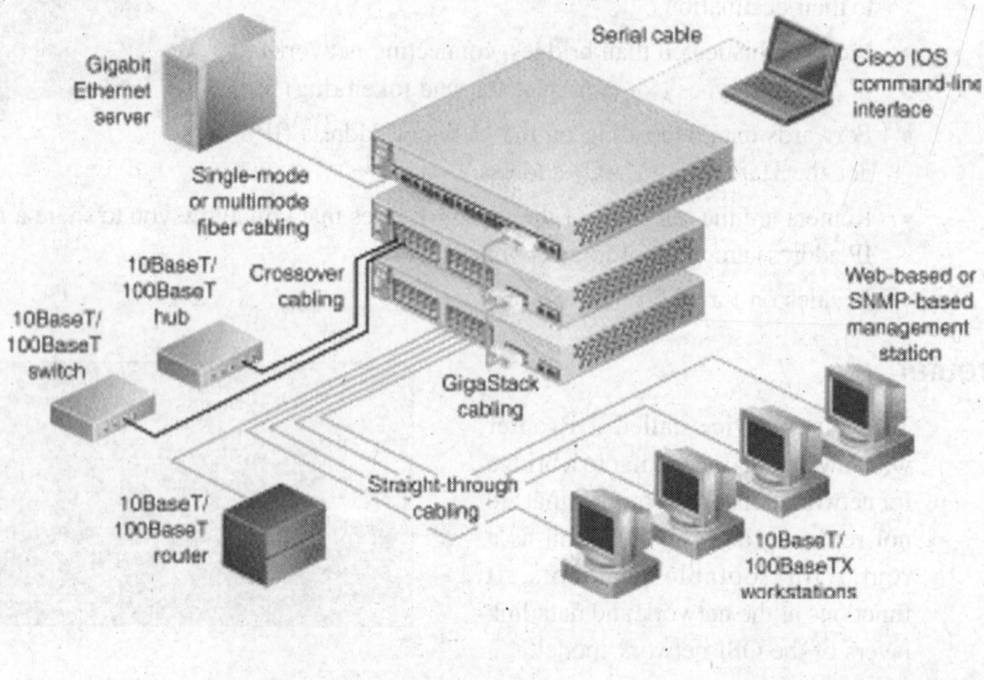

Address Resolution Protocol

ARP and RARP Address Translation

Address Resolution Protocol (ARP) provides a completely different function to the network than Reverse Address Resolution Protocol (RARP). ARP is used to resolve the ethernet address of a NIC from an IP address in order to construct an ethernet packet around an IP data packet. This must happen in order to send any data across the network. Reverse address resolution protocol (RARP) is used for diskless computers to determine their IP address using the network.

Address Resolution Protocol (ARP)

Let us take an example of a chat program used to communicate between two servers. When the user type's text into a dialog box and hit send in order to communicate between two servers to send data, the following happens:

1. The program passes the typed text in a buffer, to the socket.
2. The data is put inside a TCP data packet with a TCP header added to the data. This header contains a source and a destination port number along with some other information and a checksum.
3. The TCP packet is placed inside an IP data packet with a source and destination IP address along with some other data for network management.
4. The IP data packet is placed inside an ethernet data packet. This data packet includes the destination and source address of the network interface cards (NIC) on the two computers. The address here is the hardware address of the respective cards and is called the MAC address.
5. The ethernet packet is transmitted over the network line.
6. With a direct connection between the two computers, the network interface card on the intended machine, recognizes its address and grabs the data.
7. The IP data packet is extracted from the ethernet data packet.
8. The TCP data packet is extracted from the IP data packet.
9. The data is extracted from the TCP packet and the program displays the retrieved data (text) in the text display window for the intended recipient to read.

In step 4 above, the IP data was going to be placed inside an ethernet data packet, but the computer constructing the packet does not have the ethernet address of the recipient's computer. The computer that is sending the data, in order to create the ethernet part of the packet, must get the ethernet hardware (MAC) address of the computer with the intended IP address. This must be accomplished before the ethernet packet can be constructed. The ethernet device driver software on the receiving computer is not programmed to look at IP addresses encased in the ethernet packet. If it did, the protocols could not be independent and changes to one would affect the other. This is where address resolution protocol (ARP) is used. The computer sends a network broadcast asking the computer that has the recipient's IP address to send its ethernet address. This is done by broadcasting. The ethernet destination is set with all bits on so all ethernet cards on the network will receive the data packet. The ARP message consists of an ethernet header and ARP packet.

Reverse Address Resolution Protocol (RARP)

Reverse address resolution protocol (RARP) is used for diskless computers to determine their IP address using the network. The RARP message format is very similar to the ARP format. When the booting computer sends the broadcast ARP request, it places its own hardware address in both the sending and receiving fields in the encapsulated ARP data packet. The RARP server will fill in the correct sending and receiving IP addresses in its response to the message. This way the booting computer will know its IP address when it gets the message from the RARP server.

NETWORK ADDRESSING

IP addresses are broken into 4 octets (IPv4) separated by dots called dotted decimal notation. An octet is a byte consisting of 8 bits. The IPv4 addresses are in the following form:

192.168.10.1

There are two parts of an IP address: a Network ID and a Host ID.

The various classes of networks specify additional or fewer octets to designate the network ID versus the host ID.

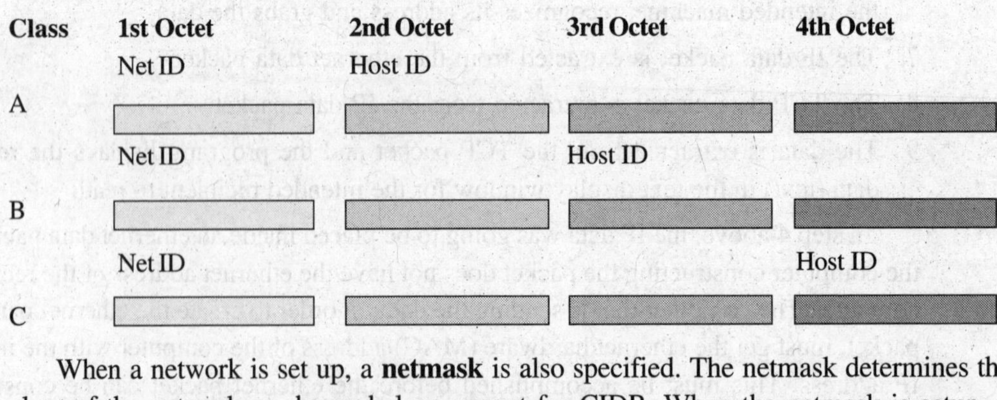

When a network is set up, a **netmask** is also specified. The netmask determines the class of the network as shown below, except for CIDR. When the netmask is setup, it specifies some number of most significant bits with a 1's value and the rest have values of

0. The most significant part of the netmask with bits set to 1's specifies the network address, and the lower part of the address will specify the host address. When setting addresses on a network, remember there can be no host address of 0 (no host address bits set), and there can be no host address with all bits set.

Class A-E networks

The addressing scheme for class A through E networks is shown below. Note: We use the 'x' character here to denote doesn't care situations which include all possible numbers at the location. It is many times used to denote networks.

Network Type	Address Range	Normal Netmask	Comments
Class A	001.x.x.x to 126.x.x.x	255.0.0.0	For very large networks
Class B	128.1.x.x to 191.254.x.x	255.255.0.0	For medium size networks
Class C	192.0.1.x to 223.255.254.x	255.255.255.0	For small networks
Class D	224.x.x.x to 239.255.255.255		Used to support multicasting
Class E	240.x.x.x to 247.255.255.255		

RFCs 1518 and 1519 define a system called Classless Inter-Domain Routing (CIDR) which is used to allocate IP addresses more efficiently. This may be used with subnet masks to establish networks rather than the class system shown above. A class C subnet may be 8 bits but using CIDR, it may be 12 bits.

There are some network addresses reserved for private use by the Internet Assigned Numbers Authority (IANA) which can be hidden behind a computer that uses IP masquerading to connect the private network to the internet. There are three sets of addresses reserved. These addresses are shown below:

- 10.x.x.x
- 172.16.x.x - 172.31.x.x
- 192.168.x.x

To further illustrate, a few examples of valid and invalid addresses are listed below:

1. Valid addresses:
   - o 10.1.0.1 through 10.1.0.254
   - o 10.0.0.1 through 10.0.0.254
   - o 10.0.1.1 through 10.0.1.254
2. Invalid addresses:
   - o 10.1.0.0 - Host IP can't be 0.
   - o 10.1.0.255 - Host IP can't be 255.
   - o 10.123.255.4 - No network or subnet can have a value of 255.

- o 0.12.16.89 - No Class A network can have an address of 0.
- o 255.9.56.45 - No network address can be 255.
- o 10.34.255.1 - No network address can be 255.

Network/Netmask specification

Sometimes we see a network interface card (NIC) IP address specified as 192.168.1.1/24.

The first part indicates the IP address of the NIC which is "192.168.1.1" in this case. The second part "/24" indicates the netmask value meaning in this case that the first 24 bits of the netmask are set. This makes the netmask value as 255.255.255.0. If the last part of the line above were "/16", the netmask would be 255.255.0.0.

Subnet masks

Subnetting is the process of breaking down a main class A, B, or C network into subnets for routing purposes. A subnet mask is the same basic thing as a netmask with the only real difference being that you are breaking a larger organizational network into smaller parts, and each smaller section will use a different set of address numbers. This will allow network packets to be routed between sub networks. When doing sub netting, the number of bits in the subnet mask determines the number of available subnets. Two to the power of the number of bits minus two ($2^{\text{number of bits}} - 2$) is the number of available subnets. When setting up subnets the number of segments as well as the hosts per segment must be determined.

Subnetting provides the following advantages:

- Network traffic isolation - There is less network traffic on each subnet.
- Simplified Administration - Networks can be managed independently.
- Improved security - Subnets can isolate internal networks so they are not visible from external networks.

A 14 bit subnet mask on a class B network only allows 2 node addresses for WAN links. A routing algorithm like OSPF or EIGRP must be used for this approach. These protocols allow the variable length subnet masks (VLSM). RIP and IGRP don't support this. Subnet mask information must be transmitted on the update packets for dynamic routing protocols for this to work. The router subnet mask is different than the WAN interface subnet mask.

One network ID is required by each of:

- Subnet
- WAN connection

One host ID is required by:

- Each NIC on each host.
- Each router interface.

Types of subnet masks:

- Default - Fits into a Class A, B, or C network category
- Custom - Used to break a default network such as a Class A, B, or C network into subnets.

IPv6

IPv6 is 128 bits. It has eight octet pairs, each with 16 bits and written in hexadecimal as follows:

2b63:1478:1ac5:37ef:4e8c:75df:14cd:93f2

Extension headers can be added to IPv6 for new features.

Supernetting

Supernetting is used to make up for some of the shortage of IP addresses for the internet. It uses Classless Inter-Domain Routing (CIDR). If a business needs a specific number of IP addresses such as 1500, rather than allocating a class B set of addresses with the subnet mask of 255.255.0.0, a subnet mask of 255.255.248.0 may be allocated. Therefore the equivalent of eight class C addresses can be allocated. 8 times 254 is equal to 2032. With supernetting, the value of 2 is not subtracted from the possible number of subnets since the router knows that these are contiguous networks.

The message order of bits transmitted is 0-7, then 8-15, in network byte order. Fragmentation is handled at the IP network layer and the messages are reassembled when they reach their final destination. If one fragment of a datagram is lost, the entire datagram must be retransmitted. This is why fragmentation is avoided by TCP. The data on the last line, item 14, is ethernet data, or data depending on the type of physical network. The header is followed by data. TCP data is full duplex.

User Datagram Protocol

User Datagram Protocol (UDP) supports the network at the transport layer. User Datagram Protocol (UDP) is an unreliable connection-less protocol and is defined by RFC 768 and 1122. It is a datagram service and there is no guarantee that the data will reach its intended destination. UDP is meant to provide service with very little transmission overhead. It adds very little to IP data packets except for some error checking and port direction (Remember, UDP encapsulates IP packets). The following protocols or services use UDP:

- DNS
- SNMP
- BOOTP
- TFTP
- NFS
- RPC
- RIP

UDP Message Format The UDP header includes the following:

1. Source port number (16 bits) - An optional field
2. Destination port number (16 bits)
3. UDP length (16 bits)
4. UDP checksum (16 bits)

This is followed by data. The UDP checksum includes UDP data and not just the header, as with IP message formats. For UDP and TCP checksum calculation, a 12 byte pseudo header is included which contains some fields from the IP message header. This header is not transmitted as part of UDP or TCP, but is only used to help compute the checksum as a means of being sure that the data has arrived at the correct IP address. The TCP/UDP pseudo header includes:

1. Source IP address (32 bits)
2. Destination IP address (32 bits)
3. blank filler(0) (8 bits)
4. Protocol (8 bits)
5. UDP length (16 bits)

ICMP is used for many different functions, the most important of which is error reporting. Some of these are "port unreachable", "host unreachable", "network unreachable", "destination network unknown", and "destination host unknown". The functions that are not related to errors are:

- **Timestamp request and reply** allows one system to ask another one for the current time.
- **Address mask and reply** is used by a diskless workstation to get its subnet mask at boot time.
- **Echo request and echo reply** is used by the ping program to test to see if another unit responds or not.

NETWORK CABLING

This section may be skipped by those more interested on the software aspects of networking or those learning networking, but all readers should at some time be aware of the terminology used in this section since they are used with regard to cabling. This section should be read by those who plan to physically install their own network.

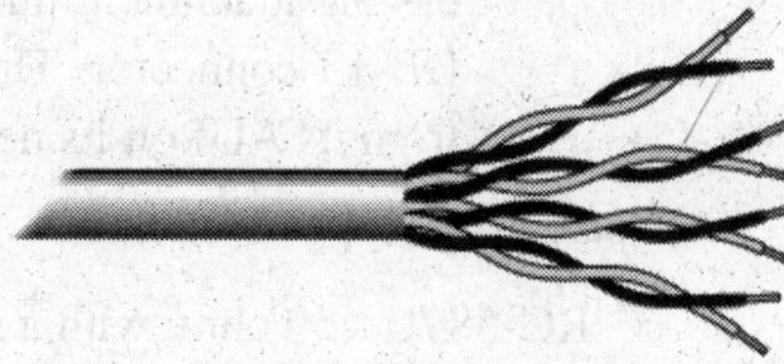

Types of Transmission It includes:

1. **Baseband** - Data bits are defined by discrete signal changes.
2. **Broadband** - Uses analog signals to divide the cable into several channels with each channel at its own frequency. Each channel can only transmit one direction.

Physical media

1. **Twisted pair** - Wire is twisted to minimize crosstalk interference. It may be shielded or unshielded.

o UTP-Unshielded Twisted Pair. Normally UTP contains 8 wires or 4 pair and has a maximum length of 100 meter. Data rate ranges from 4-100 Mbps.

o STP-Shielded twisted pair. Shielded twisted pair has a maximum cable length of 100 meters (328 feet). Its data rate ranges from 16 to 155 Mbps. Cables require special connectors for grounding but this cabling method resists electrical interference and is less susceptible to eavesdropping. It costs more than UTP or Thin net, but not as much as Thick net or Fiber-optic.

1. **Coaxial** - Two conductors separated by insulation such as TV 75 ohm cable. Maximum length of 185 to 500 meters.

(a) Thin net – Thin net uses a British Naval Connector (BNC) on each end. Thin net is part of the RG-58 family of cable*. Maximum cable length is 185 meters. Transmission speed is 10Mbps. Thin net cable should have 50 ohms impedance and its terminator has 50 ohms impedance. A T or barrel connector has no impedance.

(b) Thick net - Half inch rigid cable. Maximum cable length is 500 meters. Transmission speed is 10Mbps. Expensive and is not commonly used. (RG-11 or

RG-8). A vampire tap or piercing tap is used with a transceiver attached to connect computers to the cable. 100 connections may be made. The computer has an attachment unit interface (AUI) on its network card which is a 15 pin DB-15 connector. The computer is connected to the transceiver at the cable from its AUI on its network card using a drop cable.

Coax cable types It includes:

- o RG-58 /U - 50 ohm, with a solid copper wire core.
- o RG-58 A/U* - 50 ohm, with a stranded wire core.
- o RG-58 C/U* - Military version of RG-58 A/U.
- o RG-59 - 75 ohm, for broadband transmission such as cable TV.
- o RG-62 - 93 ohm, primarily used for ARCnet.
- o RG-6 - Used for satellite cable (if you want to run a cable to a satellite!).

*Only these are part of the IEEE specification for ethernet networks.

3. **Fiber-optic** - Data is transmitted using light rather than electrons. Usually there are two fibers, one for each direction. Cable length of 2 Kilometers. Speed from 100Mbps to 2Gbps. This is the most expensive and most difficult to install, but is not subject to interference. Two types of cables are:

0. Single mode cables for use with lasers.
1. Multimode cables for use with Light Emitting Diode (LED) drivers.

Cable Standards

The Electronic Industries Association and Telecommunications Industries Association (EIA/TIA) defined a standard called EIA/TIA 568 which is a commercial building wiring standard for UTP cable. It defines transmission speed and twists per foot.

Category	Speed	Notes
1	None	Used for old telephone systems
2	4Mps	
3	10Mps	The minimum category for data networks
4	16Mps	
5	100Mps	Cat 5 network cable, used by most networks today
6	Data patch,	Two pair with foil and braided shield
7		Undefined
8		Flat cable for under carpets with two twisted pair
9		Plenum cable with two twisted pair. It is safe incase of fire.

The maximum transmission length is 100 meters. This cable is susceptible to interference.

WIRELESS NETWORKING

This section may be skipped by all readers and used by those interested in wireless network technology. Transmission of waves takes place in the electromagnetic (EM) spectrum. The carrier frequency of the data is expressed in cycles per second called hertz (Hz). Low frequency signals can travel for long distances through many obstacles but can not carry a high bandwidth of data. High frequency signals can travel for shorter distances through few obstacles and carry a narrow bandwidth. Also the effect of noise on the signal is inversely proportional to the power of the radio transmitter, which is normal for all EM transmissions. The three broad categories of wireless media are:

1. **Radio** - 10 KHz to 1 GHz. It is broken into many bands including AM, FM, and VHF bands. The Federal communications Commission (FCC) regulates the assignment of these frequencies. Frequencies for unregulated use are:
   - o 902-928 MHz - Cordless phones, remote controls.
   - o 2.4 GHz
   - o 5.72-5.85 GHz
2. **Microwave** – This includes
   - o Terrestrial - Used to link networks over long distances but the two microwave towers must have a line of sight between them. The frequency is usually 4-6GHz or 21-23GHz. Speed is often 1-10Mbps. The signal is normally encrypted for privacy.
   - o Satellite - A satellite orbits at 22,300 miles above the earth which is an altitude that will cause it to stay in a fixed position relative to the rotation of the earth. This is called a geosynchronous orbit. A station on the ground will send and receive signals from the satellite. The signal can have propagation delays between 0.5 and 5 seconds due to the distances involved. The transmission frequency is normally 11-14GHz with a transmission speed in the range of 1-10Mbps.
3. **Infrared** - Infrared is just below the visible range of light between 100 GHz and 1000 THz. A light emitting diode (LED) or laser is used to transmit the signal. The signal cannot travel through objects. Light may interfere with the signal. The types of infrared are
   - o Point to point - Transmission frequencies are 100GHz-1,000THz. Transmission is between two points and is limited to line of sight range. It is difficult to eavesdrop on the transmission.
   - o Broadcast - The signal is dispersed so several units may receive the signal. The unit used to disperse the signal, may be a reflective material or a transmitter that

amplifies and retransmits the signal. Normally the speed is limited to 1Mbps. The transmission frequency is normally 100GHz-1,000THz with transmission distance in 10's of meters. Installation is easy and cost is relatively inexpensive for wireless.

Terms

- AMPS - Advanced Mobile Phone Service is analog cellular phone service.
- CDMA - Code division multiple access allows transmission of voice and data over a shared part of radio frequencies. This is also called spread spectrum.
- CDPD - Cellular Digital Packet Data will allow network connections for mobile users using satellites.
- Cellular - An 800 MHz band for mobile phone service.
- D-AMPS - Digital AMPS using TDMA to divide the channels into three channels.
- FDMA - Frequency Division Multiple Access divides the cellular network into 30 KHz channels.
- GSM - Global System for Mobile Communications.
- HDML - Handheld Device Markup Language is a version of HTML only allowing text to be displayed.
- MDBS - Mobile Data Base Station reviews all cellular channels at cellular sites.
- PCS - Personal communications Service is a 1.9 GHz band.
- TDMA - Time Division Multiple Access uses time division multiplexing to divide each cellular channel into three sub channels to service three users at a time.
- Wireless bridge - Microwave or infrared is used between two line of site points where it is difficult to run wire.
- WML - Wireless markup language is another name for HDML.

Categories of LAN Radio Communications

1. Low power, single frequency – Its features are
   - Distance is in 10s of meters.
   - Speed ranges from 1-10Mbps.
   - Susceptible to interference and eavesdropping.
2. High power, single frequency – Its features are
   - Requires FCC licensing and high power transmitter.
   - Speed ranges from 1-10Mbps.
   - Susceptible to interference and eavesdropping

3. Spread spectrum - It uses several frequencies at the same time. The frequency is normally 902-928MHz with some networks at 2.4GHz. The speed of 902MHz systems is between 2 and 6Mbps. If frequency-hopping is used, the speed is normally lower than 2Mbps. Its two types include:
   (a) Direct sequence modulation - The data is broken into parts and transmitted simultaneously on multiple frequencies. Decoy data may be transmitted for better security. The speed is normally between 2 to 6 Mbps.
   (b) Frequency hopping - The transmitter and receiver change predetermined frequencies at the same time (in a synchronized manner). The speed is normally 1Gbps.

Network WAN Connections

Three options for connecting over a telephone service are:

1. Dial-up connections.
2. Integrated Services Digital Network (ISDN) - A method of sending voice and data information on a digital phone line. Two types of ISDN includes:
   (a) Basic ISDN - Two 64Kbps B-channels with one 16Kbps D channel is provided. The D-channel is used for call control and setup. Basic ISDN can provide 128Kbps speed capability.
   (b) Primary ISDN - 23 B-channels and one D channel is provided.
3. Leased Lines - This involves the leasing of a permanent telephone line between two locations.

Remote Communication Protocols

1. **Serial Line Internet Protocol (SLIP)** – It allows computers to connect to the internet with a modem. No error checking or data compression is supported. Only the TCP/IP protocols are supported.
2. **Point to Point Protocol (PPP)** – It provides error checking and data compression. PPP supports multiple network protocols such IPX/SPX and NetBEUI in addition to TCP/IP. It also supports dynamic allocation of IP addresses.

Remote Access Service

Remote Access Service (RAS) with Windows NT allows users to connect to the network using a modem in order to use network resources. RAS may be called dial up networking (DUN), depending on the version of Windows you are using. The NT RAS server can handle 256 connections. Windows NT RAS servers provide the following security features:

1. User account security
2. Encryption between the DUN (dial up networking) client and the server
3. Callback capability

The client software is called Dial up networking (DUN) in windows NT4 and Windows95. For NT 3.51 and Windows 3.1 it is called a RAS client. These clients may be used to connect to the internet through an internet service provider (ISP).

Ethernet

The IEEE 802.3 standard defines ethernet at the physical and data link layers of the OSI network model. Most ethernet systems use the following:

- Carrier-sense multiple-access with collision detection (CSMA/CD) for controlling access to the network media.
- Baseband broadcasts
- A method for packing data into data packets called frames
- Transmission at 10Mbps, 100Mbps, and 1Gbps.

Ethernet Specifications

- **10BaseT** is the Ethernet specification for unshielded twisted pair cable (category 3, 4, or 5). It transmits signals at 10 Mbps (megabits per second) with a distance limit of 100 meters per segment.
- **10BaseF** is the Ethernet specification for fiber optic cable. It transmits signals at 10 Mbps (megabits per second) with a distance limit of 2000 meters per segment.
- **100BaseT** is the Ethernet specification for unshielded twisted pair cabling that is used to transmit data at 100 Mbps (megabits per second) with a distance limit of 100 meters per segment.

The figure below describes the characteristics of different cable types.

Cable Types Characteristics

IEEE 802.3 Values

	10BaseT	10BaseFL	100BaseT	100BaseFX
Data Rate	10Mbps	10Mbps	100Mbps	100Mbps
Signaling Method	Base Band	Base Band	Base Band	Base Band
Media Type	CAT5 Unshielded Twisted Pair	Fiber Optic	CAT5 Unshielded Twisted Pair	Multi. Method Fiber (2 Strands)
Max Length	100 Meters	2,000 Meters	100 Meters	400 Meters

Types of Ethernet

Before looking at different types of Ethernet, let us take a quick look at the naming conventions followed by IEEE for different Ethernet types. The IEEE naming convention for different types of Ethernet is as follows:

1. The transmission speed in Mbps
2. Baseband (base) or Broadband data transmission
3. The maximum distance a network segment could cover in hundreds of meters.

Different types of Ethernet are as follows:

1. **10Base5** uses thick net coaxial cable which requires a transceiver with a vampire tap to connect each computer. There is a drop cable from the transceiver to the Attachment Unit Interface (AIU). The AIU may be a DIX port on the network card. There is a transceiver for each network card on the network. This type of ethernet is subject to the 5-4-3 rule which means that there can be 5 network segments with 4 repeaters, and 3 of the segments can be connected to computers. It uses the bus topology. Maximum segment length is 500 Meters with the maximum overall length at 2500 meters. Minimum length between nodes is 2.5 meters and maximum node per segment is 100.
2. **10Base2** uses thin net coaxial cable. It uses a BNC connector and bus topology which requires a terminator at each end of the cable. The cable used is RG-58A/U or RG-58C/U with an impedance of 50 ohms. RG-58U is not acceptable. This type of Ethernet is subject to the 5-4-3 rule which means that there can be 5 network segments with 4 repeaters, and 3 of the segments can be connected to computers. The maximum length of one segment is 185 meters. Barrel connectors can be used to link smaller pieces of cable on each segment, but each barrel connector reduces signal quality. The minimum length between nodes is 0.5 meters.
3. **10BaseT** uses Unshielded Twisted Pair (UTP) cable and is based on the star topology. Shielded twisted pair (STP) is not a part of the 10BaseT specification. This type of Ethernet is not subject to the 5-4-3 rule. They can use category 3, 4, or 5 cables, but perform best with category 5 cable. Category 3 is the minimum. It requires only 2 pairs of wire and cables in ceilings and walls must be plenum rated. The maximum segment length is 100 meters and minimum length between nodes is 2.5 meters. The maximum number of connected segments is 1024 and maximum number of nodes per segment is 1 (star topology). 10baseT uses RJ-45 connectors.
4. **10BaseF** uses Fiber Optic cable and can have up to 1024 network nodes. The maximum segment length is 2000 meters. It uses specialized connectors for the fiber optic. The three categories of 10BaseF includes:

(a) 10BaseFL – It is used to link computers in a LAN environment, which is not commonly done due to high cost.

(b) 10BaseFP – It is used to link computers with passive hubs to get cable distances up to 500 meters.

(c) 10BaseFB – It is used as a backbone between hubs.

5. **100BaseT** is also known as fast Ethernet and uses RJ-45 connectors and the star topology. 100BaseT uses CSMA/CD media access. The minimum length between nodes is 2.5 meters and the maximum number of connected segments is 1024. The maximum number of nodes per segment is 1 (star topology). Its IEEE802.3 specification includes:

   (a) 100BaseTX – It requires category 5 cable with two pair and the maximum distance is 100 meters.

   (b) 100BaseT4 – It requires category 3 cable with 4 pair and the maximum distance is 100 meters.

   (c) 100BaseFX – It can use fiber optic to transmit up to 2000 meters and requires two strands of fiber optic cable.

6. **100VG -AnyLAN** – This type of Ethernet requires category 3 cable with 4 pair. The maximum distance is 100 meters with cat 3 or 4 cable and can reach 150 meters with cat 5 cables. It can also use fiber optic to transmit up to 2000 meters. This ethernet type supports transmission of Token-Ring network packets in addition to ethernet packets. Its IEEE 802.12 specification includes:

   (a) Demand-priority media access control.

   (b) Star topology.

   (c) Series of interlinked cascading hubs and RJ-45 connectors.

Types of Ethernet frames Mentioned below are the different types of Ethernet frames.

- **Ethernet 802.2** - These frames contain fields similar to the ethernet 802.3 frames with the addition of three Logical Link Control (LLC) fields. Novell NetWare 4.x networks use such frames.
- **Ethernet 802.3** - It is mainly used in Novell NetWare 2.x and 3.x networks. The frame type was developed prior to completion of the IEEE 802.3 specification and thus may not work in all ethernet environments.
- **Ethernet II** - This frame type combines the 802.3 preamble and SFD fields and includes a protocol type field where the 802.3 frame contains a length field. TCP/IP networks and networks that use multiple protocols normally use such type of frames.

- **Ethernet SNAP** - This frame type builds on the 802.2 frame type by adding a type field indicating what network protocol is being used to send data. This frame type is mainly used in AppleTalk networks.
- The packet size of all the above frame types is between 64 and 1,518 bytes.

Network Routing

Simple Networking Routing and Routers

Each network interface card (NIC) has a specific address which is an IP address or number. When data is sent between two computers, the data must be sent in a package that has the address of the intended receiver (IP) on it. It is like an envelope (ethernet) with the sender's and recipient's address on it. There is somewhat of a difference, however. When the computer intends to send a packet, it first checks its routing table to see if the intended data must be sent through a gateway. Many computers only have a simple routing table, which is built from the network mask and the gateway information entered, when you set up your computer to do networking. The computer, when set up for networking, must be assigned an IP address, netmask, and default gateway. This may be done manually or done automatically using Dynamic Host Configuration Protocol (DHCP) to assign this information to the computer when it boots. DCHP is described in another section. If the computer determines that the packet must be sent to a gateway, it puts it in a special packet (ethernet) for that gateway, with the actual recipient's address wrapped inside.

The data packets are equated to a letter with an envelope. For this type of thinking, the envelope would be similar to the ethernet, SLIP, or PPP packet which encapsulates the IP packet. The IP packet and its encapsulated data would be similar to a letter. Here's generally what happens when a package is sent:

The sending computer checks the IP part of the package to see the sender's IP address, and based on the address and instructions in its routing table will do one of the following:

1. Send the packet to the ethernet address of the intended recipient. The following will happen:
   (a) The ethernet card on the receiving computer will accept the packet.
   (b) The other network levels (IP, TCP) will open the packet and use it according to filtering and other programming instructions.
2. Send the packet to the ethernet address of a router, depending on the instructions in the routing table. The following will happen:
   (a) The ethernet card on the router will accept the packet.

(b) The IP level of the router will look at the packet's IP address and determine according to its routing table where to send the packet next. It should send it to another router or to the actual recipient.

(c) The router will encapsulate the IP packet in another ethernet packet with the ethernet address of the next router or the intended recipient.

(d) Router hops will continue until the packet is sent on a network where the intended recipient is physically located unless the packet expires.

(e) The ethernet card on the receiving computer will accept the packet.

(f) The other network levels (IP, TCP) will open the packet and use it according to filtering and other programming instructions.

Let's say that you enter an IP address of 10.1.20.15 and a netmask of 255.255.0.0. This means that you are on the network 10.1.0.0. The machine's IP address and net mask, together define the network that its NIC is on. Therefore any machine that fits in the address range provided under 10.1.x.x can be accessed directly from your NIC, and machines that are not in this number range, such as 10.3.34.27 cannot be accessed directly and must be sent to a gateway machine since it is on another network. Typically most machines will use their netmask to make this determination which means if the address does not match their known network, the package will be sent to that machine's default gateway in a special package meant for a router. It works similar to a post office. When you send a letter in your town, you put it in the local slot. It can be delivered to someone else in your town (network), but if you are sending to another town (network), you put the letter in the out of town slot (default gateway), then the mail personnel puts it in a special container or box and send it to a main town (gateway), which then decides where to send it based on its address. Although this simple network and default gateway may be common, specific computers or gateways can have much more complex rules for routing that allow exceptions to this example.

Please be aware that in order to be forwarded, data packets must be addressed to a router. They cannot just be sent out to the recipient's address to a network. The router does not pick packets off the network and forward them. If a packet is sent on a network and a valid recipient is not on that network, there will be no response.

To keep routing simple, most networks are structured as shown below. Generally, the higher networks are 10.x.x.x, and then the next are 10.0-254.x.x, then 10.0-254.0-254.x. The number 10 is used as an example of Class A network. This numbering scheme keeps routing simple and is the least confusing, but networks can be set up in other ways as well. In the diagram below, only gateways and their networks are shown.

Typical Network Structured Addressing Scheme

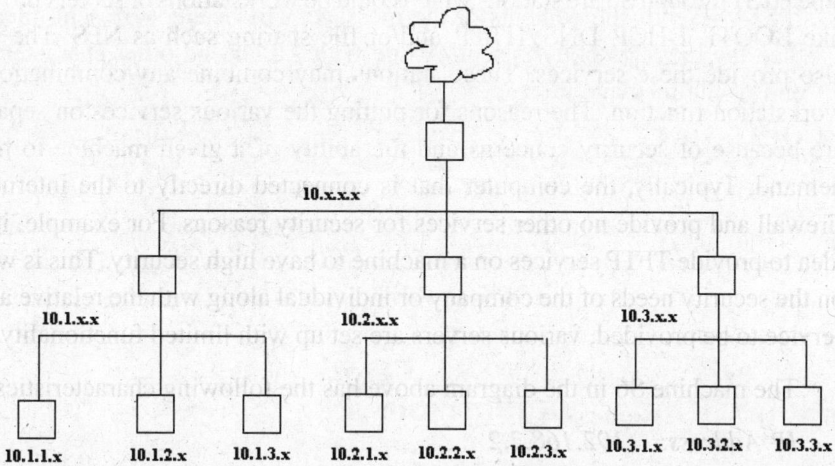

In the simple network example below, I vary from convention and make network 192.168.2.x be below network 192.168.1.x. causing traffic between the internet and 192.168.2.x to go through the network 192.168.1.x. Normally the network 192.168.1.x would be 192.168.x.x, but this will show you that there can be many variants that will work as long as you have thought your layout through well, and set your routing tables up in your gateways correctly.

A Small Network with Two Gateways

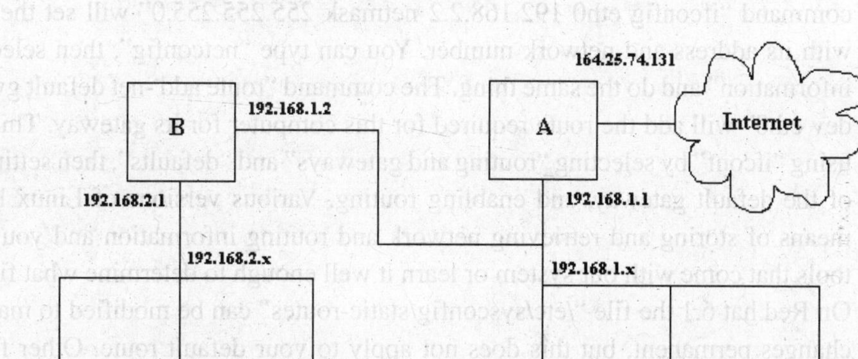

The boxes labeled as A and B must be gateways or routers in order for anyone on networks 192.168.2.x or 192.168.1.x to talk to any other network or internet. The boxes labeled S1 through S6 are stations which could be workstations or servers providing services like BOOTP, DHCP, DNS, HTTP, and/or file sharing such as NFS. The gateways may also provide these services. These stations may combine any combination of server or workstation function. The reasons for putting the various services on separate machines are because of security concerns and the ability of a given machine to handle specific demand. Typically, the computer that is connected directly to the internet would be a firewall and provide no other services for security reasons. For example, it is not a good idea to provide TFTP services on a machine to have high security. This is why, depending on the security needs of the company or individual along with the relative amount of each service to be provided, various servers are set up with limited functionality.

The machine S6 in the diagram above has the following characteristics:

IP Address: *192.168.2.2*

Network: *192.168.2.0*

Netmask: *255.255.255.0*

Gateway: *192.168.2.1*

In Linux, the "ifconfig" command is used to configure the NIC and the command "route" is used to set up routing tables for that machine. Please note that in Red hat Linux, the GUI interface programs "netconf" and "linuxconf" may also be used to set this. These GUI interface programs will set these changes to be permanent by writing them to files that are used to configure network information. Changes made with "route" without adding the changes to permanent files will no longer be valid when you reboot the machine. The command "ifconfig eth0 192.168.2.2 netmask 255.255.255.0" will set the NIC card up with its address and network number. You can type "netconfig", then select "basic host information" and do the same thing. The command "route add -net default gw 192.168.2.1 dev eth0" will add the route required for this computer for its gateway. This can be done using "ifconf" by selecting "routing and gateways" and "defaults", then setting the address of the default gateway, and enabling routing. Various versions of Linux have different means of storing and retrieving network and routing information and you must use the tools that come with our system or learn it well enough to determine what files to modify. On Red hat 6.1 the file "/etc/sysconfig/static-routes" can be modified to make your route changes permanent, but this does not apply to your default route. Other files are "/etc/sysconfig/routed" and "/etc/sysconfig/network". Other files include "/etc/gateways", "/etc/networks", "/proc/net/route", "/proc/net/rt_cache", and "/proc/net/ipv6_route". The file "/etc/sysconfig/network-scripts" is a script file that controls the network setup when the system is booted. If you type "route" for this machine, the routing table below will be displayed:

Destination	Gateway	Genmask	Flags	Metric	Ref	Use	Iface
192.168.2.2	*	255.255.255.255	UH	0	0	0	eth0
192.168.2.0	*	255.255.255.0	U	0	0	0	eth0
127.0.0.0	*	255.0.0.0	U	0	0	0	lo
Default	192.168.2.1	0.0.0.0	UG	0	0	0	eth0

Here is a simple explanation of routing tables and their purpose. All computers that are networked have a routing table in one form or another. A routing table is a simple set of rules that tell what will be done with network packets. In programming language it is easiest to think of it as a set of instructions, very similar to a case statement which has a "default" at its end. It can also be thought of as a series of if..then..elseif..then..else statements. If the lines above are labeled A through C and a default (the last line), an appropriate case statement would be: (Don't count the header line)

```
switch(address){
    case A: send to me;
            break;
    case B: send to my network;
            break;
    case C: send to my local interface;
            break;
    default: send to gateway 192.168.2.1
```

An appropriate if statement would be:

```
if (address=me)
    then send to me;
elseif (address=my network)
    then send to my network;
elseif (address=my local)
    then send to my local interface;
else send to my gateway 192.168.2.1;
```

In everyday terms this is similar to a basic decision process. Imagine you are holding a letter. If it is addressed to you, you keep it, if it is addressed to someone in your town, you drop it in the local slot at the post office, but if it is addressed to someone out of town, you would drop it in the out of town slot.

Note how the routing table is arranged. It is arranged from the most specific to the least specific. Therefore as you go down the table, more possibilities are covered. You will notice the first Genmask is 255.255.255.255 and the last is 0.0.0.0. There can be no doubt that the last line is the default. The genmasks between the start and the end have a decreasing number of least significant bits set.

So the Iface specifies the card where packets for this route will be sent. The address of eth0 is 192.168.2.2. The NIC card addresses could have easily been switched. Line 1 (above) provides for the eth0 address. The last line is the default line which specifies that any packet will be sent to the gateway 192.168.2.1. This is how the internet access can be attained, though IP masquerading will probably be used.

The flags above mean the following:

- U - Route is up
- H - Target is a host
- G - Use gateway

There are other flags, you can look up by typing "man route". Also the metric value above, indicating the distance to the target, is not used by current Linux kernels but may be needed by some routing daemons. If route knows the name of the gateway machine, it may list its name rather than the IP address. The same is true for defined networks. Networks may be defined in the file "/etc/networks".

FIREWALLS

Firewalls are mainly used as a means to protect an organization's internal network from those on the outside (internet). It is used to keep outsiders from gaining information to secrets or from doing damage to internal computer systems of the organization. Firewalls are also used to limit the access of individuals on the internal network to services on the internet along with keeping track of what is done, through the firewall.

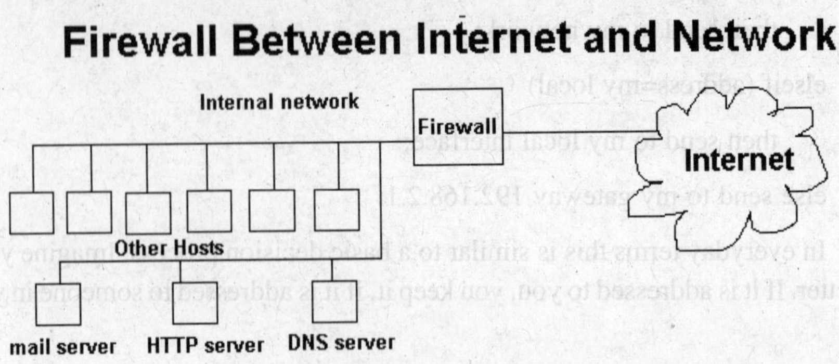

Types of Firewalls Different types of firewalls include the following:

1. **Packet Filtering** - In a packet filtering firewall, data is forwarded based on a set of firewall rules. This firewall works at the network level. Packets are filtered by type, source address, destination address, and port information. These rules are similar to the routing rules explained in the earlier section and may be thought of as a set of instructions similar to a case statement or if statement. This type of firewall is fast, but cannot allow access to a particular user since there is no way to identify the user except by using the IP address of the user's computer, which may be an unreliable method. Also the user does not need to configure any software to use a packet filtering firewall such as setting a web browser to use a proxy for access to the web. The user may be unaware of the firewall. This means the firewall is transparent to the client.
2. **Circuit Level Relay** - A circuit level relay firewall is also transparent to the client. It listens on a port such as port 80 for http requests and redirects the request to a proxy server running on the machine. Basically, the redirect function is set up using ipchains and then the proxy filters the package at the port that received the redirect. SOCKS is an example of this type of firewall. This type of proxy is not aware of applications but just cross links your connects to another one outside connection. It can log activity, but not as detailed as an application proxy. It only works with TCP connections, and doesn't provide for user authentication.
3. **Application Proxy Gateway** - The users connect to the outside using the proxy. The proxy gets the information and returns it to the user and can record everything that is done. This type of proxy may require a user login to use it. Rules may be set to allow some functions of an application to be done and other functions denied. The "get" function may be allowed in the FTP application, but the "put" function may not.

Proxy Servers can be used to perform the following functions.

1. Control outbound connections and data.
2. Monitor outbound connections and data.
3. Cache requested data which can increase system bandwidth performance and decrease the time it takes for other users to read the same data.

Application proxy servers can perform the following additional functions:

1. Provide for user authentication.
2. Allow and deny application specific functions.
3. Apply stronger authentication mechanisms to some applications.

Domain Name Service

Host Names

Domain Name Service (DNS) is the service used to convert human readable names of hosts to IP addresses. Host names are not case sensitive and can contain alphabetic or numeric letters or the hyphen, though one should avoid using underscore. A fully qualified domain name (FQDN) consists of the host name plus domain name as in the following example: computername.domain.com

The part of the system sending queries is called the resolver and is the client side of the configuration. The nameserver answers the queries. Read RFCs 1034 and 1035. These contain the bulk of the DNS information and are superceded by RFCs 1535-1537. Naming is in RFC 1591. The main function of DNS is the mapping of IP addresses to human readable names.

So the three main components of DNS are

1. resolver
2. name server
3. database of resource records(RRs)

Domain Name System

The Domain Name System (DNS) is basically a large database which resides on various computers and it contains the names and IP addresses of various hosts on the internet and various domains. The Domain Name System is used to provide information to the Domain Name Service when queries are made. The service is the act of querying the database, and the system is the data structure and data itself. The Domain Name System is similar to a file system in Unix or DOS starting with a root. Branches are attached to the root to create a huge set of paths. Each branch in the DNS is called a label. Each label can be 63 characters long, but most are less. Each text word between the dots can be 63 characters in length, with the total domain name (all the labels) limited to 255 bytes in overall length. The domain name system database is divided into sections called **zones**. The name servers in their respective zones are responsible for answering queries for their zones. A zone is a subtree of DNS and is administered separately. There are multiple name servers for a zone. There is usually one primary nameserver and one or more secondary name servers. A name server may be authoritative for more than one zone.

DNS names are assigned through the Internet Registries by the Internet Assigned Number Authority (IANA). The domain name is a name assigned to an internet domain. For example, mycollege.edu represents the domain name of an educational institution. The names tscpl.com and 3Com.com represent the domain names of those commercial companies. Naming hosts within the domain is up to individuals administering their domain.

Access to the Domain name database is through a resolver which may be a program or part of an operating system that resides on users workstations. In Unix the resolver is accessed by using the library functions "gethostbyname" and "gethostbyaddr". The resolver will send requests to the name servers to return information requested by the user. The requesting computer tries to connect to the name server using its IP address rather than the name.

Structure and message format

The drawing below shows a partial DNS hierarchy. At the top is what is called the root and it is the start of all other branches in the DNS tree. It is designated with a period. Each branch moves down from level to level. When referring to DNS addresses, they are referred to from the bottom up to the root designator (period) at the far right. Example: "myhost.mycompany.com.".

DNS is hierarchical in structure. A domain is a subtree of the domain name space. From the root, the assigned top-level domains in the U.S. are:

- GOV - Government body.
- EDU - Educational body.
- INT - International organization
- NET - Networks
- COM - Commercial entity.
- MIL - U. S. Military.
- ORG - Any other organization not previously listed.

Partial DNS Hierarchy

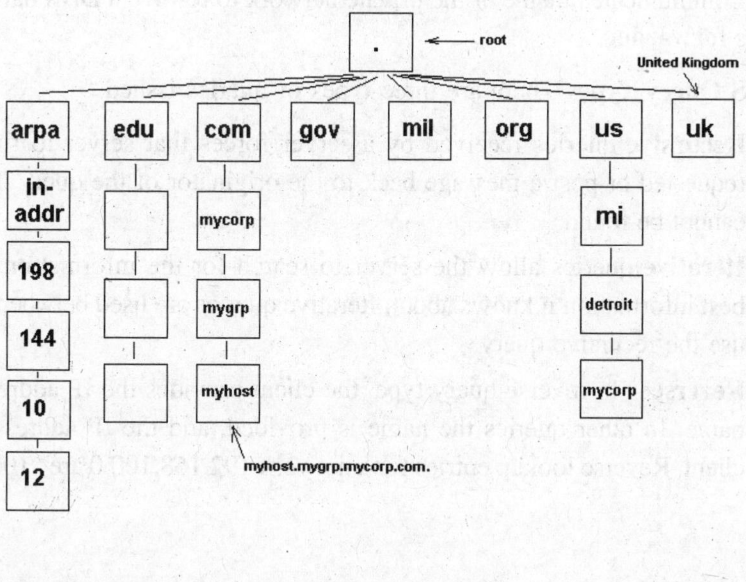

Outside this list are top level domains for various countries. Each node on the domain name system is separated by a ".". Example: "mymachine.mycompany.com.". Note that any name ending in a "." is an absolute domain name since it goes back to root.

Usage and file formats

If a domain name is not found when a query is made, the server may search for the name elsewhere and return the information to the requesting workstation, or return the address of a name server that the workstation can query to get more information. There are special servers on the Internet that provide guidance to all name servers. These are known as root name servers. They do not contain all information about every host on the Internet, but they do provide direction as to where domains are located (the IP address of the name server for the uppermost domain, a server is requesting). The root name server is the starting point to find any domain on the Internet.

Name Server Types There are three types of name servers:

1. **The primary master** builds its database from files that were preconfigured on its hosts, called zone or database files. The name server reads these files and builds a database for the zone it is authoritative for.
2. **Secondary masters** can provide information to resolvers just like the primary masters, but they get their information from the primary. Any updates to the database are provided by the primary.
3. **Caching name server** - It gets all its answers to queries from other name servers and saves (caches) the answers. It is a non-authoritative server.

The caching only name server generates no zone transfer traffic. A DNS Server that can communicate outside of the private network to resolve a DNS name query is referred to as **forwarder**.

DNS Query Types There are three types of queries issued:

1. **Recursive** queries received by a server forces that server to find the information requested or post a message back to the originator of the query that the information cannot be found.
2. **Iterative** queries allow the server to search for the information and pass back the best information it knows about. Iterative queries are used between servers and clients use the recursive query.
3. **Reverse** – In reverse query type, the client provides the IP address and asks for the name. In other queries the name is provided, and the IP address is returned to the client. Reverse lookup entries for a network 192.168.100.0 are "100.168.192.in-addr".

Generally a server-to-server query is iterative and a client-resolver-to-server query is recursive. You should also note that a server can be queried or it can be the person placing a query. Therefore, a server contains both the server and client functions. A server can transmit either type of query. If it is handed a recursive query from a remote source, it must transmit other queries to find the specified name, or send a message back to the originator of the query that the name could not be found.

DNS Transport protocol

DNS resolvers first attempt to use UDP for transport and then use TCP if UDP fails.

The DNS Database A database is made up of records and the DNS is a database. Therefore, common resource record types in the DNS database are:

- A - Host's IP address. Address record allowing a computer name to be translated into an IP address. Each computer must have this record for its IP address to be located. These names are not assigned for clients that have dynamically assigned IP addresses, but are a must for locating servers with static IP addresses.
- PTR - Host's domain name, host identified by its IP address
- CNAME - Host's canonical name allows additional names or aliases to be used to locate a computer.
- MX - Host's or domain's mail exchanger.
- NS - Host's or domain's name server(s).
- SOA - Indicates authority for the domain
- TXT - Generic text record
- SRV - Service location record
- RP - Responsible person
- HINFO - Host information record with CPU type and operating system.

When a resolver requests information from the server, the DNS query message indicates one of the preceding types.

DNS Files

CACHE.DNS - The DNS Cache file - This file is used to resolve internet DNS queries. On Windows systems, it is located in the WINNTROOT\system32\DNS directory and is used to configure a DNS server in order to use a DNS server on the internet to resolve names not in the local domain.

BOOTP

BOOTP (Boot Protocol) may be used to boot remote computers over a network. BOOTP messages are encapsulated inside UDP messages and therefore its requests and replies are forwarded by routers. BOOTP is defined by RFCs 951 and 1542. The figure below illustrates the BOOTP data encapsulation:

BOOTP Data Encapsulation

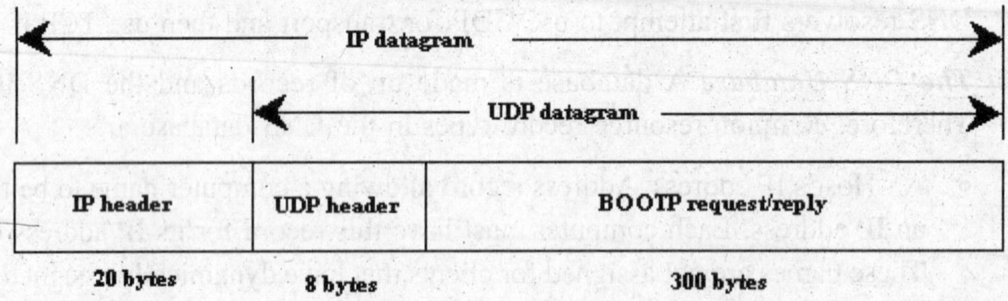

The diskless system reads its unique hardware address from its network interface card and then sends a BOOTP request. The BOOTP server uses port 67 and the BOOTP client uses port 68. The following is a brief explanation of what happens when a remote client boots:

1. **BOOTP request** The client sends a BOOTP request from 0.0.0.0.68 to 255.255.255.255.67 with its ethernet address and number of second's fields filled in.
2. **BOOTP reply** The server responds with the client's IP address, the server's IP address (it's own), and the IP address of a default gateway.
3. **ARP request** The client issues an ARP to tell if the IP address it just received is being used. It uses 0.0.0.0 as it's own address
4. **ARP request** The client waits 0.5 seconds and repeats the same ARP request.
5. **ARP request** The client waits another 0.5 seconds and repeats the ARP request with its own address as the senders address.
6. **BOOTP request** The client waits 0.5 seconds and sends another BOOTP request with its own IP address in the IP header
7. **BOOTP reply** The server sends the same BOOTP reply it sent the last time.
8. **ARP request** The client outputs an ARP request for the server hardware address
9. **ARP reply** The server replies with its own ethernet address.
10. **TFTP read request** The client sends a TFTP read request asking for its specified boot file.

NETWORK BROADCASTING AND MULTICASTING

Network interface cards are usually programmed to listen for three types of messages. They are the messages sent to their specific address, the messages broadcast to all NICs, and the messages that qualify as a multicast for the specific card. There are three types of addressing:

1. **Unicast** - A transmission to a single interface card.
2. **Multicast** - A transmission to a group of interface cards on the network.
3. **Broadcast** - A transmission to all interface cards on the network. RFC 919 and 922 describe IP broadcast datagrams. The two types of broadcast addressing are:
   - Limited Broadcast - Sent to all NICs on the same network segment as the source NIC. It is represented with the 255.255.255.255 TCP/IP address. Since this broadcast is not forwarded by routers it will only appear on one network segment.
   - Direct broadcast - Sent to all hosts on a network. Routers may be configured to forward direct broadcasts on large networks. For network 192.168.0.0, the broadcast is 192.168.255.255.

All other messages are filtered out by the NIC software unless the card is programmed to operate in promiscuous mode to perform network sniffing.

Broadcasting The different types of broadcasting uses on TCP/IP are:

- ARP on IP
- DHCP on IP
- Routing table updates. Broadcasts sent by routers with routing table updates to other routers.

The Ethernet broadcast address in hexadecimal is FF:FF:FF:FF:FF:FF. There are several types of IP broadcasting:

- The IP limited broadcast address is 255.255.255.255. This broadcast is not forwarded by a router.
- A broadcast directed to a network has a form of x.255.255.255 where x is the address of a Class A network. This broadcast may be forwarded depending on the router program.
- A broadcast sent to all subnetworks. If the broadcast is 10.1.255.255 on network 10.1.0.0 and the network is subnetted with multiple networks 10.1.x.0, then the broadcast is a broadcast to all subnetworks.
- A broadcast sent to a subnet in the form 10.1.1.255 is a subnet broadcast if the subnet mask is 255.255.255.0.

Multicasting may be used for streaming multimedia, video conferencing, shared white boards and more as the internet grows. Multicasting is still new to internet and not widely supported by routers. New routing protocols are being developed to enable multicast traffic to be routed. Some of these routing protocols are:

- Hierarchical Distance Vector Multicast Routing Protocol (HDVMRP)
- Multicast Border Gateway
- Protocol Independent Multicast

Since IP is not a reliable network protocol, a new reliable multicast protocol that works at the transport layer and uses IP at the network layer has been developed. It is called Multicast Transport Protocol (MTP)

Ethernet Addressing: The internet assigned numbers authority (IANA) allocates ethernet addresses from 01:00:5E:00:00:00 through 01:00:5E:7F:FF:FF for multicasting. This means there are 23 bits available for the multicast group ID.

IP Addressing: An IP multicast address is in the range 224.0.0.0 through 239.255.255.255. In hexadecimal that is E0.00.00.00 to EF.FF.FF.FF. To be a multicast address, the first three bits of the most significant byte must be set and the fourth bit must be clear. In the IP address, there are 28 bits for multicasting. Therefore there are 5 multicasting bits that cannot be mapped into an ethernet data packet. The 5 bits that are not mapped are the 5 most significant bits.

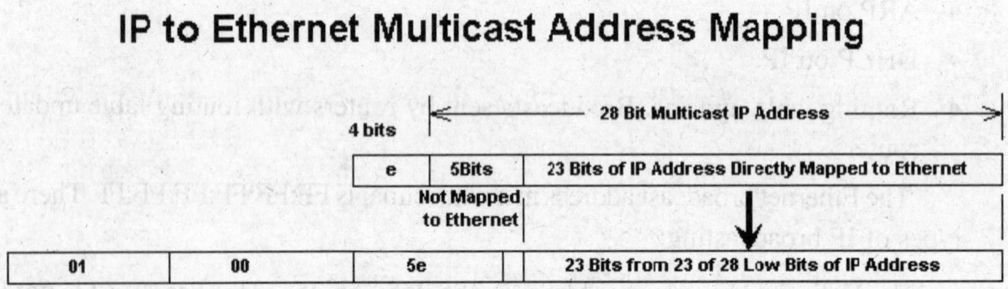

The 28 IP multicast bits are called the multicast group ID. A host group listening to a multicast can span multiple networks. There are some hostgroup addresses assigned by the internet assigned numbers authority (IANA). Some of the assignments are listed below:

- 224.0.0.1 = All systems on the subnet
- 224.0.0.2 = All routers on the subnet
- 224.0.1.1 = Network time protocol (NTP)
- 224.0.0.9 = For RIPv2
- 224.0.1.2 = Silicon graphic's dogfight application

Being on the MBONE means you are on a network that supports multicasting. Usually you must check with your internet service provider (ISP) to see if you have this capability. IGMP described in the next section is used to manage broadcast groups.

Internet Group Management Protocol

Internet Group Management Protocol (IGMP) is the protocol used to support multicasting. To use multicasting, a process on a host must be able to join and leave a group. A process is a user program that is using the network. Group access is identified by the group address and the network interface card (NIC). A host must keep track of the groups that at least one process belongs to and the number of processes that belongs to the group. IGMP is defined in RFC 1112.

IGMP messages are used by multicast routers to track group memberships on each of its networks. It uses these rules:

1. The first time a process on a host joins a multicast group, the host will send an IGMP report. This means that every time the host needs to receive messages from a new group to support its processes, it will send a report.
2. Multicast routers will send IGMP queries regularly to determine whether any hosts are running processes that belong to any groups. The group address of the query is set to 0, the TTL field is set to 1, and the destination IP address is 224.0.0.1 which is the all hosts group address, which addresses all the multicast capable routers and hosts on a network.
3. A host sends one IGMP response for each group that contains one or more processes. The router expects one response from each host for each group that one or more of its processes require access to.
4. A host does not send a report when its last process leaves a group (when the group access is no longer required by a process). The multicast router relies on query responses to update this information.

IGMP is defined in RFC 1112. Hosts and routers use IGMP to support multicasting. Multicast routers must know which hosts belong to what group at any given point of time. The IGMP message is 8 bytes, consisting of:

1. Bits 0 to 3 - IGMP version number
2. Bits 4 to 7 - IGMP type. 1=query sent by a multicast router. 2 is a response sent by a host.
3. Bits 8 to 15 - unused
4. Bits 16 to 31 - Checksum
5. The last 4 bytes - 32 bit group address which is the same as the class D IP address.

IGMP message formats are encapsulated in an IP datagram which contain a time to live (TTL) field. The default is to set the TTL field to 1 which means the datagram will not leave its subnetwork. An application can increase its TTL field in a message to locate a server distance in terms of hops. Addresses from 224.0.0.0 to 224.0.0.255 are not forwarded by multicast routers since these addresses are intended for applications that do not need to communicate with other networks. Therefore these addresses can be used for group multicasting on private networks with no concern for addresses being used for multicasting on other networks.

Dynamic Routing

Dynamic routing performs the same function as static routing except it is more robust. Static routing allows routing tables in specific routers to be set up in a static manner so that the network routes for packets are set. If a router on the route goes down, the destination may become unreachable. Dynamic routing allows routing tables in routers to change as the possible routes change. There are several protocols used to support dynamic routing including RIP and OSPF.

Routing cost Counting route cost is based on one of the following calculations:

- Hop count - How many routers the message must go through to reach the recipient.
- Tic count - The time to route in 1/18 seconds (ticks).

Dynamic routing protocols do not change how routing is done. They just allow for dynamic altering of routing tables. There are two classifications of protocols:

1. IGP - Interior Gateway Protocol. The name is used to describe the fact that each system on the internet can choose its own routing protocol. RIP and OSPF are interior gateway protocols.
2. EGP - Exterior Gateway Protocol. It is used between routers of different systems. There are two of these, the first having the same name as this protocol description:
    - EGP - Exterior Gateway Protocol
    - BGP - Border Gateway Protocol.

The daemon "routed" uses RIP. The daemon "gated" supports IGP's and EGP's.

Route Discovery Methods

- Distance vector - Periodically sends route table to other routers. It works best on LANs, not WANs.
- Link-state - Routing tables are broadcast at startup and then, only when they change. OSPF uses link-state.

Routing Information Protocol (RIP) The RIP RFC is 1058. The routing daemon adds a routing policy to the system. If there are multiple routes to a destination, it chooses the best one. The RIP message can contain information on up to 25 routes. The RIP message contains the following components:

1. Command
2. Version - Normally 1 but set to 2 for RIP version 2.
3. family - Set to 2 for IP addresses.
4. IP address - 32 bit IP address
5. Metrics - Indicate the number of hops to a given network, the hop count.

RIP periodically broadcasts its routing table to neighboring routers. The RIP message format contains the following commands:

- 1 - request
- 2 - reply
- 3 & 4 - obsolete
- 5 - poll entry
- 6 - Asks for system to send all or part of routing table

When the daemon "routed" starts, it sends out a request to all its interfaces for other router's routing tables. The request is broadcast if the network supports it. For TCP/IP the address family in the message is normally 2, but the initial request has address family set to 0 with the metric set to 16.

Regular routing updates are sent every 30 seconds with all or part of the route table. As each router sends routing tables, routes are determined to each network.

Drawbacks of RIP:

- RIP has no knowledge of subnet addressing
- It takes a long time to stabilize after a router or link failure.
- Uses more broadcasting than OSPF thus requiring more network bandwidth.

RIP Version 2 Defined by RFC 1388, it passes further information in some of the fields that are set to 0 for the RIP protocol. These additional fields include a 32 bit subnet mask and a next hop IP address, a routing domain, and route tag. The routing domain is an identifier of the daemon, the packet belongs to. The route tags support EGPs.

Open Shortest Path First (OSPF) OSPF (RFC 1257) is a link state protocol rather than a distance vector protocol. It tests the status of its link to each of its neighbors and sends the acquired information to them. It stabilizes after a route or link failure faster than a distance vector protocol based system. OSPF uses IP directly, not relying on TCP or UDP. OSPF can:

- Have routes based on IP type of service (part of IP header message) such as FTP or Telnet.
- Support subnets.
- Assign cost to each interface based on reliability, round trip time, etc.
- Distribute traffic evenly over equal cost routes.
- Uses multicasting.

Costs for specific hops can be set by administrators. Adjacent routers swap information instead of broadcasting to all routers.

Border Gateway Protocol (BGP) Described by RFC 1267, 1268, and 1497 it uses TCP as a transport protocol. When two systems are using BGP, they establish a TCP connection, and send each other their BGP routing tables. BGP uses distance vectoring. It detects failures by sending periodic keep-alive messages to its neighbors every 30 seconds. It exchanges information about reachable networks with other BGP systems including the full path of systems that are between them.

Simple Mail Transfer Protocol

Simple Mail Transfer Protocol (SMTP) is used to send mail across the internet. There are four types of programs used in the process of sending and receiving mail. They are:

- MUA - Mail users agent. This is the program a user will use to type e-mail. It usually incorporates an editor for support. The user types the mail and it is passed to the sending MTA.
- MTA - Message transfer agent is used to pass mail from the sending machine to the receiving machine. There is a MTA program running on both the sending and receiving machine. Sendmail is a MTA.
- LDA - Local delivery agent on the receiving machine receives the mail from its MTA. This program is usually procmail.
- Mail notifier - This program notifies the recipient that they have mail. Normally this requires two programs, biff and comsat. Biff allows the administrator or user to turn on comsat service.

The MTA on both machines use the network SMTP (simple mail transfer protocol) to pass mail between them, usually on port 25.

Other components of mail service include:

- Directory services - A list of users on a system. Microsoft provides a Global Address List and a Personal Address Book.
- Post Office - This is where the messages are stored.

Mail Protocols

- **SMTP** - Simple Mail Transport Protocol is used on the internet. It is not a transport layer protocol but an application layer protocol.
- **POP3** - Post Office Protocol version 3 is used by clients to access an internet mail server to get mail. It is not a transport layer protocol.
- **IMAP4** - Internet Mail Access Protocol version 4 is the replacement for POP3.
- **MIME** - Multipurpose Internet Mail Extension is the protocol that defines the way files are attached to SMTP messages.
- **X.400** - International Telecommunication Union standard defines transfer protocols for sending mail between mail servers.
- **MHS** - Message Handling Service by Novell is used for mail on Netware networks.

Directory Services

- Lightweight Directory Access Protocol (LDAP)
- X.500 - This is a recommendation outlining how an organization can share objects and names on a large network. It is hierarchically similar to DNS, defining domains consisting of organizations, divisions, departments, and workgroups. The domains provide information about the users and available resources on that domain. This X.500 system is like a directory. Its recommendation comes from the International Telegraph and Telephone Consultative Committee (CCITT)

Mail API Mail application programming interfaces (APIs) allow e-mail support to be integrated into application programs.

- MAPI - Microsoft's Messaging API which is incorporated throughout Microsoft's office products supports mail at the application level
- VIM - Vendor-Independent Messaging protocol from Lotus is supported by many vendors exclusive of Microsoft.

Three parts of a mail message are:

1. Envelope - Includes recipient and sender addresses using the MAIL and RCPT commands.
2. Headers - Each header has a name followed by a colon and its value. Some headers are From, Date, Reply To, Received, Message ID, To, and Subject.
3. Body - The contents of the message sent in 7 bit ASCII code.

SMTP Commands

- **HELLO** - Sent by client with domain name such as mymachine.mycompany.com.

- **MAIL** - From <myself@mymachine.mycompany.com>
- **RCPT** - To <myfriend@theirmachine.theirorg.org>
- **DATA** - Sends the contents of the message. The headers are sent, then a blank line, then the message body is sent. A line with "." and no other characters indicates the end of the message.
- **QUIT**

The host dept1.mycompany.com may not be directly connected to the internet or network but may be connected periodically using a PPP line. The server mail, mail1, and mail2 are used as mail forwarders to send mail to the host dept1. The one with the lowest number, 5, is normally used for sending the mail, but the others are used when the first one or ones are down.

Simple Network Management Protocol

Simple Network Management Protocol (SNMP) is used as the transport protocol for network management. Network management consists of network management stations communicating with network elements such as hosts, routers, servers, or printers. The **agent** is the software on the network element (host, router, printer) that runs the network management software. Therefore when the word agent is used it is referring to the network element. The agent will store information in a **management information base (MIB)**. Management software will poll the various network devices and get the information stored in them. RFC 1155, 1157, and 1213 define SNMP with RFC 1157 defining the protocol itself. The manager uses UDP port 61 to send requests to the agent and the agent uses UDP port 62 to send replies or messages to the manager. The manager can ask for data from the agent or set variable values in the agent. Agents can reply and report events.

There are three supporting pieces to TCP/IP network management:

1. Management Information BASE (MIB) specifies variables the network elements maintain.
2. A set of common structures and a way to reference the variables in the database.
3. The protocol used to communicate between the manager and the network element agent which is SNMP.

SNMP collects information in two ways:

1. The devices on the network are polled by management stations.
2. Devices send alerts to SNMP management stations. The public community may be added to the alert list so all management stations will receive the alert.

SNMP must be installed on the devices to do this. SNMP terms:

- Baseline - A report outlining the state of the network.

- Trap - An alert that is sent to a management station by agents.
- Agent - A program at devices that can be set to watch for some event and send a trap message to a management station if the event occurs.

The network manager can set the threshold of the monitored event that will trigger the sending of the trap message. SNMP enables counters for monitoring the performance of the network used in conjunction with Performance Monitor.

SNMP Communities An SNMP community is the group that devices and management stations running SNMP belong to. It helps to define where the information is sent. The community name is used to identify the group. A SNMP device or agent may belong to more than one SNMP community. It will not respond to requests from management stations that do not belong to one of its communities. SNMP default communities are:

- Write = private
- Read = public

SNMP Security SNMP should be protected from the internet with a firewall. Beyond the SNMP community structure, there is one trap that adds some security to SNMP.

- Send Authentication Trap - When a device receives an authentication that fails, a trap is sent to a management station.

Other configuration parameters that affect security are:

- Accepted Community Names - Only requests from computers in the list of community names will be accepted.
- Accept SNMP Packets from Any Host - This is checked by default. Setting specific hosts will increase security.
- Only Accept SNMP Packets from These Hosts - Only requests from hosts on the list of IP addresses are accepted. Use IP, or IPX address or host name to identify the host.

Network Drivers

Driver interfaces allow multiple protocol stacks to use one network interface card. The two in use today are listed below. They are not compatible with each other.

Open Driver Interface (ODI) ODI is normally found on NetWare networks and was developed by Novell and Apple. It consists of:

- Multiple Protocol Interface - Provides connectivity from the data link layer to the network layer.
- Link Support Layer - It includes functions for managing protocol stack assignments and coordinating numbers assigned to MLIDs.

- Multiple-Link Interface Driver (MLID) - Passes data between the data link layer and the hardware or the network media. The drivers are protocol-independent.

ODI allows multiple drivers to be used on one card and lets one protocol use multiple cards.

Network Driver Interface Specification (NDIS) NDIS, from Microsoft, is used on Microsoft networks. It allows multiple protocols to be used on a network card and supports the data link layer of the network model.

Transport Driver Interface (TDI) This is a standard for passing messages between the drivers at the data link layer and the protocols working at the network layer such as IP or NetBEUI. It was produced by Microsoft.

Network Operating Systems

Network operating systems (NOS) typically are used to run computers that act as servers. They provide the capabilities required for network operation. Network operating systems are also designed for client computers and provide same functions so the distinction between network operating systems and stand alone operating systems is not always obvious. Its installed components include client functionality and server functionality. The functions provided by NOS are: Account Administration for users, Security and File and print sharing. The network services include File Sharing, Print sharing, User administration and Backing up data. Network operating systems provide the following functions:

- File and print sharing.
- Account administration for users.
- Security.

Universal Naming Convention (UNC) A universal naming convention (UNC) is used to allow the use of shared resources without mapping a drive to them. The UNC specifies a path name and has the form: \\servername\pathname

Network Applications

There are three categories of applications with regard to networks:

1. Stand alone applications - Includes editors
2. Network versions of stand alone applications - May be licensed for multiple users.
3. Applications only for a network that includes databases, mail, group scheduling, groupware.

Models for network applications

1. Client-server - Processing is split between the client who interacts with the user and the server performing back end processing.

2. Shared file systems - The server is used for file storage and the processing of the file is done on the client computer.
3. Applications that are centralized - Telnet session. The data and the program run on the central computer and the user uses an interface such as the Telnet client or X server to send commands to the central computer and to see the results.

E-mail Systems

- Novell GroupWise - Also called Windows Messaging
- Microsoft Mail
- Microsoft Exchange - This is for the Microsoft Exchange Server. There is a Microsoft Exchange client for the Microsoft Exchange server and a client for an internet mail account only.
- Lotus Notes
- cc:Mail - From Lotus and IBM

There are several types of programs used in the process of sending and receiving mail. They are:

- MUA - Mail users agent. This is the program a user will use to type e-mail. It usually incorporates an editor for support. The user types the mail and it is passed to the sending MTA. This may also be called the user agent (UA).
- MTA - Message transfer agent is used to pass mail from the sending machine to the receiving machine. There is a MTA program running on both the sending and receiving machine. Sendmail is a MTA.
- MS - Message Store is a storage area for messages that can't be delivered immediately when the recipient is off-line.
- AU - Access Unit provides access to resources like fax, telex, and teletex.
- LDA - Local delivery agent on the receiving machine receives the mail from its MTA. This program is usually procmail.
- Mail notifier - This program notifies the recipient that they have mail. Normally this requires two programs, biff and comsat. Biff allows the administrator or user to turn on comsat service.

Message Handling Service (MHS)

- MHS and Global MHS by Novell
- MHS by OSI - It is called MOTIS (message-oriented text interchange system).

Scheduling systems

- Microsoft Schedule+
- Lotus Organizer

Groupware are used for various electronic communications to enable a group to work together better. Its functions may include group discussion, submission of reports and time sheets electronically, an online helpdesk database, forms design and access, and creating a document as a group such as configuration management.

Database Management Systems (DBMS) They are used to share data on a network. DBMS standards for distributed databases are:

- SQL - Structured Query Language is a database access language. It is used by most client/server database applications.
- ODBC - Open Database Connectivity (ODBC) from Microsoft lets application developers integrate database connections in applications. It is an application programming interface (API). ODBC drivers convert an application's query into SQL and send it to the database engine program.
- DRDA - Distributed Relational Database Architecture is from IBM.

When information is processed in a distributed database, it is called a transaction. The two phases of a transaction are:

1. Write or Update - The data is temporarily updated. An abort can cancel what this phase did by removing the changed data from a temporary storage area.
2. Commit - The changed data is made permanent in the database.

Databases store multiple copies of the data which is called replication. They must be sure that the various copies of the database on various servers is accurate with identical data. Data is also partitioned into smaller blocks of data.

Wide Area Networks

Wide Area Networks (WAN) refers to the technologies used to connect offices at remote locations. The size of a network is limited due to size and distance constraints. However networks may be connected over a high speed communications link (called a WAN link) in order to link them together and thus become a WAN. WAN links are usually:

1. Dial up connection
2. Dedicated connection - It is a permanent full time connection. When a dedicated connection is used, the cable is leased rather than a part of the cable bandwidth and the user has exclusive use.
3. Switched network - Several users share the same line or the bandwidth of the line.

There are two types of switched networks:

- Circuit switching - This is a temporary connection between two points such as dial-up or ISDN.
- Packet switching - This is a connection between multiple points. It breaks data down into small packets to be sent across the network. A virtual circuit can improve performance by establishing a set path for data transmission. This will shave some overhead of a packet switching network. A variant of packet switching is called cell-switching where the data is broken into small cells with a fixed length.

WAN Connection Technologies

1. **X.25** - This is a set of protocols developed by the CCITT/ITU which specifies how to connect computer devices over an internetwork. These protocols use a great deal of error checking for use over unreliable telephone lines. Their speed is about 64Kbps. Normally, X.25 is used on packed switching PDNs (Public Data Networks). A line must be leased from the LAN to a PDN to connect to an X.25 network. A PAD (packet assembler/disassembler) or an X.25 interface is used on a computer to connect to the X.25 network. CCITT is an abbreviation for International Telegraph and Telephone Consultative Committee. The ITU is the International Telecommunication Union.
2. **Frame Relay** - Error checking is handled by devices at both sides of the connection. Frame relay uses frames of varying length and it operates at the data link layer of the OSI model. A permanent virtual circuit (PVC) is established between two points on the network. Frame relay speed is between 56Kbps and 1.544Mbps. Frame relay networks provide a high-speed connection up to 1.544Mbps using variable-length packet-switching over digital fiber-optic media.
3. **Switched Multi-megabit Data Service (SMDS)** - Uses fixed length cell switching and runs at speeds of 1.533 to 45Mbps. It provides no error checking and assumes devices at both ends provide error checking.
4. **Telephone connections**

   (a) Dial up

   (b) Leased lines - These are dedicated analog lines or digital lines. Dedicated digital lines are called digital data service (DDS) lines. A modem is used to connect to analog lines, and a Channel Service Unit/Data Service Unit or Digital Service Unit(CSU/DSU) is used to connect to digital lines. The DSU connects to the LAN and the CSU connects to the line.

   (c) T Carrier lines - Multiplexors are used to allow several channels on one line. The T1 line is basic T Carrier service. The available channels may be used separately for data or voice transmissions or they may be combined for more transmission bandwidth. The 64Kbps data transmission rate is referred to as DS-0 (Digital Signal level 0) and a full T1 line is referred to as DS-1.

Signal	System	Total Kbps	Channels	Number of equivalent T1 lines
DS-1	T1	1544	24	1
DS-2	T2	6312	96	4
DS-3	T3	44736	672	28
DS-4	T4	274760	4032	3668

(d) T1 and T3 lines are the most common lines in use today. T1 and T2 lines can use standard copper wire. T3 and T4 lines require fiber-optic cable or other high-speed media. These lines may be leased partially called fractional T1 or fractional T3 which means a customer can lease a certain number of channels on the line. A CSU/DSU and a bridge or router is required to connect to a T1 line.

(e) Integrated Services Digital Network (ISDN) - Comes in two types and converts analog signals to digital for transmission.

- Basic Rate ISDN (BRI) - Two 64Kbps B-channels with one 16Kbps D channel. The D-channel is used for call control and setup.
- Primary Rate ISDN (PRI) - 23 B-channels and one D channel.

A device resembling a modem (called an ISDN modem) is used to connect to ISDN. The comput er and telephone line are plugged into it.

(f) Switched-56 - A switched line similar to a leased line where customers pay for the time they use the line.

5. **Asynchronous Transfer Mode (ATM)** - May be used over a variety of media with both baseband and broadband systems. It uses fixed length data packets of 53 bytes called cell switching. 5 bytes contain header information. It uses hardware devices to perform the switching of the data. Speeds of up to 622 Mbps can be achieved. Error checking is done at the receiving device, not by ATM. A permanent virtual connection is established (PVC).

6. **Synchronous Optical Network (SONET)** - A physical layer standard that defines voice, data, and video delivery methods over fiber optic media. It defines data rates in terms of optical carrier (OC) levels. The transmission rate of OC-1 is 51.8 Mbps. Each level runs at a multiple of the first. The OC-5 data rate is 5 times 51.8 Mbps which is 259 Mbps. SONET also defines synchronous transport signals (STS) for copper media which use the same speed scale of OC levels. STS-3 runs at the same speed of OC-3. Mesh or ring topology is used to support SONET. SONET uses multiplexing. The ITU has incorporated SONET into their Synchronous Digital Hierarchy (SDH) recommendations.

5 Microsoft Windows

INTRODUCTION TO WINDOWS

Until a couple of years ago, Windows predecessor MS DOS (Microsoft Disk Operating System) used to rule the roost. Because of its numerous drawbacks (as discussed in the previous chapter), a new class of system software emerged. Windows, which was a product of this class, was based on a radically different approach called Graphical User Interface (GUI). With a Graphical User Interface, the various commands and options are represented on the screen in the form of small images called Icons. The user is not expected to remember or type any command, all he is required to do is to click on the appropriate picture (icon) with the help of a small hand-held device called a mouse. Since using a mouse is considerably easier than using a keyboard- and clicking on an icon is much easier than having to type out commands through a keyboard—GUI-based interfaces are much more user friendly. And since GUI based interfaces work on WYSIWYG (What You See Is What You Get) technology, the work of the user is made that much more easy.

With Windows, Microsoft has successfully addressed all the limitations of MS DOS in addition to new user-friendly features. Incidentally, Windows is so called because it allows users to work on several Windows at the same time. There are many operating systems in the market, but MS Windows (with its various versions like Windows 3.1, Windows 3.11, Windows 95, Windows 98, Windows NT, Windows 2000, Windows XP etc.) are the most widely used and have a phenomenal and near monopolistic market share.

Overview of Different Versions of Windows

Windows 1.0: Microsoft released the first version of Windows way back in 1985. It marked a major breakthrough in as much as it allowed users to switch from character based (CUI)/non-graphical MS DOS to the GUI based operating system. The product included a set of desktop applications, including the MS-DOS file management program, and value additions such as a calendar, card file, notepad, calculator, clock, and telecommunications programs. It allowed users to work with multiple applications at the same time (multitasking).

Windows 2.0: Microsoft released its second version of Windows in 1987. It allowed users to overlap windows, control screen layout, and use various keyboard combinations (shortcut keys or keyboard shortcuts) to move rapidly through Windows operations. It included support for inter-application communication using Dynamic Data Exchange (DDE). DDE is the basic foundation for inter-process communication between applications.

Windows 3.0: Microsoft released this version of Windows in 1990. Some of its main features were:

- 32 bit operating system with support for advanced graphics.
- Inclusion of Program Manager, File Manager, and Print Manager.
- A completely rewritten application development environment with new capabilities and native support for applications running in extended memory, and fully pre-emptive MS-DOS multitasking. (In pre-emptive multitasking, once a task is assigned to CPU, it can be taken away from the CPU during its execution. This would ensure optimum utilisation of CPU resources.)
- Inclusion of Windows software development kit (SDK), which helped software developers focus more on writing applications and less on writing device drivers.
- An improved set of Windows icons.

Windows 3.1/3.11: Microsoft released this version of Windows in 1993. It provided several additional utilities like sending a fax (Microsoft Fax), hooking up computers in a network (network), linking up to an outside information service (terminal) etc.

Windows NT 3.1: Microsoft released this version of Windows on July 27, 1993. This OS marked an important milestone for microsoft. Some of its main features were:

- it was the first Windows operating system to combine support for high-end client/server business applications.
- it included new features for security, operating system power, performance, desktop scalability, and reliability.
- it included support for multiprocessor (more than one CPU) architecture.
- Windows NT was geared towards business users and had a rich Application Programming Interface (API), which made it easier to run high-end engineering and scientific applications.

Windows 95: Microsoft released this version of Windows in 1995. Some of its main features were:

- true 32 bit operating system with built in Internet-support.
- facilitated easy installation of hardware peripherals and software applications through plug and play capabilities.

- enhanced multimedia capabilities, more powerful features for mobile computing, and integrated networking.

Windows NT 4.0: Microsoft released this version of Windows in 1996. It was an upgrade to Microsoft's business desktop operating system with increased ease of use and simplified management. It used the Windows 95 interface and included improved networking support, easy access to the Internet and corporate intranets.

Windows 98: Microsoft released this version of Windows in 1998. It is often described as an operating system that "Works Better, Plays Better". Some of its main features were:

- New features were added to enable easy access to Internet related information.
- Multiple display support – allowed using several Visual Display Units (VDU) simultaneously to increase the capacity of the desktop and to allow running of different programs on separate monitors.
- USB Support – the Universal Serial Bus made a computer easier to use, with advanced plug-and-play capabilities. It allowed adding devices to your computer without having to restart each time a device is added to the computer.
- Accessibility wizard – made it easier for people with disabilities to operate a computer without installing any special software.
- Help – an extensive and easy-to-use self-help system was provided.

Windows Millennium Edition (ME): Microsoft released this version of Windows in 2000. It was the last Microsoft operating system to be based on the Windows 95 technology. Windows ME offered consumers numerous music, video, and home networking enhancements and reliability improvements.

Windows 2000 professional: Microsoft released this version of Windows in 2000. It was an upgrade to Windows NT 4.0. It was designed with the aim to replace Windows 95, Windows 98, and Windows NT 4.0 on all business desktops and laptops. It added major improvements in reliability, ease of use, Internet compatibility, and support for mobile computing. It made hardware installation much easier by adding support for a wide variety of new Plug and Play hardware, including advanced networking and wireless products, USB devices and infrared devices.

Windows XP: Microsoft released this version of Windows in 2001. It was a major breakthrough for desktop operating systems. Two main versions of Windows XP were released, viz., Windows XP Home Edition and Windows XP Professional Edition.

Windows XP home edition: Windows XP Home Edition offers a clean, simplified visual design that makes frequently accessed features more accessible. The product offers many enhancements aimed at home users such as the Network Setup Wizard, Microsoft Windows Media Player (allowed users to easily find, organise, and play digital media), Windows Movie Maker (provided users with the tools to digitally edit, save, and share home videos), and enhanced digital photo capabilities.

Windows XP Professional

- Benefits from the long track record of Microsoft Windows NT technology: superior operating system performance including preemptive multitasking, fault tolerance, and system memory protection.
- A redesigned interface that includes features for business and advanced home computing. It included support for Remote Desktop, file, system restore and advanced networking features (Wireless Networking Support). System Restore is a very useful feature that allows users to roll back their PC software configuration to a date or time before a problem occurred.

Basic Elements of Windows

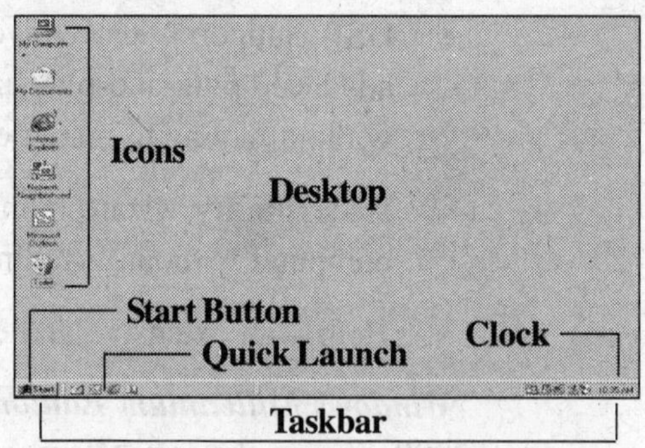

Figure 5.1 *An overview of Windows Desktop showing its major elements*

Once Windows is loaded into the memory of the computer, the focus is placed on the desktop. The desktop is designed to act just like an actual desktop. The desktop is a window that covers your entire computer screen. It is the interface through which all of the programs are accessed. All other programs run on the top of the Windows desktop. A typical Windows 98 desktop contains a series of labeled pictures referred to as 'Icons'. These icons represent the applications loaded onto your computer and clicking on the icon launches the associated application. The desktop can contain icons, files and folders. Desktop can be customised according to the users requirements by adding or deleting icons, inserting background picture or by changing color schemes. Therefore, the number of icons displayed on the desktop could vary from computer to computer, depending on users' choices.

Key Elements of the Windows Desktop

While there may be more or less options enabled on a particular display, we would discuss the basic elements. The Windows desktop is comprised of three key elements:

1. Icons
2. Start Menu
3. Taskbar

Icons Icons can be further classified into five categories:

i. ***Folder Icons:*** When a folder icon is double clicked, a folder window is opened displaying the contents of the folder (folders are explained later in this section).

ii. ***Program Icons:*** When a Program icon is double clicked, the corresponding program is loaded into the memory of the computer and the application starts running in a Window.

iii. ***Document Icons:*** When a document icon is double clicked, the document itself is opened. Windows starts the application (Word processing program, spreadsheet, database, or whatever) in which the document was created, and then opens the document (data file) itself.

iv. ***Shortcut Icons:*** Shortcut icons provide an alternate way to open programs, documents, and folders. Shortcut icons are indicated by a little curved arrow in a box in the lower left hand corner of the icon and their labels generally begin with "Shortcut to." Deleting a shortcut icon does not delete the program or file; only the shortcut that leads to it is deleted.

v. ***System Icons:*** System icons are mandatory programs or files that are located on your desktop. User is not allowed to delete the system icon, since deleting the system icon would mean deleting the actual program from the hard drive of the computer. Examples of System Icons are Recycle Bin, MyComputer, Network Neighborhood etc.

a. *Recycle Bin:* Any file that is deleted from the hard disk of the computer is moved to a separate folder called Recycle Bin. The files stored in the bin can be restored to their original location by using the 'Restore' option of Recycle Bin. 'Restore' option can be accessed by right clicking on Recycle Bin icon. This feature is useful if any of the files/folders/ shortcuts are accidentally deleted. The file remains in the Recycle Bin, until the bin is emptied explicitly. To empty the Recycle Bin, simply right click on this icon and select 'Empty Recycle Bin' option. To permanently delete files from the

hard disk without moving them to the bin, use a combination of the shift and del keys while deleting the files (deletion of files explained later in this section.) Any files that are deleted from a floppy are not stored in the Recycle Bin.

b. *My Computer:* Double-clicking on the "My Computer" icon will open a window that displays the contents of the computer. All the files and folders available in the computer can be viewed here. It also allows you to display the system and hardware information.

c. *Network Neighborhood:* If your computer is connected to a network, then the "Network Neighborhood" icon will be displayed on the desktop. Double-clicking this icon will open a Window that displays other computers and resources, like printers, connected to the network.

Start Menu Clicking on the Start button gives access to the 'Start Menu'. All the applications and tools available in the computer can be accessed from this menu. The menu choices may vary for different versions of Windows. The standard options are discussed below:

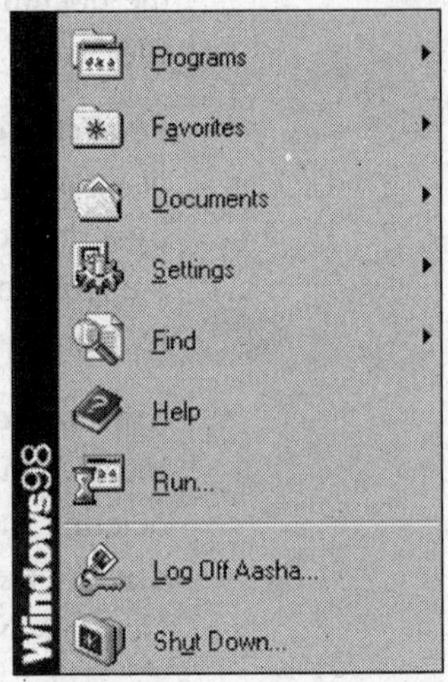

i. ***Programs:*** Opens a series of menus for starting the programs and applications installed on the computer. Programs can be added/deleted from this menu. A link is added to this menu for any new application that is installed on the computer.

ii. ***Favorites:*** Opens the web pages that have been marked as favorites. While surfing the Internet, it is possible to record the addresses of frequently visited websites using 'Favorites' option of the browser.

iii. ***Documents:*** Opens a menu containing the shortcuts to the most recent documents or data files. The list of files displayed in the Documents menu can also be cleared. To delete a file from this menu simply right click on the file name and press the 'Del' key from the keyboard.

iv. ***Settings:*** Opens a menu for customising Windows, the Taskbar, the Start menu and the printers. It gives access to 'Control Panel'. Control Panel contains utilities for customising the Windows interface, adding/removing installed components, changing number, date, time and currency formats, assigning sounds to program events and many more.

v. ***Find:*** Opens a dialogue box that allows users to search for files, folders located anywhere within the computer or within the network. (If the computer is connected to network). Files can be searched by name, location, date, type, content etc.

vi. ***Help:*** Opens the Windows Help topics. An extensive and easy to use Help system with informative screens and tools is provided for navigating and finding the required information. A table of contents displaying all the topics as well as a search facility is provided for quick access to the desired information.

vii. ***Run:*** Opens a dialogue box that allows you to run programs and commands directly by typing in the name of the command/program rather than clicking an icon or shortcut.

viii. ***Shut down:*** Opens a dialogue box that permits you to shut down, restart, or log off/on the computer.

Taskbar The Windows taskbar is the grey bar located at the bottom of the desktop. The taskbar usually stays on the screen all the time. It is comprised of several elements. Start button is also an element of the taskbar. The other elements of Taskbar are Quick Launch Toolbar and System Tray.

Quick Launch may or may not be available in all computers. The Quick Launch allows for immediate access to a variety of elements through a mouse click. On clicking the icon the associated program or Windows tool will be launched. Icons for different programs can be added to the quick launch toolbar.

The System Tray contains icons for applications that are running in the background of the computer. Programs such as anti-virus, task scheduler, etc., may be running in the System Tray. It also includes a clock that displays the current date and time as set by the user.

In addition to these elements, the taskbar also contains buttons for each application that is actively running on the computer. For example, if the user is working on a document in Microsoft Word, then there will be a corresponding button on the taskbar for Microsoft Word.

ANATOMY OF AN APPLICATION WINDOW

Most programs designed to run on Windows look and behave similarly. Application windows, folder windows and files windows have several common features. A brief summary of the common features is discussed below:

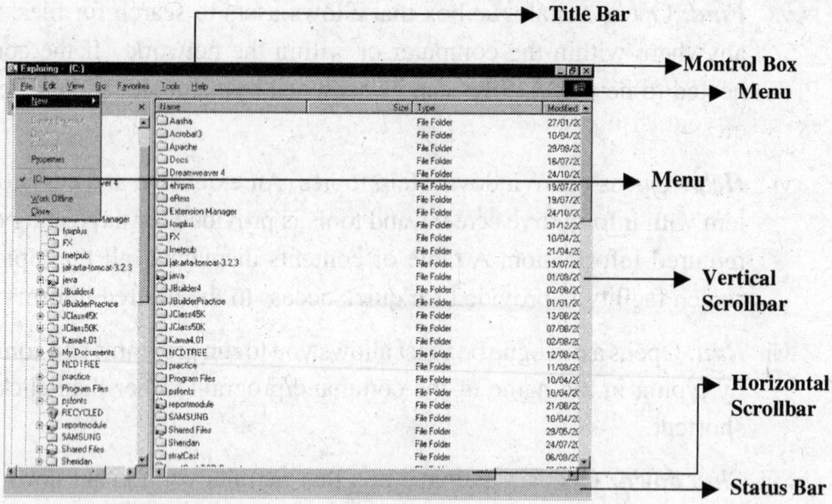

Fig. 5.2 Overview of a Windows Explorer Window

(Windows Explorer explained later in the section)

Title Bar The Windows Title bar is displayed at the top of the window. It usually tells something about the contents of the window. For application programs name of the document along with the program name is displayed in the title bar.

Control Box

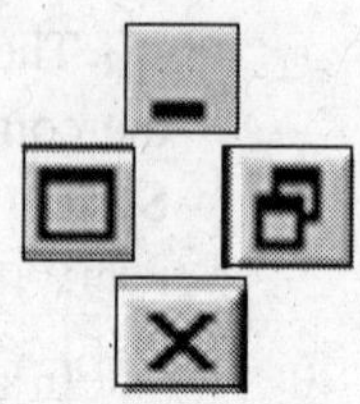

i. ***Minimize window:*** When the minimize button is clicked, the window disappears and is replaced by a button in the Taskbar. Clicking on this button again will restore the Window to its previous size. Minimising a Window does not close an application, it simply removes it from the user's view.

ii. ***Maximize/Restore Window:*** When the maximize button is clicked, the window is expanded to fill the screen. Once a Window is maximized, the restore button replaces this icon. Clicking on the restore button will restore the window to its previous size.

iii. ***Close Window:*** When the close button is clicked, the window/application is closed.

Menu Bar It is located just below the title bar. The menu bar generally comprises a set of words, such as File, Edit, View, and Help, laid out horizontally starting at the left edge of the screen. All Window applications utilise menus in some form or the other. In the

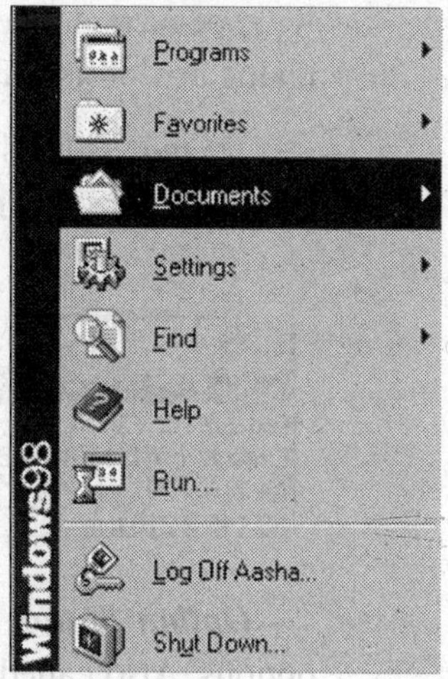

picture shown above (Windows Explorer) 'File', 'Edit', 'View' etc. are referred to as menus and the items within each menu are referred to as menu items. 'New', 'Open', 'Save', 'Exit', etc., form the menu items for the 'File' menu. Menu items can be invoked by clicking on the desired menu item. Menu items within a menu can be navigated using 'Up' and 'Down' arrow keys.

Shortcut keys: If a menu item has a letter in it that is underlined, the item may be selected by holding down the Alt key on the computer and pressing the underlined key whenever the menu is visible. For example, pressing 'Alt' and the 'D' key can open 'Documents' shown in the Screen Shot below. This combination is usually written as 'Alt+D'.

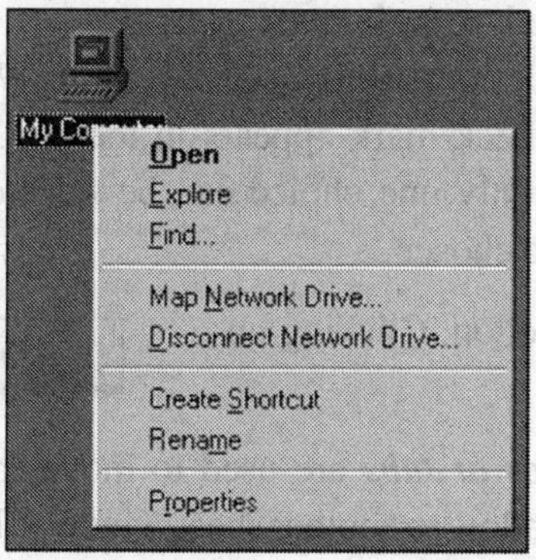

Sub-menu: A little arrow after a menu item, like the one after the "Settings" item, indicates that this option has several sub-options. Menu options that lead to sub-menus typically have arrows to their right. Items on that second menu can be linked to yet another menu. Nesting of menus extending to several layers is possible, and often encountered.

Context menu: If an object is right clicked, a menu is displayed, this menu is referred to as context or shortcut menu. The menu displays a list of options for that objects, the contents of the list could vary depending upon the object. For example, if you right click on the 'My Computer' icon, a menu is displayed showing options related to 'My Computer'.

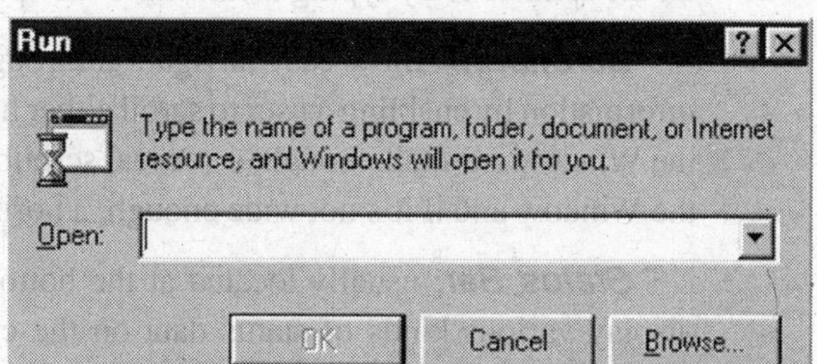

Dialog boxes: Dialog boxes are small windows that appear when a program needs more information before it can complete an operation. A dialog box is used to capture user preferences and when the user has entered his preferences he can put his preferences into effect by clicking on the 'OK' button. The user can click on the 'Cancel' button to cancel the operation. If a menu item has ellipses (...) after it, it indicates that selecting the item will open a dialogue box. For example, clicking on 'Run' in the Start Menu will display a dialog box prompting the user to enter the desired information.

Textbox is used to enter any information (numbers, alphabets, special characters etc). Typically they hold a single line of text.

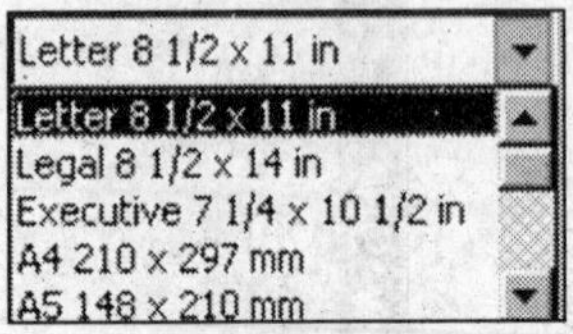

Drop down box/list box is used to make a selection from a list of options. Displays a set of options when the down arrow key is clicked. The list box has a scroll bar (discussed later in the section), if there are more options than the list has room to show.

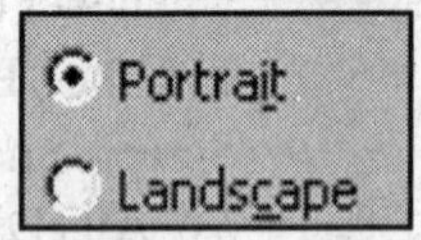

Option button is used to select one option among several options. Also called as a radio button. It appears as a small circle that, when selected, has a smaller, filled circle inside it.

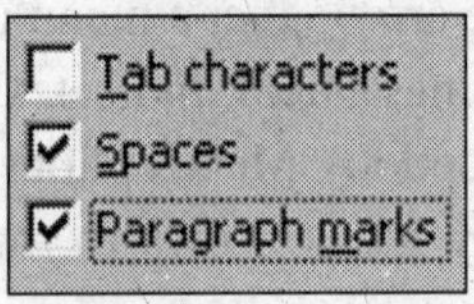

Checkbox is used to select or deselect one or more options from a set of options. When an option is selected, a check mark appears in the box. Unlike option buttons where only one choice can be selected, here multiple options can be chosen.

Command button is used to carry out some action. Clicking on the command button will carry out some action.

Folios or tabs are used to move from one sheet/window to another sheet/window. They are analogous to a set of dividers in a notebook.

Spinners are used to choose from a range of numeric values by 'spinning' through the values by clicking the up or down arrows on the spinner or by typing a value into the spinner box.

Scrollbars Allow easy navigation through a long list of items or a large amount of information by enabling a user to scroll either horizontally or vertically within a Window. If the Window isn't tall enough, a vertical scrollbar will be displayed along the right edge of the Window and if it's not wide enough, a horizontal one will be displayed.

Status Bar: usually located at the bottom of an application Window. It is used to display various kinds of status data on the current environment; it can contain text or pictures.

Customising Windows

Creating Shortcuts Shortcuts are icons that provide a quick way to start a program or open a file or folder without having to go to its permanent location in Windows Explorer. Windows Explorer can be accessed using Start ® Programs ® Windows Explorer. (Explained in detail later in this section). Shortcuts are useful for programs, files, and folders that are used frequently.

Creating a shortcut for file/folder/program

i. Select the file/folder/program from the Windows Explorer. For programs the '.exe' (Executable) file has to be selected from the Windows Explorer, in order to create a shortcut.

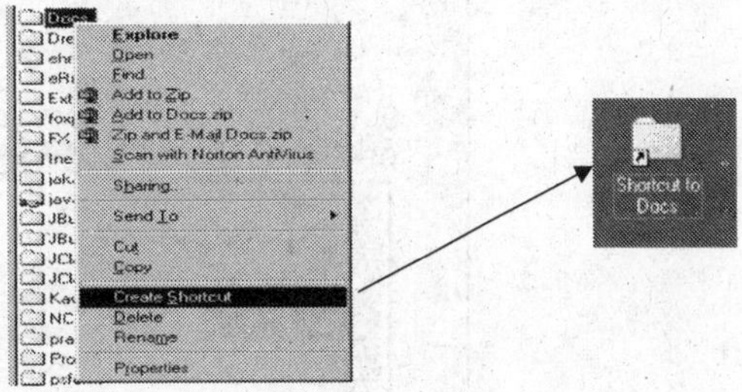

ii. Right click on the file/folder/program and select 'Create Shortcut' from the context menu. This would create the shortcut in the same folder as that of file/folder/program.

iii. Drag the newly created shortcut to the desired place. You can drag the shortcut to the Desktop also.

Deleting a shortcut: Deleting a shortcut will not delete the actual file/folder/program from the computer. When a shortcut is deleted, the set of directions pointing towards the file/folder/program is deleted; the actual file/folder/program stays in its usual location. Follow the steps below to delete a shortcut:

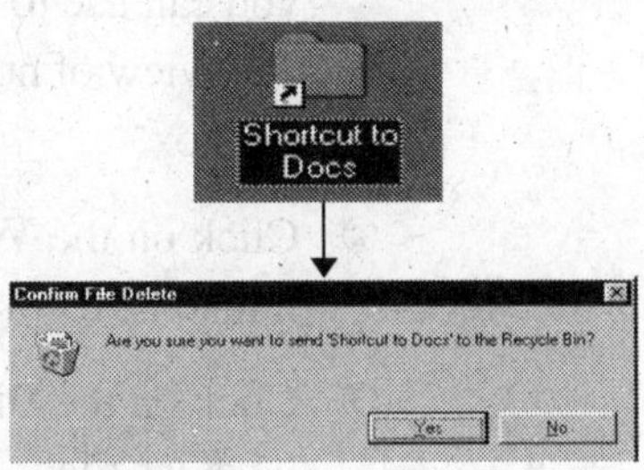

i. select the shortcut by clicking on it.

ii. press 'Del' key from the keyboard.

iii. a dialog box is displayed asking for confirmation for deleting this shortcut.

iv. click on the 'Yes' button to confirm deletion.

Inserting background picture: Desktop Wallpapers do exactly what your room wall paper does–decorates your surroundings and adds colour and fun to your life. Use this option to modify and apply different pictures and images as your desktop wallpapers. You can also use repetitive designs called Patterns to get a woven fabric or block printed look on your desktop.

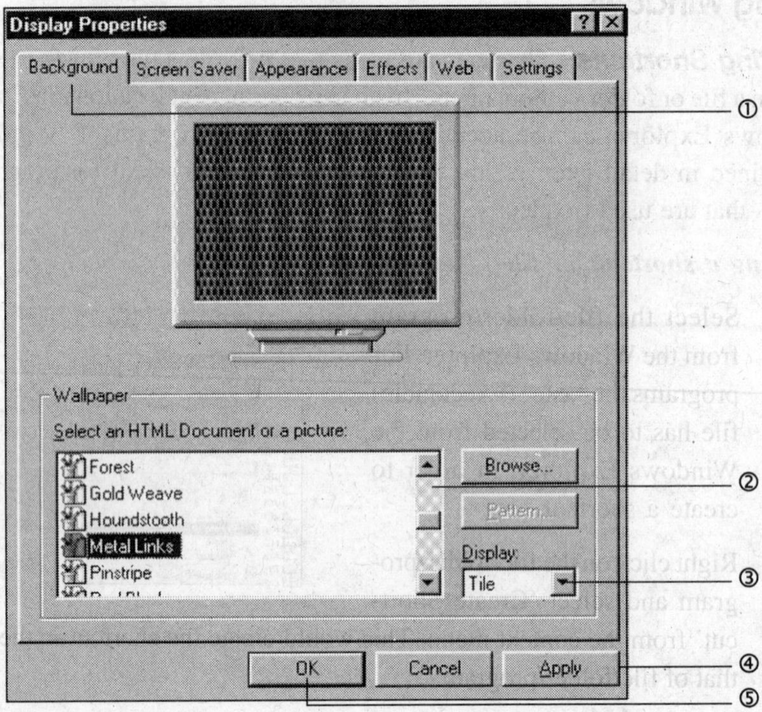

Right click on the Windows desktop, select Properties option from the Context menu, the following screen will be displayed:

① Click once on **Background folio/tab**. Background lists the available wallpapers you can use to decorate your desktop. When you click on a wallpaper in this list, a preview of how the wallpaper will look appears on the monitor simulated within the box.

② Click on the **Wallpaper** or HTML document from the list given that you would like to be displayed on your desktop.

③ Click on the **Display** box to choose how you want the wallpaper to be displayed–whether tiled, stretched or centered.

④ Click on **Apply** button to apply the settings that you have changed.

⑤ Click on **OK** button to continue.

Screen saver A screen saver is a moving image or pattern that appears on your monitor when you have left your computer idle for a specified limit. Screen saver serves four main functions:

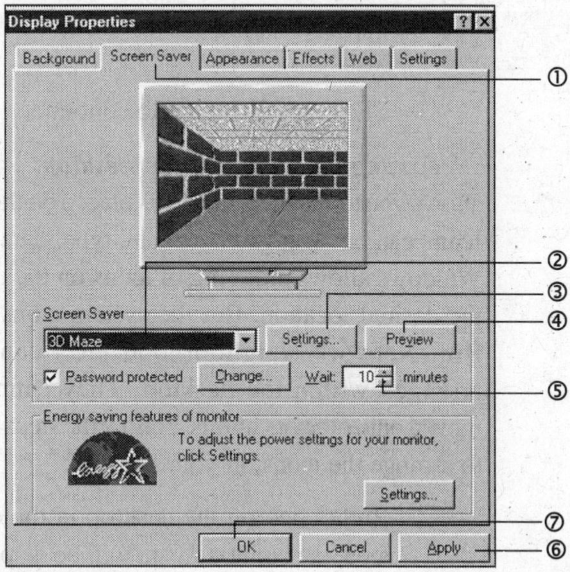

a. Most of them are interesting and provide fun and entertainment.

b. When the same static image stays on a screen for a long period of time it can burn the delicate phosphors on the inside surface of the picture of your monitor. This can leave a permanent ghost of the image on the screen, thereby damaging your monitor.

c. Many newer computers have inbuilt power saving option built into them (e.g. EPA energy star, VESA etc.) which powers down the monitor as soon as the screen saver comes into effect, thereby saving on your electricity bills.

d. The screen saver also has an optional security feature. Through this option you can define a password. Once the screen saver is activated it requires the user to type in the correct password before he can resume working. This makes sure nobody peeps into and or messes around with someone's computer file while she is away from her desk.

Right click on the Windows desktop the following screen will be displayed:

① Click on **Screen Saver** folio/tab. The Screensaver lists the available screen savers.

② Click on the **Screen saver** roll-down list and choose the screen saver that you want to apply.

③ Click on the **Settings** button to change the settings.

④ Click on **Preview** button to preview the screen saver before applying it.

⑤ Click here to increase or decrease the time after which the screen saver would appear.

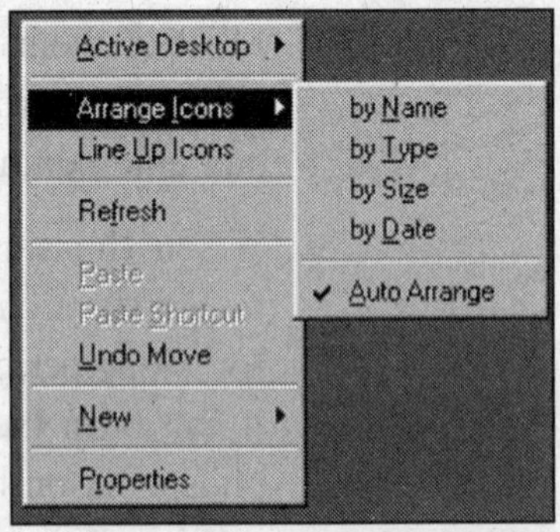

⑥ Click on **Apply** button to apply the changes made.

⑦ Click on **OK** button to continue.

Arranging icons on the desktop: Windows allows you to organize the icons placed on the desktop. Icons can be arranged by name, type, date and size. Windows allows dragging of icons on the desktop to the desired location. But the system icons (Recycle Bin, Network Neighborhood etc.) can only be arranged within the desktop. They cannot be moved onto other locations. Follow the steps below to arrange the icons on your desktop:

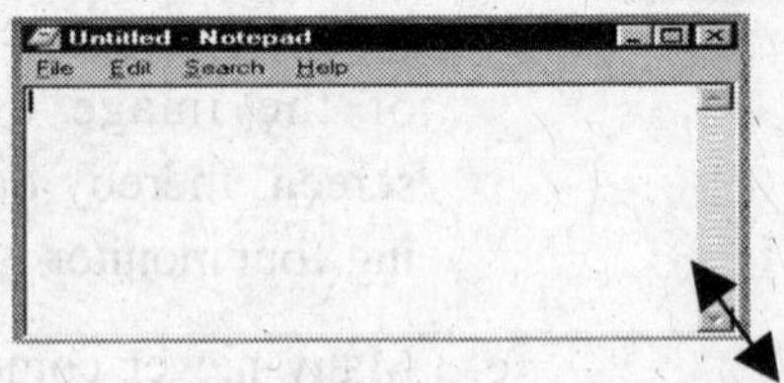

i. Right click on the desktop in the empty area, the context menu will be displayed.

ii. Select 'Arrange Icons' ® Name.

iii. Icons will be arranged accordingly.

Working with Windows

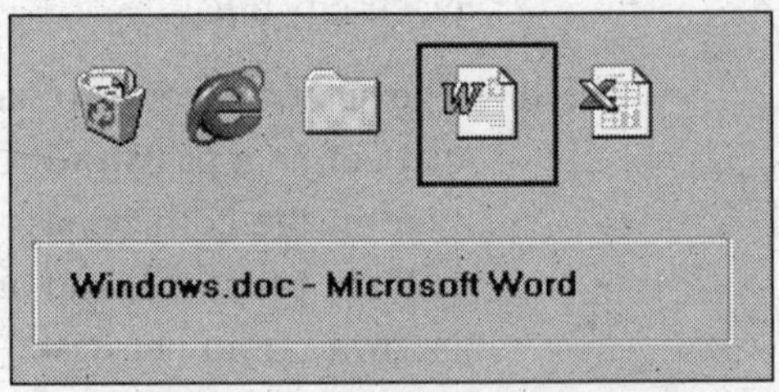

Moving Windows: You can move a window on the screen (if it is not maximized) by left clicking on and dragging its title bar with the mouse.

Resizing Windows Start by slowly moving the mouse pointer across the border until the pointer changes into a double-headed arrow. Then press the left mouse button and hold it down as you drag the border of the Window. When the window is the desired size, release the mouse button.

Switching between multiple Windows: Most Window applications allow opening of multiple document Windows, but only one among them can be active at a time. The active Window is said to have the focus. Follow the steps below to switch between multiple documents:

i. Press 'Alt +Tab' from the keyboard. Icons representing each program you're running are displayed at the center of the screen.

ii. Hold down Alt and continue to press Tab, Windows cycles through the programs, enclosing one after another within a box, and listing its name at the bottom of the window.

iii. Release both the keys when the desired program receives focus.

Minimizing all Windows: When multiple document Windows are opened, all of them can be minimised using a single command rather than clicking on the minimise button for each window that is opened. Follow the steps given below to minimise all Windows at one go:

i. Click on the task bar in the empty area.

ii. Select 'Minimise all Windows' from the context menu.

iii. All the open Windows will be minimised. The windows can be restored to their original positions by selecting 'Undo Minimise All' from the context menu.

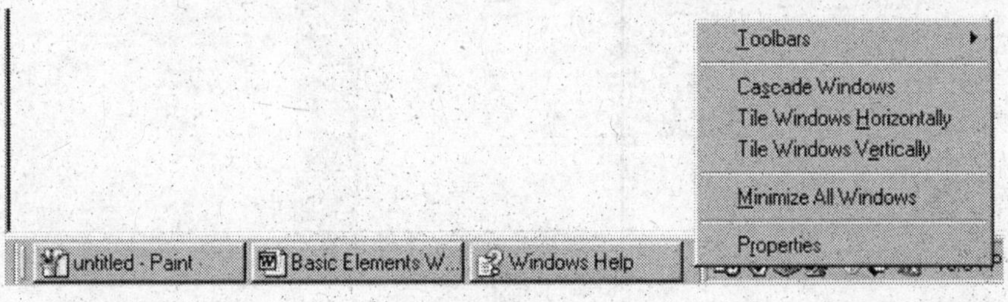

Arranging Windows: Windows provides three options for displaying all the open Windows namely Cascade, Tile Horizontally and Tile Vertically. Follow the given below steps to display all open Windows:

i. Click on the task bar in the empty area.

ii. Select 'Cascade' or 'Tile Horizontally' or 'Tile Vertically' from the context menu.

iii. All the open Windows will be arranged according to the selected option. The Windows can be restored to their original positions by selecting 'Undo Cascade' or 'Undo Tile' from the context menu.

Exploring Control Panel

Control panel contains utilities for customising the Windows interface. Through Control Panel you can define what colour scheme would be used by Windows (Colour), what fonts would be available (Fonts), what currency format would you be using (International), which events would generate which sound (Sounds), how fast or slow your mouse would work (Mouse), what is the current date and time (Date/Time) etc.

Some of the utilities contained in the Control panel are explained below. Control Panel can be accessed from:

Start → Settings → Control Panel

Installing or Removing Programs

A Select Add/Remove Programs option by double clicking on it. The following screen ('B') would be displayed:

A Install/Uninstall: Select this option if you want to install/uninstall any programs into/from your computer.

1. **CD or Floppy:** Select this option if you want to install any programinto your computer. A new program can be installed using either a CD or a floppy.

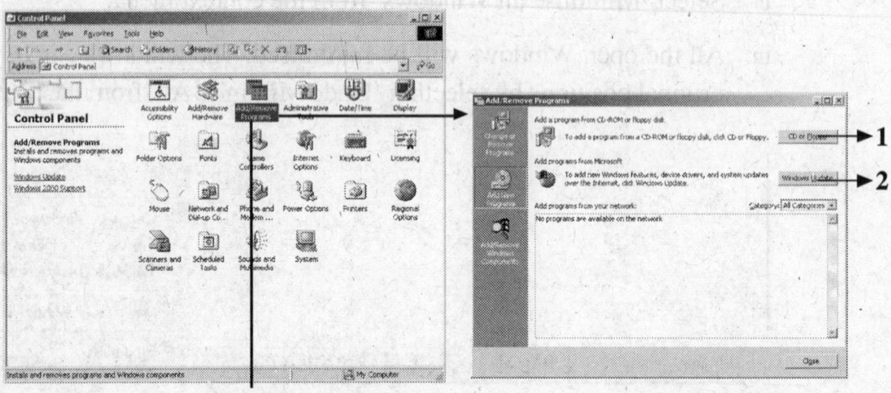

A ('B')

2. **Update:** You can choose Windows Update to add new Windows features or system updates over the Internet.

B Windows Setup: Select this option for installing/uninstalling specific components or sub-components of Windows.

1. Displays the list of currently installed components of Windows in your computer.
2. **Details:** It gives the details of the selected component. You can add or remove individual sub-components contained in the selected component group.
3. **Have Disk:** Click on 'Next' button to install the component.

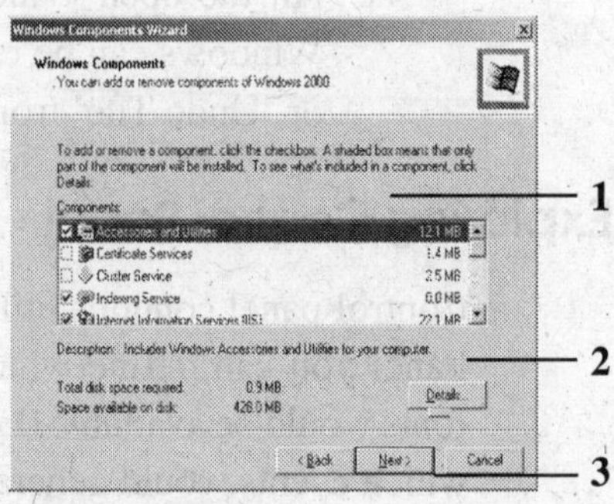

Date and Time

Inside your computer there is a small component called a Real Time Clock (RTC). This RTC and CMOS set up powered by a battery cell ensures that the basic settings of your computer are not lost when you switch off your computer. RTC stores the current date and time in your computer and passes on this information to put a date and time stamp on all file operations. The date and time option lets you adjust the system's date and time to correct settings. It is important that your computer works on the correct clock and calendar timings, so that your computer uses current date and time information to create and update your files.

A Select 'Date/Time' from the control panel.

① Click once on the Date & Time folio/tab.

② Click on the month roll-down list to change the month.

③ Click on this button to change the year.

④ Click on any of the dates to change the date.

⑤ Click on this Window to change the time.

⑥ Click on Apply button to apply the changes you have made.

⑦ Click on OK button to continue.

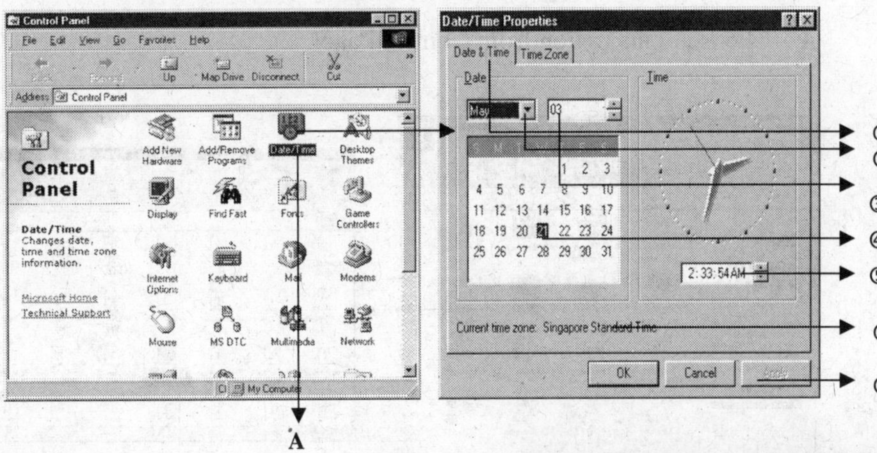

Time Zone

This option determines which time zone you are in. Especially for Laptop users who zip across many countries (and time zones) frequently, this is a great boon and helps them maintain the computer date and time as per the local settings. For India the time zone is GMT+ 05:30 Mumbai, Calcutta, Chennai, New Delhi.

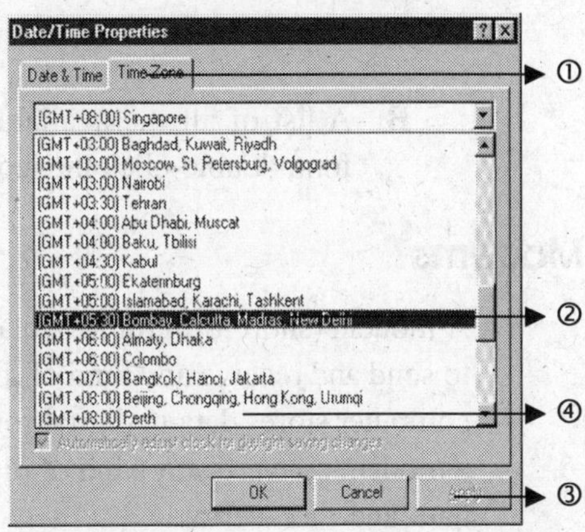

① Click once on **Time Zone** folio/tab.

② Choose the time zone you want to change to by scrolling up or down in the list displayed here.

③ Click on **Apply** button to apply the changes you have made.

④ Click on **OK** button to continue.

Fonts

Fonts are like having different handwritings available on your computer. Fonts are type faces that you can use to pep up your work and change the appearance of characters on your screen and on the printed paper. Fonts help you to express your message more clearly and emphatically. Broadly, there are two types of fonts Serif and Sanserif. A serif is a short stroke at the end of, or at an angle to, the letter form. An example of Serif is Times New Roman font and Sanserif is Arial font. Windows comes bundled with a large number of fonts, which are automatically installed (depending upon your monitor and printer type) during the Windows setup installation. You can install additional fonts from other softwares, as and when required.

A Choose Fonts option from Control Panel.

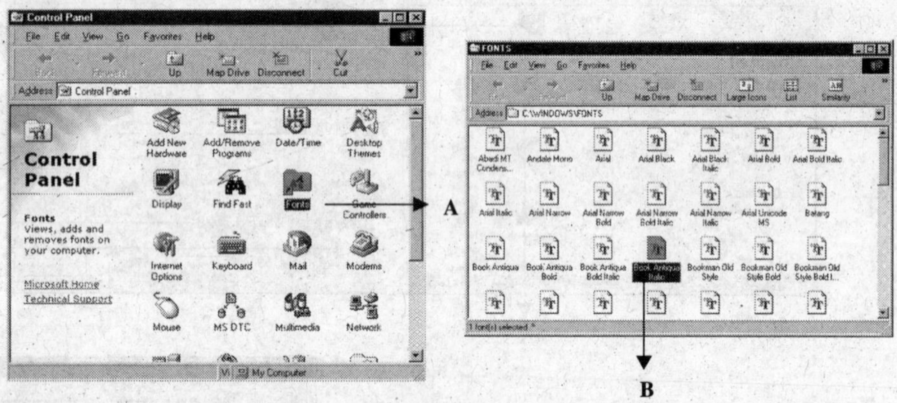

B A list of all the available fonts would be displayed. To look at a sample of a font, double-click the icon for the font.

Modems

A modem (short form for Modulator DeModulator) is an electronic device that allows you to send and receive any kind of digital data through the normal telephone line. Since your computer stores data in digital format and your telephone line transmits only analog data, a modem converts any kind of digital data (text, pictures, sound, movies etc.) into analog data and vice versa.

You can use the Modem option from Control Panel to install new modems or to check the performance and settings of pre installed modems.

A Choose **Modem** from **Control Panel**.

① Click on the **Modems** folio/tab.

② Click on the modem to highlight it.

③ Click on the **Add** or **Remove** button to add or remove the modem.

④ Click on the **Properties** button to configure the modem.

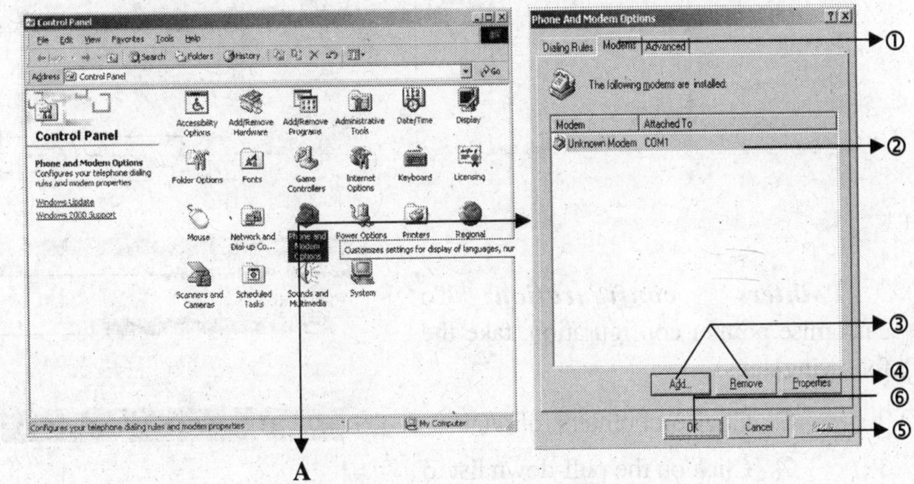

⑤ Click on the **Apply** button to apply the changes made.

⑥ Click on **OK** button to continue.

Mouse

As explained earlier, a mouse is a small hand held device through which you can quickly and easily navigate the different parts of the screen. You can customise the various aspects of mouse to make them work the way you prefer. You can control the mouse pointer speed, shape, button configuration, double click speed etc. You can even swap the left and right buttons. If you frequently lose track of where your mouse pointer is, you can choose to have a mouse trail effect, which will make the mouse pointer more visible.

A Choose Mouse option from Control Panel.

Button configuration: To customise button configuration, take the following steps:

① Click on the **Buttons** folio/tab.

② Click on **Right handed** radio button of the **Button configuration** option to convert your left mouse button into right button, and vice versa.

③ Drag this button to increase or decrease the clicking speed of the mouse.

④ Click on **Apply** button to apply the changes that you have made.

⑤ Click on **OK** button to continue.

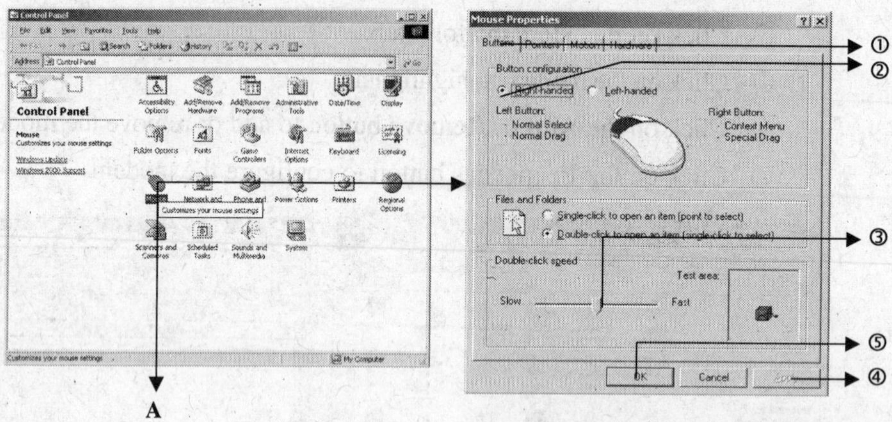

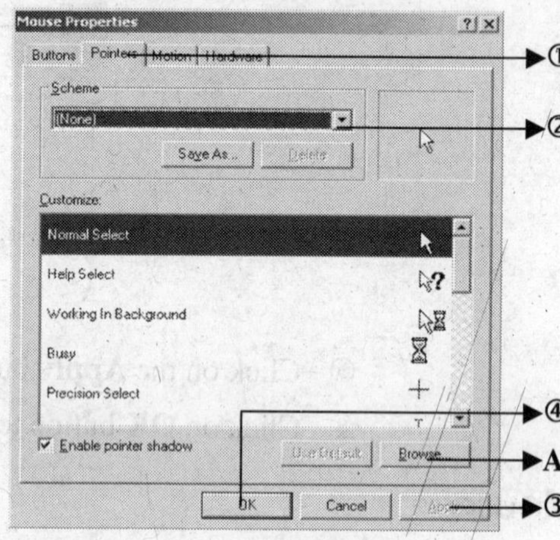

Pointers configuration: To customise pointer configuration, take the following steps:

① Click on Pointers folio/tab.

② Click on the pull-down list to choose the scheme that you want to apply.

A You can choose a scheme from another location by clicking on the Browse button.

③ Click on Apply button to apply the chosen scheme.

④ Click on the OK button to continue.

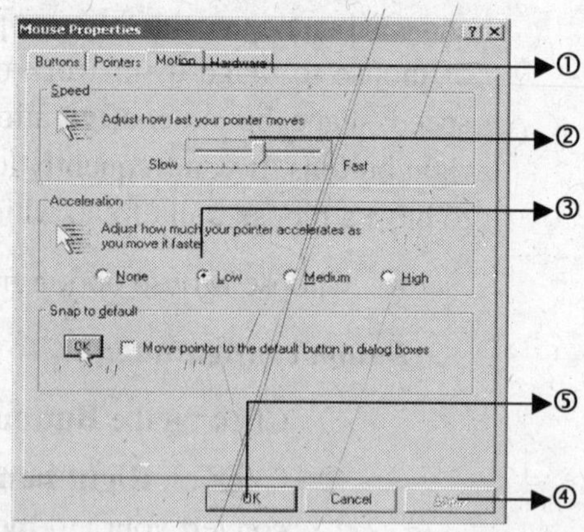

Motion configuration: To customise motion configuration, take the following steps:

① Click on the Motion folio/tab.

② Click on this button to increase or decrease the pointer speed.

③ You can also click on the pointer trails radio buttons to make them look long or short.

④ Click on Apply button to apply the changes you have made.

⑤ Click on the OK button to continue.

Mouse pointers At this stage, it is important to understand the various mouse pointers that would be shown to you at different times. In short, the mouse pointer gives you a clue about the work that Windows is either doing, or expecting you to do. Let us see these pointers one by one:

Vertical Resize: Whenever you move the cursor on the top or bottom boundary of a Window/object, your Mouse Pointer would turn into this shape.

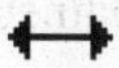

Horizontal Resize: Whenever you move the cursor on the left or right boundary of a Window/object, your mouse pointer would turn into this shape.

Diagonal Resize 1: Whenever you move the cursor on the upper left or lower right diagonal corner of a window/object, your mouse pointer would turn into this shape.

Diagonal Resize 2: Whenever you move the cursor on the upper right or lower left diagonal corner of a window/object, your mouse pointer would turn into this shape.

Move: Whenever you have selected an object for moving, your mouse pointer would turn into this shape.

Normal Select: Whenever you normally point the mouse pointer at any object or icon, scroll bar or menu, the mouse pointer would turn into this shape.

Help Select: Whenever you press the Help Icon to get help on a specific topic, the mouse pointer would turn into this shape. Once you get this mouse pointer, simply click on the icon for which you want help and Windows will show you the help text.

Working: Whenever you have executed a command which takes a couple of moments, Windows would display this mouse pointer. This means that Windows is processing your request in the background.

Busy: Whenever Windows is trying to load some information into the computer memory or is busy trying to open or save a file, this mouse pointer would be displayed. At this stage, you would not to be able to execute any other command.

Text Select: Whenever and wherever you can work on some text matter or some typed input is required from the user (usually in a Word processor like Note Pad or MS Word), this mouse pointer would be displayed.

Printers

Use this option to install new printers. You would need Windows 2000 CD or the Printer Installation CD to run this option. Windows 2000 installation CD includes many printer drivers from various well-known printer manufacturers. However, if your printer or it's exact model is not listed in the driver's list provided by Windows 2000, you don't need to worry. Simply insert CD or floppy (which must have come along with the printer) and complete the printer installation procedure.

A Select **Printers** option from **Control Panel.**

B Double click on the **Add Printer** button and follow the steps explained in the wizard to install a new printer.

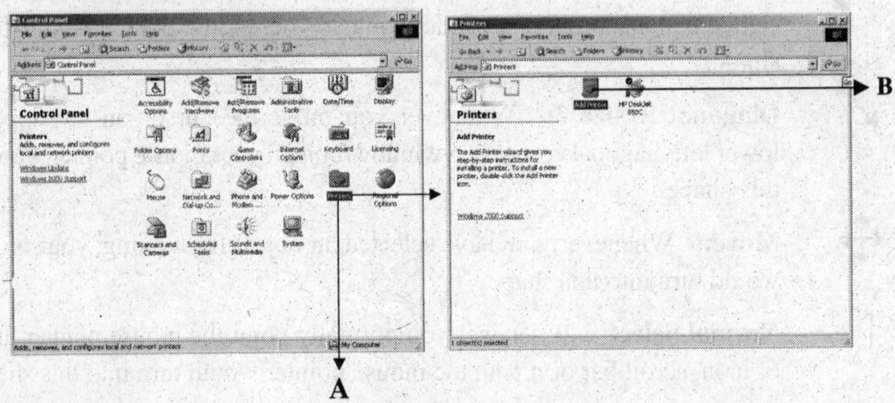

Regional Settings

If you are using Windows 2000 in any country other than USA or are using any language other than American English, you need to go to this option to define the various regional settings like language, number formatting, currency, date and time format.

A Select **Regional Settings** option from **Control Panel.**

① Click on the **General** folio/tab.

② Click on this roll-down list to choose the regional settings. Choosing a regional setting automatically changes settings on the Number, Currency, Time and Date tabs.

③ Click on **Apply** button to apply the changes you have made.

④ Click on the **OK** button to continue.

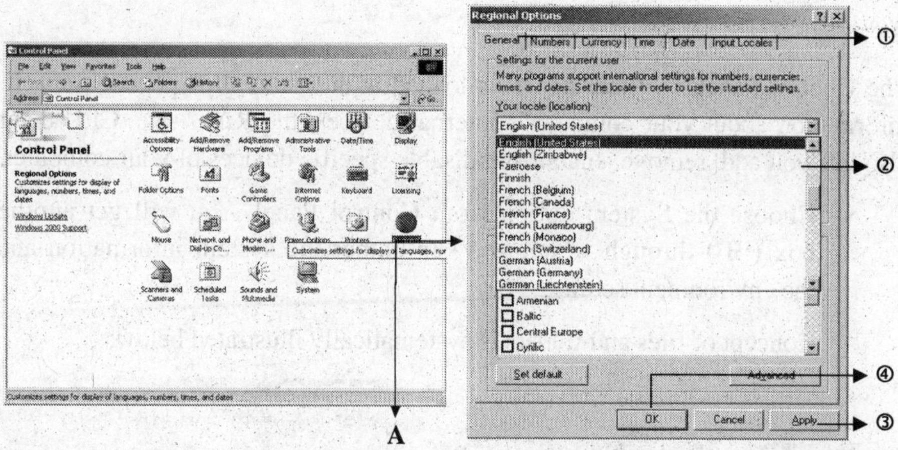

Sounds

You can use this option for assigning different sounds to various system events such as error messages, warning dialog boxes, starting and exiting Windows etc. Needless to say, this option will work only if you have a Sound Card and Speakers installed.

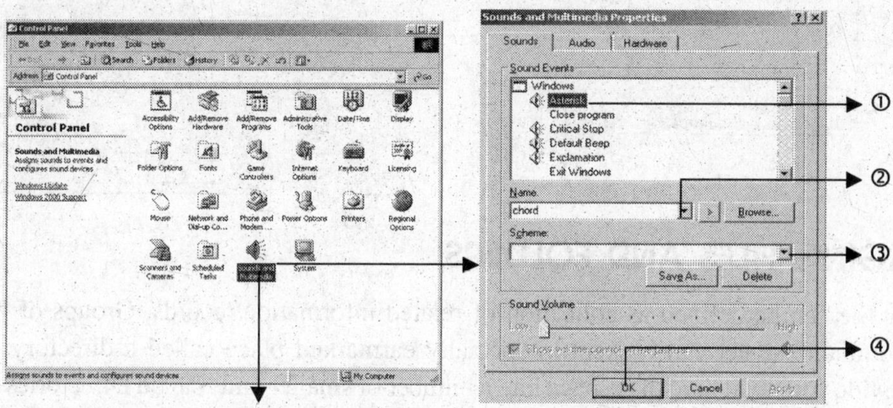

A Choose **Sounds and Multimedia** option from **Control Panel**.

① Choose the sound type.

② Click on the **Name** roll-down list to choose from the various instruments from which you can assign sounds.

③ Click on the Schemes roll-down list to choose a scheme. This list displays schemes that you can use to simultaneously change the sounds assigned to many system events.

④ Click on OK button.

System

The Control Panel's System applet is loaded with features for power users. It displays information about your computer's internal devices, the RAM size, CPU details etc. It also lets you add, remove, enable and disable specific devices of your computer.

A Choose the System option from Control Panel. You will get another dialog box (**'B'**) through which you can gather the system information and change the environment settings.

Concept of files and folders is systematically illustrated below:

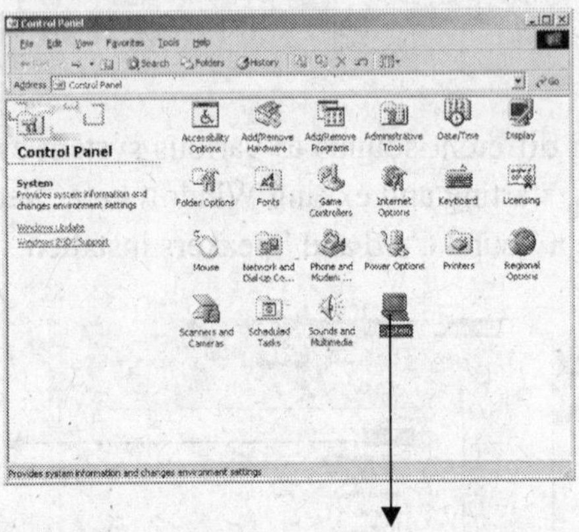

A

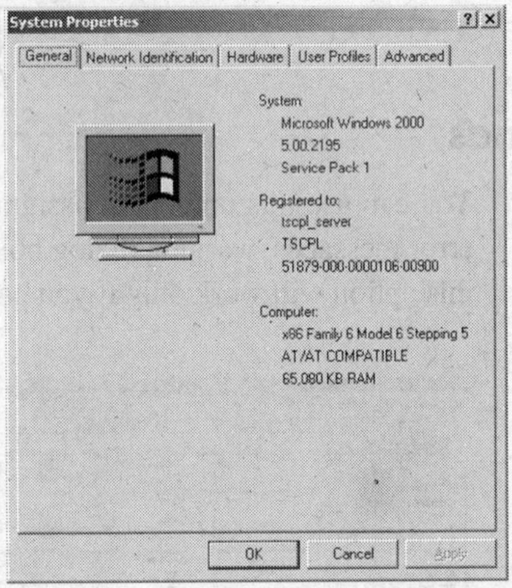

MANAGING FILES AND FOLDERS

A file can be defined as collection of related information/records. Groups of files on a common subject can be kept in specially earmarked place called a directory. You can divide your total hard disk space into a number of smaller units called Directories and Sub-directories.

Basically all the files are maintained on your hard disk in the form of an inverted tree like structure. At the top is the root directory under which there are sub-directories and sub-sub-directories. Each of these directories or sub-directories may contain one or many files. Microsoft decided that Folders is a more helpful word than directories and therefore they are called **Folders and Sub-folders**. A folder can consist of files as well as sub-folders. It is also possible to have an empty folder. The number of files in a folder or sub-folder is limited only by your hard disk capacity. File names should convey some sense of their contents (for instance you would not like to call your love letter that you wrote to your girlfriend/boyfriend - **The National Charter of Demands!!!**)

Whenever the user creates a new file, an extension is automatically appended to it. The extension of file tells about the type of the file and the program(s) through which the file can be opened and viewed.

For example, Hello.txt ('Hello' is the file name and .txt is the extension, which indicates that 'Hello' is a text file).

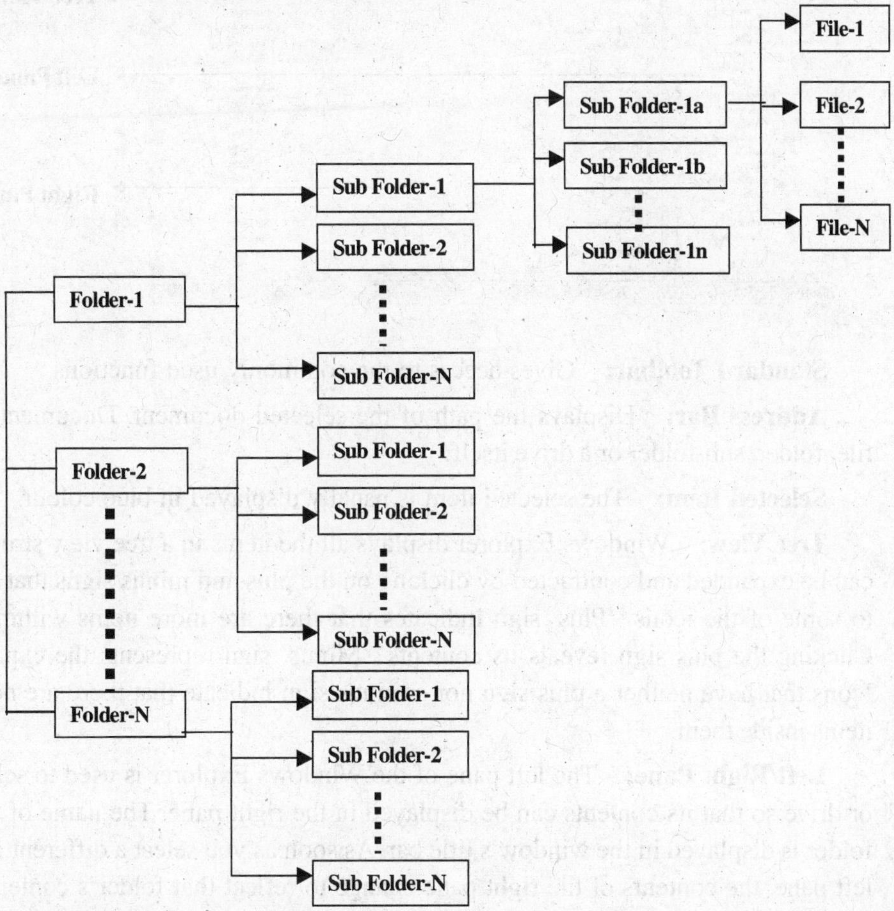

Overview of Windows Explorer

Windows Explorer is a utility that represents the contents of your computer in a graphical form. It allows you to do various file and disk management tasks like copy, rename, move and delete file(s) and create folder(s) and sub-folder(s), format floppies etc. It is the quickest way to get a complete view of the contents of your computer. You can take its help to quickly determine which files are available and where it. Windows Explorer can be accessed:

Start → Programs → Windows Explorer

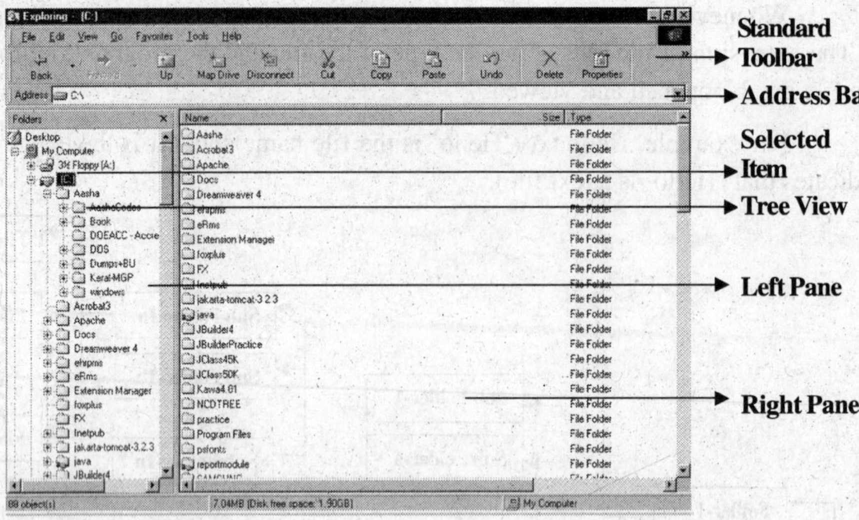

Standard Toolbar: Gives access to the commonly used functions.

Address Bar: Displays the path of the selected document. Document could be a file, folder, sub-folder or a drive itself.

Selected Item: The selected item is usually displayed in blue colour.

Tree View: Windows Explorer displays all the items in a tree view structure. Items can be expanded and contracted by clicking on the plus and minus signs that appear next to some of the icons. 'Plus' sign indicates that there are more items within the folder. Clicking the plus sign reveals its contents. 'Minus' sign represents the expanded view. Icons that have neither a plus sign nor a minus sign indicate that there are no additional items inside them.

Left/Right Pane: The left pane of the Windows Explorer is used to select a folder or drive so that its contents can be displayed in the right pane. The name of the selected folder is displayed in the window's title bar. As soon as you select a different folder in the left pane, the contents of the right pane change to reflect that folder's contents.

Creating Folders

Follow the steps below to create a new folder:

1. Select the drive ('C' or 'D' or 'A' etc.) in Windows Explorer where you want to create the new folder. A drive can be selected by clicking on its name. If desired, desktop can also be selected for creating a new folder. The selected drive will be displayed on the Address bar of the Windows Explorer.
2. On the **File** menu, point to **New**, and click on **Folder**. The new folder appears with a temporary name in the same location as that of the selected drive/folder.
3. Type a name for the new folder, and then press ENTER.

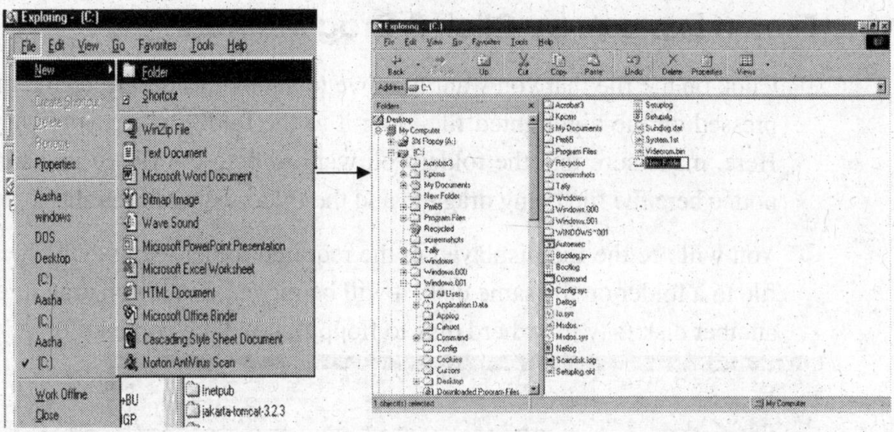

Note A file name can contain up to 255 characters, including spaces. It cannot contain the following characters:’ \’,’ /’,’:’,’ *’ ‘? ‘,’”’,’ < >’,’ | ‘. Since it may be difficult for you to remember which symbols are allowed and which are not, it is best to avoid all symbols while giving any folder and file names.

Creating Sub-folders Follow the steps below to create a sub-folder:

1. Select the folder within which you want to create a sub-folder.
2. Repeat Steps ‘2 ‘ and ‘3’ explained in ‘Creating Folders’.

Opening folders Follow the steps below to view the contents of a folder:

1. In the left pane, select the drive in which the folder is located.
2. Click on the folder name to view its contents. The contents of the folder will be displayed in the right pane.

Opening files As a general rule a file can be opened only through the application program through which it was created. The extension name of a file indicates the program through which it was created. There are exceptions to this rule also – for instance, files created in one type of word processor (say Word Perfect) can be opened in another word processor (say MS Word) provided necessary conversion tools are installed.

Follow the steps given below to open a file:

1. Select the desired file from the Windows Explorer. If the file is stored within a folder then open that folder using the steps explained above.
2. Double click on the file name.
3. The desired file will be opened using the associated program.

Copying Files in Explorer by Click & Drag Method

① Click on the file that you want to move to another folder. Keep the mouse button pressed on the highlighted file, drag it to the folder where you want to copy it. Here, make sure that the folder you want to drag the file to is visible. You will notice here the file being dragged and the folder being highlighted.

② You will see the file displayed in the required folder. Note that when you drag a file to a folder on the same disk, it will be moved, but if you drag it to a folder on another disk (say from hard disk to floppy), it will be copied.

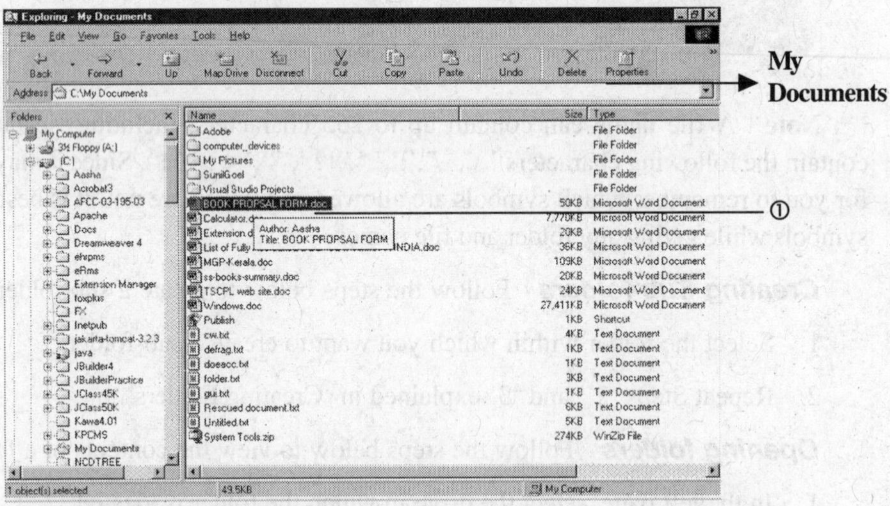

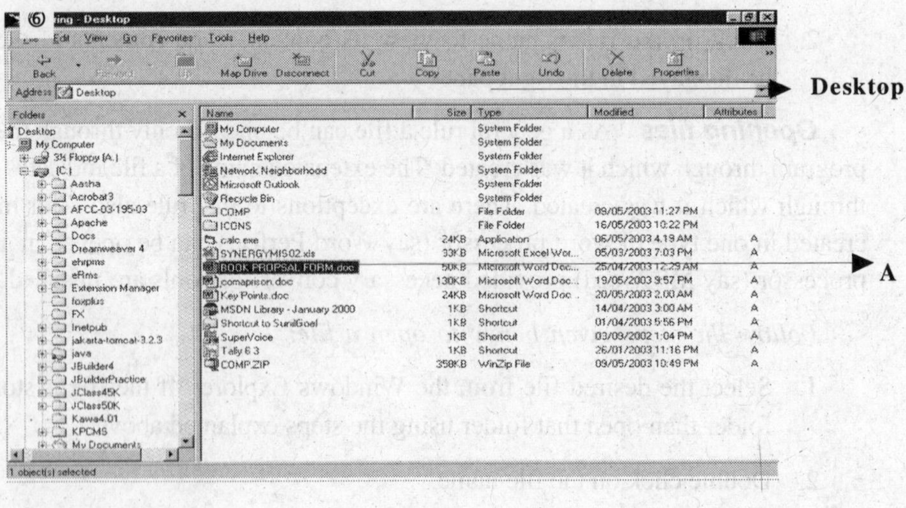

Notes:

1. When a file is copied from one location to another then the file is available in the original location and a copy of it is saved at the destination. But when a file is

moved from one location to another location then the file is available only at the destination.

2. To copy a file using Click and Drag method from one folder to another (both located in the same disk), select the desired file, drag the file using the right mouse button and when you reach the destination, simply right click and select 'Copy here' option.

Copying Files Discontinuously

① Click on a file that you want to copy and press the CTRL key.

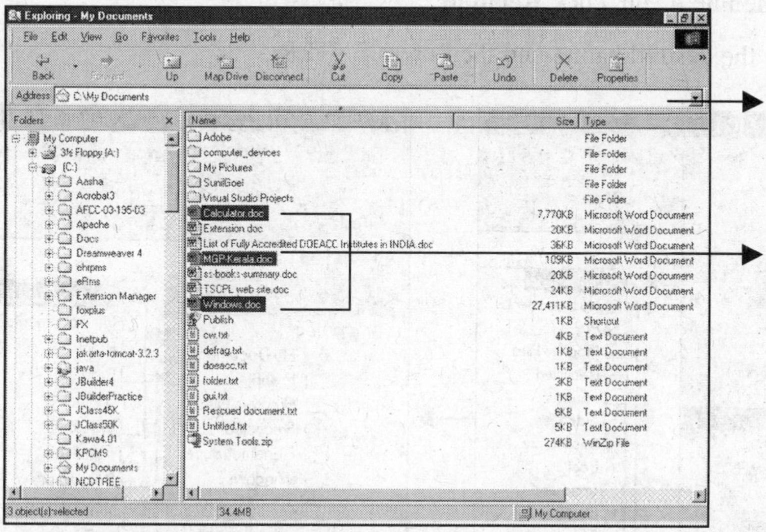

My Documents

A total of 3 files are selected

② Keeping the CTRL key pressed, click on another file. After that simply follow the steps that you take to copy a file to another folder. This is easier in the sense that you do not have to copy the required files one by one.

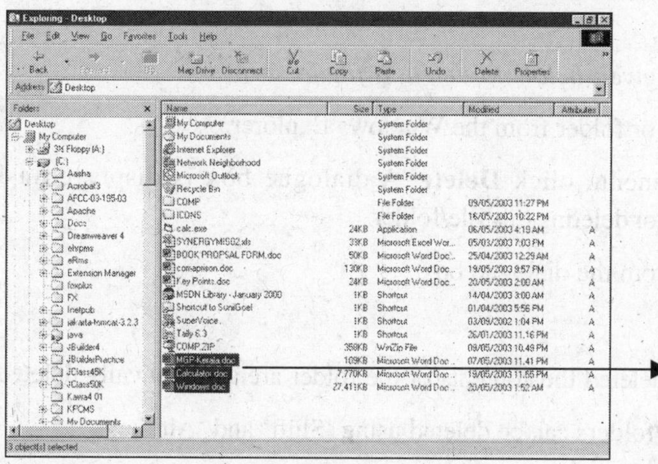

3 files copied from C:\My Documents to Desktop

Copying a Continuous Range of Files

You can also select a continuous range of files by using the SHIFT key. Click on the first file, press and hold the SHIFT key and click on the last file of the range to highlight a range of files. After that you can Cut or Copy them in any other folder.

Renaming Files/Folders

Follow the steps given below to rename a file/folder:

1. Select the file or folder from the Windows Explorer.
2. On the File menu, click **Rename**.
3. Type the desired name, and then press ENTER.

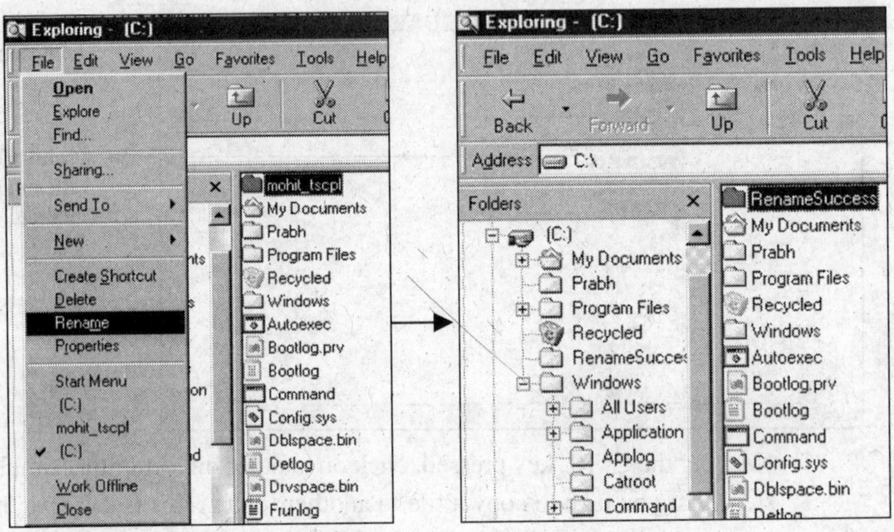

Deleting Files/Folders

Follow the steps given below to delete a file/folder:

1. Select the file or folder from the Windows Explorer.
2. On the File menu, click **Delete**. A dialogue box is displayed asking for confirmation for deleting this file/folder.
3. Select 'Yes' from the dialogue box.

Notes:

- If a folder is deleted the contents of the folder are automatically deleted.
- Multiple files/folders can be deleted using 'Shift' and 'Alt' keys.

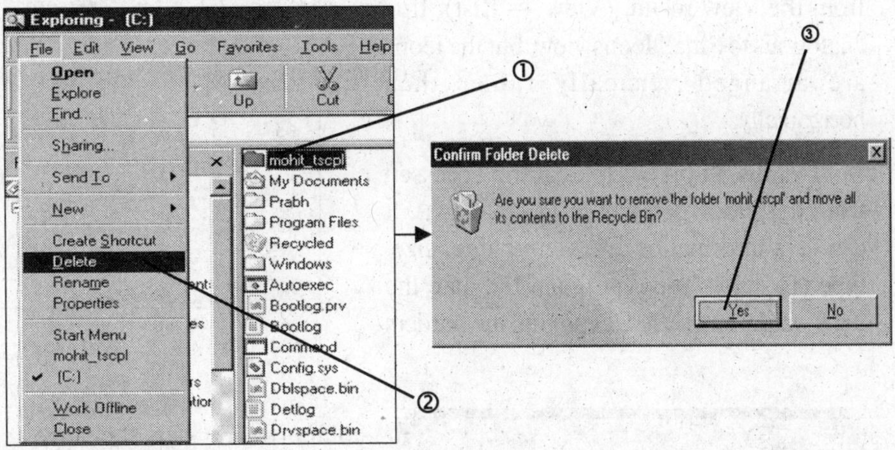

Notes: Copy, Rename, Delete command can also be accessed by right clicking on the file name.

Changing the Folder Views

The folders in the Windows Explorer can be displayed in several views. Below is a brief description of these views:

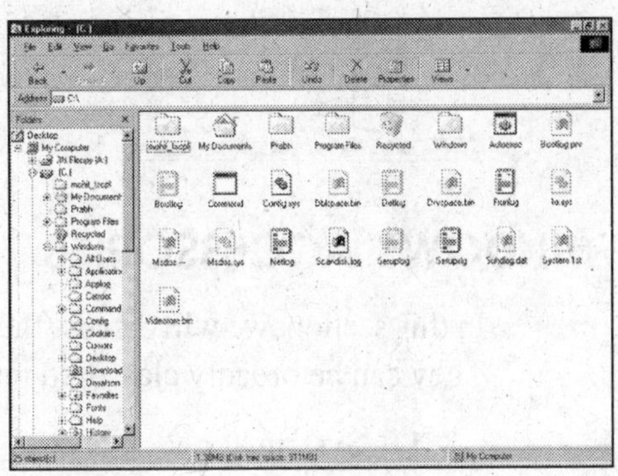

Large Icons View: This can be accessed from the View menu. (View — Large Icons). In this view each drive, folder, or file is shown as a large icon with a name or description underneath.

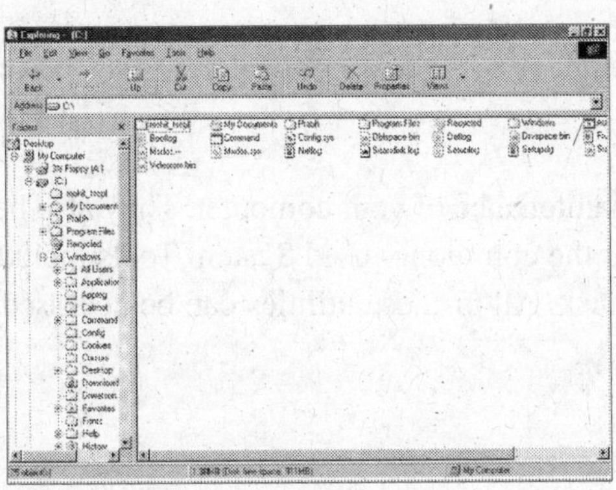

Small Icons View: This can be accessed from the View menu. (View — Small Icons). In this view each drive, folder, or file is shown as a small icon with a name or description to its right. The items are arranged horizontally in this view.

List View: This can be accessed from the View menu. (View — List). It is analogous to Small Icons view, but the icons are arranged vertically rather than horizontally.

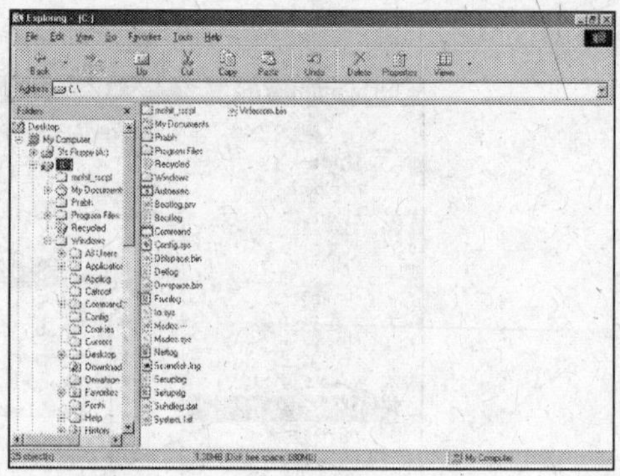

Details View: This can be accessed from the View menu. (View — Details). It displays information like item name, size, type (folder or file type), and the date the item was last modified. Dragging the borders column headings will change column widths in the details view. To sort the items by Name or Size or Type or Modified simply click on the corresponding column heading. For example, if you want to sort the items by name then simply click on the 'Name' column. All the items will be displayed in the ascending order of their names.

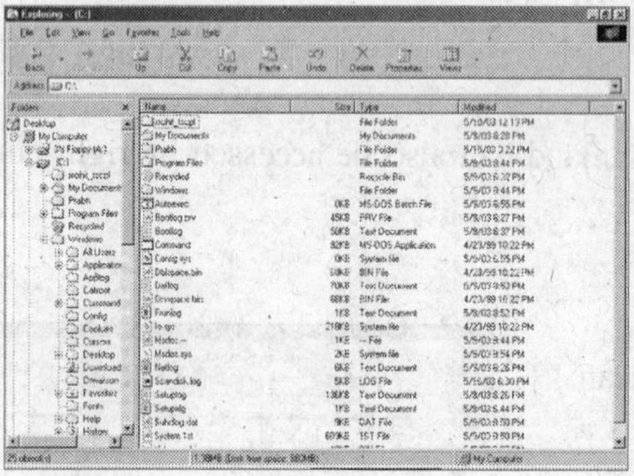

WINDOWS ACCESSORIES

In this section, we will discuss the commonly used accessories that are built into Windows. They can be broadly classified into the following categories:

1. System Tools
2. Entertainment Utilities
3. Miscellaneous Accessories

System Tools

These built-in tools aid in the easy maintenance of your computer. They also help you to troubleshoot minor problems. Some of the commonly used System Tools include Disk Cleanup, Disk Defragmenter and Scan Disk. All of these utilities can be accessed from:

Start ⟶ Programs ⟶ Accessories ⟶ System Tools

Disk Cleanup This utility helps to free up space on your hard disk. It first searches the entire hard disk and then lists temporary files, Internet cache files, downloadable program files (These are ActiveX controls and other Java Applets that are automatically downloaded from the Internet and stored onto the hard disk of your computer.), contents of Recycle Bin and unnecessary program files that can be safely deleted. Disk cleanup should be periodically used to free up the space in the hard disk. It cannot be used for CD-ROM's or Network Drives. It can be accessed from:

Start ⟶ Programs ⟶ Accessories ⟶ System Tools ⟶ Disk Cleanup

a. The following screen will be displayed. All the hard drives of the computer will be displayed in the drop down box. The desired drive can be selected and then 'OK' button should be pressed to start the disk clean up.

b. Process of disk clean up will be displayed to the user and in the end a dialog box is prompted to the user asking for confirmation for deleting the list of unnecessary files. If desired the user can view the list of files that would be deleted. It will also display the amount of space that will be freed.

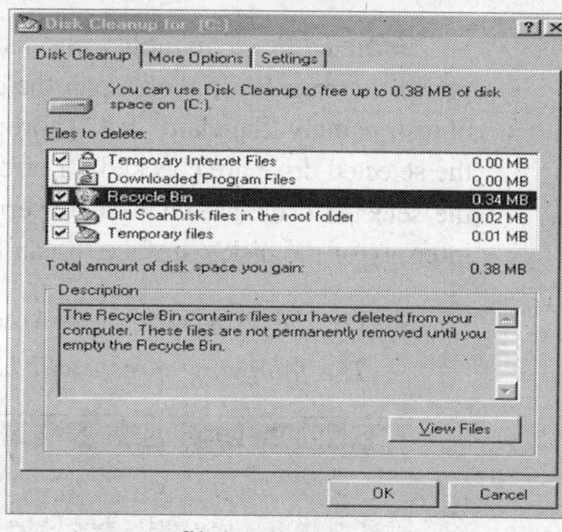

Disk defragmenter This utility helps to rearrange files and unused hard disk space to enable programs run faster. Large files that cannot be accommodated in a single location on the hard disk are usually fragmented and are stored at the nearest available free space on the hard disk. System takes more time to access fragmented files. This utility rearranges all such free spaces on the hard disk; as a result, files become quickly accessible. The defragmenter arranges them in adjacent units and consolidates all the free spaces recovered from various locations of the hard disk. It is always advisable to close other programs while the disk is being defragmented, because defragmenter restarts each time whenever other programs write to the disk. It can be accessed from:

Start → Programs → Accessories → System Tools → Disk Defragmenter

a. The following screen will be displayed. All the hard drives of the computer will be displayed in the drop down box. The desired drive can be selected and then 'OK' button should be pressed to start the process of defragmentation.

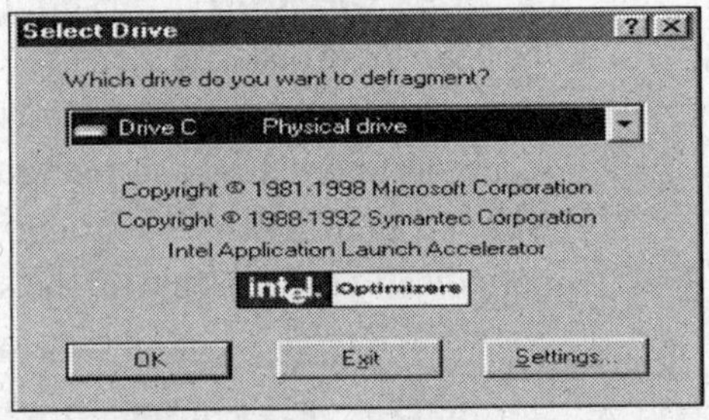

b. Progress of defragmentation is displayed to the user. For graphical view of this process 'Show Details' button can be pressed. When the progress reaches 100%, it indicates that defragmentation is complete. 'Pause' button can be pressed to temporarily stop disk defragmenter.

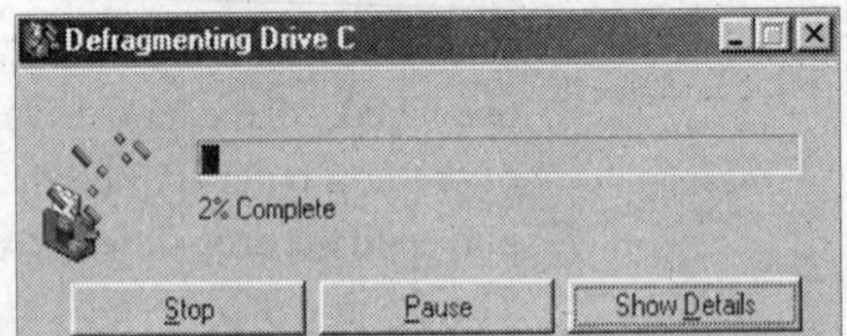

Scan Disk This utility checks the hard disk and removable disk for logical and physical errors. It can then repair the damaged areas. It can be used to perform two types of tests namely 'Standard' and 'Thorough'. In 'Standard' testing all the files and folders of the selected drive are checked for errors. In 'Thorough' testing all the files and folders of the selected drive are checked for errors. In addition to that it also checks the physical integrity of the disk's surface. It can be accessed from:

Start → Programs → Accessories → System Tools → Scan Disk

The following screen will be displayed:

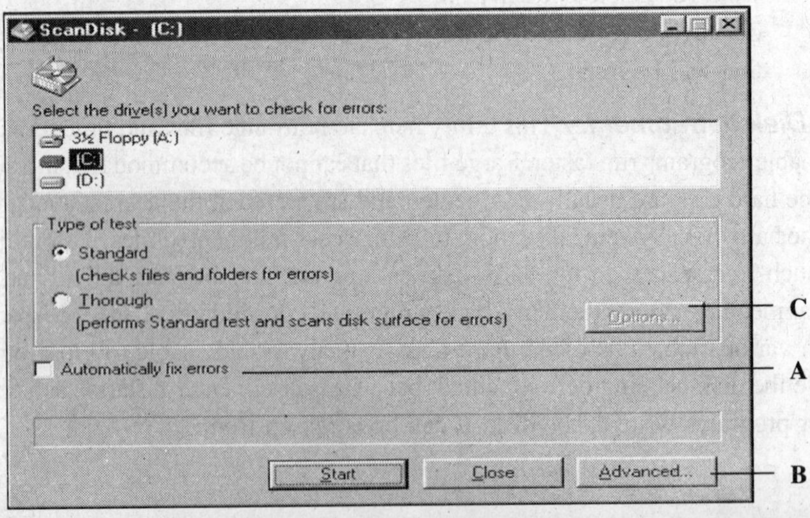

A If this option is selected then scan disk will automatically repair the errors using pre-defined settings (Settings can be changed by clicking on the 'Advanced' button). Otherwise the scan disk would prompt the user to specify how the errors should be corrected.

B This button is used to change the settings the scan will use while checking the drives for errors.

C This button will be enabled only for 'Thorough' testing. It allows you to specify the settings the scan disk will use while checking the disk surface for errors.

The scanning process will start as soon as the 'Start' button is clicked. After the scanning is completed, a summary report detailing total disk space, disk space occupied by bad sectors, files, and folders will be displayed. The summary report is displayed only if 'Display Summary' is enabled in settings.

Entertainment Utilities

Some of the commonly used Entertainment Tools include CD Player, Sound Recorder, Volume Control and Windows Media Player. All of these utilities can be accessed from:

Start ⟶ Programs ⟶ Accessories ⟶ Entertainment

CD player It can be used to play audio compact discs on a CD-ROM drive connected to your computer. CD player can be used to play multiple CDs provided your computer has a multidisk player. You can listen to a CD over your speaker system provided your computer has a sound card. It can be accessed from:

Start ⟶ Programs ⟶ Accessories ⟶ Entertainment ⟶ CD Player

The following screen will be displayed:

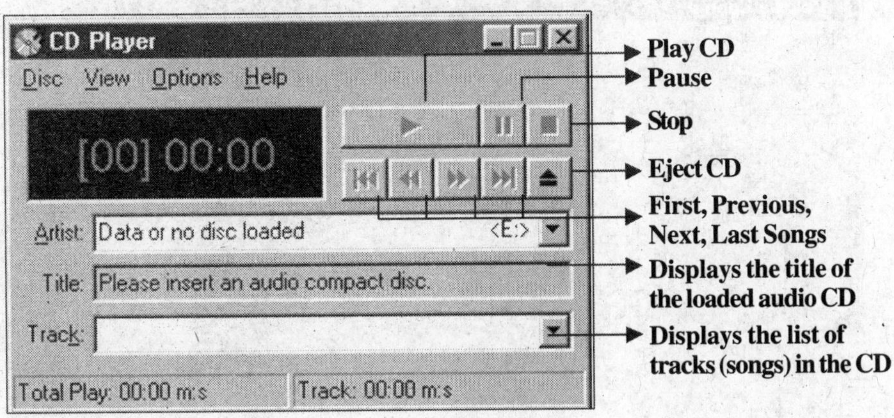

Sound recorder It can be used to record, edit and play ound files. The computer must have a microphone for recording and a sound card and speakers for listening to sound files. It can be accessed from:

Start ⟶ Programs ⟶ Accessories ⟶ Entertainment ⟶ Sound Recorder

The following screen will be displayed:

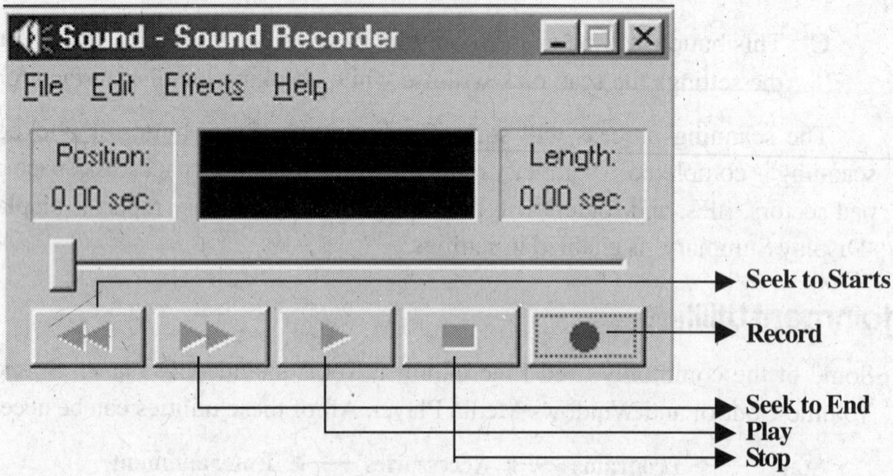

Volume control It can be used to adjust the volume when playing audio files. It can be used to adjust the recording volume as well as the playback volume. It has a facility that allows muting of all or some volumes. It can be accessed from:

Start ⟶ Programs ⟶ Accessories ⟶ Entertainment ⟶ Volume Control

The following screen will be displayed:

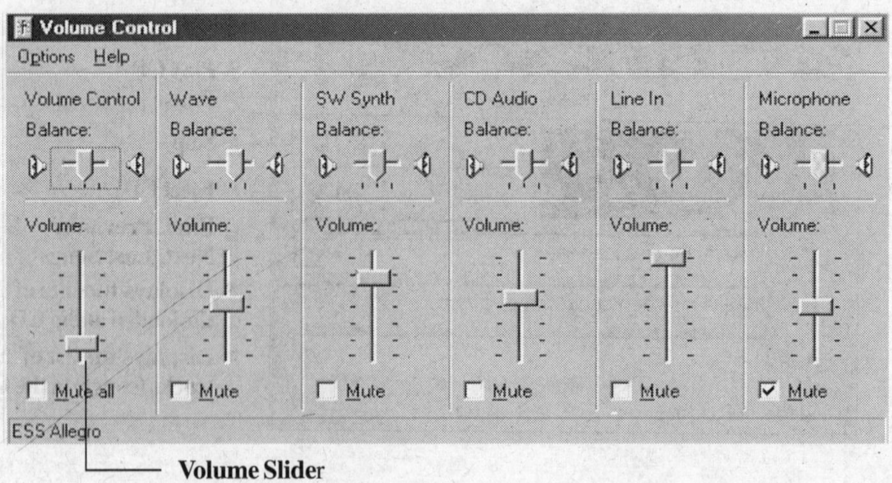

Windows media player It is an efficient and simple media player that can be used to play audio, video or animation files. It allows playing of streaming media files from the Internet in addition to the media files stored on your computer. It supports multiple media formats (.mp3, .mpeg, .wav, .avi etc.). It is flexible enough and can be customised according to your preferences. You can quickly change the size of the video window and even enlarge it to full-screen size. It provides continuous viewing even when playing a file that consists of multiple media types. In addition, it supports intelligent streaming, which monitors network conditions and automatically makes adjustments to ensure the best reception and playback. It can be accessed from:

Start ⟶ Programs ⟶ Accessories ⟶ Entertainment ⟶ Media Player

The following screen will be displayed:

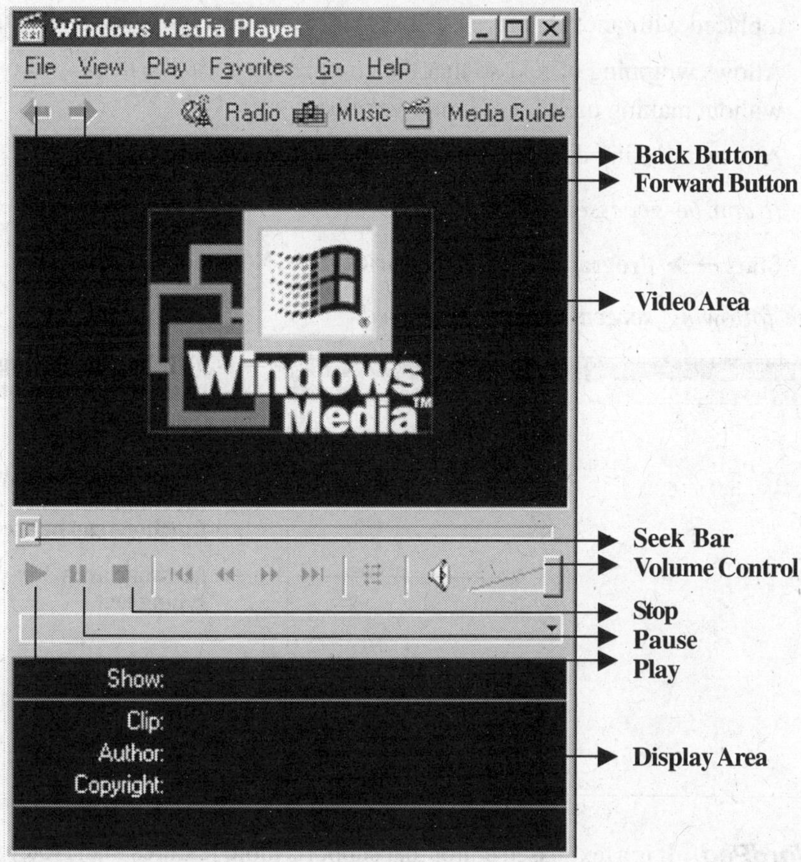

Miscellaneous Accessories

Some of the commonly used Windows accessories include Notepad, Wordpad, Calculator, Imaging, Paint and Games.

Notepad It is a simple text based editor that can be used for creating and editing text files that do not require any special formatting. Files larger than 64 KB cannot be created or edited in Notepad. Some of the features of Notepad are as follows:

- It opens and saves text in ASCII (text-only) format only.
- A simple search facility is built into the editor that allows searching for words in the current document.
- Supports cut, copy and paste operations. Text can be copied from one location and can be pasted to another location. This is accomplished with the help of Windows clipboard. (A clipboard is a temporary storage location for the information you cut or copy). It is always comes into play whenever you cut, copy or paste information. Information moved to the clipboard remains there until it is replaced with another piece of information, or the computer is switched off.
- Allows wrapping of text so that the complete text can be displayed on the screen without making use of horizontal scrollbars.
- Allows inserting date and time into the current document.

  It can be accessed from:

  Start ⟶ Programs ⟶ Accessories ⟶ Notepad

The following screen will be displayed:

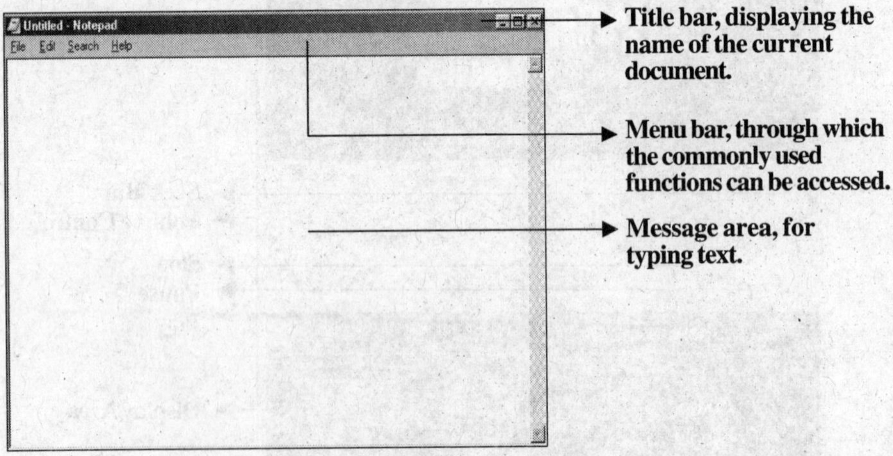

WordPad It is a text based editor that supports more features than Notepad. Wordpad can be used for files larger than 64 KB. It supports all the features of Notepad. Some of the features specific to Wordpad are as follows:

- Allows formatting of text using different font styles, colours and bullets.
- Different alignment options (Left, Right, Center) are provided for the paragraphs.

- Allows to set page margins and a preview of the page can be seen of how document would appear in print.
- Toolbars are provided that provide quick access to commonly used functions. User has the option to view/hide the toolbars.
- Allows to embed/link an object into a WordPad document from another file.

It can be accessed from:

Start ⟶ Programs ⟶ Accessories ⟶ Wordpad

The following screen will be displayed:

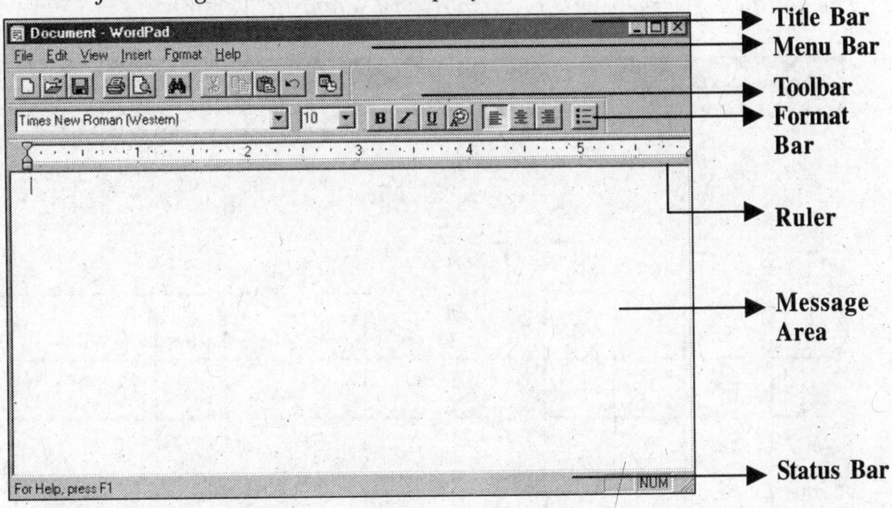

Imaging It allows you to view, annotate, and perform basic tasks with image documents, including fax documents and scanned images. It can be used for scanning documents, defining image resolution and supports image compression. It can be accessed from:

Start ⟶ Programs ⟶ Accessories ⟶ Imaging

The following screen will be displayed:

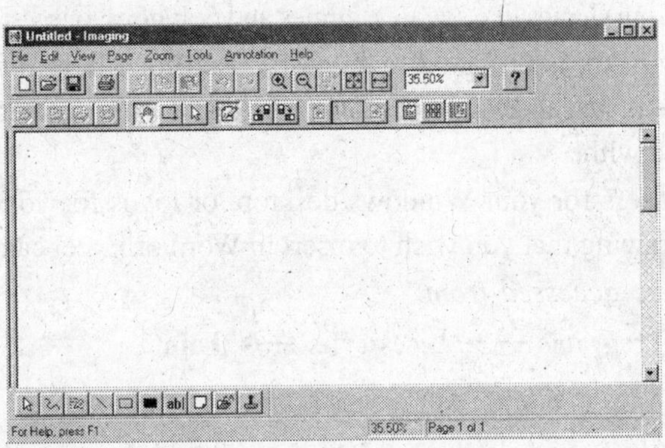

Calculator A full-fledged calculator is provided through which you can perform various calculations. You have the option of using the scientific (With Cos, Sin, Tan, log, Square-Root, Cube-Root functions etc.) or the standard calculator having basic mathematical functions. You can use either the keyboard or the mouse to enter numbers and operators into the calculator. In case you need the result of your calculations somewhere in your document, you can use the copy command provided along with the calculator to copy the result at the desired place. It can be accessed from:

Start ⟶ Programs ⟶ Accessories ⟶ Calculator

The following screen will be displayed (Scientific Version):

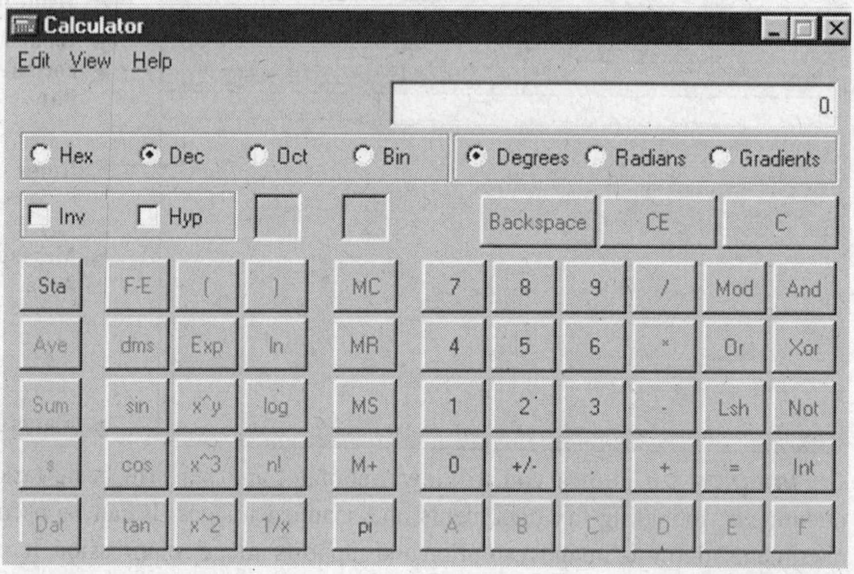

Paint Allows you to create, edit and view pictures. Some of the features of Paint are as follows:

- Allows to create or "assemble" pictures by drawing straight, wavy or curved lines, using shapes like squares, circles and polygons, or by simply free hand drawing.
- A colour box is provided that can be used for filling different colors into your document. It can even erase any portion of your masterpiece that you are not satisfied with.
- Wall papers for your Windows desktop, or logos for your company, or any free hand drawing that you wish to insert in Word or Excel can be created using paint.

It can be accessed from:

Start ⟶ Programs ⟶ Accessories ⟶ Paint

The following window will be displayed:

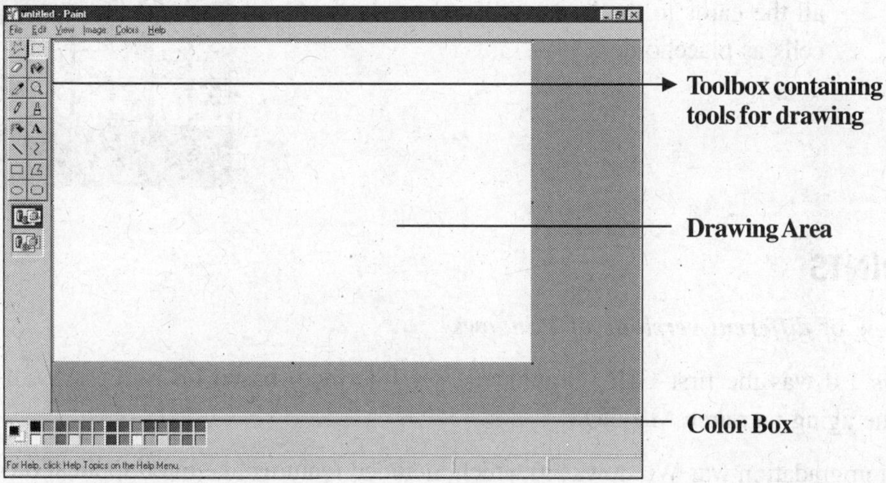

Games Windows contains some standard games – Solitaire, Minesweeper, Hearts and FreeCell. Games can be accessed from:

Start ⟶ Programs ⟶ Accessories ⟶ Games

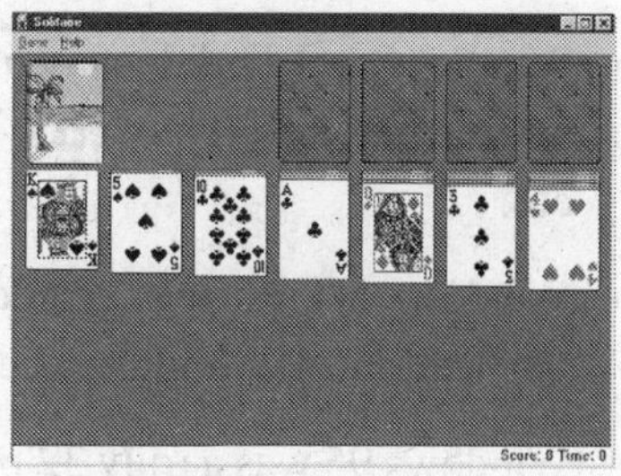

i. **Solitaire** The object of this game is to use all the cards in the deck to build up the four suit stacks from ace to king.

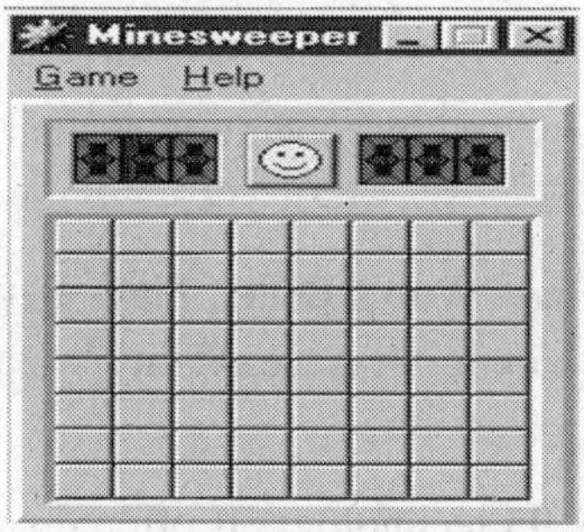

ii. **Minesweeper** The object of this game is to find all the mines on the playing field as quickly as possible without uncovering any of them.

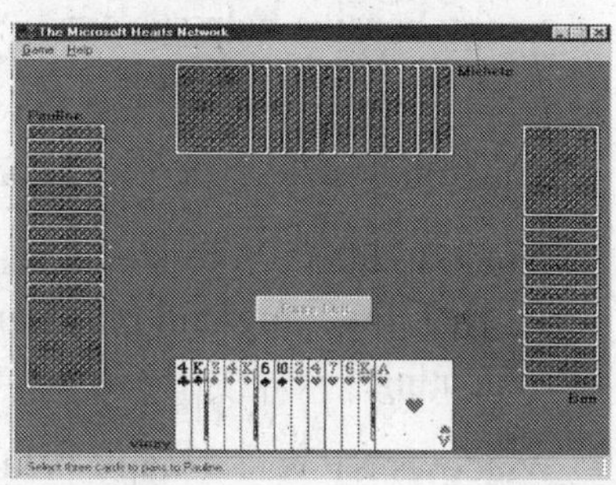

iii. **Hearts** The object of Hearts is to have the lowest score at the end of the game.

iv. **FreeCell** The object of FreeCell is to move all the cards to the home cells, using the free cells as placeholders.

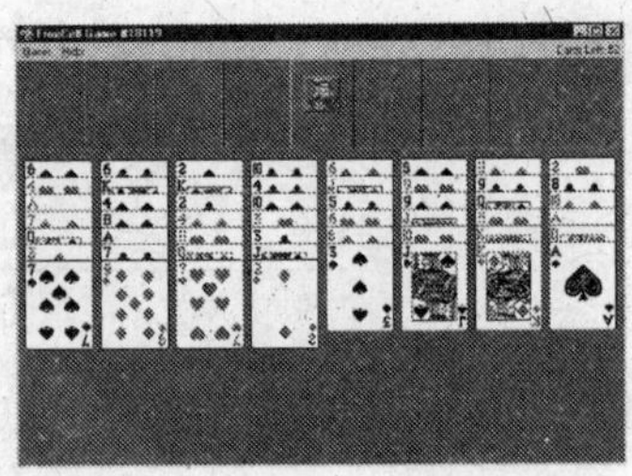

KEY POINTS

Overview of different versions of Windows

- Windows 1.0 was the first GUI (Graphical User Interface) based operating system that replaced the aging patriarch MS-DOS.
- The next upgradation was Windows 2.0 which included features like inter-application communication, use of keyboard shortcuts for switching between windows etc.
- Windows 3.0 was a 32 bit operating system that included Program Manager, File Manager, Printer Manager, improved set of icons and a powerful application development environment.
- Window 3.1/3.11 did many miscellaneous operations like sending a fax (Microsoft Fax, hooking up to a network (Network), linking up to an outside information service company (Terminal) etc.
- Windows NT 3.1 was geared towards business users and it included support for Client/Server applications and multi-processor architectures.
- Windows 95 was a truly 32 bit operating system with built in Internet-support and plug and play capabilities.
- Windows NT 4.0 was an upgrade to Microsoft's business desktop operating system with increased ease of use and simplified management.
- Windows 98 is often described as an operating system that "Works Better, Plays Better". Its main features were multiple display support, USB support, an Accessibility wizard and a comprehensive help system.
- Windows ME was the last OS to be based on Windows 95 technology. It offered consumers numerous music, video, and home networking enhancements and reliability improvements.
- Windows 2000 Professional was an upgrade to Windows NT 4.0. It added major improvements in reliability, plug and play hardware, ease of use, Internet compatibility, support for mobile computing.
- Windows XP was a major breakthrough for desktop operating systems. Two main versions of

Windows XP were released namely Windows XP Home Edition and Windows XP Professional Edition.

Basic Window Elements

- Once Windows is loaded into the memory of the computer, the user works on the Windows Desktop. Desktop comprises of icons that represent various applications loaded onto your computer. Icons are further classified into five categories namely Folder Icons, Document Icons, Program Icons, Shortcut Icons and System Icons.
- System Icons are actual programs or files that are located on your desktop. Examples of System Icons – Recycle Bin, My Computer, Network Neighborhood etc.
- Other elements of Desktop are Start button and Taskbar. Standard items included in the Start menu are 'Programs', 'Favorites', 'Documents', 'Settings', 'Find', 'Help', 'Run' and 'Shut Down'. Start button is also an element of the Taskbar.
- The other elements of taskbar are Quick Launch Toolbar and System Tray. The Quick Launch allows for immediate access to a variety of elements through a mouse click. The System Tray contains icons for applications that are running in the background of the computer.
- A typical Application Window in Windows contains the following elements - Title Bar, Menu Bar, Control box (Minimize button, Maximize/Restore button and Close button), Scroll bars and a Status bar.
- Menus can be classified into Sub-Menus and Context Menus. Clicking on some menu items may lead to a Dialogue box. Dialog boxes are small Windows that appear when a program needs more information before it can complete an operation.
- Some frequently used controls in Windows are Textbox, Drop down box, Option button, Check box, Command button, Tab and Spinners.
- Windows can be customised according to user preferences. Shortcuts can be created/deleted, Background pictures and Screen Savers can be added.
- Control panel contains utilities for customising the Windows interface, adding/removing installed components, changing number, date, time and currency formats, changing desktop display, configuring modems, customising mouse, defining regional settings, assigning sounds to program events and many more.

File Management

- The contents of a hard disk can be organised in different folders. Each of the folders can contain any number of sub-folders or files. The number of files in a folder or sub folder is limited only by your hard disk capacity.

- Windows Explorer is a utility that represents the contents of your computer in a graphical form. It allows you to do various file and disk management tasks like copy, rename, move and delete file(s) and create folder(s) and sub-folder(s), format floppies etc.
- Windows Explorer contains various functions that can be used to create, rename and delete files as well as folders in the hard disk.
- Multiple files from one folder can be copied to different locations at one go using 'Ctrl' and 'Shift' keys of the keyboard.
- Files/Folders once created can be renamed or deleted. Deleting a folder will automatically delete all its contents.
- Files/Folders can be displayed using different views in Windows Explorer – Small Icons View, Large Icons View, List View and Details View.

Windows Accessories

- Windows has many built in accessories. Some of the commonly used accessories can be classified into three categories, viz., System Tools, Entertainment and miscellaneous utilities.
- Some of the commonly used System Tools include Disk Cleanup, Disk Defragmenter and Scan Disk. Disk Cleanup frees up space on your hard disk by deleting all temporary cache files. Defragmenter rearranges files and unused hard disk space to enable programs run faster. Scan Disk checks the hard disk and removable disk for logical and physical errors.
- Entertainment Tools include CD Player, Sound Recorder, Volume Control and Windows Media Player. CD Player is used to play audio compact discs on a CD-ROM drive connected to your computer. Sound Recorder is used to record, edit and play sound files. Volume Control is used to adjust the volume when playing audio files. Media player can be used to play audio, video or animation files.
- Some of the commonly used Windows accessories include Notepad, Wordpad, Calculator, Imaging, Paint, and Games. Notepad is a simple text-based editor with limited features. Wordpad is a text-based editor that supports text formatting using different fonts and styles. Calculator can be used for performing mathematical as well as scientific calculations. Paint is used to create, edit and view pictures. Windows contains some standard games – Solitaire, Minesweeper, Hearts and FreeCell.

REVIEW QUESTIONS

1. Choose the appropriate answer:

i. Microsoft Windows 2000 is an up gradation of

(a) Windows 98 (b) Windows NT
(c) Windows ME (d) None of the above

ii. Which type of icons cannot be deleted from the desktop?

(a) Folder Icons (b) System Icons
(c) Program Icons (d) Document Icons

iii. Which of the following is a system icon?

(a) MS Word (b) Windows Explorer
(c) My Computer (d) None of the above

iv. Which control is used by Windows for viewing text beyond the screen?

(a) Status Bar (b) Task Bar
(c) Title Bar (d) Scroll Bar

v. The menu that displays a list of options when a particular item is right clicked is referred to as:

(a) Main Menu (b) Sub Menu
(c) Context Menu (d) None of the above

vi. Which of the following utilities displays the contents of your computer in graphical form?

(a) Start Menu (b) Desktop
(c) Internet Explorer (d) Windows Explorer

vii. Which of the following combination of keys can be used to delete a continuous range of files that are stored in the same folder?

(a) 'Alt+Del' (b) 'Shift+Del'
(c) 'Ctrl+Del' (d) None of the above

viii. Which type of folder view displays complete information about a folder?

(a) List View (b) Large Icons View
(c) Details View (d) None of the above

ix. This utility rearranges discontiguous files and free space on your computer so that your files are stored in contiguous units and free space is consolidated in one contiguous block.

(a) Disk Cleanup (b) Patch
(c) Logical addressing (d) Defragmenter

x. Find the odd one out:

(a) Scan Disk (b) CD Player
(c) Volume Control (d) Media Player

2. Enter True or False:

i. Windows is a single task operating system.

ii. Desktop consists of a series of icons and a taskbar placed at the bottom of the screen.

iii. All files that are deleted from the computer are stored in Recycle Bin.

iv. Windows Explorer contains utilities for customising the Windows interface, adding/removing installed components, changing number, date, time and currency formats, assigning sounds to program events and many more.

v. Dialog boxes are small windows that appear when a program needs more information before it can complete an operation.

vi. In a GUI a list box can be used for displaying a list of values.

vii. Deleting a shortcut for a folder would actually delete the folder itself.

viii. A folder can consist of any number of sub-folders.

ix. Address bar of the Windows explorer is used to display the path of the selected document.

x. Scan disk is used to delete temporary cache files from your computer.

3. Match the following:

	X	Y
1.	For application programs name of the document along with the program name is displayed here.	(a) Start Button
2.	Quick Launch Toolbar and System Tray	(b) Folder
3.	Provides a quick way to start a program or open a file or folder without having to go to its permanent location in Windows Explorer.	(c) Windows 98
4.	Switching between multiple Windows Saver.	(d) Screen
5.	Gives access to a series of menus like 'Programs', 'Documents', 'Settings', 'Shut Down' etc.	(e) Elements of Task Bar..
6.	A collection of files.	(f) Title Bar

7.	A text based editor.	(g) Wordpad
8.	A moving page or a pattern that appears on your monitor when you have left your computer idle for a specified limit.	(h) 'Alt + Tab'
9.	A GUI based multitasking operating system.	(i) Scan Disk
10.	Checks hard disk for logical and physical errors and then repairs the damaged areas.	(j) Shortcuts

4. Fill in the blanks with the appropriate choices listed below

(i) Start Button (ii) Search (iii) Shift +Del (iv) Shortcut (v) Icons (vi) Windows Explorer (vii) Taskbar (viii) Calculator (xi) Alt + Del (x) CD Player (xi) Pictures (xii) Find (xiii) Media Player (xiv) Details View (xv) Scan Disk

1. Desktop contains a series of labeled pictures referred to as ____________.
2. To permanently delete files from the hard disk without moving them to the bin use ____________ while deleting the files.
3. All the applications and tools available in the computer can be accessed from ____________.
4. ____________ allows searching for files, folders located anywhere within the computer or within the network.
5. Buttons are placed on the ____________ for each application that is actively running on the computer.
6. If a menu item has a letter in it that is underlined, the item may be selected by holding down the Alt key on the computer and pressing the underlined key whenever the menu is visible. This type of keys are referred to as ____________ keys.
7. ________________ allows you to do various file and disk management tasks like copy, rename, move and delete file(s) and create folder(s) and sub-folder(s), format floppies etc.
8. ________________ for folders displays information like item name, size, type (folder or file type), and the date the item was last modified.
9. ________________ can be used for performing mathematical calculations.
10. ____________ can be used to play audio and video files of multiple formats.

5. Give a brief overview of different versions of Windows.

6. Write short notes on Windows Explorer.

7. Explain briefly the basic elements of Windows Desktop.

8. Write short notes on

(a) Disk Defragmenter (b) Scan Disk

9. Write short notes on

(a) CD Player (b) Windows Media Player

10. Discuss in brief the main features of Word Pad.

6

Word Processing

WORD BASICS

Microsoft Word is a full-featured word processing program which can be used for any work involving creating and managing text. You can use it for the simplest to the most complex word processing applications. Using Word, you can write letters and reports, prepare bills and invoices, prepare office stationery–letter heads, envelopes and forms, design brochures, pamphlets, newsletters, magazines, etc.

In short, you would find it extremely difficult to think of a word processing feature not available in Microsoft Word. For most tasks, Word offers several ways of doing the same thing. It is up to the user to find which method is more preferable to him. Since covering all the different methods for doing the same task would require a book running into a thousand pages, I have taken the liberty of illustrating the method(s) I considered most user-friendly. As you gain more proficiency in using Word, you will yourself discovering other methods of doing your tasks, some of them perhaps more personally preferable to you than the ones I have selected.

STARTING WORD

To start **Word** click once on the **Start** button, choose **Programs** and click once on **Microsoft Office** and then once on **Microsoft Word.**

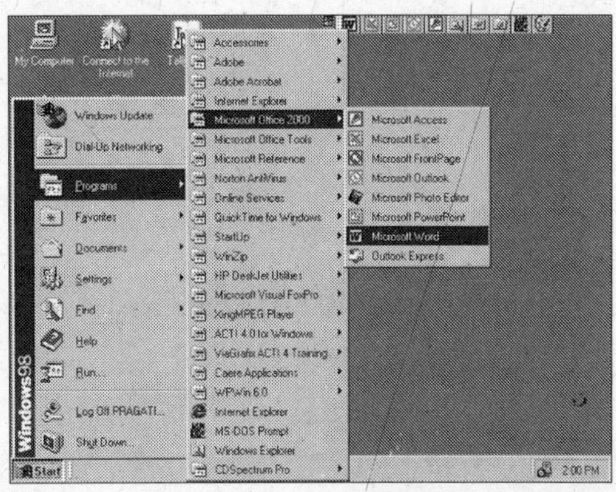

On starting Word you would see a Word main screen with the Tip of the Day. These tips are Word's way of teaching you new tricks and techniques while you work. Most of these tips are quite informative and some are even entertaining.

Read the tip, if you have the time and the inclination, then click once on Close OK button in the dialogue box to start working on the document.

Word always starts by opening an untitled "normal" document so that you can begin from scratch. This "normal" document is based upon all the default values (another name for pre-defined settings) provided by Word, i.e., standard page size, standard margins, font type and size etc. These settings can also be changed, details of which have been covered later in the book.

Different Views of Word

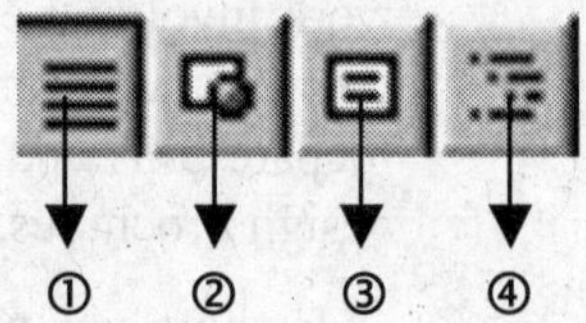

Any Word document can be viewed in four different types of views namely **Normal** View, **Web Layout** View, **Print Layout** View and **Outline** View. You can switch from one view to another by simply clicking on the corresponding icon.

① **Normal View:** This is the default view.

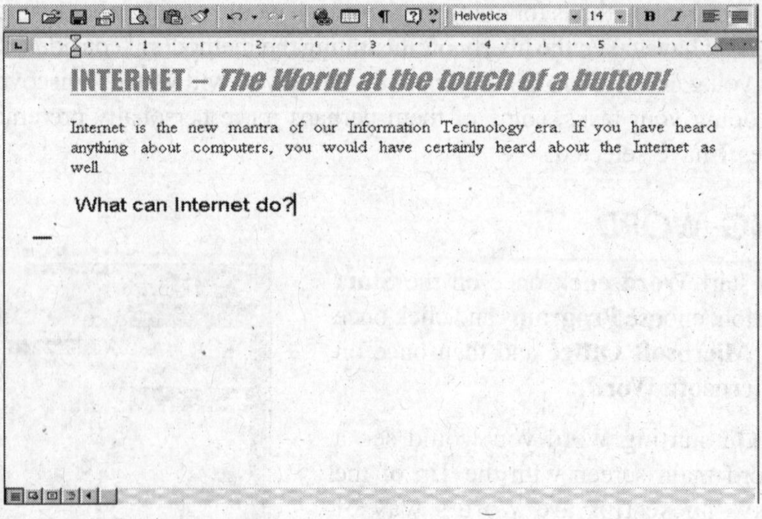

② **Web Layout View**: In this view you can preview your page, as it will appear in a web browser.

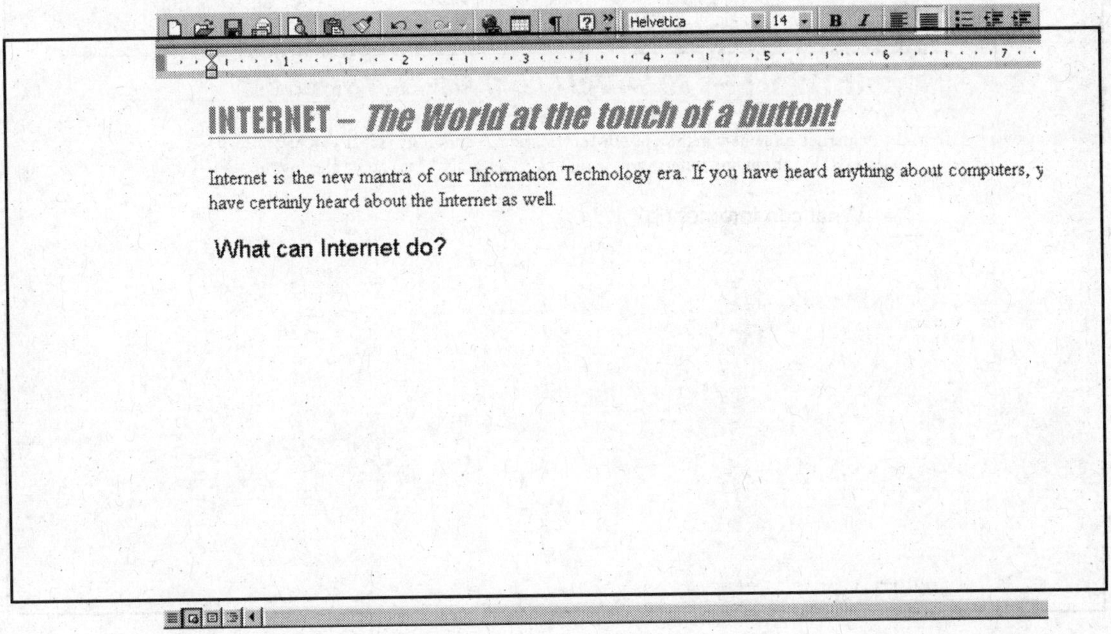

③ **Print Layout View:** In this view you can preview your page, as it will appear when printed. You can see the page margins and borders.

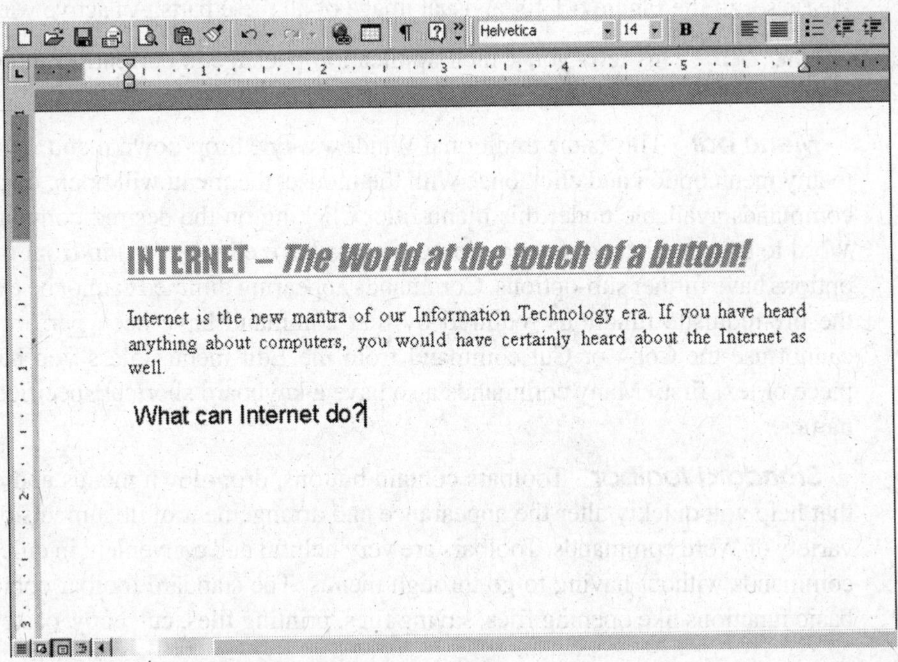

④ **Outline View:** In this view you can specify upto seven levels of headings. You can rearrange both the headings as well as its content to revise the structure of the document.

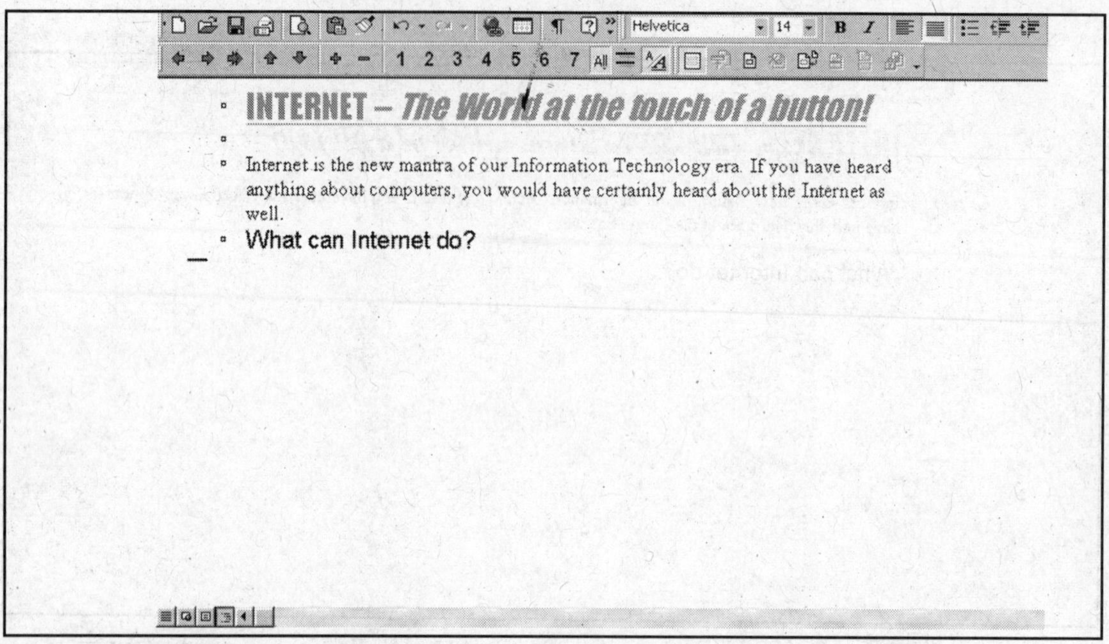

PARTS OF WORD WINDOW

Please see in the Figure 6.1 for a visual image of all these parts. An active window has:

Title bar This tells you which application package is currently running and which document is currently open.

Menu bar This is the traditional Windows style drop-down menu. When you point to any menu option and click once with the mouse, the menu will open, displaying all the commands available under this menu title. Clicking on the desired command would tell Word to execute that command. Some options have ellipses (…) in front of them. These options have further sub-options. Commands appearing dimmed cannot be executed unless the pre-requisite functions required by that command have been performed, e.g., you cannot use the Copy or Cut command from the Edit menu unless you have selected a piece of text first. Many commands also have a keyboard shortcut specified against their names.

Standard toolbar Toolbars contain buttons, drop-down menus and other controls that help you quickly alter the appearance and arrangement of documents by executing a variety of Word commands. Toolbars are very helpful and convenient in quickly executing commands without having to go through menus. The standard toolbar contains icons for basic functions like opening files, saving files, printing files, cut, copy, paste etc.

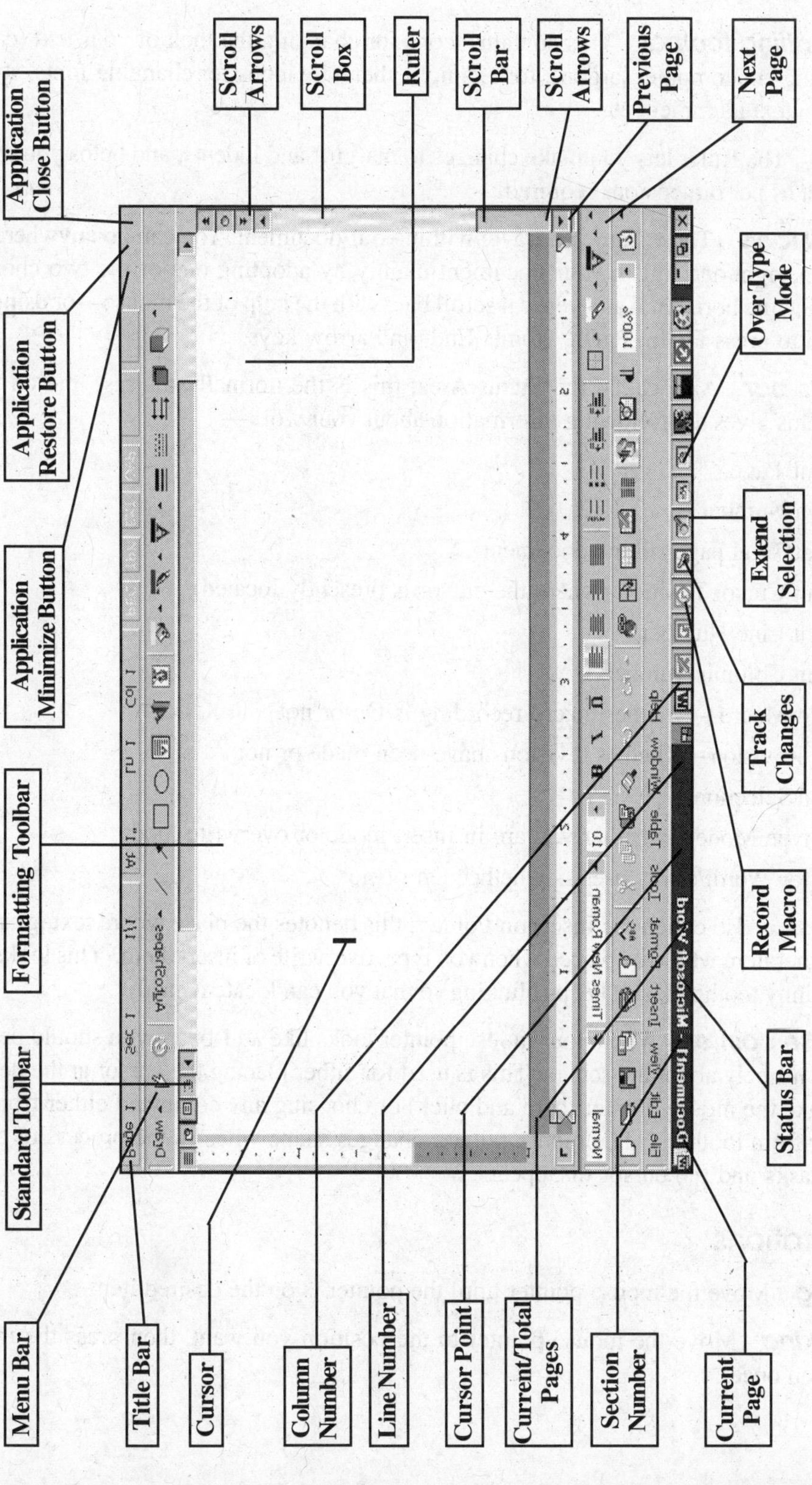

Fig. 6.1 Parts of a Word Window

Formatting toolbar This contains icons for changing the look of your text (called "formatting" in computer jargon); for example, there are icons for changing fonts, styles, font sizes, text alignment etc.

Ruler The Ruler lets you make changes to margins and indents, and helps you create document as per dimensions required.

Scroll tools These help you travel within your document. You can go anywhere, up and down, right and left in your document mainly by adopting one of the two choices: either using the horizontal and vertical scroll bars with the help of the mouse—or using the keyboard to press PgUp, PgDn, Home, End and arrow keys.

Status bar Also called the Status Area, this is the normally the last line on your screen. This gives the following information about your work—

- Current Page
- Section Number
- Current/Total pages in the document
- Current Cursor Position (where the cursor is presently located)
- Current Line Number
- Current Column Number
- Record Macro—whether macro recording is On or not
- Track Revision—whether revisions have been made or not
- Extend Selection
- Over type Mode—whether you are in Insert mode or overwrite mode
- Help for WordPerfect users—whether On or not.

Cursor Also called the Insertion Pointer, this denotes the place where text, graphics or any other item would be placed when you type, overwrite or insert them. This looks like a tall, skinny toothpick and keeps blinking so that you can locate it easily.

Mouse pointer When your mouse pointer looks like an I-beam you should be able to move it freely about the screen. This is used for either placing the cursor at the desired place (take the mouse pointer there and click) or choosing any command either from the menu or from toolbars. The mouse pointer changes shape when in the process of doing certain tasks and the cursor disappears.

Mouse Operations

Pointing Move the mouse pointer until the pointer is on the desired item.

Clicking Move the mouse pointer to the position you want, then press the mouse left button once.

Double-clicking Move the mouse pointer to the position you want, then press the mouse left button twice in rapid succession. Alternatively, if your mouse has been so installed, you can also click the middle button once, instead of pressing the left button twice.

Right-clicking In some cases like changing the properties of an object, or for correcting a mis-spelt word, or even for cut, copy and paste—the mouse right button can be used. In such cases, simply select the object and click once on the mouse right button.

Dragging Move the mouse pointer to the right place, highlight the desired text by clicking once in the beginning and releasing the left button at the end, then click once again in the highlighted block, keep the mouse left button pressed and roll the mouse to move the block to a new location by releasing the left button at the desired location.

At first, using the mouse may be difficult (particularly double-clicking and dragging). However, learning to use it is worth the trouble because many of the advanced tools in modern programs are only operated with the mouse. In any case most operations are much simpler and faster to execute through the mouse rather than through the keyboard.

Keyboard Operations

Typing keys The part of the keyboard which is used to type letters, numbers and other characters. The alphabets layout resembles a standard typewriter keyboard exactly. However there are some extra keys for entering commands, e.g., *Ctrl* key, *Alt* key, *Shift* key, *Enter* key etc. On most keyboards, these extra keys are grey in colour whereas the alphabet, number, symbol and punctuation keys are white in colour. The *Ctrl*, *Alt* and *Shift* key is always used in conjunction with some other key.

Shift and Caps Lock key The *Shift* key is used to type capital letters, i.e., if you want to type the letter "F", you have to press the *Shift* key, keep it pressed with one finger and press "f" key with the other. However, if you want to type an entire word or a sentence in capital letters, use the *Caps Lock* key instead. Unlike the *Shift* key, *Caps Lock* key is a toggle key and does not need to be pressed continuously. Press it once and it becomes *On* (you will see the Caps Lock indicator on the keyboard lighting up when you do this) and thereafter whatever you type would be in capital letters; press it again and it becomes *Off*.

Function keys The row of 10–12 keys—*F1* to *F12* above the typing keys are called the Function keys and are used to execute special commands or as shortcut keys. The use of these keys varies from program to program, however within MS Office some degree of standardisation has been achieved. In Word, the function keys are used alone or together with the *Shift, Alt* and *Ctrl* keys to give commands.

Cursor control keys A group of special keys used to control and navigate the cursor - arrow keys (Up ↑, Down ↓, Left ←, Right →). *Home* and *End* are used to quickly place the cursor in the beginning or end of a line. To delete an alphabet to the left of the cursor press the *Backspace* key ← (normally above the *Enter* key), to delete an alphabet to the right of the cursor press the *Del* key.

Numeric keypad The keys on the extreme right of the keyboard (resembling a calculator's keyboard), which can be used both to enter numbers (when the *Num Lock* is *On*) as well as to move the cursor (when the *Num Lock* is *Off*). The *Num Lock* key is located above the number 7 (Home) key on the Numeric keypad and its *On* or *Off* status is displayed by the *Num Lock* indicator light on your keyboard. Since *Num Lock* is also a toggle key, pressing it once makes it *On* and pressing it again makes it *Off*.

Note: Press the keys briefly with a light pressure, unless you want repeated characters.

The Most Important Keys

Alt and Ctrl The command keys are used in combination with another key or with the mouse. For example, the Alt+F4 key combination (press down the Alt key, hold it down and press the F4 function key briefly and then release both) closes the program.

Shift Like Alt and Ctrl, the Shift key is also used in commands in combination with other keys. In typing, it is used in the same way as on a typewriter – to produce capital letters.

Enter When typing text, press Enter when you want to produce a forced line feed (e.g., at the end of a paragraph and to create blank lines). Enter is also used in combination with other keys to execute a few commands. On some keyboards, this key is named Return instead of Enter.

Esc The Esc key is located to the left of the function keys, in the upper left corner of the keyboard. It can be used to Cancel selection in a menu.

Backspace Pressing this key deletes the character to the left of the cursor.

Del (Delete) This key deletes the character to the right of the cursor.

How to type in Word Once Word has been started, you can immediately start typing. When you press character keys on the keyboard, you can see the corresponding characters appear in the Word window. Use the Spacebar when you want to separate characters and words from each other. Use the Tab key when you want to move the cursor or text from one Tab stop to another, and also when you want to create a blank longer than one space between words. Use 'Enter' key when you want to start a new paragraph.

Insert and Overtype modes Word normally uses the insert mode. In this mode, Word does not overtype the existing text but pushes it forward. By pressing the Ins key, you can switch to overtype mode. In this mode, the new text replaces the old text after the cursor. To switch between Overtype/Insert modes press the *Insert* key. In the Insert mode, when you place the cursor in the middle of two words and start typing, the new text is inserted between the two words and all the text below this line is automatically adjusted.

In the Overtype mode, when you place the cursor in the middle of two words and start typing, the new text overwrites the previous text.

SOME 'DON'TS'

- Don't use the Spacebar to indent paragraphs. Instead, use the Tab key for the indent control in Word's ruler (the top handle on the left hand side)
- Don't use Spacebar to centre or otherwise position text. Use the Left, Right and Center alignment buttons from Formatting bar instead.
- Don't use Spacebar to create columns. Use Word's Table or Column command instead.
- Don't hit Enter key repeatedly for starting the matter on new page. Use Insert Page break command instead.

MENUS, COMMANDS, TOOLBARS AND THEIR ICONS

Till some years ago, users used to type long string of code words, called **Commands**, for making the computer do anything. The user had to remember these coded commands for each step that he wished to execute. Each command had an appropriate grammar, called **Syntax**. This meant that even if you made the slightest mistake in typing the command, it would not work.

Fortunately things have changed dramatically now. Users are not expected to be trained parrots that can reproduce phrases or sentences verbatim! Now, all Windows based software have a Graphical User Interface, consisting of icons and menus. Simply click on the desired icon through your mouse and presto – the command would be executed. To make sure that icons look different from each other, they have small pictures on them, e.g., the icon which prints your documents has a picture of a printer on it, the icon which saves your work has a picture of floppy on it, and so on. This makes it very easy to recognise and remember the individual use of these icons. To make things still simpler, whenever you leave your mouse pointer on the top of any icon, for a couple of seconds, the icon's name is shown below it, so that you know what this particular icon does for you.This text is reffered to as **Tool Tip** text.

In MS Word, groups of icons, which perform related tasks, are placed together in a ribbon, called a *Toolbar*. There are many toolbars available in Word—Standard toolbar, Formatting toolbar, Drawing toolbar, Tables and Borders toolbars etc. Each of these contain an assortment of related icons, specific to that toolbar. For executing most tasks, the user has three options:

1. Choose the desired command from the Menu options provided by either using the mouse or using cursor movement keys, or
2. Press the appropriate shortcut keys combination from the keyboard, or
3. Click once on the relevant icon from the displayed toolbars.

Although there is no wrong or right approach, most users find the third option simplest and fastest.

The present section deals in detail with toolbars and icons. It deals with all the Word toolbar–the names of icons within each toolbar, it's purpose and usage, it's menu equivalent option and it's keyboard shortcut, if any.

You are advised to just go through the pages in this section once. Do not worry if you do not understand everything and, most importantly—do not try to memorise anything. Mugging up is no substitute for actual practice. In the next section, when we do exercises based upon these menu options and icons, these would automatically become second nature to you. Later, this section may be used by you to refer to any specific command or icon's usage.

TOOLBARS AND THEIR ICONS

Word Standard Toolbar

New

Creates a new document based on normal template.
Alternative: File→New
Shortcut→Ctrl+N

Open

Opens an existing document or template.
Alternative: File→Open
Shortcut→Ctrl+O

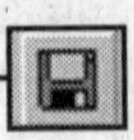

Save

Saves the active document or template
Alternative: File→ Save
Shortcut→Ctrl+S

E-Mail

It sends the contents of the document as the body of the e-mail message.
Alternative: File→ Send To→ Mail

Print

Prints the active document using current defaults.
Alternative: File→ Print
Shortcut→Ctrl+P

Print Preview

Displays full page as they are printed.
Alternative: File→ Print Preview
Shortcut→Ctrl+F2

Spelling

Checks the spelling in the active document
Alternative: Tools→Spelling and Grammar
Shortcut→F7

Cut

Cuts the selection and puts it on the Clipboard.
Alternative: Edit→Cut
Shortcut→Ctrl+X

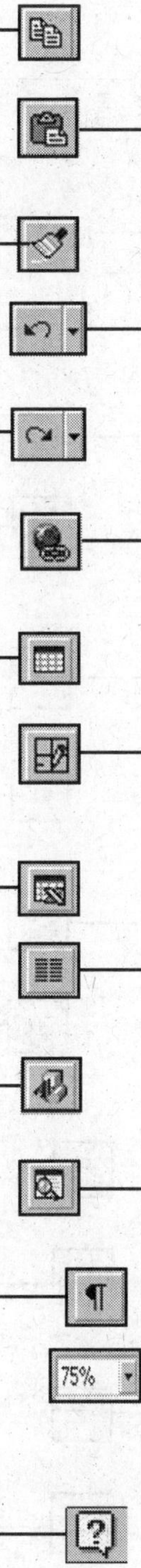

Copy
Copies the selection and puts it on the clipboard.
Alternative: Edit→Copy
Shortcut→Ctrl+C

Paste
Inserts the clipboard contents at the insertion point.
Alternative: Edit→Paste
Shortcut→Ctrl+V

Format Painter
Copies the formatting of the selection to a specified location.
Shortcut→Ctrl+Shift+C

Undo
Reverses certain commands.
Alternative: Edit→Undo
Shortcut→Ctrl+Z

Redo
Reverses the action of the Undo command.
Alternative: Edit→Repeat
Shortcut→Ctrl+Y

Insert Hyperlink
Displays the destination object, document or page.
Alternative: Edit→Repeat
Shortcut→Ctrl+K

Insert Table
Inserts a table
Alternative: Table→Insert Table

Tables and Borders
Displays the tables and borders toolbar.
Alternative:
View→Toolbars→Tables and Borders

Insert Excel Worksheet
Inserts Microsoft Excel Worksheet.
Alternative: Insert→File

Columns
Changes the column format of the selected sections.
Alternative: Format→Columns

Drawing
Shows or hides the Drawing Toolbar.
Alternative: View→ Toolbars →Drawing

Document Map
Shows an outline of a document heading and helps to quickly navigate around the document.
Alternative: View→Document Map

Show/Hide
Shows/hides non-printing characters.
Shortcut→Ctrl+*

Zoom Control
Scales the editing view (Zoom).
Alternative: View→Zoom

Office Assistant
Provides help topics and tips to accomplish your task.
*Alternative:*Help→ Microsoft Word Help
Shortcut →F1

Word Formatting Toolbar

Style
Applies a style or records a style by example.
Alternative: Format→Style
Shortcut→Ctrl+Shift+S

Font
Changes the font of the selection.
Alternative: Format→Font
Shortcut→Ctrl+Shift+F

Font Size
Changes the font size of the selection.
Alternative: Format→Font→Size
Shortcut→Ctrl+Shift+P

Bold
Makes the selection Bold.
Alternative: Format→Font→Font style
Shortcut→Ctrl+B

Italic
Makes the selection Italics.
*Alternative:*Format→Font→Font style
Shortcut→Ctrl+I

Underline
Formats the selection with continuous underline.
Alternative:
Format→Font→effects
Shortcut→Ctrl+U

Align Left
Aligns the paragraph at left indent.
Alternative:
Format→Paragraph→Alignment
Shortcut→Ctrl+L

Centre
Centres the paragraphs between the indents.
Alternative :
Format→Paragraph→Alignment
Shortcut→Ctrl+E

Align Right
Aligns the paragraph at right indent.
Alternative:
Format→Paragraph→Alignment
Shortcut→Ctrl+R

Justify
Aligns the paragraph at both right and left indent.
Alternative:
Format→Paragraph→Alignment
Shortcut→Ctrl+J

Numbering
Creates a numbered list based on the current defaults.
Alternative:
Format→Bullets and Numbering

Bullets
Creates a bulleted list based on the current defaults.
Alternative:
Format→Bullets and Numbering

Decrease Indent

Decreases or promotes the selection one level.

Alternative:

Format→Paragraph→Indentation

Increase Indent

Increases indent or demotes the selection one level.

Alternative:

Format→Paragraph→Indentation

Borders

Shows or hides the border toolbar.

Alternative:

Format→Borders and Shading

Highlight

Highlights a selected piece of text in the chosen color.

Font Color

Selects and applies Font Color.

Alternative:

Format→Font→Color

Word Tables and Borders Toolbar

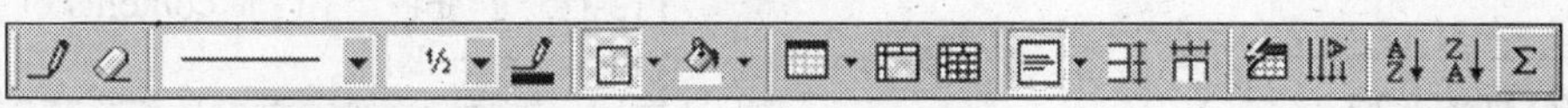

Draw Table

Inserts a table where you drag in the document. After you drag to insert the table, drag inside the table to add cells, columns, or rows.

Eraser

Removes a table cell line and merges the contents of the adjacent cells. If the cell has a border, Word removes the border but does not merge the cells. Click Eraser, and then drag the eraser pointer over the table cell lines or borders you don't want.

Line Width

Click the width you want for the border on the selected object.

Border Color

Click on the border color you want.

Border Style

Click the style and thickness you want for the selected line.

Fill Color

Adds, modifies, or removes the fill color or fill effect from the selected object. Fill effects include gradient, texture, pattern, and picture fills.

Outside Border

Adds or removes a border around the selected text, paragraphs, cells, pictures, or other object.

Insert Table
Inserts a table in the document with the number of columns and rows you specify.

Merge Cells
It combines the contents of the selected adjacent cells into a single cell.

Split Cells
It splits the selected cells into the number of rows and columns you enter.

Align Top Left
Aligns horizontally oriented text with the top of the table cell. Similarly you can choose from the various options to align the text differently.

Distribute Rows Evenly
Changes the selected rows or cells to equal row height.

Distribute Columns Evenly
Changes the selected columns or cells to equal column width.

Table AutoFormat
It automatically applies formats, including predefined borders and shading, to a table. Automatically resizes a table to fit the contents of the table cells.

Change Text Direction
Orients selected text in a text box, cell, or frame horizontally, left to right.

Sort Ascending
Sorts the selected items in order from the beginning of the alphabet, the lowest number, or the earliest date, using the column that contains the insertion point. If you previously set other sorting options, those options are still in effect.

Sort Descending
Sorts the selected items in order from the end of the alphabet, the highest number, or the latest date, using the column that contains the insertion point. If you previously set other sorting options, those options are still in effect.

AutoSum
Inserts a = (Formula) field that calculates and displays the sum of the values in table cells above or to the left of the cell containing the insertion point.

Word Drawing Toolbar

Draw

Activates the Draw Menu

Free Rotate

Rotates the selected object to any degree. Select the object, click on the icon and then drag a corner of the object in the direction you want to rotate it.

Line

Draws a straight line where you click or drag in the active Window. To constrain the line to draw at 15-degree angle from its starting point, hold down SHIFT as you drag.

Rectangle

Draws an rectangle where you click or drag in the active Window. To draw a square, press SHIFT and drag.

Text Box

Draws a text box where you click or drag in the active Window. Use a text box to add a text—such as captions or callouts—to your pictures or graphics.

Alternative: Insert→TextBox

Clip Art

Opens the Clip Gallery where you can select the clip art image you want to insert in your file or update your clip art collection.

Alternative: Insert→Picture →Clip Art

Select Objects

Changes the pointer to a selection arrow so that you can select objects in the active window. To select a single object, click the object with the arrow. To select one or more objects, drag the arrow over the objects you want to select.

Auto Shapes

Activates the AutoShapes menu.

Arrow

Inserts a line with an arrowhead where you click or drag in the active Window. To constrain the line to draw at the 15-degree angle from its starting point, hold down SHIFT as you drag.

Oval

Draws an oval where you click or drag in the active Window. To draw a circle, press SHIFT and drag.

Word Art

Creates text effects by inserting a Microsoft Office drawing object.

Alternative: Insert→Picture →Word Art

Fill Color

Adds, modifies, or removes the fill color or fill effect from the selected object. Fill effects include gradient, texture, pattern and picture fills.

Font Color

Formats the selected text with the color you click.

Line Color
Adds, modifies, or removes the line color from the selected object.

Line Style
Click the width you want for the selected line.

Dash Style
Click the dashed line or dashed-dot line style you want for the selected shape or border. Click the solid line if you don't want the dotted line.

Arrow Style
Click the arrowhead style you want for the selected line.

3-D
Click the 3-D style you want for the selected object.

Shadow
Click the shadow style you want for the selected object.

Note: Although by default the Standard and Formatting toolbars are normally displayed below the Menubar, it is the user who decides which toolbars he wants to be displayed while working. To display or remove any toolbar from the users view, click on the **View** menu, choose **Toolbars** and click on the desired toolbar.

The following exercise (Word Exercise - 1) explains the basic Word processing concepts.

- Creating a New Document
- Saving a Document
- Closing a Document
- Opening an Existing Document
- Selecting Text
- Editing Text
- Finding and Replacing Text
- Formatting Features
- Page Design and Layout
- Printing a Document

WORD EXERCISE 1

INTERNET – *The World at the touch of a button!*

Internet is the new mantra of our Information Technology era. If you have heard anything about computers, you would have certainly heard about the Internet as well.

What is Internet after All?

The Internet is a world - wide network of computer networks. Imagine a network of five computers in your office that are linked up together in such a manner that you can exchange data, correspondence (mail) and even software between these computers. Now imagine that you have a business associates or friends who also have several computers in their homes or offices organised pretty much like yours. Now imagine all these computers spread over different locations linked up in manner so that they (meaning you!) can communicate between each other. This is what Internet is all about. Internet is a global network linking millions of computers and people cutting across all barriers and boundaries of countries, race, class or sex. Internet can also be described as a collection of government, academic, commercial and individual's sites.

What can Internet do?

- E-Mail
- E-Commerce
- E-Chat
- Central Repository of Data
- Advertisement Billboard
- Distance learning
- Shareware Software
- Wide Area Networks and much more.

1. **E-Mail** Through E-mail (Electronic Mail), mail messages can be sent to or received from anywhere in the world, in a matter of minutes and even fewer rupees!
2. **E-Commerce** Through Internet you can shop for various products and pay through your credit card, ask your bank to transfer money from account of yours to another; all this without leaving your desk!
3. **E-Chat** Nowadays you can even make national and international telephone calls through the Internet at practically the cost of a local call.
4. **Central Repository of Data** The Internet is like a huge central ware house of data that can be accessed and queried by people from all over the world.

5. **Advertisement Billboard** You can launch your own site on the Internet or put up banner ads on other people's sites.
6. **Distance Learning** Several distance learning courses are available on the Internet through which you can study and complete courses on different subjects.
7. **Shareware Software** Internet is also a great place from where you can download shareware (free) software, games and utilities.
8. **Wide Area Networks** Using the Internet, organisations can collect and compile information from their offices spread over a huge geographical area.

CREATING A NEW DOCUMENT

① Choose **New** command from the **File Menu.** You can activate the menu in two ways:

1. Press ALT-F Key (or any Key underlined in Menu line to activate that menu list) and use the Keyboard to move up and down within the various options under the file menu and press Enter to select an option.
2. Use a mouse. Move the mouse pointer to File and click, this will open the menu list. Use the mouse to choose between various options and click once on the desired option.

② Click on the **General** folio.

③ Click here to choose **Blank Document**.

④ Click once on the **OK** button.

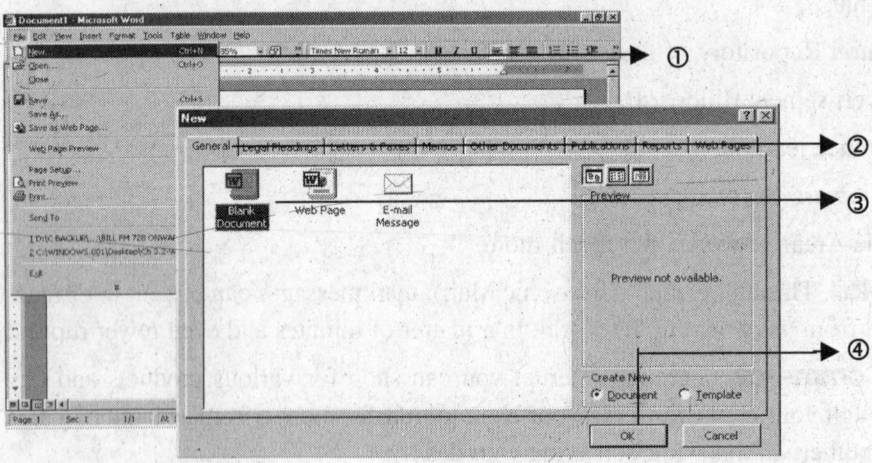

Entering Text

The blank white area is the place where you would be typing your matter. Notice the toothpick cursor at the beginning of first line, when you start typing, your text would appear from this point onwards. So let's begin. Start typing the text given in Sample Exercise 1. Type only till "Wide Area Networks, and much more" as shown below:

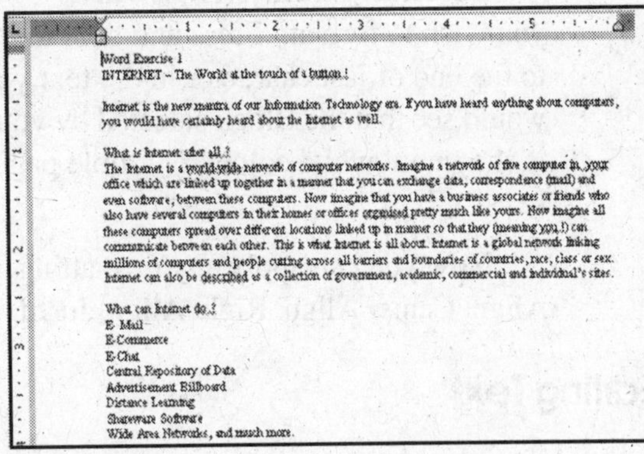

Word Exercise 1
INTERNET – The World at the touch of a button !

Internet is the new mantra of our Information Technology era. If you have heard anything about computers, you would have certainly heard about the Internet as well.

What is Internet after all.?
The Internet is a world-wide network of computer networks. Imagine a network of five computer in your office which are linked up together in a manner that you can exchange data, correspondence (mail) and even software, between these computers. Now imagine that you have a business associates or friends who also have several computers in their homes or offices organised pretty much like yours. Now imagine all these computers spread over different locations linked up in manner so that they (meaning you.!) can communicate between each other. This is what Internet is all about. Internet is a global network linking millions of computers and people cutting across all barriers and boundaries of countries, race, class or sex. Internet can also be described as a collection of government, academic, commercial and individual's sites.

What can Internet do.?
E-Mail
E-Commerce
E-Chat
Central Repository of Data
Advertisement Billboard
Distance Learning
Shareware Software
Wide Area Networks, and much more.

While typing do not bother about how your text looks, simply go ahead and type in continuity. One of the basic features of Word is Word-Wrap. This feature allows you to type in continuity without bothering about your line running out of right margin of your page. While you are typing as soon as you approach the end of a line (right side of your paper), Word automatically figures out whether the last word that you have typed can fit within the current line. If it will, fine, otherwise Word automatically picks up the whole word and places it in the next line.

When you reach the end of a paragraph or a paragraph heading (like – What is Internet after all?) press **Enter** to place your cursor in the next line. If you need a blank line then press **Enter** once more to create some blank space between two paragraphs. This point is so important that I am going to repeat it once again. Never press Enter after every line, but only at the end of a paragraph or a paragraph heading.

Paragraph Marks ¶

If this option is turned on then the paragraph symbol is displayed at the end of each paragraph. It helps in undestanding the formatting of your document. However this is a non-printable character, which means that when you print a document this symbol does not get printed. To turn off this option, click again on this symbol.

Selecting Text

All the formatting features offered by Word require pre-selection of a piece of text. This piece of text, also called a 'Block' or a 'Range' in computer speak, could be a single word, a phrase, a sentence, a paragraph, a page or the entire document. For applying various formatting commands this Block has to be specified first before choosing the desired formatting command.

Selecting text (Mouse) Place the mouse pointer at the beginning of the text that you wish to format. Click once, keep the left mouse button pressed and drag till the end of the Block. Release the mouse button and you would see that the Block selected by you has been highlighted in black colour and the text is shown in white colour. To select a word in a document simply double click on it and to select an entire paragraph use triple click.

Selecting text (Keyboard) Place the cursor at the beginning of the text that you wish to format. Press and hold the Shift key then use arrow keys to move the cursor to the end of last character in the text you wish to select. Release the arrow keys and you would see that the Block selected by you has been highlighted in black colour and the text is shown in white colour. Multiple pages can be selected by using 'Shift' + 'PageDown' keys.

Now you can apply any formatting command like Bold faced, Italics, Underline, Left Align, Center Align, Right Align, Justify, etc. by simply clicking on the correct icon.

Editing Text

If you make any mistakes while typing, use the **Backspace** and **Del** key to delete the incorrect text. **Backspace** key deletes a character to the left of the current cursor position whereas **Del** key deletes a character to the right of the current cursor position.

Finding Text

This utility can be used for searching for a word or a phrase in a document. Choose **Find** from the **Edit** Menu to access this utility.

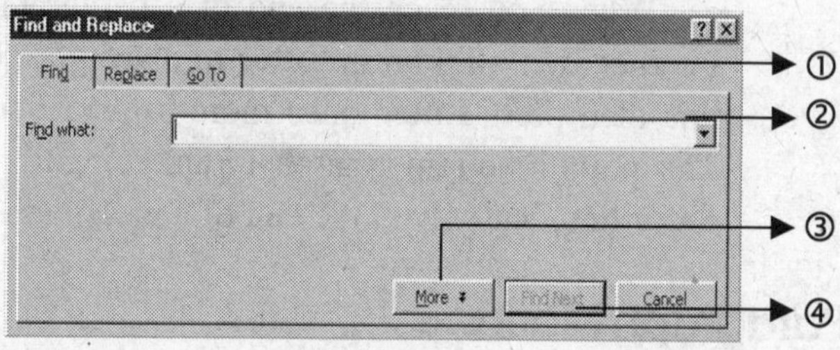

① Click on the **Find** tab/folio (or Ctrl + F keys).

② Enter the word/phrase that you want to search for in the document.

③ Click on this option if you want to specify more advanced options for performing the search.

④ Click here to locate the typed word in the document.

Replacing Text

This utility helps to replace a single or all instances of any word/phrase with another word/ phrase. For example, you can replace all occurrences of 'Word97' in a document with 'Word2000' at one click using this feature.

① Click on the **Replace** tab/folio.

② Enter the word/phrase that you want to search for in the document.

③ Enter the replacement word/phrase.

④ Click on this option if you want more advanced options.

⑤ Click here to locate the typed word in the document.

⑥ Click here to replace the found text or click on Find Next to skip to the next occurrence.

⑦ Click here to replace all occurrences of found text in the entire document.

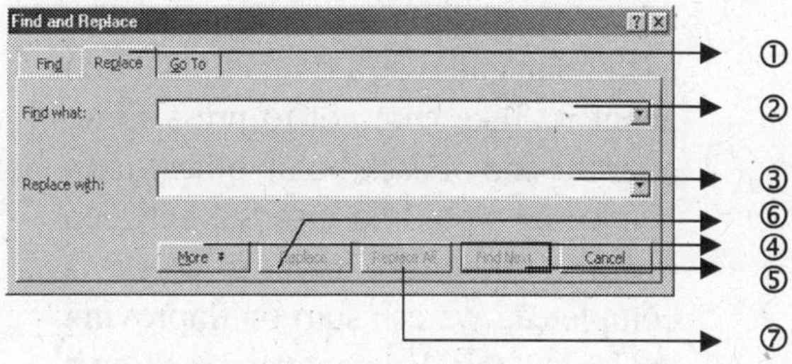

Undo Mistakes

Undo command can be used to undo the effect of recent commands or actions taken by the user. Redo command can be used to redo something that the user has undone. Redo undoes an Undo.

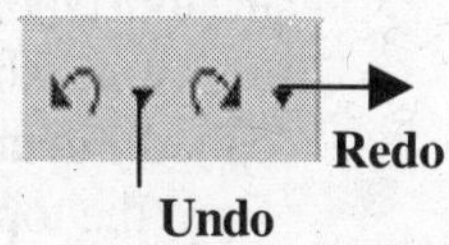

Undo and Redo command can be accessed from the Standard toolbar.

Note: Click the arrow button next to Undo button to view the list of recent actions that the user has undone.

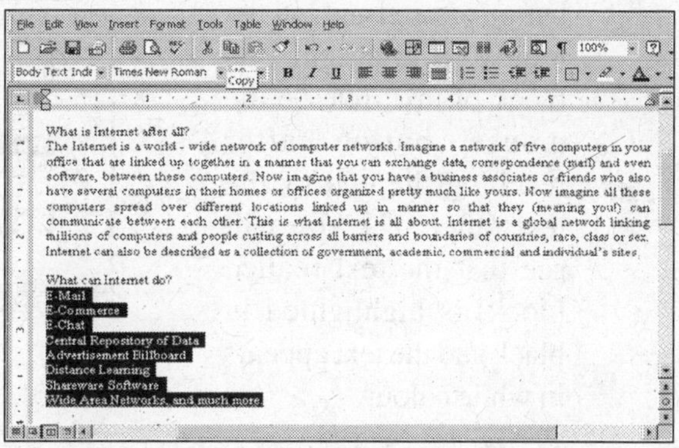

Coming back to our exercise, you will notice that the remaining text is a repetition of the same points about Internet, which have been briefly explained in the next section. This brings us to an interesting and very useful group of commands - Cut, Copy and Paste. Through **Cut** command you can move a block of text from one place to another. Through **Copy** command you can copy a block of text from one place to another such that the text appears at both the places. **Paste** command is used to insert the block of text, which has been either Cut or Copied. In the present example we will use the Copy and Paste command to copy the Internet features. Highlight all the Internet points by placing the cursor before "E-Mail", clicking on the mouse's left button, keeping it pressed and rolling the mouse till the end of "Wide Area Networks, and much more" release the mouse button now. This highlighted text, called a block can be either cut or copied. At the moment, since we want to copy, click once on **Copy** icon. Press Enter twice to come to a new paragraph and click once on **Paste** icon to get the same block of text here. Any block of text that is copied or cut is stored in a temporary location called **Clipboard** and whenever a paste command is issued the copied block of text is pasted into the selected location from the clipboard.

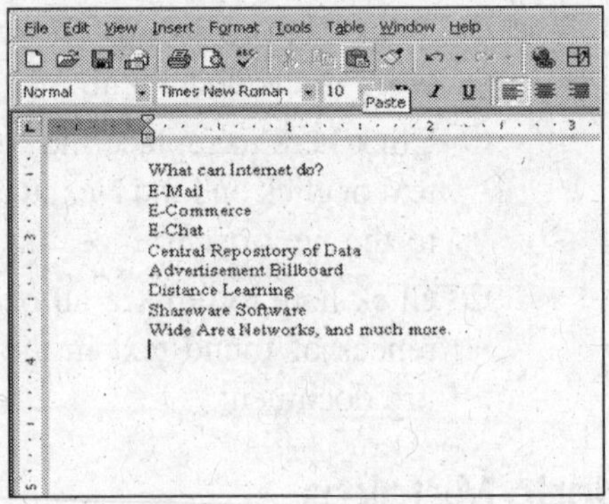

Now that you have a second block of text, you can place the cursor after each point and type a brief explanation about it. Take care not to press Enter after the end of each point, otherwise a blank line would be inserted between points. Once the typing work is completed, we can start on improving the look of this document and making it look exactly like the sample exercise page. This process involving changing the font type, font size, alignment of text, applying shades and colours etc. is called **Formatting**. So let us now start from the top of the document and move our way down.

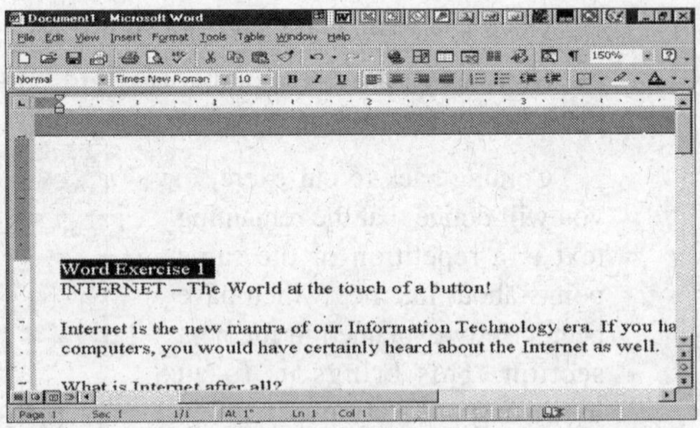

Place the mouse pointer before 'W' of 'Word Exercise 1', click once, keep the mouse button pressed and roll the mouse to highlight this block of text, release the mouse button after reaching the end of the text (after '1'). You will see that the text (called block) is highlighted in black and the text appears in white colour.

Now we have to make this text bigger, thicker and aligned to the right side. This would be done by three commands

- Increasing the font size,
- Applying Bold font style, and
- Right Aligning, respectively.

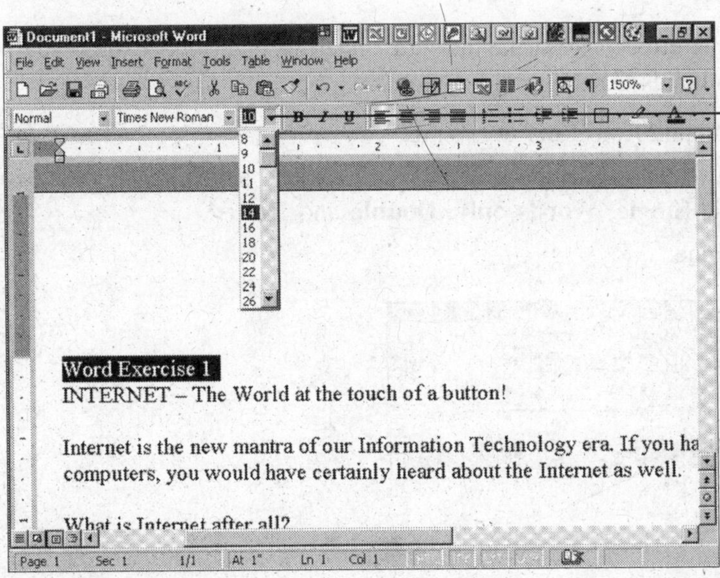

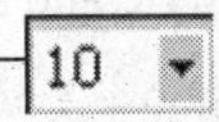

Click here once to see a pull down list of font sizes available. The bigger the font size, the bigger would be the text.

Alternative Method

There is an alternative method to change the font. Highlight the text as explained earlier by ‘blocking’. Choose **Font** from the **Format** menu. A window will appear.

This is a very compact and feature rich dialog box. Through this you can change not only the fonts and point size, but also the styles like **Bold**, *Italics*, ***Bold Italics***, Regular etc.

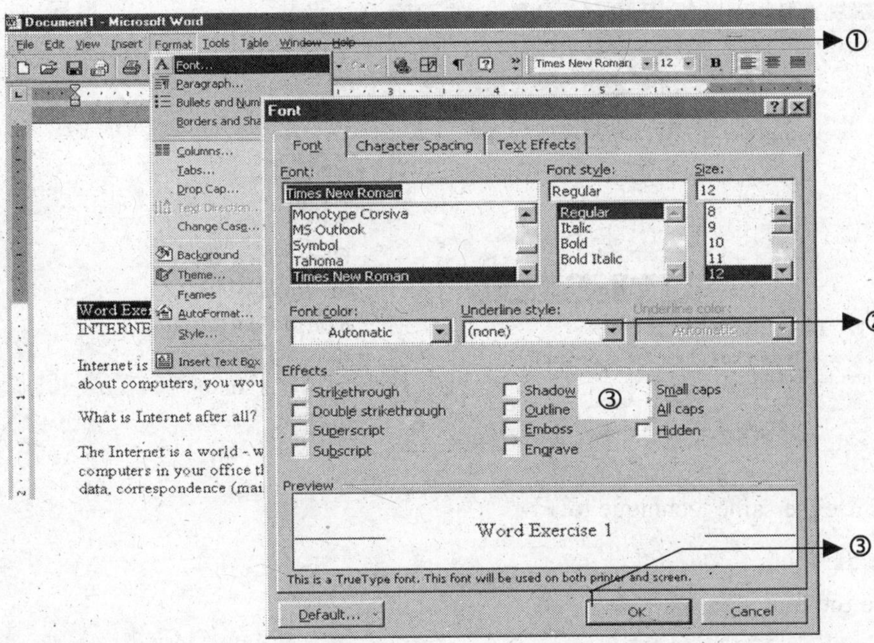

You can also apply other effects like strike through, underline etc. Choose the desired font, font style and size and click **OK** button to continue.

① Choose **Font** command from **Format** menu.

② In case you wish to underline the selected text, choose from the alternatives given here—**None**, **Single**, **Words only**, **Double** and **Dotted**.

③ Click **OK** to continue.

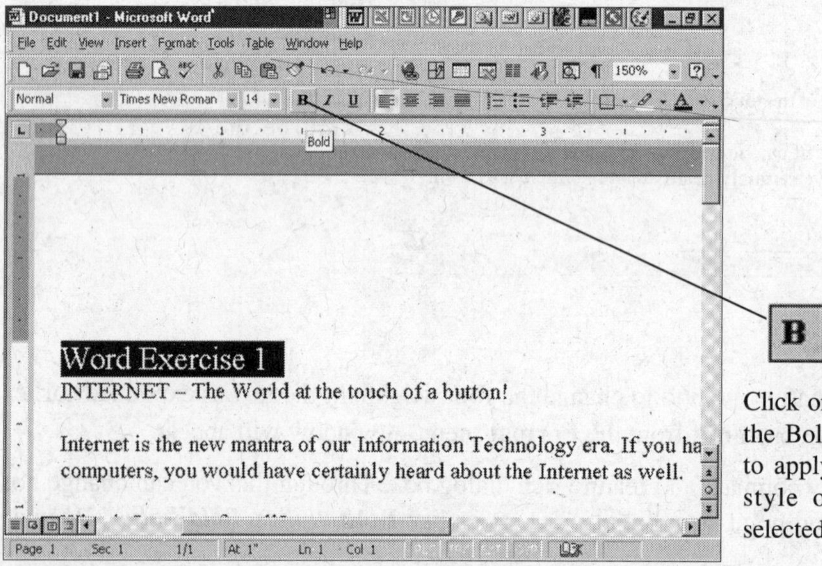

Click once on the Bold icon to apply bold style on the selected text.

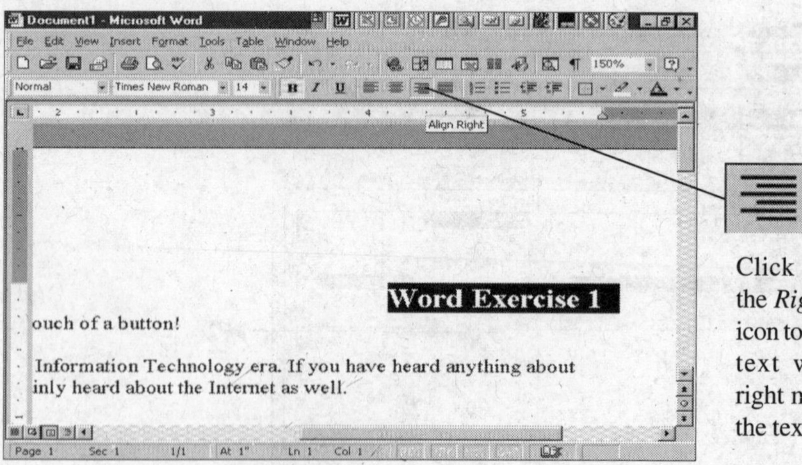

Click once on the *Right Align* icon to align the text with the right margin of the text.

Now let us use the same technique to:

- Change the font,
- Increase the font size,

- Italicise the selected text,
- Underline the selected text, and
- Centre the heading horizontally between the pages.

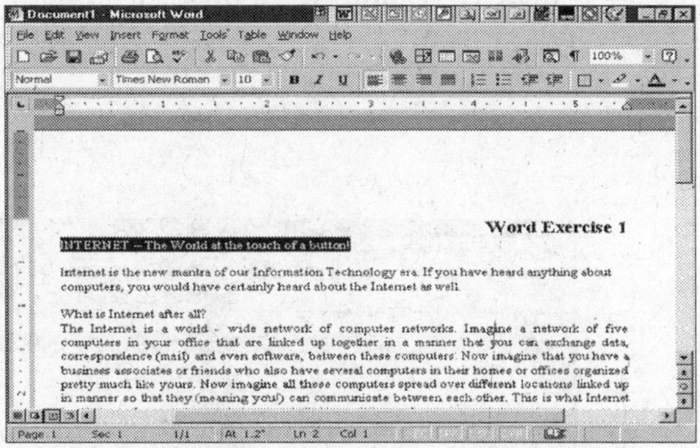

Fonts are like different handwriting scripts available to you. Just as different people write the same alphabets differently, similarly using the font facility of MS Word, you can choose the way in which your alphabet script is displayed and printed. You can have the same font for the entire document or you could apply different fonts for different pieces of text to make your document appear more interesting and appealing.

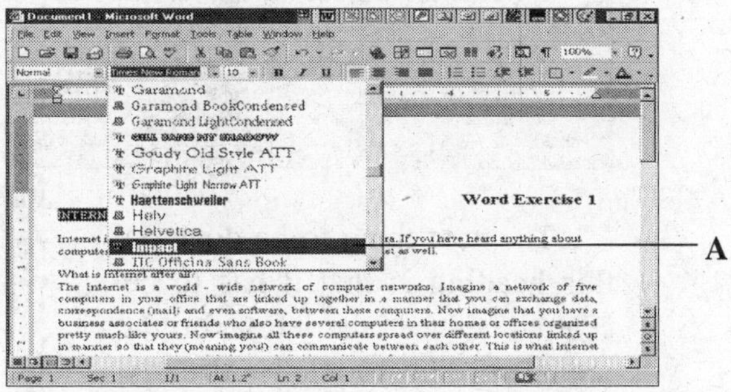

Highlight the document heading "Internet – The world at the touch of a button!" using the technique explained earlier to mark a block.

Click here once to get a pull down list of all the fonts available to you. Choose the *Impact* font by clicking on it.

A Notice that each font is displayed in its own unique font style, so before you apply the font you can get to see what it looks like.

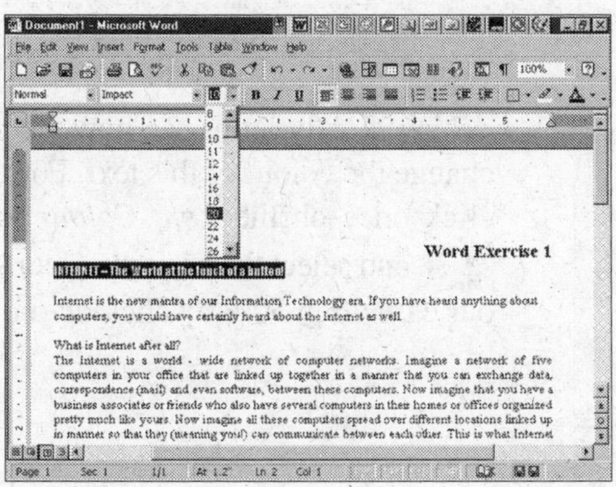

Click here once to increase the font size to 20.

Now since we want to Italicise only "The world at the touch of a button!" and not the entire heading, highlight only this portion, leaving out the word "Internet", and click once on the *Italics* icon.

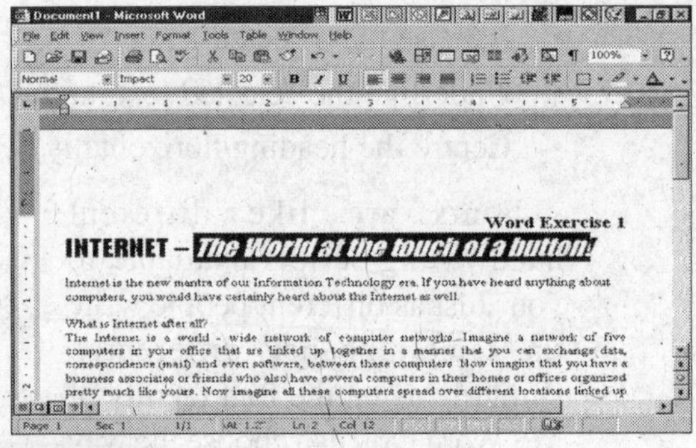

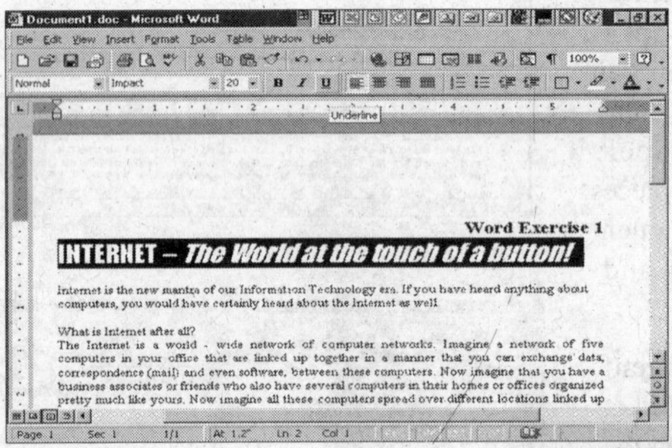

Now highlight the entire heading once again and click once on the *Underline* icon U to apply underline style.

The next thing to be done on this heading is that it has to be centred between the left and right margins. The block is already highlighted, just click once on the *Centre Align* icon.

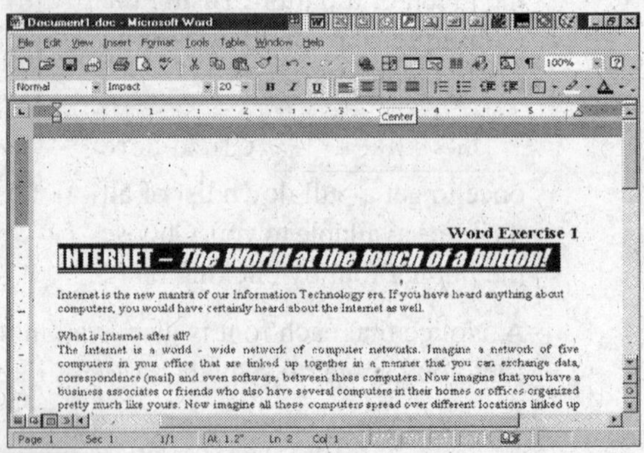

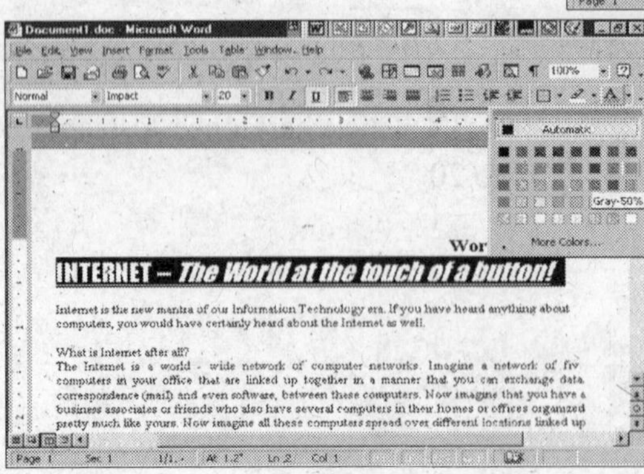

Now finally let us see how we can change the colour of this text. For this click once on the *Font Colour* icon A and select the desired colour - in our case Grey 50% by clicking on it.

Now let us move ahead. You would have noticed that typically the first line of a paragraph is slightly indented, i.e., it begins not from the extreme left but slightly ahead. For doing this, place the cursor at the beginning of the first paragraph and press Tab key. You will see that the first line has got indented. Take care not to use the Space Bar to create this space, since this is not only more tedious and time consuming but may also result in different paragraphs having different indent spaces.

Let us now highlight the paragraph heading "What is Internet after all?" Click here once,  use the scroll bar to scroll down to the font "Helvetica", click on it to apply it to the selected block.

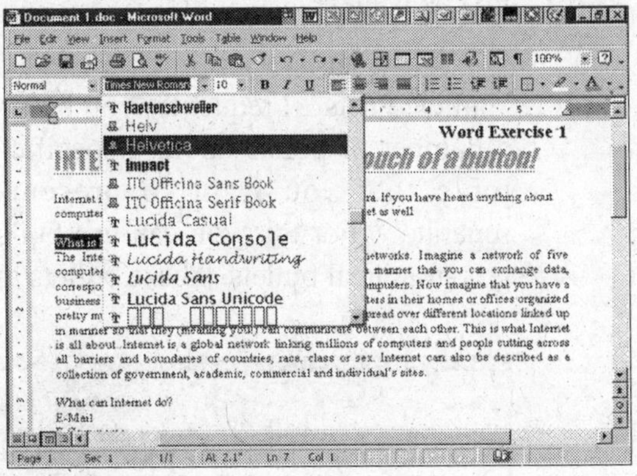

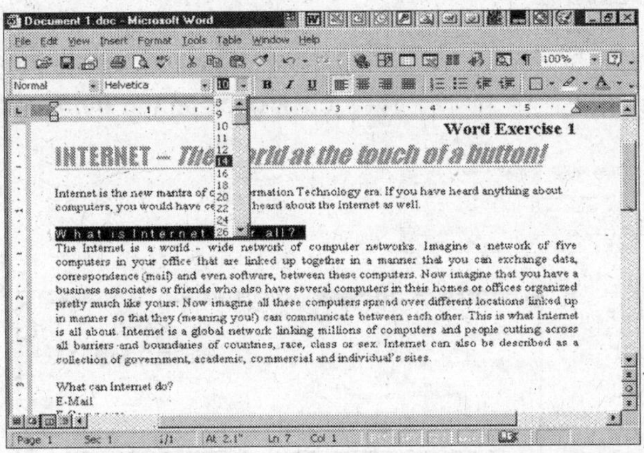

Click here once to get the font size pull down list and select point **14** by clicking on it once. Notice, the text would become bigger.

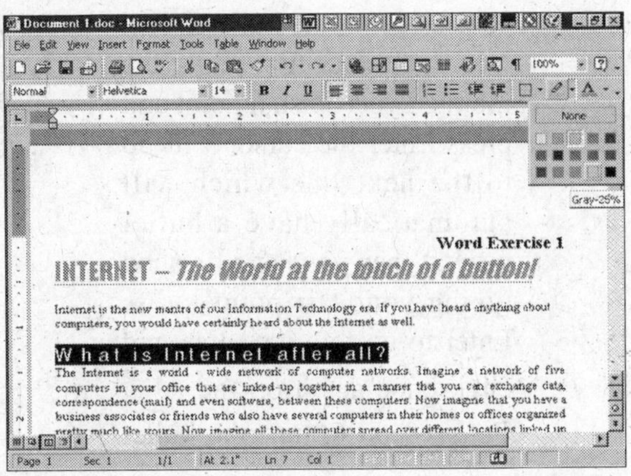

To give a highlight effect to any block of text, highlight the text and click here once  and select the desired highlight by clicking on it.

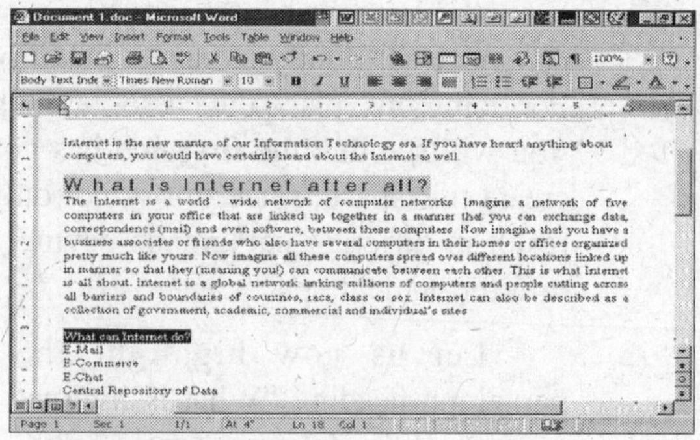

Now move to the next paragraph heading "What can Internet do?" and use the same techniques just learnt to increase the font size, change the font and apply the highlight effect on this text as well.

Now let us learn how to create "bulleted lists". Frequently you have a number of points about a specific topic that you want to present separately. For this you can use bullets. No, not the ones that you put in a revolver but typographical bullets. These bullets are small marks at the beginning of each new point.

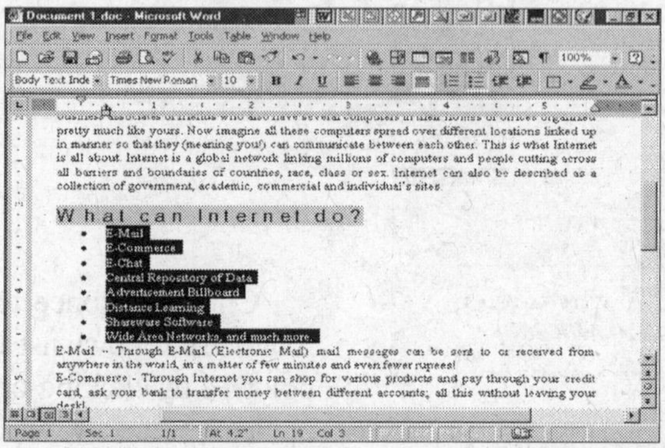

For applying bullets to points that already exist, highlight all the points (like in our case, starting from "E-Mail" and ending with "Wide Area Networks, and much more") and click once on the *Bullets* icon

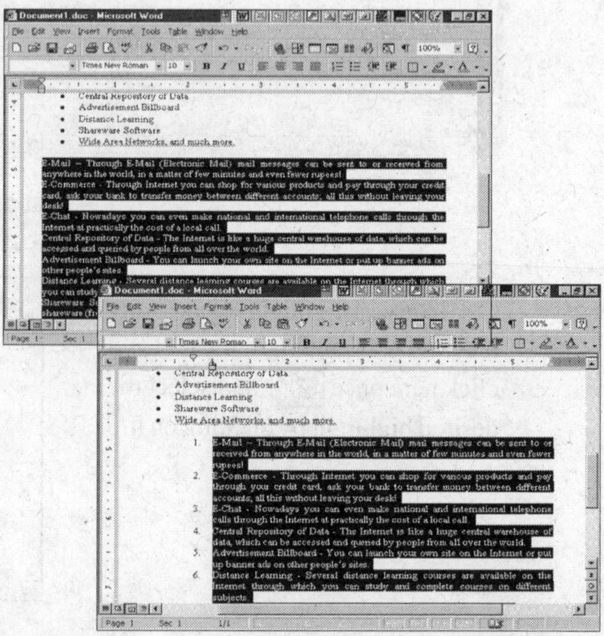

Alternatively you can also have bullet marks appear automatically when you begin a new point. For this, place the cursor in a new blank line and click once on the bulleted list. Now type your first point, the moment you finish a point and press Enter the cursor will go to the next line which will automatically have a bullet mark. When you have finished typing your last point, press Enter to go to a next line and click once again on the *Bullets* icon to turn the bullet list off. *Bullet* icon like most other icons on the *Formatting Tool* bar is a "toggle switch", which means that if you click on it once, it becomes *On* and if you click again on it becomes *Off*.

Similar to the bulleted list is the numbered list. In case of a numbered list each point starts with a point number (1, 2, 3... or A, B, C... I, II, III... etc.) instead of a bullet mark. The procedure for this is similar to that of bullet list. Highlight all the points and click once on the *Numbered List* icon .

Note: Bullets/Numbering can be customised by clicking **Bullets** and **Numbering** from the **Format** menu.

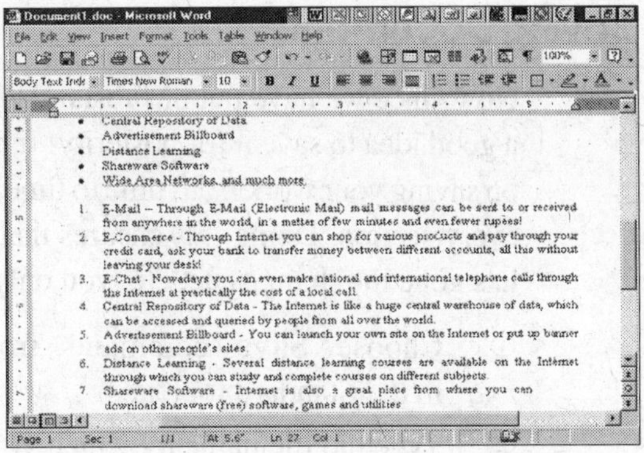

As we can see here that Word is taking the next matter as a part of the above matter, therefore, it is showing the numbered list as sub-points of the above bulleted list. To correct this you indent these points to the left, click once on the *Left Indent* icon . You will notice that all the points have moved to the left by one tab position. In case you want to further indent click on the *Left Indent* icon again. If not satisfied with the results you can always use the *Right Indent* icon to bring back the text by one tab position at a time.

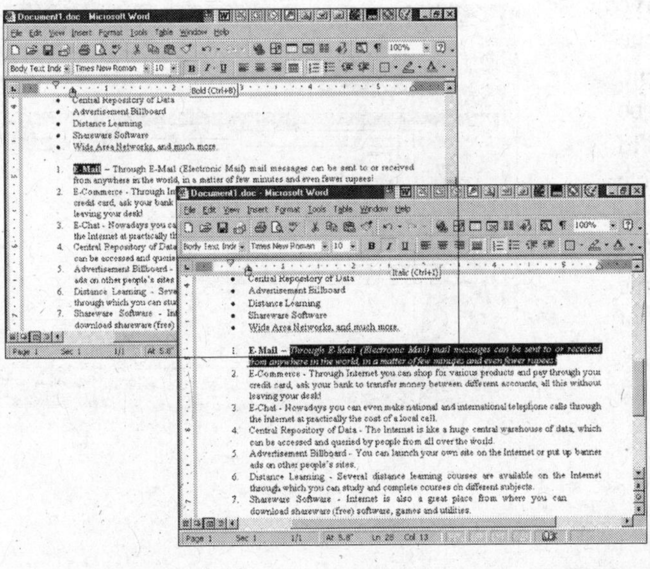

Notice all the points have a running number against them and the matter starts from a neatly aligned straight line. Try doing this manually by typing the numbers and using spacebar to create perfectly aligned text and it might take you more than fifteen minutes to achieve this perfectly, whereas through *Numbered List* icon it is a matter of seconds. Remember computers are all about saving time!

Now take a look at the Exercise 1 format given and apply *Bold* and *Italics* formatting on all the points.

Congratulations! With this step you have completed your first exercise in MS Word. It may have taken you a bit of time to do it the first time but with practice you would become much faster, efficient and hopefully more innovative.

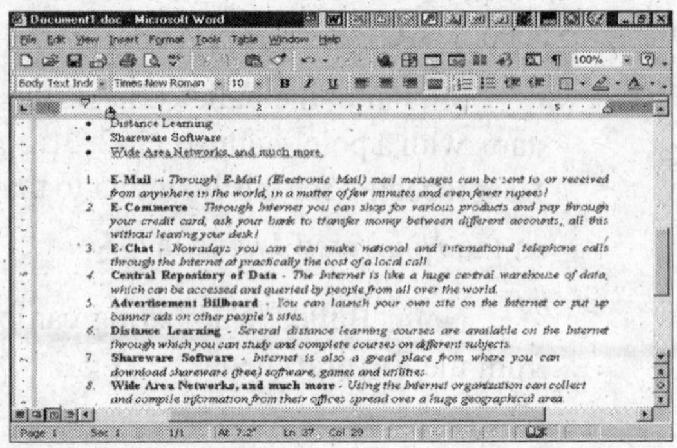

Saving Documents

Now since we have put in substantial amount of work creating this document, it might be a good idea to save it for posterity! In fact, for all your subsequent documents you must go on saving your work from time to time, let us say every 15 minutes or so, or after completing every section. Doing this ensures that if there is problem like power off or your machine has gone into hung state, etc. you only lose minimal work.

① Choose **Save** command from **File** menu or click the Save command icon in the Standard toolbar.

② Type the file name by which you wish to save your file.

③ Specify where you want to save your document. By default MS Word saves your documents in the default My Documents folder.

④ Click on the **Save** button.

Note: In the **Save As** dialog box specify the name of your document. Although this name can be anything, but it would make a lot of sense to give a meaningful name to your documents, so that just by reading the name you can have the idea of its contents.

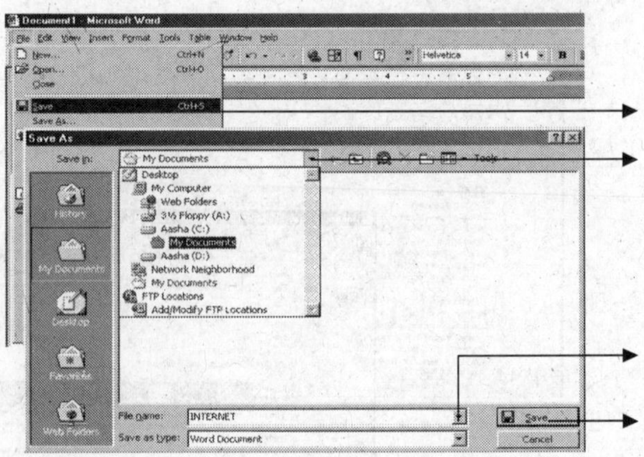

Closing the Document

Once your work is completed and you do not wish to continue working with a particular document then you can close that file.

① Choose **Close** command from **File** menu.

A You will notice the exit screen of **MS Word**. If you wish to work on any other file, follow the steps explained later for opening files.

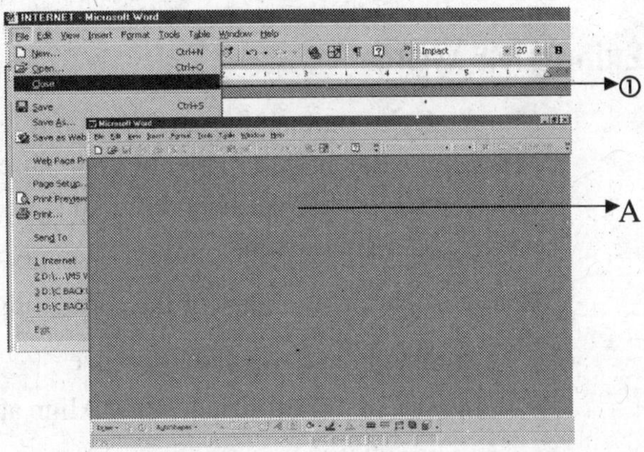

Opening the Document

Once a file is saved and closed, it can be again reopened and used at any time using the open command.

① Choose **Open** command from **File** menu or click the Open command icon in the Standard toolbar.

② Select the correct tory path where your file is stored.

③ Choose the desired file by clicking it once with the mouse.

④ Click once on **Open** button to open the chosen file. You can also double click on the file in rapid succession to op

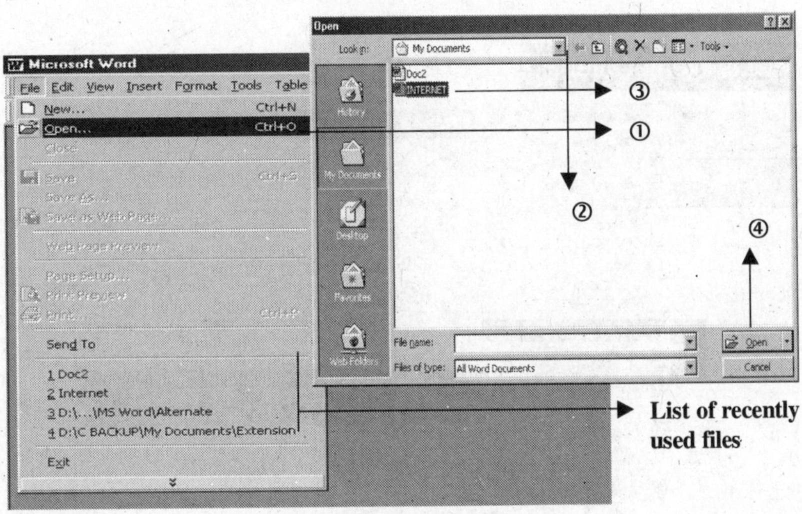

Note: If the file you wish to open is one of the last four files used by you, then that file will be displayed in the list of recent documents at the bottom of the File menu. You can simply click that file to open it.

Exiting MS Word

Choose **Exit** command from **File** menu to end your MS Word session. Alternatively you can click on the Close button of the Word window. And you are back to where you started from.

Click here to quit MS Word

Below is a brief summary of the formatting commands covered in Word Exercise 1:

- changing Font Style and Font Size
- aligning Text (Left Align, Right Align and Center Align)
- justifying Text
- boldfacing, Italicising and Underlining
- indenting paragraphs using the Tab key and 'Increase Indent' and 'Decrease Indent' icons located on the Formatting toolbar
- creating Bulleted Lists
- numbering Lists
- changing the text colour
- highlighting the text

Some additional formatting commands of MS Word are explained below:

Changing Text Case After having typed a particular piece of text, Word allows you to change the text case to lower case, upper case or a combination of both.

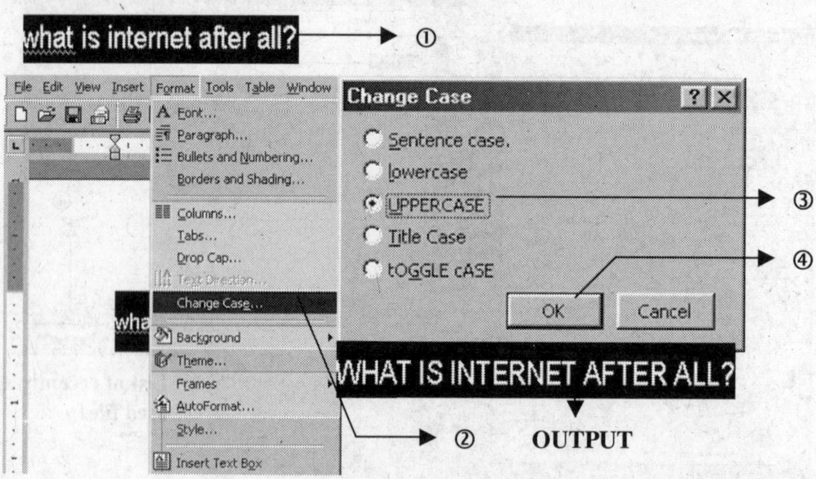

① Select the desired text.

② Select **Change Case** from the **Format** menu. A dialogue box will be displayed to the user.

③ Select an appropriate choice from the dialogue box.

④ Click on the **OK** button to apply the changes.

Paragraph spacing By default paragraphs are single spaced. This spacing can be customised according to the users preference. Paragraph spacing is used to create spaces between paragraphs. It is also possible to create additional spacing between lines of a paragraph. This is called as **Line Spacing**. As discussed earlier, formatting a block of text requires pre-selection of that block. So do not forget to select a block of text before you apply any formatting features.

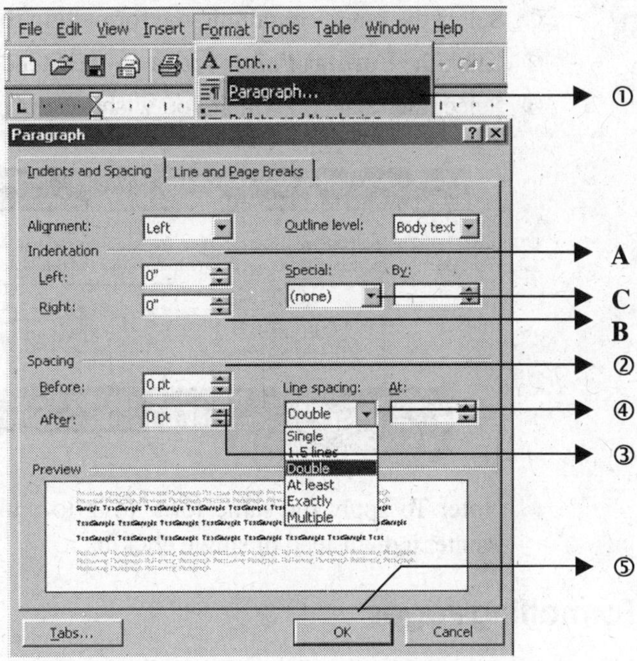

① Select **Paragraph** from the **Format** menu, a dialogue box will be displayed.

② Specify the amount of space you wish to leave before the start of a paragraph by clicking on the spinner or by directly typing a value.

③ Specify the amount of space you want to leave after the end of a paragraph by clicking on the spinner or by directly typing a value.

④ From the line spacing drop down box select the desired spacing. You can also choose 'Multiple' line spacing by selecting 'Multiple' from the drop down box and specifying the desired number of lines in the adjacent box **('At')**.

⑤ Click on the **OK** button to apply the changes.

Indenting using paragraph dialogue box Paragraphs can be indented by specifying the desired indent measurements in the paragraph dialogue box. (Please refer the screenshot)

A Specify the left indentation by clicking on the spinner or by directly typing a value.

B Specify the right indentation by clicking on the spinner or by directly typing a value.

C If you want a first line or hanging indent then select this option using the **Special** drop down box. You can then set the amount of the desired indent in the adjacent box (**By**).

Format Painter

Format Painter is used to transfer formatting from one range of text to another. The range could be a word, a line, a paragraph or a table.

① Select the range containing the formatting that you wish to apply to another block.

② Click the **Format Painter** icon on the Standard toolbar.

③ Select the range on which you wish to apply the formatting.

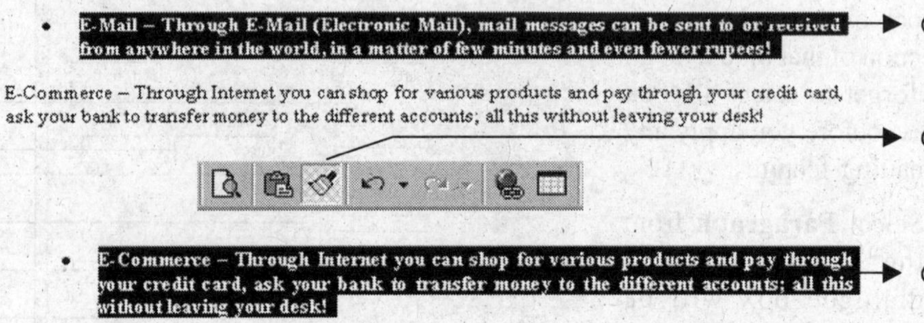

Note: To apply the same formatting to multiple locations, double click the Format Painter icon instead of single clicking it.

Formatting Pages

Page formatting involves setting the page margins, page size, page orientation etc. It is usually a good practice to specify the page settings before you start working on your document. MS Word adjusts the text in your document to fit in the specified page margins. By default whenever you create a new document, the document is created with predefined page settings. **Page Setup** can be accessed from the **File** menu.

Changing Page Margins

① Click on the **Margins** tab/folio.

② Specify the **Top**, **Bottom**, **Left** and **Right** margins, to specify how much blank space you wish to leave on the sides, top and bottom of each page.

③ Specify the **Gutter** margin.

④ Specify the **Header** and **Footer** positions. They are measured from the edge of the page (Header and Footer discussed later in the chapter).

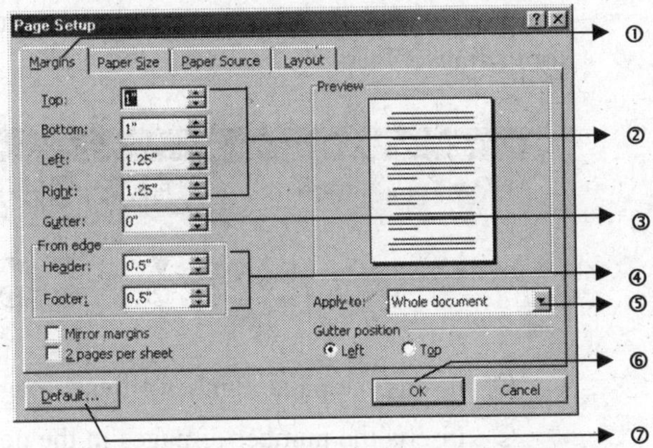

⑤ Settings can be applied for all the pages in a document or for a particular page. Select **Whole Document** if you wish to apply the settings for the entire document or **This Point Forward** if you wish to apply the settings for the text after the current cursor position.

⑥ Click on the **OK** button to apply the changes.

⑦ Click on the **Default** button if you wish to restore the original settings of MS Word.

Changing Page Size and Orientation

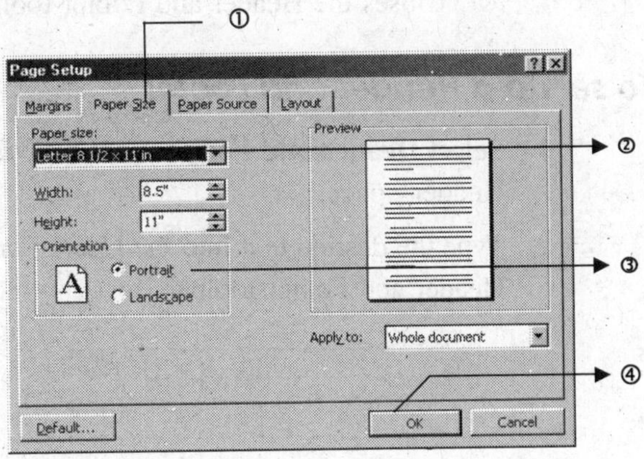

① Click on the **Paper Size** tab/folio.

② Specify the paper size by clicking on the **Paper Size** drop down box. If the paper size desired by you is not available in the drop down box then you can define the desired paper size dimensions by selecting **Customize** from the drop down box. After selecting customize from the drop down box, enter the width and height of the paper in the **Width** and **Height** boxes. Select the page orientation - **Portrait** for Vertical or **Landscape** for Horizontal.

④ Click on the **OK** button to apply the changes.

Setting up Header and Footer Another helpful feature of Word is Header and Footer. Using this features you can print a standard piece of text and /or an image at the top or end of each page of your document. Headers appear at the top of each page and footers appear at the bottom of each page. The most common use of Headers and Footers is to print page numbers and reference titles. It can be accessed by clicking on **Header**

and Footer from the **View** menu. A header and footer toolbar will be displayed below the formatting toolbar.

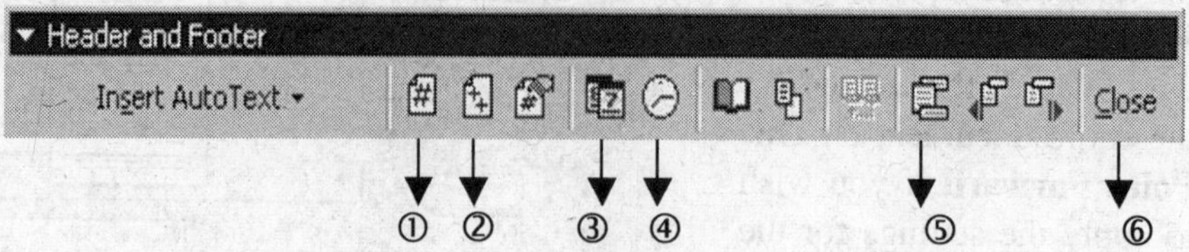

① Inserts the page number on each page.

② Inserts the number of pages in the document.

③ Inserts the current date.

④ Inserts the current time.

⑤ Allows the user to switch between Header and Footer.

⑥ Closes the Header and Footer toolbar.

To set up a Header and Footer

1. Select **Header and Footer** from the **View** menu. Word places the cursor in the blank Header space.
2. Type the desired text into the Header or insert any of the standard functions from the Header and Footer toolbar.

3. Click on the **Switch between Header and Footer** icon to switch to the Footer.
4. Type the desired text into the Footer or insert any of the standard functions from the Header and Footer toolbar.

5. Click on the **Close** icon of the Header and Footer toolbar to close the toolbar.

Inserting Page Numbers Page Numbers can be inserted by making use of Headers and Footers. Alternatively page numbers can be inserted directly by selecting **Page Numbers** from the **Insert** menu. A dialogue box is displayed as shown below:

① Select the **Position** where you want the page number to app,,ear (Top or Bottom).

② Specify the **Alignment** of the page number in the selected position (Left, Right or Center).

③ Click on this button for formatting the appearance of page number in the document.

④ Click on the **OK** button to apply the changes.

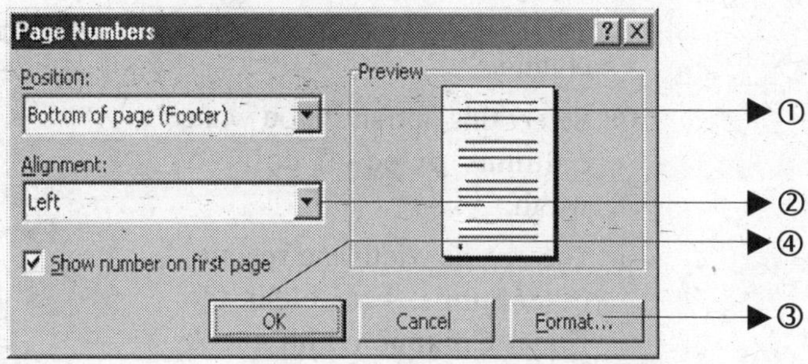

Creating multiple sections By default a new document contains only one section. (If no section break has been inserted explicitly.) Word allows inserting multiple sections into the same document. This feature allows the user to apply different formatting styles within the same document. Follow the steps below to insert a new section:

1. Place the cursor at which you wish to start a new section.
2. Select **Break** from the **Insert** menu.
3. Select one of the section break options from the dialogue box.

① Starts a section at the top of the next page.

② Starts a section without moving the following text to the next page.

③ Starts a section on the next even numbered page. If required it leaves a blank odd page.

④ Starts a section on the next odd numbered page. If required it leaves a blank even page.

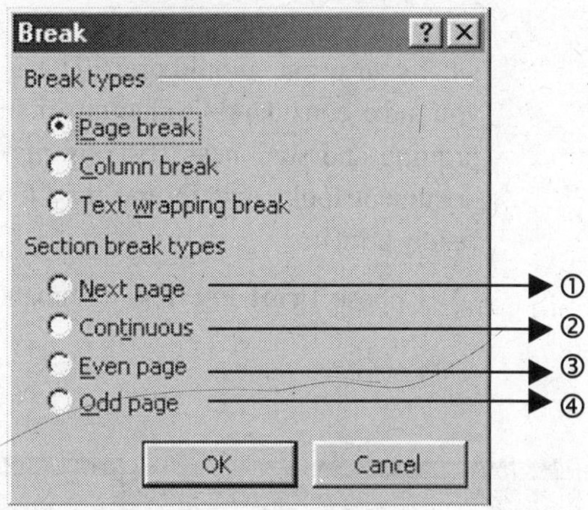

Setting up Multiple Columns

Word allows you to arrange your text in newspaper like columns. To set the number of columns for your document, follow the steps below:

1. Choose **Columns** from the **Format** menu.
2. Select the number of columns and then click on the **OK** button to split your document into the specified number of columns.

① You can specify the number of columns here or select any one option from the **Presets**.

② Select this option to add a vertical line between the columns.

③ Select this option if you want columns of equal column width.

④ To vary the width and spacing of columns, first clear the Equal Column Width check box and then enter the **Width** and **Spacing** for individual columns.

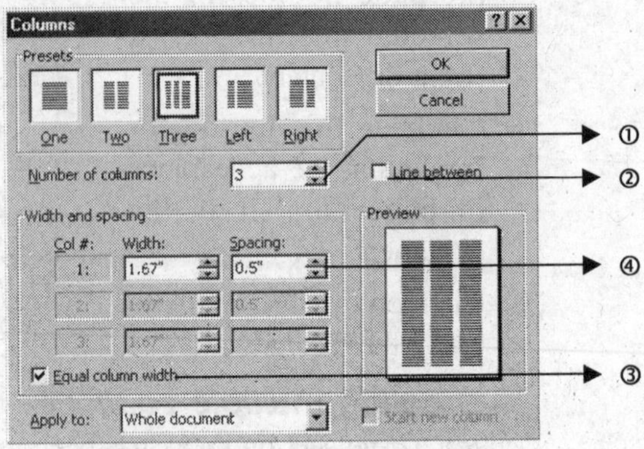

Print Preview

Because of advanced *WYSIWYG* feature (**W**hat **Y**ou **S**ee **I**s **W**hat **Y**ou **G**et) in-built in MS Office, you can see a preview, on screen of what you wish to print. In most cases, this preview would give you an exact replica of what your printer would print. This is very helpful, since you save considerable amount of time and money (in printing and stationery cost) by making sure that your document looks exactly the way it should, before you finally print it.

① Choose **Print Preview** command from **File** menu.

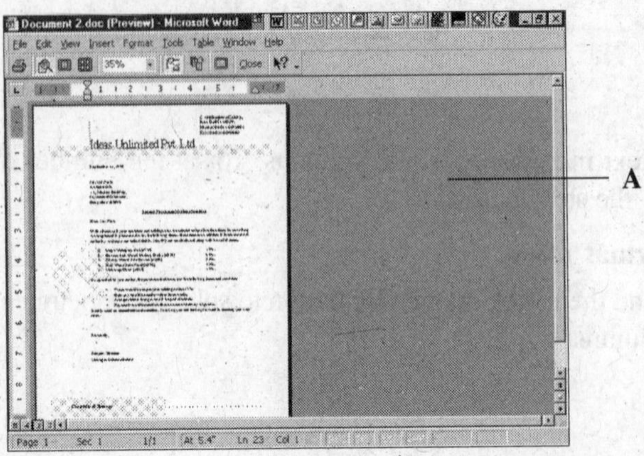

A This is what appears on the screen. An exact copy of the page, which your printer would print. If you are happy with what you see, go ahead and print the document. If not, go back to the main screen by clicking on **Close** button and make necessary changes.

Icons for Printing Toolbar

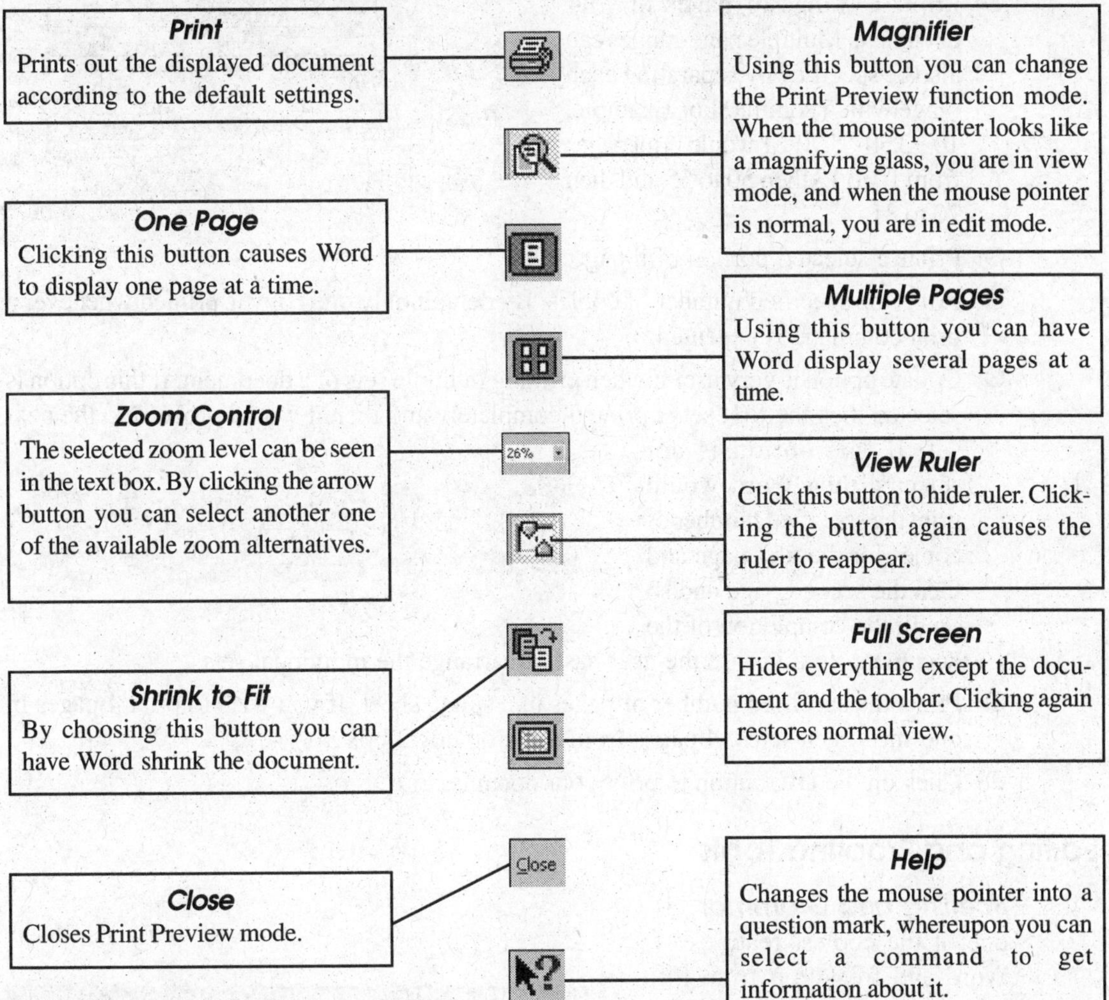

Printing Documents

Print command can be accessed from the **File** menu. Alternatively you can click on the Print icon from the Standard toolbar. A Print dialogue box is displayed to the user where different print options can be set.

① Select your printer from this list. In most of the cases default printer would be the right one. All the printers attached to your computer will be displayed in the drop down box.

② Prints all the pages in the document.

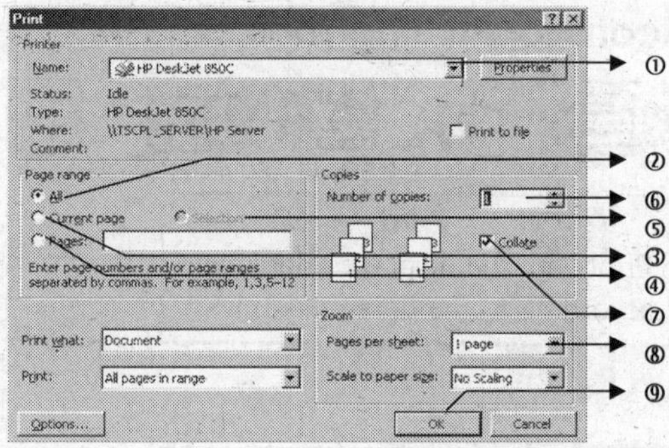

③ Prints only the current page; current page is the page where the cursor is currently placed.

④ Prints a range of pages in your document. Multiple page-ranges can also be specified by separating each range with a comma. For Example, 10-13,50-55,70-81 would print pages from 10 to 13 then 50 to 55 and then 70 to 81.

⑤ Prints a selected portion of a page.

⑥ Prints the specified number of copies. By default only one copy is printed whenever a print command is executed.

⑦ Collate option is very useful when printing multiple sets of a document. If this option is selected then the first set is printed completely and then it would proceed to the next set. If this option is not selected then Word would print the specified number of copies for the first page and then the second page and so on till the completion of the document. In this case the user has to rearrange the individual sets.

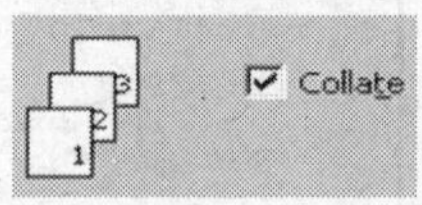

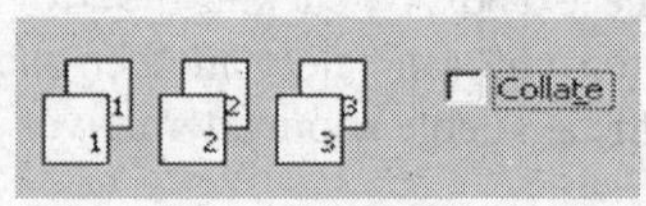

⑧ Prints the specified number of pages in a single sheet. If you wish to print 4 pages in one sheet then select 4 pages from the drop down box.

⑨ Click on the **OK** button to print your document(s).

Editing and Proofing Tools

Spelling and Grammar is one of the coolest features of Word and frees you from the bother of concentrating on the spelling and grammar of your text. Spell checker compares the words in your document with those in its main dictionary (inbuilt in MS Word). The main dictionary contains most common words, but it might not include proper names, technical terms, acronyms, and so on.

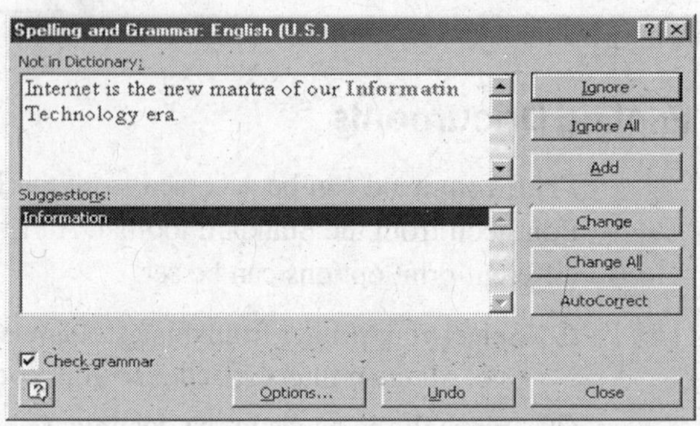

Spelling and Grammar can be accessed by choosing **Spelling and Grammar** from the **Tools** menu. A dialogue box will be displayed to the user.

Explanations for some of the options in the spell-check program are given below:

Suggestions	Based upon the misspelt word, Word would try to think of all possible suggestions for the correct word. You may either choose from the words suggested or simply type the correct word and click once on the change button.
Ignore	Though this word is not found in the dictionary, leave it unchanged.
Ignore all	Ignore this word for all subsequent occurrences.
Change	Change this word with the suggestion specified.
Change all	Change this word for all subsequent occurrences, with the suggestion specified.
Add	Add this word to the dictionary.
Auto-Correct	Add the suggested correction to Auto-Correct. AutoCorrect feature allows to automatically detect and correct typos, misspelled words, grammatical errors, and incorrect capitalisation. For example, if you type **teh** plus a space, then AutoCorrect replaces what you have typed with "the."
Options	For changing Spell Check's default settings.
Undo Last	Cancel one of the previous replacements.
Cancel	Terminate Spell Check and return to the document.

Spell Check's Default Settings

These can be accessed by clicking on the options button in the Spell Check dialogue box or by choosing **Options** from the **Tools** menu. By default the spelling and grammar checks are enabled. This is the reason we often find red and green wavy underlines in our word document. A red wavy underline indicates a spelling mistake where as a green one indicates a grammatical mistake. Various settings for Spelling and Grammar are displayed in the given below screenshot. However, they can be customised according to the users requirement.

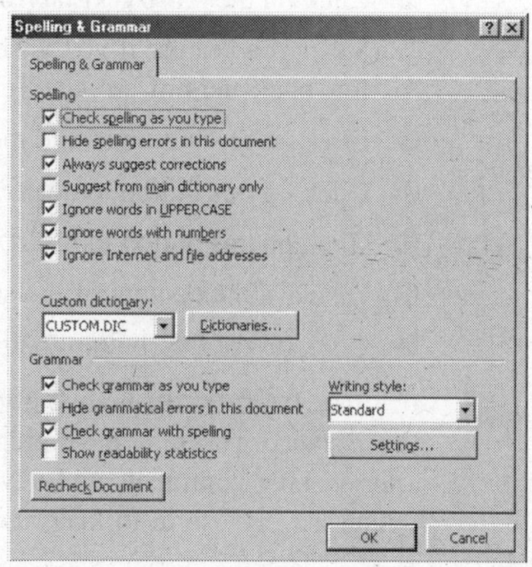

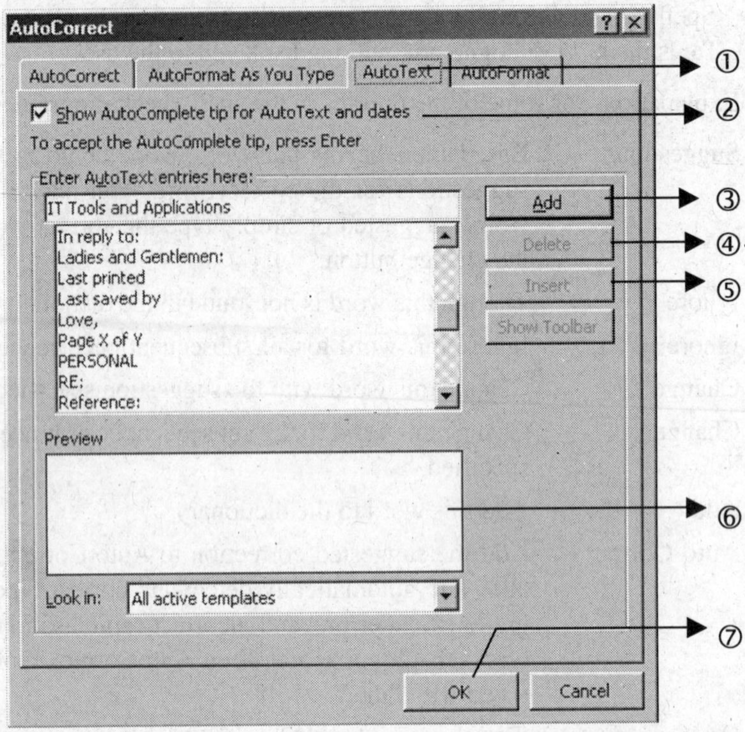

AutoText MS Word displays a Tool tip text when you type the first few characters of a date or an AutoText entry, at which point you can insert the entry by pressing the Enter key or continue typing. You can define your own entries and then add them to the AutoText entry list. This would help in minimising typing as well as typing errors. This feature can be accessed by choosing **Autotext** from the **Insert** menu.

① Click on the **AutoText** tab/folio.

② Select this feature if you wish the tooltip text to be displayed when you type the first few characters of an AutoText entry.

③ Click on this button to add the entry typed in the textbox to the AutoText list.

④ Click on this button to delete the selected autotext entry from the drop down box.

⑤ Click on this button to insert the selected autotext entry into your document.

⑥ Displays the content of the selected autotext entry.

⑦ Click on the **OK** button to apply the changes.

Track Changes Frequently several people collaborate to finalise a single document. For instance, you may have prepared a contract agreement and then want to finalise it after seeking comments and advice from several people. In such cases Track Changes option is very useful to keep track of who has made which changes to the document.

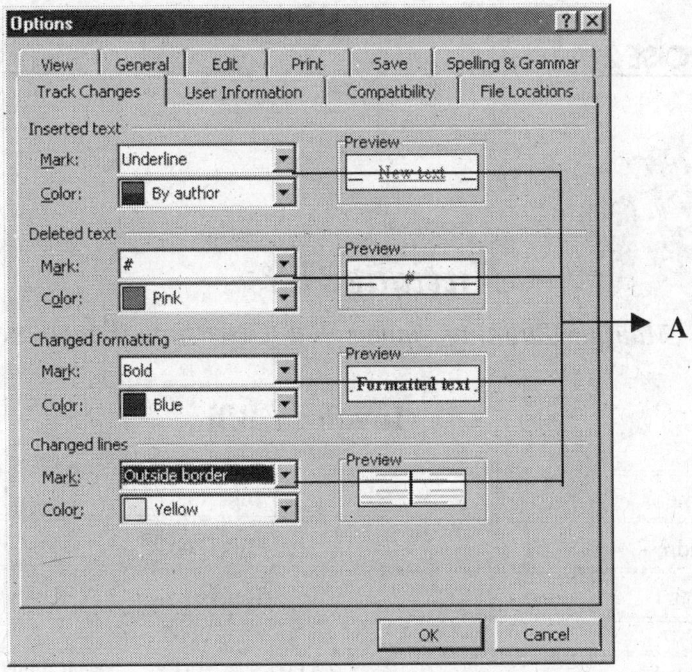

Once enabled, Word tracks all the changes made to your document. Changes could include insertion/deletion of text, formatting or moving text from one place to another in the document. Word makes use of revision marks to show the tracked changes to the user. A revision mark shows where an insertion, deletion or any other editing change has been made in the document. Word allows you to specify how the inserted or deleted text should appear in your document. These settings can be customised by clicking on the **Track Changes** tab/folio in the **Options** dialogue box from the **Tools** menu.

A You can specify the revision marks as well as the colour for various changes (Inserted text, Deleted text, Changed Formatting and Changed Lines). Clicking on **OK** button will then apply the specified settings.

Steps for Tracking changes in a document:

1. Open the desired file.
2. Click on the **Track Changes** icon from the Reviewing toolbar. If the Reviewing toolbar is not visible then select the **Reviewing** toolbar by choosing **Toolbars** from the **View** menu.
3. Make the changes you want by inserting, deleting, or moving text or graphics.

Tracked changes would appear as follows:

> ***Internet*** is the new mantra of our I# Technology era. If you have heard anything about computers, you would have # as well IT TOOLS AND APPLICATION

WORD EXERCISE 2

Antique Arts

13 Mayfair Building, Jayamahal Extension, Bangalore 560046

Invoice / Bill

Customer Name		Bill. No.		
Customer Address		Bill. Date.		
Kind Attention		Ref. No.		

SL.NO	DETAILS	RATE	QTY	AMOUNT

Taxes	
Delivery Status	
Warranty Period	
Payment Period	

<u>For Customer</u>

Name

Designation

Company Seal

<u>For AntiqueArts</u>

Name

Designation

Company Seal

The following exercise makes use of two new features of Word:

Creating Tables A table is made up of a grid of cells that you can fill with text and graphics. Horizontal grid of cells is called a Row and vertical grid of cells is called a column. Tables are often used to organise and present information, but they have a variety of other uses as well. Word allows you to create tables and format tables.

Inserting Graphics There are two basic types of graphics that you can use to enhance your MS Word documents – Drawing Objects and Pictures. Drawing objects include textboxes, curves, lines, and other objects. These objects can be accessed from the Drawing toolbar. Pictures are graphics that have been created using any graphics software. They include bitmaps, scanned pictures and photographs, and MS Word's inbuilt Clipart gallery. You enhance these objects with colors, patterns, borders, and other effects.

Creating Tables

① Type the name of the Company, Address and Document heading. Place the cursor after the line 'Invoice / Bill'.

② Keep the table icon pressed and a grid line box would appear. Drag the mouse. Highlight the number of rows and columns that you wish to have. In our example, 3 rows and 4 columns are selected. A table with the required number of rows and columns with dotted lines would appear.

③ In case the table goes beyond the right margin line, place the mouse on the right most column edge and drag it so that the last column fits within the right margin of the page.

④ Repeat step ③ for fitting the table within the page left margin.

⑤ Type the column titles.

Notes :

1 Use the same technique explained in step ③ to size individual columns width.

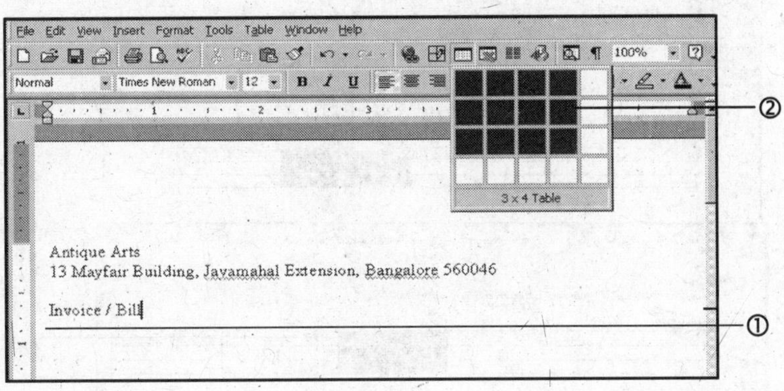

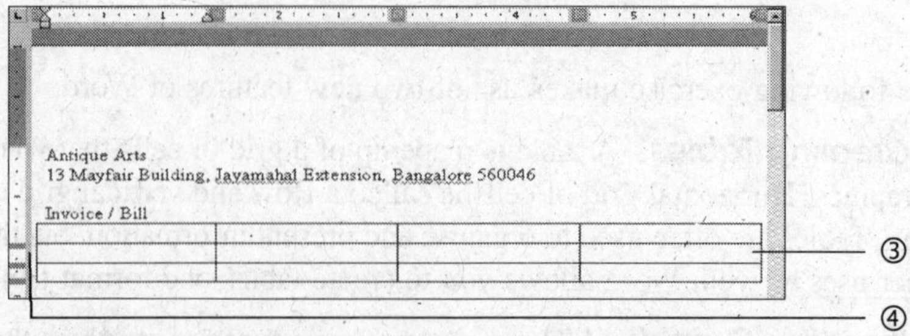

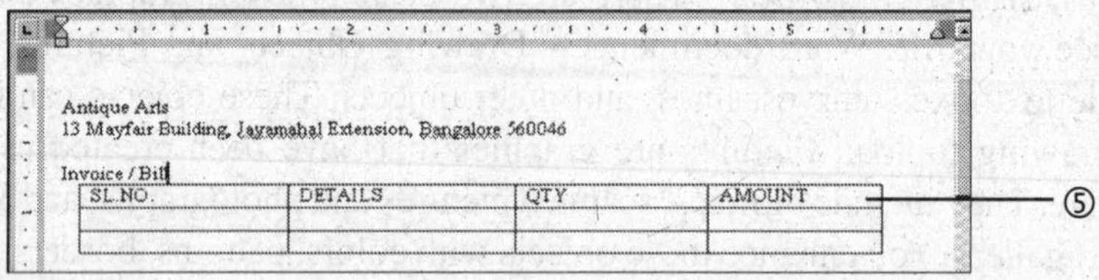

2 You can move from one cell to another by pressing Tab key or arrow keys from the keyboard.

Inserting Columns

① In case you wish to insert another column called 'Rate' before the 'Qty' column; you can highlight an entire column by simply placing the cursor at the top of the column so that it looks like a thick arrowhead. Clicking once would automatically highlight the entire column. Alternatively, you can place the cursor inside any row in the desired columns (the column before which you wish to insert another column) and choose the option **Select column** from the **Table** menu. The selected area is shown in dark background.

② Choose **Columns to the left** from **Insert Command** from the **Table** menu.

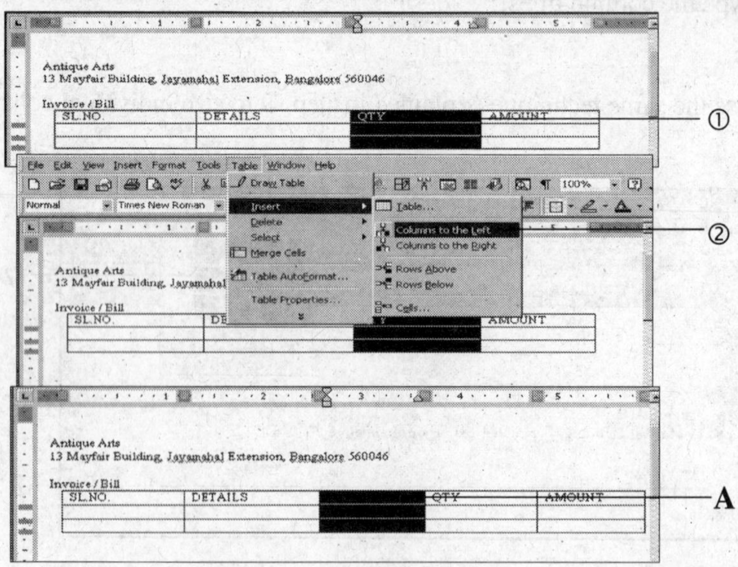

A Another blank column would automatically be inserted before the 'Qty' column. Type the column heading 'Rate'.

Inserting Rows

Now we would need more rows for typing the details in the bill.

① Highlight any blank row by choosing the option **Select Row** from **Table** menu.

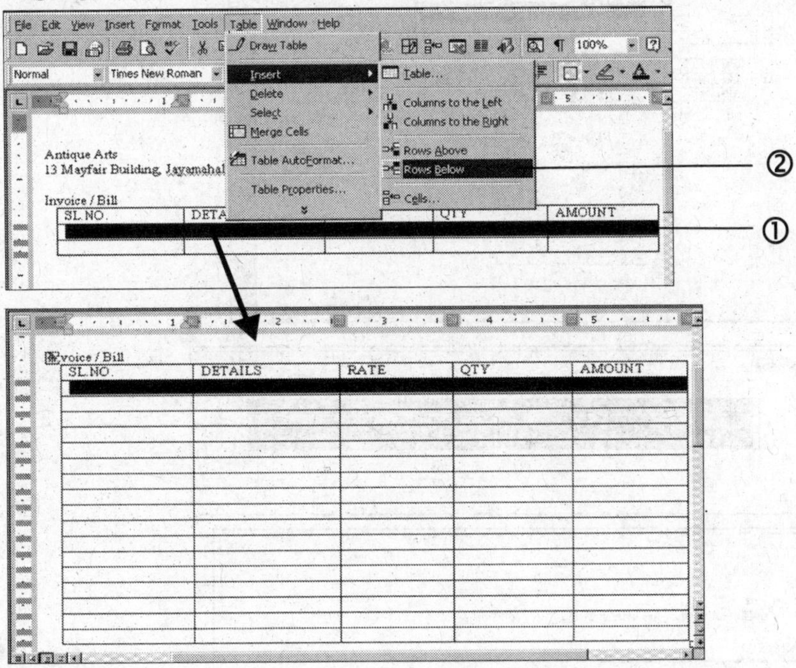

② Click on this icon repeatedly or choose **Insert Row** from **Table menu** to insert as many rows you want.

Creating Tables

① Using the technique learnt in earlier pages, let us now try to create another table like the one shown here. Enter the data. Now, if you realise that this table should have been placed on top of the table created before, there's no problem. Follow the following steps to move it to its right place.

② Place the cursor anywhere inside the new table.

③ Choose **Table** command from **Select** option from **Table** menu. The entire matter would be highlighted.

④ Click on **Cut** icon from Standard Toolbar to cut the table or alternatively choose the **Cut** command from the **Edit** menu. The customer details table would no longer be visible here.

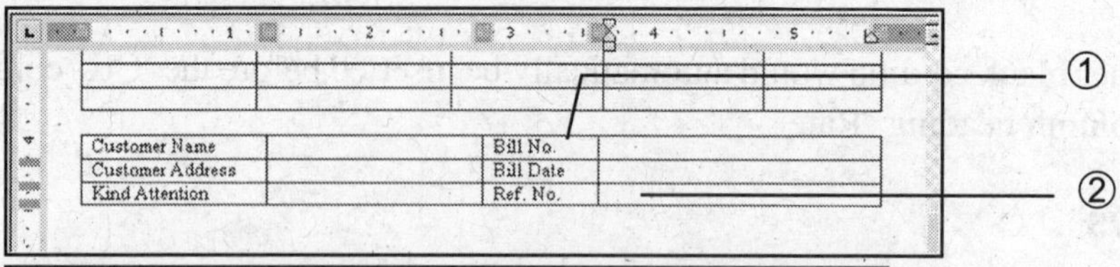

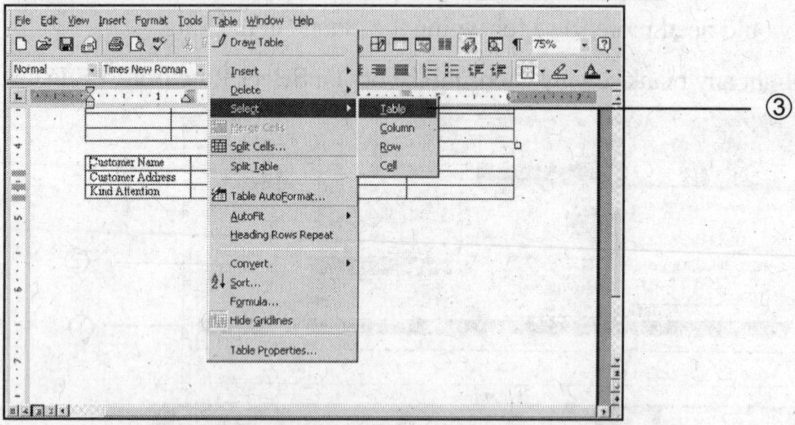

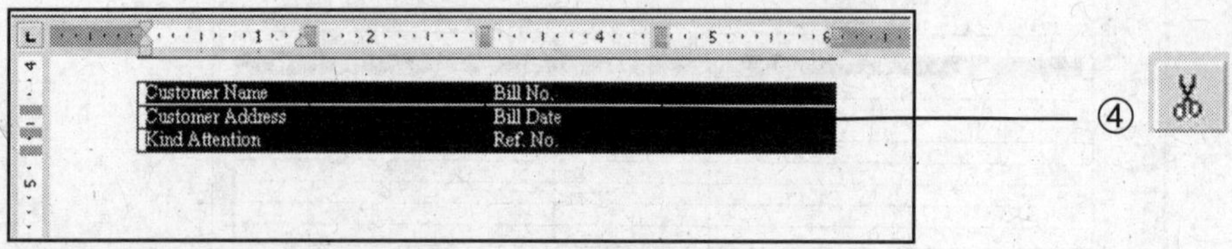

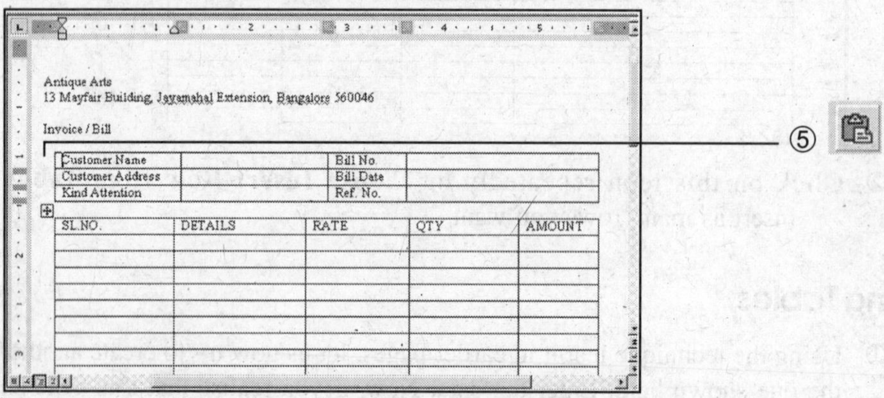

⑤ Place the cursor above the table on top of which you wish to have the latter one and click on **Paste** icon or choose **Paste** command from **Edit** menu. The customer details table would now appear here.

Creating More Tables

① Let's create the last table required in our example. Move the cursor to the place where you want the new table.

② Choose **Insert Table** from **Table** menu.

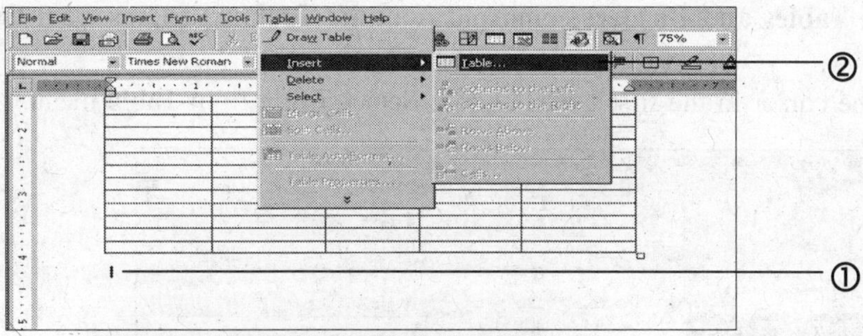

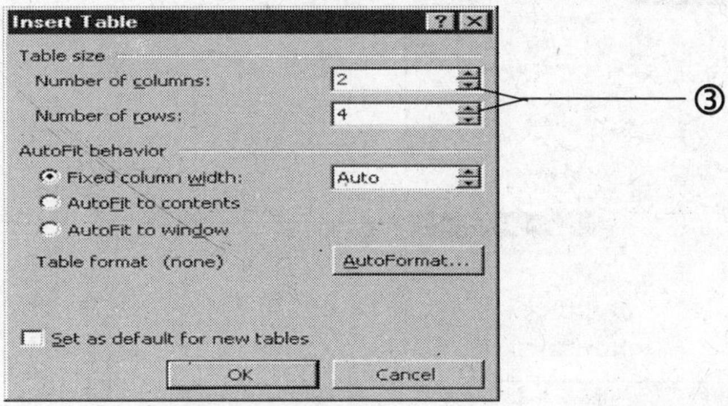

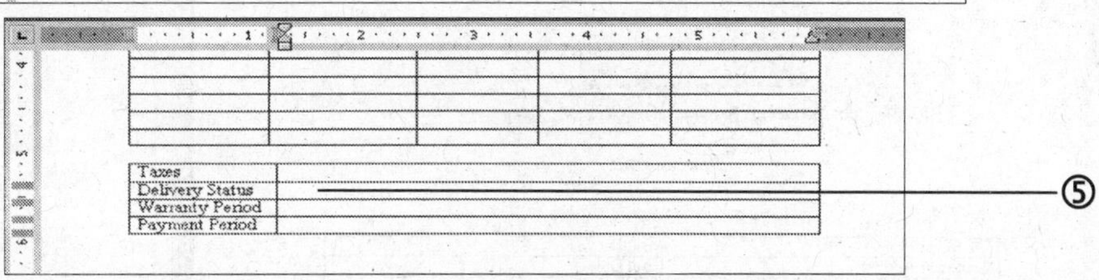

③ Specify the number of rows and columns required by you, say 2 columns and 4 rows for our example, and click on **OK** button.

④ Change the column width as per your requirement.

⑤ Type the required data as shown in the screen shot below:

Since the structure of the table is now ready, you can simply type the required matter and do the necessary text formatting.

Borders

Now, let us start formatting. In order to start formatting our table we would need the Borders Toolbar.

① Choose **Tables and Borders** command from the **Toolbar** options from the **View** menu.

② Place the cursor in the first table. Choose **Select Table** from **Table** menu.

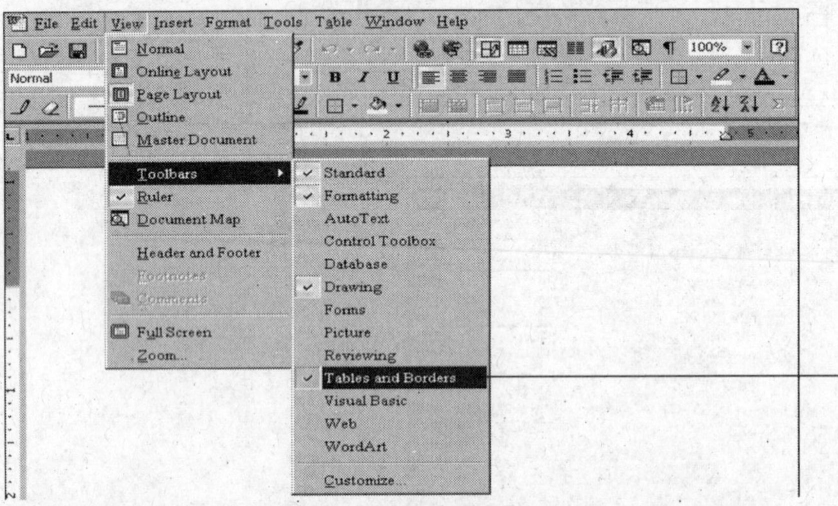

①

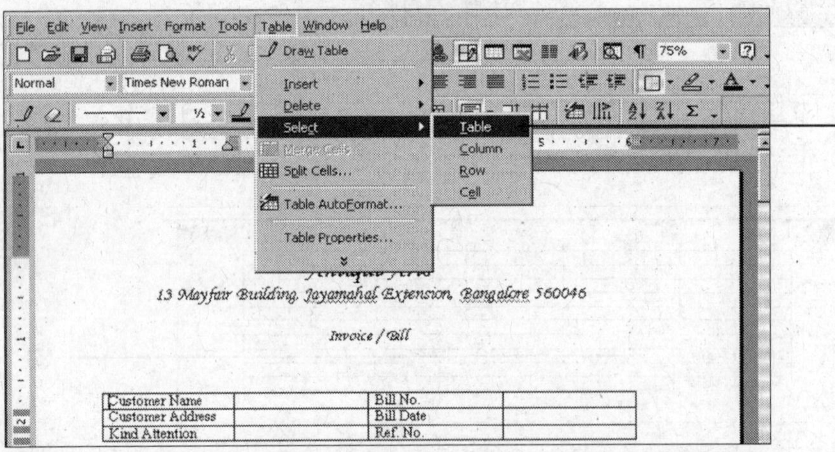

②

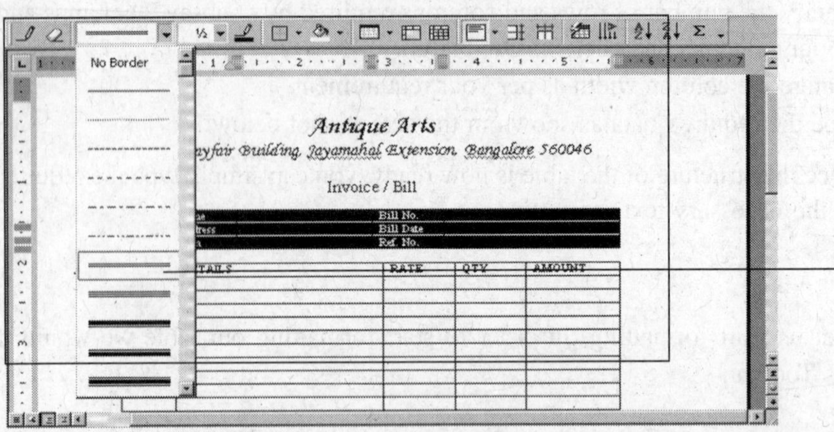

③

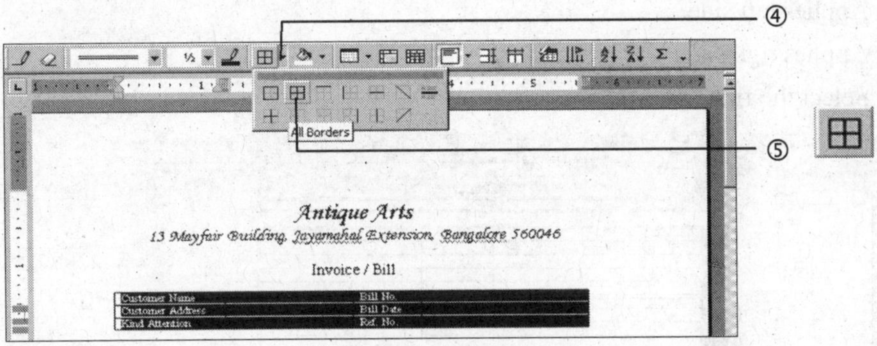

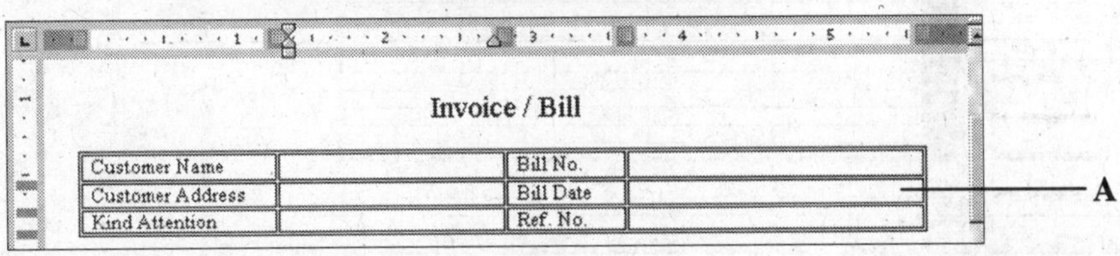

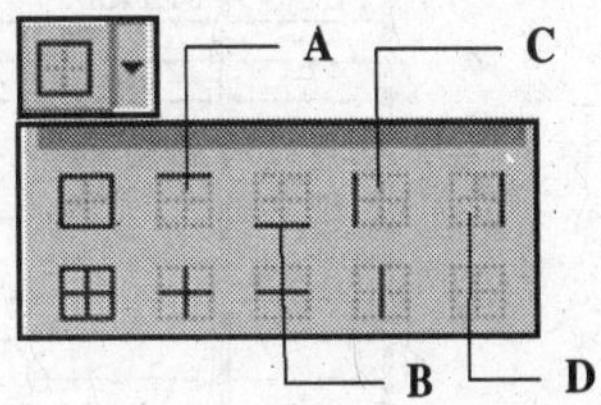

③ Select the line style that you like.

④ Click here to open borders frame.

⑤ Click here to apply style to '**All**' border frame.

A Final Result!

More Borders

For Qty, Rate and Amount Table, we wish to apply only column border and not the row border. Therefore, border command would have to be applied individually to each column.

① Choose the Table by clicking **Select Table** from **Table** menu. Click this icon to apply the outside border.

A Applies top line border for the selected range.

B Applies bottom border.

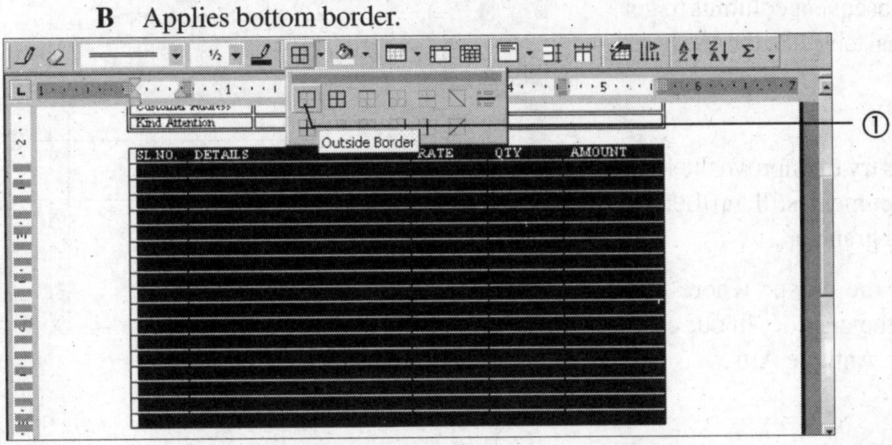

C Applies left side.

D Applies right side.

② Select the first column.

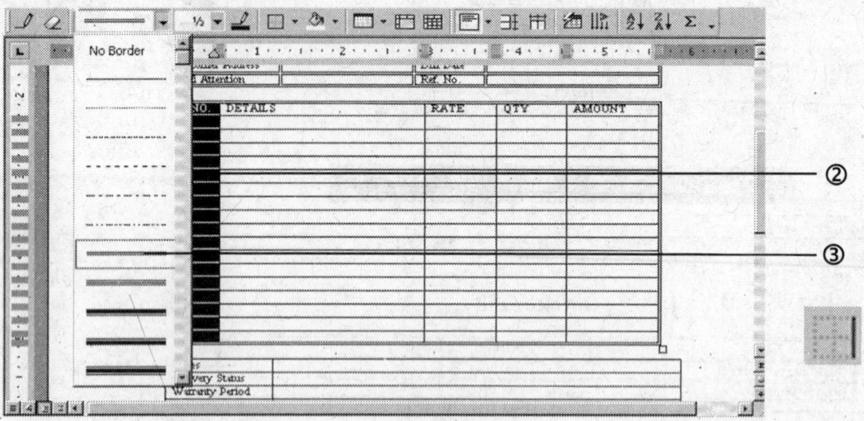

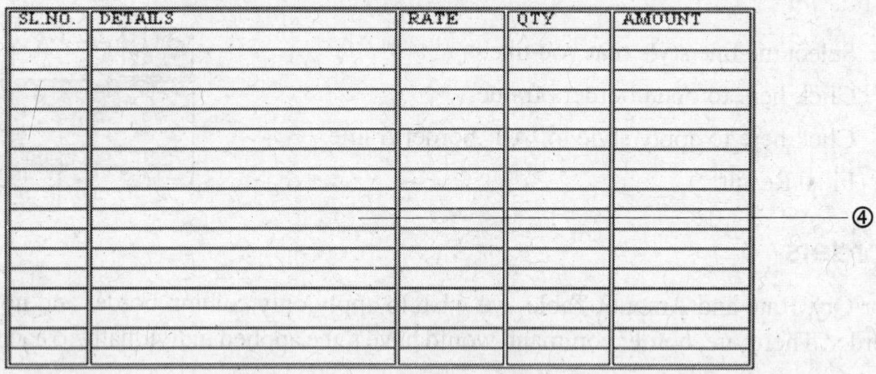

③ Select the line style and click on Right Side Border icon to apply.

④ Repeat steps ② and ③ for all the subsequent columns to get the final table like the one here.

Insert Picture

Now let us try to improve the look of the document still further by inserting a graphic.

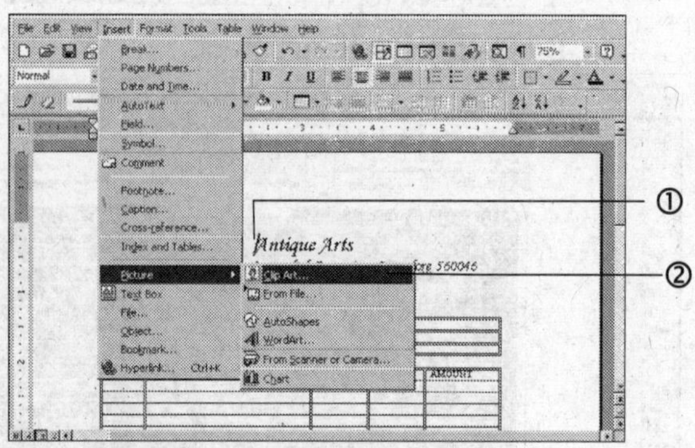

① Place the cursor where you want the graphic. In our case, before Antique Arts.

② Select **Picture** command from **Insert** menu.

③ Click on a Clip Art category from which you can select an individual clip art image. In

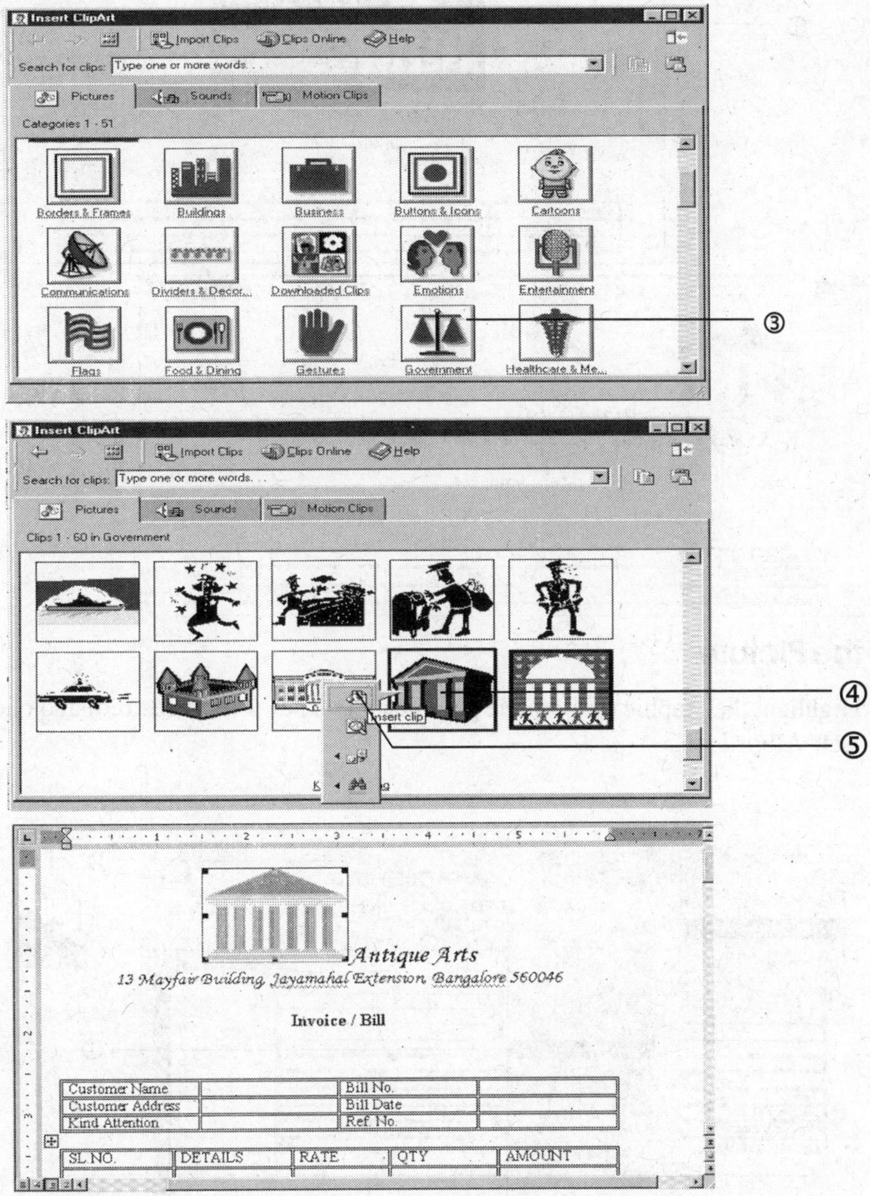

this case click on Government category.

④ Click on the picture that you want to insert.

⑤ Choose **Insert Clip** command from the options given.

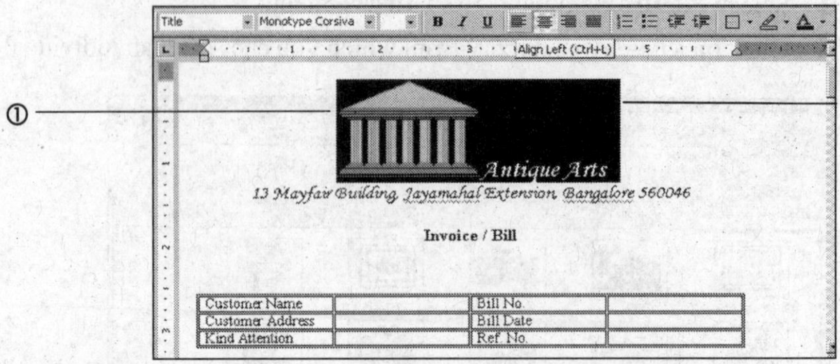

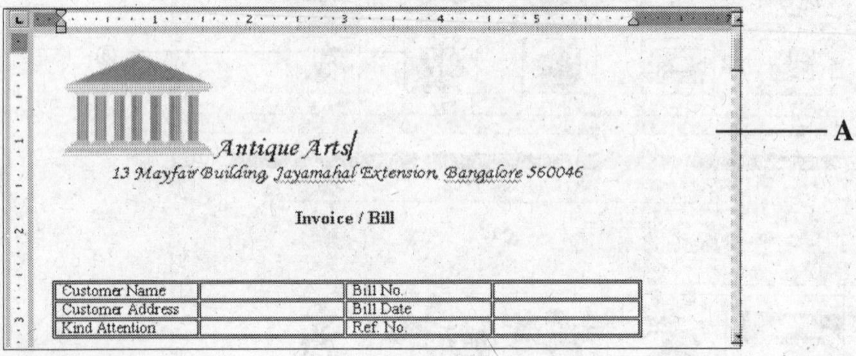

Aligning the Picture

① Highlight the graphic (or both the graphic and text as well, if desired) and click on the **Left Align** icon.

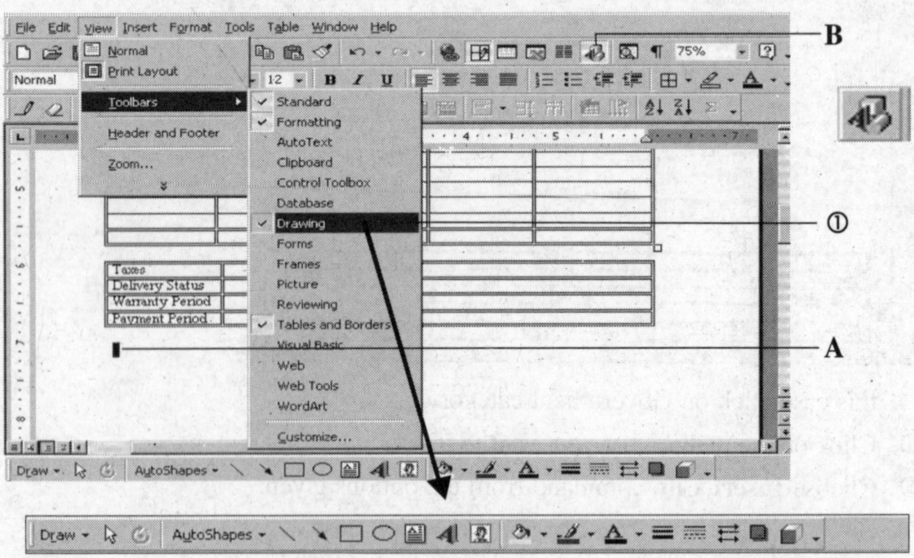

A Final result!

Text Box

Now let us try to create two text boxes below the tables, as shown in the sample exercise.

A First, place the cursor right at the end of the document.

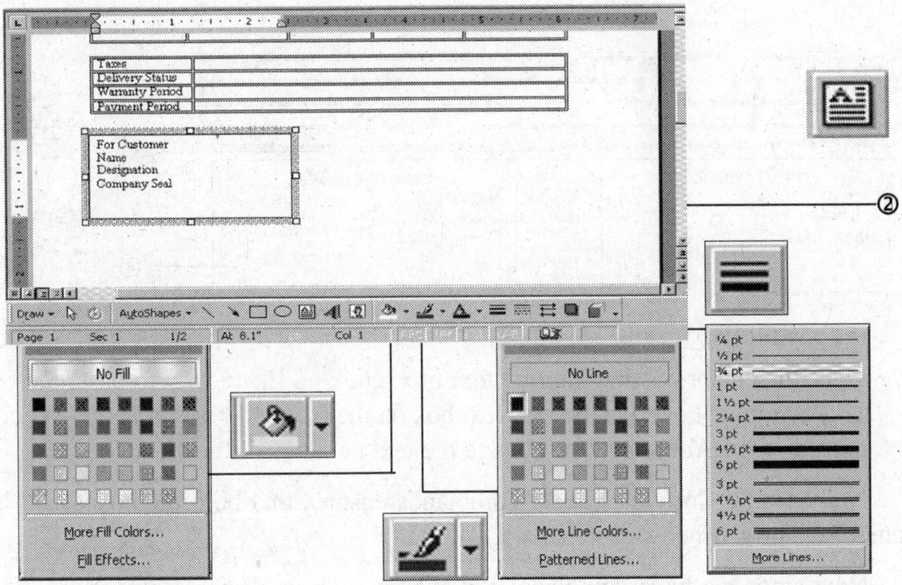

Box Fill Color | Line Color | Line Style and Thickness

① Activate the Drawing Toolbar by choosing **Drawing** command from **Toolbar** option of **View** menu.

B Alternatively, you could activate **Drawing** Toolbar by directly clicking on this icon.

② Click here to create text box. Size it according to your requirement by dragging the mouse. Type the matter and format. You can also set the line thickness; line color and box fill colours.

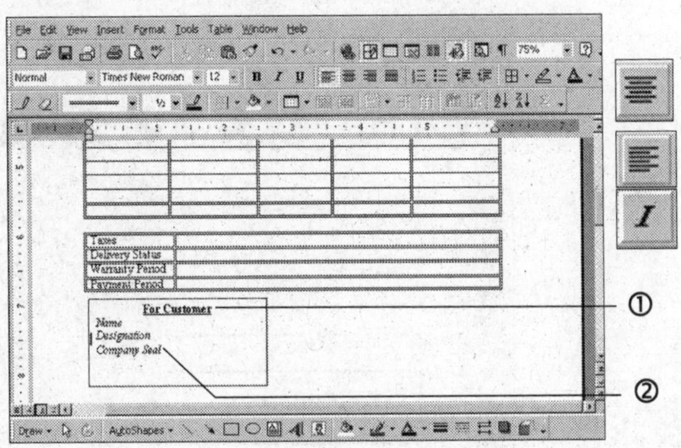

Formatting

Now, let us start formatting the text box.

① Highlight the first line and click on this icon to centre the text.

② Highlight the rest of the matter in the box, click the **Left Align** icon to left align the text. Also click on the **Italics** icon to italicise the text.

③ Click on the border of the text box so that the box is selected, click on the icon shown

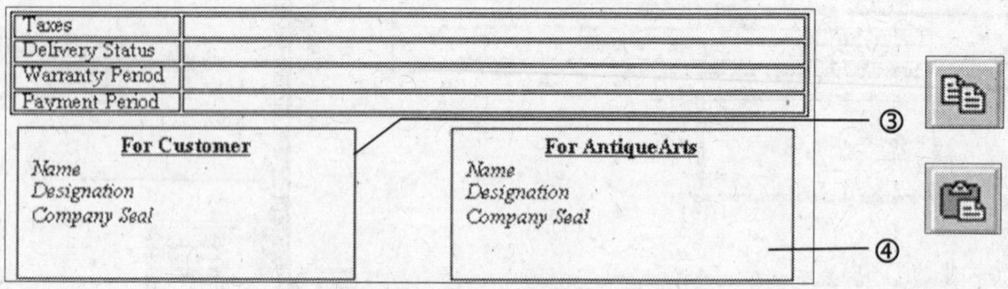

to copy this box.

④ Place the cursor outside the first text box, click on **Paste** icon to paste the box here. This action will overlap the new text box on the first text box. Drag the text box to the new location. You may now change the text contents of this box.

Note: Using **Copy** and **Paste** commands ensures that both the boxes will have the same size and attributes.

Now since we have completed our exercise, let us discuss some more features of Word Tables:

Deleting Table Follow the steps below to delete a table:

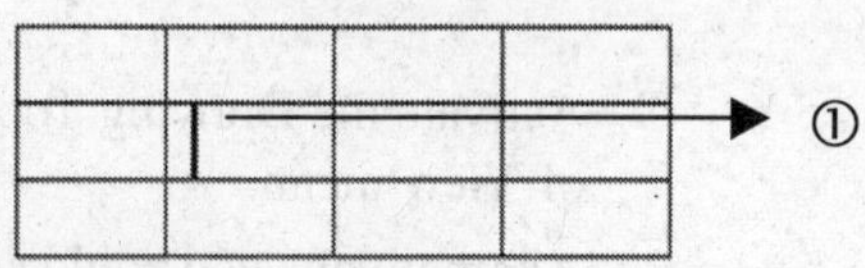

① Place the cursor anywhere within the Table.

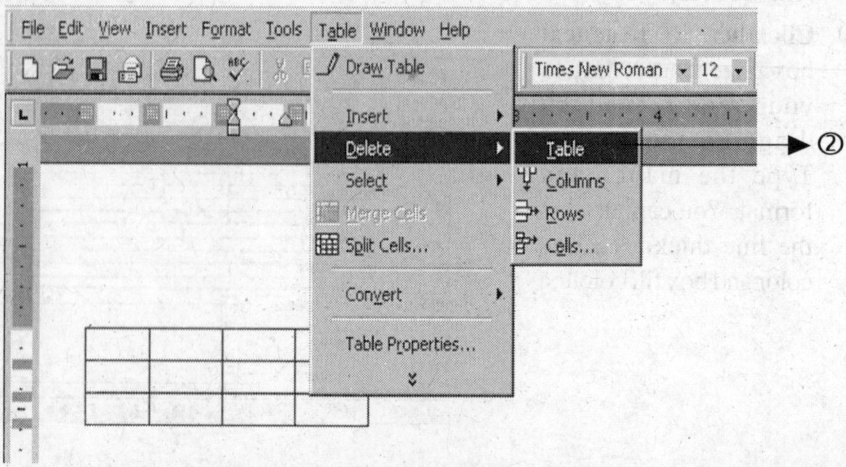

② Choose **Delete (Table)** from the **Table** menu.

Note: If you wish to delete a particular row or column or cell of a table, you can use the same command. The only difference would be you will have to choose Delete (Row/Column/Cell whichever is applicable) from the Table menu. The row or column or cell having the focus will be deleted.

Merging Cells Word allows you to combine two or more cells in the same row or column into a single cell. For example, you can merge several cells horizontally to create

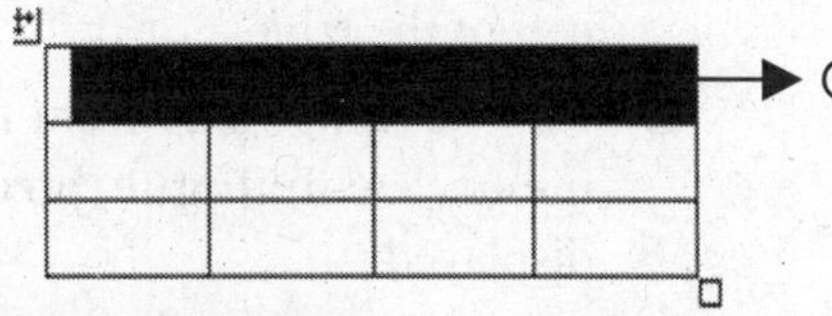

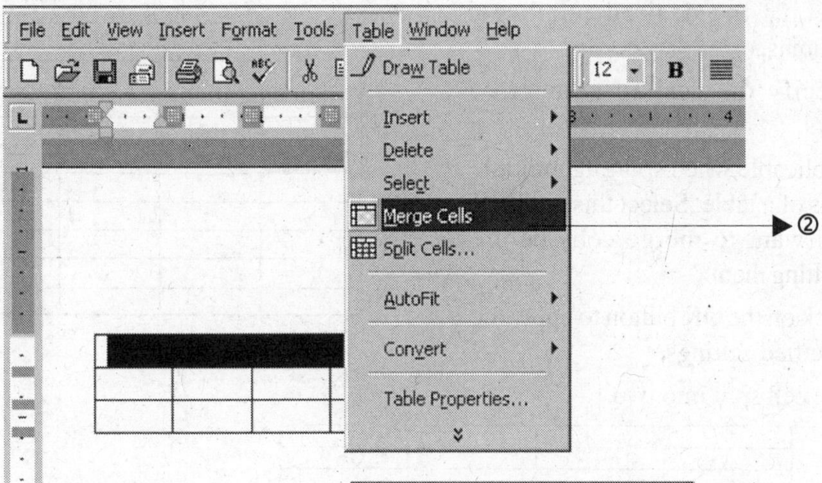

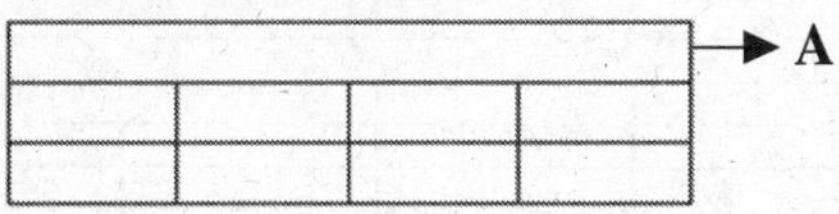

a table heading that spans several columns.

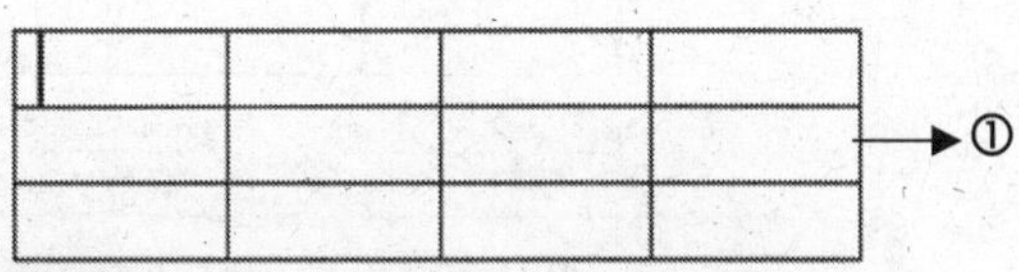

Follow the steps below to merge the cells of a table:

① Select all cells in a row or a column that you wish to merge.

② Choose **Merge Cells** from the **Table** menu.

A Merged Cells

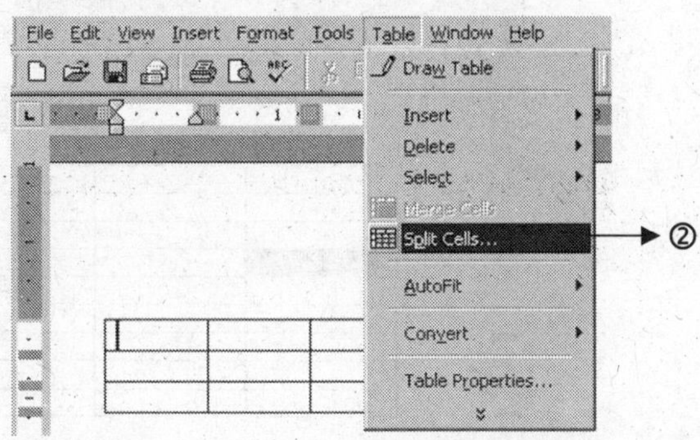

Splitting Cells Word allows splitting a cell of a table into multiple cells.

Follow the steps below to split the cells of a table:

① Place the cursor inside the desired cell of the table.

② Choose **Split Cells** from the **Table** menu. A dialogue box will be displayed.

③ Specify the desired number of columns.

④ Specify the desired number of rows.

⑤ Applicable when splitting multiple cells of a table. Select this option if you want to merge cells before splitting them.

⑥ Click on the OK button to apply the specified settings.

A One cell split into two.

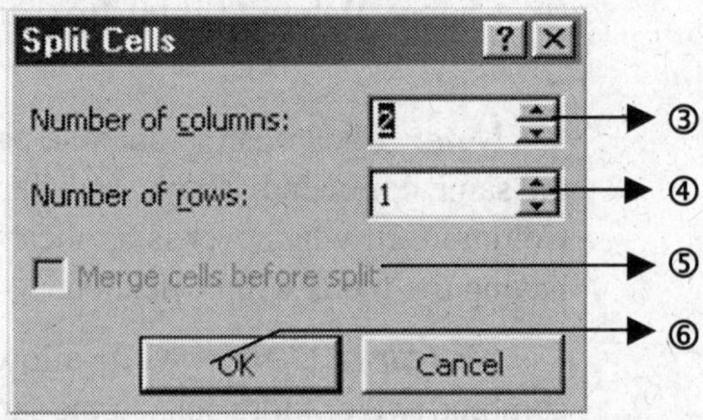

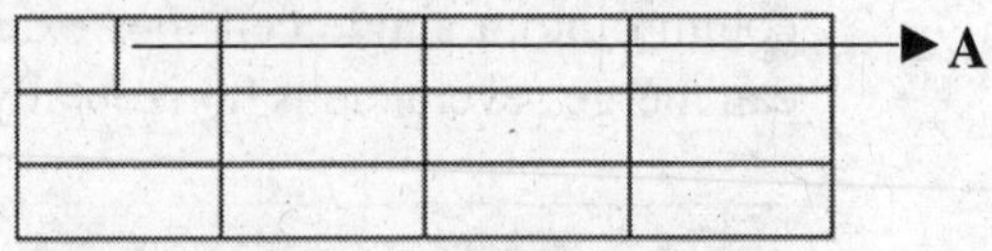

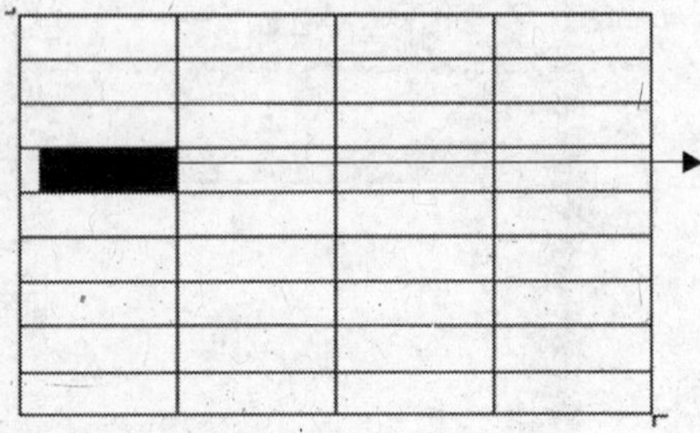

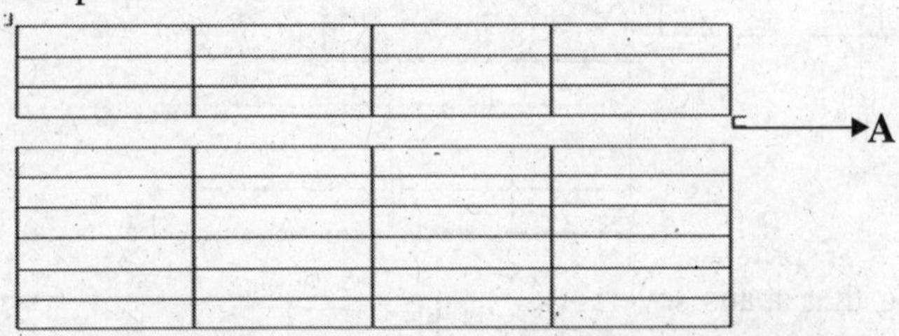

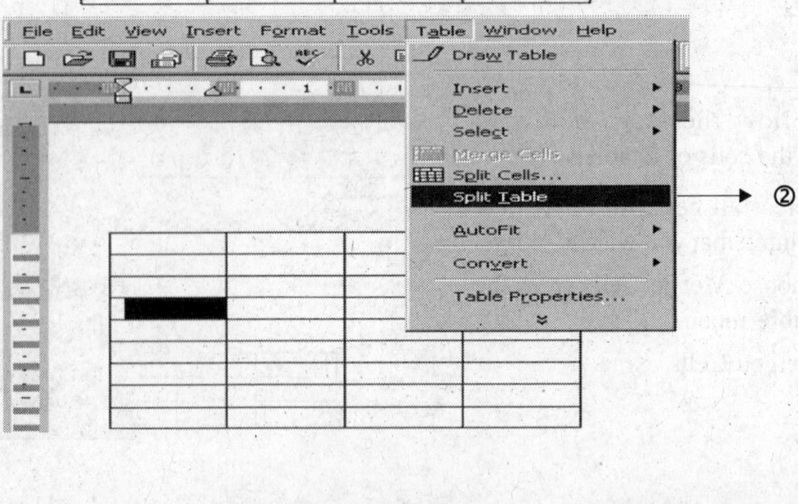

Splitting Tables Follow the steps below to split a table in two tables:

① Click the row that you want to be the first row of the second table.

② Choose **Split Table** from the **Table** menu.

A Two separate tables split from one.

MAIL MERGE

Mail Merge does what it says - merges mail! To explain further, let me give you some examples. Sometime or other you must have had the need to send the same document to a large number of people. This document could be a pleasant one, like a mailer informing people of new products and services, or informing people about change of your address or phone numbers, or informing people that they do not have to pay their rent any longer (I wish I received one like that!) etc. It could even be an unpleasant one, like asking people to pay up their dues promptly (I'm sure some of us have already received lots of these!) or, informing people about some bad news (withdrawal of a faulty product, or death of a person) etc.

Now, what is common in all these letters is that the SAME matter has to be sent to a number of people. In the days of typewriters (for some of you - presently) what you did was something like this–you typed the main body of the letter on your typewriter, leaving out space for the name and address of the recipients, ran your office boy to the nearest photostat shop asking him to get 100 copies made. Then you picked up each of these copies and either manually wrote the recipient's name and address (which is more common) or if you are more meticulous, asked your secretary (in some cases yourself!) to type out the recipient's name and address separately on each of these photocopies.

This works fine, except for two things. One, the end product (your letter) doesn't exactly look beautiful (the recipient can make out exactly what you have done) and two, next time you have to send another (similar) letter to these people, the entire exercise has to be done again.

Fortunately, Mail Merge overcomes both these problems. Because of skills learnt through the preceding exercises, producing beautiful looking letters can't exactly be called difficult. Secondly, with Mail Merge facility you can create a database of your contacts (including friends, relatives, acquaintances etc.) and automatically merge the main body of letters, this database in such a manner that many personalised letters would be generated. Each of these letters would be addressed individually to different people and all the recipients would feel as if you have personally written the letter to him or her.

The file that contains the form letter is called the *main document* and the file containing the database (names, addresses and other information) is called the *data source*. Each entry in the database file (data source) containing details about one person is called a *record* and each item of detail in this record (like name, phone number, subscription number etc.) is called a *field*. So, put simply, many related fields put together form a record and many records put together is called a database.

Enough of theory. Let's get down to actually doing mail merge. As I said earlier, for mail merge we have to create two files – main document and data source. Let's begin with the main document first (although there is no hard and fast rule for this). Before you begin, take a look at the sample letter shown on the next page. In our present exercise we shall use the Mail Merge option to prepare personalised letters like this and see how, with very little additional work, we can create 20 or 200 or even 2000 such letters.

Another great advantage in using the mail merge is that the next time you want to send the same or another letter to the same group of people, all you need to do is to create the main letter and merge it with the existing database, which already contains the names and addresses of the recipients.

WORD EXERCISE 3

Synergy Solutions

142A Greater Kailash I,
New Delhi 110048
Ph: 6482922 Fax: 6228363
E Mail: sanjeev@synergy.com

Dr. Mike Rodell,

Financial Consultant,
IHS,
Suite No. 202, Hotel Southern Star,
Mysore, Karnataka

Customer ID : 124779

Subject : <u>Renewal of your subscription for Cyber Mate - Internet Help Line for 2000</u>

Dear Mr. Rodell,

Warmest greetings for the year! I hope the New year brings you less problems than the one gone by (but not so less that you do need our Cyber Mate Help Line!). With a view to improve the quality and extent of services provided to you, we are pleased to launch a new release of our Internet based Help line Software, (you guessed it right!) called **Cyber Mate 2000.**

Cyber Mate 2000 has the following new features:

☺ Totally new and extremely user-friendly graphics User Interface.

☺ Provision for sending and receiving Emails - **Free** !

☺ Provision for participating in E-Chats, on latest trends and products in IT -**Free !**

☺ And several other features which make it even simpler (and you thought it couldn't be done!) to ask **Cyber Mate 2000** about any technical questions about computers.

And of course all this at no extra cost!

So don't miss out. Please fill up the enclosed form and send it across with your subscription no. (which we remember as) latest by 15th July 2000.

And by the way, **the first hundred subscribers would get free tickets to The Michael Jackson Show to be held in Delhi on the 15th of August 2000.**

So hoping to see you at the MJ show. Happy surfing and Happy New Year.

Please feel free to ring me up for any clarifications.

Yours sincerely 30th June 2000

Monica Dhaul
Director - Customer Relations

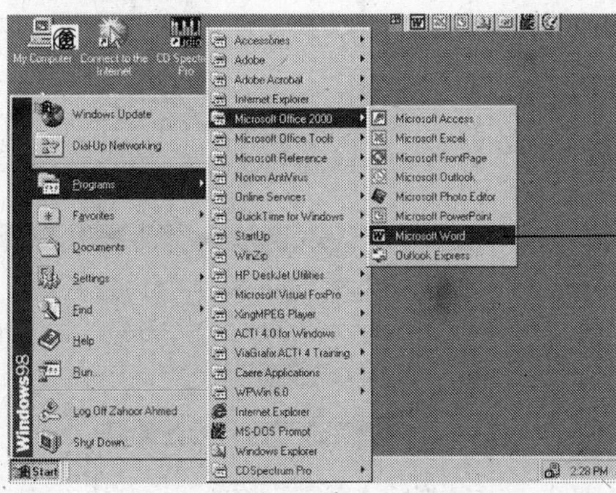

①

Creating the Main Document

① Start Word by choosing **Microsoft Word** from **Programs** option.

② Type the complete body of the letter first. It is always preferable

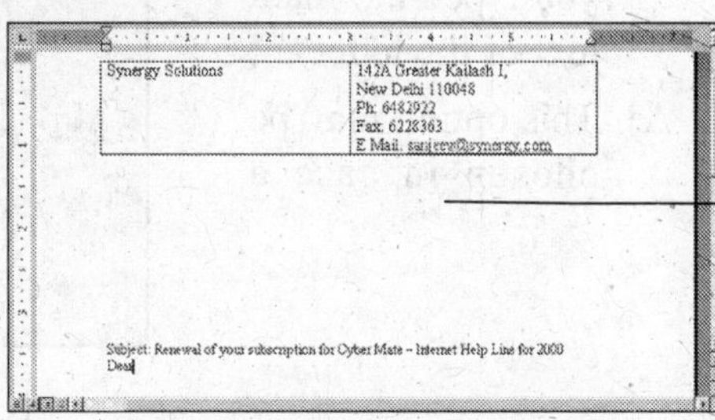

②

to type the body of the letter first and then apply the formatting styles later. This results in great savings in time.

Create the letterhead with a single row, two-column table.

Also ensure that sufficient space is left in the beginning of the letter for names, addresses and other details of the recipients.

③ Once having typed the entire matter, apply the fonts, point sizes, alignment, and other attributes to the text, based upon sample provided.

Now that you have put in some bit of work, let us save the file with any name. Since the steps involved in saving a file have already been explained to you, I'm going to move ahead to the next steps.

Now let us start Mail Merging.

Creating Data Source

① Choose **Mail Merge** from **Tools** menu. The following Window will be displayed.

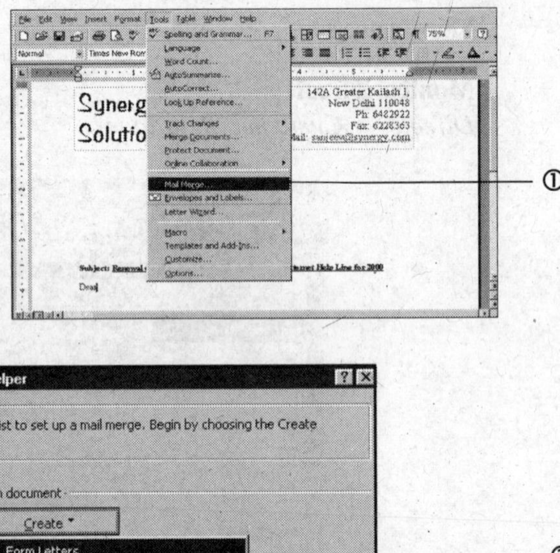

② Click on **Create** button.

③ Choose **Form letters** option.

The following Window would be displayed.

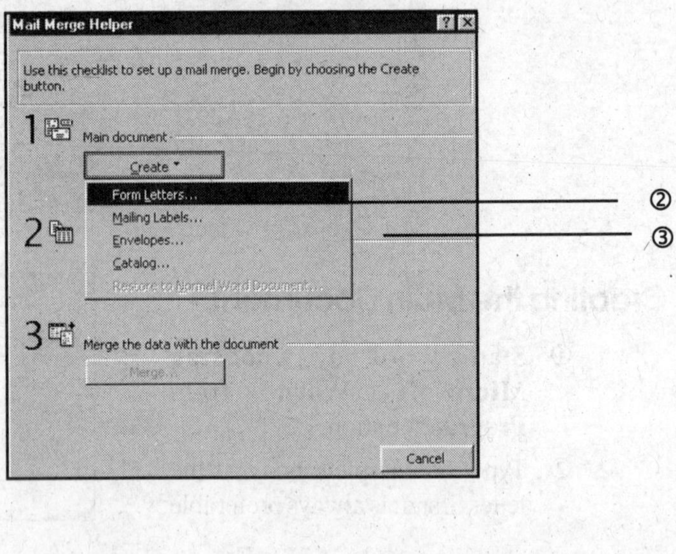

④ Click here to choose the currently active document (in which you typed the main text of the letter).

A This option may be chosen in case a

new document (i. e. other than the one that is currently open) has to be used for mail merging.

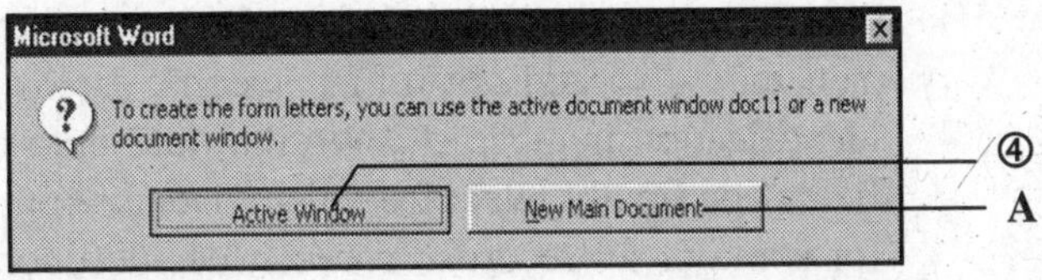

⑤ Click on **Get Data.**

⑥ Choose **Create Data Source** option.

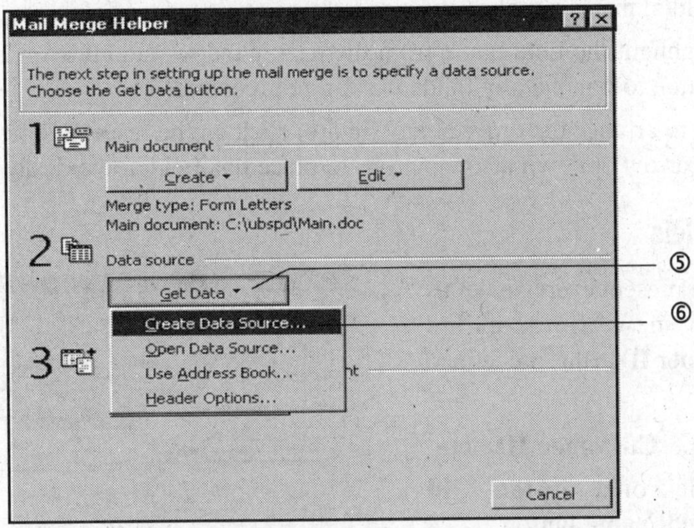

A Window for customising the Database Structure (header row) appears, as shown below.

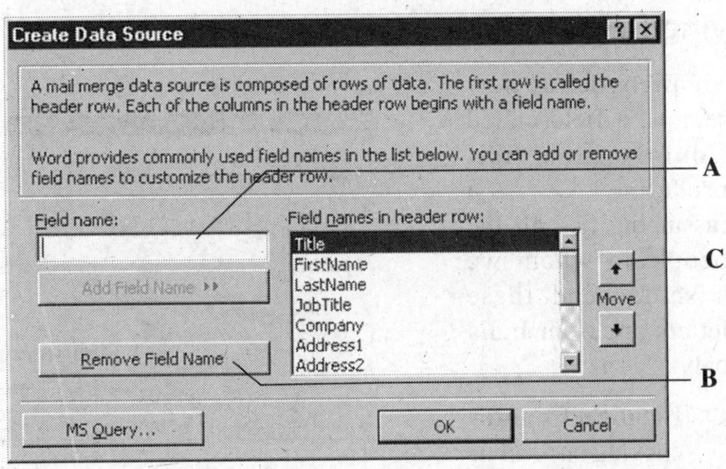

Now is the time to do some serious thinking! At this stage you have to decide about what all information you wish to store in the data file. Typically this file contains the names, address details, contact numbers, etc., of people that you wish to send letters to. (Though the phone and fax numbers are only required for sending the letters through courier, nonetheless it is helpful to store them here so that your contact database is complete). You may also add any other specific fields that you may require, like the customer identification number etc. Word would auto-matically create a data file with whatever fields you finally select from here. Do not bother if you do not have any data for any field for some or all records. You can decide upon the final shape of this file now and can always fill up the missing information as and when it becomes available to you.

A Type the desired field name and click on **Add Field Name** button to add any additional field(s) that is not already provided.

B Highlight the field name from the next Window and click on **Remove Field Name** button to remove any fields that are not required.

C To re-arrange the order of any field(s) click on the respective field name and click on up arrow or down arrow buttons to place this field at the desired place.

Adding Fields

For the present exercise, let us add a new field called **Customer ID** to this predefined list.

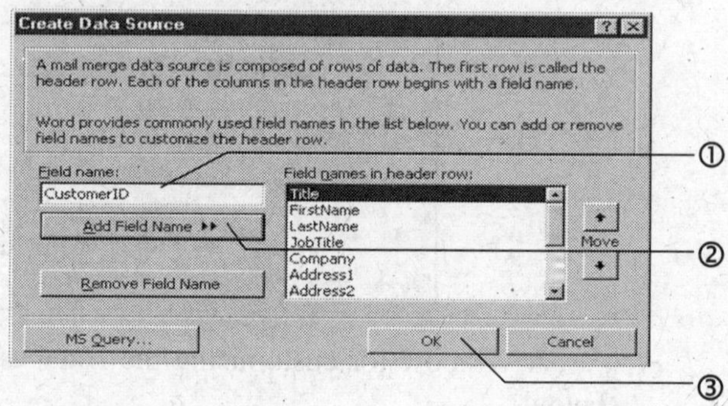

① Type **Customer ID** here.

② Click once on the **Add Field Name** button.

③ Click once on **OK** button.

Removing Fields

Similarly, let us now remove a field called **Country** from this predefined list (assuming that all the people to whom we wish to send these letters are from India only).

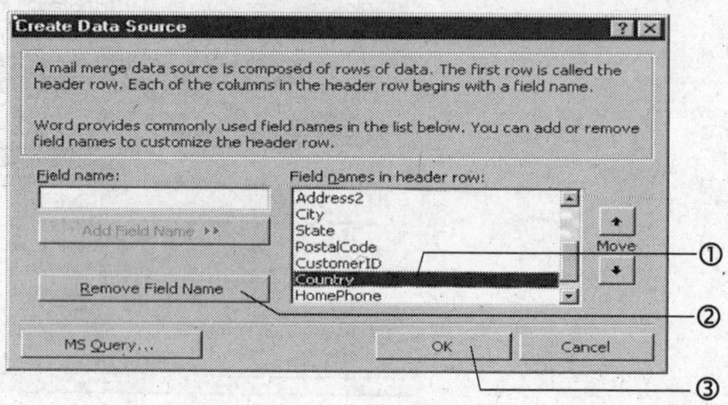

① Highlight **Country** clicking once on it.

② Click once on **Remove Filed Name** button.

③ Click on **OK** button to finalize the list of fields.

The following window will be displayed.

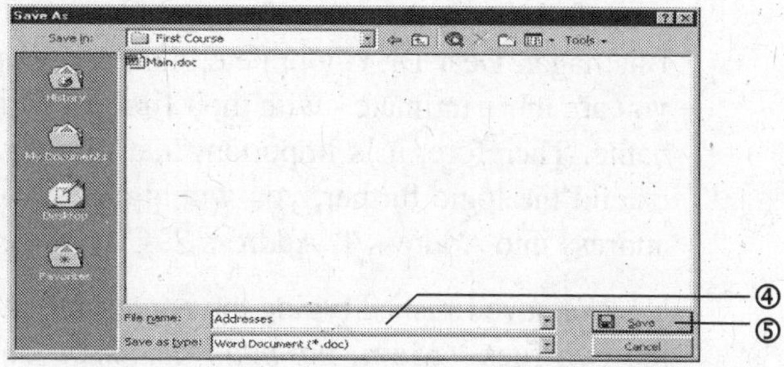

④ Type **Addresses** as the file in which you wish to save the customer details

⑤ Click on **Save** button.

The following Window would be displayed.

⑥ Click once on **Edit Data Source** to start typing the name and addresses to people to whom this letter has to be sent. The following Window will be displayed.

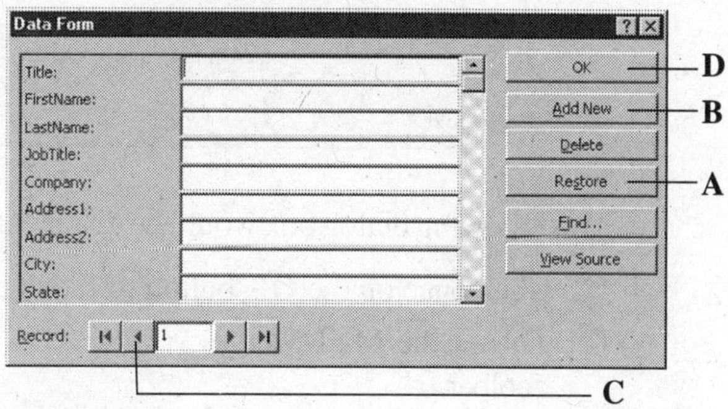

A Notice that the various items of information chosen or specified by you earlier appear here as field names.

B You can see all the fields by scrolling down with the help of scroll bars shown here

C Through these buttons you can travel through the different records in the database. Clicking once on left arrow button you can go to the previous record and by clicking on the right arrow button it would take you to the next record.

D Also notice that **Add**, **Delete**, **Restore**, **Find** and **View** options are available here. Through these options you can create and modify your database file.

Now type the details for ten people to whom this letter has to be sent. After typing details about one person (one record), click once on the **Add New** button to add the next record. Take care to fill up the information in the right fields, e.g., the field 'Title' has been created so that you can type salutations for different people like Mr., Mrs., Dr, Major General, etc. Similarly, all first names must go to the First Name field and all last names to Last Name. You might be wondering why have I split the name into three different parts - Title, First Name and Last Name. Splitting the names in this manner gives you complete control over which part of the name you use where. For instance, you are sending this letter to all you customers with whom you maintain a cordial and professional relationship (hopefully!). In that case you would normally address the letter to them as Dear Mr. Bhatnagar, Dear Dr. Chopra etc., i.e., you would address them with their last name or, if you are more intimate - with their first name. In any case you would not use the complete name. Therefore, it is important that two separate fields are specified for name. If you extend the logic further, you would also understand the need for splitting the complete address into Address 1, Address 2, City, State etc.

We have finished typing the names and addresses. Let us now see how we can merge the two files - **Main**, *the main document* and **Addresses**, *the data source*, to produce personalised letters.

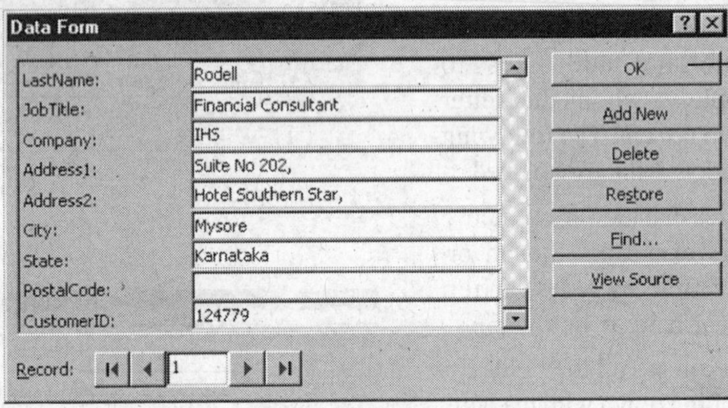

①

The following dialog box would be displayed.

① Click once on the **OK** button to finish entering the records.

② This is the Mail Merge Toolbar.

③ Place the cursor at the place where you wish to insert the names.

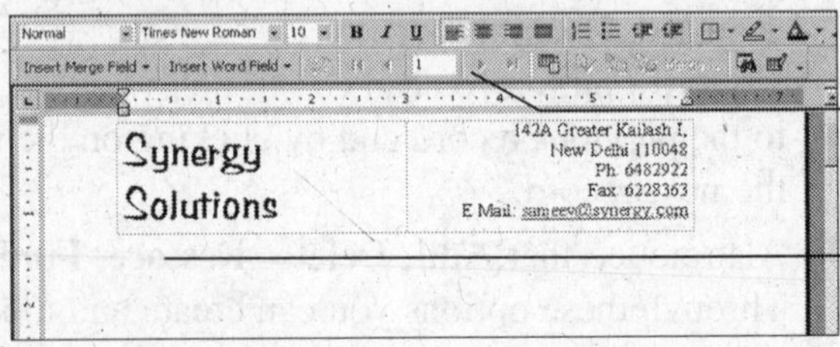

②
③

④ Click once on **Insert Merge Field** button. A drop down list displaying all the fields that you created would be shown. Now by highlighting the desired field and clicking on it once, we can insert the field into the main document. Choose **Title** and click on it once.

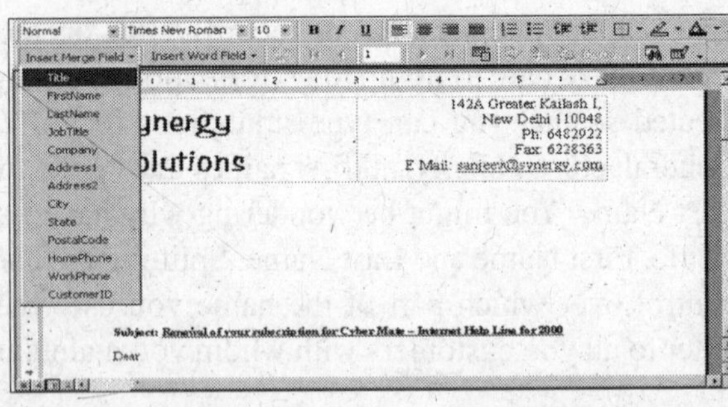

④

A Notice that the Title field has been inserted here. The effect of this would be that when you give the mail merge command, the field contents of the field 'title' (i.e., Dr. or Mr. or Ms. etc.) would get substituted at this place. Therefore, it is important that before you insert a field you must place your cursor at the right place, i.e., at the place you wish the field contents to be inserted.

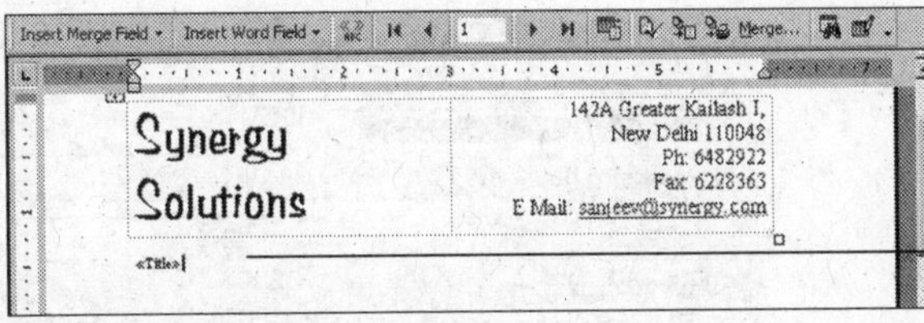

Now use the same technique to insert all other fields as shown below.

B Please note that wherever required, blank spaces, commas and hyphen marks have been typed while inserting different fields. For instance, if you do not give a space between Title, First name and Last name the actual output (after merging) would be something like this: *Mr.MikeRodell.*

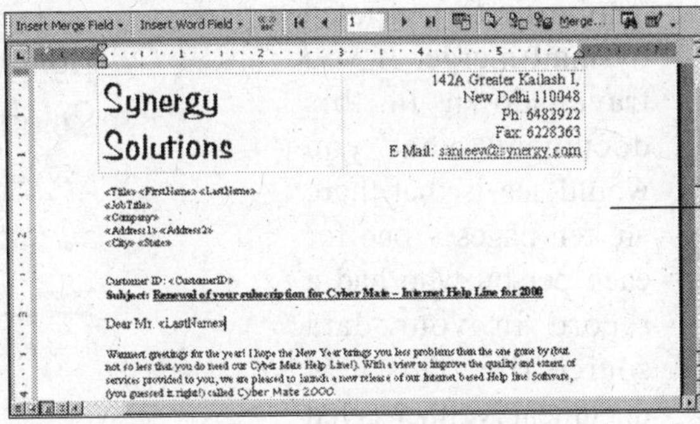

Obviously this would not be acceptable. Therefore just visualise the output first and then insert the fields.

⑤ Now to begin mail-merging, click once on the **Mail Merge** Icon.

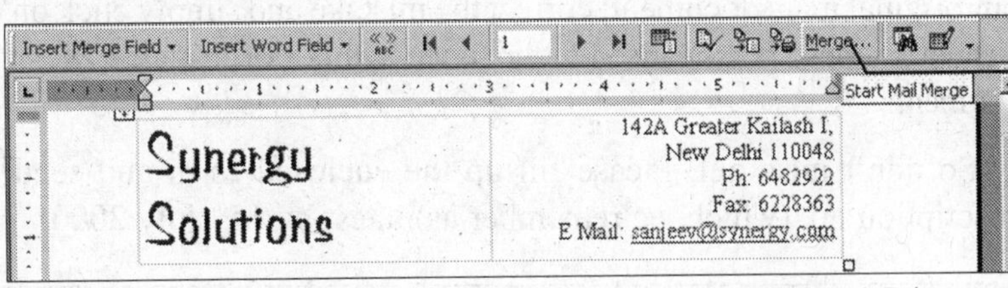

The following window would be displayed.

⑥ Simply click once on the **Merge** button to generate letters for all the records in your data source file.

A You may specify a range of records here, in case you wish to generate letters only for some selected people.

B Click here in case you do not wish to leave blank lines for those fields that are empty.

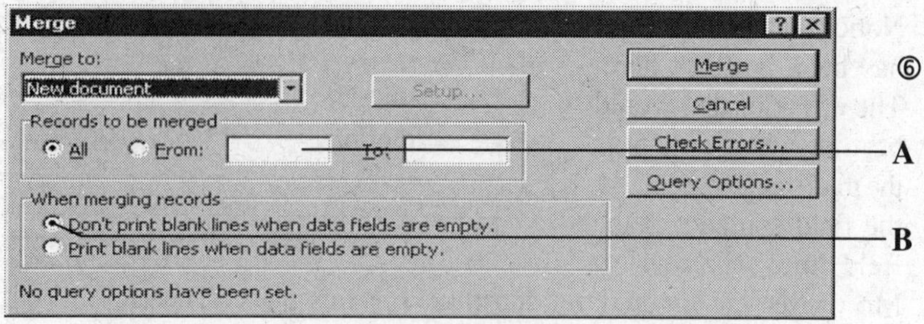

The following results would be displayed.

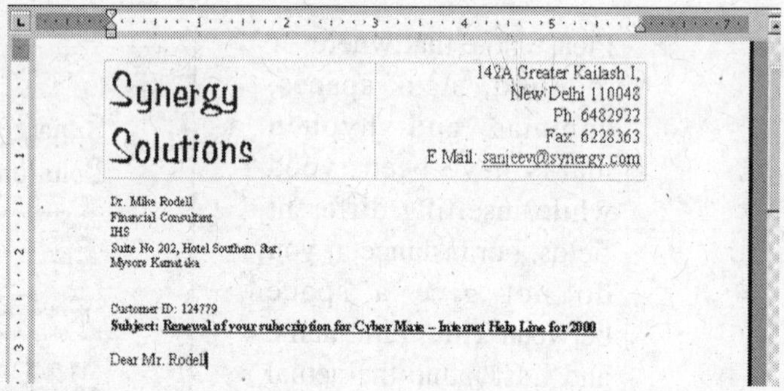

Bravo! What you now see is the first letter auto-matically generated by mail merge. If you travel down in this document what you would see is that there are ten pages – one for each person who had a record in your data source file. This new document is either saved under any file name specified by you or can simply be printed and closed without saving. Since we would be saving our original main document, this new document containing the letters can always be generated again by a click at Mail Merge Icon.

If you find any mistake in these letters, simply close this file without saving, go back to your original main document; correct the mistake and simply click on the Mail Merge icon to generate these personalised letters once again. For instance, we had a line in our main document:

So don't miss out. Please fill up the enclosed form and send it across with your subscription no. (which we remember as) latest by 15th July 2000.

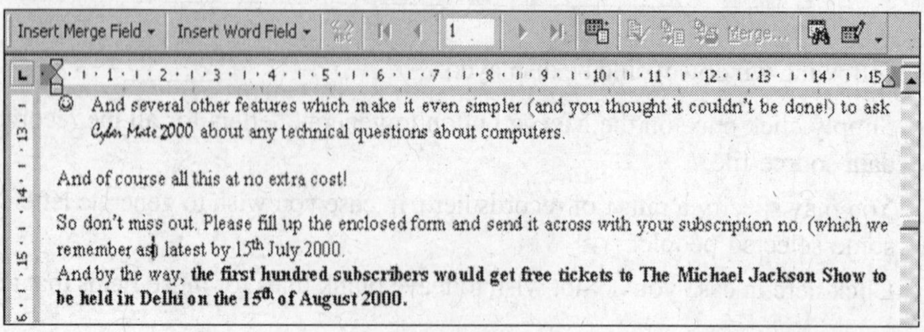

Here we want to insert the CustomerID inside the parentheses, simply place the cursor after 'as' and insert the field **CustomerID.** You may then apply the Bold attribute to this number to make the number more prominent.

So don't miss out. Please fill up the enclosed form and send it across with your subscription no. (which we remember as_**«CustomerID»**) latest by 15th July 2004.

You will notice that after mail merging, again this number would be inserted and shown as below:

So don't miss out. Please fill up the enclosed form and send it across with your subscription no. (which we remember as **124779**) latest by 15th July 2000.

So hurry now, dig out all the visiting cards of all the people you know and surprise them by sending them a mail-merged greeting/letter!

MACROS

Now that you've done a fair bit of work in Microsoft Word, let's now move on to do something more advanced. By now you have learnt to execute many commands and get the desired result one by one. It's a bit like having to explain to your servant all the steps on how to make a cup of tea - over and over again. Possible, but a bit tedious! Sooner or later you're bound to get frustrated and wish that your servant was a bit smarter and could learn from experience. In simple words, you would want that having once explained in simple and precise steps to him the process of making a cup of tea, he should be able to follow the explained steps and make a perfect cup of tea every time you ask him to.

If you like to do things the right way, better write down all the steps involved in it. This process of writing down many commands together in a logical and sequential manner is called Programming in computer jargon. Programming enables you to group many commands together and execute them at a press of a button. In Microsoft Word you can create your programs which automate any repetitive tasks involving several steps. These programs are called **Macros.**

A macro is a small software program. A program is a series of instructions written in a computer language to execute a specific task or tasks. It enables the execution of a series of sequential and logical commands without having to give those commands one by one.

A macro is a series of Word commands which have been grouped together as a single command. Any repetitive operation which involves executing a number of sequential steps can be automated by creating a macro for it. In other words, if you perform any operation repetitively, involving many commands and / or steps, you can group these together into a single command, such that by giving one command all these grouped commands / steps are executed automatically. It is a bit like having a very faithful and obedient servant – just show him how to do anything once and he will faultlessly do it again whenever asked to do so. In short, Macros can save you considerable time and effort by automating your repetitive tasks.

There are two stages in using macros:

- Creating Macros, and
- Running Macros

While creating a macro, you require two things:

- The actual commands/steps which are to be grouped together to run as one, and
- Assigning the macro. 'Assigning' means specifying to the computer how you would prefer to run this macro.

You can create the macros in two ways:

- Record a series of steps / actions using the keyboard and mouse, or
- Type a macro directly into a macro editing Window using Visual Basic programming language.

Needless to say, the first option is easier, while the second is more powerful and flexible. For creating complex and sophisticated macros you can combine the two approaches – record as much as you can, and then edit the result using Visual Basic editor.

You can assign a macro as follows:

- An option in any menu, or
- As an icon in a toolbar, or
- To a button, or
- To a shortcut key (like function keys), or
- To a key combination.

Given below are the steps involved in recording a macro.

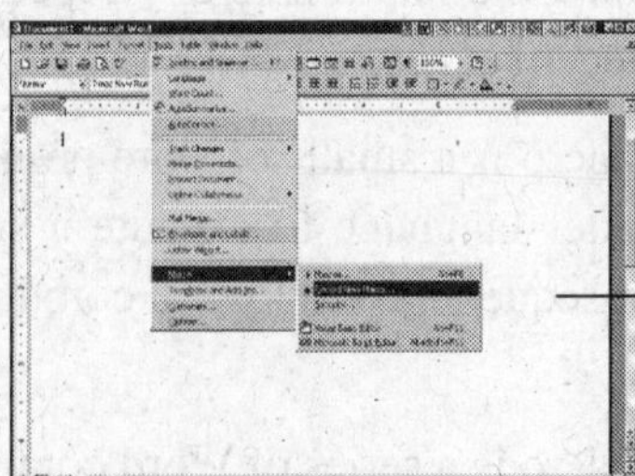

①

① Choose **Re-cord New Macro** com-mand from **Macro** option, in the **Tools** menu.

The following dialog box would be displayed.

② Click on the **Keyboard** button to define the macro from the keyboard. The following dialog box would be displayed.

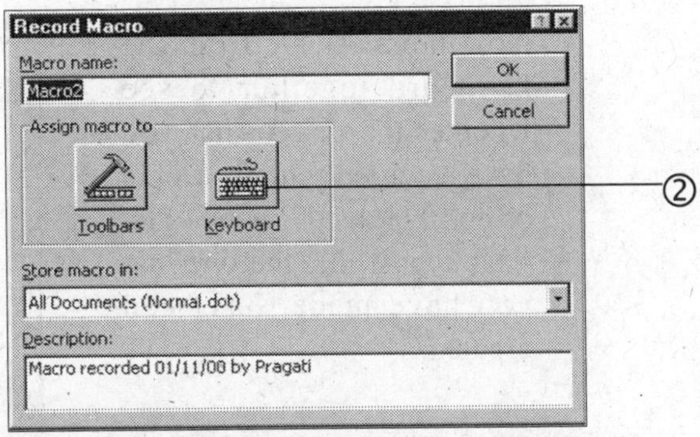

③ Click in this box and press **Alt** and **X** keys from the keyboard together. This is now the macro shortcut.

④ Click on **Assign** button to assign the macro to these two keys.

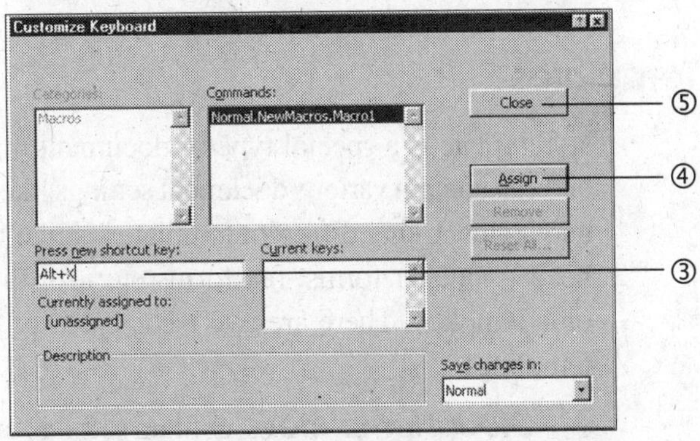

⑤ Click on **Close** button to close this dialog box.

You would notice the small macro box on the left side.

⑥ Choose a table with the dimension of **4 rows and 5 columns** from **Insert Table** icon on the Standard Toolbar.

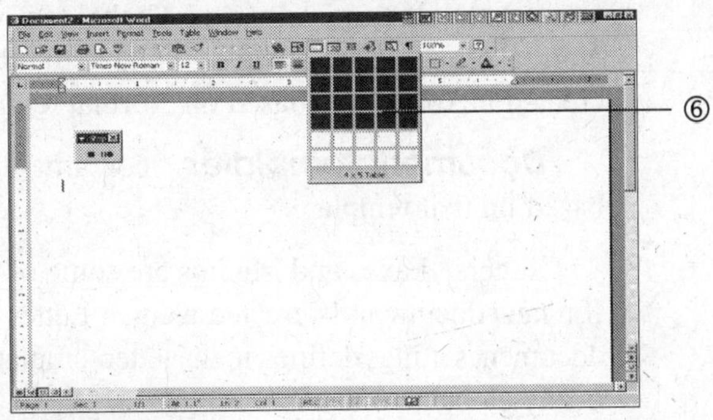

⑦ Fill in the details of the columns as shown below.

⑧ Click on the **Stop Recording** button to stop recording the macro.

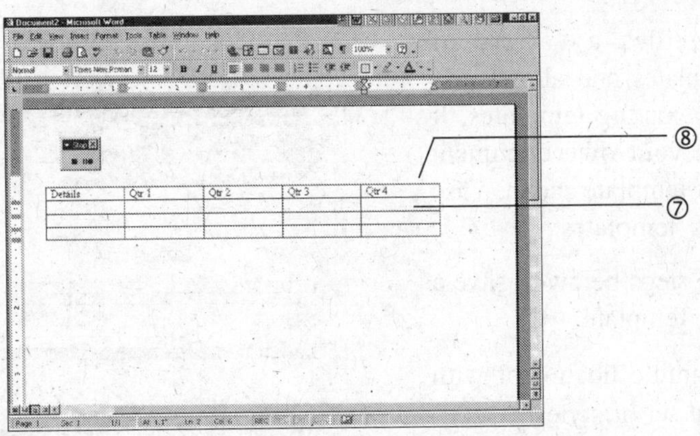

A Now press Alt+X from the keyboard together to see whether the macro that you have recorded actually works or not. You would notice that a table, just like the one that you have made, has been created.

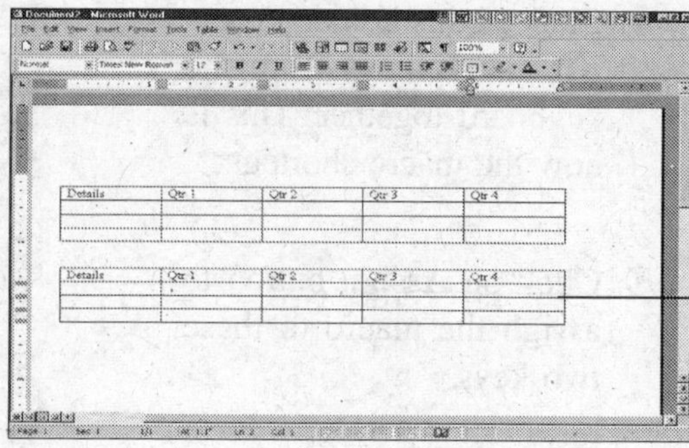

A

Templates

A Template is a special type of document that determines the basic layout of a document and can contain various document settings like fonts, page layout, toolbars, special formatting and styles. Using different templates is like having pre-printed stationery (Example letter heads, voucher forms, fax forms etc.) for different uses. Every Word document is based on a template. There are two basic types of templates – Global templates and Document templates.

Global templates contain settings that are available to all documents. The Normal template by design is always a Global template; this is because any settings added to the Normal template are always available to other documents. Whenever a new document is created in Word, it is based on Normal template.

Document templates contain settings that are available only to documents based on that template.

Letters, Faxes and Memos are some of the in-built document templates of MS Word. If a new document is created using a Letter template then that document will have all the document settings defined in the letter template as well as all the document settings contained in any global template.

Word provides a variety of document templates and allows you to modify the existing templates. It allows to save your own document design as a new template and then use it to create new templates.

Follow the steps below to save a document as a Template:

A Create a sample document with the required set of styles.

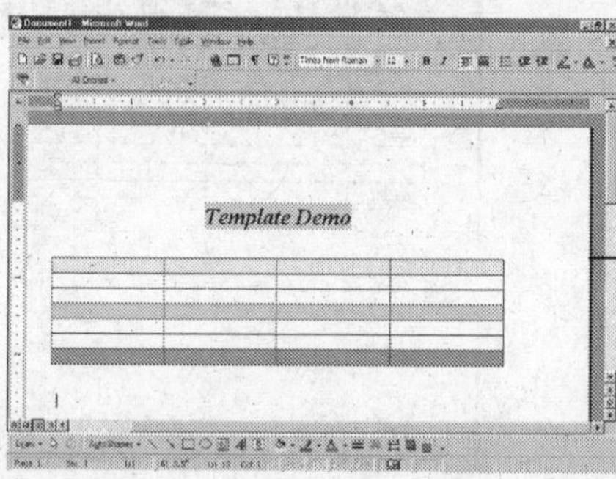

A

B Choose **Save as** from the **File** menu.

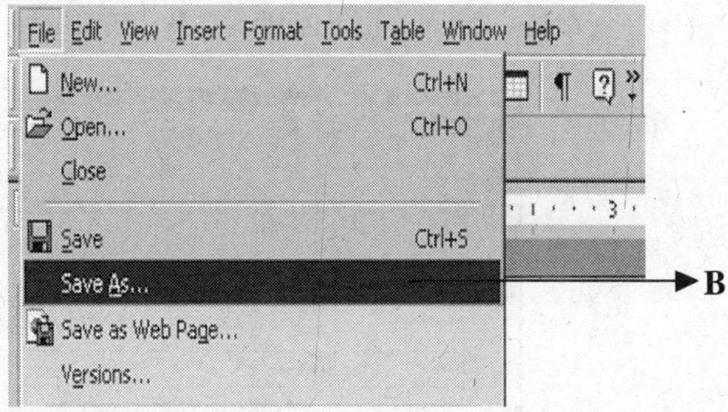

C In the Save drop down box choose **Document Template.** All templates have their extension name as .DOT unlike Word files that have .DOC as their extension name.

D Type a name for your template. All the templates must be stored in the **Template** directory so that they can be used as a base for creating new documents. In Windows 95 or 98, the **Templates** folder is located by default in either the C:\Windows_folder/ Application Data/ Microsoft folder or the C:\Windows_folder/ Profiles/User_name/ Application Data/ Microsoft folder.

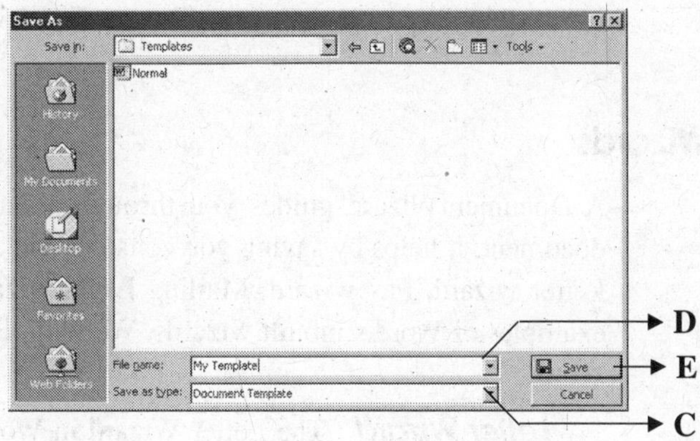

E Click on the **Save** button to save your template.

Follow the steps below to create a new document based on.

① Choose **New** com-mand from **File** menu, a dialog box will be displayed to the user.

② Select **My Template**.

③ Click on **Document** to create document based on My Template.

④ Click on the **OK** button.

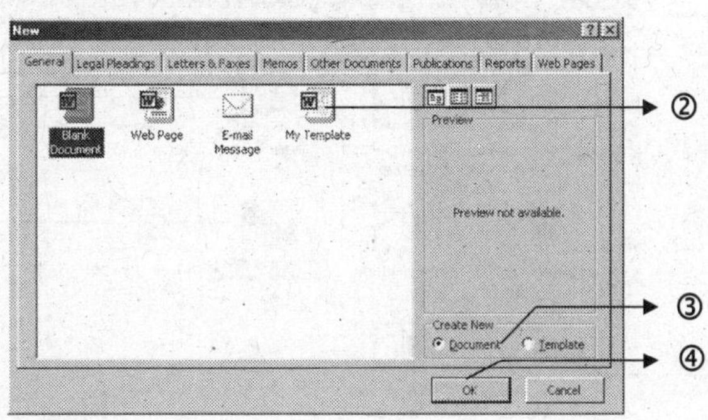

A New document based on **My Template**.

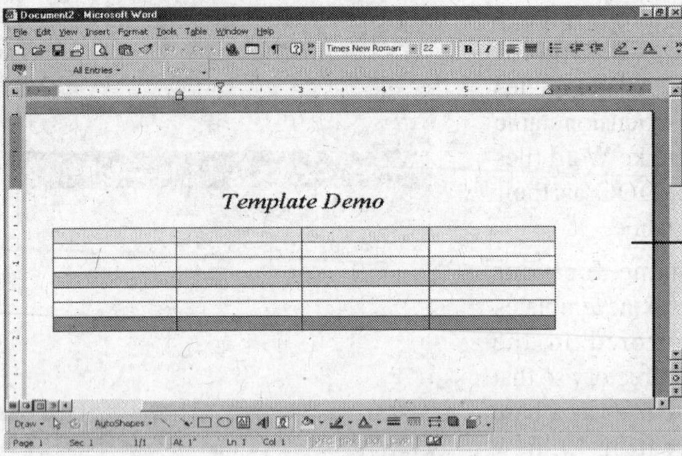

Wizards

A DocumentWizard guides you through a series of instructions to help you create a document. It helps by saving you considerable amount of effort as well as precious time. Letter wizard, Fax wizard, Mailing Label wizard, Envelope wizard, Memo wizard are examples of Word's inbuilt wizards. We will discuss the most commonly used wizard of Word:

Letter Wizard The Letter Wizard in Word can help you write letters quickly and easily. It provides frequently – used letter elements – such as date, reference lines, salutations, and closings – that you can select from lists. It also helps you structure your letters based on frequently – used letter styles.

Follow the steps below to create a letter using a Letter Wizard:

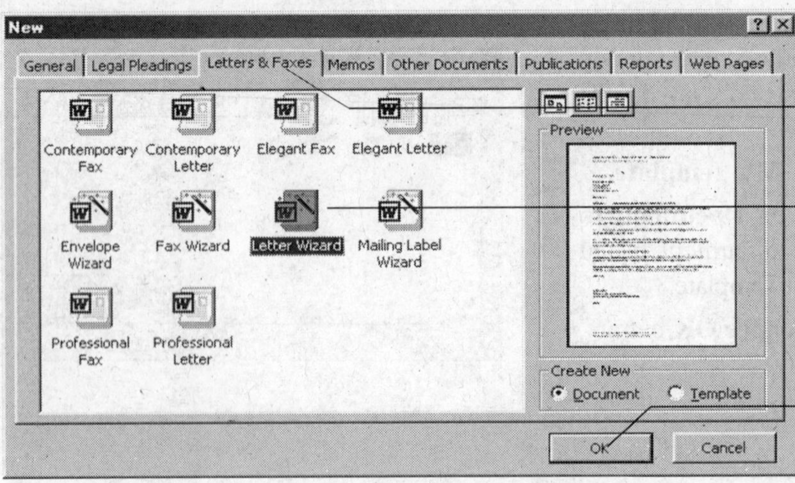

① Choose **New** from the **File** menu. Click on Letters and Faxes in the New file dialogue box.

② Choose Letter wizard.

③ Click on the **OK** button to open the Letter wizard.

Letter Wizard – Step 1

① Choose **Date Line** to insert date in the selected format as shown in the drop down box.

② Choose the type of letter you wish to create (Contemporary, Normal, Professional or Elegant). Preview of the selected type will be displayed.

③ Choose **Include Header and Footer** if you wish to insert any header or footer to your letter.

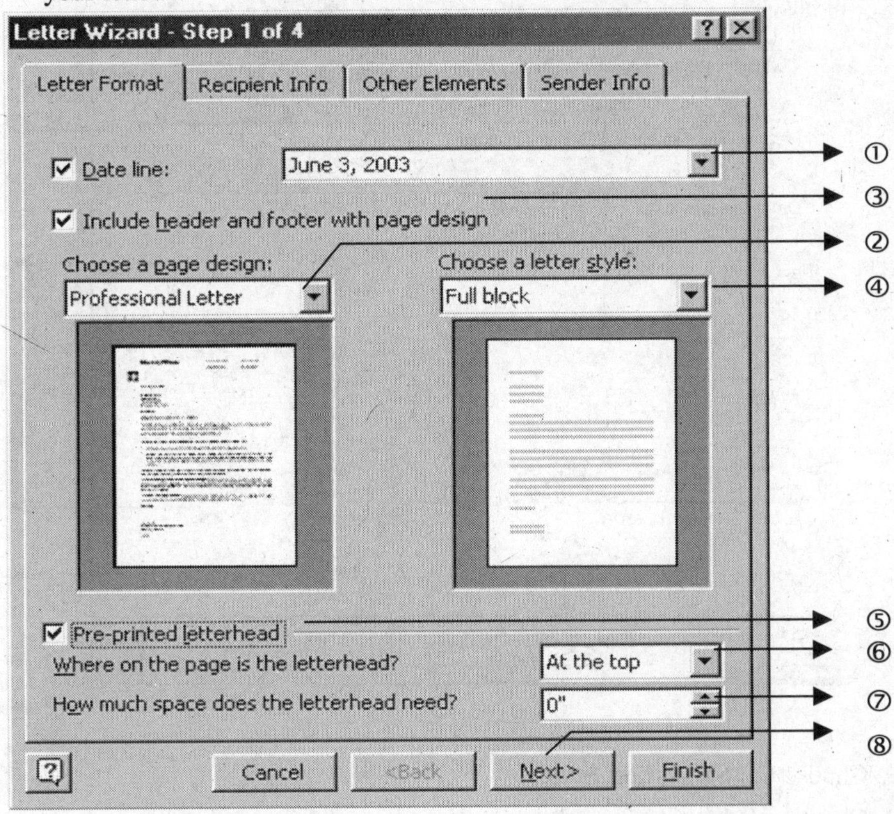

④ Choose the **Letter Style** from the drop down box. Preview of the selected type will be displayed.

⑤ Choose **Preprinted letterhead** if you wish to leave space for your letter head.

⑥ Select the position of the letterhead (Top, Bottom, Left or Right) from the drop-down box.

⑦ Select the space required by the letterhead on the page.

⑧ Click on the **Next** button to continue. The following screen will be displayed:

Letter Wizard – Step 2

① Type the **Recipient's Name** or select from the drop down box.

② Type the **Delivery** address for this letter.

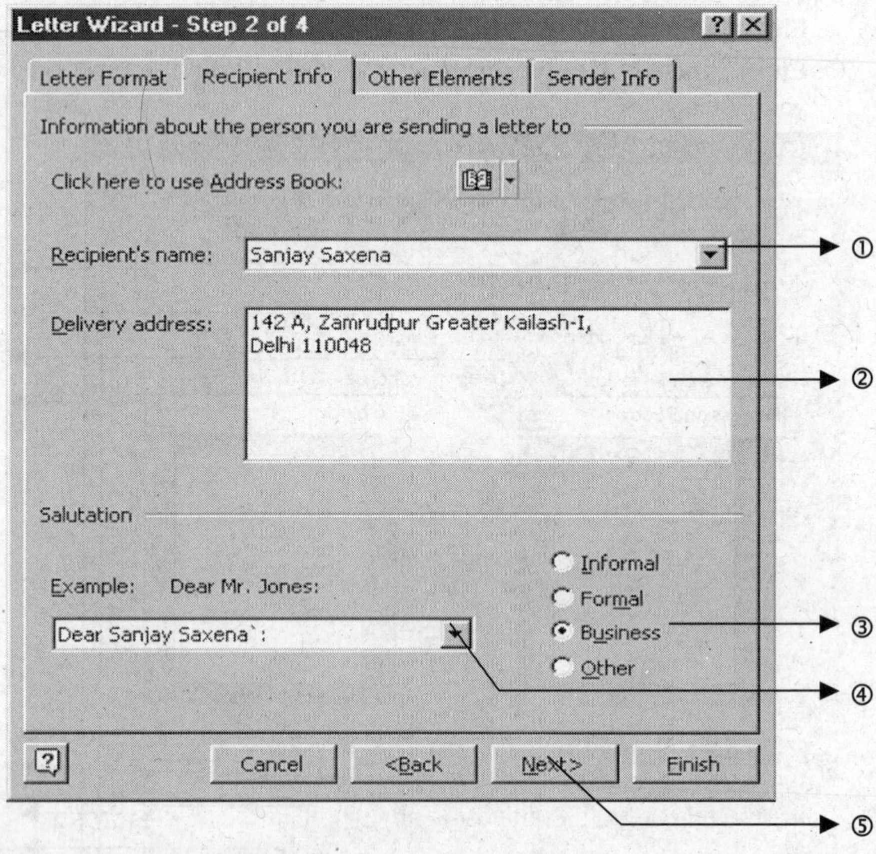

③ Choose the **Salutation Style**.

④ Choose a Salutation from the drop down box or type a value.

⑤ Click on the **Next** button to continue. The following screen will be displayed:

Letter Wizard – Step 3

① Click once on the check box to add **Reference Line.** It can be selected from the drop down menu or a value can be typed.

② Click once on the check box to add **Mailing Instructions**.

③ Click once on the check box to add **Attention** line.

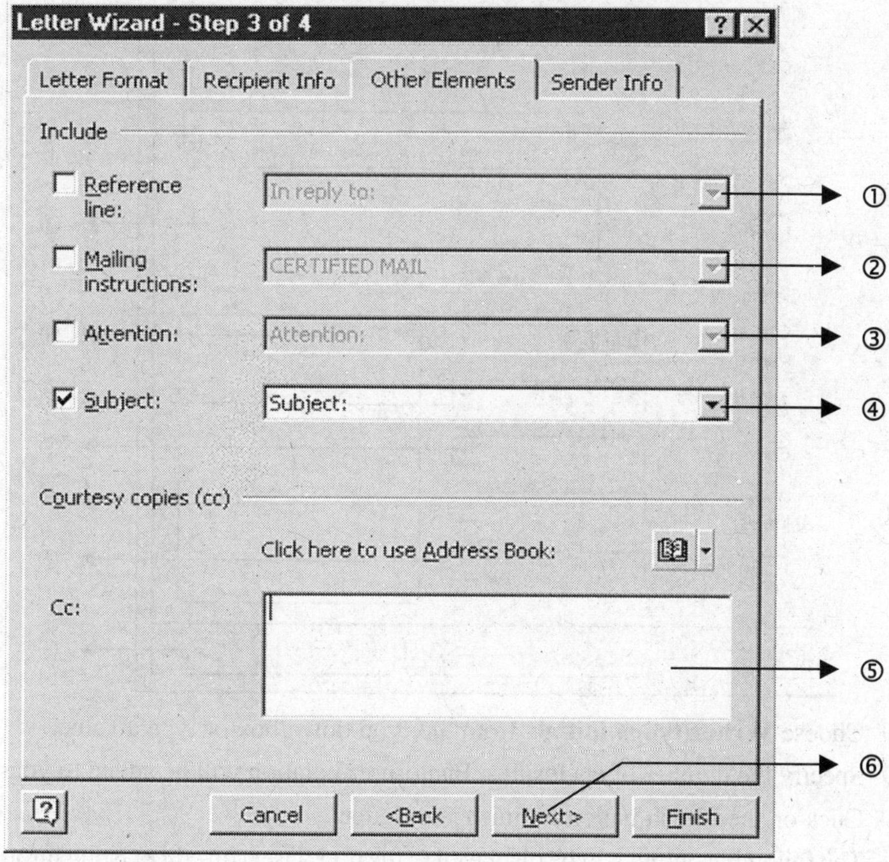

④ Select the check box to add **Subject** line.

⑤ If you wish to send a courtesy copy of the letter then specify the recipient's name and address in the **cc** box.

⑥ Click on the **Next** button to continue. The following screen will be displayed:

Letter Wizard – Step 4

① Enter the **Sender's** name.

② Select **Omit** if you do not wish to specify the **Return** address. Clear Omit if you wish to specify the Return address.

③ Choose **Complementary Closing** from the drop down box.

④ Choose **Job Title** from the drop down box or type a value.

⑤ Choose **Company** from the drop down box or type a value.

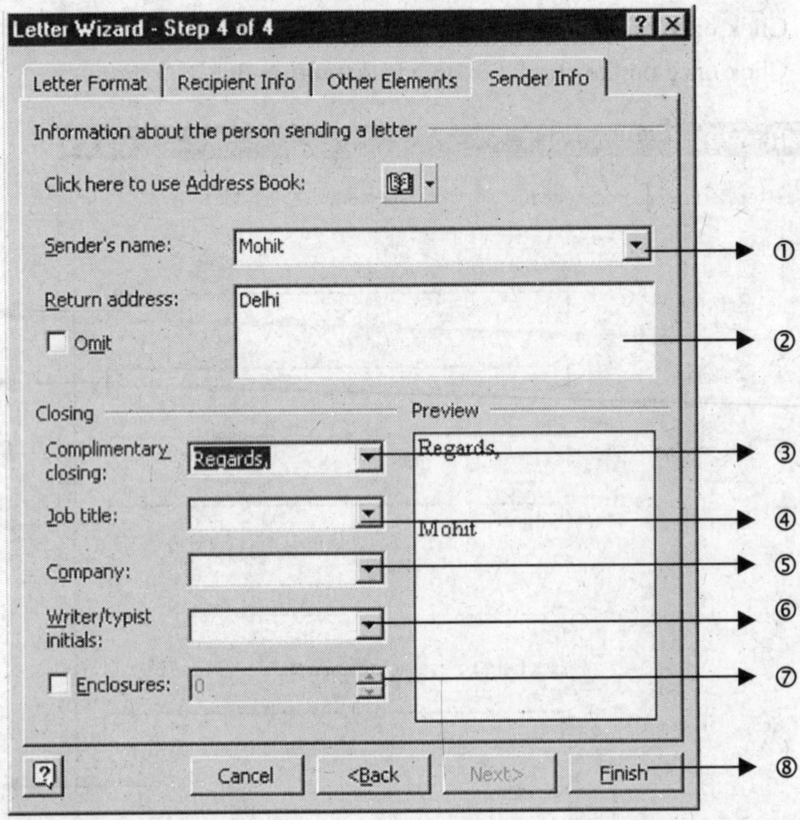

⑥ Choose **Writer/typist initials** from the drop down box or type a value.

⑦ Specify the number of enclosures. Enclosures notation will be added to your letter.

⑧ Click on the **Finish** button to finish your letter.

A The following output will be displayed to the user. User can edit existing information as well as add new information to the letter.

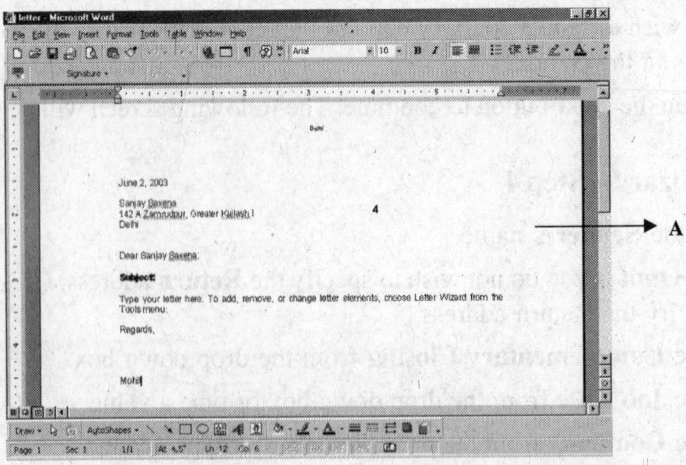

KEY POINTS

Word Basics and formatting features

- Microsoft Word is a full-featured word processing program that can be used to write letters and reports, prepare bills and invoices, prepare office stationery – letter heads, envelopes and forms, design brochures, pamphlets, newsletters, magazines and many more.
- Any Word document can be viewed in four different types of views viz., Normal View, Web Layout View, Print Layout View and Outline View. Normal view is the default view. In Web Layout View you can preview your page as it will appear in a web browser. In Print Layout view you can preview your page as it will appear when printed. In Outline view you can specify upto seven levels of headings. You can rearrange both the headings as well as its content to revise the structure of the document.
- Title bar, Menu bar, Standard toolbar, Formatting toolbar, Scroll bars and Status bar are the key elements of a Word Window. Standard toolbar contain icons that help you quickly alter the appearance and arrangement of documents by executing a variety of Word commands. Formatting toolbar contains icons for changing the formatting of your text. Status bar displays information like Current Page, Section Number, Current/Total pages in the document, Current Line Number etc.
- For executing most tasks in MS Word, the user has three options:
  1. Choose the desired command from the Menu options provided, by either using the mouse or using cursor movement keys, or
  2. Press the appropriate shortcut keys combination from the keyboard, or
  3. Click once on the relevant icon from the displayed toolbars.
- One of the basic features of Word is Word-Wrap. This feature allows you to type in continuity without bothering about your line running out of right margin of your page.
- The process of changing the appearance of text by changing the font type, font size, alignment of text, applying shades and colours etc. is called Formatting. All the formatting features offered by Word require pre-selection of a piece of text.
- Fonts are like different handwriting scripts available to you. Just as different people write the same alphabets differently, the font facility of MS Word enables you to choose the way in which your alphabet script is displayed and printed.
- The last four files that have been used recently are displayed in the list of recent documents at the bottom of the File menu. Simply click on that file name to open it.
- Paragraph spacing is used to create spaces between paragraphs. It is also possible to create additional spacing between the lines of a paragraph. This is known as Line Spacing.
- Page formatting involves setting the page margins, page size, page orientation etc. By default, whenever you create a new document, the document is created with predefined page settings.

- Header and Footer allow you to print a standard piece of text and/or an image at the top or end of each page of your document. Headers appear at the top of each page and footers appear at the bottom of each page.
- By default a new document contains only one section. (If no section break has been inserted explicitly.) Word allows inserting multiple sections into the same document. This feature allows the user to apply different formatting styles within the same document.
- Word allows to preview on screen what you wish to print. In most cases, this preview would give you an exact replica of what your printer would print.

Editing and Proofing Tools

- Spelling and Grammar is one of the coolest features of Word and frees you from the bother of concentrating on the spelling and grammar of your text. Word contains an inbuilt dictionary, but it does not always include proper names, technical terms and acronyms.
- AutoText – MS Word displays a Tool tip text when you type the first few characters of a date or an AutoText entry, at which point you can insert the entry by pressing the Enter key, or ignore it and continue typing.
- MS Word allows you to track the changes made to your document. Word makes use of revision marks to show the tracked changes to the user. A revision mark shows where an insertion, deletion or any other editing change has been made in the document.

Tables and Pictures

- Tables are often used to organise and present information, but they have a variety of other uses as well. Word allows you to create and format tables. The following operations can be performed for a Word table:
  - i. Deletion of a Row, Column, Cells, Table.
  - ii. Insertion of Rows, Columns, Cells.
  - iii. Merging multiple rows or columns into a single row or column.
  - iv. Splitting a cell into multiple rows and columns.
  - v. Formatting a table – Changing the border colour, border width, border style, text colour, background colour and many more.
- There are two basic types of Graphics in MS Word – Drawing Objects and Pictures. Drawing objects include textboxes, curves, lines, and other objects. These objects can be accessed from the Drawing toolbar. Pictures are graphics that have been created using any graphics software. They include bitmaps, scanned pictures and photographs, and MS Word's inbuilt Clipart gallery. You can enhance these objects with colors, patterns, borders, and other effects.

Mail Merge, Macros and Templates

- Mail Merge does what it says – merges mail! It is useful for sending the same matter to a number of people, with each letter addressed individually.
- Mail Merge facility allows you to create a database of your contacts (including friends, relatives, customers, acquaintances etc.) and automatically merges the main body of letter, and this database to generate personalised letters.
- The file that contains the form letter is called the main document and the file containing the database (names, addresses and other information) is called the data source. Each entry in the database file (data source) containing details about one person is called a record and each item of detail in this record (like name, phone number, subscription number etc.) is called a field.
- A macro is a small software program that enables the execution of a series of sequential and logical commands without having to give those commands one-by-one.
- There are two stages in using macros – Creating Macros and Running Macros.
- You can create the macros in two ways:

  i. Record a series of steps/actions using the keyboard and mouse, or

  ii. Type a macro directly into a macro-editing window using Visual Basic programming language.
- A template is a special type of document that determines the basic layout of a document and can contain various document settings like fonts, page layout, toolbars, special formatting and styles. Using different templates is like having pre-printed stationery for different uses.
- There are two basic types of templates – Global templates and Document templates. Global templates contain settings that are available to all documents. Document templates contain settings that are available only to documents based on that template.
- A Document Wizard guides you through a series of instructions to help you create a document. It helps you in saving a considerable amount of your work as well as your precious time. Letter wizard, Fax wizard, Mailing Label wizard, Envelope wizard, Memo wizard are examples of Word's inbuilt wizards.
- A brief summary of all the Commands covered in this chapter are outlined below:

Action	Command	Icon
To create a new document	Choose **New** from the **File** menu.	
To open an existing document	Choose **Open** from the **File** menu.	
To Save a document	Choose **Save** from the **File** menu.	
To make a copy of the entire document	Choose **Save As** from the **File** menu.	
To set Page margins and Page size	Choose **Page Setup** from **File** menu.	
To print a document	Choose **Print** from **File** menu.	
To preview document before printing	Choose **Print Preview** from **File** menu.	
To close a document	Choose **Close** from the **File** menu.	
To close MS Word	Choose **Exit** from the **File** menu.	
To cancel your last action	Choose **Undo** from the **Edit** menu.	
To redo an undone action	Choose **Redo** from the **Edit** menu.	
To copy a block of text	Choose **Copy** from the **Edit** menu.	
To cut a block of text	Choose **Cut** from the **Edit** menu.	
To paste a block of copied/cut text	Choose **Paste** from the **Edit** menu.	
To search for a word or a phrase in a document	Choose **Find** from the **Edit** menu.	
To replace a single or all instances of any word/phrase with another word/phrase	Choose **Replace** from the **Edit** menu.	
To change the Font style, size and other formatting styles	Choose **Font** from the **Format** menu.	
To highlight the text	Click on the Highlight icon from the **Formatting** toolbar.	
To align (Left, Center, Right) the text/paragraph	Click on the desired Alignment icon from the **Formatting** toolbar.	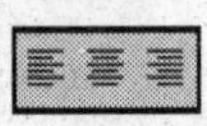
To justify the text	Click on the Justify icon from the **Formatting** toolbar.	
To insert bullets/numbers	Choose **Bullets** and **Numbering** from the **Format** menu.	

Action	Command	Icon
To indent the text	Click on left and right indent icons from the **Formatting** toolbar.	
To change the text case (Capitals to Lower or vice versa)	Choose **Change Case** from the **Format** menu.	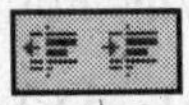
To change paragraph and line spacing	Choose **Paragraph** from the **Format** menu.	
To create newspaper-like columns.	Choose **Columns** from **Format** menu.	
To transfer formatting from one range of text to another.	Click on the **Format Painter** icon from the **Formatting** toolbar.	
To insert header and footer	Choose **Header and Footer** from the **View** menu.	
To insert page numbers	Choose **Page Numbers** from the **Insert** menu.	
To view all the toolbars	Choose **Toolbars** from the **View** menu. Click on the desired toolbar that you wish to be displayed.	
To insert multiple sections into the same document	Choose **Break** from the **Insert** menu.	
To check spelling and grammar	Choose **Speelling** and **Grammar** from the **Tools** menu.	
To access Autotext	Choose **Auto Text** from the **Insert** menu.	
To track the changes in your document	Choose **Track Changes** in the Options dialogue box from the **Tools** menu.	
To insert table	Choose **Insert (Table)** from the **Table** menu.	
To delete table	Choose **Delete (Table)** from the **Table** menu.	
To Select table	Choose **Select (Table)** from the **Table** menu.	
To insert picture from the clipart gallery.	Choose **Picture (Clipart)** from the **Insert** menu.	
To insert picture from a file	Choose **Picture (From File)** from the **Insert** menu.	
To merge mail	Choose **Mail Merge** from the **Tools** menu.	
To create a macro	Choose **Record New Macro** command from **Macro** option from **Tools** menu.	

REVIEW QUESTIONS

1. Choose the most appropriate answer:

i. Which of the following is a Word Processing program?

(a) MS Windows (b) MS Access
(c) MS Outlook (d) MS Word

ii. This toolbar contains icons for changing the look/style of your text:

(a) Reviewing Toolbar (b) Standard Toolbar
(c) Formatting Toolbar (d) None of these

iii. This command displays a preview on screen of what you wish to print:

(a) Preview (b) Print Preview
(c) Page Preview (d) Document Preview

iv. In mail merge the file that contains the form letter is referred to as:

(a) Data source (b) Record
(c) Field (d) Main document

v. A series of word commands that have been grouped together as a single command:

(a) Macro (b) Menu
(c) Function (d) None of these

vi. This tool can be used to print a standard piece of text at the top and bottom of each page:

(a) Title (b) Message Box
(c) Header & Footer (d) None of these

vii. This is a special type of document that determines the basic layout of a document and can contain various document settings like fonts, macros, page page layout, toolbars, special formatting and styles:

(a) Table (b) Page Layout
(c) Template (d) None of these

2. Enter True or False:

i Toolbars contain buttons and dropdown menus that can be used for quickly executing the commands without having to go through the menus.

ii. All the formatting features offered by Word require pre-selection of a piece of text.

iii. Whenever a copy command is issued, the copied text is placed in Windows clipboard.

iv. Paragraph symbol is a non-printable character.

v. Once bullets are added to a paragraph, they cannot be removed from that paragraph.

vi. Word allows opening the recent documents without having to go to the open command.

vii. Scanned pictures can be inserted inside a Word table.

viii. Data source in the mail merge contains the names and addresses of recipients.

ix. Every Word document is based on some template.

x. Document templates contain settings that are available to all documents.

3. Match the following:

	X		Y
1.	Proofing Tool.	a.	Track Changes
2.	Combining two or more cells in the same row or column into a single cell.	b.	Mail Merge
3.	Allows to change the page margins, orientation and paper size.	c.	Spell Checker
4.	This feature can be used to track the changes (insertion/deletion of text, formatting or moving text from one place to another in the document) in your document.	d.	Merging cells
5.	This feature can be used to send the same matter to multiple people	e.	Page Set up

4. Fill in the blanks with the appropriate choices listed below:

(i) Format Painter (ii) Break (iii) Change (iv) Collate (v) Revision marks (vi) Undo (vii) Datasource (viii) Landscape (ix) Template (x) Format (xi) Replace (xii) Web Layout (xiii) Global (xiv) Redo.

1. In ________ view you can preview your page, as it will appear in a web browser.
2. A document can be printed in portrait or ______________ mode.
3. Changes in a document can be reverted by using the ______________ feature.
4. ___________ can be used to replace all occurrences of one word with another.
5. ________ can be used to transfer formatting from one object to another object.
6. ___________ command is used to create multiple sections within a document.
7. _____________ is a useful feature when printing multiple sets of a document.
8. Word makes use of _____________ to show the tracked changes to the user.
9. Mail merge requires two things; creating main document and creating _________________.
10. All the templates must be stored in _____________ directory so that they can be used as a base for creating new documents.

5. **Explain the various uses of MS Word.**
6. **Write short notes on:**

   i. Tables ii. Macros
7. **Discuss the different types of templates in MS Word, and their specific advantages.**
8. **Discuss the Editing and Proofing tools available in MS Word.**

7 Spreadsheet Package

EXCEL BASICS

If the job at hand requires lot of lists, tables, financial calculations, analysis and graphs, Excel is just the package for you.

Excel is great at organising all types of data, but it is the numerical data where Excel is on its home turf. If you not only need a tool for storing and managing data—and also analysing and querying it—Excel's powerful features help you do all this and more effortlessly. Excel, besides offering simple database capabilities, also allows you to create documents for the World Wide Web (WWW) also.

The menus, toolbars and icons of MS Excel are very similar (though not the same; after all, if they were the same, why would you need two different packages!) to MS Word. This is keeping in line with Microsoft's much hyped philosophy and strategy of offering users a totally integrated office suite pack. From the user point of view, this means less time spent in learning the second package, once you know the first, and almost effortless and seamless exchange of data between various components.

Excel—or for that matter any spreadsheet—essentially comprises of a grid of rows and columns. Intersection of a row and a column is called a cell. Typically, rows are numbered numerically, i.e., 1, 2, 3… and so on, and columns are labeled alphabetically, i.e., A, B, C… and so on. Of course columns do not end at Z, after Z they start as AA, AB, AC… and then BA, BB, BC… and so on.

A workbook is similar to a notebook, containing numerous individual pages. Each workbook is stored as a separate file in Excel. Each page/sheet in a workbook is called a worksheet. You can enter and edit data on several worksheets simultaneously, and perform calculations based on data from multiple worksheets. The names of the sheets appear on tabs at the bottom of the workbook window.

Each spreadsheet (also called a worksheet) contains 65536 rows and 256 columns. That makes 16,777,216 cells (65536 *256), each holding either text or numbers or formulas.

And this is not all; each workbook can contain 16 or numerous such worksheets (limited only by your computer's memory and storage capacity)! Huge, isn't it?

So much for facts and figures. In spite of these impressive statistics, the real power of Excel—member-crunching apart—lies in it's cool graphical user interface and user friendliness, even while performing some very sophisticated tasks.

Starting Excel

To start MS Excel choose **MS Excel** from **Programs** option from **Start** button.

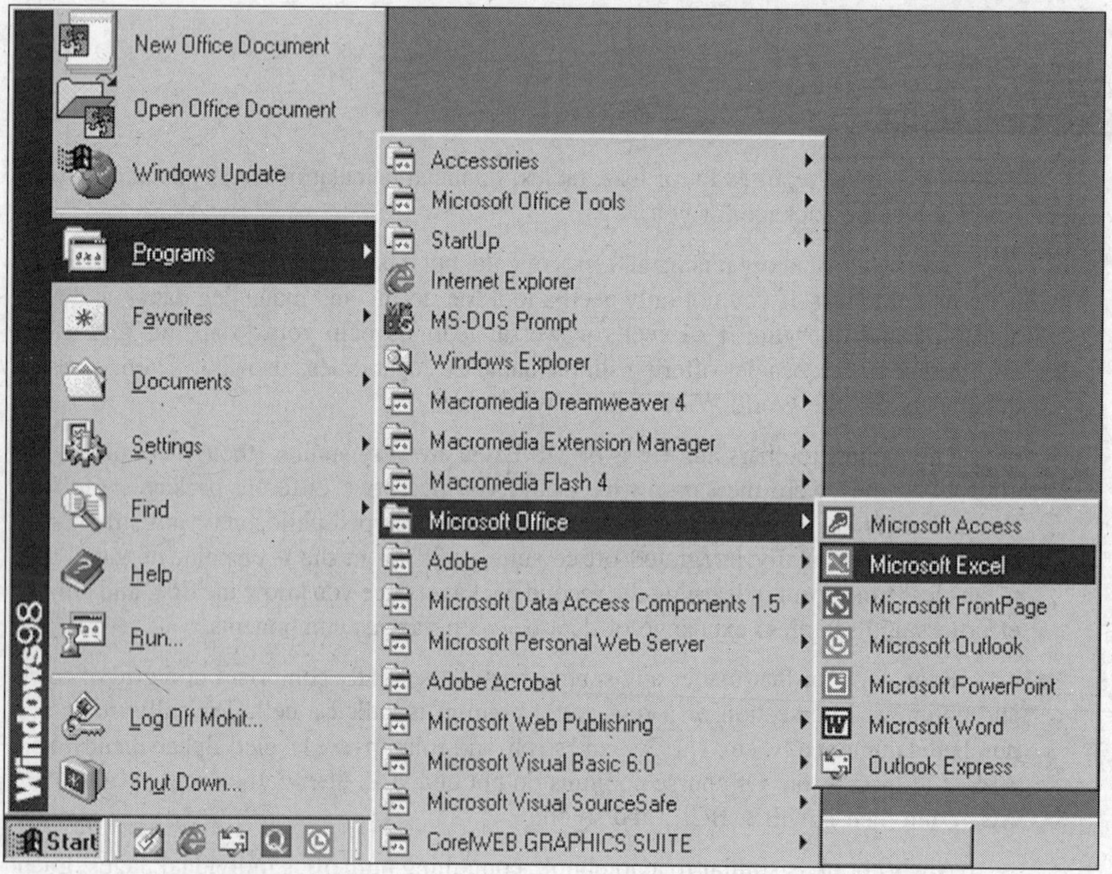

Elements of an Excel Window

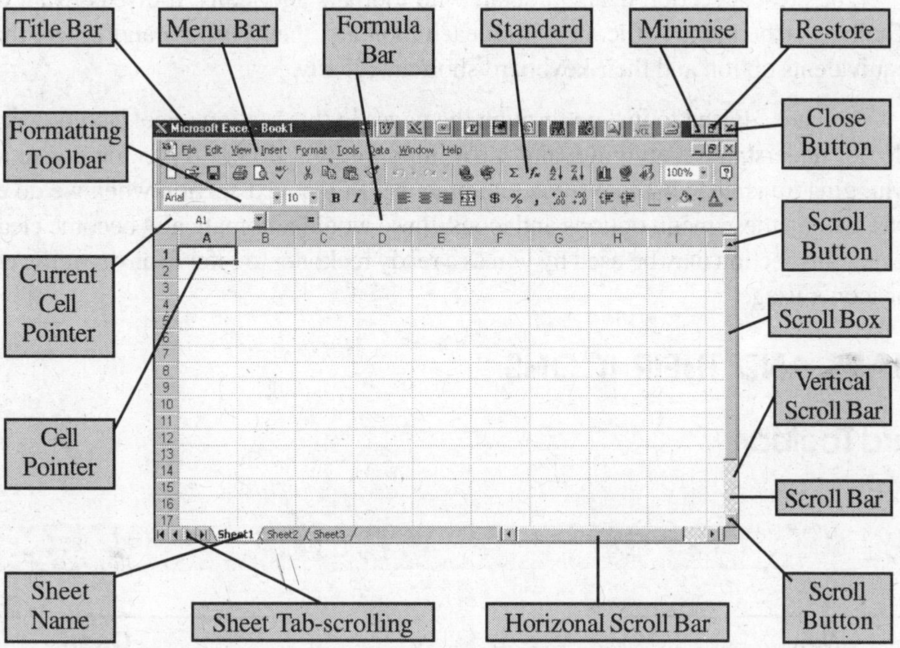

MENUS, COMMANDS, TOOLBARS AND THEIR ICONS

Most mechanics or technicians have a special box in which they keep their tools (working mechanics, that is!). This box normally has separate sections for keeping different kinds of tools, based upon their usage and size. This helps in selecting the right tool easily and quickly.

For MS Excel these physical tools are replaced by commands. As has been explained earlier in the Word section, commands are executed by clicking on their specific icons. Groups of icons that perform related tasks, are placed together in a ribbon, and called a Toolbar. There are many toolbars available in Excel – Standard toolbar, Formatting toolbar, Drawing toolbar etc. Each of these contains an assortment of related icons, specific to that toolbar. For executing most tasks, the user has three options:

1. Choose the desired command from the Menu options provided – either using the mouse or using keyboard cursor movement keys, or
2. Press the appropriate shortcut keys combination from the keyboard, or
3. Click once on the relevant icon from the displayed toolbars.

Although there is no wrong or right approach, most users find the third option simplest and fastest. Especially, for most commonly used commands, it is much simpler to use the

Standard Toolbar and Formatting Toolbar icon, than using the menu options or keyboard shortcuts (which in any case are not available for all the commands).

The present section deals in detail with toolbars and icons. It discusses all the Excel Toolbars – the names of icons within each toolbars, their purpose and usage, their menu equivalents option and their keyboard shortcuts, if any.

You are advised to just go through the pages in this section once. Do not worry if you do not understand everything, and most importantly – do not try to memorise anything. Mugging up is no substitute for actual practice. In the next section when we do exercises based upon these menu options and icons, these would automatically become clear to you. Later, this section may be used by you as a ready reckoner to refer to any specific command or icon's usage.

TOOLBARS AND THEIR ICONS

Standard Toolbar

New
Creates a new blank file.
Alternative: File→New
Shortcut→Ctrl+N

Open
Opens or finds a file.
Alternative: File→Open
Shortcut→Ctrl+O

Save
Saves the active file.
Alternative: File→ Save
Shortcut→Ctrl+S

E-mail
Sends contents of the current worksheet as body of the e-mail message.

Print Preview
Displays full page as they are printed.
Alternative: File→Print Preview
Shortcut→Ctrl+F2

Print
Prints the active file using current defaults.
Alternative: File→Print
Shortcut→Ctrl+P

Cut
Cuts the selection and puts it on the Clipboard.
Alternative: Edit→Cut
Shortcut→Ctrl+X

Spelling
Checks the spelling in the active file.
Alternative: Tools→Spelling
Shortcut→F7

Paste

Inserts the Clipboard contents at the insertion point.
Alternative: Edit→Paste
Shortcut→Ctrl+V

Undo

Reverses certain last commands.
Alternative: Edit→Undo
Shortcut→Ctrl+Z

Insert Hyperlink

Displays the destination object, document or page.
Shortcut→Ctrl+K

AutoSum

Adds numbers automatically with the SUM function. Excel suggests the range of cells to be added. If the suggested range is incorrect, drag through the range you want, and then press ENTER.

Sort Ascending

Sorts the selected items in order from the beginning of the alphabet, the lowest number, or the earliest date, using the column that contains the insertion point. If you previously set other sorting options, those options are still in effect.
Alternative: Table→Sort →Ascending

Chart Wizard

Starts the Chart Wizard, which guides you through the steps for creating an embedded chart on a worksheet or modifying an existing chart.

Zoom Control

Scales the editing view (Zoom).
Alternative: View→Zoom

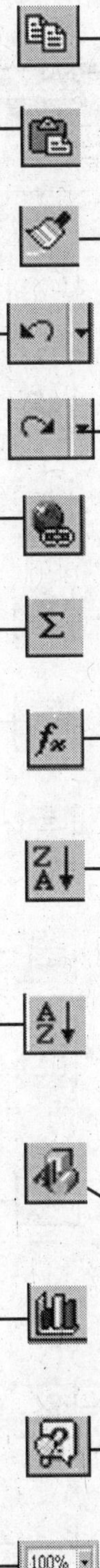

Copy

Copies the selection and puts it on the clipboard.
Alternative: Edit→Copy
Shortcut→Ctrl+C

Format Painter

Copies the formatting of the selection to a specified location.
Shortcut→Ctrl+Shift+C

Redo

Reverses the action of the Undo command.
Alternative: Edit→Repeat
Shortcut→Ctrl+Y

Paste Function

Displays a list of functions and their formats and allows you to set values for arguments.

Sort Descending

Sorts the selected items in the order from the end of the alphabet, the highest number, or the highest date, using the column that contains the insertion point. If you previously set other sorting options, those options are still in effect.
*Alternative:*Table→Sort→ Descending

Drawing

Shows or hides the Drawing Toolbar.
*Alternative:*View→Toolbars→Drawing

Microsoft Excel Help

Provides help topics and tips to accomplish your task.
Alternative: Help→ Microsoft Word Help
Shortcut →F1

Formatting Toolbar

Font

Changes the font of the selection.
Alternative: Format→Font
Shortcut→Ctrl+Shift+F

Font Size

Changes the font size of the selection.
Alternative: Format→Font→Size
Shortcut→Ctrl+Shift+P

Bold

Makes the selection Bold.
Alternative: Format→Font→Font style
Shortcut→Ctrl+B

Italic

Makes the selection Italics.
Alternative: Format→Font→Font style *Shortcut*→Ctrl+I

Underline

Formats the selection with continuous underline.
*Alternative:*Format→Font→effects
Shortcut→Ctrl+U

Align Left

Aligns the paragraph at left indent.
Alternative:
Format→Paragraph→Alignment
Shortcut→Ctrl+L

Align Right

Aligns the paragraph at right indent.
Alternative:
Format→Paragraph→Alignment
Shortcut→Ctrl+R

Centre

Centres the paragraphs between the indents.
Alternative:
Format→Paragraph→Alignment
Shortcut→Ctrl+E

Merge and Centre

Combines two or more selected adjacent cells to create a single cell. The resulting merged cell contains only the upper left most data in the selection, which is centered within the cell. The cell reference for a merged cell is the upper left cell in the original selected range.

Currency

Applies on International currency style to the selected cells. Depending on the country selected in the **Windows Regional Settings** dialog box, the **International Currency Style** button might appear instead of the **currency style** button.

Percent Style

Applies the percent style to the selected cells. To change the Percent Style, use the **Style** command on the **Format** menu.

Comma Style

Applies the comma style to the selected cells. To change the comma style, use the **Style** command on the **Format** menu.

Increase Decimal
Increases the number of digits displayed after the decimal point in the selected cells.

Decrease Decimal
Decreases the number of digits displayed after the decimal point in the selected cells.

Decrease Indent
Decreases or promotes the selection one level.
Alternative:
Format→Paragraph→Indentation

Increase Indent
Increases indent or demotes the selection one level.
Alternative:
Format→Paragraph→Indentation

Borders
Shows or hides the border toolbar.
Alternative:
Format→Borders and Shading

Fill Color
Adds, modifies, or removes the fill color or fill effect from the selected object. Fill effects include gradient, texture, pattern or picture fills.

Font Color
Selects and applies Font Color.
Alternative: Format→Font →Color

Drawing Toolbar

Draw
Activates the Draw Menu.

Select Objects
Changes the pointer to a selection arrow so you can select objects in the active Window. To select a single object, click the object with the arrow. To select one or more objects, drag the arrow over the objects you want to select.

Free Rotate
Rotates the selected object to any degree. Select the object, click on the icon and then drag a corner of the object in the direction you want to rotate it.

AutoShapes
Activates the AutoShapes menu.

Line
Draws a straight line where you click or drag in the active Window. To constrain the line to draw at the 15-degree angles from its starting point, hold down SHIFT as you drag.

Arrow
Inserts a line with an arrowhead where you click or drag in the active Window. To constrain the line to draw at the 15-degree angles from its starting point, hold down SHIFT as you drag.

Rectangle
Draws an rectangle where you click or drag in the active Window. To draw a square, press SHIFT and drag.

Oval
Draws an oval where you click or drag in the active Window. To draw a circle, press SHIFT and drag.

Text Box
Draws a text box where you click or drag in the active Window. Use a text box to add a text – such as captions or callouts to your pictures or graphics.
Alternative: Insert→TextBox

WordArt
Creates text effects by inserting a Microsoft Office drawing object.

Insert Clip Art
Inserts existing picture into the file at the desired position from the picture gallery.
Alternative: Insert→Picture →ClipArt

Line Color
Adds, modifies, or removes the line colour from the selected objects.

Font Color
Formats the selected text with the colour you click.

Fill Color
Adds, modifies, or removes the fill colour or fill effect from the selected object. Fill effects include gradient, texture, pattern or picture fills.

Dash Style
Click the dashed line or dashed-dot line style you want for the selected shape or border. Click the solid line if you don't want the dotted line.

Line Style
Click the width you want for the selected line.

Shadow
Click the shadow style you want for the selected object.

Arrow Style
Click the arrowhead style you want for the selected line.

3-D
Click the 3-D style you want for the selected object.

Navigating

To move around the spreadsheets, either use the keyboard keys ↑ for going up, ↓ for going down, ← for going left, → for going right, Page Up for going one screen up, Page Down for going one screen down, and other related keys; or use mouse to traverse the different parts of the worksheet through scroll bars. You can also type the desired cell address directly in the Address name box to randomly go anywhere in the worksheet.

Selecting Cells

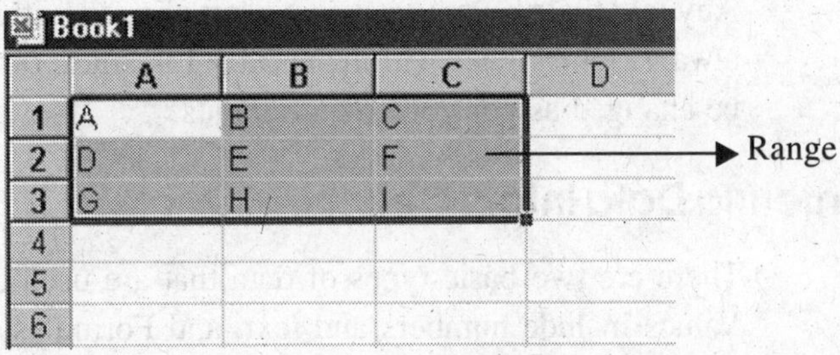

Before entering, editing or formatting cells, they need to be selected. You can select a single cell, or a group of continuous cells or even a discontinuous group of cells. This selection is called a range. A range is a rectangular group of cells that is referred to by its diagonal corners (top-left cell address and bottom-right cell address separated by a colon). Example A1:C3 implies a rectangle covering all the 9 cells from A1 to C3, i.e., A1, B1, C1, A2, B2, C2, A3, B3 and C3.

Selecting Cells with Mouse

1. To select a single cell, simply point and click on it to make it active.
2. Click on a row number to select the entire row.
3. Click on a column alphabet to select the entire column.
4. Click and drag to select a range of cells.
5. Click on the empty button at the intersection of the column and row numbers to select the entire worksheet.

Selecting Sheets

1. To select a single sheet, click on the desired sheet tab.
2. To select multiple adjacent sheets, select the first sheet by clicking on its tab, and then hold down the **Shift** key and click on the tab for the last sheet.
3. To select multiple non-adjacent sheets, select the first sheet by clicking on its tab, and then hold down the **Ctrl** key and click on the tabs for other sheets.
4. To select all the sheets in a workbook, right click on any sheet tab and choose **Select All Sheets** from the pop up menu.

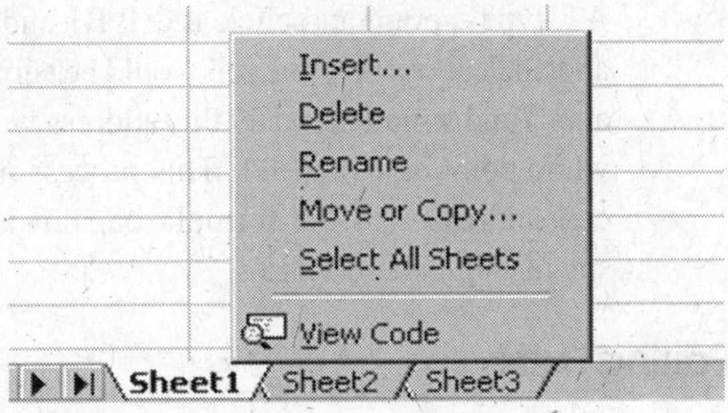

Alignment

Any text that you type is always left aligned within the cell. Any number that you type is always right aligned within the cells. Like most other default settings, these alignments can be changed as per your requirements.

Entering Data into a Cell

There are two basic types of data that are used in a spreadsheet: Values and Formulas. Values include numbers and text, and Formulas are arithmetic calculations that change based on the input given to them. To enter values, simply select the desired cell and start typing. Press Enter key to conclude an entry. As you start typing, the text would appear in the active cell and in the formula bar. The data is not considered to be entered into your worksheet until the Enter key is pressed. When you press the Enter key, you may find that you are automatically moved one cell down on your worksheet.

If you wish to enter data into a range of cells, then it is advisable to select the entire range first and then use the Tab key to navigate within the selected range of cells.

Entering Formulas

The real power of Excel lies in it being able to store complex formulas. You can either build formulas using absolute numbers (like = 4+2) or use relative cell address (like = A1+B1). As a rule of thumb, you must always use relative cell referencing because in case the values change in future, the formulas based upon these values would automatically show the updated results. You place the formula in the cell in which you want to see the result. Start by activating the cell where you wish to place the formula, begin by typing either an equal sign (=) or plus sign (+) to tell Excel that you are about to start a formula. You can then either type the formula, one character at a time in the formula bar, or assemble it using mouse or keyboard. For instance, you could either type =A1-B1 in the cell C1 and press Enter, or place the mouse pointer in cell C1 and type = sign, point and click the cell A1, type -, point and click at cell B1 and press Enter. During this process when you point and click at cell A1, this cell would be surrounded by a dashed outline (some call it marching ants!) and simultaneously this address would appear in the formula bar. The same happens while pointing to cell B1. This process not only makes it unnecessary for you to type the cell addresses in the formula bar but also ensures that no mistakes are committed in specifying cell addresses.

Editing Data

Once you have entered a value or a formula into a cell, you may need to change it. If you make a mistake while typing and before pressing Enter, simply press Backspace Key to erase the present contents and type the correct text. If you notice an error after finishing the entry, activate the relevant cell and press F2 Function Key. The current contents of the cell would be displayed in the formula bar, now you can correct the entry and press Enter to conclude. If you wish to replace the entire text, activate the relevant cell and simply type the new text. The new text would automatically replace the old text.

Editing a cell's contents is very similar to editing data in any Word document. You can use the arrow keys to navigate between the cells of a worksheet.

Creating a New Workbook

Workbooks are named consecutively, starting with Book1, Book2 and so on. By default a workbook contains three sheets. However, as many sheets can be added to the workbook as required.

Follow the steps below to create a workbook:

① Choose **New** from the **File** menu.

② Click on **Workbook** in the **New** dialogue box.

③ Click on **OK** button to create the workbook.

A Workbook

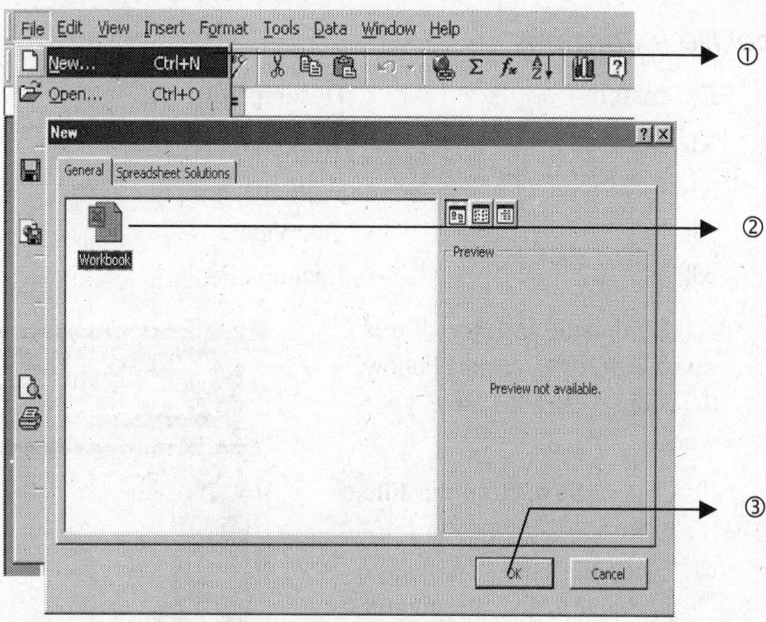

Note: You can also create new workbooks on existing templates. A template in Excel is a special type of workbook with pre-defined formats and controls that can be used as a base for creating other workbooks. To create a workbook based on an existing template,

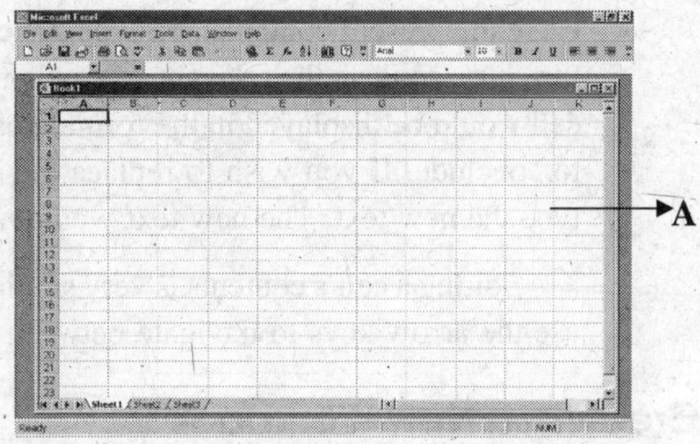

simply select the desired template from the Spread-sheet Solutions tab and click the **OK** button to create the desired template based work-book.

As explained earlier, a cell is an intersection of a vertical column identified by a column letter (A, B, C…) and a horizontal row identified by a row number (1, 2, 3…). This unique location (for each cell) is called the Cell Address (e.g., cell B3 means column B and third row, A27 means column A, row twenty-seven. The cell, which you are presently working on (where your cursor is presently placed), is called the Active or the Current cell.

Saving a Workbook

You must save your work so that it can be used again. It is usually a good practice to save your work frequently so that, in case of a power failure, you would loose only a minimal amount of work.

Excel file extensions

Extension	Description
.xls	Workbook
.xlw	Workspace
.xlt	Template
.xlk	Backup File

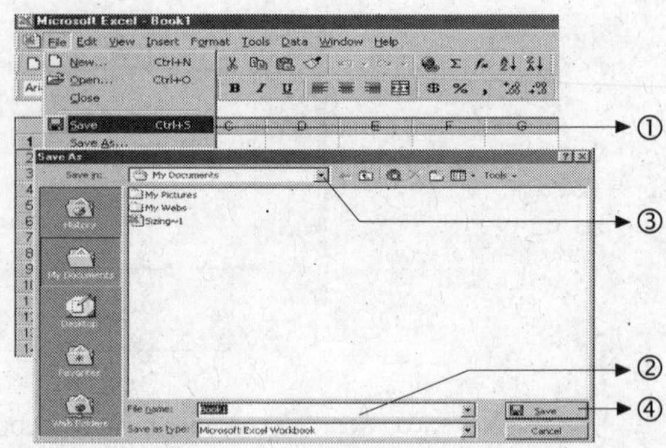

By default an Excel file is saved with .xls extension. Follow the steps below to save your work:

① Choose **Save** from the **File** menu.

② Type a file name, it is always advisable to give meaningful file names.

③ Specify the path or location where you wish to save your work. By default your workbook is saved in **My Documents** folder.

④ Click on the **Save** button to save your file.

Closing Workbooks

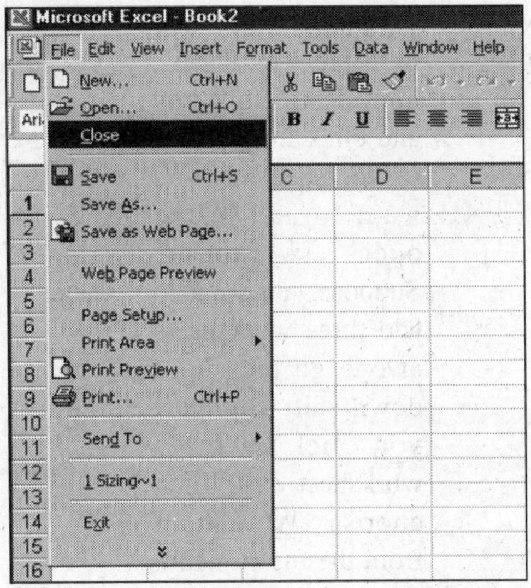

Choose **Close** from the **File** menu to close an active workbook. If you have made changes since the last time you saved your work then you will be prompted to save your changes. To close all open workbooks, hold down the Shift key before you click the File menu. The close command of the File menu changes to Close All. Click on this option if you wish to close all open workbooks at one go.

Closing Excel

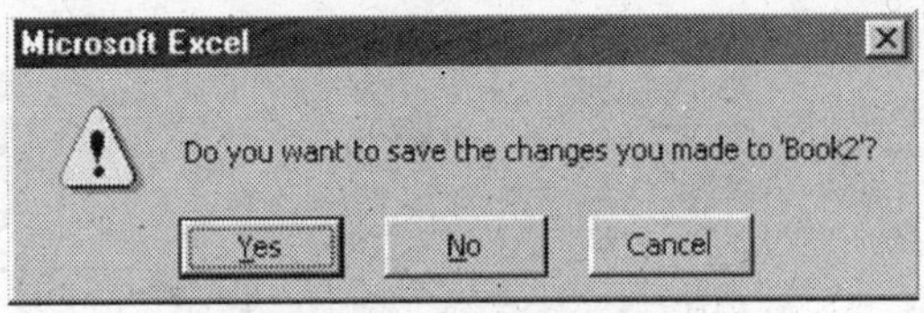

To quit Excel, Choose **Exit** from the **File** menu. If you have been working in a workbook that has not been saved then a dialogue box is displayed to the user, asking whether the user would like to save the changes.The user has three options – he can choose **Yes** to save the chang in the workbook, **No** to discard the changes or Cancel to return to working in Excel.

Alternate Methods

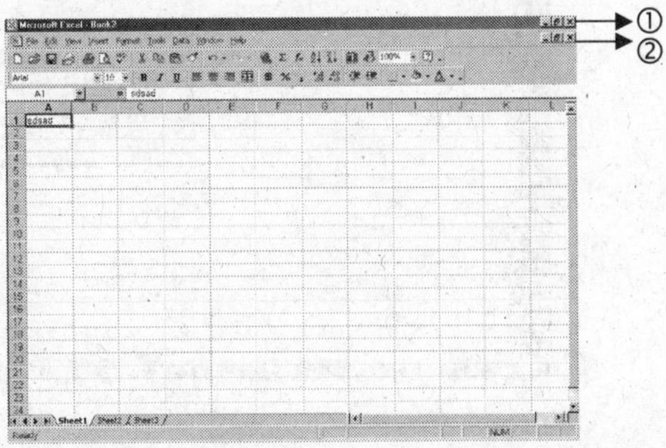

1. Press Alt key along with the function key F4 to close any active window.
2. **Close Button**: Click on the cross (X) mark in the upper right corner of the Excel Window to close Excel.

① Quits Excel.

② Closes the active workbook.

Working with Workbooks and Worksheets

Inserting Worksheets To add a new worksheet into your workbook, choose **Worksheet** from the **Insert** menu. Worksheet will be added to the left of active sheet.

Note: To add multiple worksheets, hold down Shift key and click the number of worksheet tabs you want to add in the open workbook. Suppose you want to add three worksheets at one go then hold down shift key until you click on three worksheet tabs. Then choose Worksheet from the Insert menu.

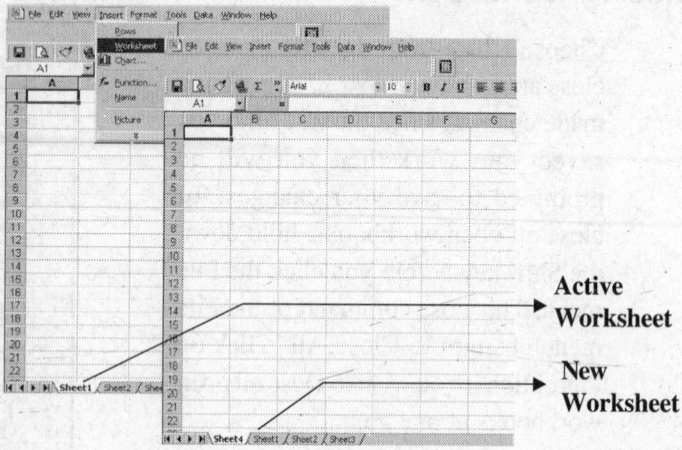

Deleting Worksheets Select the sheet(s) you want to delete and choose **Delete Sheet** from the **Edit** menu. Choose **OK** from the dialog box to delete the selected sheet.

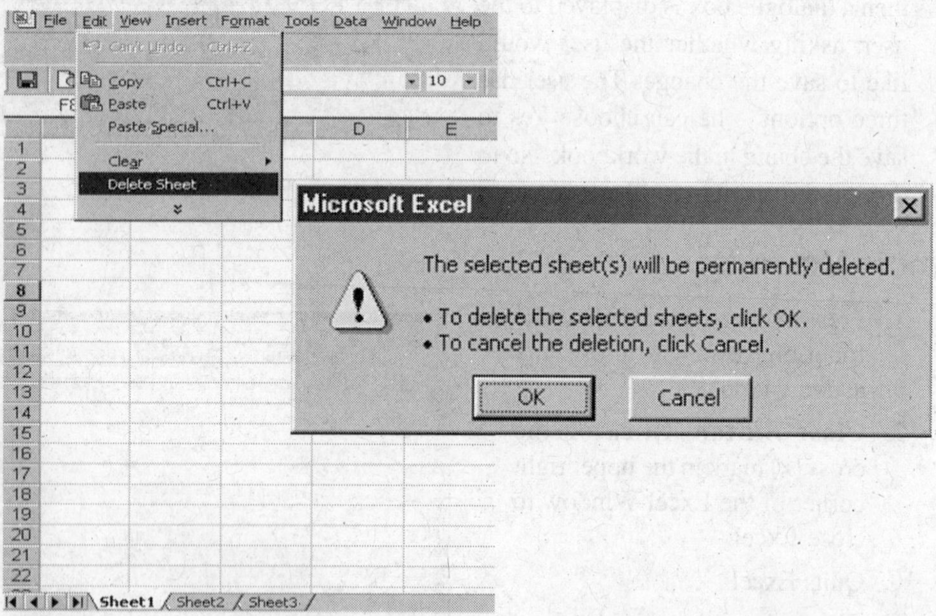

Renaming Worksheets You can Rename a worksheet to make it more user-friendly. To rename a worksheet, select the sheet and choose **Rename** from **Sheet** command from the **Format** menu. Alternatively, you can double click on the desired sheet tab and type the new worksheet name.

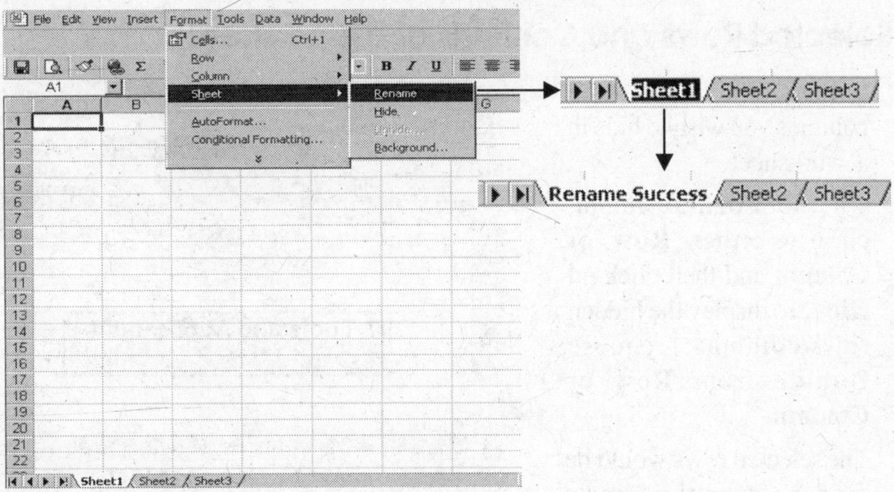

Moving Worksheets To move sheets within the current workbook, drag the desired sheet along the row of sheet tabs to the desired position. Alternatively, you can choose **Move or Copy Sheet** from the **Edit** menu. A dialog box as shown below is displayed to the user.

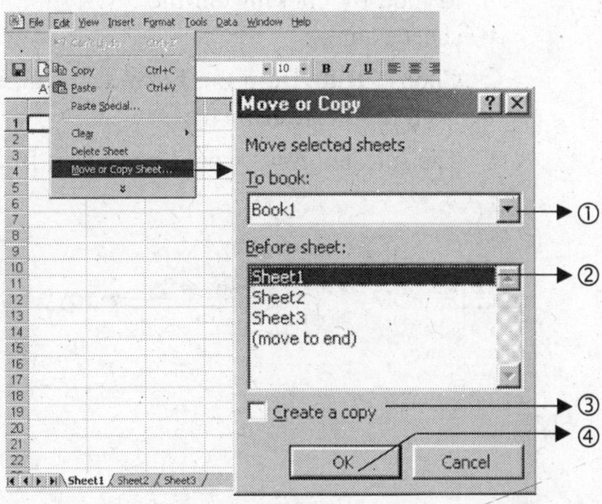

① The drop down box will contain the list of all open workbooks; the current workbook will be displayed at the first position. In case you wish to move the sheet to a different workbook, choose the desired workbook from the drop down box.

② Choose the new position of your sheet. In the **Before sheet** box, click the sheet before which you want to insert the moved or copied sheets.

③ Select this option if you want to create a copy of your sheet instead of moving it.

④ Click on the **OK** button to perform the selected options.

Hiding Workbooks/Worksheets A Workbook/Worksheet can be hidden from the user's view. Hiding a workbook/sheet does not delete its data. Hiding the worksheet(s) reduces the number of sheets on the screen. It is useful to hide the sheets that contain sensitive data to prevent unwanted changes.

Hiding Selected Rows and Columns of a Worksheet

① Selects the rows and columns you wish to hide in a worksheet.

② On the **Format** menu, choose either **Row** or **Column** and then click on **Hide.** To display the hidden rows/columns, choose **Unhide** from **Row** or **Column.**

A The selected rows would be hidden from the user's view.

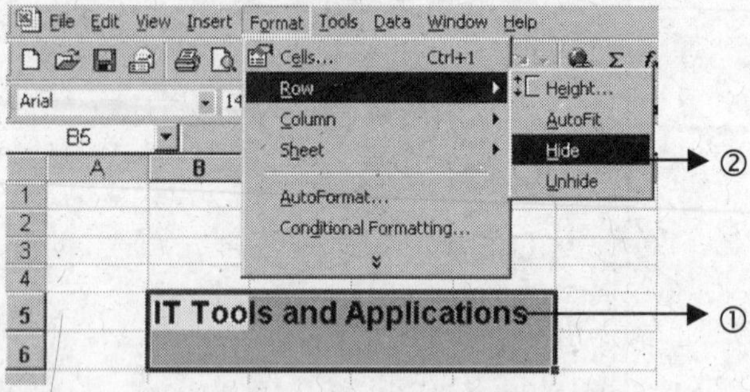

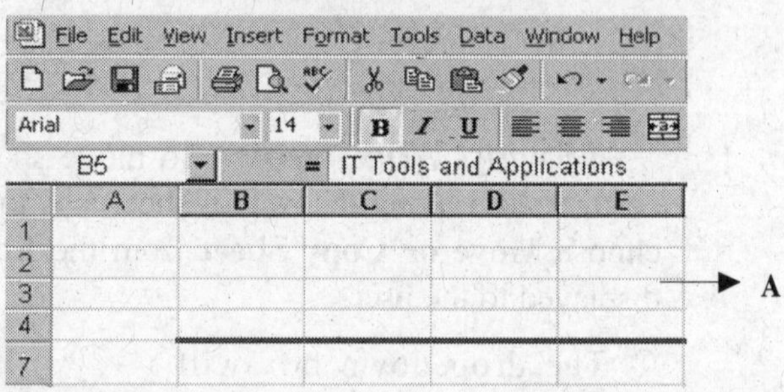

Hiding a Worksheet

① Selects the sheets you wish to hide by clicking on the sheet name.

② Choose **Hide** from the **Format** menu. To display the hidden sheets, choose **Unhide** from the **Format** menu.

A The selected rows would be hidden from the user's view.

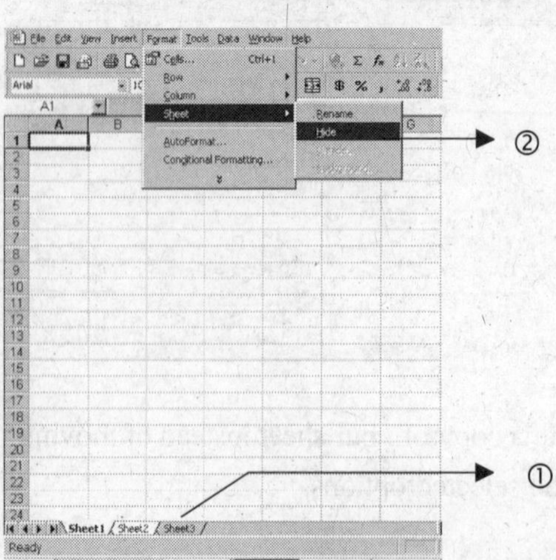

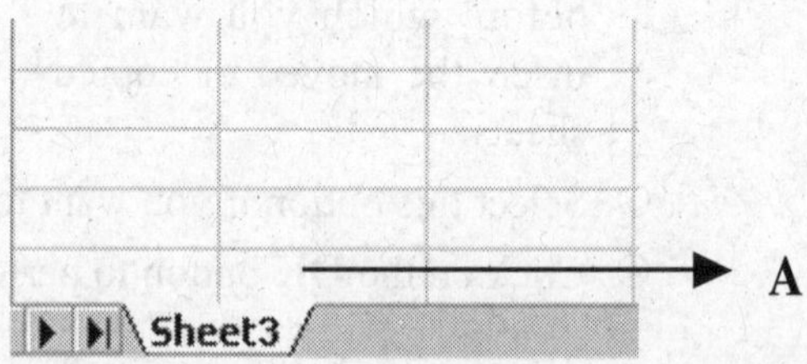

Hiding a Workbook

① Open the work-book(s) you wish to hide.

② Choose **Hide** from the **Window** menu. To display the hidden workbook(s), choose **Unhide** from the **Window** menu.

A Workbook(s) sele-cted in ① will be hidden from the user's view.

Entering Formulas

A formula is an equation that can be used to perform simple as well as complex operations on worksheet data. A formula in Excel always begins with an equal sign (=). If you leave the '=' sign then your formula will be treated as text. Following the equal sign are the elements to be calculated (the operands), which are separated by calculation operators. Formulas can contain constant values, valid cell references, operators, or worksheet functions (Functions are explained in the next section).

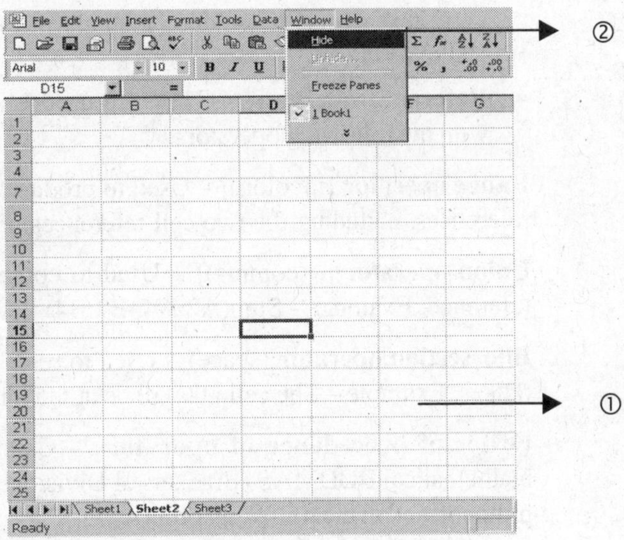

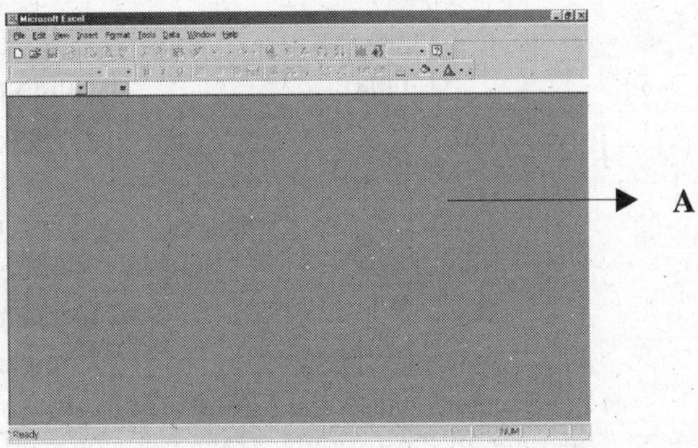

Note: Formulas can refer to other cells on the same worksheet, cells on other sheets in the same workbook, or cells on sheets in other workbooks.

Handling Operators in Formulae

Operators define the calculation to be performed by the formula. Calculation operators in Excel can be broadly classified into four categories:

1. **Arithmetic operators** – They are used to perform basic mathematical operations such as addition, subtraction, or multiplication or division. Examples: + (Addition), - (Subtraction), * (Multiplication), / (Division), ^ (Exponentiation) etc.
2. **Comparison operators** – They are used to compare two values and the result of comparison is a logical value (true or false). Examples: = (Equal To), > (Greater than), < (Less than), >= (Greater than or Equal to), <= (Less than or equal to), <> (Not Equal to)
3. **Text concatenation operator** (&) – They are used to join, or concatenate, one or more text strings to produce a single piece of text. Example: "Hello" & "World" = HelloWorld
4. **Reference operators** – They are used to combine ranges of cells for calculations with the following operators:

Range operator [: (colon)] – Used to produce one reference to all the cells between two references, including the two cell references. Example - A2:A20

Union operator [, (comma)] – Used to combine multiple cell references into a single reference. Example – Sum(A2:A4, B2:B4)

Intersection operator (space) – Used to refer to the cell at the intersection point of two ranges. Example – The cell D2 will be at the intersection of the ranges D2:D4 and C2:E2.

Order of precedence of operators – Calculates the formula as per the standard mathematical BODMAS (Brackets of Division, Multiplication, Addition and Subtraction) protocol, and in the following order:

Operator	Description
: (colon)	
(single space)	
, (comma)	Reference Operators
%	Percent
^	Exponentiation
/ and *	Division and Multiplication
+ and –	Addition and Subtraction
&	Concatenation Operator
= < > <= >= <>	Comparison Operators

Excel calculates the formula from left to right, according to a specific order for each operator in the formula. However, you can change the order of operations by using parentheses. Operations within parenthesis to take precedence in calculations. Example: the following two formulas are identical, with the exception of parenthesis.

2+(6/3) = 4 and (2+6)/3 = 2.7

Now let us learn how to create formulas in Excel using an example. The following example explains:

- How to define a formula
- Some of the commonly used formatting features in MS Excel
  - Changing Data alignment
  - Changing Font Style and Font Size
  - Changing Date, number and currency format.
- Previewing and Printing Worksheets.

Excel Exercise I

Ideas Unlimited Pvt. Ltd.

C-100 Defence Colony, New Delhi, India

<u>Payroll for the month of January 1997</u>

Figures in '000

SI.No.	Employee Name	Joining Date	Basic	DA	HRA	CCA	PF	I.Tax	Net Salary
1	Bill Hates	1-Dec-92	5000.00	1666.50	999.98	597.99	742.97	826.45	6695.04
2	Binder Gujral	5-Feb-97	8500.00	2833.05	1699.96	1016.57	1263.06	1404.96	11381.57
3	J.R.D. Bata	30-Mar-87	7500.00	2499.75	1499.96	896.98	1114.46	1239.67	10042.56
4	Lorry Ellison	30-Jun-86	9000.00	2999.70	1799.96	1076.37	1337.35	1487.60	12051.07
5	Manwoman Singh	5-Nov-81	6500.00	2166.45	1299.97	777.38	965.87	1074.38	8703.55
6	Only Birla	19-Feb-76	6700.00	2233.11	1339.97	801.30	995.59	1107.44	8971.35
7	Scot Really	27-Jan-95	4500.00	1499.85	899.98	538.19	668.68	743.80	6025.54
8	Steve Knobs	30-Sep-86	9100.00	3033.03	1819.95	1088.33	1352.21	1504.13	12184.97
9	Tea Chidambaram	15-Oct-95	10000.00	3333.00	1999.95	1195.97	1485.95	1652.89	13390.08
10	Witch Kapoor	15-Jun-87	2900.00	966.57	579.99	346.83	430.93	479.34	3883.12
	Totals		69700.00	23231.01	13939.65	8335.91	10357.07	11520.66	93328.84

<u>Instructions for filling up various columns:</u>

Dearness Allowances (DA) is paid @ 33.33% of Basic Salary.

House Rent Allowance (HRA) is paid @ 15% of Basic Salary + DA combined together.

City Compensatory Allowance (CCA) is paid @ 7.8% of Basic Salary + DA + HRA combined together.

Provident Fund (PF) is deducted @ 8.99% of Basic Salary +DA + HRA + CCA combined together.

Income Tax (I.Tax) is deducted @ 10% of Basic Salary + DA + HRA + CCA combined together.

Net Salary is summation of Basic Salary + DA + HRA + CCA less PF and I.Tax.

ENTERING TEXT IN CELLS

① Create a new worksheet and start typing the text in this blank worksheet. You would find it slightly different than typing in Word. Here, each piece of text is typed in a different cell. Type only till what is shown here and for the time being don't bother about the way it looks. Notice that columns for Employee Name and Joining Date appear trimmed off, we will see later how we can rectify this.

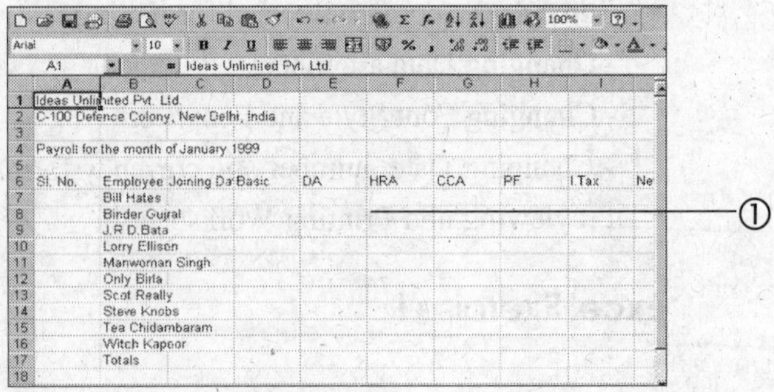

② Type the Joining Date of all the employees in American mm/dd/yy (month/date/year) format. Don't worry, we can always change this later to our Indian dd/mm/yy (date/month/year) format. Type the Basic Salaries in the next column.

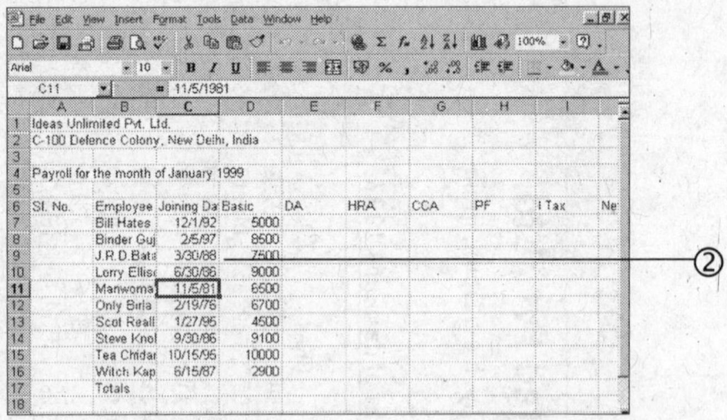

ColumnWidth

Now is the time to rectify the problems. To begin with, presently the employee names are not fitting within the current column width.

① Click once on the column label (B) to select the entire column.

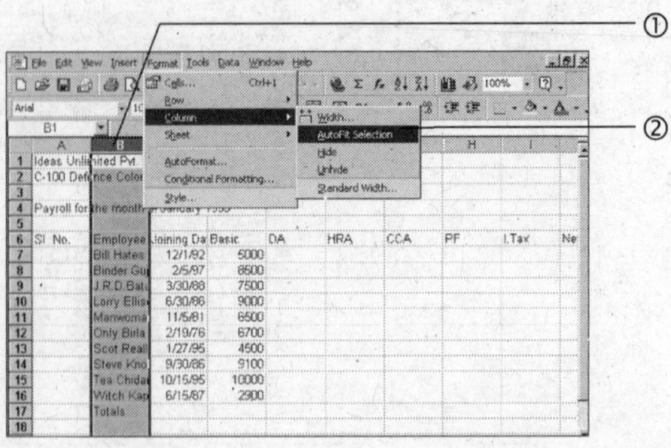

② Choose **AutoFit Selection** from **Column** command from **Format** menu. This command would check for the longest entry in the selected column and based upon that entry, would automatically adjust the column width accordingly, so that even the longest entry is displayed fully in the column width.

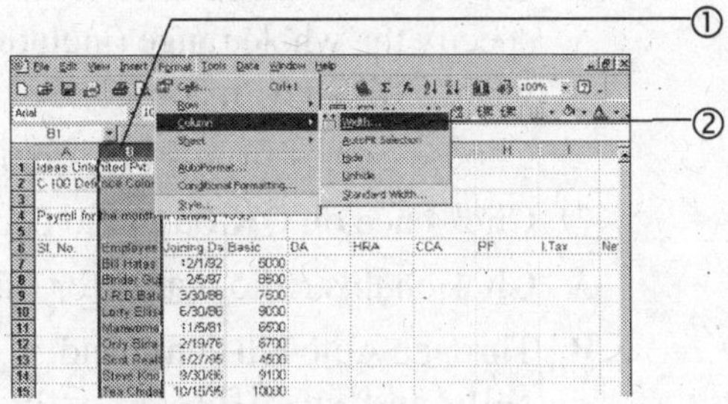

Alternate Method

① Click here to select the column.

② Choose **Width** from **Column** command from **Format menu.**

③ A dialogue box like this would pop-up. Specify the desired column width.

④ Click once on **OK** button to execute the command.

Series Fill

Now let us use another of Excel's many helpful features. One of the most common things that we do while preparing worksheets is that we have a range of cells in a column or a row, which we wish to fill up with consecutive and incremental numbers. For example, you might wish to prepare a column in which running Serial Numbers are filled up (that is what we wish to do now) or with continuous dates like 1 Jan, 2 Jan, 3 Jan, or with a list of all Mondays in a year like 4 May, 11 May, 18 May,... and so on. For such cases, you need not waste your time in doing these things manually. You can ask Excel to do it for you. There is only one prerequisite, the common

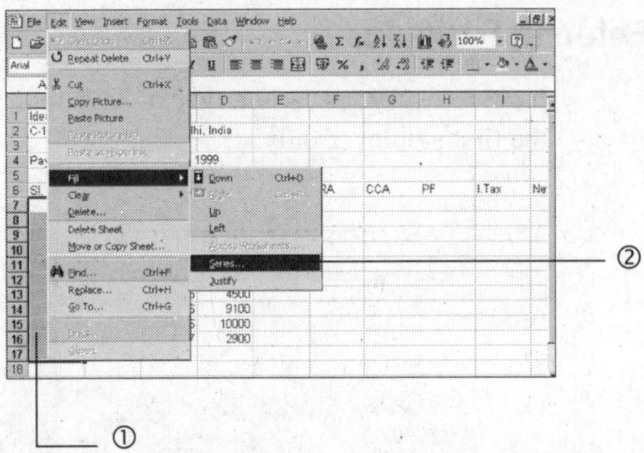

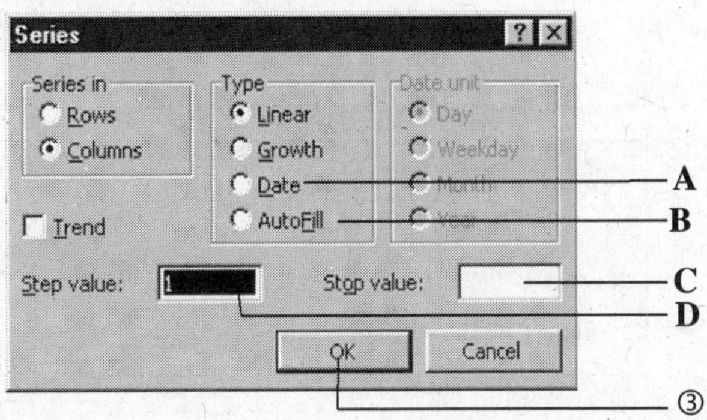

difference between any two consecutive numbers must be common throughout this series: 1, 1 and 7 in case of our three examples mentioned above, respectively.

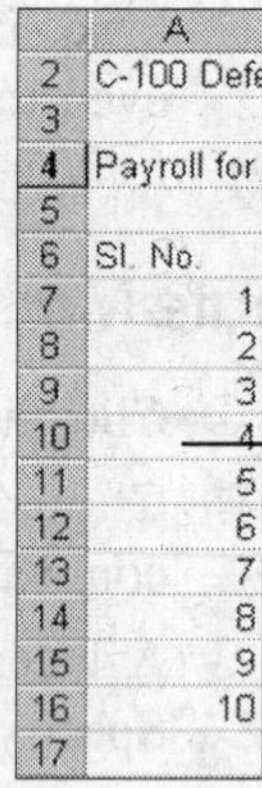

① Type 1 in the place of first SL. No. Use the mouse and specify the whole range (including Sl. No. 1), which you wish to fill up with consecutive nos.

② Choose **Series** from **Fill** command from **Edit** menu.

③ Click once on **OK** button to continue.

A Click on this radio button for filling up for Dates.

B Through Auto Fill command, if you type Jan., Feb. in two cells and specifies a further range, Excel would automatically fill in March to December. Same for Sunday to Monday and so many more examples.

C Stop value need not be specified, since the length of range specified would automatically determine the last value.

D Common increment between two consequent numbers in the desired series.

E All serial numbers filled up automatically.

Entering Formulas

Now, as explained earlier, type or "assemble" the formulas for the subsequent columns for the first employee only.

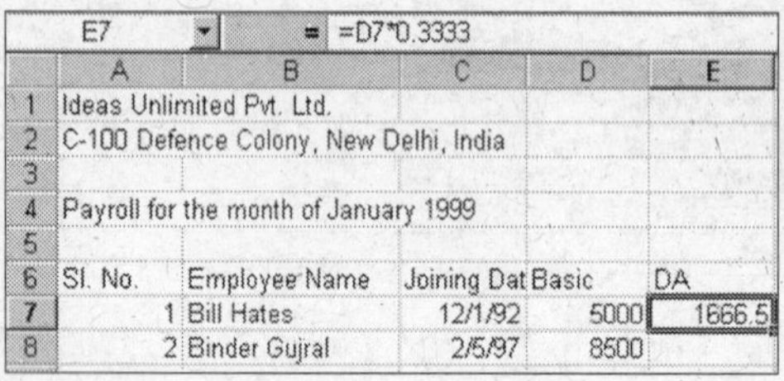

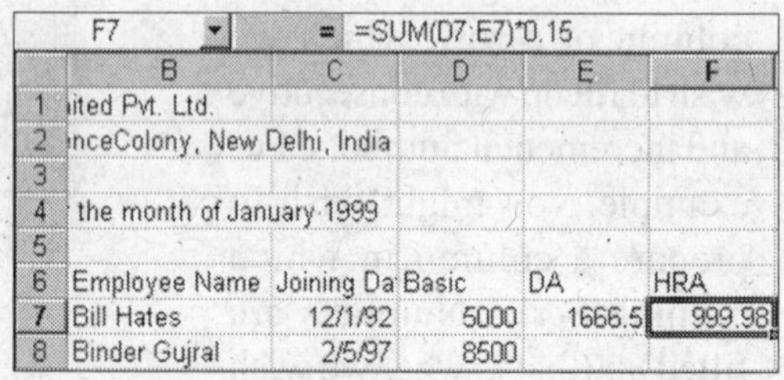

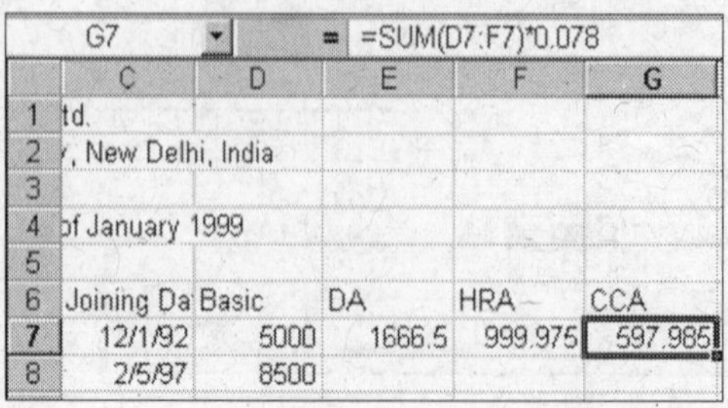

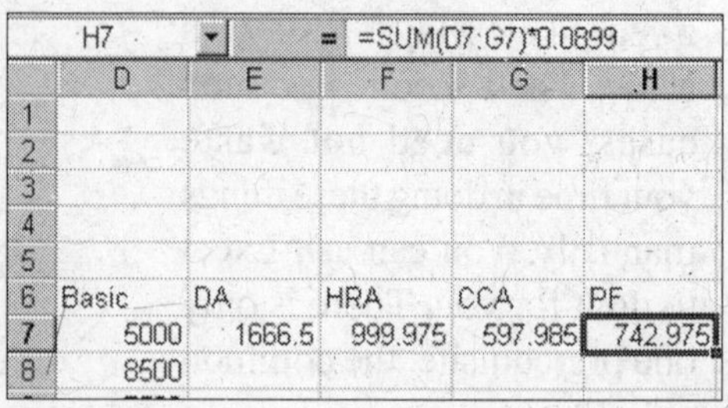

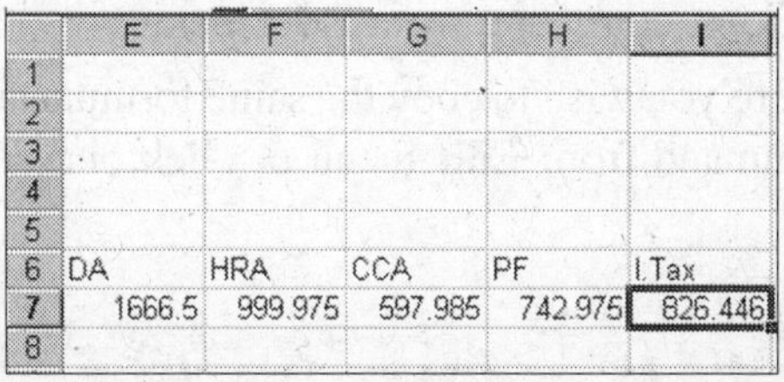

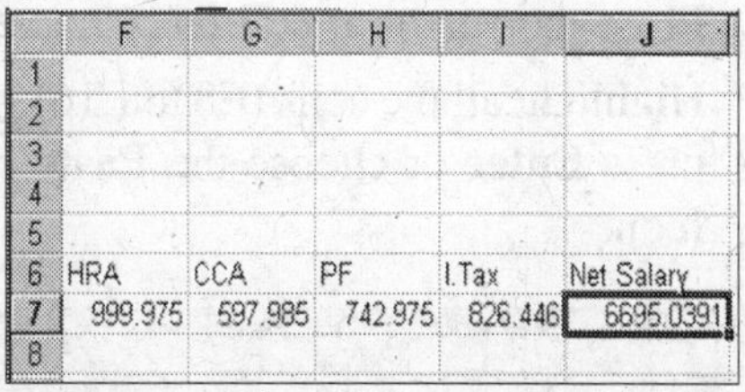

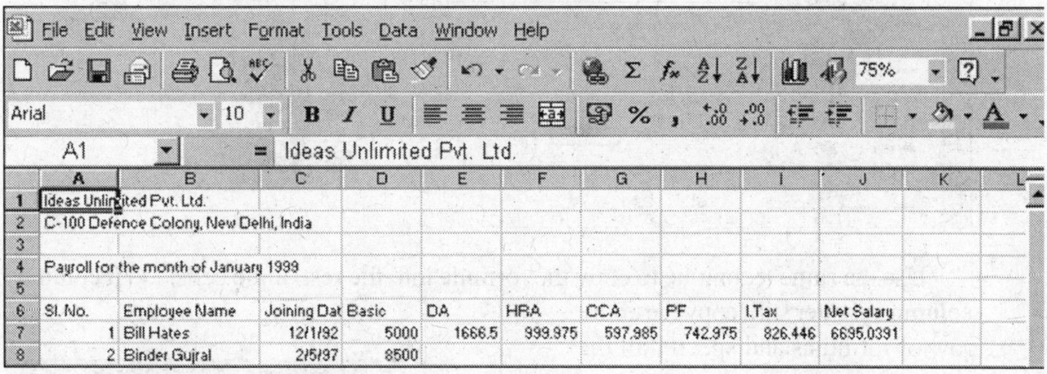

Copying and pasting the formula Once all the formulas have been created for the first employee, all you need to do now is copy these to the rest of the cells. That's right, simply copy! Excel does a very smart thing while copying formulas. It changes them based upon the relative positioning of cells. Let me explain this in more detail. When Excel builds a formula like =A1+B1 in cell C1, the computer does not understand A1, B1 or C1. What it does understand is "I'm in a cell called C1, go two cells to the left (i.e., A1) and go one cell to the left (i.e. B1), add up the contents of these two cells and show me the answer here (i.e. the cell C1)". The important thing here is the relative positions of cells A1, B1 and C1 to each other and the logic of the formula. What actually gets copied, when you copy cells with formulas in them, is that – instead of the absolute contents getting copied, the logic (in terms of relative cell positions) gets copied and therefore you get the right answer. Similarly, now, when Excel copies cell E7 to cell E8 what happens is something like this: cell E7 contains a formula go one cell to the left (i.e., cell D7) and multiply the contents of this cell with 0.3333 (to get 33.33% of Basic salary). Now, when the cell is copied to cell E8 (or for that matter to any other cell in the same column), the logic that gets copied is go one cell to left (i.e., cell D8, and not D7) and multiply with 0.3333 and therefore, you get the correct answer. Now you know how it works!

It is most important to properly understand this concept, because frequently you would be copying all kinds of complex formulas from one place to other. You must remember that the relative relationship between the cells from the place that you want to copy from, must be same as that of cells that you wish to copy to. If this relationship is changed even slightly, obviously you would get wrong answers.

① Place the cursor at cell E7. Choose **Copy** command from **Edit** menu.

② Highlight all the cells (E8 to E16) where you wish to copy the same formula and either press **Enter** or choose the **Paste** command from **Edit** menu or click once on **Paste** Icon.

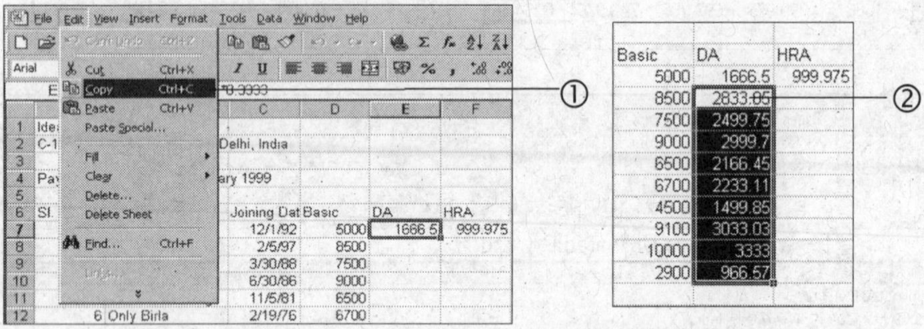

Use the same technique to copy the formula into the rest of the cells. Do it column-by-column or better still, copy the entire row of formulas and specify all the subsequent rows to copy to, in a single command.

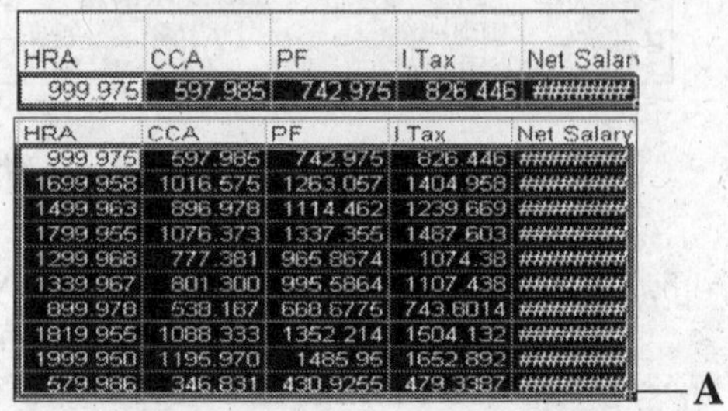

A Notice that in some places instead of numbers you are getting hash symbols (#), it means that the current column width is not sufficient to display the entire contents.

③ Simply use the **AutoFit selection** command from the **Column** command from **Format** menu to adjust the column width of Net Salary.

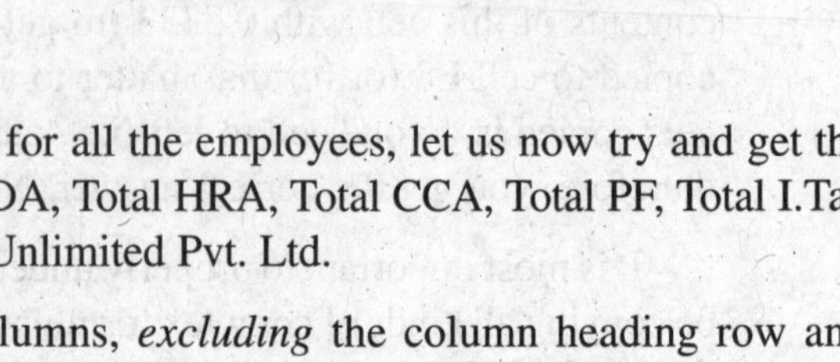

Summation

Once all the values have been filled up for all the employees, let us now try and get the column sum, i.e. Total Basic, Total DA, Total HRA, Total CCA, Total PF, Total I.Tax and Total Net Salary paid by Ideas Unlimited Pvt. Ltd.

① Highlight all the Salary related columns, *excluding* the column heading row and *including* a blank row at the bottom, where you want the totals to appear.

② Click on **AutoSum** icon  to get an AutoSum of all columns total.

A Notice this row has automatically been filled in with the totals of all the salary items.

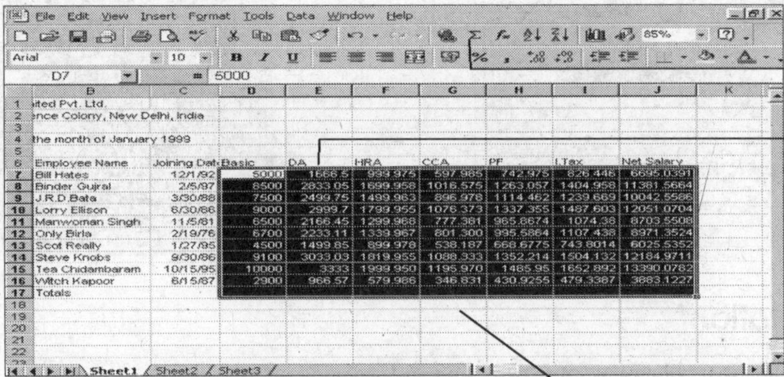

Basic	DA	HRA	CCA	PF	I.Tax	Net Salary
5000	1666.5	999.975	597.985	742.975	826.446	6695.0391
8500	2833.05	1699.958	1016.575	1263.06	1404.96	11381.5664
7500	2499.75	1499.963	896.978	1114.46	1239.67	10042.5586
9000	2999.7	1799.955	1076.373	1337.35	1487.6	12051.0704
6500	2166.45	1299.968	777.381	965.867	1074.38	8703.5508
6700	2233.11	1339.967	801.300	995.586	1107.44	8971.3524
4500	1499.85	899.978	538.187	668.677	743.801	6025.5352
9100	3033.03	1819.955	1088.333	1352.21	1504.13	12184.9711
10000	3333	1999.950	1195.970	1485.95	1652.89	13390.0782
2900	966.57	579.986	346.831	430.925	479.339	3883.1227
69700.00	23231.01	13939.652	8335.912	10357.07	11520.66	93328.8449

A

Formatting Cells

You might have noticed by now that some columns have decimal places and some do not. Also, it is not very easy to read long numbers without comma (,) marks. So to solve this problem, let us format the range.

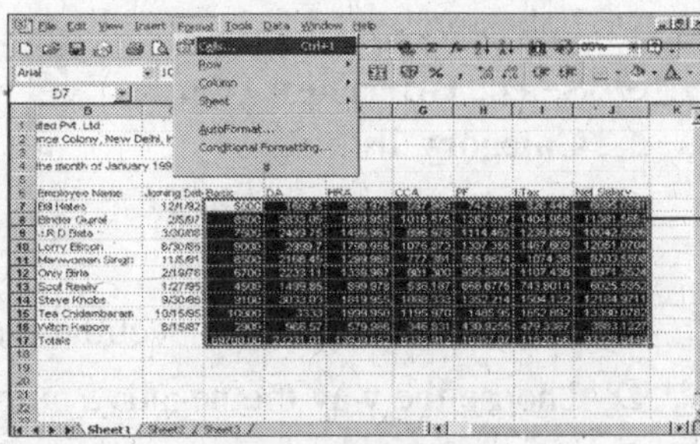

① Highlight all the columns containing numbers.

② Choose **Cells** command from **Format** menu.

③ Choose **Number** Folio.

④ Choose **Number** from **Category** list.

⑤ Specify 2 decimal places.

⑥ Click here to have (,) after every 3rd digit in each numbers

⑦ Click once on **OK** button to execute the command.

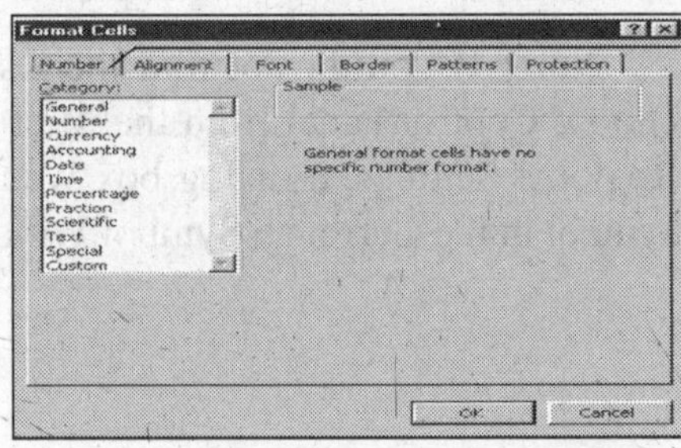

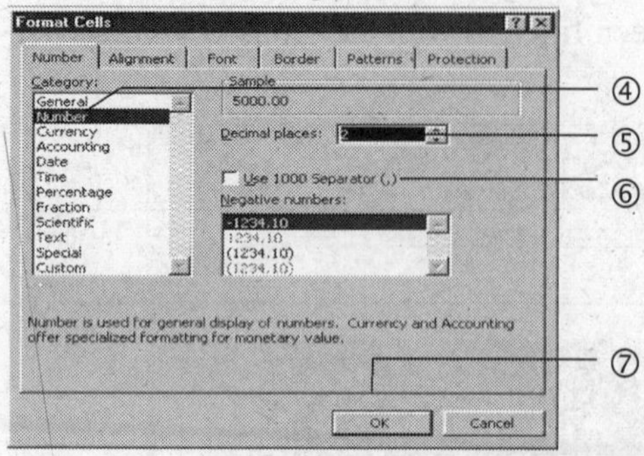

Basic	DA	HRA	CCA	PF	I.Tax	Net Salary
5,000.00	1,666.50	999.98	597.99	742.97	826.45	6,695.04
8,500.00	2,833.05	1,699.96	1,016.57	1,263.06	1,404.96	11,381.57
7,500.00	2,499.75	1,499.96	896.98	1,114.46	1,239.67	10,042.56
9,000.00	2,999.70	1,799.96	1,076.37	1,337.35	1,487.60	12,051.07
6,500.00	2,166.45	1,299.97	777.38	965.87	1,074.38	8,703.55
6,700.00	2,233.11	1,339.97	801.30	995.59	1,107.44	8,971.35
4,500.00	1,499.85	899.98	538.19	668.68	743.80	6,025.54
9,100.00	3,033.03	1,819.95	1,088.33	1,352.21	1,504.13	12,184.97
10,000.00	3,333.00	1,999.95	1,195.97	1,485.95	1,652.89	13,390.08
2,900.00	966.57	579.99	346.83	430.93	479.34	3,883.12
69,700.00	23,231.01	13,939.65	8,335.91	10,357.07	11,520.66	93,328.84

Currency Notation

Next, let us say, we want that the Net salary should display the currency symbol as a prefix for all the numbers. Here, we have derived this Net Salary as a formula, so it is treated as a number, however even if you had typed certain numbers (e.g., Basic Salary) and wanted these to be displayed in currency format, NEVER type the currency symbol before the numbers. This would cause Excel to understand these values as text and not as numbers and as a result, you would not be able to do any calculation on these values.

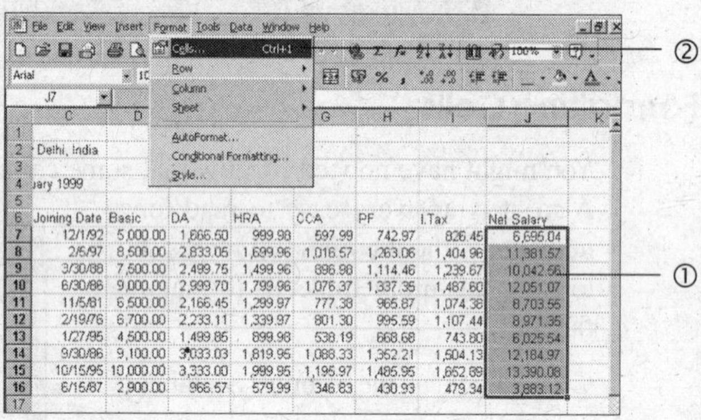

① Highlight the column range you wish to format.

② Select **Cells** command from **Format** menu.

③ Select **Number** from the Folios presented.

④ Select **Currency** from **Category** list.

⑤ Choose the symbol that you want.

⑥ Choose the number of decimal places.

⑦ Choose the way the negative numbers are to be displayed.

⑧ Click on **OK** button to execute the command.

Note: If you do not find the Rs. currency symbol in the available options, then choose Control Panel from the Microsoft Office shortcut toolbar. Double click on the Regional Settings, a dialog box would appear. Click on the Currency folio. Type Rs. symbol in the Currency Symbol Window and click on OK button.

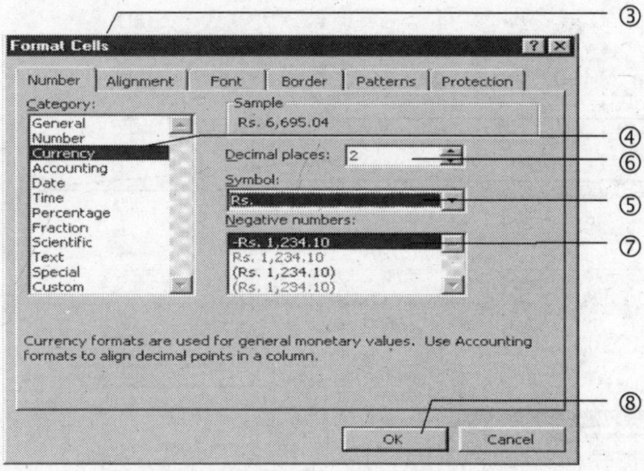

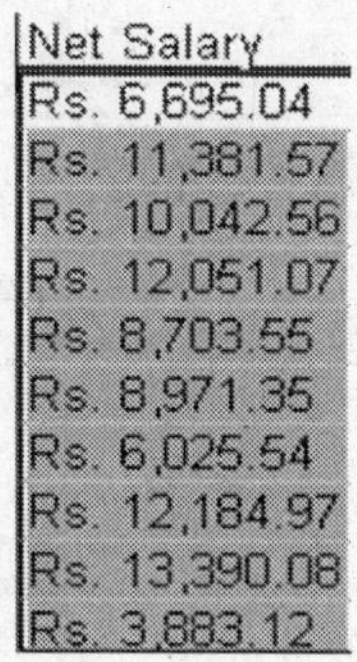

Centering Across Selection, Changing Font and Size

① Select the text as well as all the columns across which you wish to center this text.

② Click the **Center Across** icon  to center text.

A Repeat the process 1 & 2 to center across other rows.

Changing Fonts in Excel is exactly the same as in Word.

③ Highlight the text.

④ Click on this roll-down list to get a list of all available fonts. Choose the one desired by clicking it once.

Now let us change the character (font) sizes.

⑤ Click here to see a list of point size. Click on the desired one.

Similarly, use Bold, Underline or Italic icon on any piece of worksheet. Do this by simply highlighting the desired area and click once on 

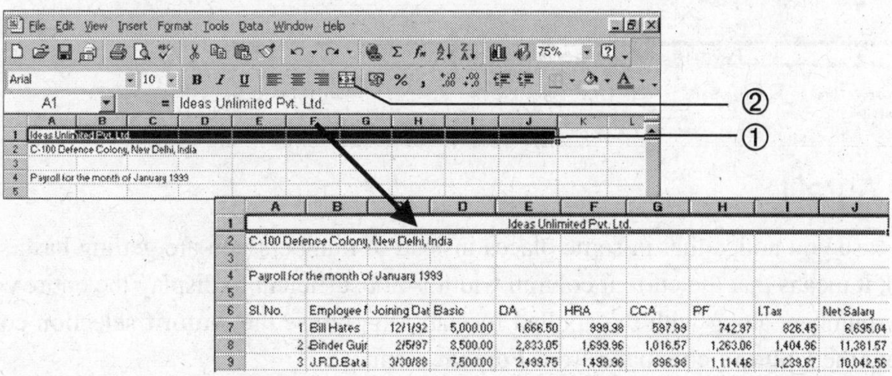

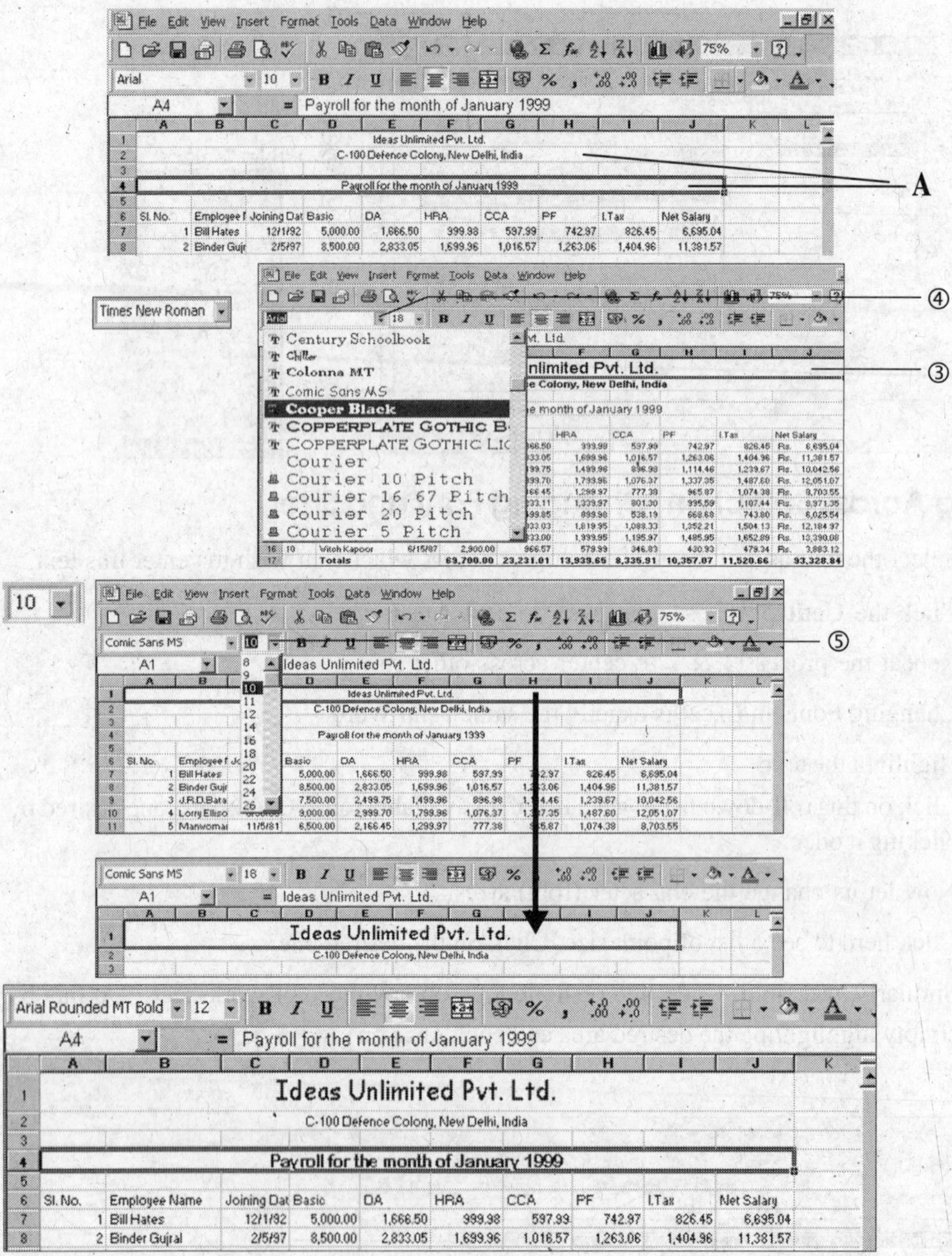

Column Autofit

In case you notice that in some places instead of numbers you are getting hash symbols (#), it means that the current column width is not sufficient to display the entire contents, i.e. numbers along with the applied format. Simply use the **Autofit** selection command from the **Column** command from **Format** menu.

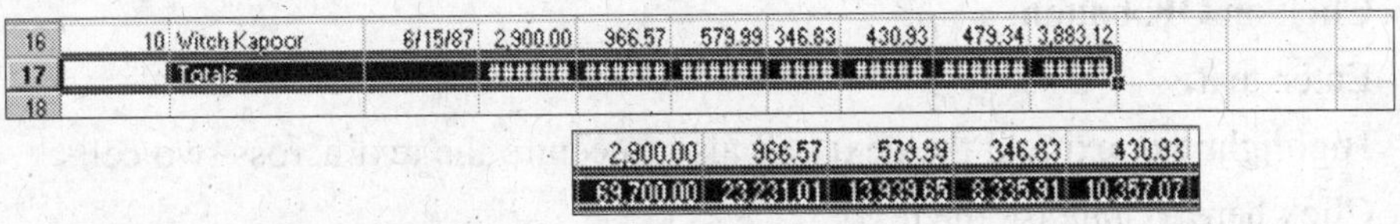

Formatting Text (Bold, Italic)

① Highlight the text.

② Choose **Cells** command from **Format** menu.

③ Choose Font Folio.

④ Choose the desired font.

⑤ Choose the font style, whether you need Regular, **Bold**, *Italics* or ***Bold Italics***. Some of the fonts might not have all these choices.

⑥ In case you wish to underline the text, choose from one of the choices, single, i.e., underline single line, double, i.e., underline data with a double line etc.

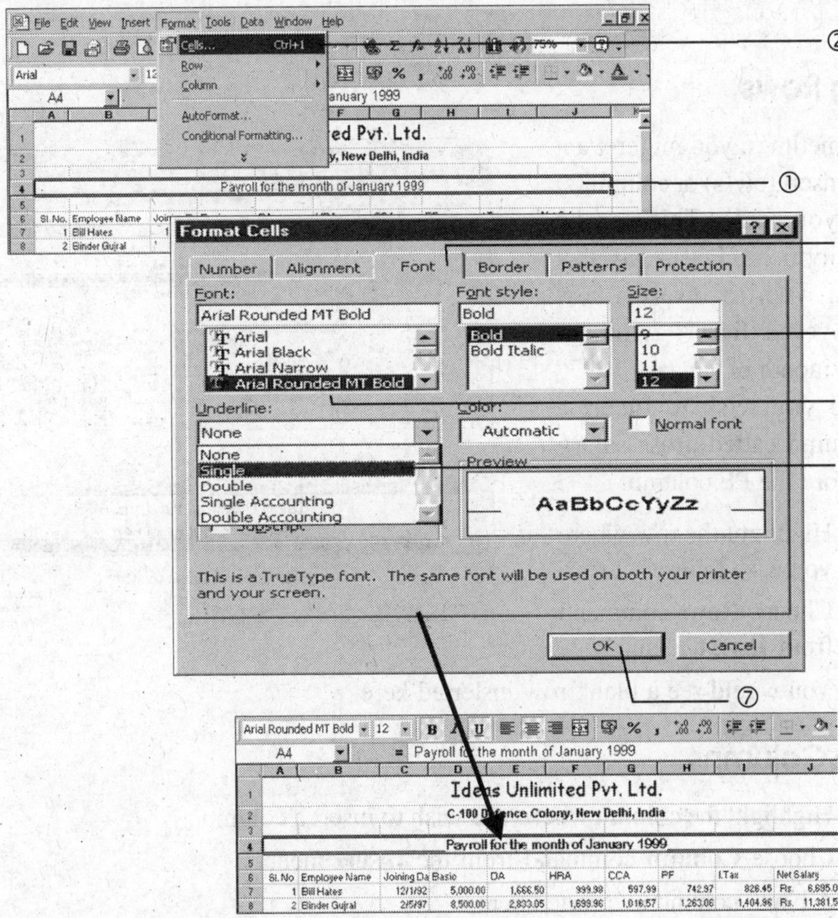

⑦ Click on **OK** button.

⑧ Enter text.

⑨ Highlight the text and the next cell also to centre the text across two cells.

⑩ Click here to italicise the text.

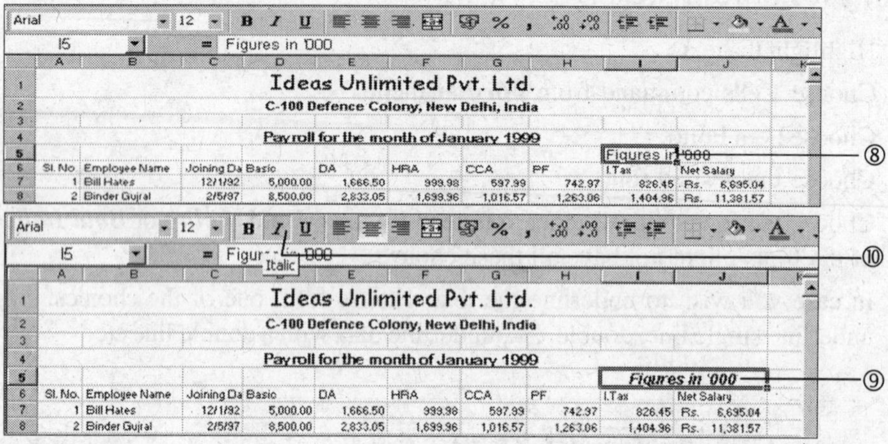

Inserting Rows

Sometimes, you might want to insert row(s) or column(s) in your data. This can be easily done. Let us say that you wish to insert a row above the line "Payroll for the month of January 1997" and you wish to insert a column called gross salary before the PF column.

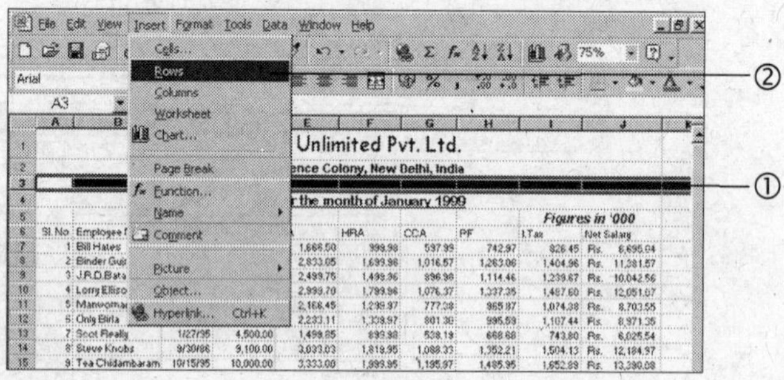

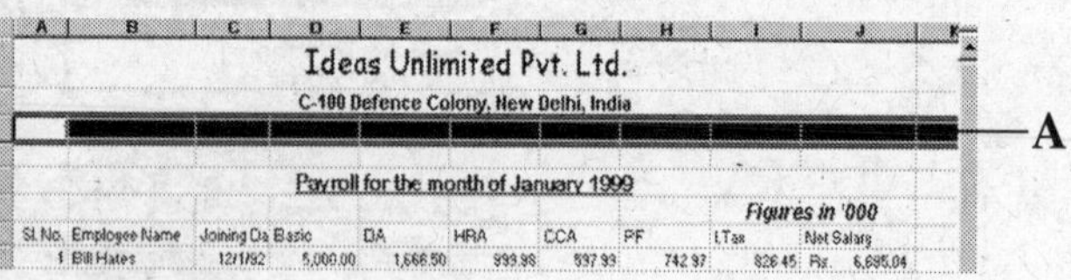

① Highlight the row where you wish to insert a row.

② Choose **Rows** command from **Insert** menu.

A You would see a blank row insterted here.

Inserting Columns

① Highlight the column where you wish to insert a column.

② Choose **Column** command from the **Insert** menu.

A A blank column is inserted here.

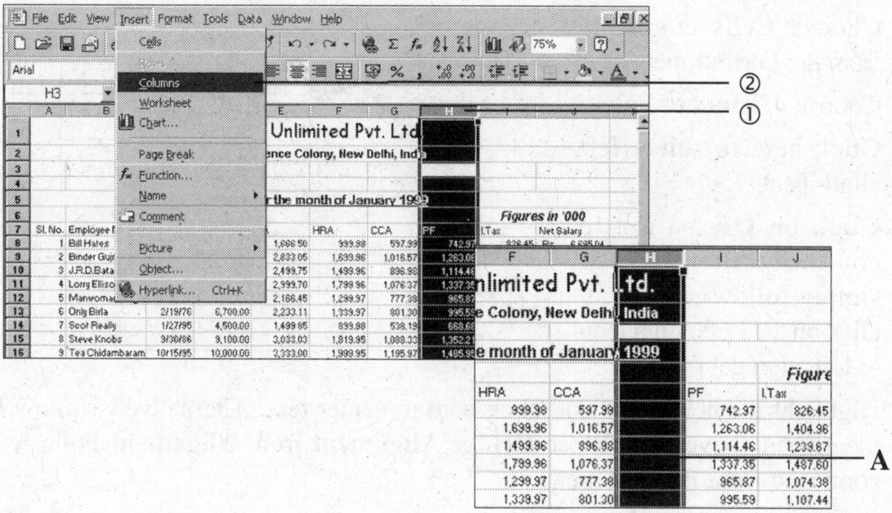

Formula

Now let us fill this column with Gross Salary, i.e., Summation of basic, DA, HRA and CCA. For this you may either use the AutoSum technique explained earlier in the exercise or alternatively, type =SUM (D8:G8) and press Enter in cell H8. In this formula, D8:G8 specifies that you wish to add all the value in the range starting from D8 and ending at G8.

① Type the formula and press Enter.

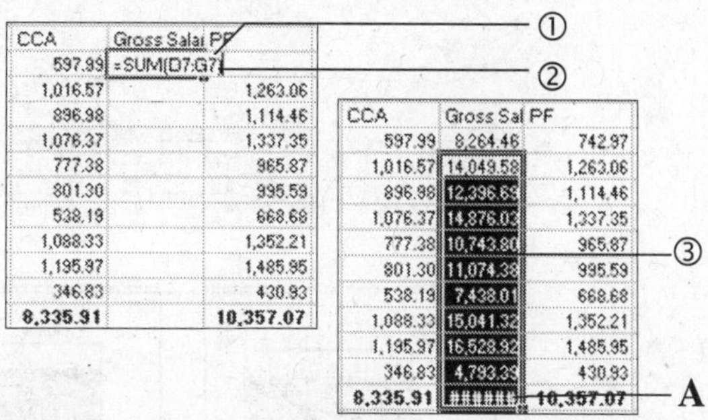

② Remaining in the cell where you have given the formula, click on **Copy** icon.

③ Highlight the range where you want to copy this formula, i.e., from H9 to H17 and Press **Enter** or click on **Paste** icon.

A This indicates that the value cannot fit within the current cell width. Use AutoFit selection to increase the width of the column.

Aligning the Data

As you would have noticed by now, all text entries are left aligned and all numeric entries are automatically right aligned within the cells. The default alignment can be changed in the following way.

① Highlight the range for which you wish to change the alignment.

② Choose **Cells** command from the **Format** menu

③ Choose **Alignment** Folio.

④ Click here to select left align-ment.

⑤ Click on **OK** button to continue. Alternatively, simply follow step no.① click on the Left Align icon to left align data.

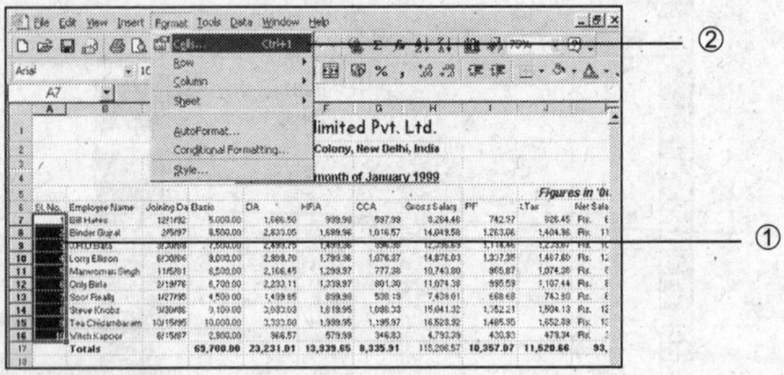

⑥ Highlight the new range and click here to center text. Alternatively, follow the step mentioned above and choose **Center Alignment** from **Alignment** Folio from **Cell** command from **Format** menu.

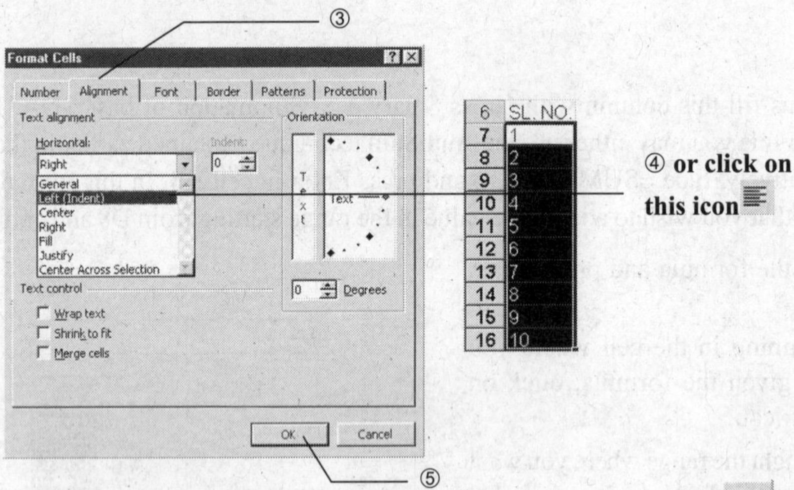

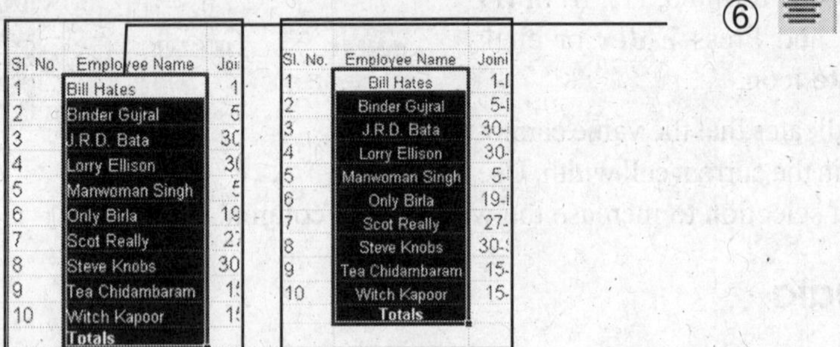

Formatting Date Range

① Highlight date range.

② Choose **Cells** command from **Format** menu.

③ Choose **Number** Folio.

④ Choose the **Date** category.

⑤ Choose the desired type.

⑥ Click on **OK** button to apply the chosen Format.

A Final Result!

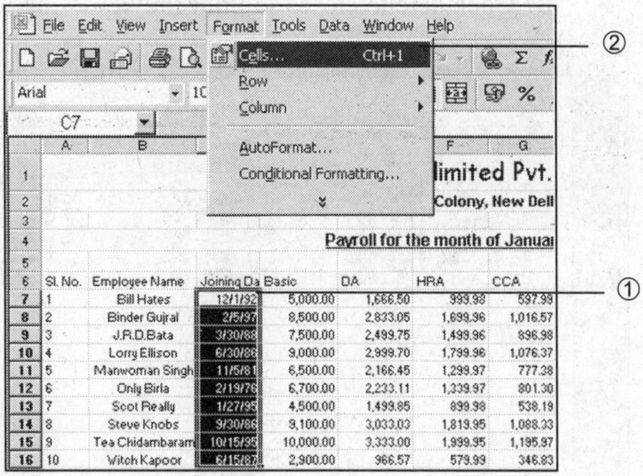

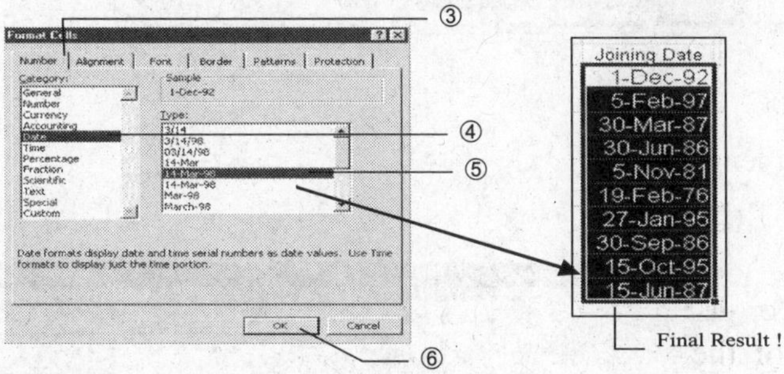

Preview

Now that you have done considerable work on the worksheet, it is time to sit back and take stock of your work. It might be a good idea to see a Print Preview of your work, i.e., take a look at a near exact replica of the Page that your printer would eventually print out.

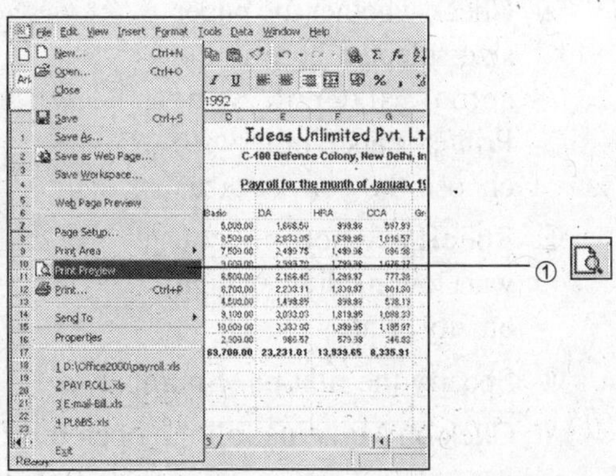

① Either click the **Print Preview** icon or choose **Print Preview** command from the **File** menu.

A This is what your screen would look like and also what your current page would look like, when printed.

① Click here to specify the print settings.

B Click here to close the Print Preview window without printing the document.

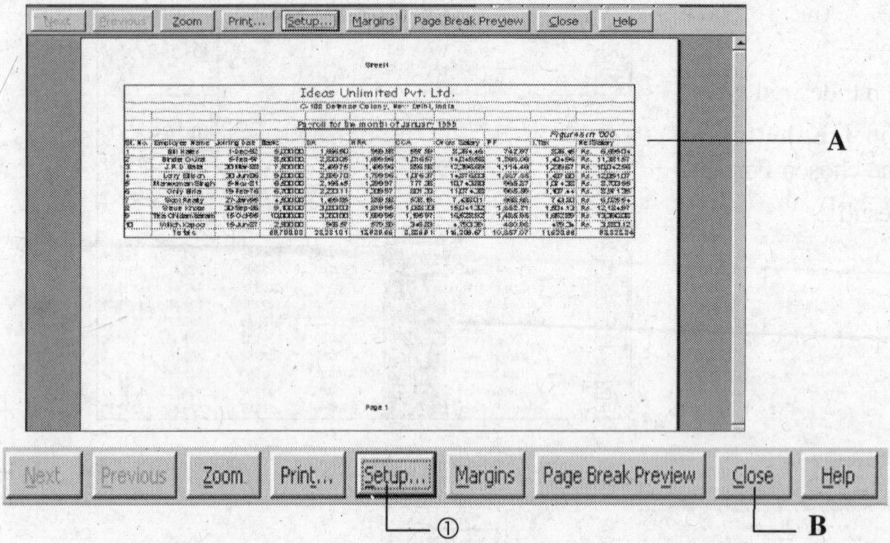

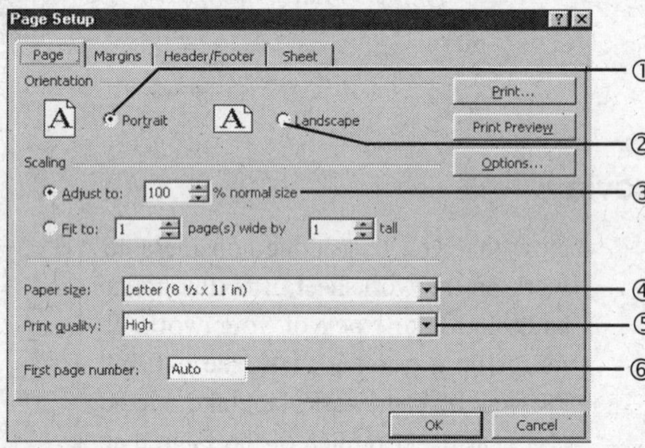

① Click here to Print lengthwise.

② Click here to Print widthwise.

③ You can increase or decrease the size of the printed matter by specifying the scaling percentage.

④ Check whether the paper size selected here is the actual size of your Printer paper, otherwise choose the correct size.

⑤ Specify whether you want low, medium or high quality print.

⑥ Specify the first page number.

A Click on **Margins** folio to open this dialog box.

B Specify the header and footer margin.

C Specify the top, bottom, left and right margin.

D Specify whether you wish to center the data, horizontally or vertically or both, within the page.

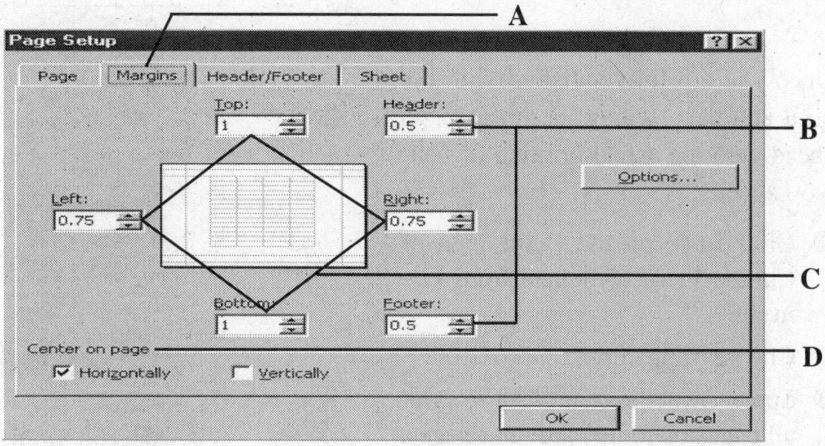

① Click on the **Header and Footer** folio to open this dialog box.

② Click on this roll-down list to choose from already given header matters, or you can create your own by clicking on the **Custom Header** button and define it.

③ Click on this roll-down list to choose from samples footer of textual/other matter, or you can create your own by clicking on the **Custom Footer** button and define it.

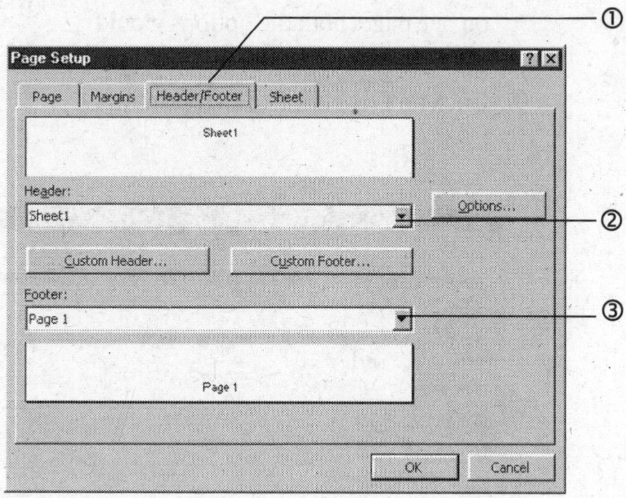

① Click on **Sheet** folio to open this dialog box.

② Click here to print the grid lines along with the data.

③ Click on OK butt-on.

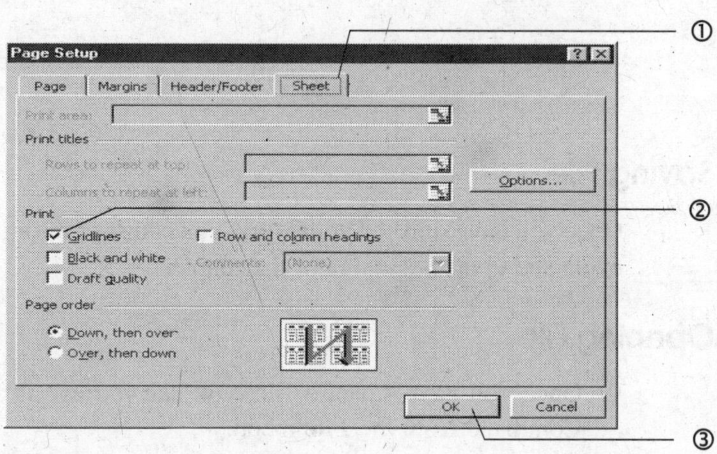

Print

Once you are fully satisfied with the print and page setting, you should go ahead with the actual printing of your worksheet.

① Click once on the **Print** icon or Choose **Print** command from **File** menu.

② Choose your Printer.

③ Specify whether you wish to print all pages or some particular pages. Since the present example has data on one page, both the options would give the same results.

④ Click on **OK** button to start printing.

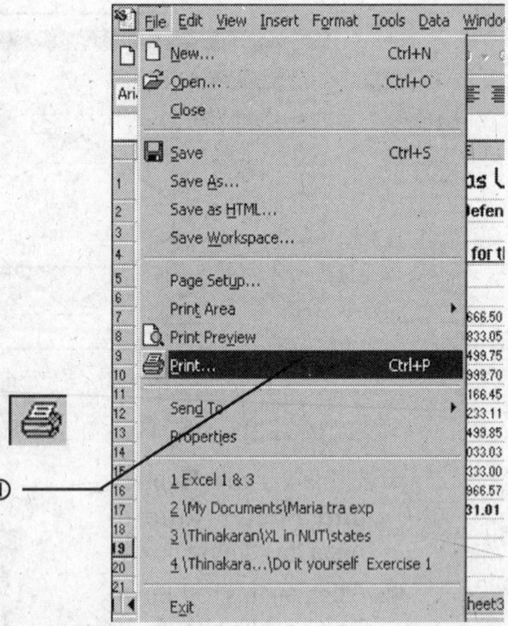

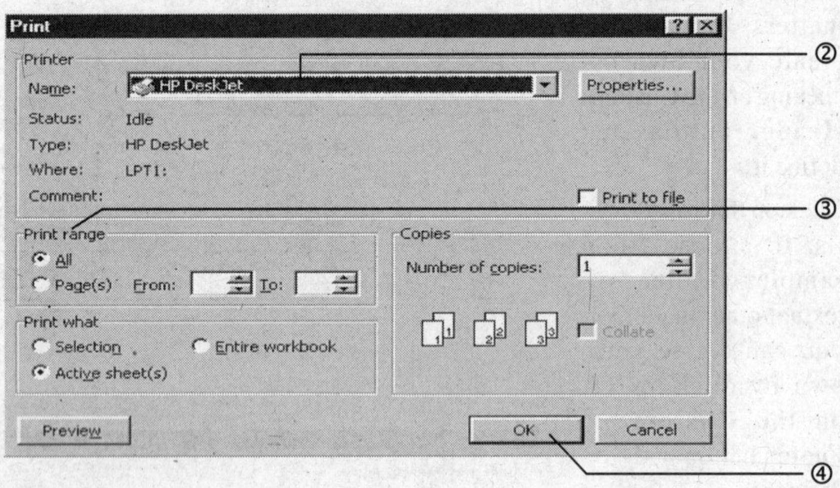

Saving File

Once you have finished your work, you can save it for your record (Saving a file has been explained in the beginning of the chapter).

Opening File

① Once you have saved a file, you can retrieve it any time. For this, choose **Open** Command from the **File** menu.

② Type the file name or choose the file from the list shown.

③ Click on **Open** button to open the selected file.

A Make sure that you have specified the correct path for the directory in which your file is stored.

B The requested file would open up.

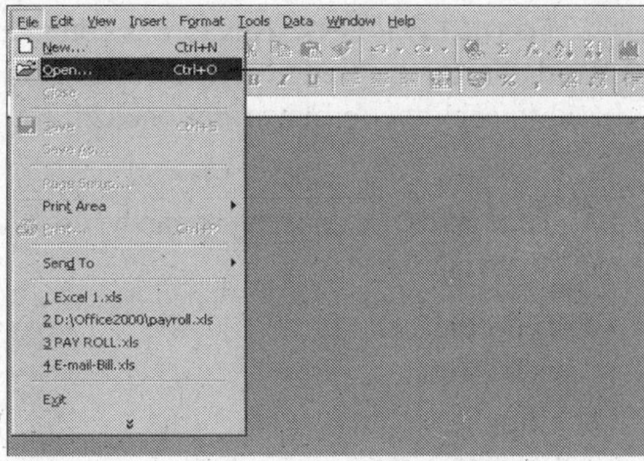

①

A

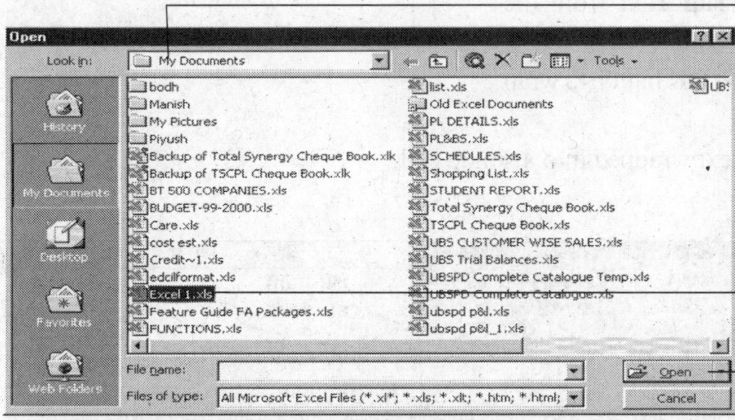

②

③

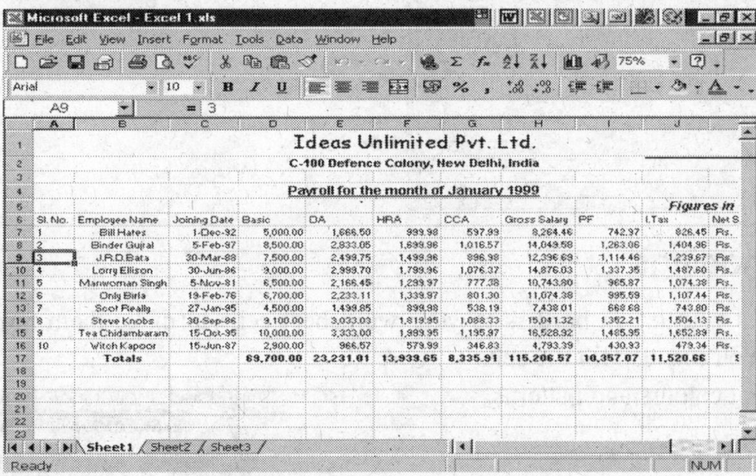

B

Excel offers a unique set of formatting features that can be used to effectively display your data. Now that we have completed our exercise, let us explore some more formatting features of Excel:

Format Painter This tool is common to all MS office packages. As discussed in Word, this can be used to copy formatting of one object into another. In Excel, this can be used to copy the formats from one cell (or a group of cells) to another cell or group of cells.

Text Wrap This feature can be used to display multiple lines of text within a single cell. To wrap the text:

① Type the desired text in the usual way.

② Choose **Cells** from the **Format** menu.

③ Under the **Alignment** tab, choose **Wrap Text** from the **Text Control.**

④ Click on the **OK** button to wrap the text.

A Output—text wrapped into a single cell.

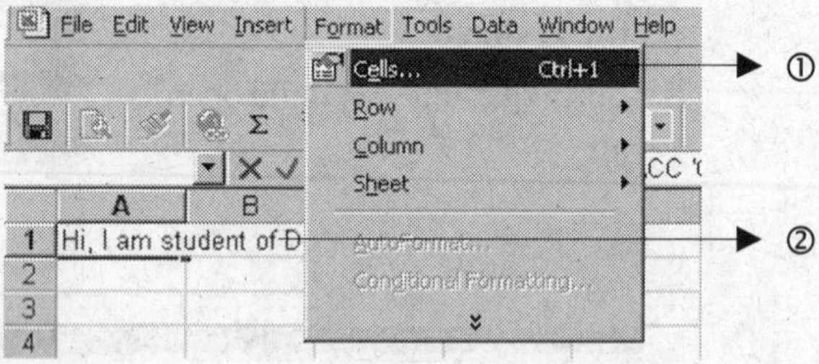

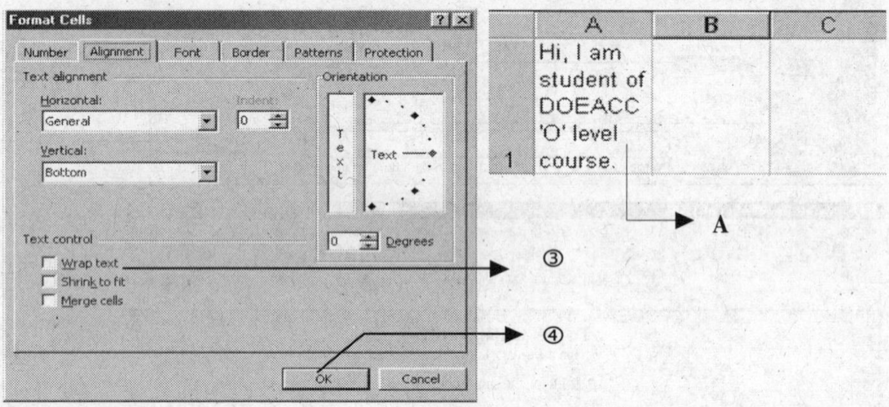

Borders and Shadings

Excel allows you to add borders to your worksheet cells to make them more visually appealing. You can also fill the cells with different colours and patterns.

To add borders

① Select the range of cells for which you wish to add border.

② Choose **Cells** from the **Format** menu.

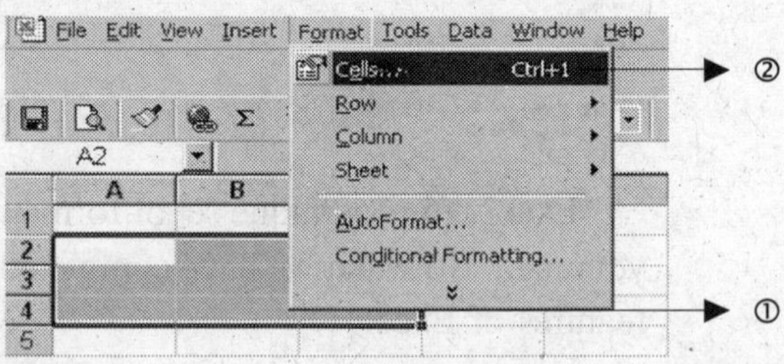

③ Under the **Border** tab, choose the desired **Border Style** from one of the presets. You can also choose a different **Line Style** and **Color** for your selected border style.

④ Click on the **OK** button to apply your changes

A Output—range of cells selected in ① with border.

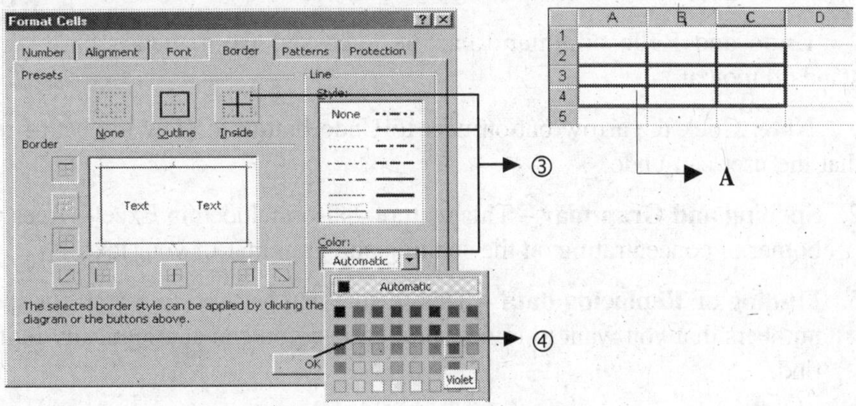

To add shading

① Select the range of cells that you wish to shade.

② Choose **Cells** from the **Format** menu.

③ Under the **Format** tab, choose the desired **Color** and shade **Pattern.**

④ Click on the **OK** button to apply your changes

A Output—range of cells selected in ① with shading.

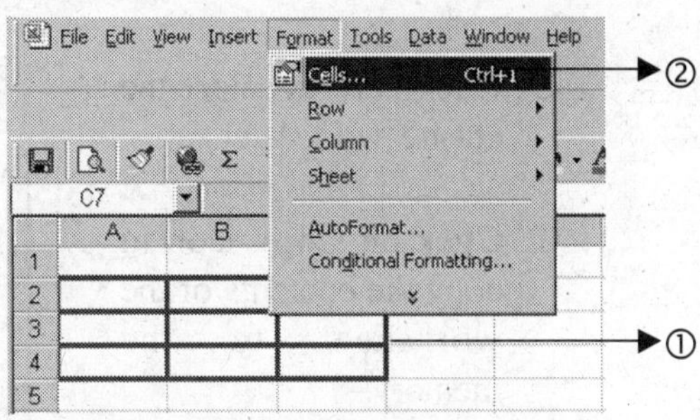

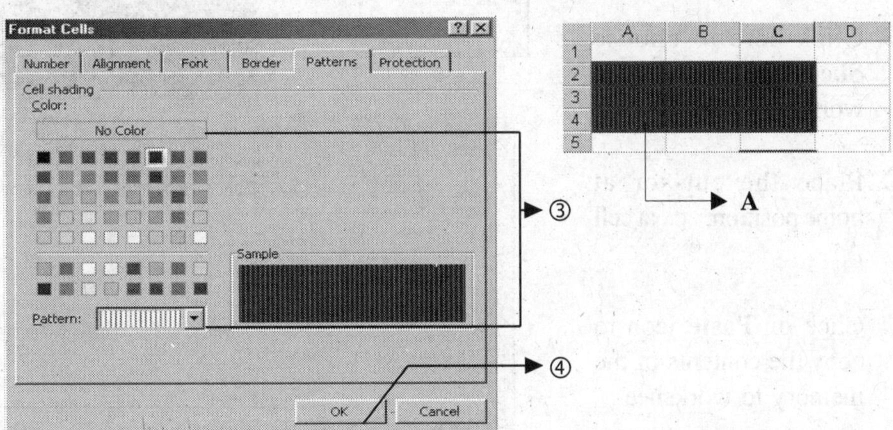

Editing Workbooks

1. **Undo** command can be used to undo the effect of recent commands or actions taken by the user. Redo command can be used to redo something that the user has undone. Redo undoes an Undo!

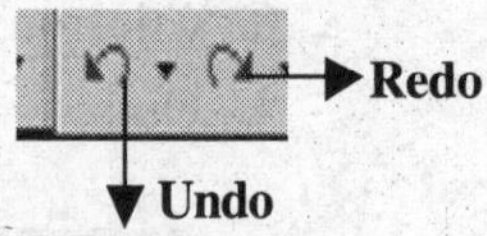

Undo and Redo command can be accessed from the standard toolbar.

Note: Click the arrow button next to Undo button to view the list of recent actions that the user can undo.

2. **Spelling and Grammar** – This feature—also included in Excel—frees you from the bother of concentrating on the spelling and grammar of your text.

3. **Finding or Replacing data** – This feature can be used to search for specific text or numbers that you want to review or edit, and you can automatically replace data you find.

All the three editing features explained above are common to MS word as well. For details, refer to the chapter on Word processing.

4. **Copying Text between Worksheets** – Copy & Paste commands can also be used to copy the entire contents of one worksheet into another sheet.

① Click here to select the ent-ire worksheet.

② Click on **Copy** icon to copy the contents of the worksheet to the memory.

③ Click here to choose **Sheet 2** within the same work-book file.

④ Place the cur-sor at home position, i.e., at cell A1.

⑤ Click on **Paste** icon to copy the contents of the memory to worksheet.

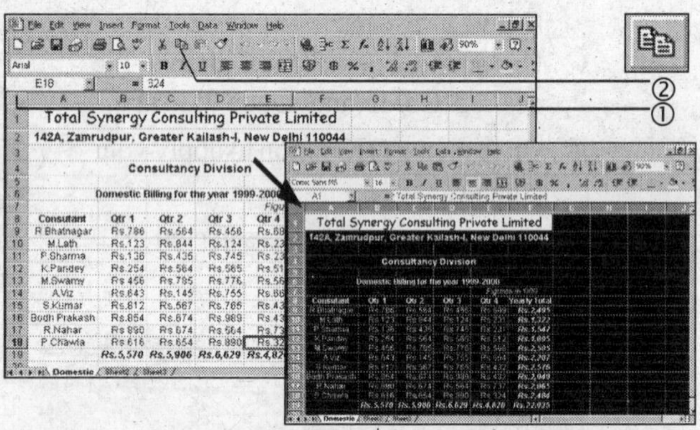

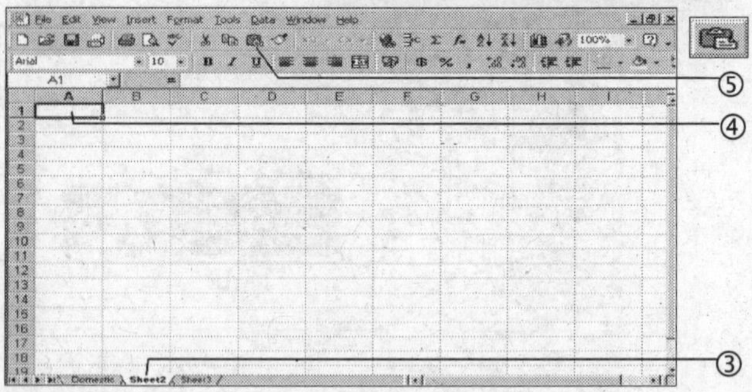

A You will see that the Domestic Billing sheet has been copied, below.

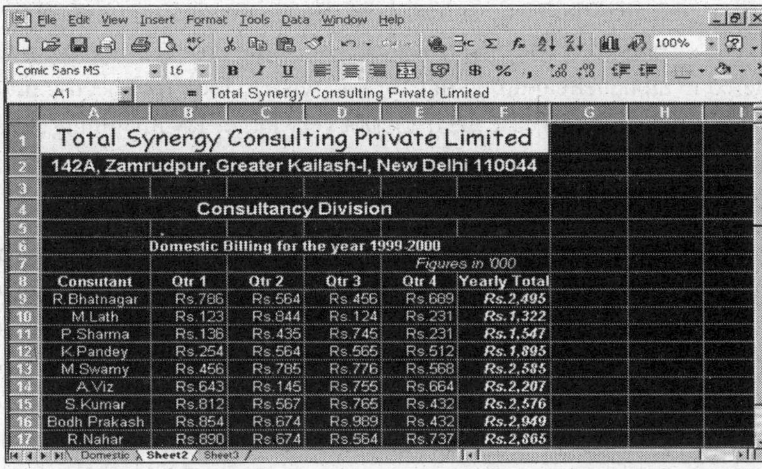

Total Synergy Consulting Private Limited

142A, Zamrudpur, Greater Kailash-I, New Delhi 110044

Consultancy Division

Domestic Billing for the year 1999-2000

Figures in '000

Consultant	Qtr 1	Qtr 2	Qtr 3	Qtr 4	Yearly Total
R.Bhatnagar	Rs.786	Rs.564	Rs.456	Rs.689	*Rs.2,495*
M.Lath	Rs.123	Rs.844	Rs.124	Rs.231	*Rs.1,322*
P.Sharma	Rs.136	Rs.435	Rs.745	Rs.231	*Rs.1,547*
K.Pandey	Rs.254	Rs.564	Rs.565	Rs.512	*Rs.1,895*
M.Swamy	Rs.456	Rs.785	Rs.776	Rs.568	*Rs.2,585*
A.Viz	Rs.643	Rs.145	Rs.755	Rs.664	*Rs.2,207*
S.Kumar	Rs.812	Rs.567	Rs.765	Rs.432	*Rs.2,576*
Bodh Prakash	Rs.854	Rs.674	Rs.989	Rs.432	*Rs.2,949*
R.Nahar	Rs.890	Rs.674	Rs.564	Rs.737	*Rs.2,865*

A

5. **Clear contents, formats, or comments from cells - Clear** command can be used to:

   a. Clear the cell formats,

   b. Clear the comments, or

   c. Clear the cell contents - When the contents of a cell are deleted, only its contents are removed but the cell formats, comments remain intact.

   d. Clear all the three at one go.

① Select the cells, rows, or columns you want to clear.

② On the **Edit** menu, point to **Clear**, and then click **All**, **Contents**, **Formats**, or **Comments**, whichever is applicable

A Output

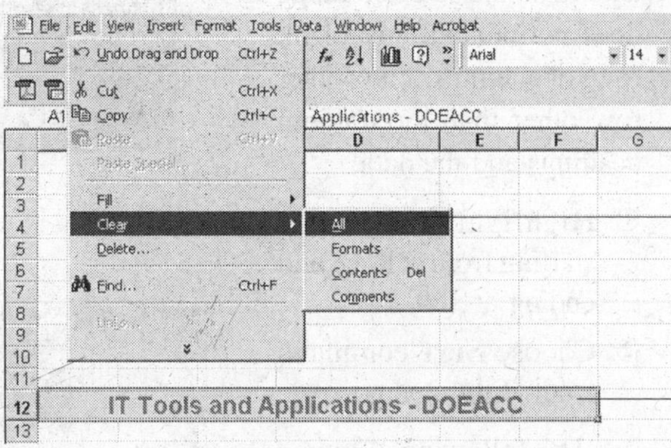

② ①

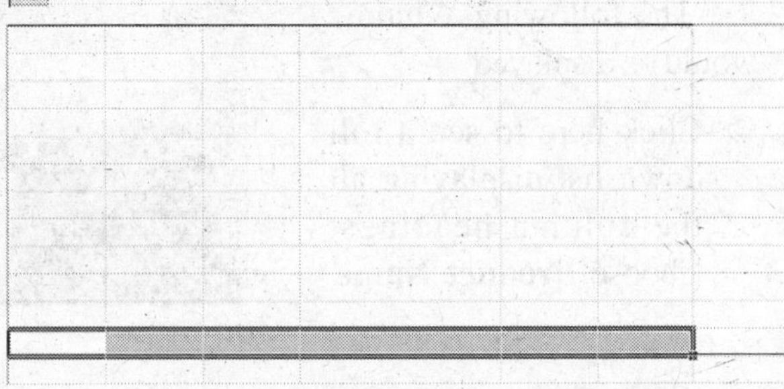

A

DATA SORT

Having once prepared the basic spreadsheet, let us now learn a few new commands. As you would notice, in the present spreadsheet, since the products and their details have not been entered in alphabetical order, in case you wish to look for specific product you have to read the entire list. In this case the list is not very large. Try imagining a real life scenario where the number of products could well run into hundreds, if not thousands. It would be simply maddening to hunt for any product!

Fortunately Excel has a simple solution (in fact, there are several solutions, but for the time being we shall confine ourselves to one) called **Data Sort.** Simply put, this command allows you to alphabetically rearrange any type of data, either in ascending (*A to Z or 1 to 10 or 1st January 1999 to 31st December 1999*) or descending (*Z to A or 10 to 1 or 31st December 1999 to 1st January 1999*) order. This frees you from the bother of having to arrange data while typing. Just enter the data in random order and apply Data Sort to rearrange it for you.

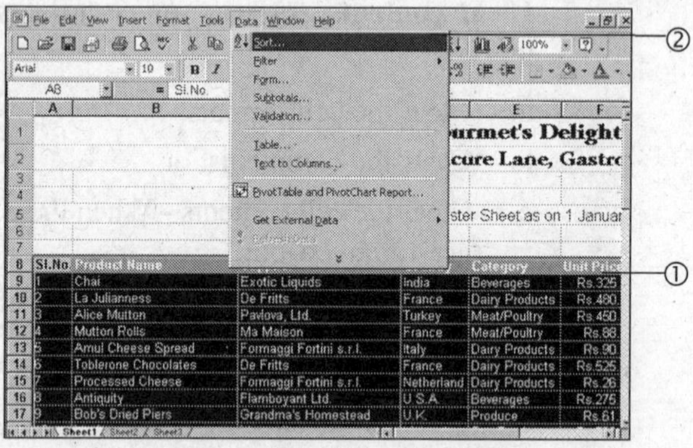

Note: While using Data Sort command the entire table, including the column headings, has to be selected for this command to work properly. Care should also be taken that the selected range does not contain any blank rows or columns or any other row other than the column headings and the data.

① Highlight the range starting from cell **A8** and ending at **J60.**

② Choose **Sort** command from **Data** menu.

The following Window would be displayed:

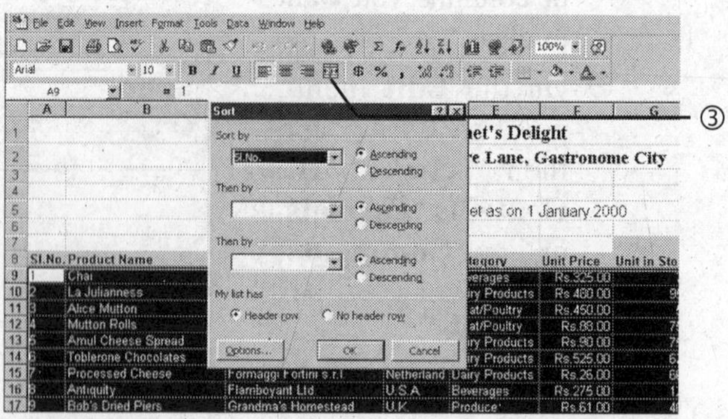

③ Click here to see a roll down list displaying all the column headings. Choose **Product Name**.

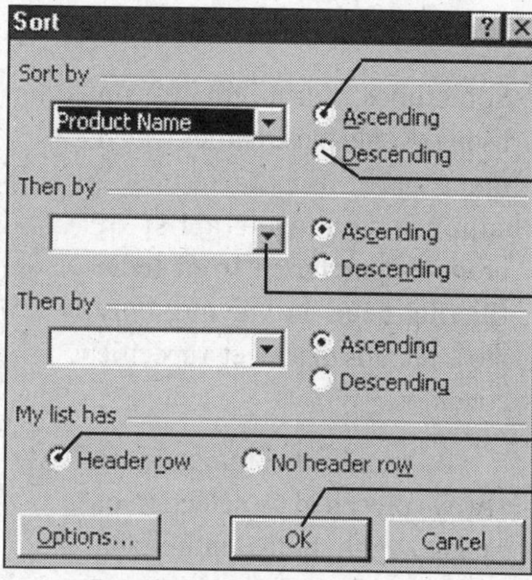

④ Click here once to choose the **Ascending Order** radio button.

⑤ Click on **OK** to execute the data sort command.

A If you want to do a reverse sort, i.e., on descending order, choose this option.

B While highlighting we had also included the column header row, therefore click here to choose the **My list has Header Row** radio button.

C If you wish to apply a sort within sort, choose this option. This means that the data would first be sorted on the basis of the primary column (Sort By) specified above, and only if there is a tie for that column, the data would sorted based upon the secondary column (Then By) chosen here.

For instance if the primary column chosen is Product Name and the secondary column chosen is country and if there are two products both called "Chocolate Candy" one coming from Italy and one coming from France, the one coming from France will be listed first (presuming that ascending order has been chosen for secondary column).

Once having clicked on OK button from the data sort Window the following results will be shown.

Using the same technique you can sort this table in ascending or descending order on the basis of any column.

A Notice that the entire table has been rearranged based upon the **Product Name** column and now it is obviously much easier to look up a specific item. In our present example, since serial numbers were also assigned initially in ascending order, this column hence also gets rearranged.

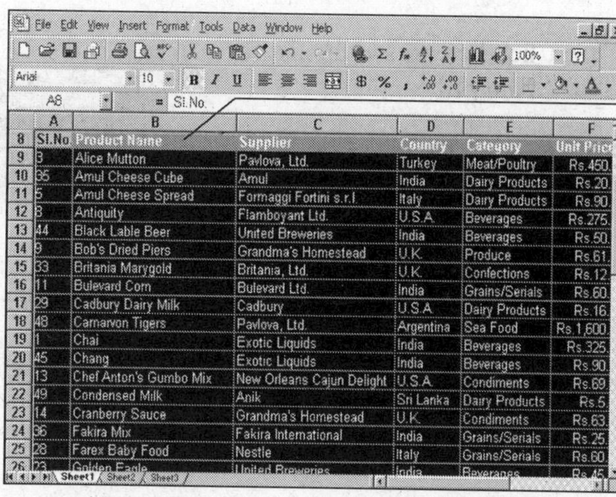

Data Filters

Sometimes you might want a listing of only those entries which meet certain criteria, e.g., suppose you want a list of products purchased from India filtering helps in viewing only those records that meet a specific condition.

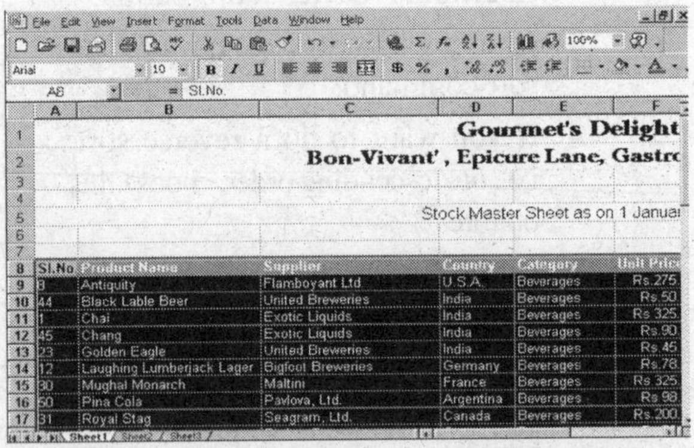

As usual, all commands are always preceded by selection of range. Highlight the entire table including the column headings and data rows.

① Choose **Auto Filter** command from the **Filter** option from the **Data** menu.

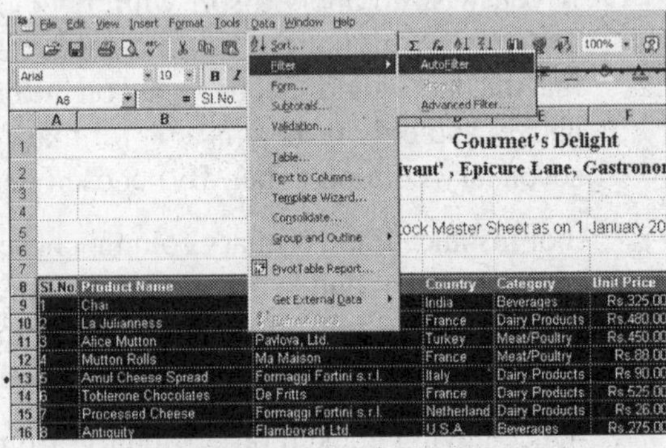

A Notice that the drop-down list buttons begin shown against each column heading. Now with the help of these buttons you can apply various conditions and get the desired output.

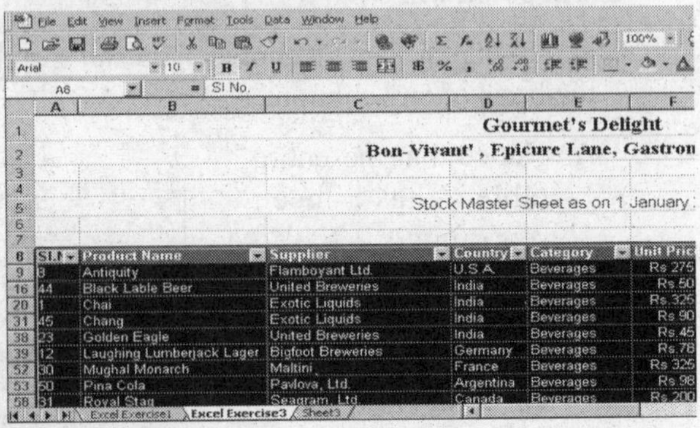

① Click here to see the list for country filter.

② Select U.S.A. [Use scroll bar (if provided) to travel in this list].

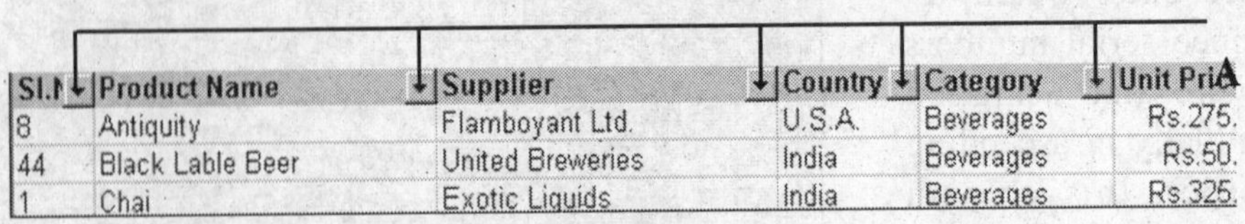

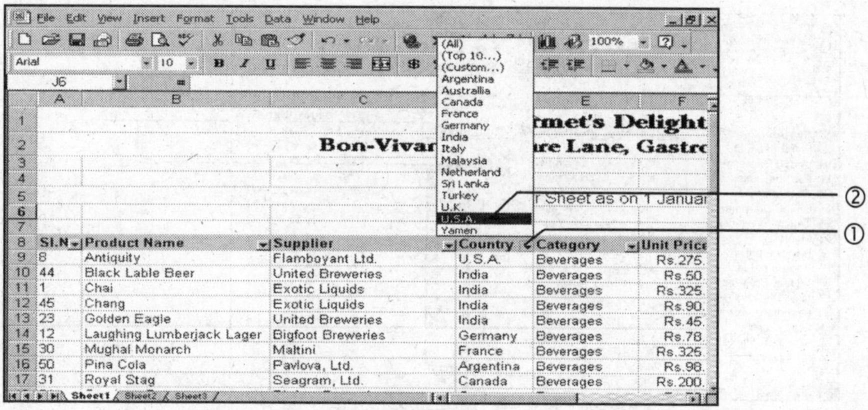

A Do not worry, the rest of the items have not been deleted or lost! They have simply been hidden from display and can be got back by simply clicking on the **Country filter** and selecting **All.**

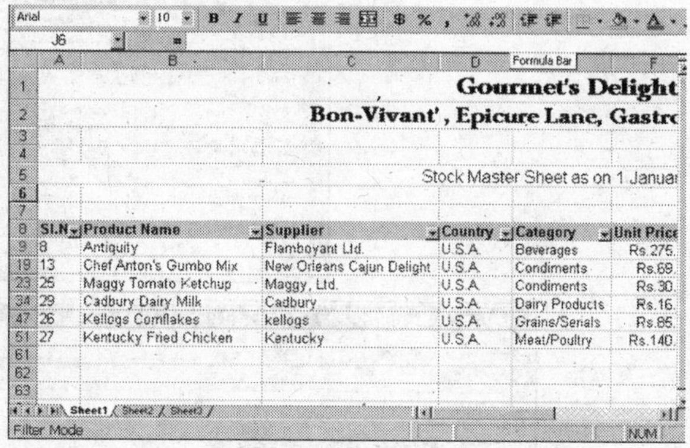

Note: All is very helpful feature. Whenever you get stuck or have given a wrong filter selection, use this option to get back to the complete table.

Custom Data Filters

Filters can be used to pull out records based upon a mathematical criteria (condition). In our present example let us try to filter records for those products which have a unit price of more than Rs. 200.

① Click once on the **Unit Price** Filter and choose **Custom** option. Through this option you can specify various criteria which, if met, ought to yield the results sought.

A You will get this dialog box.

② Through this drop-down list, you can select the operator that you want to use for specifying your criteria.

③ Either you can make a selection from this drop-down list, which displays all possible entries existing in the current filter column; or you can type the desired figure straight away. In most cases, the second alternative is easier. Click on the "**is greater than or equal to**" option.

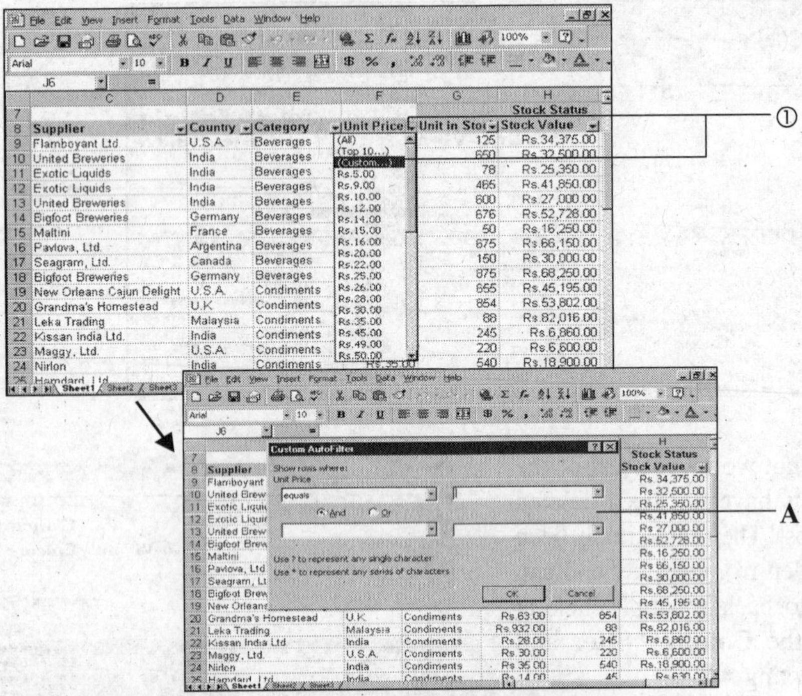

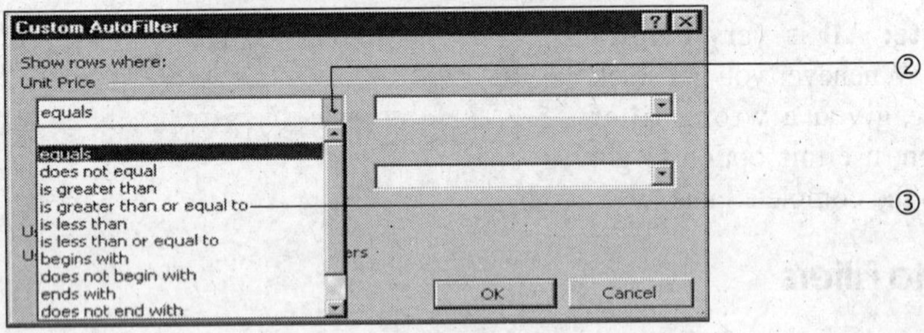

④ Click on the second window to type the Unit Price.

⑤ Click on **OK** button to view the desired result.

Using **And** between two conditions means *both the conditions must be satisfied by a record for it to be eligible for selection.* Using **Or** between two conditions means that *even if one of the two conditions is satisfied by a record, it would be eligible for selection.*

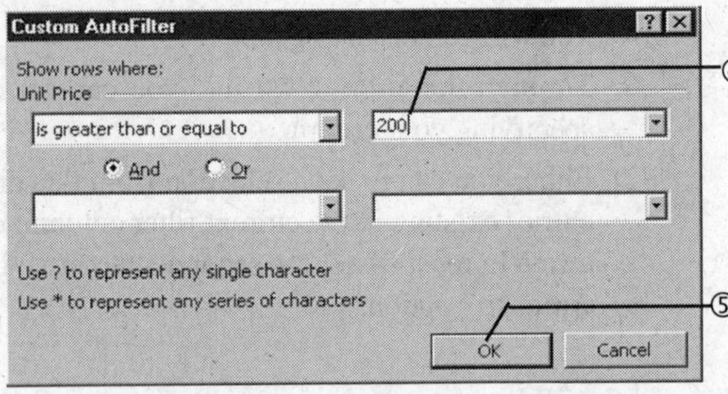

To make it still clearer, let us take a look at a few valid and invalid multiple criteria statements (conditions).

Valid Criteria

- '>=200' **And** '<=500', i.e., *all values between 200 and 500, both figures inclusive.*
- '>200' **Or** '<100', i.e., *all values greater than 200 and all values less than 100.*

Invalid Criteria

- '>=200' **Or** '<=500', i.e., all values either greater than or equal to 200 or all values less than or equal to 500. Since all values will be either >=200 or <=500 these multiple conditions have the effect of including all the values in our data range.
- '>200' **And** '<100' i.e. *all the values greater than 200 but also less than 100.* A value if greater than 200 cannot be less than 100 and vice versa, therefore this is an invalid criterion.

FUNCTIONS

Let us now move to yet another powerful feature of Excel, called Functions. **Functions** are powerful tools that help you perform complex computations–easily and quickly. Functions are like predefined formulas in which the user has to simply provide the values based upon which the calculations are done.

Typically, a function consists of two parts–**function name** and **arguments**. Arguments (or values) may in some cases be mandatory and in some cases optional. Even within a function, one of the arguments may be mandatory and another optional. Functions always return a result.

There are hundreds of worksheet functions that come along with your Excel package; we shall be restricting ourselves to only a few commonly used ones. Once you get the hang of it, you should be able to figure out the rest yourself without much difficulty. Excel also allows you to create your own functions using VBA (Visual Basic for Applications).

Worksheet functions in Excel can be broadly classified into:

1. Mathematical Functions
2. Statistical Functions
3. Logical Functions
4. Financial Functions
5. Text Functions
6. Date and Time Functions

Mathematical Functions

Excel provides many mathematical functions for performing different arithmetical operations. Some of the commonly used functions are explained below:

ROUND( ) The ROUND( ) function rounds off a number to the specified number of decimal places. In our present example, we have a number 3.786 which we want to round off to only two decimals. This can be done as shown.

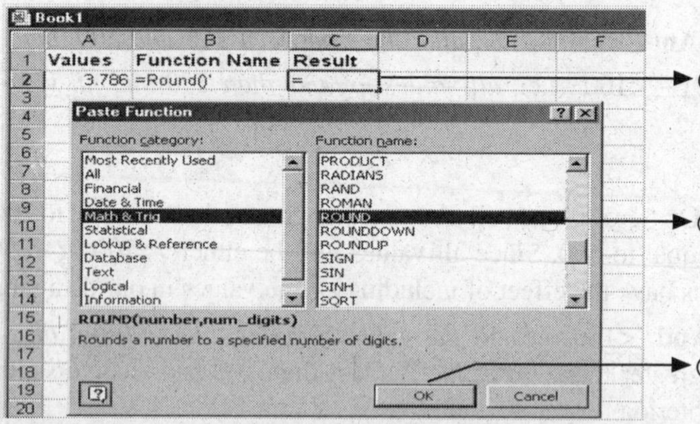

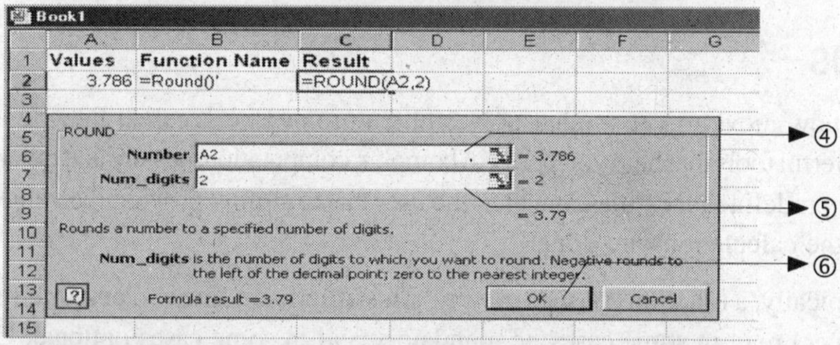

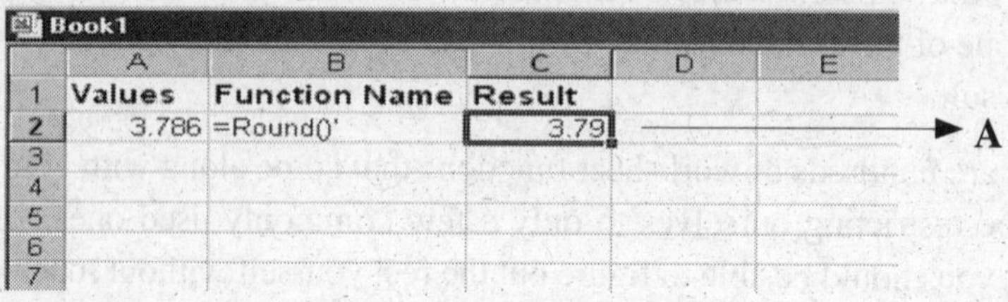

(1) Place the cursor where you want the function result to appear and choose **Function** from the **Insert menu.**

(2) Choose the **Math & Trigo** from the **functions Catagory** and **Round** from the **functions name.**

(3) Click once on the **OK** button.

(4) Type or point on the Cell number which has to be rounded off.

(5) Type the number of digits you want its round off.

(6) Click once on the **OK** button.

A The result would be displayed in the cell where you had initially placed the cursor.

Other Mathematical Functions

S.No.	Function	Description	Example
1.	ABS **(number)**	Returns the absolute value of a number, a number without plus or minus sign.	ABS(-45) = 45
2.	FACT **(number)**	Returns the factorial of a number, equal to number * number-1…. * 1.	FACT(5) = 120
3.	INT **(number)**	Rounds a number down to the nearest integer.	INT(4.9) = 4
4.	MOD **(number, divisor)**	Returns the remainder after a number is divided by a divisor.	MOD(10,3) = 1
5.	ROMAN **(number,** from)	Converts an arabic numeral to roman, as text. Form is a number specifying the type of roman numeral you want. Form can take values from 0 to 4.	ROMAN(4,0) = IV ROMAN(-4,0) = If number is negative, the #VALUE! error value is returned.
6.	SIGN **(number)**	Returns the sign of a number, 1 if positive, 0 if the number is zero, or -1 if the number is negative.	SIGN(-5) = -1
7.	SQRT **(number)**	Returns the square root of a number.	SQRT(9) = 3
8.	SUM **(number1,** number2.....)	Adds all the numbers in a range of cells. Number1, number2, ... are 1 to 30 arguments for which you want the total value or sum.	SUM(3,2,3) = 8
9.	SUMIF **(range, criteria,** sum_range)	Adds the cells specified by a given criteria. Sum_range are the actual cells to sum, if omitted the cells in range will be added.	Suppose A1:A4 contain 1,2,3,3 then SUMIF(A1:A4,">1") = 8
10.	TRUNC **(number,** num_digits)	Truncates a number to an integer by removing the fractional part of the number. Num_digits specify the position of truncation.	TRUNC(5.999,1) = 5.9

Notes:

1. An argument in bold letters indicates that it is mandatory; it must be supplied to view the output of a function.
2. Follow the steps explained for **ROUND( )** function to work with the above functions.

Statistical Functions

Excel provides many functions that can be used for analysing and summarising data.

AVERAGE ( ) The AVERAGE ( ) function calculates the average of a series of specified numbers. Let us see how this can be done:

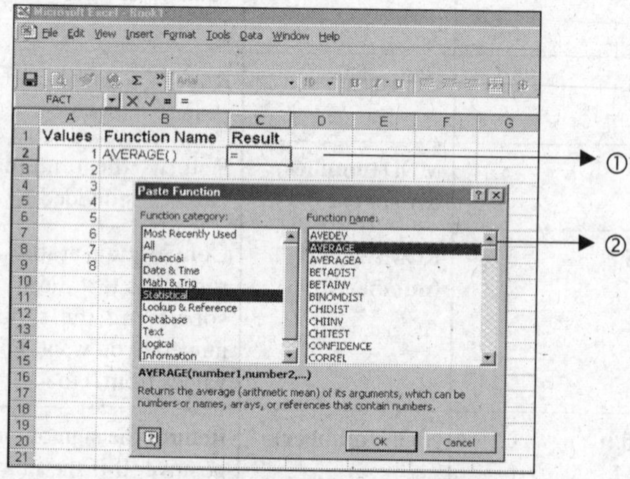

① Place the cursor where you want the function result to appear and choose **Function** from the **Insert Menu.**

② Choose **Statistical** from the **Function Category** and **AVERAGE** from the Function Name. Click once on the OK button.

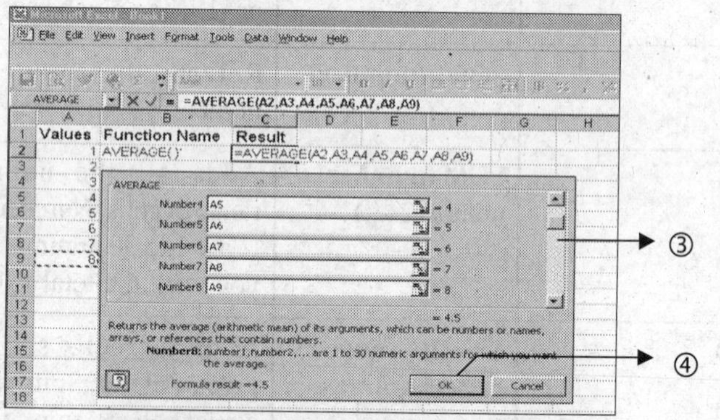

③ Either type the range or point to the cells (with the mouse) which contains the numbers for which average has to be calculated.

④ Click once on the OK button.

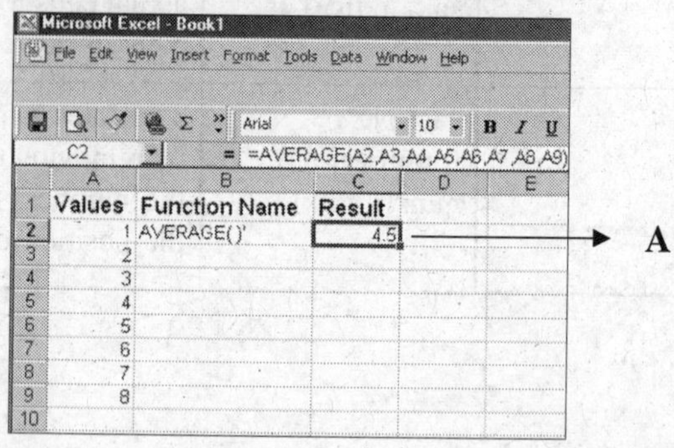

A The result would be displayed in the cell where you had initially placed the cursor.

Other Statistical Functions

	Function	Description	Example
1.	COUNT **(value1,** value2....)	Returns the number of entries in a specified range. Value1, value2, are 1 to 30 arguments that can contain or refer to a variety of different types of data, but only numbers are counted.	Suppose A1 contains 'Hello', A2 contains 20 and A3 contains' 20-11-1978' then COUNT (A1:A3) = 3
2.	COUNTBLANK **(range)**	Returns the number of empty cells within the specified range. Cells with zero values are not counted.	Suppose A1 contains 1, A2 = 0, A3 = "and A4 =" then COUNTBLANK (A1:A4) = 2
3.	COUNTIF **(range, criteria)**	Returns the number of cells within the range that meets the specified criteria/condition.	Suppose A1 contains 1, A2 contains 20 and A3 contains 25 then COUNTIF (A1: A3,">20") = 2
4.	MAX **(number1,** number2,.....)	Returns the largest value in a set of values. Ignores logical values and text. Number1, number 2,...are 1 to 30 numbers for which you want to find the maximum value.	IF A1:A5 contain 1, 2, 3, 4, 5, then MAX (A1:A5) = 5 MAX (A1:A5,75) = 75
5.	MIN **(number1,** number2,.....)	Returns the smallest value in a set of values. Ignores logical values and text. Number 1, number 2,...are 1 to 30 numbers for which you want to find the minimum value.	If A1:A5 contain 1,2,3,4,5 then MIN (A1:A5) = 1 MIN (A1:A5,-1) = -1

Notes:

1. An argument in bold letters indicates that it is mandatory; it must be supplied to view the output of a function.
2. Follow the steps explained for AVERAGE( ) function to work with the above functions.

LOGICAL FUNCTIONS

They use True and False statements to evaluate a condition or return information. 'IF' is the most commonly used logical function. Excel also provides 'AND', 'OR', 'NOT' operators that can be used in conjunction with the 'IF' function.

IF ( ) The IF ( ) function is one of the most useful and powerful functions available in Excel. Through this function you can conduct conditional tests on values and formulas and execute some operation based upon the result of that text. If the specified criterion or condition is satisfied IF returns a value T (for True) otherwise F (for False). In our present example we have a number in cell A2. Based upon the number in this cell we want to write down 'Century' or 'Better Luck Next Time' in cell C2. Let us see how this can be done.

(1) Place the cursor where you want the function result to appear and choose **Function** from the **Insert** menu.

(2) Choose the **logical** from the **Function category** and **IF** from the **Function name.** Click once on the **OK** button.

(3) Type the 'logical-test' value.

(4) Type the 'Value-if-true'.

(5) Type the 'Value-if-false'.

(6) Click on the **OK** button.

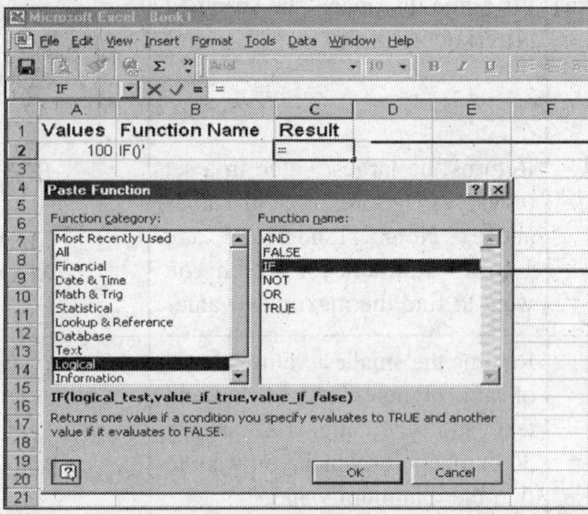

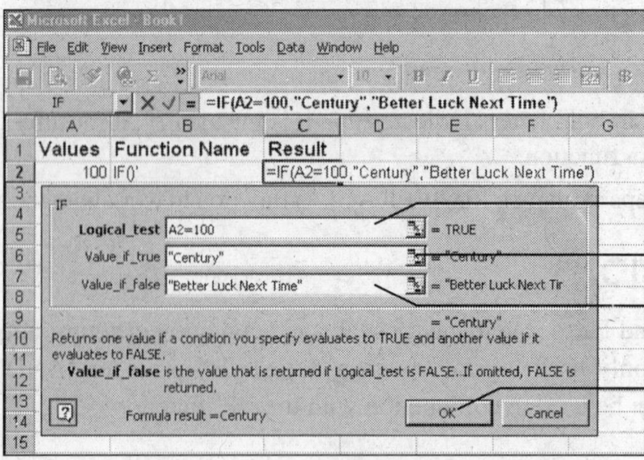

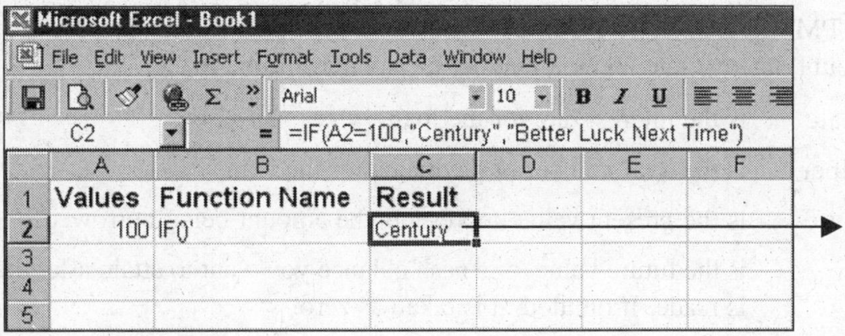

A

Other Logical Functions

S.No.	Function	Description	Example
1.	AND (**logical1, logical2,....**)	Return true if all the arguments are true. Returns false if any argument is false. Logical1, logical2, ... are 1 to 30 conditions you want to test that can be either TRUE or FALSE.	AND (true, true) = TRUE AND (true, false) = FALSE AND (false, false) = FALSE
2.	OR (**logical1, logical2,....**)	Return true if any argument is true. Return false if all the arguments are false. Logical1, lofical2,... are 1 to 30 conditions you want to test that can be either TRUE or FALSE.	OR (true, true) = TRUE OR (true, false) = FALSE OR (false, false) = FALSE
3.	NOT (**logical**)	Reverses the logic of its argument, i.e., if the argument is TRUE it returns FALSE and vice versa.	NOT (TRUE) = FALSE NOT (FALSE) = TRUE

Notes:

1. An argument in bold letters indicates that it is mandatory; it must be supplied to view the output of a function.
2. Follow the steps explained for IF( ) function to work with the above functions.

Financial Functions

Excel's financial functions can be used to perform the commonly required financial calculations. They can be used to calculate information such as interest, principal amount etc.

PMT(rate, nper, pv, fv, type) — Calculates the payment amount for the specified loan amount, interest rate and the number of payments to be made.

Rate	is the interest rate for the loan.
Nper	is the total number of payments for the loan.
Pv	is the present value, represents the amount being borrowed.
Fv	is the future value, or a cash balance you want to attain after the last payment is made. If omitted, it is taken as zero.
Type	It can be 0 (payments are due at the end of the year) or 1 (payments are due at the beginning of the year). If omitted, it is taken as zero.

Let us calculate the monthly payment on a loan of $3000 for 3 months at an annual interest of 10 per cent.

① Place the cursor where you want the function result to appear and choose **Function** from the Insert menu.

② Choose **Financial** from the function category and **PMT** from the function name. Click on the **OK** button.

③ Supply appropriate values for all the arguments.

④ Click once on the **OK** button.

A The result would be displayed in the cell where you had initially placed the cursor.

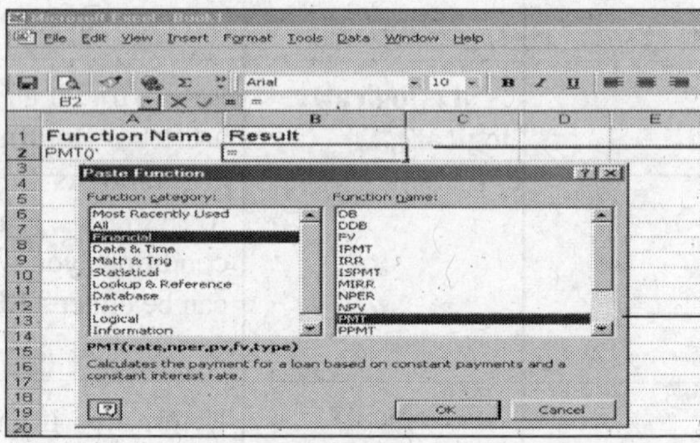

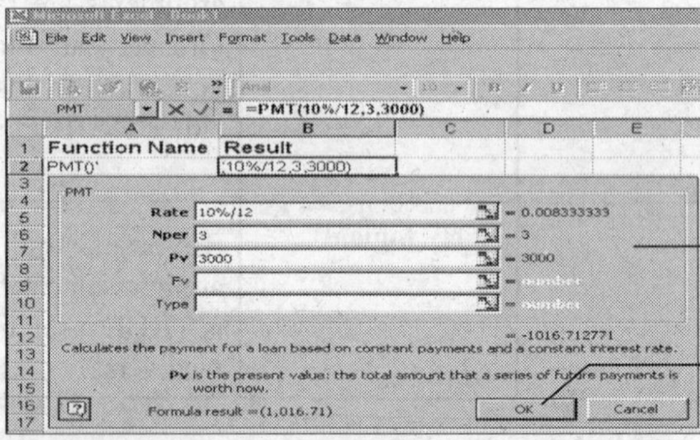

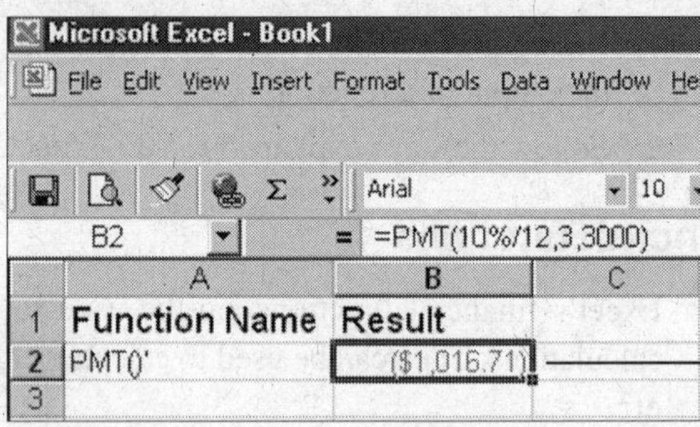

Other Financial Functions

S.No.	Function	Description	Example
1.	IPMT (**rate, per, nper, pv**, fv, type)	Returns the interest payment for a given period for an investment based on constant payments and a constant interest rate. Rate, nper, pv, fv and type will have the same meaning as they had in PMT(). Per is the period for which you want to find the interest and must be in the range 1 to nper.	To determine the interest due in the first month of a 3 month $3000 at 10% annual interest- IPMT (.1/12,1,3,3000) = $25
2.	NPER (**rate, pmt, pv**, fv, type)	Returns the number of periods required to pay back a loan assuming constant payments and a constant interest rate. Rate, pv, fv and type will have the same meaning as they had in PMT() Pmt is the payment made for each period.	NPER(.1/12,-50,3000) = 83.53 pmt is negative because the cash that you pay is taken as negative. This gives the number of periods needed to pay off a loan of $3000 when $50 are paid every month and the interest rate = 10% pa.

Notes:

1. An argument in bold letters indicates that it is mandatory; it must be supplied to view the output of a function.
2. Follow the steps explained for PMT() function to work with the above functions.

TEXT FUNCTIONS

Excel provides numerous for manipulating text strings. Some of the basic text functions are explained below:

UPPER( )

The UPPER ( ) function is used to convert your case text entry into upper case, i.e. capital letters. In cell A13 there is a text entry 'big' which has to be converted to caps. Let us see how this can be done.

① Place the cursor where you want the function result to appear and choose Function from the Insert menu.

② Choose **Text** from the **Function Category** and **UPPER** from the **Function Name**. Click once on the **OK** button to continue.

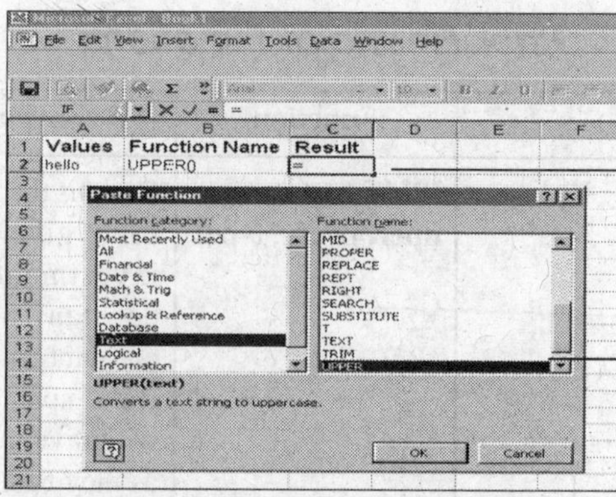

③ Type or specify (through the mouse) the cell address in which the text to be converted is there, i.e., A2.

④ Click once on the **OK** button.

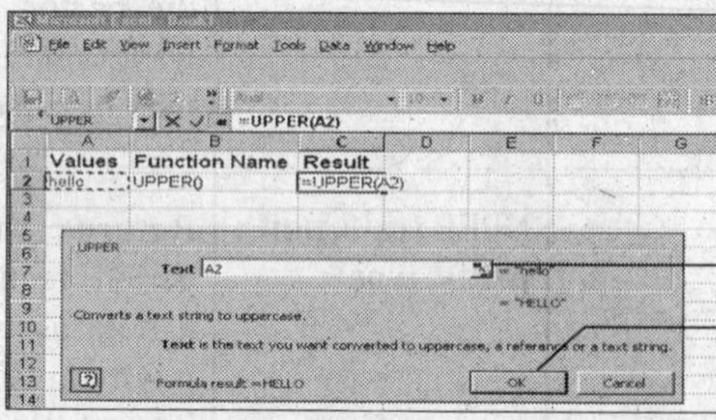

A Since the value in cell A2 was 'hello', the results would be displayed in the cell where you had initially placed the cursor.

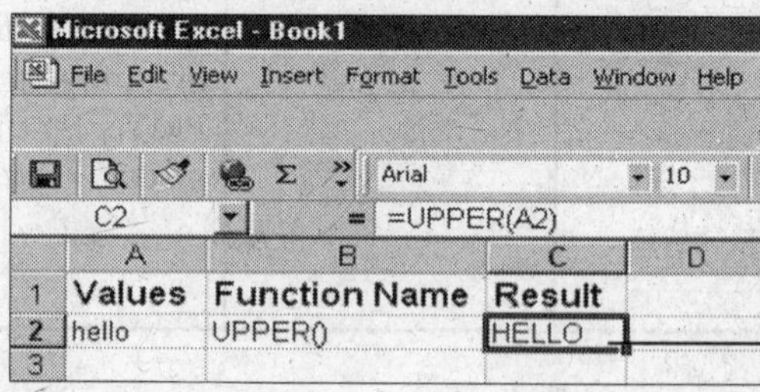

Other Text functions

Notes:

1. An argument in bold letters indicates that it is mandatory; it must be supplied to view the output of a function.
2. Follow the steps explained for UPPER() function to work with the above functions.

S.No.	Function	Description	Example
1.	CHAR (**number**)	Returns the character for the specified code number from the character set used by your computer. Number is a number between 1 and 255 specifying which character you want.	CHAR(65) = A
2.	CODE (**text**)	Returns the code number for the first character in the specified text string, in the character set used by your computer.	CODE(A) = 65 CODE(AND) = 65

S.No.	Function	Description	Example
3.	FIND (**find_text, within_txt**, start_num)	Finds one text string (find_text) within another text string (within_text) and returns the number of the starting position of the found text string. FIND is case sensitive and doesn't allow wild card characters. Start_num specifies the character at which the search should be started.	FIND("e", "hello") = 2 FIND("e", "Elate") = 5
4.	LEFT(**text**, num_chars)	Returns the specified number of leftmost characters (num_chars) from the text string.	LEFT("HELLO",4) = HELL LEFT("HELLO") = H
5.	LEN (**text**)	Returns the number of characters in the text. Blank spaces are also counted as characters.	LEN ("HELLO WORLD") = 11
6.	LOWER (**text**)	Returns the text in lower case.	LOWER("HELLO) = hello
7.	REPLACE (**old_text, start_num, num_chars, new_text**)	Replaces part of a text string(old_text), based on the number of characters you specify, with a different text string(new_text). Start_num is the position of the character in old_text that you want to replace with new_text. Num_chars is the number of characters in old_text that you want REPLACE to replace with new_text.	REPLACE("2000",4, 1,"3") = 2003 REPLACE("A*D", 2,1,"BC") = ABCD
8.	RIGHT (**text**, num_chars)	Returns the specified number of rightmost characters (num_chars) from the text string.	RIGHT("HELLO", 4) = ELLO RIGHT("HELLO") = O
9.	SEARCH (**find_text, within_text**, start_num)	Similar to FIND() except that it allows using wildcards in the text string and is case in sensitive.	SEARCH("H", "HELLO") = 1

DATE AND TIME FUNCTIONS

Date and time are internally stored as numbers in Excel. These numbers are called as Serial Numbers. Date and Time can be calculated from the serial number. Date can be calculated by counting the number of days passed since Jan. 1, 1900 and Time can be calculated as percentage of 24 hrs. Example–the serial number 37781.770833333 represents June 9, 2003 and 6.30 PM. Left portion of the decimal point indicates the date and the right portion indicates the time. Basic DATE and TIME functions are explained below:

Today ( )

The TODAY function is one of the few functions that do not require any user argument. It simply returns the current date. Let us see how this works.

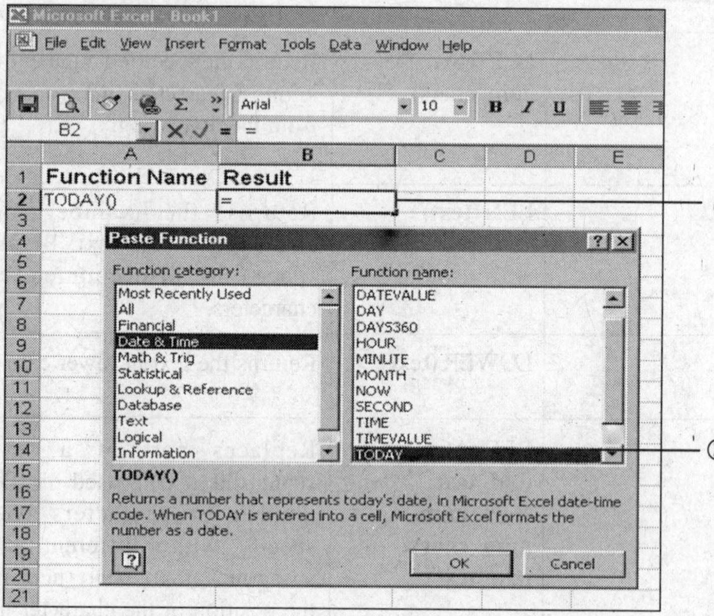

① Place the cursor where you want the function result to appear and choose Function from the Insert menu.

② Choose **Date & Time** from the **Function Category** and **TODAY** from the **Function Name**.

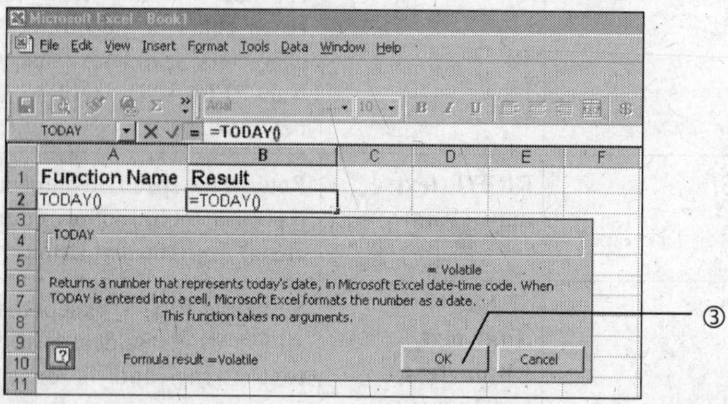

③ Click once on the **OK** button to continue.

A Output

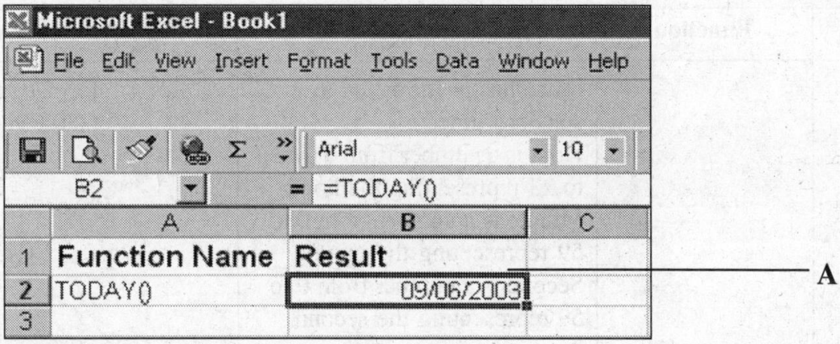

Other DATE and TIME Functions

S.No.	Function	Description	Example
1.	DATE **(year,month, day)**	Returns the serial number that represents a particular date. This serial number is immediately formatted as a standard date.	DATE(2003,5,5) returns 37746 which is automatically form-atted by Excel as 05/05/2003
2.	DAY **(serial_number)**	Returns the day of a date, represented by a serial number. The day is given as an integer ranging from 1 to 31. The argument can be a text string within quotation marks ("20/11/1978"), a serial number or a valid cell reference.	DAY("15-Apr-2003") = 15
3.	MONTH **(serial_number)**	Returns the month of a date, represented by a serial number. The month is given as an integer ranging from 1 to 12. The argument can be a text string within quotation marks ("20/11/1978"), a serial number or a valid cell reference.	MONTH("15-Apr-2003") = 4
4.	NOW()	Returns the current date and time.	NOW() = 09/06/2003 18:30
5.	TIME **(hour, minute, second)**	Returns the decimal number that represents a particular time. This decimal number is	TIME(18,30,00) returns 770833333 which is automatically

S.No.	Function	Description	Example
		immediately formatted as a standard time. Hour is a number from 0 (zero) to 23 representing the hour. Minute is a number from 0 to 59 representing the minute. Second is a number from 0 to 59 representing the second.	formatted by Excel as 6.30 PM.
6.	YEAR **(serial_number)**	Returns the year of a date, represented by a serial number. The year is returned as an integer in the range 1900-9999. The argument can be a text string within quotation marks ("20/11/ 1978"), a serial number or a valid cell reference.	YEAR("15-Apr-1978") = 1978

Notes:

1. An argument in bold letters indicates that it is mandatory; it must be supplied to view the output of a function.
2. Follow the steps explained for TODAY() function to work with the above functions.

CREATING CHARTS AND GRAPHS

It is often easy to understand information that is presented graphically. Charts make it easy for users to see comparisons, patterns, and trends in data rapidly. Excel contains powerful charting wizards and tools that can be used to build effective and impressive charts. Excel comes with a wide variety of chart styles, including bar, pie, column, scatter, bubble and many more. Once a chart is created, you can customise it to suit your requirements. You can add, edit or delete titles, labels, legends and gridlines in a chart.

You can create a chart in its own chart sheet or as an embedded chart in a worksheet. A chart sheet is a separate sheet within your workbook that has its own sheet name. An embedded chart is a chart that is displayed directly in a worksheet. A chart is always linked to the worksheet data it's created from and any changes done on the worksheet data are automatically reflected in the chart.

By default Excel creates a Column type chart. However, the default chart type can be changed to some other chart type.

Creating a Chart using the default settings:

① Select the data you wish to include in the chart.

② Press the F11 key; a column type chart will be created.

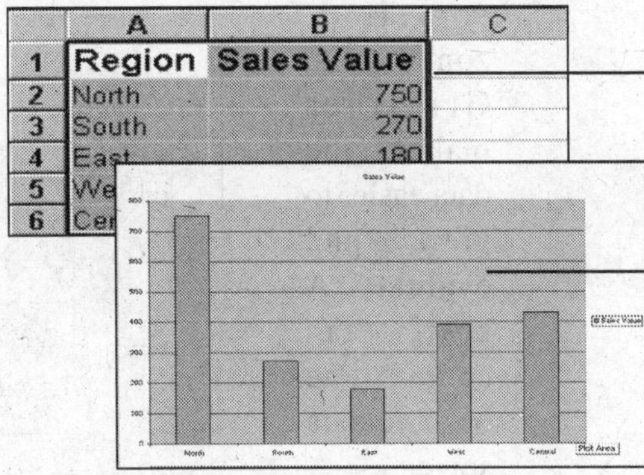

Changing the default Chart type:

① Right click on the chart and choose **Chart type** from the pop up menu.

② Select the desired chart type and click the **Set as Default Chart** button.

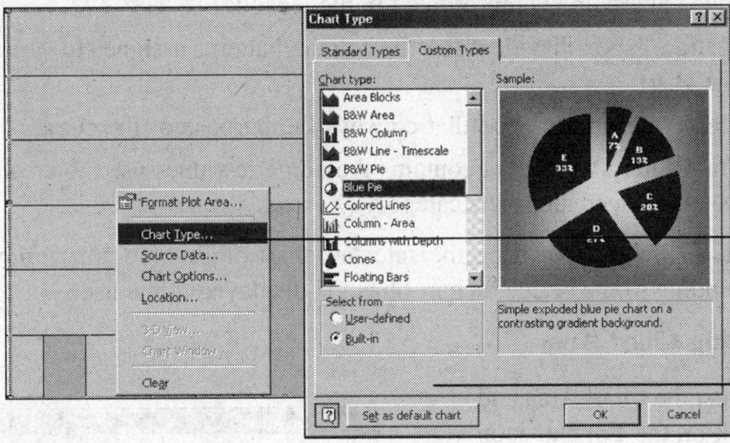

Chart Toolbar

To view the Chart toolbar Choose **Chart** from the **Toolbars** command under the **View** menu.

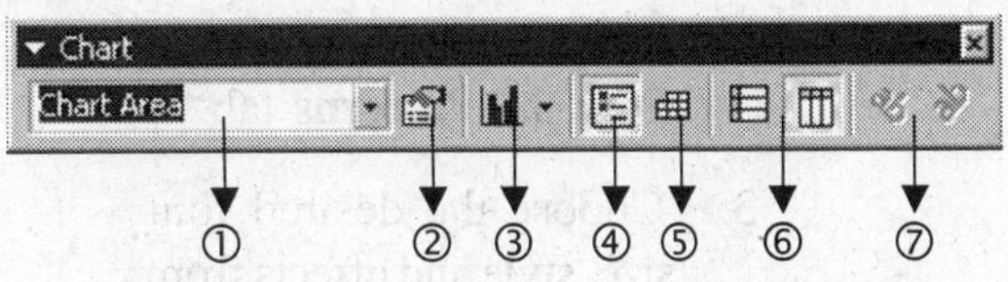

① Displays the various chart objects. A brief explanation of various chart elements/ objects is given below:

a. **Chart Area** It contains the entire chart and all of its elements. It is similar to a canvas.

b. **Plot Area** It contains the Axes, Gridlines and all Data Series. Usually values are plotted against the Y or the Vertical axis and categories are plotted ag-ainst the X

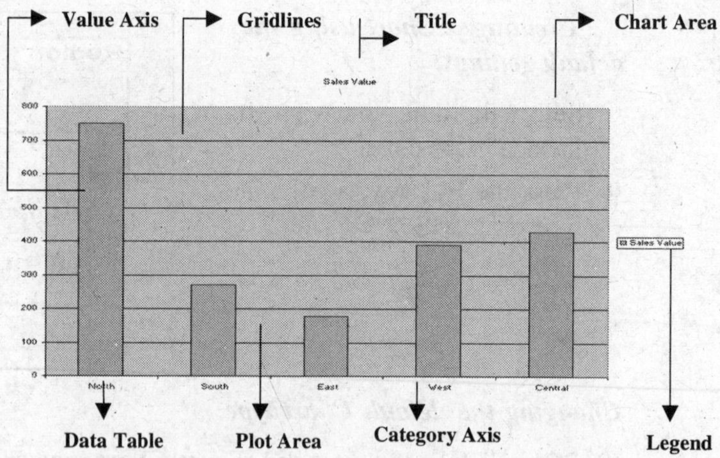

or Horizontal axis. Gridlines makes the data easier to view and evaluate. A chart can contain one or more data series. A data series is made up of an array of values and names indicating what the series represent. Each data series has a unique pattern and is represented in the legend.

c. **Legend:** A box that identifies the colours/patterns assigned to various data series in the chart.

d. **Title:** A descriptive text that conveys the purpose of the chart.

e. **Data Table:** A grid that contains the numeric values used to create the chart. It is usually placed along the category (X) axis.

② **Format** – Allows formatting the selected chart object. An appropriate dialog box corresponding to the selected chart object is displayed to the user.

a. Modifying Chart Area

1. Select the Chart Area and click on the **Format** icon from the Chart toolbar.
2. Choose the desired border style, colour and weight from the **Patterns** tab.
3. Choose the desired font size, style and effects from the **Font** tab. The Chart will use the selected font styles.
4. Click on **OK** button to apply your changes.

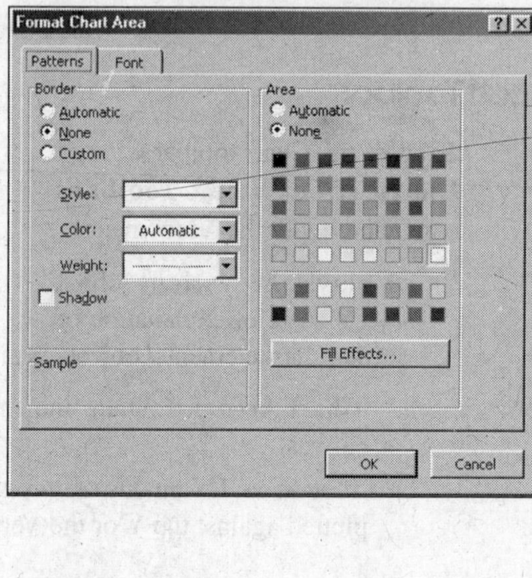

b. Modifying Plot Area

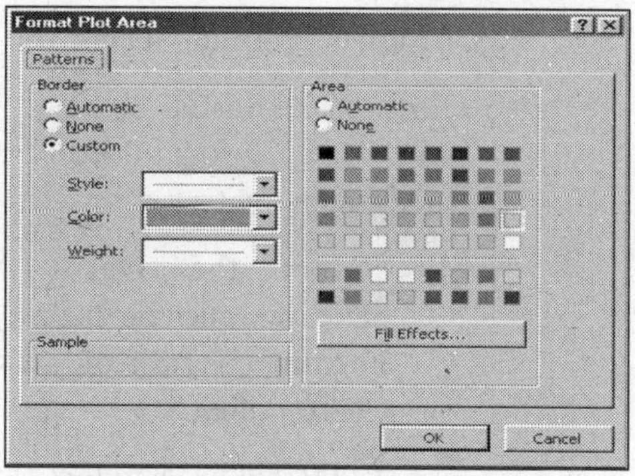

1. Select the Plot Area and click on the **Format** icon from the Chart toolbar.
2. Choose the desired border style, color and weight from the **Patterns** tab.
3. Click on **OK** button to apply your changes.

c. Modifying Axis

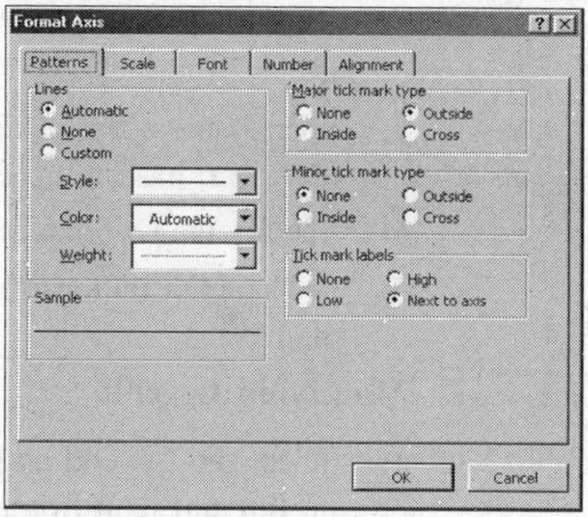

1. Select the Axis (X or Y) and click on the **Format** icon from the Chart toolbar.
2. Choose the desired line style, color and weight from the **Patterns** tab.
3. Specify the scale settings for Category and Value axis of your chart using the **Scale** tab.
4. Choose the desired font size, style and effects from the **Font** tab. The Axis will use the selected font styles.
5. Choose the desired number format for your axis labels from the **Number** tab.
6. Specify the alignment of axis labels using the Alignment tab.
7. Click on **OK** button to apply your changes.

d. Modifying Gridlines

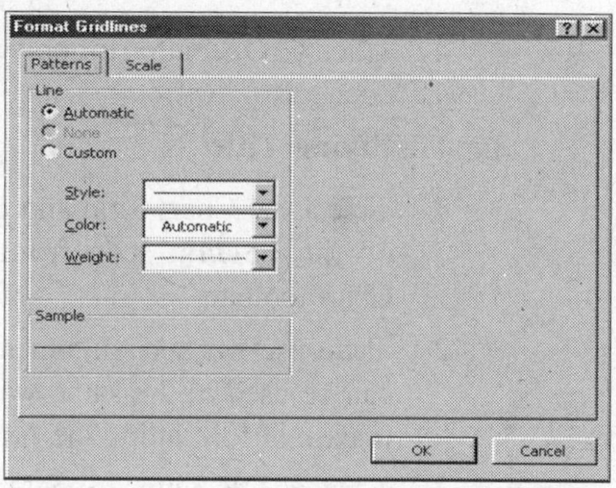

1. Select the Gridlines and click on the **Format** icon from the Chart toolbar.
2. Choose the desired line style, color and weight from the **Patterns** tab.
3. Specify the scale settings for Gridlines using the **Scale** tab.
4. Click on **OK** button to apply your changes.

e. Modifying Data Series

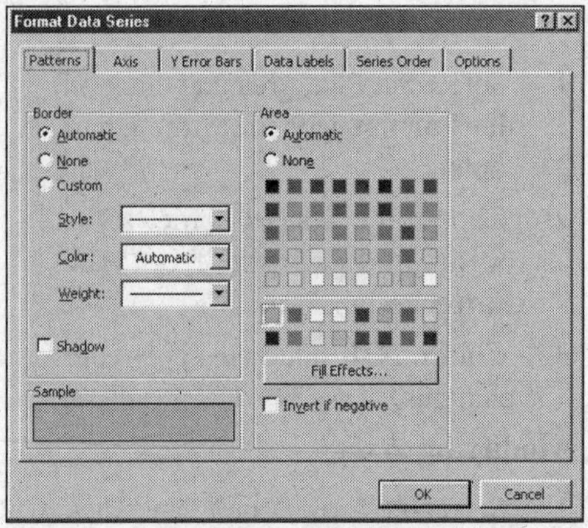

Each series in the chart can be formatted independently.

1. Select the Data Series and click on the **Format** icon from the Chart toolbar.
2. Choose label or value or per cent or both from the Data Labels tab.
3. Specify the order of data series using the **Series Order** tab. This holds good if your chart has multiple data series.
4. Specify the Overlap and Gap width using the **Options** tab.
5. Click on **OK** button to apply your changes.

f. Modifying Legend

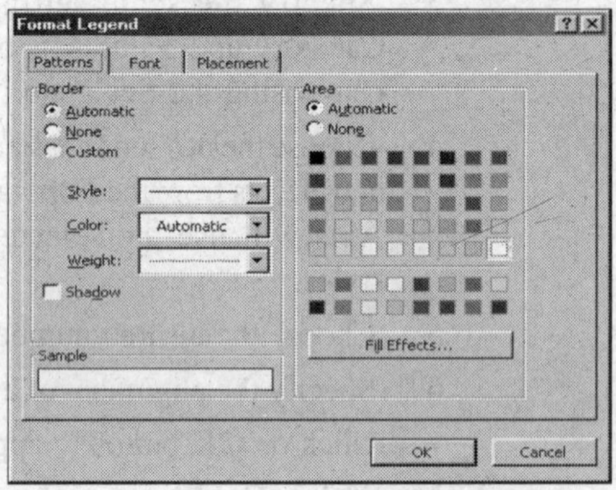

1. Select the Legend and click on the **Format** icon from the Chart toolbar.
2. Patterns and Font tab can be used in the same way as in case of formatting the Chart Area.
3. Choose the position (left/ right/ top/ bottom) of the legend in the chart.
4. Click on **OK** button to apply your changes.

g. Modifying Title

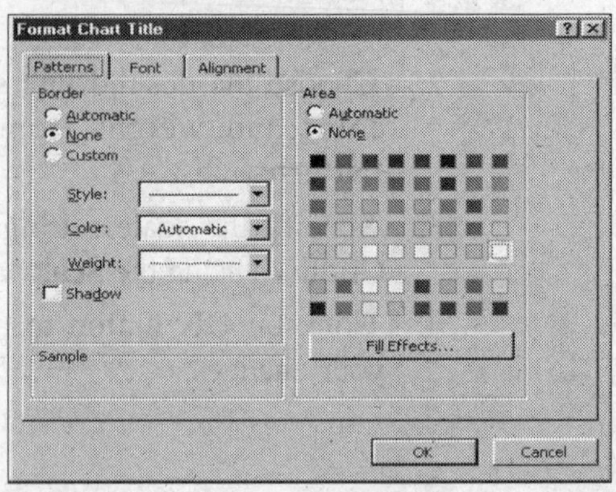

1. Select the Chart Title and click on the **Format** icon from the Chart toolbar.
2. Patterns, Font and Alignment tab can be used in the same way as in case of formatting the Axis.
3. Click on **OK** button to apply your changes.

h. Modifying Data Tables

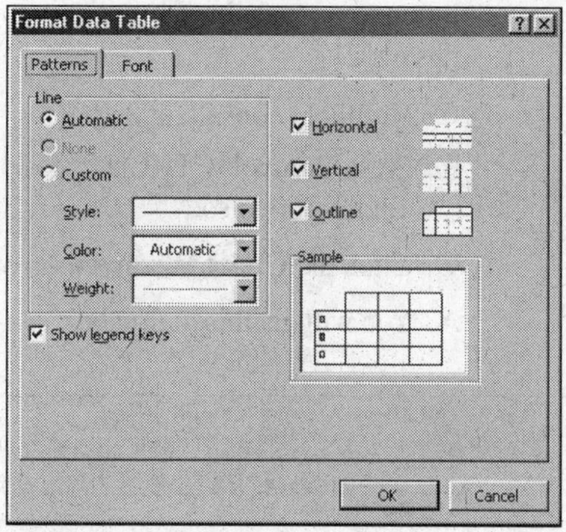

A chart may or may not have a data table. To add a data table, simply click the **Data Table** icon on the Chart toolbar.

1. Select the Data Table and click on the **Format** icon from the Chart toolbar.
2. Patterns and Font tab can be used in the same way as in case of formatting the Chart Area.
3. Click on **OK** button to apply your changes.

③ **Chart Type** Displays the available chart types in Excel. You can choose a type that that best suits your need.

④ **Legend** Displays/Hides the legend.

⑤ **Data Table** Displays/Hides the data table.

⑥ **By Row and By Column** Determines the chart's interpretation of your data.

⑦ **Angle Text Downward and Angle Text Upward** These buttons are enabled only when an object containing text is selected. They allow you to rotate text 45 degrees downward or upward.

CREATING A CHART USING CHART WIZARD

This wizard guides you through a series of steps that helps in creating your chart. Let us learn the usage of this wizard with the help of an example. The following example displays the quarterly billing of various consultants. You can calculate their annual total by defining an appropriate formula. Annual total would be sum of the four quarters.We can determine the most

Total Synergy Consulting Private Limited					
142A, Zamrudpur, Greater Kailash-I, New Delhi 110044					
Consultancy Division					
Domestic Billing for the year 1999-2000					
					Figures in '000
Consutant	**Qtr 1**	**Qtr 2**	**Qtr 3**	**Qtr 4**	**Yearly Total**
R.Bhatnagar	Rs.786	Rs.564	Rs.456	Rs.689	***Rs.2,495***
M.Lath	Rs.123	Rs.844	Rs.124	Rs.231	***Rs.1,322***
P.Sharma	Rs.136	Rs.435	Rs.745	Rs.231	***Rs.1,547***
K.Pandey	Rs.254	Rs.564	Rs.565	Rs.512	***Rs.1,895***
M.Swamy	Rs.456	Rs.785	Rs.776	Rs.568	***Rs.2,585***
A.Viz	Rs.643	Rs.145	Rs.755	Rs.664	***Rs.2,207***
S.Kumar	Rs.812	Rs.567	Rs.765	Rs.432	***Rs.2,576***
Bodh Prakash	Rs.854	Rs.674	Rs.989	Rs.432	***Rs.2,949***
R.Nahar	Rs.880	Rs.674	Rs.564	Rs.737	***Rs.2,865***
P.Chawla	Rs.616	Rs.654	Rs.890	Rs.324	***Rs.2,484***
	Rs.5,570	***Rs.5,906***	***Rs.6,629***	***Rs.4,820***	***Rs.22,925***

productive consultant by creating a chart. Follow the steps below to create a start using this data:

① Highlight consultant names.

② Press **Control** (CTRL) key to specify another discontinuous range, and highlight Yearly Total figure also.

③ Click the **Chart Wizard** icon on the **Standard Toolbar** to start the Chart Wizard.

A You will get this dialog box.

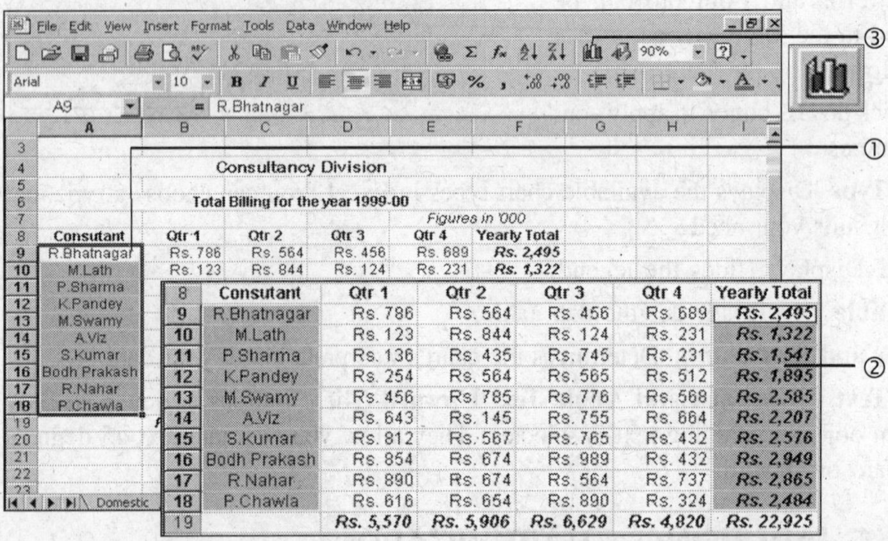

④ Select the desired chart type.

⑤ Select the 3D Chart sub type.

⑥ Click on 'Next' tab to continue.

B You will get this dialog box.

C The range of cells, which you have highlighted earlier, would be selected here automatically.

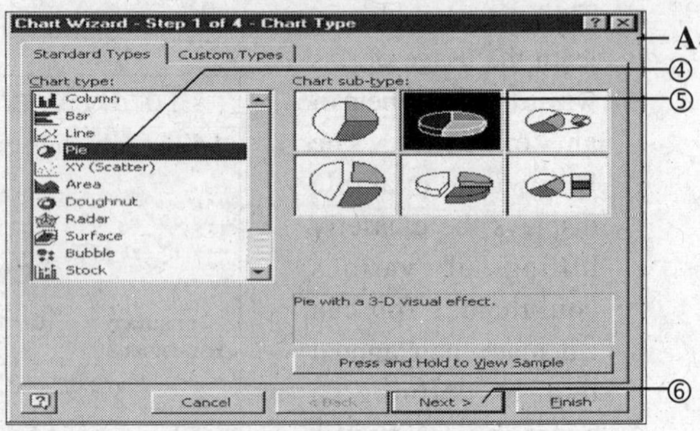

D This signifies that your data series is in columns and not rows.

⑦ Click here to continue.

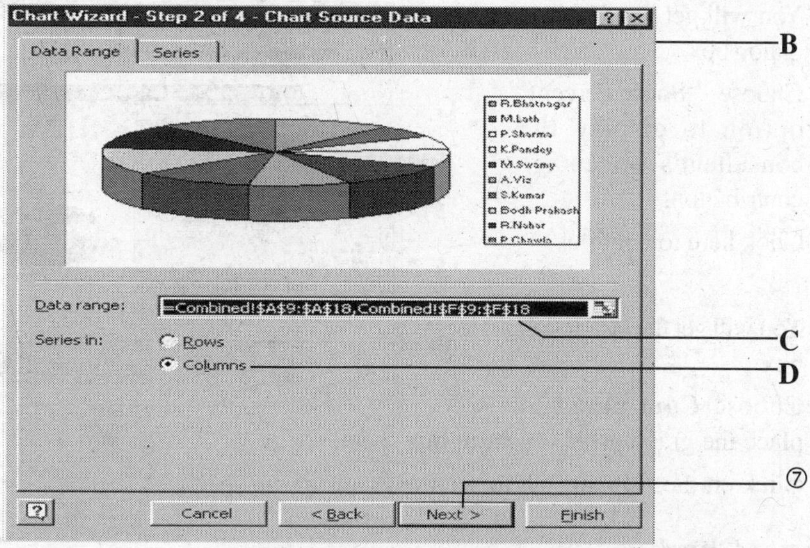

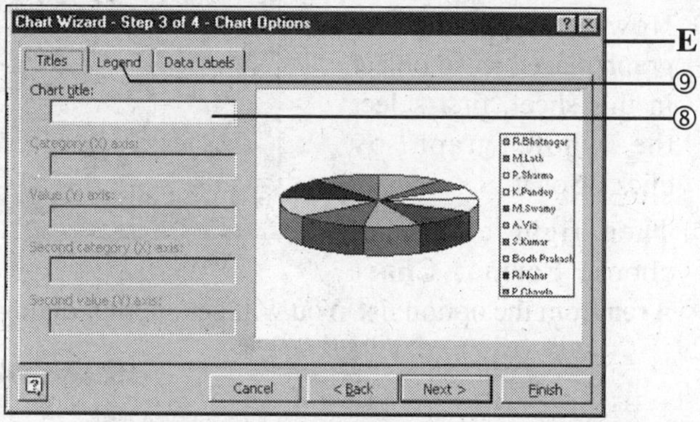

E You will get this dialogue box.

⑧ Type the Graph Title as 'Consultant's Contribution to Total Billing' after choosing **Title** folio.

⑨ Choose the **Legend** folio.

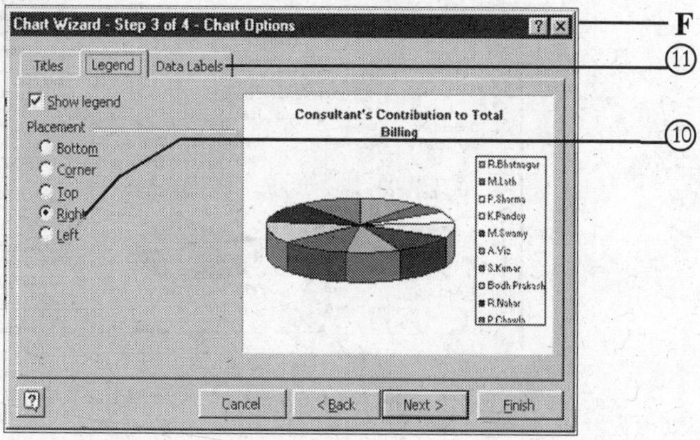

F Now you will get this dialogue box.

⑩ Click here once to specify the data legends to appear on any side of graph you desire (Here we let it remain on right side).

⑪ Choose **Data Labels** folio.

G You will get Data Labels dialog box.

⑫ Choose 'Show Percent' option to display the consultant's percentage contribution.

⑬ Click here to continue.

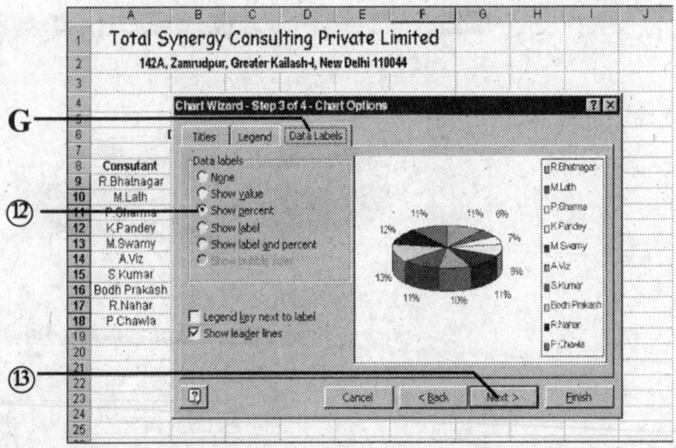

H You will get the last dialog box.

⑭ Choose **Com-bined** to place the graph as an object in this sheet.

⑮ Click on the **'Finish'** tab to see the graph.

Modifying a Chart

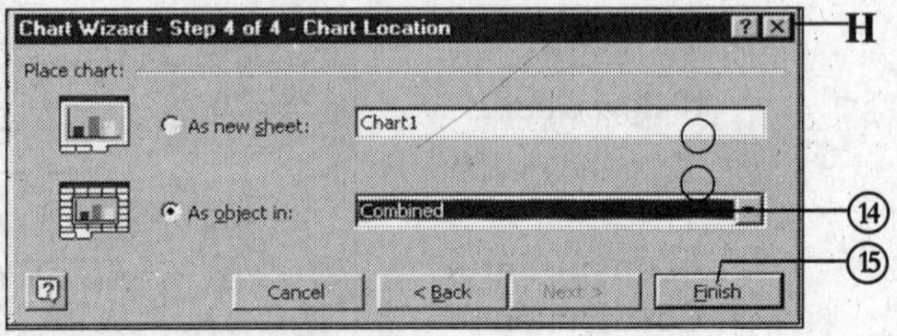

① Now after getting the graph placed as an object in this sheet, first select the whole graph by clicking on it.

② Then right click and choose **Format Chart Area** from the option list. You will get another dialog box.

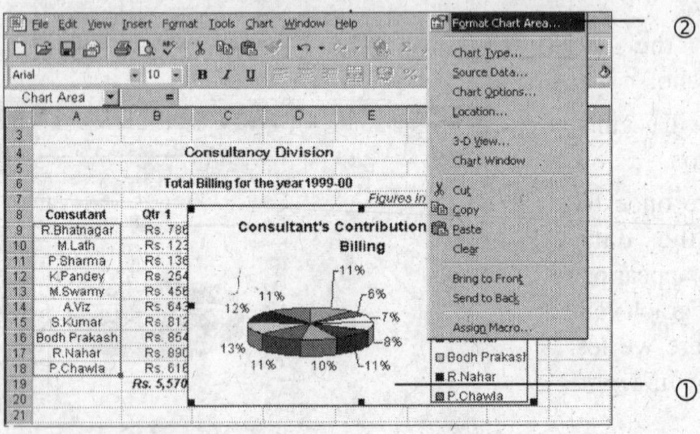

③ Choose the desired font.

④ Choose the font style.

⑤ Choose the font size.

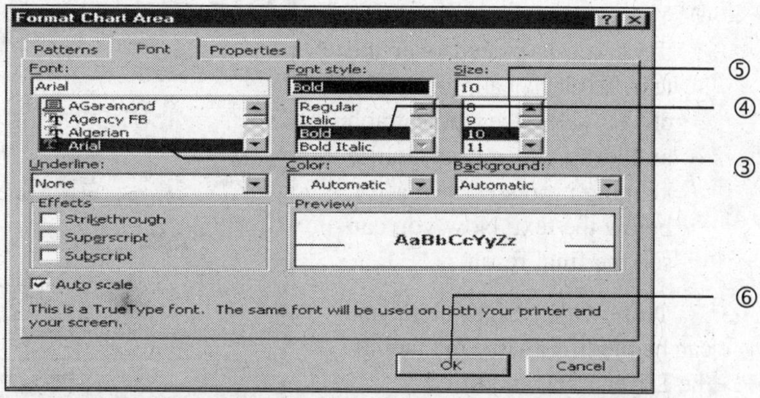

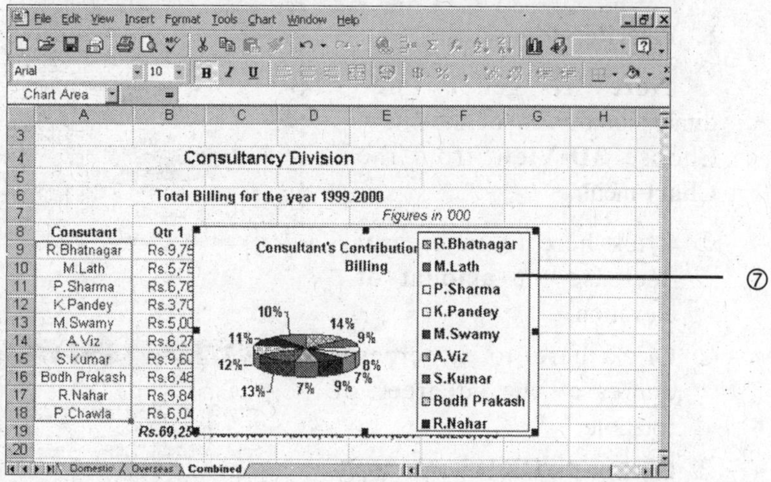

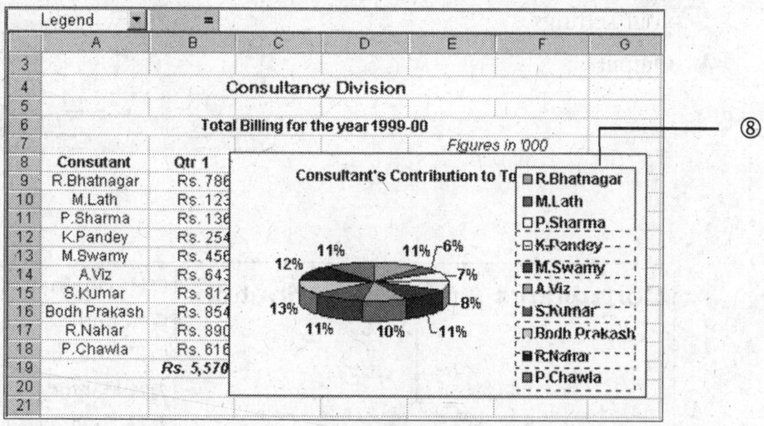

⑥ Click on OK button to get the formatted graph.

⑦ Since the legend is large, it needs to be resized. So select only the legend by clicking on it.

⑧ Click here and drag the mouse so that this box becomes smaller. Now it will appear on the lower right corner.

⑨ You would have noticed that the graph is placed over the text. To place it appropriately, click to select the whole graph and drag the mouse while keeping it pressed to place it below the text. Now you can see the final result.

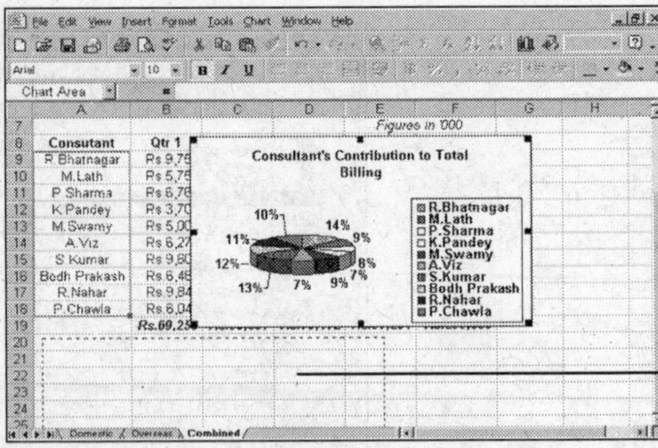

Note: Other Chart elements can be modified same manner as the Legend was modified.

I Final Result!

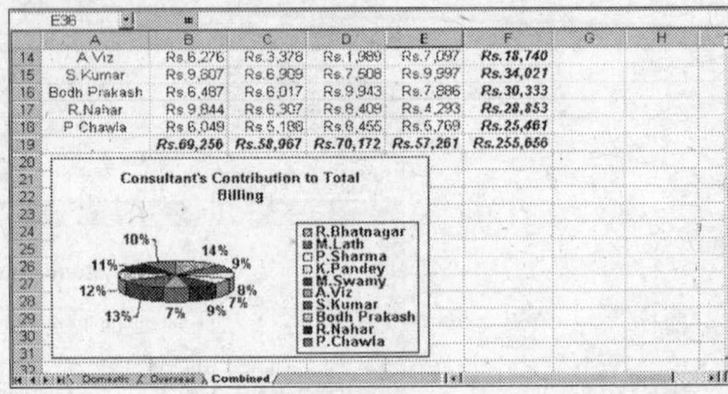

Note: To get a three dimensional view of the chart, Choose **3D-View** from the **Chart** menu.

① Click here to in crease/ decrease the amount of elevation.

② Click here to in crease/ decrease the degree of rotation.

③ Click on the **OK** button to apply your settings.

A Output

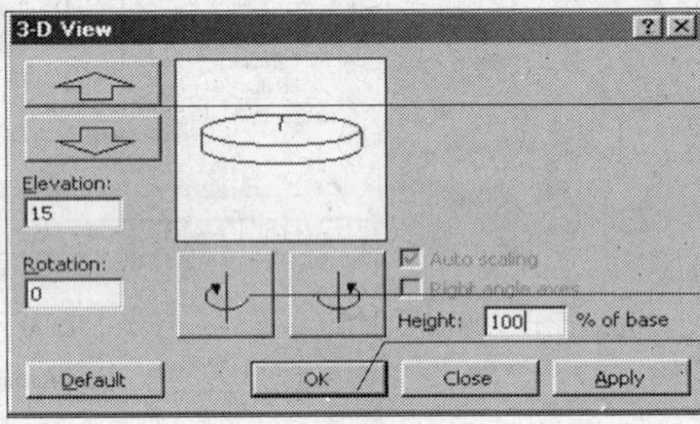

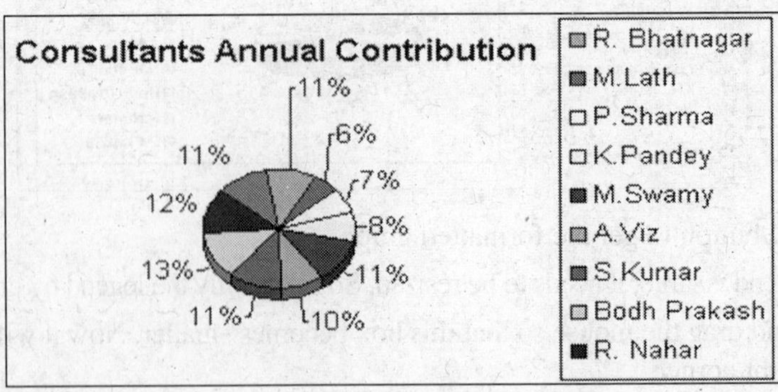

ADDING TRENDLINES

Trendlines are used to graphically display trends in data. As the name suggests, it shows the general trend, such as growth or decline that occurs in the data. Excel comes with six different types of trendlines:

1. **Linear** — It usually shows that something is increasing or decreasing at a steady rate.
2. **Logarithmic** — It is useful when the rate of change in the data increases or decreases quickly and then levels out. It can use negative and/or positive values.
3. **Polynomial** — It is a curved line that is used when data fluctuates. It is useful, for example, for analysing gains and losses over a large data set.
4. **Power** — It can be used with data sets that compare measurements that increase at a specific rate. It cannot be used for data that has zero or negative values.
5. **Exponential** — It is most useful when data values rise or fall at increasingly higher rates. It cannot be used for data that has zero or negative values.
6. **Moving Average** — It smoothes out fluctuations in data to show a pattern or trend more clearly. It uses a sequence of averages to reduce the effect of fluctuation from one data point to another.

To Add a Trendline

1. Select the data series for which you wish to add a trend line.
2. Choose **Add Trendline** from the **Chart** menu. Whenever a chart is created, the Chart menu is auto-matically added to the menu bar.
3. Specify the type of trendline you want for your data series in **Add Trendline** dialogue box.
4. Click the **OK** button to apply your changes.

A Output for the data series used in the first example for creating a chart using the default chart type.

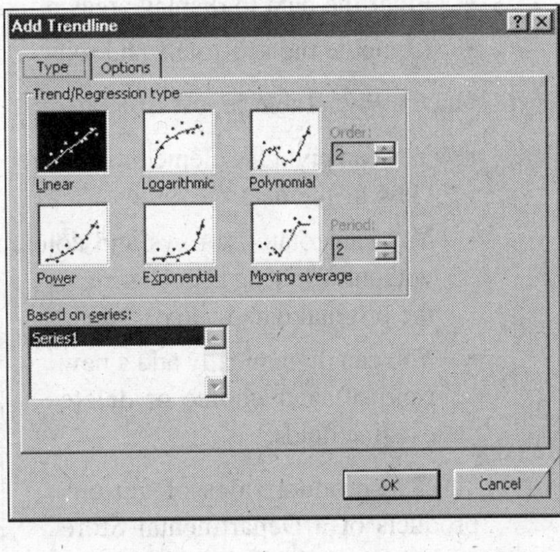

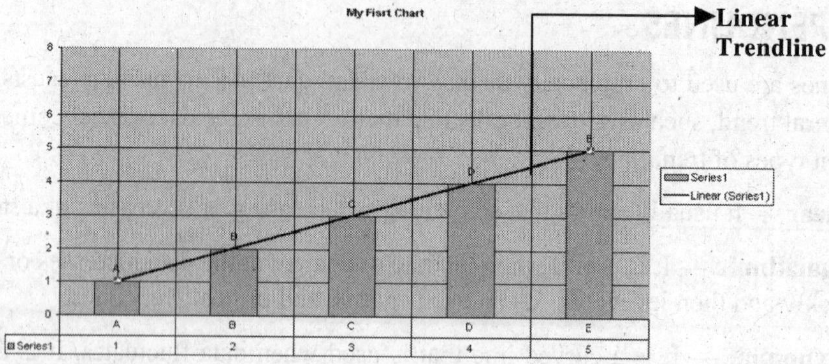

PivotTable Reports

These reports can be used in almost any environment to simplify data analysis but their real use is appreciated when dealing with large amounts of data. You can create a PivotTable report from an Excel worksheet or using an external source. An external source could be any source that exists outside MS Excel, such as a database (Access, Oracle or SQL Server), Text file or a source on the Internet. Some of the advantages of using PivotTable Reports are outlined below:

A PivotTable report can be used to:

- Summarise large amounts of data into a flexible format.
- Compare field/column values across multiple categories.
- Filter the data to display areas of concern.
- Compute the sub-totals and totals.

Once a PivotTable report is created:

- You can pivot the elements of the report to new positions within the table for a different view of the data.
- You can rotate its rows and columns to see different summaries of the source data without worrying about harming the original data source.
- You can dynamically add a new field of your choice or delete existing fields.

The product sales of various products of a Departmental Store are displayed in the following example. Let us understand the usefulness of a PivotTable report by taking this example:

	A	B	C	D	E	F
1						
2	**Needs Departmental Store - Quarterly Sales (2003)**					
3						
4	**Product Name**	**Category**	**Month**	**Quantity**	**Unit Price**	**Sales (Rs.)**
5	Pens	Stationary	April	50	25	1000
6	Pens	Stationary	May	55	25	1000
7	Pens	Stationary	June	40	25	875
8	Pencils	Stationary	April	100	12	720
9	Pencils	Stationary	May	96	12	960
10	Pencils	Stationary	June	86	12	960
11	SketchPens	Stationary	April	20	55	550
12	SketchPens	Stationary	May	18	55	550
13	SketchPens	Stationary	June	26	55	1100
14	Perfumes	Gift Items	April	35	190	3800
15	Perfumes	Gift Items	May	45	190	7600
16	Perfumes	Gift Items	June	52	190	7600
17	Wrist Watches	Gift Items	April	10	550	5500
18	Wrist Watches	Gift Items	May	8	550	2750
19	Wrist Watches	Gift Items	June	12	550	5500
20	Teddy Bears	Gift Items	April	5	300	1500
21	Teddy Bears	Gift Items	May	4	300	600
22	Teddy Bears	Gift Items	June	8	300	1500

Creating a PivotTable report using PivotTable wizard:

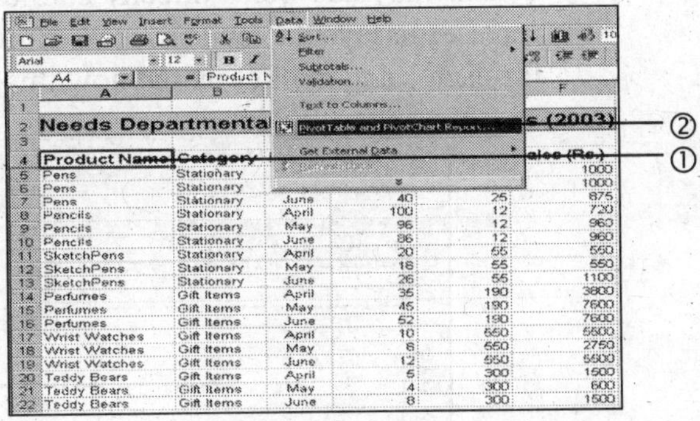

① Open the workbook where you wish to create the PivotTable report. Select a cell in your data range.

② Choose **Pivot Table** and **Pivot-Chart Report** to start the PivotTable wizard.

③ Choose **Microsoft Excel list** as your data source. If your data is stored in an Excel Workbook then you can choose this option. If your data is stored in a database then you can choose External Data Source option.

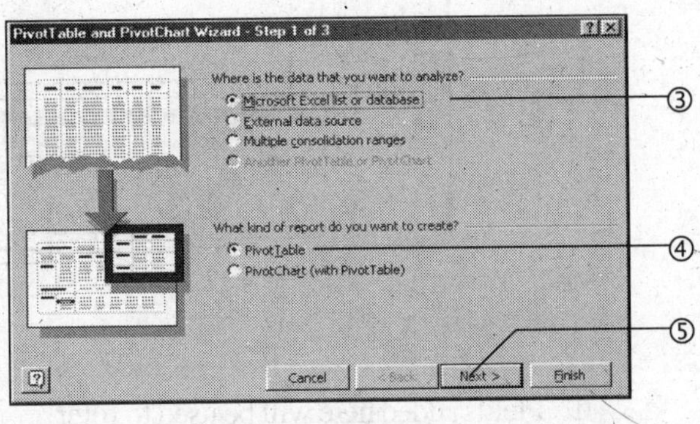

④ Specify the kind of report (PivotTable or PivotChart) you wish to create.

⑤ Click on the **Next** button to continue.

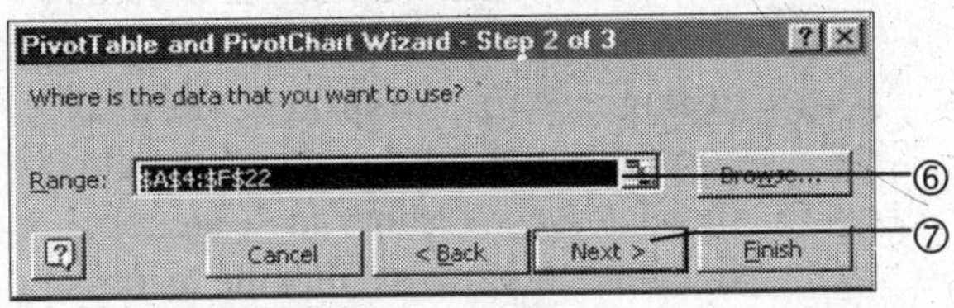

⑥ Indicate the location of the source data. If you have selected a cell in the data range prior to starting the wizard then Excel would automatically select the entire range, including the column headings.

⑦ Click on the **Next** button to continue.

⑧ Specify the location of the PivotTable report. You can choose to place the report in the existing workbook or a new workbook.

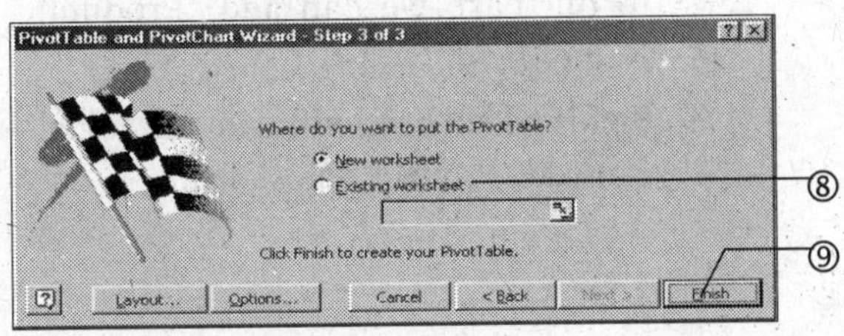

⑨ Click on the **Finish** button to create the PivotTable report.

A Output–This kind of output is referred to as **OnScreen Layout**, which allows you to dynamically add fields directly onto the worksheet from the PivotTable toolbar. We can use this layout to build a report displaying the monthly sales of all/selected products for each category. Let us see how this can be done!

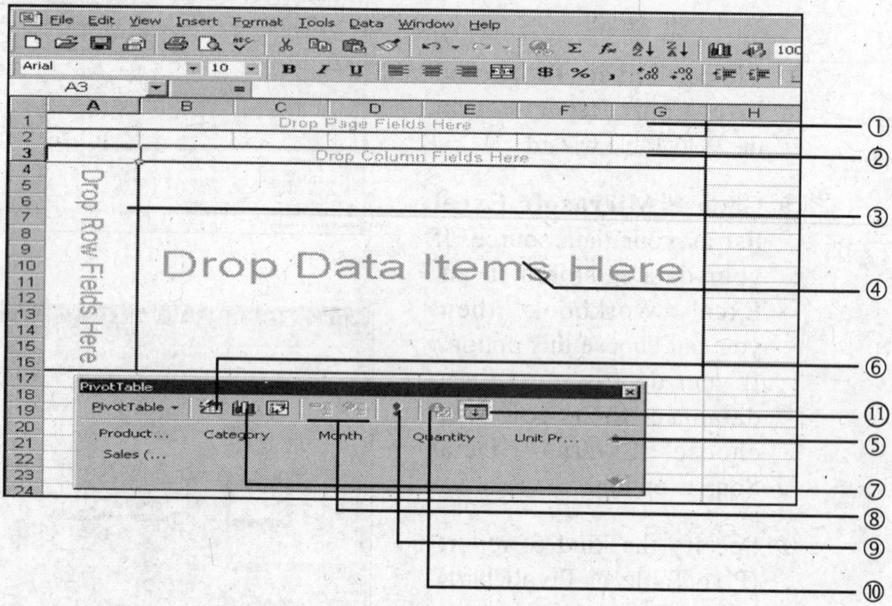

① Fields added here will be used to filter the view. When you select a value within a **Page Field**, the report changes to display records corresponding to the selected field. In our case we can add 'Category' field into this area to filter the records according to the product category.

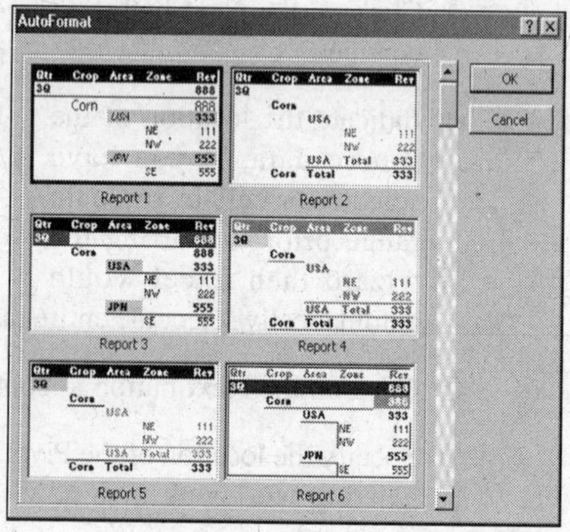

② Fields added here will serve as column headings. In our case we can add 'Month' field.

③ Fields added here will serve as headings for the rows of information. In our case we can add 'Product Name' field.

④ Fields added here will give the actual data values used in the summary. In our case we can add 'Product Sales' field.

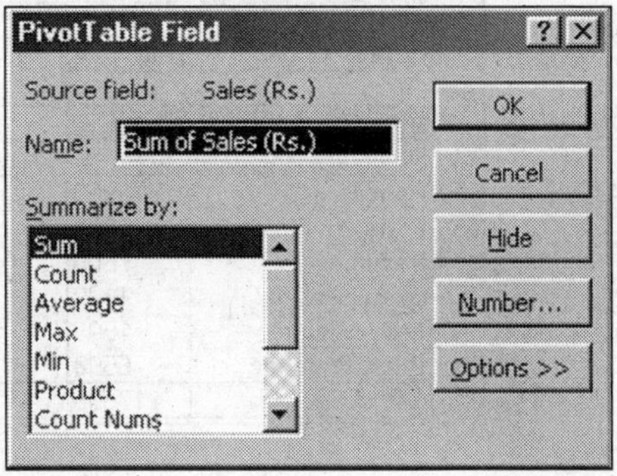

⑤ This is the **PivotTable Toolbar** displaying all the field headings used in the data source. You can drag the fields from here to various regions (Page/Column/Row/Data) of the report.

⑥ This opens an **AutoFormat** dialogue box displaying various inbuilt report formats. You can select any one format for your PivotTable report.

⑦ This opens the **Chart Wizard**, which can be used to create a PivotChart report based on the current PivotTable report.

⑧ These are **Hide** and **Show** details buttons, which can be used to hide/show the details of a particular field.

⑨ This Refreshes the PivotTable report to reflect any changes to the source data.

⑩ This opens the Field Settings dialog box, which can be used to change the summary function for a data field. By default Excel applies the Sum function if the data is numeric, or the Count function if the data is non-numeric.

⑪ This toggles the field heading area between hidden and visible.

A Final Output Once this report is created, you can pivot the table for a different view of the data. You can exchange the current row field with the current column field or you can add a new field by dragging it from the PivotTable toolbar to get whole new view of your data. You can also change the summary function with the help of Field Settings icon of the PivotTable toolbar.

	A	B	C	D	E	F
1	Category	(All)				
2						
3	Sum of Sales (Rs.)	Month				
4	Product Name	April	May	June	Grand Total	
5	Pencils	720	960	960	2640	
6	Pens	1000	1000	875	2875	
7	Perfumes	3800	7600	7600	19000	
8	SketchPens	550	550	1100	2200	
9	Teddy Bears	1500	600	1500	3600	
10	Wrist Watches	5500	2750	5500	13750	
11	Grand Total	13070	13460	17535	44065	
12						

①
②
③

	A	B	C	D	E
1	Category	Gift Items			
2					
3	Sum of Sales (Rs.)	Month			
4	Product Name	April	May	June	Grand Total
5	Perfumes	3800	7600	7600	19000
6	Teddy Bears	1500	600	1500	3600
7	Wrist Watches	5500	2750	5500	13750
8	Grand Total	10800	10950	14600	36350

① Click here to change your filter.

② Click here to change the Month

③ Click here to change the Product Name.

	A	B	C
1	Category	(All)	
2			
3	Sum of Sales (Rs.)	Month	
4	Product Name	June	Grand Total
5	Pencils	960	960
6	Pens	875	875
7	Perfumes	7600	7600
8	SketchPens	1100	1100
9	Teddy Bears	1500	1500
10	Wrist Watches	5500	5500
11	Grand Total	17535	17535

	A	B	C
1	Category	(All)	
2			
3	Sum of Sales (Rs.)	Month	
4	Product Name	June	Grand Total
5	Teddy Bears	1500	1500
6	Wrist Watches	5500	5500
7	Grand Total	7000	7000

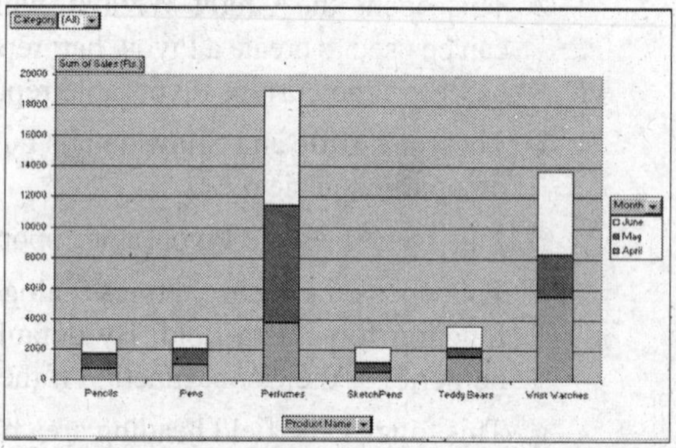

PivotChart Report, created using the ChartWizard icon of the PivotTable toolbar. Different Chart objects can be modified (as explained earlier in this section) to suit the user's need.

ANALYSING YOUR DATA

Excel provides a number of tools to formulate future performance and perform what-if analysis in your worksheets. What-if analysis, as the name suggests, is used to analyse your worksheet data to predict the future performance of your data by understanding its past behaviour, thereby assisting users in taking better decisions.

Ways to forecast values with what-if analysis:

1. Data Tables
2. Scenarios

Data Tables

A data table is a technique that can be used to view the variations in the formula result by substituting different input values in the formula. Variations can be substituted in the formula either down one column or across one row. If the variations are listed down a column, then it is known as Column-Oriented table. If the variations are listed down a row, then it is known as Row-Oriented table.

There are two types of Data Tables, viz., One-Variable Data Table and Two-Variable Data Table. A One-Variable Data table substitutes different values for one variable in the formula. A Two-variable data table substitutes different values for two variables in the same formula. For example: we can use a Two-Variable data table to determine how different interest rates and loan terms will affect a payment. Interest Rate and Loan terms would be the two variables.

Defining Formulas and Input Tables for the Data Tables For creating Data Tables, Excel needs an Input Cell. An Input cell is a blank cell lying outside the table range for holding calculations of the formula. Excel requires specific locations for the inputs and formulas used by data tables. For a column-oriented table, the formula should be defined in a cell, i.e., one cell above the first value and one column to the right of the input variable list. For a row-oriented table, the formula should be defined in a cell, i.e., is one cell below the row of values and one column to the left of the first value.

Example:

A company calculates the projected sales by using the following formula:

Project Sales for the year = PS + PS*R

where

PS = Previous Year's sales

R = Rate of growth in sales

You are given the following details:

Sales in 2001 (thousand Rs.)	:	1200
Rate of growth in sales	:	28%
Projected sales in 2002	:	1536

Let us have a better understanding of Data Tables by creating a Data Table for the above example. We shall be creating a One-Variable data table as this has only one variable namely 'R' for showing the projected sales if the growth rate is changed to 29%, 30%, 31%, 32%, 33% and 34%.

Creating a One-Variable Data Table

① Enter the data in your worksheet. Since we have entered the variables in a column, it is a column-oriented table.

② Choose an input cell for holding the calculations, as the input cell will be over written many times during the creation of the Data Table, it should be blank. Let us choose 'C1' as our input cell.

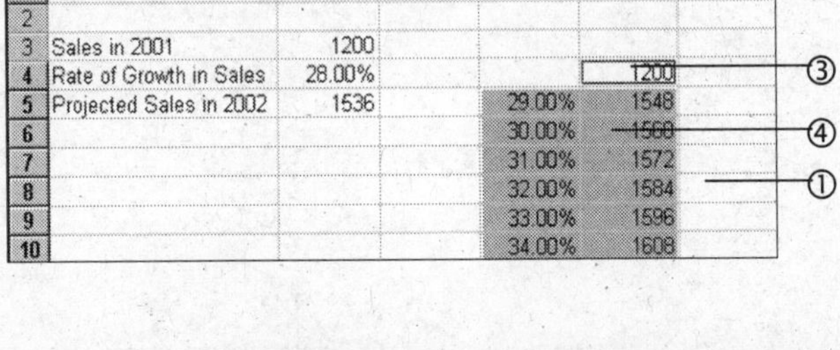

③ Enter the formula (PS+PS*C1 as C1 is our input cell). For a column-oriented table, the formula must be entered in a cell that is one row above and one column to the right of the top of the list of variations. In our case we will enter the formula in the cell E4.

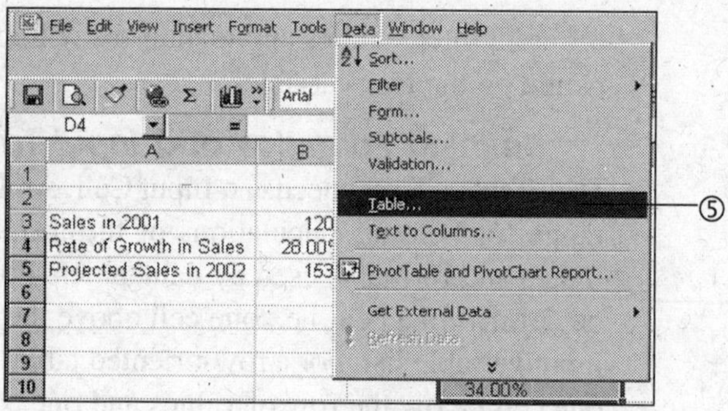

④ Select a minimum data range covering the input variables and the formula. D4:E10 would be our minimum data range.

⑤ Choose **Table** from the **Data** menu.

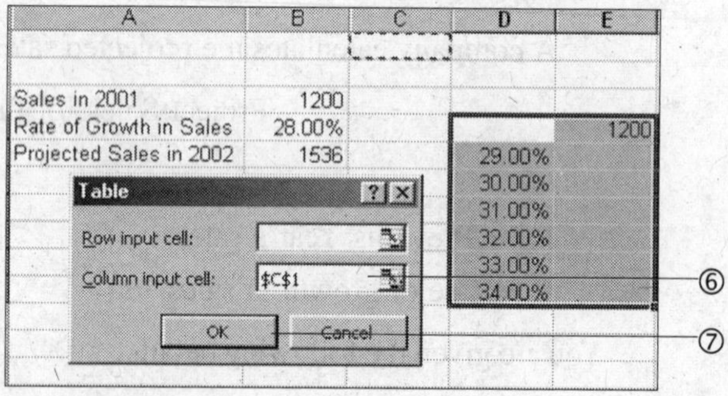

⑥ Type the cell reference for the input cell in the **Column input cell** box. For row-oriented data table, the cell reference should be typed in the **Row input cell** box.

⑦ Click on the **OK** button.

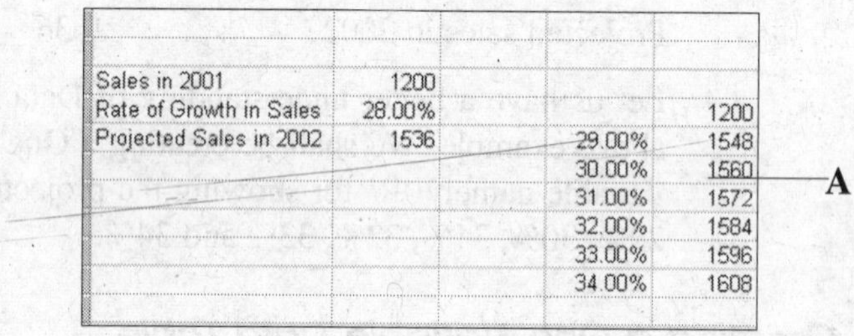

A Output–displaying the projected sales for different values of 'R'.

Notes:

1. You can change the value of the input variable(s) and accordingly view the projected sales figure.
2. To clear a data table, select the entire data range and press **Del** key. You cannot delete individual entries, as they share a common formula.

Scenario Manager

Scenario Manager, as the name suggests, assists you in managing your scenarios. It allows you to view different scenarios in a single spreadsheet so that you can switch to any of these scenarios to view different results. You can use scenarios to predict the outcome of a worksheet model.

A scenario in Excel refers to a group of changing cells, where you can create and save various sets of input values and results. A scenario must contain at least one changing cell — a cell whose contents will vary depending upon the active scenario. Scenario manager uses this changing cell reference to display the values of each scenario. You can define upto 32 changing cells per scenario.

Example

A person wants to take a loan for buying a house. He visits a bank to get the details. He is given different options which are shown in the table below.

Investment Amount	Interest Rate	Term (Months)
20000	10%	60
20000	11%	48
14000	12%	84
12000	13%	60

This example has 4 scenarios, with three changing cells namely Investment Amount, Interest Rate and Term. Let us see how we can use the Scenario Manager to evaluate the most profitable one.

Creating Scenarios

① Enter the data for the first scenario in a worksheet. And cal-culate the monthly payment amount. (Monthly Payment Amount = PMT (Interest Rate/ 12, Term, Investment Amount). (PMT function has been explained earlier in the chapter)

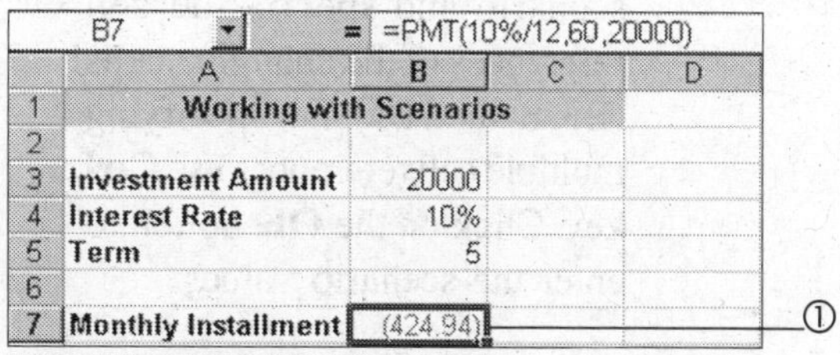

② **Naming the changing cells** — it would be more meaningful if we assign a user-friendly

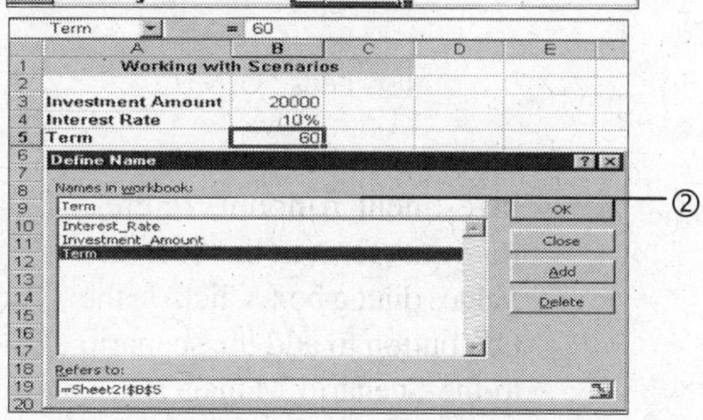

name to each changing cell rather than referring the cell by its cell address. To assign a name, select the cell, choose **Define** under the **Name** option from the **Insert** menu and type the desired name in the **Name** box.

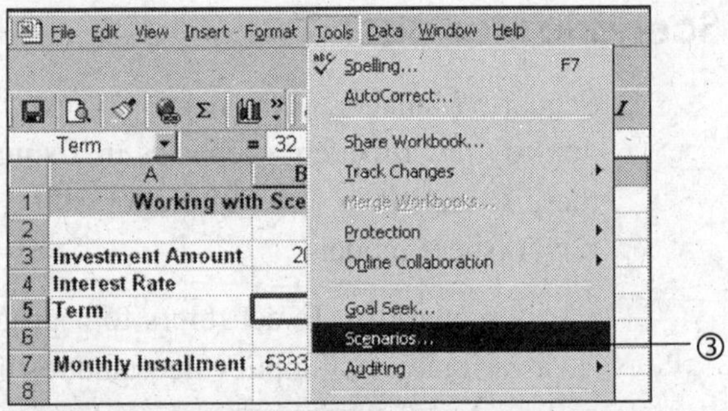

③ Choose **Scenarios** from the **Tools** menu. A **Scenario Manager** dialog box will be displayed.

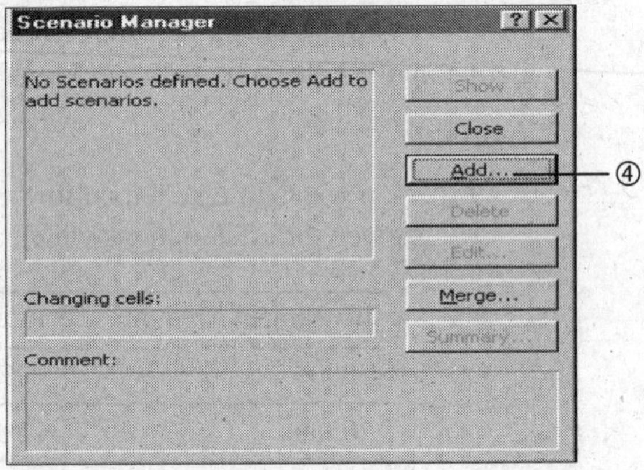

④ Click on the **Add** button from the **Scenario Manager** dialog box.

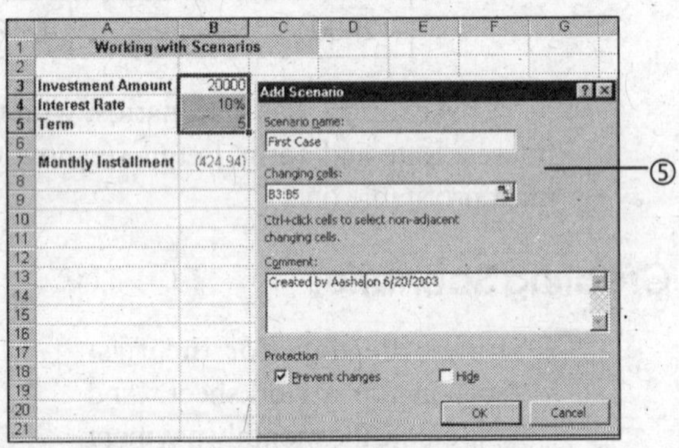

⑤ Type a name for your first scenario and specify the cell references of the changing cells (B3, B4 and B5). For specifying multiple cell references use **Ctrl** key. Click on the **OK** button to enter the scenario values.

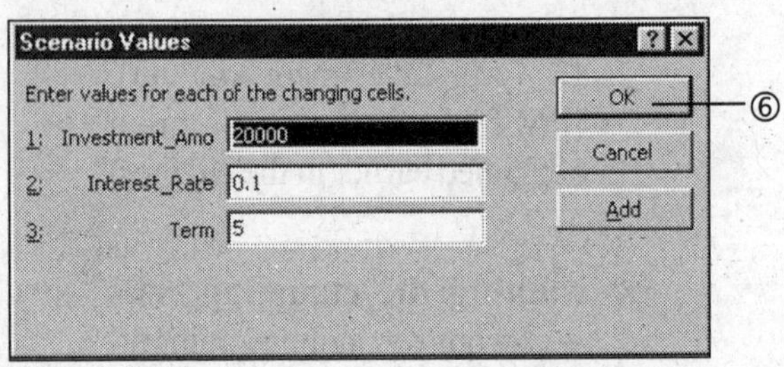

⑥ Enter the desired values for the Investment Amount, Interest Rate and Term in the Scenario Values dialog box. Click on the **OK** button to add the scenario to the Scenario Manager.

⑦ Similarly, add the remaining scenarios to the Scenario Manager. To view a particular scenario, select the scenario and click on the **Show** button.

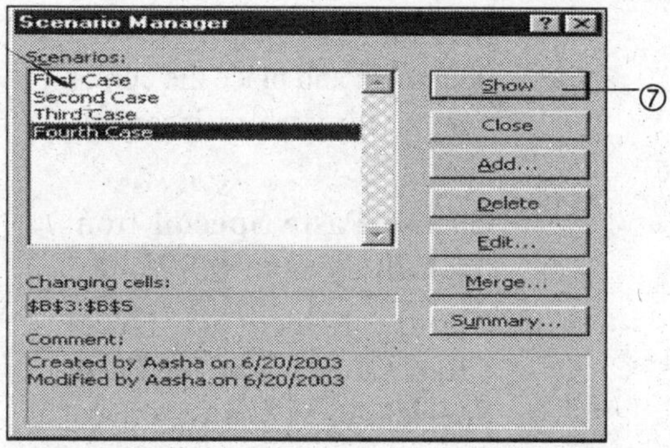

The results for the four scenarios would be as follows:

First Case = 424.94
Second Case = 516.91
Third Case = 247.14
Fourth Case = 254.96

Exchanging Data between Excel and Other Programs

You can exchange data between Excel and other MS office programs, and vice versa. You can transfer information between Excel and other applications in broadly two ways:

1. Using the Copy/Paste method.
2. Using OLE (Object Linking and Embedding) technology.

Using the Copy/Paste method This technique is used if you wish to copy information that appears in one program into another program. In this technique, the data that is pasted in the destination document is completely independent of the source document, i.e., **any changes done in the source document will not be reflected in the destination document.** The most common way to transfer information between Excel and Word or vice versa is to use the Windows clipboard. As discussed earlier in Windows chapter, a clipboard is a temporary area containing the copied or cut information and the paste function takes the information from the clipboard.

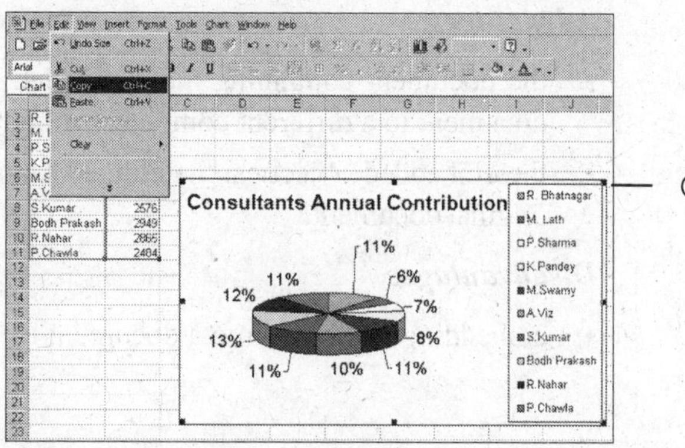

Example – Follow the steps below to copy a chart created in Excel into a Word document.

① Select the Excel chart and choose **Copy** from the **Edit** menu.

② Switch to your Word document and place the cursor where you wish to insert the chart.

③ Choose **Paste Special** from the **Edit** menu of MSWord.

④ Choose **Microsoft Excel Chart Object** from the **Paste Special** dialog box.

⑤ Click on **Paste** as you wish to paste only the information reflected in the current chart.

⑥ Click on the **OK** button to paste the selected object.

Note: The same technique can be used to copy an object from a Word document into an Excel workbook.

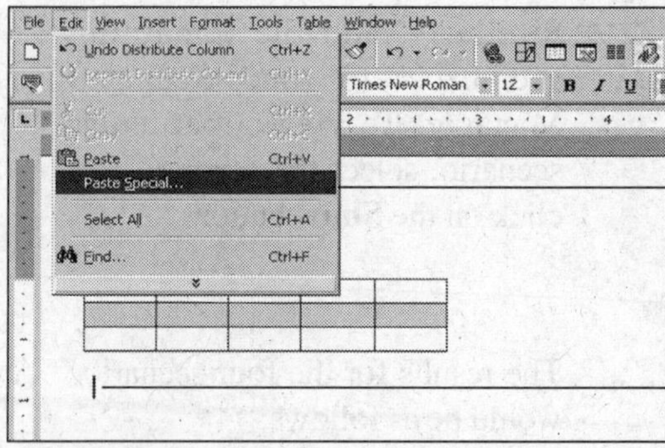

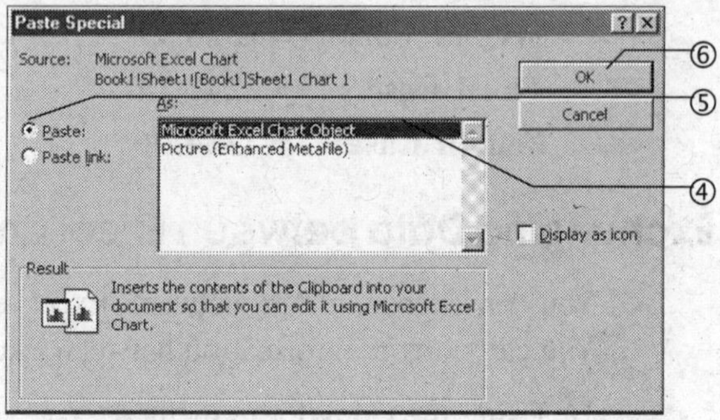

Using OLE (Object Linking and Embedding) technology

Embedded Objects An embedded object has no link to the source document so any changes done in the source document will not be reflected in the destination document. Whenever the **Paste** option from the **Paste Dialog** box is used, the object is always copied as an embedded object. In the above example, the Excel chart is copied as an embedded object into the Word document. To change an embedded object, double-click the object to open it in its source program. Once the object is opened it can be edited using its source program. The source program (or another program capable of editing the object) must be installed on your computer.

Advantages:

- the document containing the embedded object is portable, i.e., you can transfer the document to a different computer without breaking a link.
- the embedded object can be edited without affecting the content of the source or the original document.

Disadvantages:

- embedding an object into a document increases its file size.

Linked Objects A linked object maintains a link with the source document, so any changes done in the source document are automatically reflected in the destination document. Whenever the **Paste Link** option from the **Paste Dialogue** box is used, the object is always copied as a linked object. With a linked object, the original information remains stored in the source file. The destination file contains only a reference or link to the source file.

Advantages:

- It is easy to keep the linked object up to date. This feature is very helpful when multiple documents contain a link/reference to a specific object.
- Linking keeps the size of the document very small.

Disadvantage:

- The source file must remain available on your computer or network to maintain the link to the original data.

Excel and the Web

Excel (As well as other MS office programs) incorporates unprecedented support for publishing information on the web. You can save your Excel workbook as a Web page so that it can be viewed on the World Wide Web (WWW). Once you have saved your Excel workbook in HTML format (Webpage), you can rearrange the items on the WebPage, add more text or graphics, or any additional features supported by HTML. (HTML–Hypertext Markup Language–is an encoding scheme that helps in creating web-pages.) Excel also allows reading web pages, i.e., you can open a webpage as an Excel worksheet.

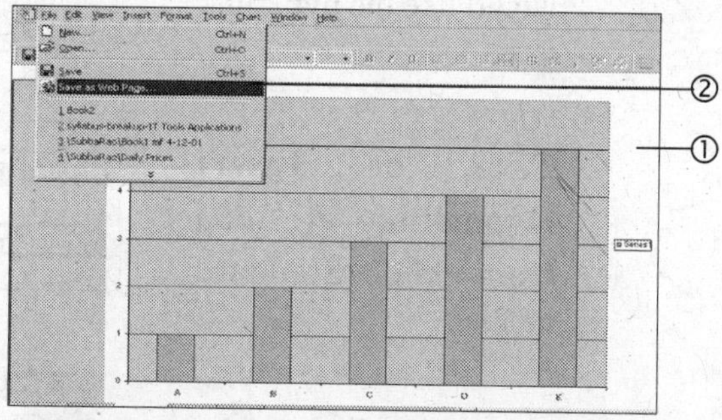

Saving an Excel Workbook as a Webpage:

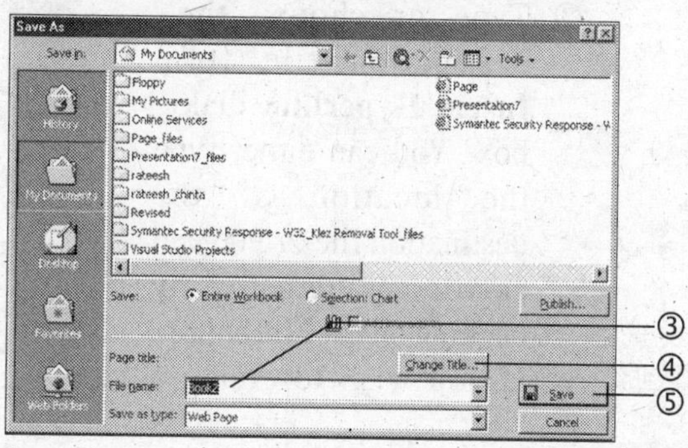

① Open the workbook that you wish to save as a Webpage.

② Choose **Save As Webpage** from the **File** menu.

③ Specify a file name in the **Save As** dialog box.

④ Click here to change the title of your webpage. This title will be displayed at the top of your browser window.

⑤ Click the **Save** button.

Notes:

1. Once a workbook is saved as a webpage, you can view it in any browser.
2. Whenever a workbook is saved as a webpage, a folder containing all the dependent files is automatically created in the same location. Example: If you saved your workbook as 'My Web Book' in C:\My Documents then a folder titled 'My Web Book_Files' will be created automatically in C:\My Documents.

Hyperlinks in Excel

Hyperlinks provide a simple way to navigate from one document to another. In Excel, a hyperlink can be used to navigate from one sheet to another within the same or a different worksheet.When you move the mouse pointer over a hyperlink, the pointer changes to a different symbol/image (usually a hand). Hyperlinked text is usually represented in blue colour.

Creating Hyperlinks

① Select the cell where you would like the hyperlink to be located.

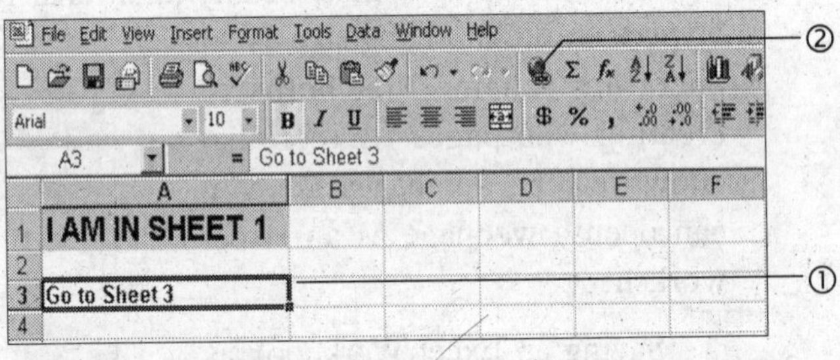

② Click on **Insert Hyperlink** icon from the Standard toolbar.

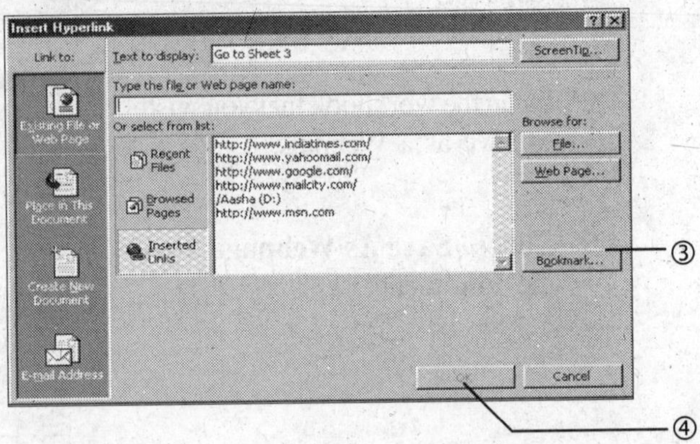

③ Type or choose the destination file from **Insert Hyperlink** dialog box. You can either type the location of the destination file or you can choose an alternative by clicking on the **File** button. If you wish to create a hyperlink within the same worksheet then click on the **Bookmark** button and select the desired sheet. Click on the **OK** button to close the Bookmark dialog box.

④ Click the **OK** button.

A Output – Clicking on the hyperlink would open the destination file.

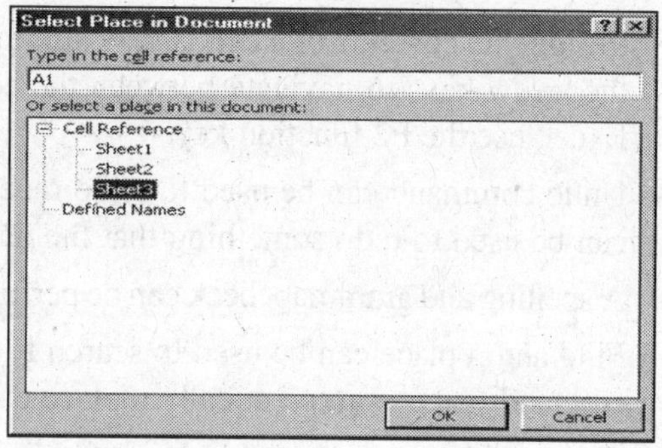

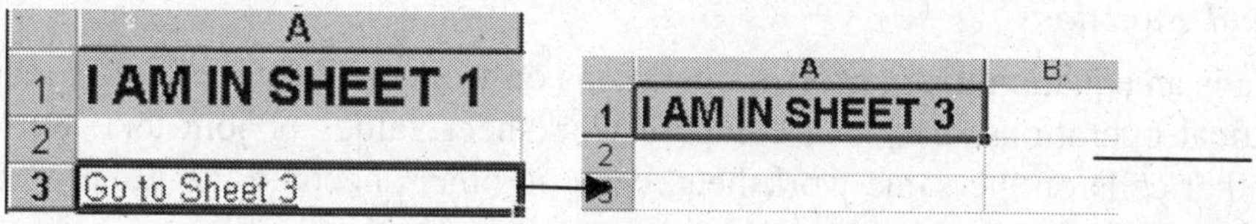

A

SUMMARY

Excel - Basics

- Excel is a spreadsheet package that can be used for financial calculations, analysis and creating graphs.
- Excel, or for that matter any spreadsheet, essentially comprises of a grid of rows and columns. Intersection of a row and a column is called a cell. Typically, rows are numbered numerically, i.e., 1, 2, 3... and so on, and columns are labeled alphabetically, i.e., A, B, C... and so on. An Excel file is always saved with .xls extension.
- There are two basic types of data that are used in a spreadsheet: Values and Formulas. Values include numbers and text and formulas are arithmetic calculations that change based on the input given to them.
- Excel allows creating template-based workbooks. A template in Excel is a special type of workbook with pre-defined formats and controls that can be used as a base for creating other workbooks.
- By default, a workbook contains three sheets. It is possible to add more sheets to a workbook as well as remove existing worksheets. Sheets can also be moved/rearranged from one location to another in a workbook. You can rename a sheet to make it more user friendly.
- Excel allows hiding a workbook/worksheet from the user's view. Hiding a workbook/sheet does not delete its data.

- Editing the contents of a cell is very similar to editing data in any Word document. You can use the arrow keys to navigate between the cells of a worksheet. To edit the contents of a cell in Excel, use the F2 function key.
- Undo command can be used to undo recent action(s)/errors done by the user. Redo command can be used to redo something that the user has undone.
- A spelling and grammar check can be performed on the data/text contained in an Excel workbook.
- Find and replace can be used to search for specific text or numbers that you want to review or edit, and you can automatically replace data you find.

Formulas and Functions

- A formula is an equation that performs operations on worksheet data. Formulas can perform mathematical operations, they can compare worksheet values or join text. Formulas can refer to other cells on the same worksheet, cells on other sheets in the same workbook, or cells on sheets in other workbooks.
- A formula in Excel always begins with an equal sign (=). Following the equal sign are the elements to be calculated (the operands), which are separated by calculation operators. Once a formula is defined for a particular row, it can be used for the rest of the rows by using a simple method of Copy and Paste.
- Operators define the calculation to be performed by the formula. Calculation operators in Excel can be broadly classified into four categories: **Arithmetic Operators** (+,-,*,/,^), **Comparison operators** (=,<>,>,<,>=,<=), **Text concatenation operator** (&) and **Reference operators** (Colon, Comma, Space).
- Excel calculates the formula from left to right, according to a specific order for each operator in the formula. You can change the order of operations by using parentheses.
- Excel contains many built-in formulas, which are known as functions. Functions are power tools that help you perform complex computations easily and quickly. Typically, a function consists of two parts–**function name** and **arguments**. Arguments (or values) may in some cases be mandatory and in some cases optional. Functions always return a result.
- Worksheet functions in Excel can be broadly classified into: Mathematical, Statistical, Logical, Financial, Text and Date and Time Functions. ABS(), FACT(), INT(), MOD(), and ROMAN() are some examples of Mathematical functions. AVERAGE(), COUNT(), COUNTIF(), MIN() and MAX() are some examples of Statistical functions. IF(), AND(), OR() and NOT() are some examples of Logical functions. PMT(), IPMT() and NPER() are some examples of Financial functions. CHAR(), CODE(), FIND(), LEFT(), RIGHT() and LEN() are some examples of Text functions. TODAY(), DATE(), TIME(), NOW() and DAY() are some examples of Date and Time functions.

Formatting Features

- Excel offers a unique set of formatting features that can be used to effectively display your data. Most of the formatting features can be accessed from the Format menu and the Formatting toolbar.

- You can format all of the text in a cell or only selected characters using different text formatting icons available in the Formatting toolbar.
- Text Wrap can be used to display multiple lines of text within a single cell.
- You can use merge and centre function to center the text across several columns.
- Autofit command can be used to adjust the column width according to its contents.
- You can format numbers by adding desired currency symbol, inserting percent symbol, increasing or decreasing the number of decimal places and much more.
- You can apply borders to a cell or range of cells. Excel allows customising the border style and colour.
- You can apply shading to a cell or range of cells. Excel allows customising the shading pattern and colour.
- Text is always left aligned within the cell and Numbers are always right aligned within the cells. These alignments can be changed as per your requirements.
- Excel allows using the existing headers and footers or you can create your own by defining custom header and custom footer.
- You can use Format Painter to copy formatting of one object into another.

Filters

- Data Sort feature can be used to alphabetically rearrange any type of data, either in ascending (A to Z or 1 to 10 or 1st January 1999 to 31st December 1999) or descending (Z to A or 10 to 1 or 31st December 1999 to 1st January 1999) order.
- While using Data Sort command, the entire table, including the column headings, has to be selected for this command to work properly. Care should also be taken that the selected range does not contain any blank rows or columns or any other row other than the column headings and the data.
- Filtering helps in viewing only those records that meet a specific condition.
- All is very helpful feature of Data Filters. Whenever you get stuck or have given a wrong filter selection, use this option to get back to the complete table.
- Excel allows defining custom data filters, which can be used to pull out records based upon a mathematical criterion (condition). You can use the 'And' and 'Or' operators for specifying the condition for filtering records.

Creating Charts and Graphs

- Charts make it easy for users to see comparisons, patterns, and trends in data rapidly. Excel contains powerful charting wizards and tools that can be used to build effective and impressive charts.
- Excel comes with a wide variety of chart styles, including bar, pie, column, scatter, bubble and many more. Once a chart is created, you can customise it to suit your requirements.

- You can create a chart in its own chart sheet or as an embedded chart in a worksheet. A chart sheet is a separate sheet within your workbook that has its own sheet name. An embedded chart is a chart that is displayed directly in a worksheet.
- By default, Excel creates a Column type chart. However the default chart type can be changed to some other chart type.
- Elements of a chart include Chart Area, Plot Area (Axes + Gridlines + Data Series), Legend, Title and Data table. All the elements of a chart can be modified using the Format icon from the Chart toolbar.
- Chart Wizard guides you through a series of steps that helps in creating a chart.
- Trendlines are used to graphically display trends in data. As the name suggests, it shows the general trend, such as growth or decline that occurs in the data.
- Excel comes with six different types of trendlines, Linear, Logarithmic, Polynomial, Power, Exponential and Moving average.
- PivotTable reports are summary reports, which can be used in almost any environment to simplify data analysis, but their real use is appreciated when dealing with large amounts of data.
- Once a PivotTable report is created, you can pivot the elements of the report to new positions within the table for a different view of the data; you can rotate its rows and columns to see different summaries of the source data without worrying about harming the original data source and you can dynamically add a new field of your choice or delete existing fields.

Analysing Your Data

- Excel provides a number of tools to formulate future performance and perform what-if analysis in your worksheets.
- A data table is a technique that can be used to view the variations in the formula result by substituting different input values in the formula. There are two types of Data Tables, viz., One-Variable Data Table and Two-Variable Data Table.
- For creating Data Tables, Excel needs an Input Cell. An Input cell is a blank cell lying outside the table range for holding calculations of the formula.
- Scenario Manager, as the name suggests, assists you in managing your scenarios. You can use scenarios to predict the outcome of a worksheet model.
- A scenario in Excel refers to a group of changing cells, where you can create and save various sets of input values and results.

Integrating Word Processor, Spreadsheets and Webpages

- You can exchange data between Excel and other MS office programs, and vice versa.
- You can use Copy/Paste technique to copy information that appears in one program into another program. When an object is copied using this technique, it is copied as an embedded object, i.e., any changes done in the source document will not be reflected in the destination document.

- A linked object maintains a link with the source document so any changes done in the source document are automatically reflected in the destination document.
- Excel (like other MS office programs) incorporates unprecedented support for publishing information on the web.
- You can save your Excel workbook as a Webpage so that it can be viewed on the World Wide Web (WWW). Excel also allows reading webpages, i.e., you can open a webpage as an Excel worksheet.
- Whenever a workbook is saved as a webpage, a folder containing all the dependent files is automatically created in the same location.
- Hyperlinks provide a simple way to navigate from one document to another. In Excel, a hyperlink can be used to navigate from one sheet to another within the same or a different worksheet.

REVIEW QUESTIONS

1. Choose the most appropriate answer:

i. Which one of the following is a spreadsheet package?

(a) MS Word (b) MS PowerPoint
(c) Windows (d) None of the above

ii. A workbook with predefined formats, controls and formulas that can be used as a base for creating other workbooks:

(a) Spreadsheet (b) Template
(c) Wizard (d) None of the above

iii. An equation that performs operations on worksheet data. It can refer to other cells on the same worksheet, cells on other sheets in the same workbook, or cells on sheets in other workbooks:

(a) Hyperlink (b) Formula
(c) Argument (d) None of the above

iv. This operator produces a single reference to all the cells between two references, including the two cell references:

(a) Range Operator (b) Union Operator
(c) Intersection Operator (d) None of the above

v. This function returns the interest payment for a given period for an investment based on constant payments and a constant interest rate:

(a) IPMT (b) NPER
(c) PMT (d) None of the above

vi. This feature can be used to alphabetically rearrange any type of data, either in ascending (A to Z or 1 to 10 or 1st January 1999 to 31st December 1999) or descending (Z to A or 10 to 1 or 31st December 1999 to 1st January 1999) order:

(a) Data Sort (b) Data Filter
(c) Arrange (d) None of the above

vii. This can be used to graphically represent the information. It can be used to view the comparisons, patterns, and trends in data rapidly.

(a) Chart (b) Table
(c) Macro (d) None of the above

viii. It contains the entire chart and all of its elements. It is similar to a canvas:

(a) Plot Area (b) Chart Area
(c) Data Table (d) None of the above

ix. This type of object maintains a link with the source document so that any changes done in the source document are automatically reflected in the destination document:

(a) Linked Object (b) Embedded Object
(c) Dependent Object (d) None of the above

x. It can be used to navigate from one sheet to another within the same or a different worksheet:

(a) Arrow Keys (b) Enter Key
(c) Hyperlink (d) None of the above

2. Enter True or False:

i. Sheets in a workbook cannot be moved/rearranged from one location to another.

ii. An Excel file is saved with .xls extension.

iii. Hiding a workbook will delete its data.

iv. Series fill can be used to fill up a range of cells with consecutive numbers.

v. All the formatting features offered by Excel require pre-selection of a piece of text.

vi. You can change the order of operations in a formula by using parentheses.

vii. An argument is compulsory for any type of function, i.e., it is not possible to have a function without any arguments.

viii. Date and Time are internally stored as serial numbers in Excel.

ix. In Excel values are plotted against the Y or the Vertical axis and categories are plotted against the X or Horizontal axis.

x. An Excel worksheet cannot be viewed on the Web.

3. Match the following:

	X	Y
1.	To edit the contents of a cell.	Legend
2.	Rectangular group of cells that is referred to by its opposite corners.	Embedded Chart
3.	This feature can be used to display multiple lines of text within a single cell.	Trendlines
4.	This command can be used to adjust the column width according to its contents.	F2 key
5.	Returns the code number for the first character in the specified text string, in the character set used by your computer.	ALL
6.	This feature of Data filters can be used to get back to the complete table.	Input cell
7.	This type of chart is displayed directly in a worksheet.	Autofit
8.	A blank cell lying outside the table range for holding calculations of the formula.	Range
9.	Displays the growth or decline that occurs in the data.	CODE()
10.	A box that identifies the colours/patterns assigned to various data series in the chart.	Text Wrap

4. Fill in the blanks with the appropriate choices listed below

(i) FIND (ii) Scenario Manager (iii) Row-Oriented table (iv) Column-Oriented table (v) Function (vi) LEN (vii) CLEAR (viii) SEARCH (ix) Del (x) COUNT

i. ________________ can be used to find one text string (find_text) within another text string. It allows using wild card characters.

ii. ________________ is a built-in formula that can be used to perform complex computations - easily and quickly.

iii. ________________ is used to return the number of characters in the text.

iv. ________________ can be used to clear the contents, formats and comments in a cell.

v. ________________ can be used to view the list of scenarios.

vi. In a ________________, the variations of a data table are listed down a column.

5. **Write short notes on:**

   i. Handling operators in Formulae.

   ii. Relative Cell Referencing

   iii. Data Filters

   iv. What-if Analysis

   v. Scenarios

6. **Explain the needs of functions in a spreadsheet package with suitable examples.**

7. **How do Charts assist as a management tool?**

8 Internet Basics

NETWORKING

In the past, the computers were stand-alone systems, and transferring information from one computer to another required a tape or a disk. Resources (like CD-ROM drive, floppy drive etc.) and peripherals (like printers, scanners, plotters, etc.) of any computer could not be shared by other computers. Networking—or interconnecting the computers—was a solution for this. A network is simply the most cost-effective way to share equipment such as computers, printers and scanners that have been connected by cables. A network helps people work collectively.

A network can be as simple as connecting two computers. A large network can link hundreds or thousands of computers and peripherals in various configurations. Computer networks are available in different types.

Local Area Network (LAN) A LAN connects network devices over a relatively short distance. An office building, or a school usually contains a LAN.

Wide Area Network (WAN) A WAN spans a large physical distance. A WAN like the **Internet** spans most of the world!

Intranet It is a network of computers within an enterprise that can share data using existing standardized www protocols. ("www and protocols" explained in detail later in the chapter.)

INTERNET

Internet is a **"network of networks"** that links computers around the world. It allows communication across networks, i.e. one can communicate between one network and another network. This allows people to have access to information from different websites, locations or machines. It literally puts a world of information and a potential worldwide audience at your fingertips.

IMPORTANT FEATURES

Some of the facilities available on the Internet are:

- **World Wide Web** The Internet application that is currently drawing the most attention is the World Wide Web. It has dramatically influenced the online world and continues to grow in popularity.
- **Direct Communication** Through email (electronic mail), messages can be sent to or received from any part of the world within a few minutes.
- **Round-The-Clock Availability** Information on the Internet is available to the users 24 hours a day.
- **Central Repository of Data** The Internet is like a huge central warehouse of data that can be accessed by people from all over the world.
- **Search Engines** They are like directories which help you get any information from all over the world within a few minutes.
- **Advertisement** A company can advertise its products/services.
- **E-Commerce** The Internet is increasingly being used for carrying out money transactions. Through the Internet you can shop and pay through your credit card or ask your bank to transfer your money to a different account, without even leaving your desk.
- **Distance Learning** Several online distance learning courses are offered by Indian and foreign universities on the Internet.
- **BBS and New Services** The Internet is perhaps the cheapest medium for online help. BBS services are available on the Net through which you can ask questions and get immediate troubleshooting assistance.
- **Wide Area Networks** Using the Internet, organizations can collect and compile information from offices spread over a large geographical area.
- **Shareware Software** Internet is also a great medium for downloading free software. You can get a truckload of free games, utilities and trail versions of softwares through the Net.

PREREQUISITES FOR INTERNET

Hardware

1. A computer with a serial port for connecting external modem or a spare expansion slot for connecting an internal modem card.
2. A modem (internal or external), ideally a faster one (with a speed of 56 KBPS [Kilo Bytes Per Second] or more), is required. A modem converts electronic

signals from your computer into analog signals (sound), which can then be sent over the telephone lines.

3. Cables with jacks and sockets to connect your modem with the computer and telephone.

Software

1. Windows—although you can use earlier versions, Windows 98 or higher version is preferable because it has inbuilt components to support Internet connectivity.
2. A web browser such as Internet Explorer or Netscape Navigator. A browser is a client software program that allows the user to navigate the web.

Internet Explorer **Netscape Navigator**

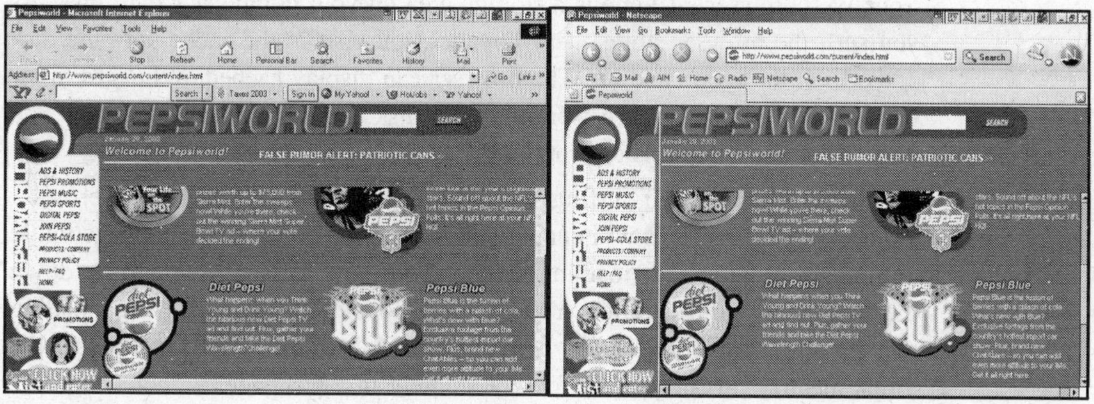

Fig 8.1 Web browsers

Others

1. A telephone connection.
2. An Internet account. If you want to have Internet access at your home, you will need to sign on with an Internet Service Provider (ISP). Some common ISPs are MTNL and VSNL.

FACTORS AFFECTING THE SPEED OF INTERNET CONNECTIVITY

1. **Speed of the modem** A modem with a minimum speed of 56 kbps or higher is recommended.
2. **Quality of phone line** Noise on the phone line running into your home can disrupt Internet connection with a modem.

3. **Internet traffic** Web traffic tends to expand throughout the day and peaks around the early evening. If you plan to download software or wish to surf faster, schedule such activities during off-peak hours.

There are **factors associated with your computer**.

- A **faster processor** (650 MHz or higher) will allow you to surf the Web faster.
- A computer with more memory **(Random Access Memory)** will help to surf faster. One way to avoid slowdowns is to avoid working with other software applications while you are surfing.
- A highly fragmented hard disk can slow down Web surfing considerably. It is a good practice to keep your hard drive defragmented and optimized.
- Your Web browser's **Cache** is a storage area on your computer's hard disk. As you surf, the browser stores the Webpages you visit in the cache upto the disk space limit that you have set. The browser can display cached Webpages faster since they may be retrieved from the hard disk and not from the Internet. You might want to increase your browser's cache limit.
- To further increase your surfing speed you can surf with two or more browser windows at a time. This will enable you to read the contents of one page while allowing another page to load in the second window. This may help to cut down the "lag time" and frustration. You may also consider turning off image loading and Java in your browser (go to **Advanced** tab of **Internet Options** in the **Tools** menu). This may not affect the content in a webpage.

INTERNET PROTOCOLS

People very often forget the basic protocols of a network. Before we understand the internet protocols, let's first discuss addresses.

The Internet has a large number of computers connected to it, from which arises the need of a proper addressing system. Each computer on the network is called a host, and has a name and a number that identifies it.

IP Address

Internet Protocol (IP) address is the numeric location of your computer so that it is an identifiable machine to all the other computers connected to the Internet. The IP address is a 32-bit number divided into four octets, and these octets are written in dotted-decimal format, e.g. 11.245.196.212.

Domain Naming System (DNS)

Domain names provide a system an easy-to-remember Internet address, which can be translated by the Domain Name System (DNS) into the numeric address (Internet Protocol number). Examples of domain names include microsoft.com, pepsi.com etc. The last three letters of the address are important as they provide information about the kind of organization to which the address belongs.

Abbreviations commonly used with the domain names

Abbreviation	Represents
com	Commercial organizations
org	Non-profit groups
net	Networking organizations
gov	Government agencies
mil	Military
edu	Educational institutions

Communication Protocols

In the context of data networking, a protocol is a formal set of rules and conventions that govern how computers exchange information over a network medium.

The Internet uses a set of communication protocols called TCP/IP (Transmission Control Protocol/Internet Protocol). These protocols enable information to be transferred between dissimilar computers, such as a PC and a Macintosh. Thus, TCP/IP binds the Internet.

TCP/IP is made up of two components – TCP and IP.

TCP – Transmission Control Protocol. When two computers want to communicate between each other reliably, they establish a connection. This is analogous to making a telephone call. If you want to speak to your uncle in New York, a connection is established when you dial his phone number and he answers. The TCP guarantees that data sent from one end of the connection actually reaches the other end in the same order it was sent. Otherwise, an error is reported.

IP – Internet Protocol. It is the basic protocol of the Internet. The task of the IP is to send a packet (In a network, information is transmitted in the form of packets.) from Computer A to Computer B. The IP does not verify that the packet really reaches its destination, nor it is the task of the IP to make sure it reached error free, and in the correct order.

Configuring the modem

As mentioned earlier, your hardware and software settings have to be properly configured for logging on to the Internet. It is quite technical which you may find rather cumbersome. Any way, let us start and go ahead.

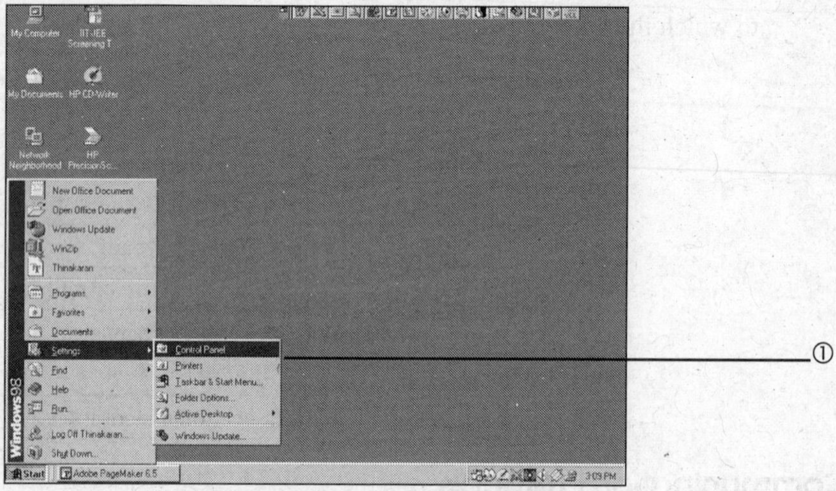

① Choose **Control Panel** from **Settings** option from **Start** menu.

The following window would be displayed:

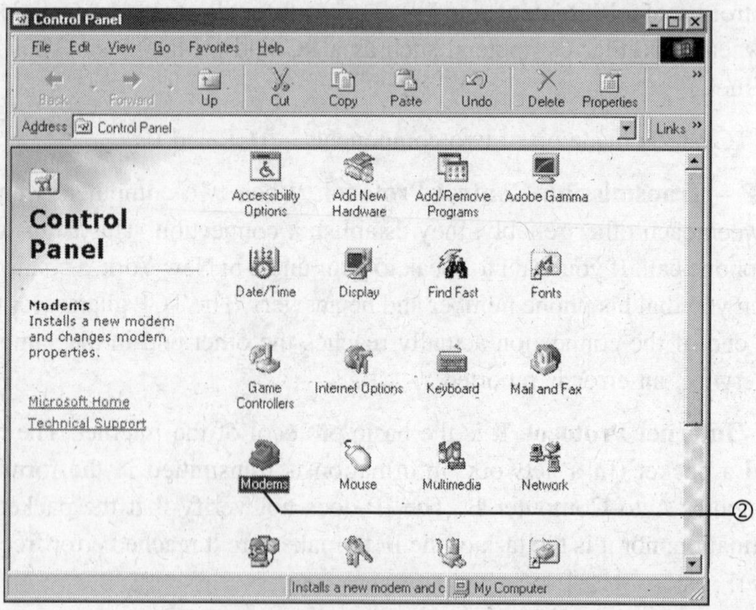

② Double click on the **Modems** icon.

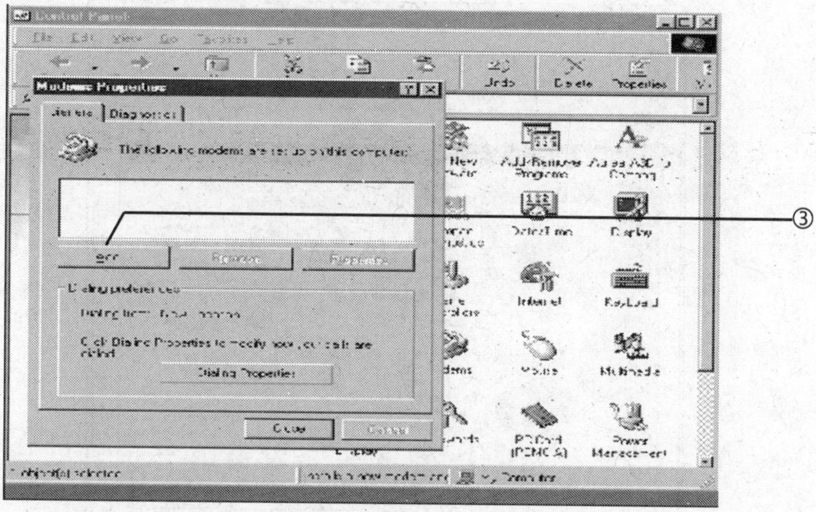

③ Click on the **Add** button.

The following window would be displayed:

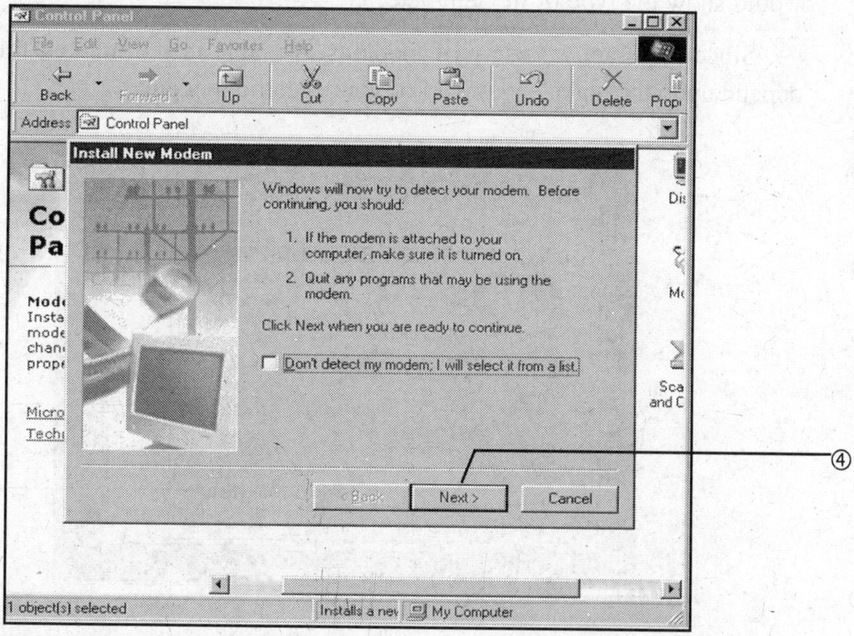

④ Click on the **Next** button.

The following window would be displayed:

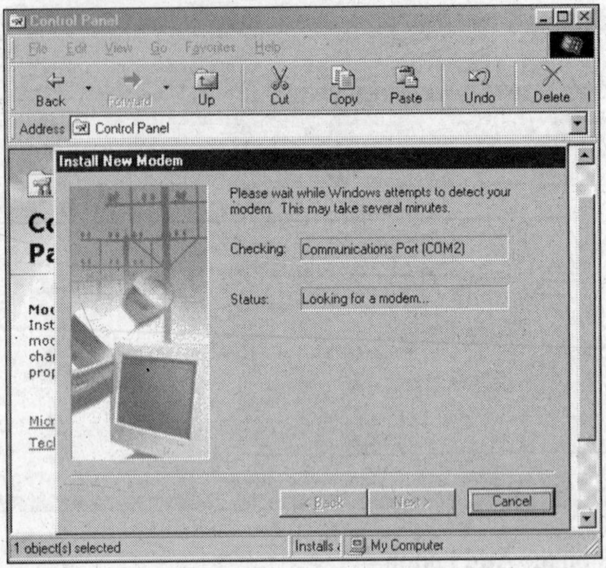

Now the computer will try to detect the type of modem attached to your computer. This step may take a few minutes. The moment the computer has detected the modem it would show the type of modem detected.

Since there are a variety of modems available in the market, this message would depend upon the make and model of your specific modem.

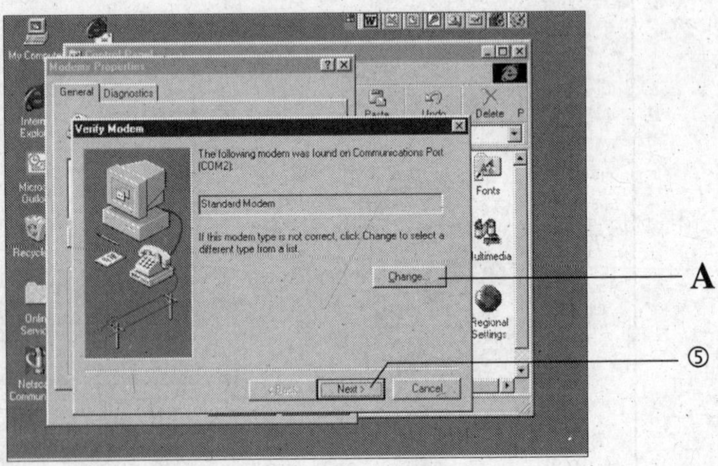

⑤ Click on the **Next** button.

A You can click on the **Change** button to change the modem.

The following window would be displayed:

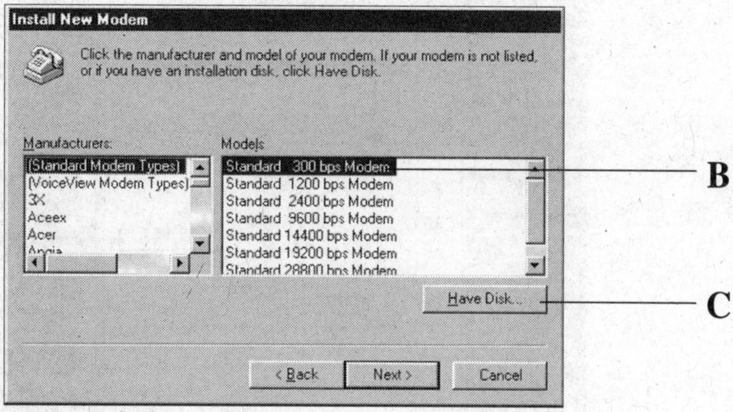

B Choose your modem by clicking on it.

C Insert the floppy that you got with your modem in the floppy drive and click on **Have Disk** button to install your modem. To finish installing click on **OK** button that will appear in the subsequent window.

Now the modem has been successfully installed.

⑥ Click on **Finish** button.

A The modem installed by you is displayed here.

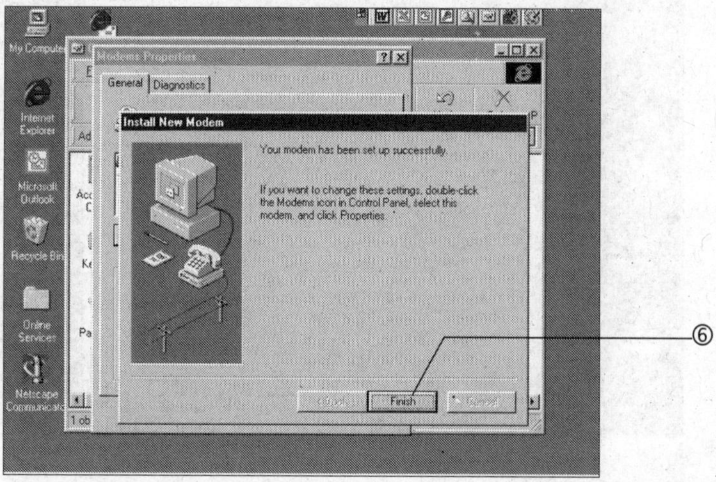

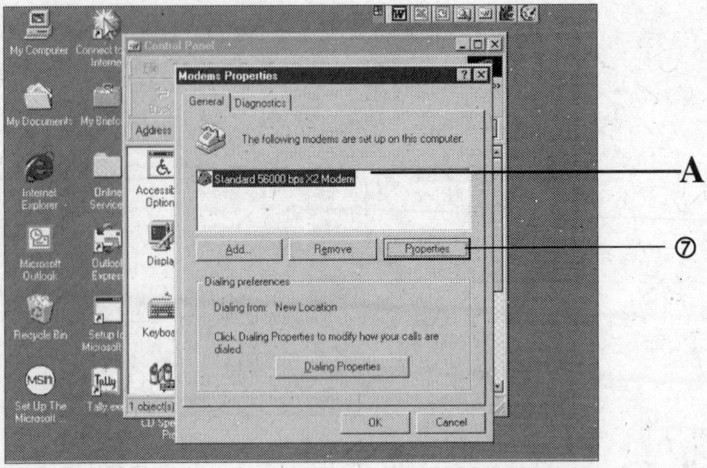

⑦ Click on the **Properties** button.

The following window would be displayed:

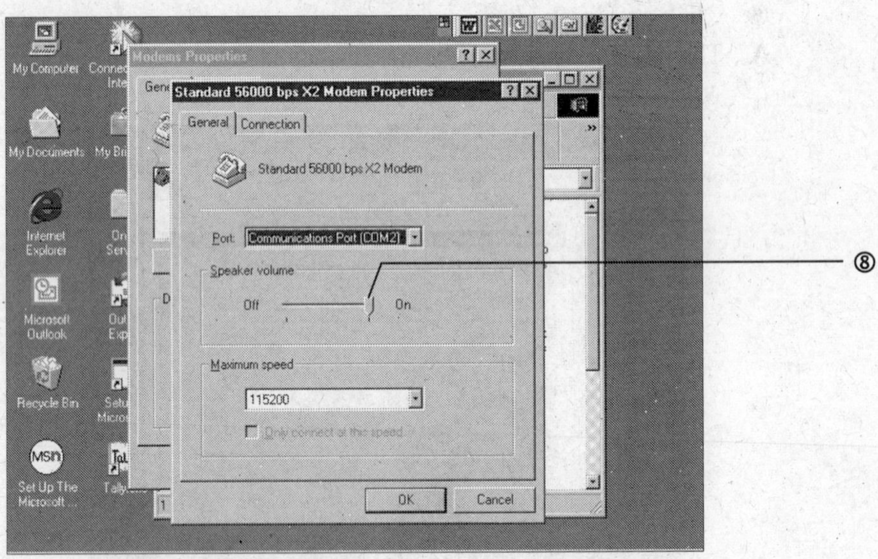

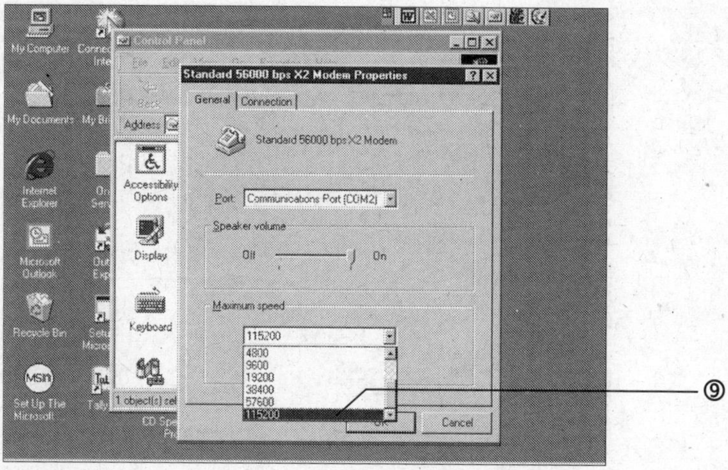

⑧ Adjust your modem's speaker volume.

⑨ Depending upon your modem's speed select the maximum speed.

If you are not sure about the maximum speed supported by your modem, select the highest speed available and run your modem. In case you face problems like frequent breaking of connection, go back to this option and reduce the speed.

⑩ Click on the **Connections** folio.

The following dialog box would be displayed. Match your computer's settings with the ones shown here.

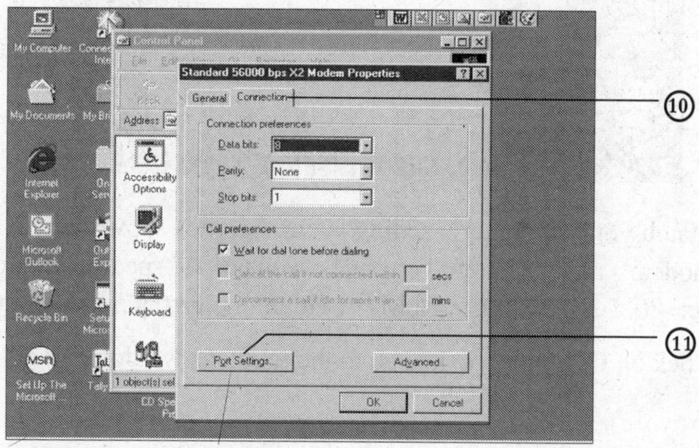

⑪ Click on the **Port Settings** button.

The following window would be displayed. Normally, the settings are automatically defined. However, you can adjust your Transmitter and Receiver buffer rates.

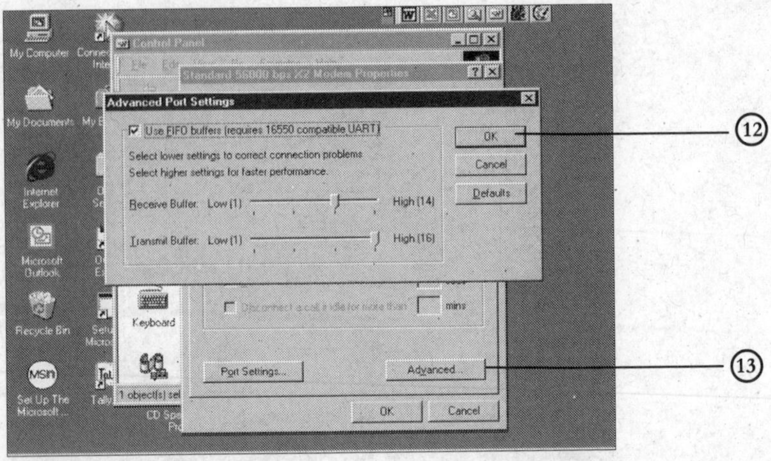

⑫ Click once on **OK** button.

⑬ Click once on **Advanced** button.

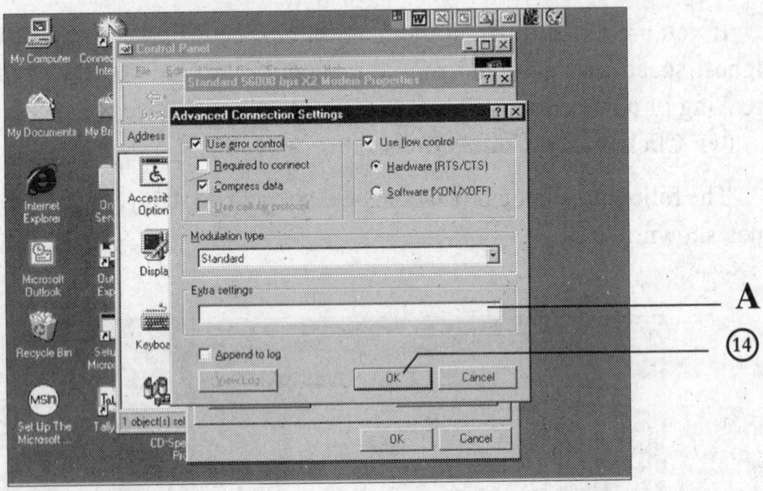

A Match your computer's settings with the ones shown here. However, read your modem's manual carefully to find if you need to specify any string like atx=100 or atx=80, L2S10=200S7=S0M1x1 etc. in the **Extra Settings** field.

⑭ Click on **OK** button to switch to the previous window.

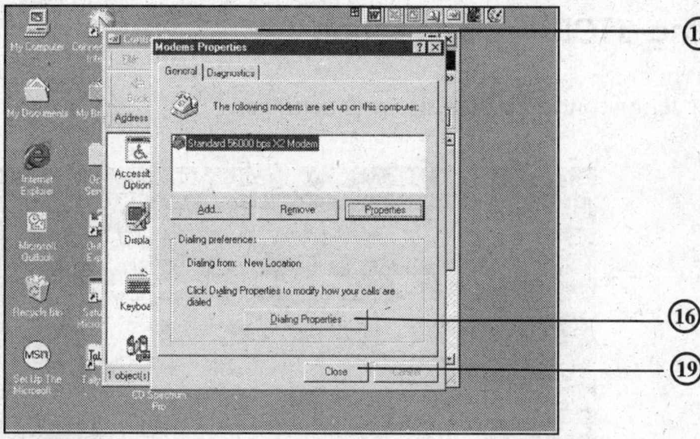

⑮ Click on **General** folio

⑯ Click on **Dialing Properties** button. The following dialog box would be displayed:

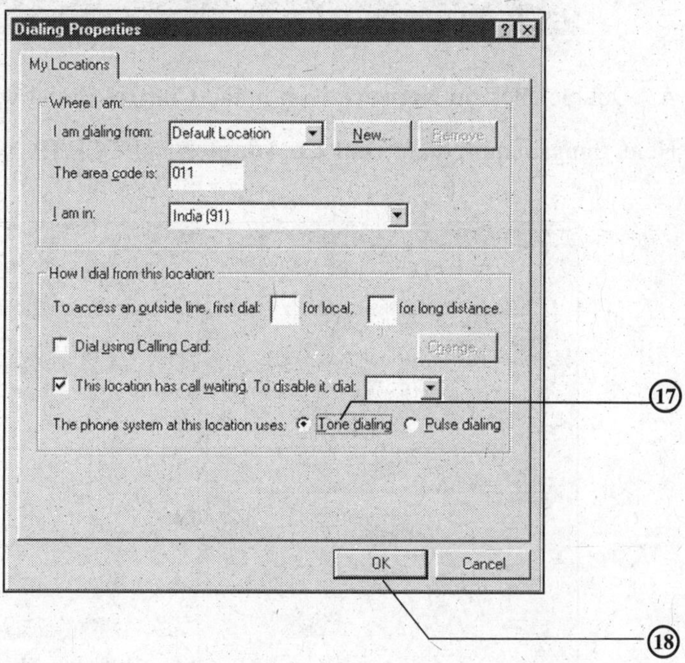

⑰ If your phone line has a fast dial then click on **Tone Dialing** radio button; otherwise click on **Pulse Dialing**.

⑱ Click on **OK** button to switch to the previous window.

⑲ Click on **Close** button.

Configuring a TCP/IP Connection

Now let us configure your network settings.

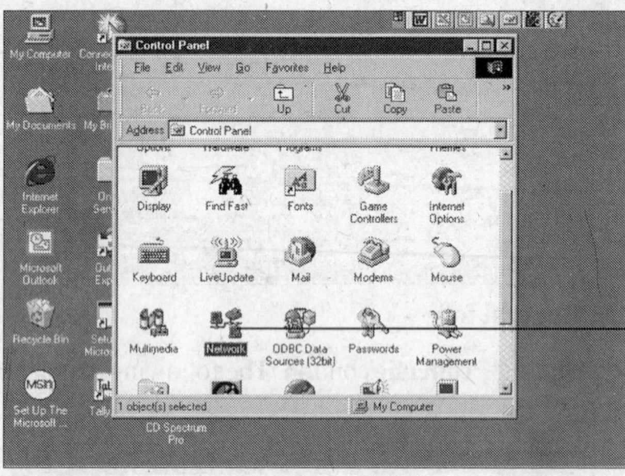

A

A Double click on **Network** icon in the **Control Panel** window.

Here, things required are **Dial Up Adapter** and **TCP/IP**.

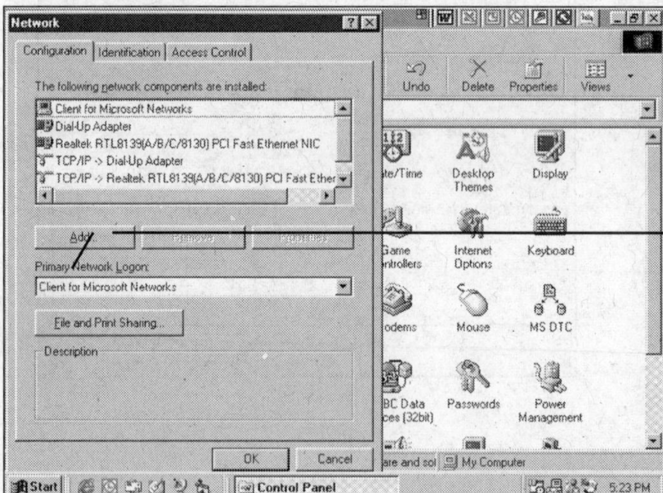

①

① Click on **Add** button.

② Choose **Protocol** option from the **Network Components** list.

③ Click on **Add** button.

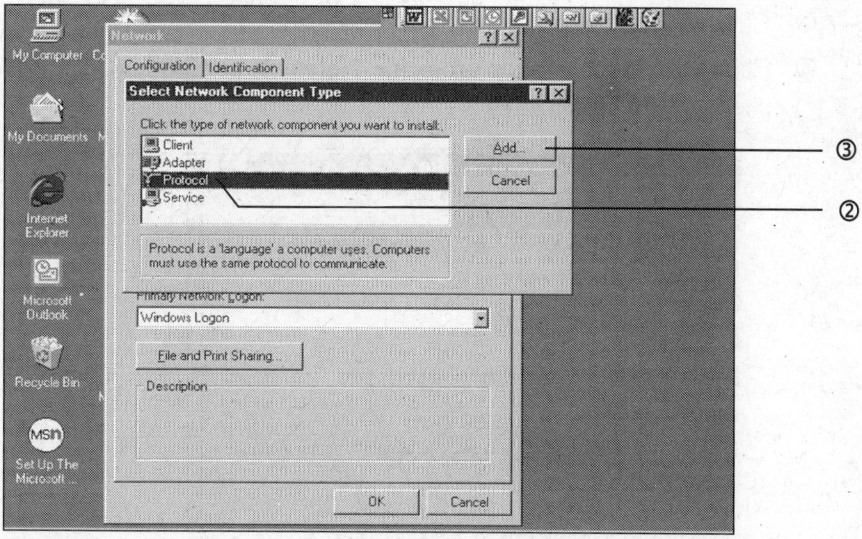

The following window would be displayed:

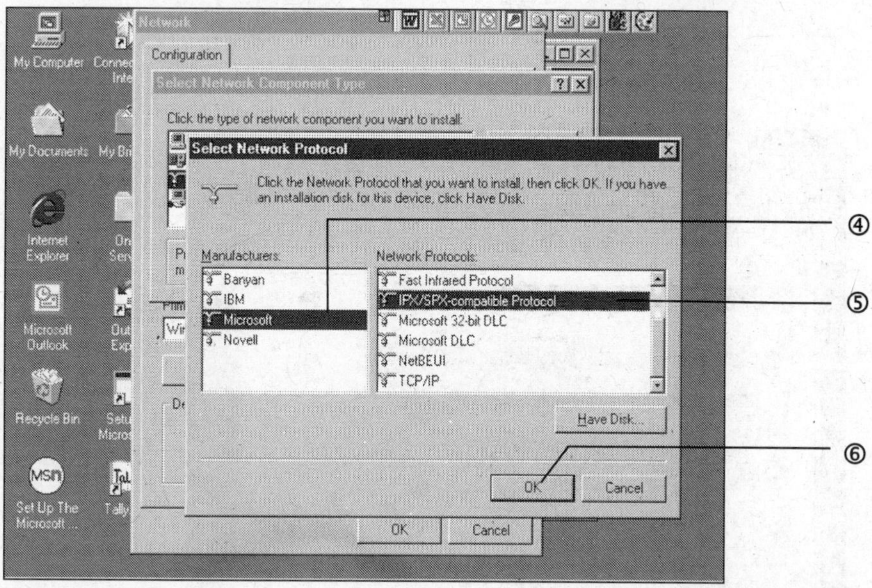

④ Choose **Microsoft** from the **Manufacturers** list.

⑤ Choose **IPX/SPX-compatible Protocol** from the **Network Protocols** list.

⑥ Click on **OK** button to switch to the previous window.

⑦ Click on **Add** button again to add a protocol.

⑧ Choose **Protocol** option from the **Network components** list given and then click on **Add** button.

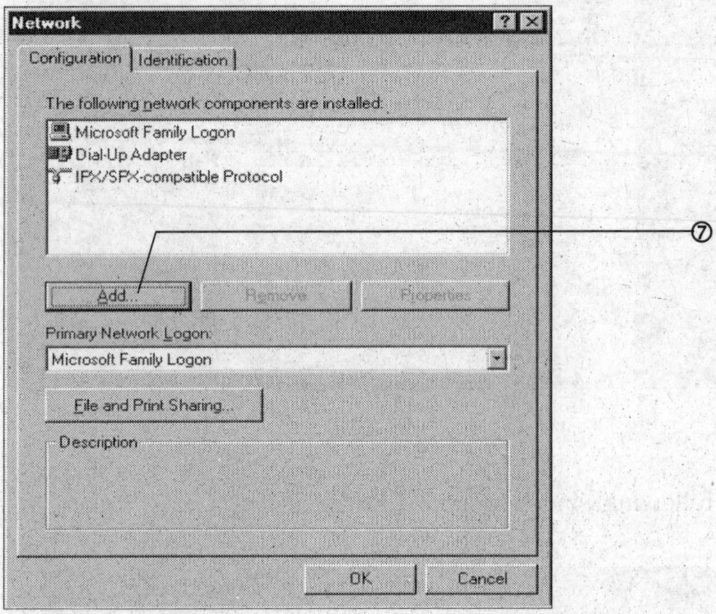

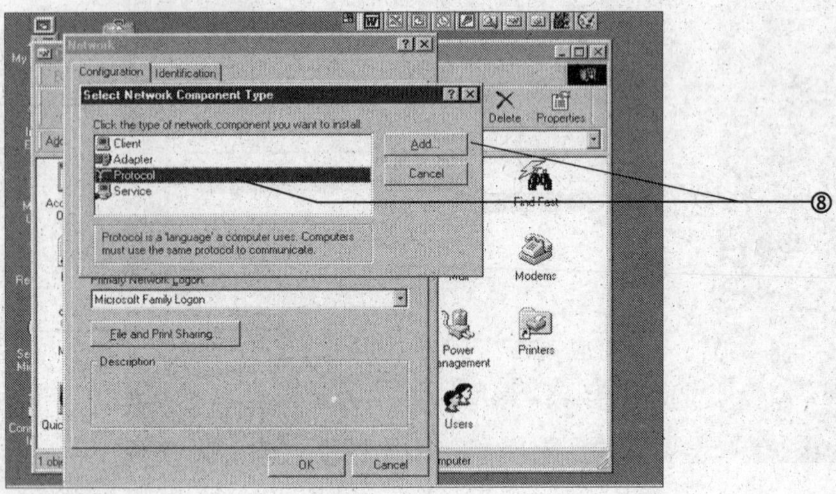

⑨ Choose **Microsoft** from the **Manufacturers** list.

⑩ Choose **TCP/IP** from the **Network Protocols** list.

⑪ Click on **OK** button to continue.

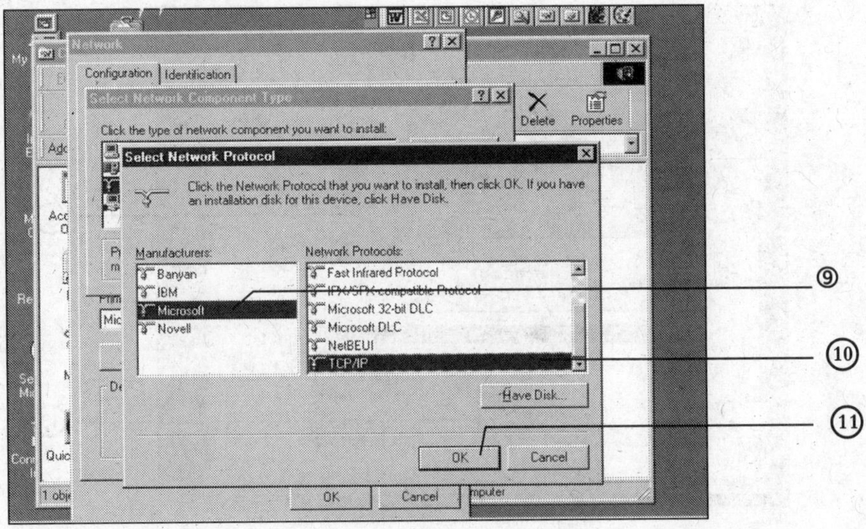

The following window would be displayed. The Dial-Up Adapter, TCP/IP, IPX/SPX-compatible Protocol and Microsoft Family Logon have been installed successfully.

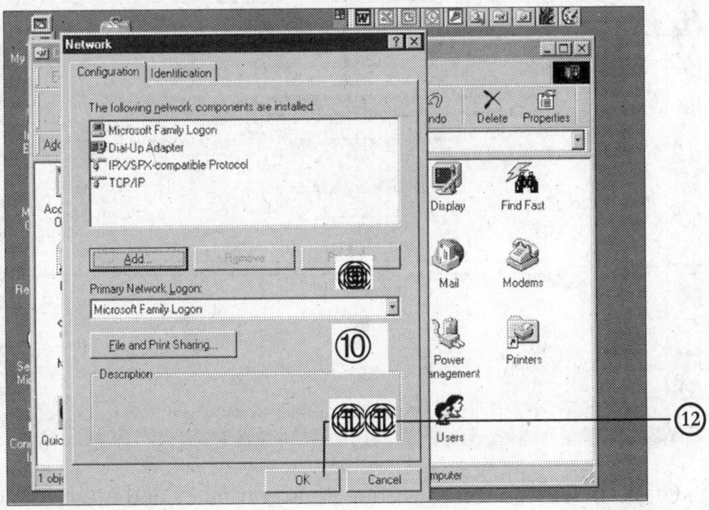

⑫ Click on **OK** button.

Ⓐ You will have to now insert the Windows 98 CD in the drive to continue.

⑬ Click on **OK** button.

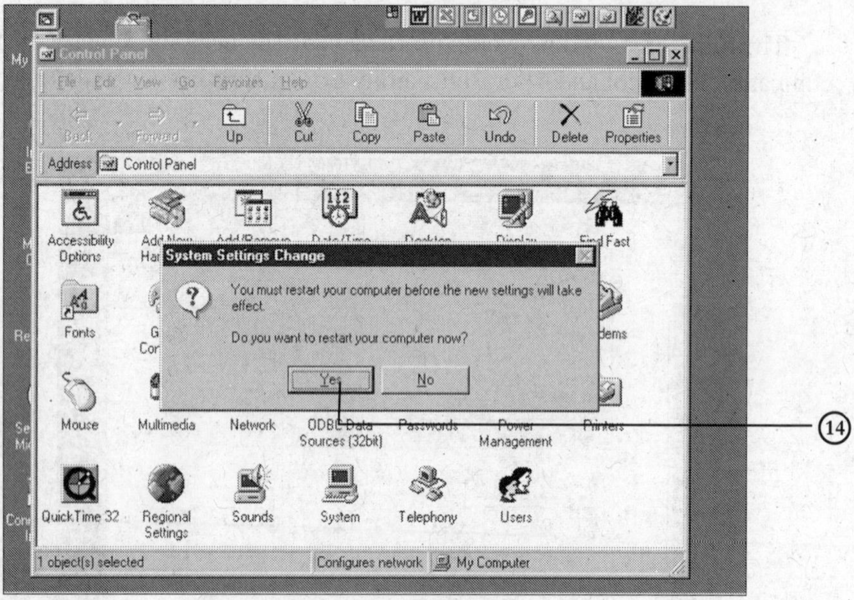

(14) Click on **Yes** button to restart your computer and apply the changes.

Now choose **Network** option from **Control Panel**.

(15) Select **TCP/IP**.

(16) Click on the **Properties** button.

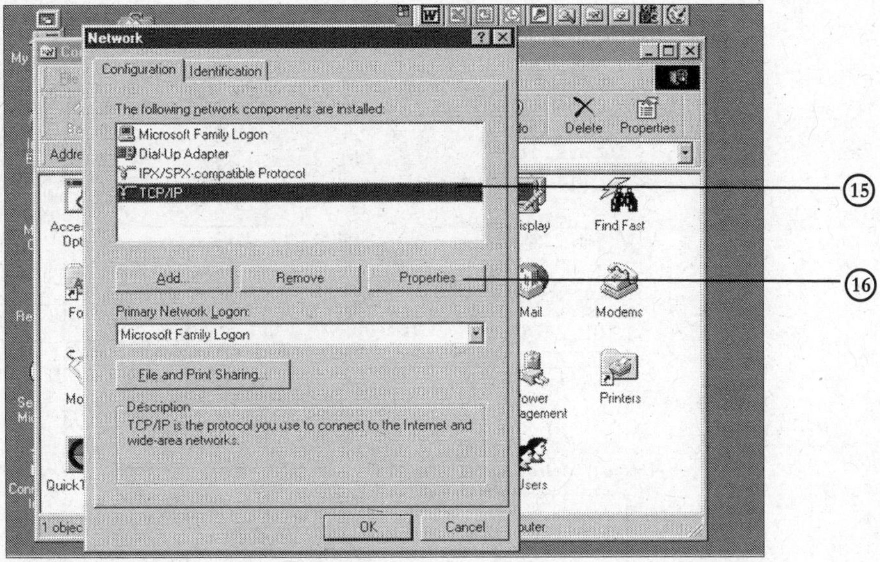

The following window would be displayed:

Match your computer's settings with the ones shown here.

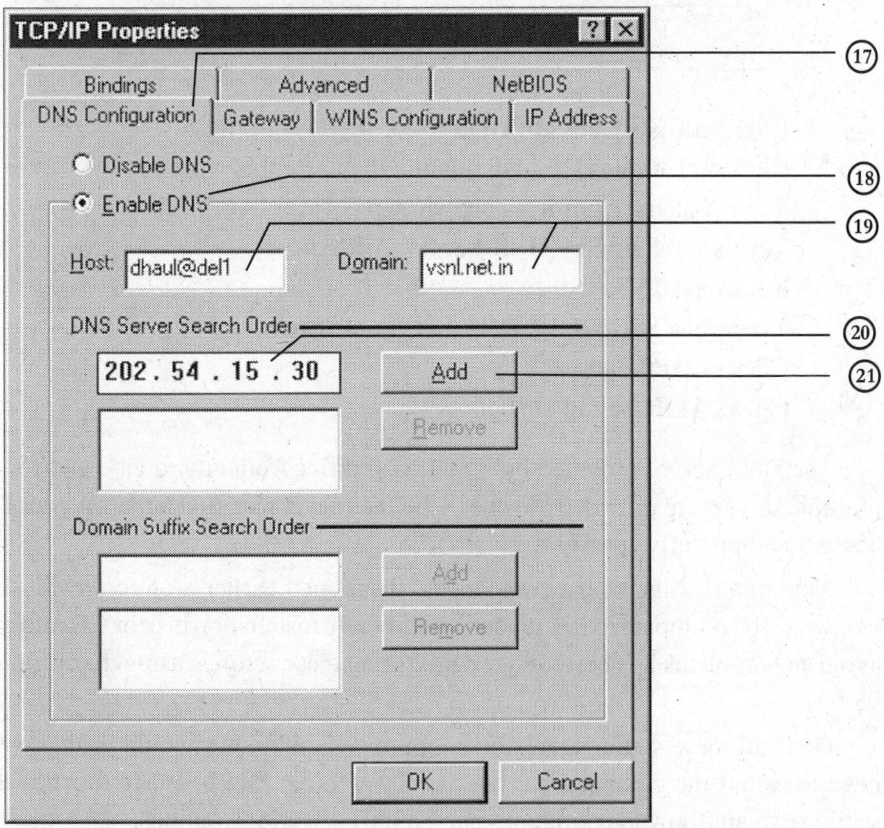

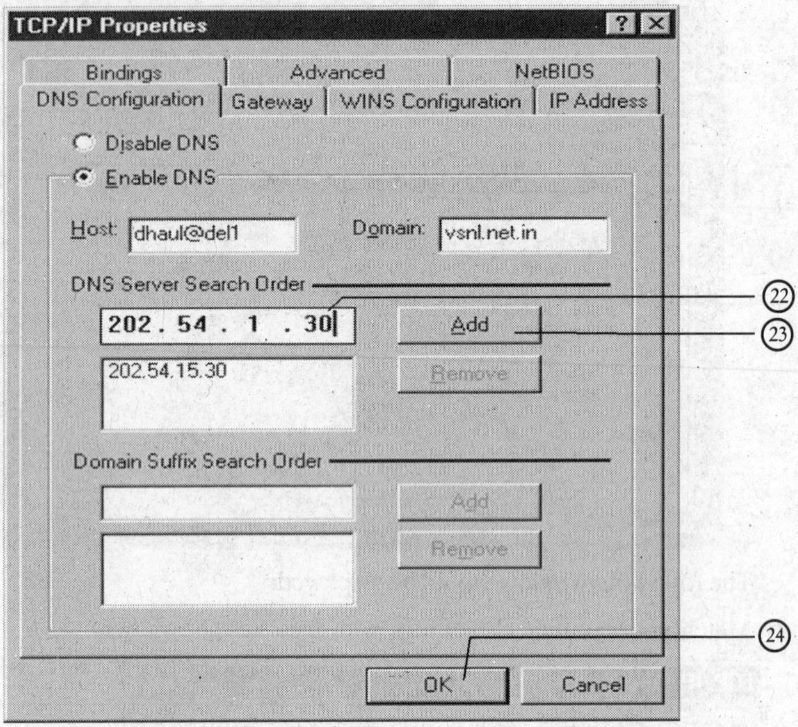

⑰ Click on **DNS Configuration** folio.
⑱ Click on **Enable DNS** radio button to enable this window.
⑲ Type your **user name** as shown here.
⑳ Type your **Primary DNS Server Address**.
㉑ Click on **Add** button.
㉒ Type your **Secondary DNS Server Address**.
㉓ Click on **Add** button.
㉔ Click on **OK** button to continue.

The DNS Server provided by VSNL will differ from city to city, and for large cities multiple servers are provided. So check the Internet connection letter for your DNS Server address and properly specify it.

Note that if some of the components mentioned earlier are not previously installed, you would be prompted to insert your Windows 98 installation disk or CD into the drive. To avoid any problems it is best to start configuring these settings using the original Windows 98 CD.

Once all these settings have been optimized, Windows would prompt you that you need to restart the computer so that the new settings can be made functional. The next section explains how to configure your dial up networking options.

Configuring Dial Up Networking

We shall now see how to configure Dial Up Networking options.

① Double click on **My Computer** icon on your desktop.

② Double click on **Dial Up Networking** icon.

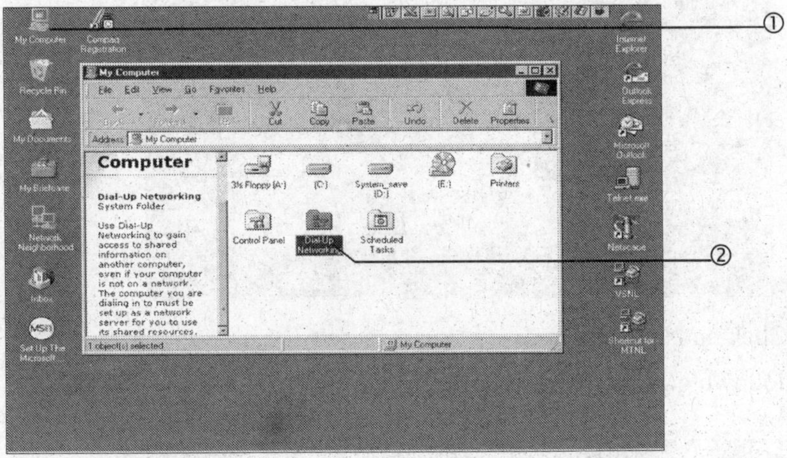

③ Double click on **Make a New Connection** icon.

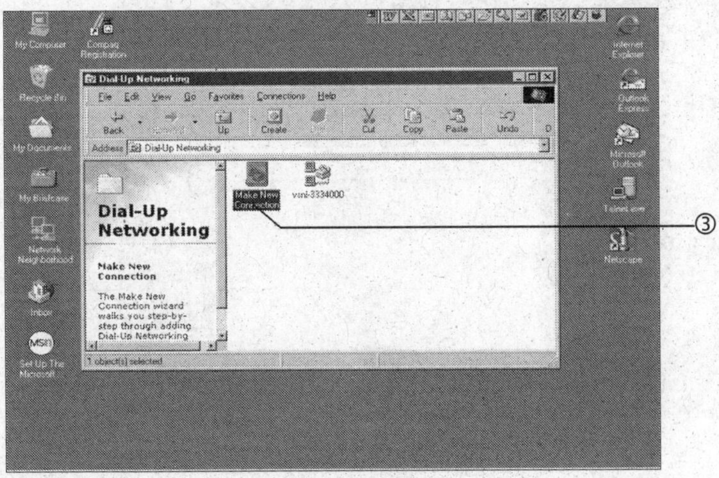

The following window would be displayed:

A Note that your modem driver name is already displayed here.

④ Specify a name for the connection in this text box.

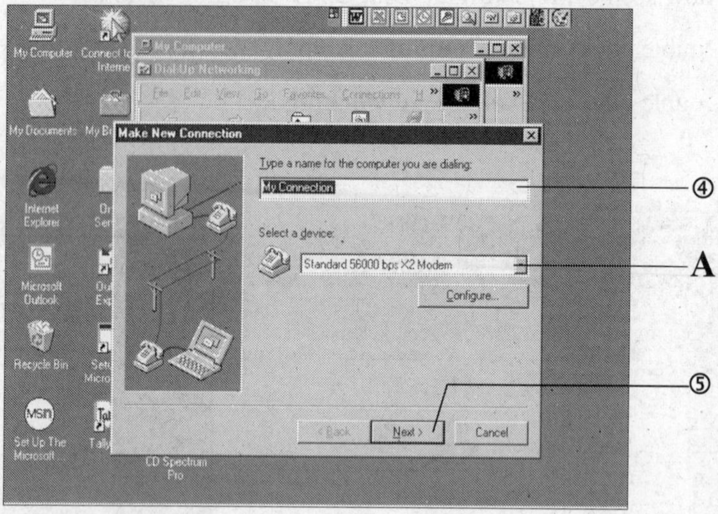

⑤ Click on **Next** button.

The following window would be displayed:

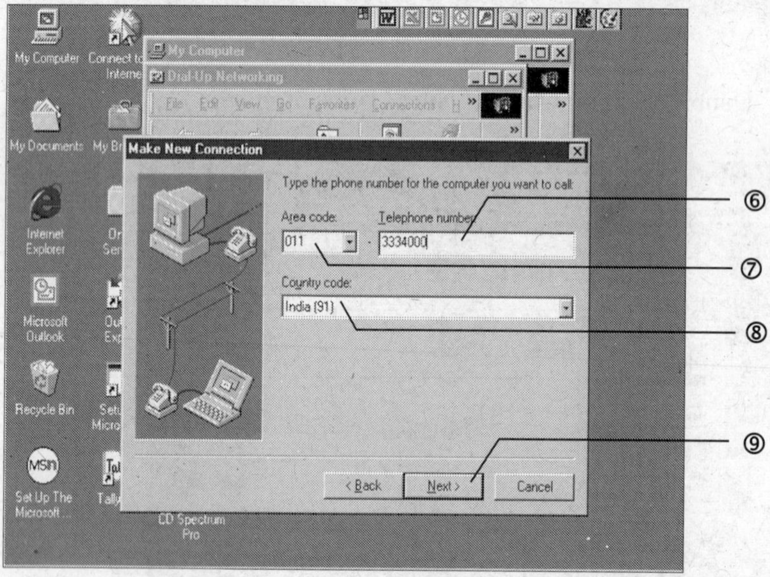

⑥ Type **VSNL's Internet telephone connection number**.

⑦ Type your city's **STD code**.

⑧ Choose your **Country** from the drop down list.

⑨ Click on **Next** button.

The following window would be displayed:

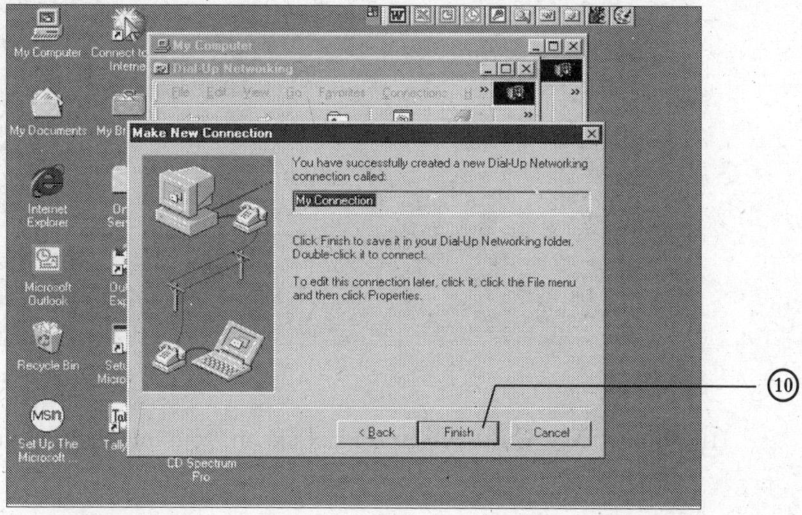

⑩ Click on **Finish** button.

Ⓐ Your dial-up connection called **My Connection** is now ready.

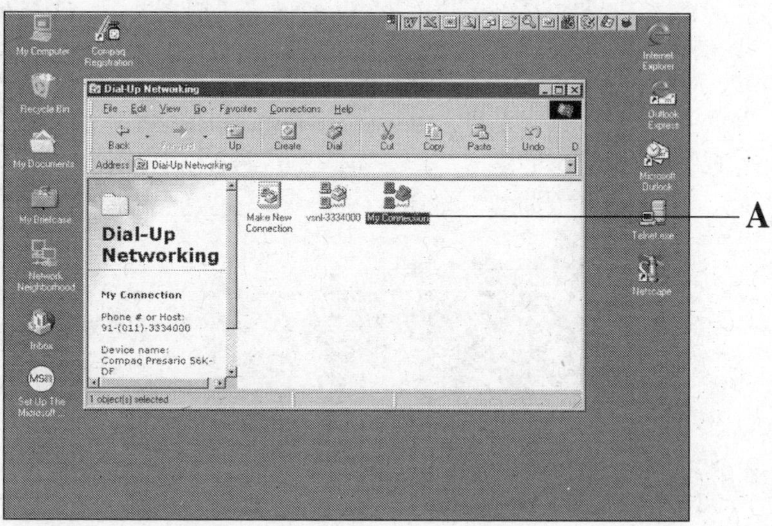

Now let us make a shortcut icon for the dial-up connection on your computer desktop.

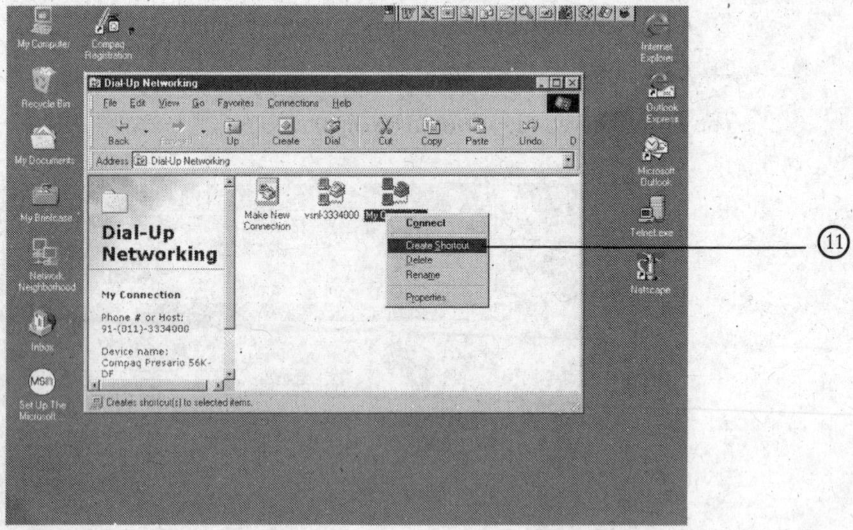

⑪ Select **My Connection** and click on your mouse's **right button** to get this menu.

The following message window would be displayed:

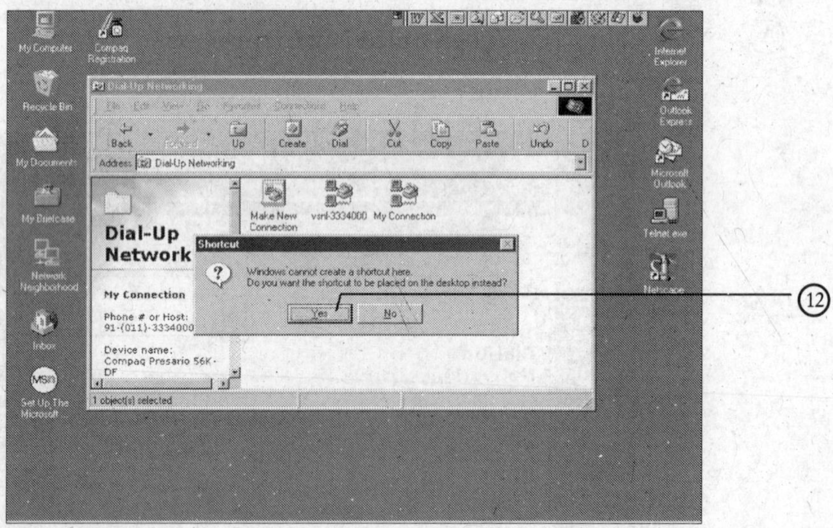

⑫ Click on **Yes** button.

A The shortcut icon for my connection has been created.

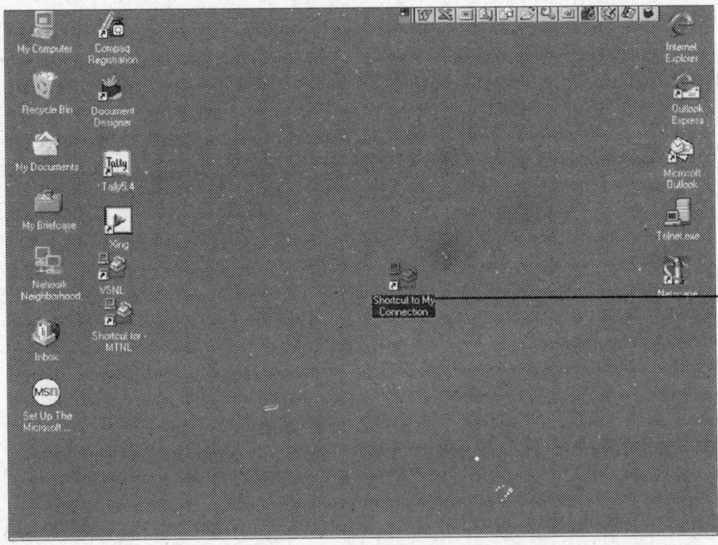

With this, you complete configuring your settings for Internet. You will now need Netscape Navigator or Internet Explorer software to be properly installed on your computer.

I know, by now, you must be thinking that if it takes so many steps to setup Internet, actually working on it would be a nightmare. Fortunately, my friend, you couldn't be more wrong! Surfing the Net is the simplest thing you have done so far if your telephone is working and you manage to get through to VSNL! So let's start surfing.

REVIEW QUESTIONS

1. **What is a Internet?**
2. **Compare shell account and TCP/IP account.**
3. **What are the activities that can be performed using Internet?**

9 Starting Internet

COMMON TERMINOLOGY

World Wide Web(WWW) It is a series of web servers (computers with 24 hours Internet connection) that are interconnected through hypertext. Hypertext is the organization of information units into connected associations that a user can choose to make. An instance of such an association is called a hyperlink. When a user clicks on such a link, more information on the particular topic is displayed. Hyperlinks allow the user to navigate from one document to another that may be located on a different web server. It is World Wide Web, which makes it possible to share information between disparate groups of users, computers and operating systems.

Website The web comprises a million of information locations called websites. Organizations and individuals who want to present information about themselves to the entire world or sell and/or buy products and services primarily create Websites. Websites comprise **web pages.** A webpage is an electronic page like any other computer document, except that it is created using **HTML (Hypertext Markup Language)**.HTML is an encoding scheme that helps in creating webpages. Webpages can contain pictures, buttons, videos, links to sound files, in addition to text , thus allowing multimedia applications.

A website includes a beginning file called a **homepage**. From the homepage, you can visit all other pages in the site. Since site implies a geographic place, a website can be confused with a web server. A server is a computer that holds the files for one or more sites. A very large website may be spread over a number of servers in different geographic locations. Microsoft is a good example; its website consists of thousands of files spread over a number of servers at various geographic locations.

Hypertext Transfer Protocol (HTTP) HTTP is a set of rules for exchanging files (text, images, sound, video, and other multimedia files) on the World Wide Web. This protocol makes the communication between your internet browser and the web possible. Relative to the TCP/IP suite of protocols (which are the basis for information exchange on the Internet), HTTP is an application protocol.

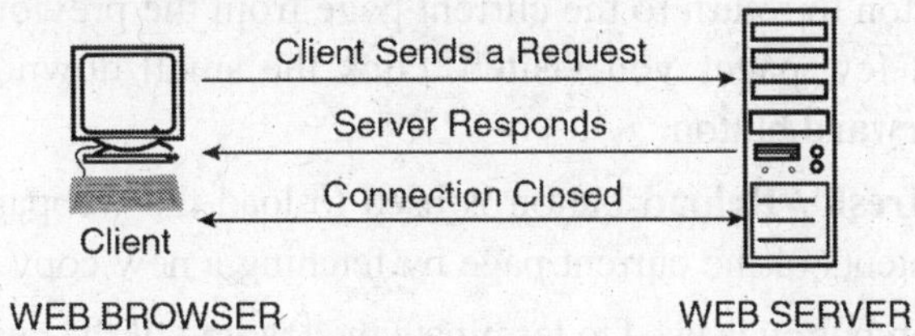

Fig. 9.1 Request Response Paradigm of HTTP

Uniform Resource Locator (URL) A URL is the Internet address of a web document. It contains information about the location of the document. The URL contains the name of the protocol required to access the resource, a domain name that identifies a specific computer on the Internet, and a hierarchical description of a file location on the computer. Any web page, not just a home page, or an individual file can have a HTTP URL.

An example of a URL is:

http://www.microsoft.com/index.html

which describes a Webpage to be accessed with an HTTP (Web browser) application that is located on a computer named www.microsoft.com. The file to be accessed is index.html.

BROWSER FUNCTIONS

Toolbar (Internet Explorer)

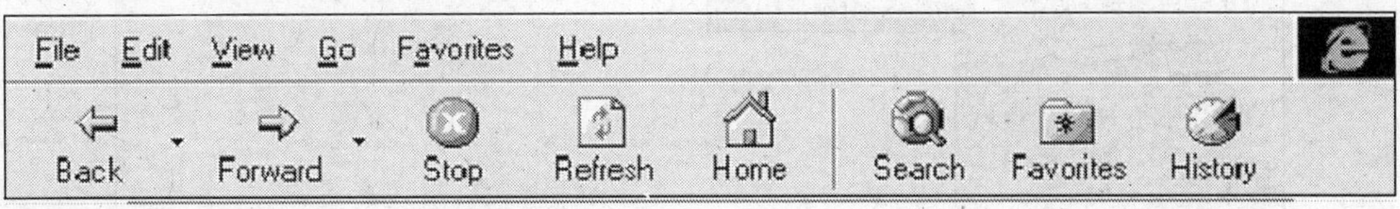

Toolbar (Netscape Navigator)

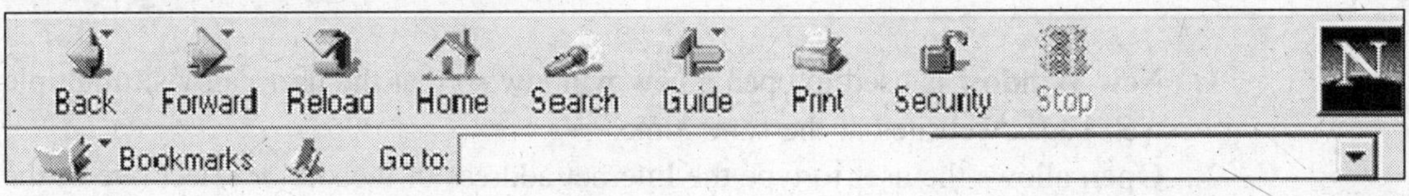

The row of buttons at the top of your web browser is known as the toolbar. Most of the options available in the menu bar are also available as icons in the toolbar. We will discuss the commonly used ones :

1. **Back** button is used to return to the page you viewed last. To view a page you viewed previously, click on the **Back** button. Similarly click on the **Forward** button to return to the current page from the previous page. To see a list of the last few pages you visited, click the small down arrow beside the **Back** or **Forward** button.
2. **Refresh / Reload** button is used to load the webpage again, i.e. refreshing the contents of the current page by fetching a new copy of it.
3. **Stop** button is used to terminate the loading of the current page. This can be used when a webpage takes a long time to download.
4. **Print** button is used to print the current webpage.
5. **Favorites/Bookmarks** is used to record the addresses of frequently visited websites. Once a webpage/website is added to this list it can be revisited by simply clicking on the link in the favorites list. This saves effort of typing the URL each time the user visits the same site.
6. **History** is a record of all pages visited during a specific period of time. Clicking on the History button will display all the webpages/websites visited recently. To revisit the page simply click on the address.

File Menu (Internet Explorer)

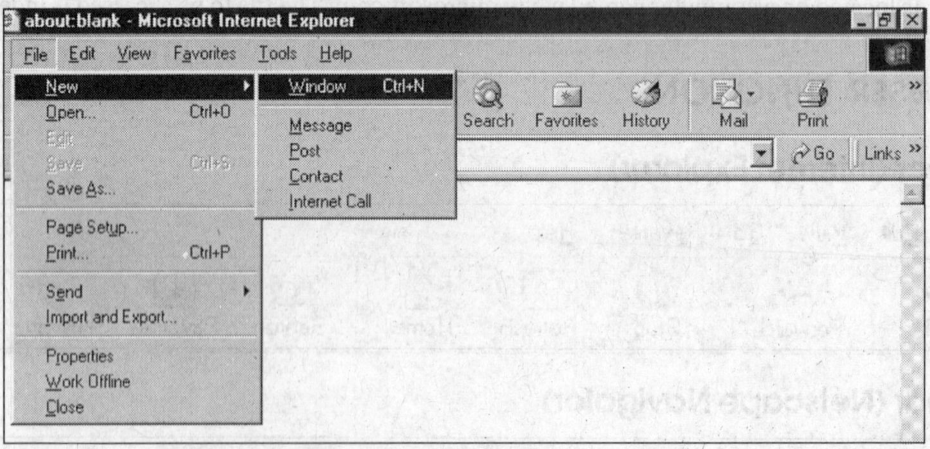

1. **New Window** is used to open a new window so that the user can visit multiple web pages/websites at the same time.
2. **Open** allows the user to type the Internet address of the site or select one of the sites already visited.

3. **Save As** allows the user to save the currently loaded webpage.
4. **Close** is used to close the current window.

View Menu (Internet Explorer)

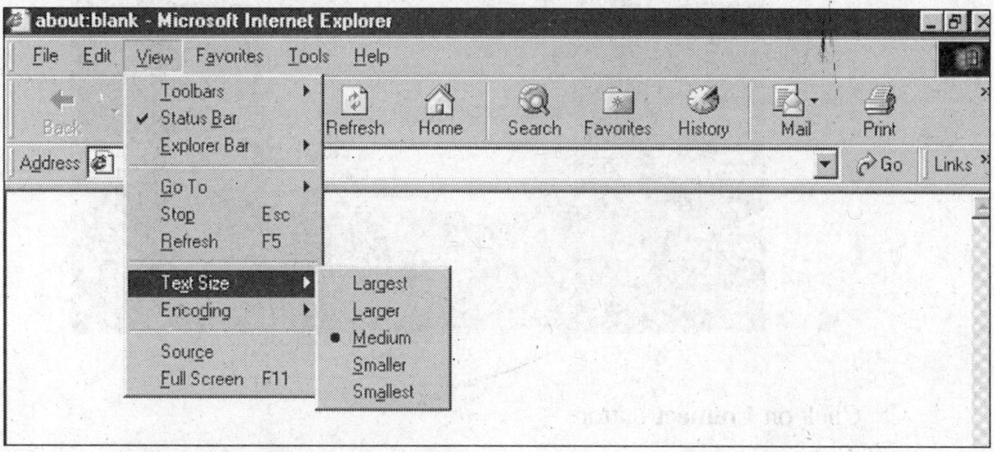

1. **Toolbars, Status Bar** allows to enable or disable the display of toolbars and status bar respectively.
2. **Text Size** allows the user to select the size of the text on pages being viewed.

By now we have properly configured our Internet connection. Let us now start working on the Internet.

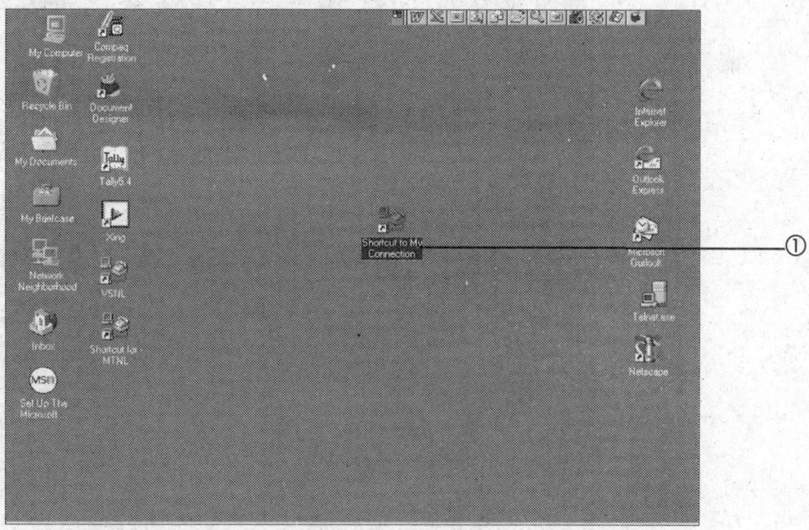

① Double click on the **My Connection** icon.

The following window would be displayed:

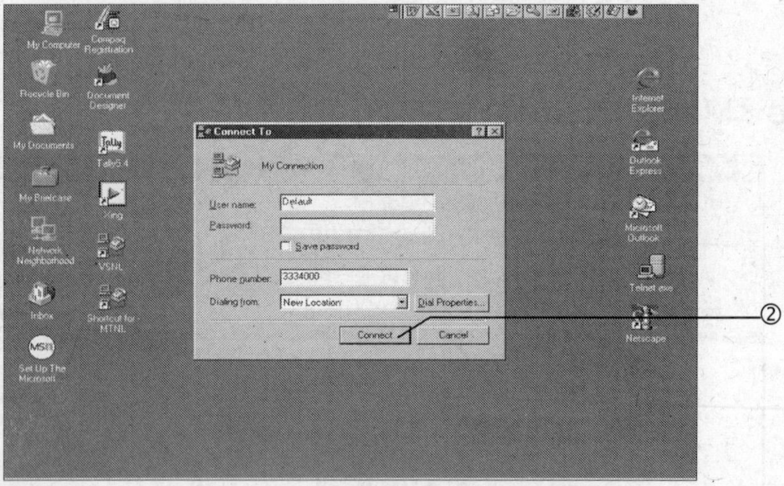

② Click on **Connect** button.

The following message window would be displayed. Your modem would start dialing the VSNL's Internet connection number and you distinctly hear the dialing tone. If this tone is not sufficiently loud or clear, adjust the modem's speaker volume (refer the previous section).

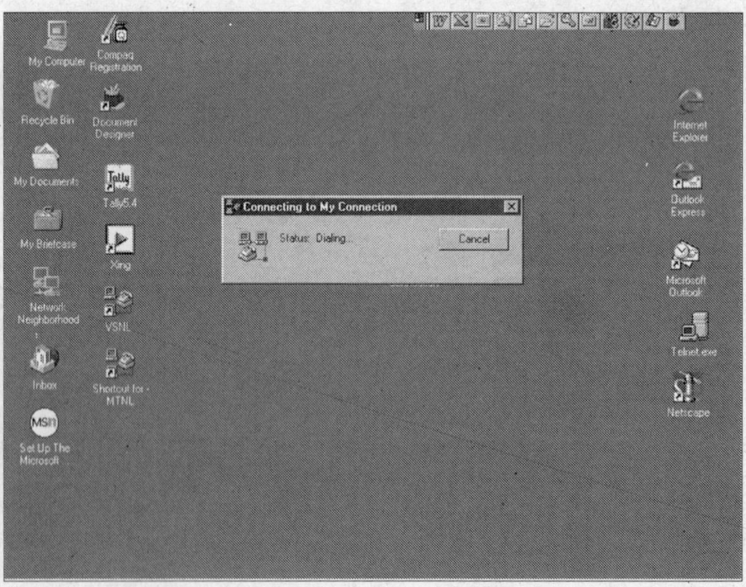

It is possible that you either get connected or get a message saying that the line is busy. If you get this message, do not lose heart, it simply means that the number you have dialed is busy.

Carefully read the letter that you received with Internet connection kit. This letter contains all the telephone numbers available to you for logging on to the Internet. It contains VSNL's helpline which you can call for assistance.

Finally, when you are persistent and lucky enough (in that order!) you would finally get through to VSNL. You would see VSNL's Internet opening screen welcoming you to the Internet fraternity.

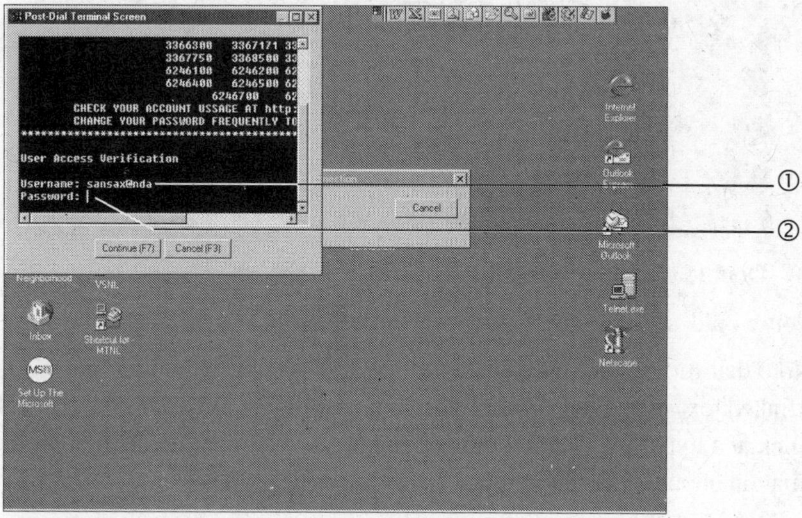

① Type your **Username** and press Enter key.
② Type your **Password** and press Enter key.

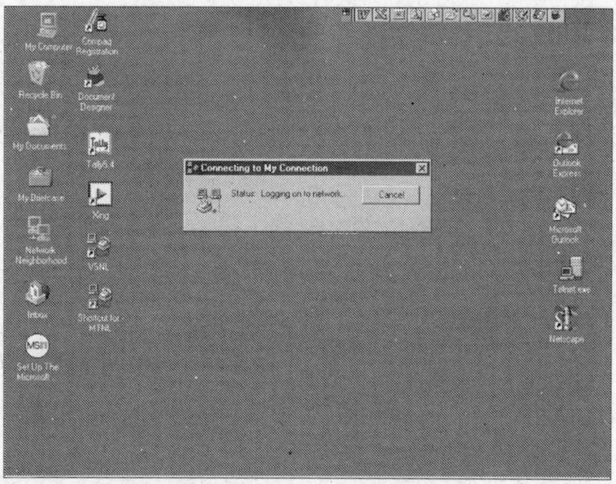

As soon as your password is verified, you will be connected to the Internet.

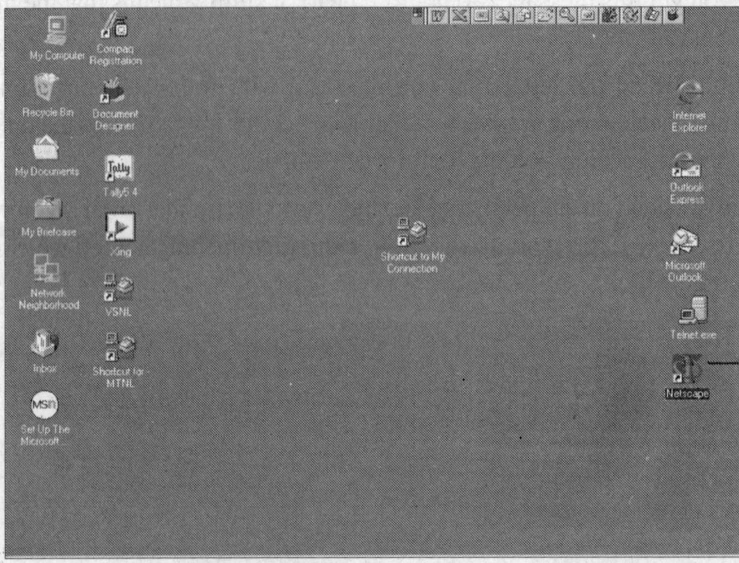

③ Double click the **Netscape** icon.

You would now see the Netscape Home Page.

Note that mouse pointer changes to a Hand symbol when you move the cursor over hyperlinked text. As stated earlier hyperlinks are links to other Web sites or documents. If you click at a hyperlink, you would be taken to a document or site that would show more information about a topic or subject.

A Type in the name of the site that you want to visit in the Address bar of the browser (e.g. let us visit an interesting site called **gobookshopping.com**) and press Enter key.

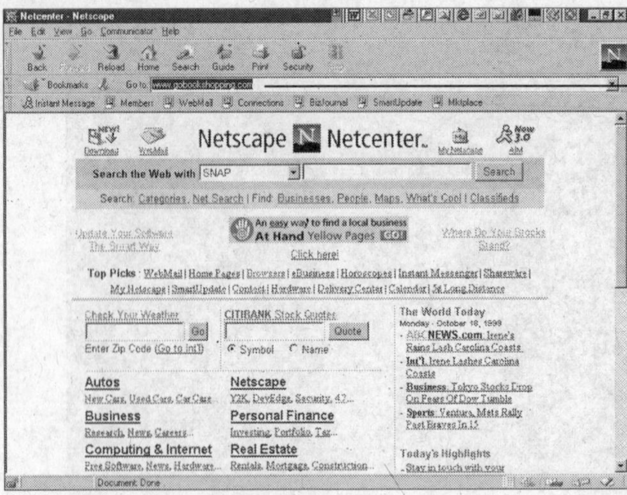

Gobookshopping's homepage would be displayed now.

When you want to visit this site again, simply Bookmark it.

B To bookmark this site click once on **Add Bookmark** from **Bookmarks** menu. A pop-up window would be displayed, containing the current webpage URL. Simply click on the **OK** button to bookmark this site.

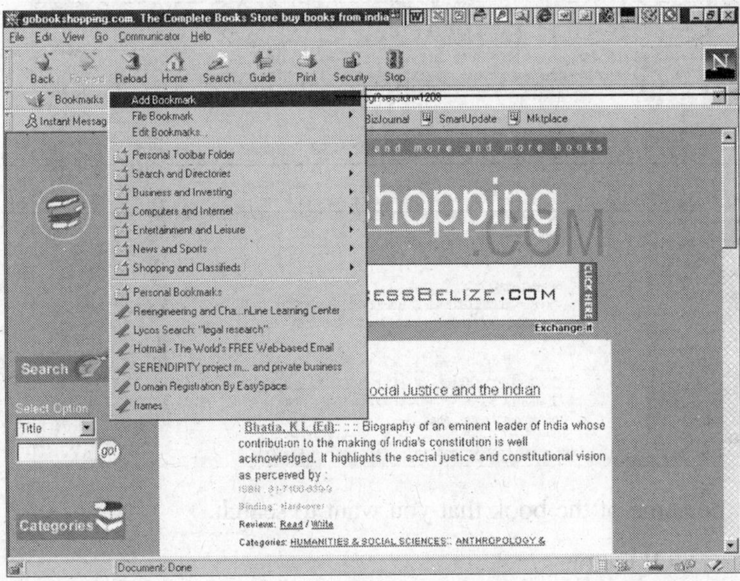

B

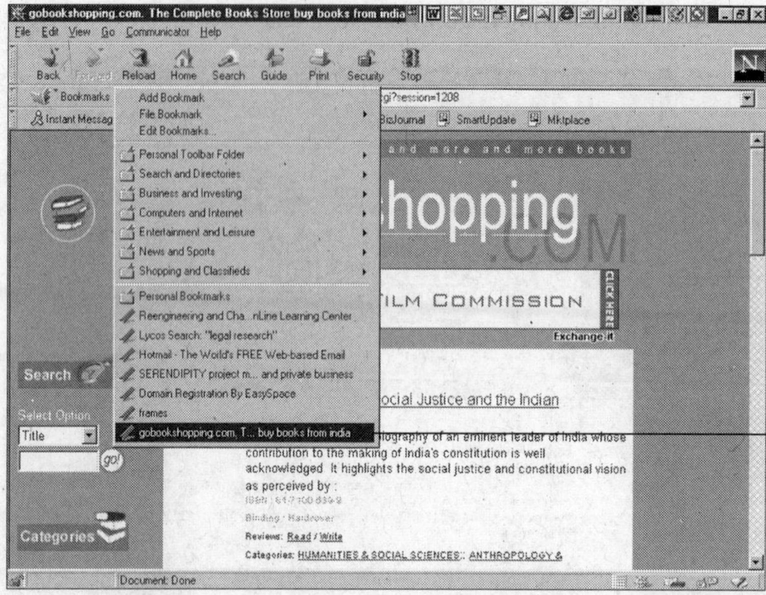

C

C Note that gobookshopping.com is added to your bookmarks list .

Now let us search a particular book, *A First course in computers* in this website.

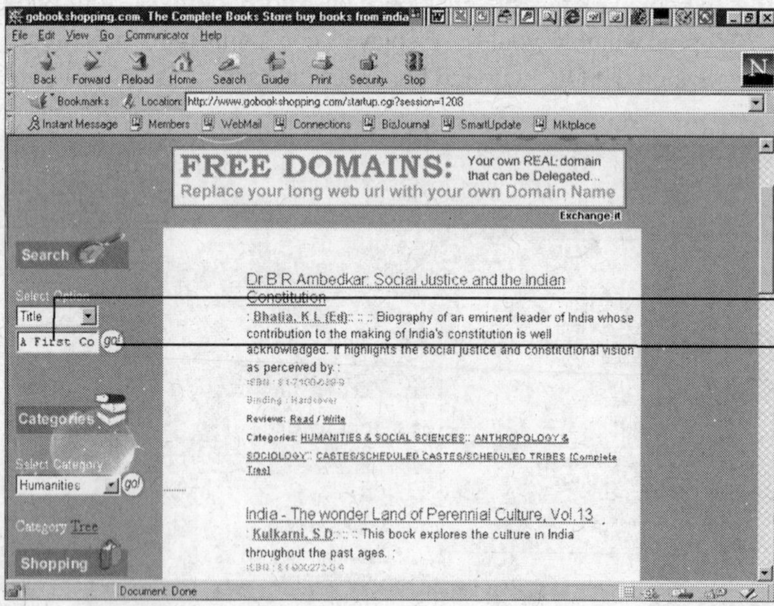

①

②

① Type the name of the book that you want to search.

② Click on **GO!** button.

The book, if listed, would appear before you.

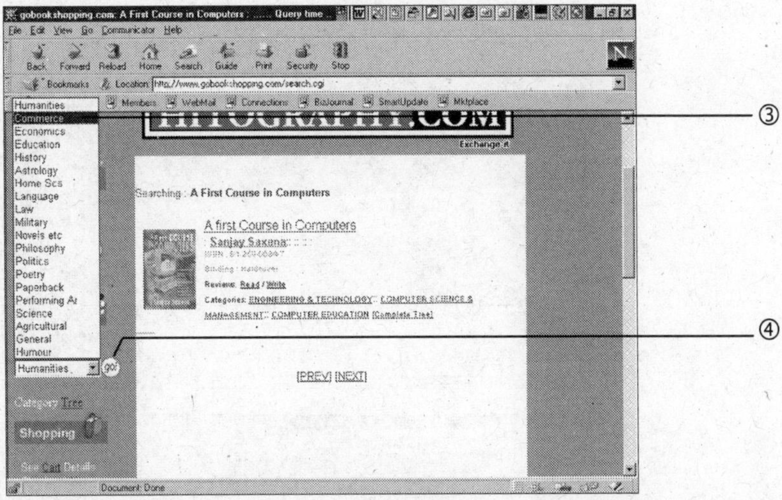

Now let us try to search all the books available on a category.

③ Choose from this roll-down list the category of books you want to search.

④ Click on **GO!** button.

A A list of books available in the category has been displayed..

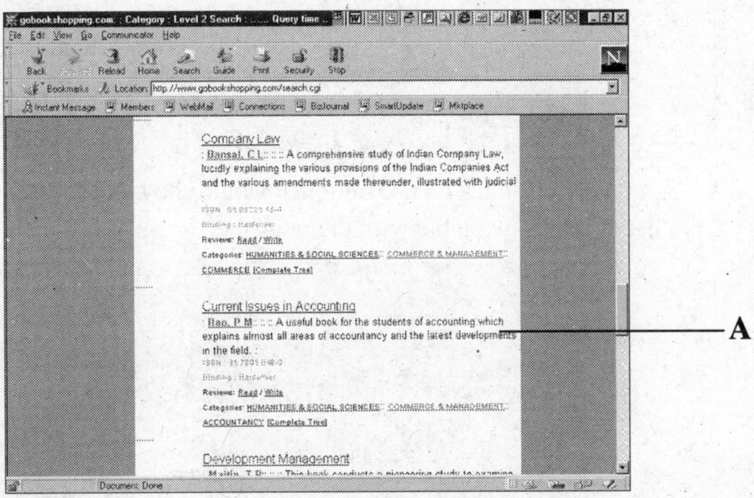

Now suppose you want a list of all books available with a particular publisher.

⑤ Click on this roll-down list and choose **Publisher**.

⑥ Type in the name of the publisher (e.g. Vikas).

⑦ Click on **GO!** button.

A As soon as you click on GO button, it would show this message and start displaying a list of books available with the publisher.

Let us visit another interesting site ubspd.com. The home page of ubspd.com.in displayed below.

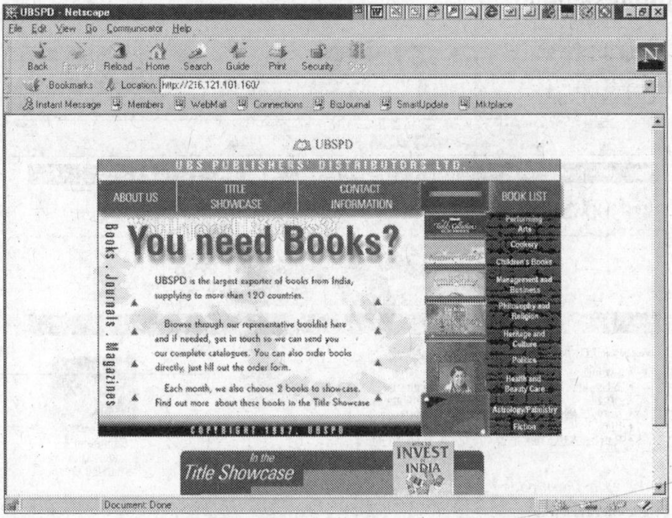

Let us now visit another interesting site called download.com. It is a largest site containing free software, games, shareware programs etc. to be downloaded at just a click of a button. The homepage of download.com. is displayed below.

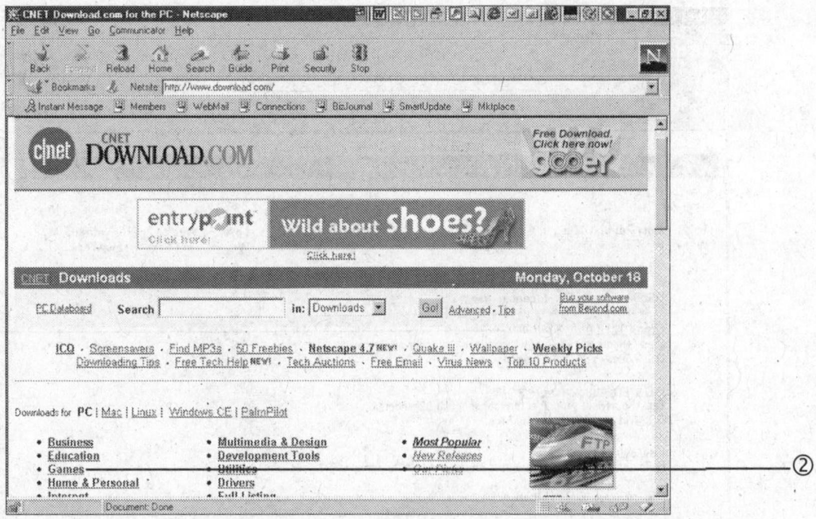

As you would notice, there are just so many things that can be downloaded. We choose to download games.

② Click on the **Games** option.

A You would see that we have a variety of games that can be downloaded. We would try to download one of the most popular games. Click on the **Most Popular** option.

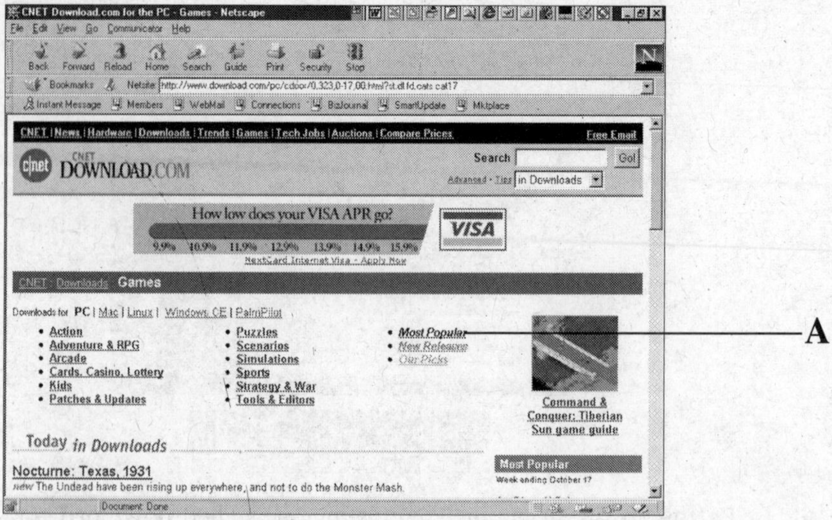

① We choose **The Grand Theft Auto 2** by clicking on it.

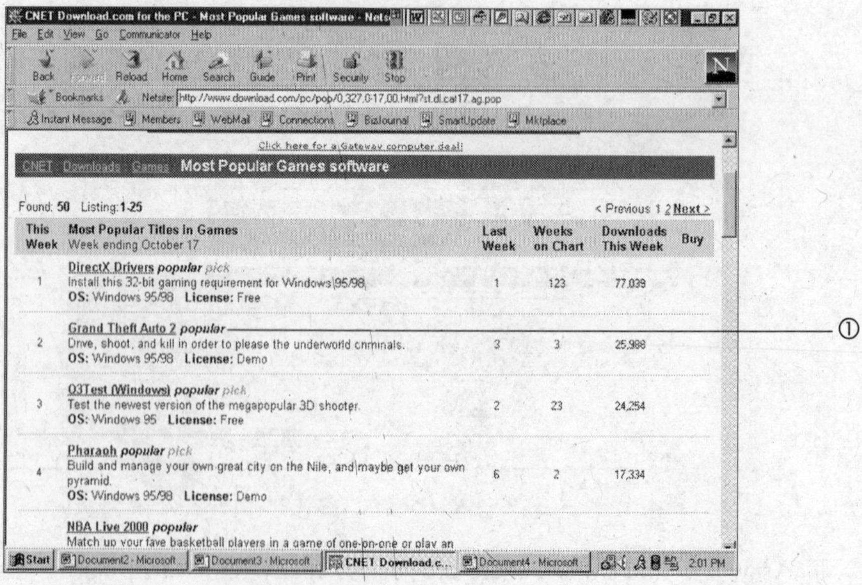

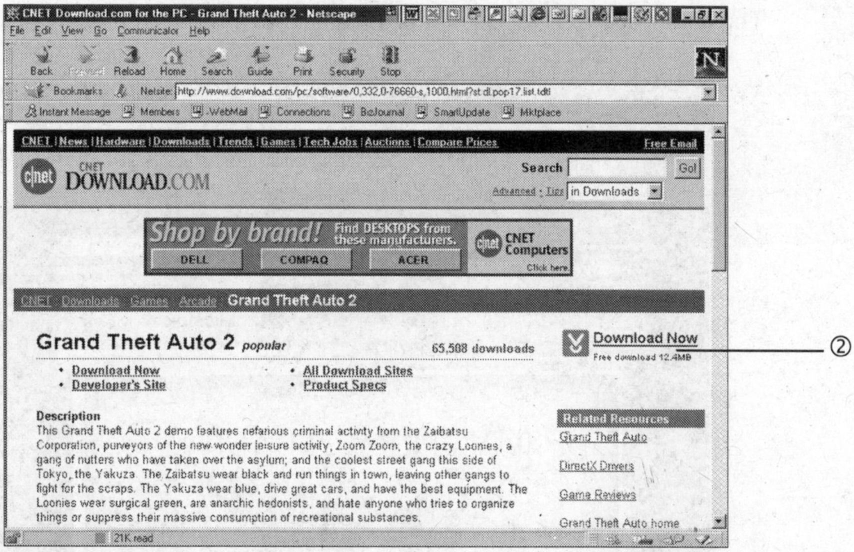

② Click here to download the game.

You would now see the message that the game is being downloaded. It will also show the directory into which the game is downloaded. At any point of time, you can cancel the download by simply clicking on the Cancel button. If you decide to proceed, then wait for the confirmation that the download is complete.

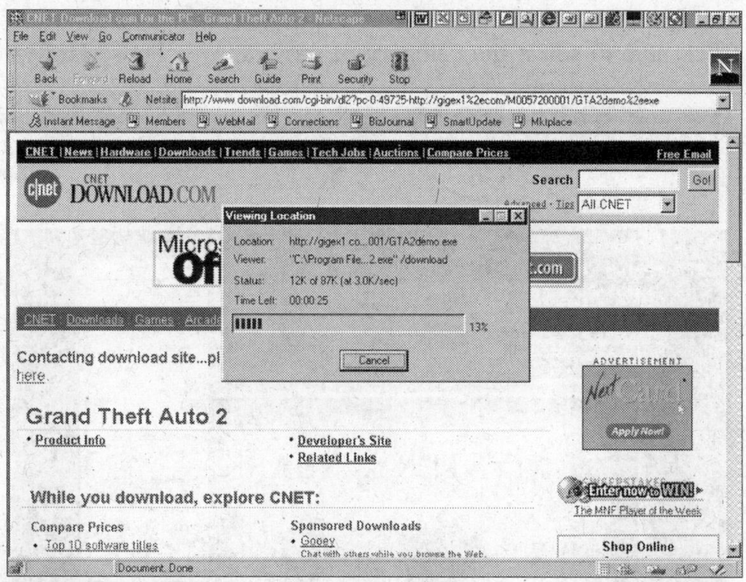

It is time to entertain ourselves by watching some movies. Let us visit a site movies.com developed for this purpose.

The homepage of movies.com is displayed below.

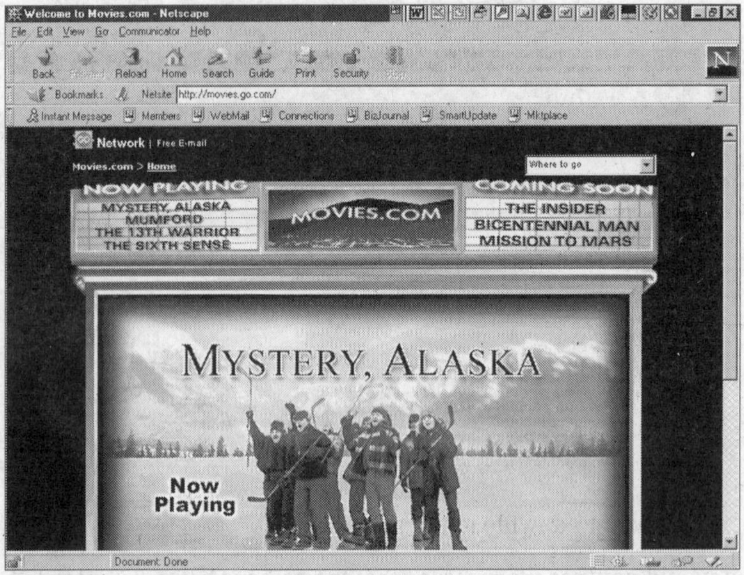

You can now see here the latest movie released in Hollywood.

You can scroll down to read about the movie, its directors, actors, scriptwriter and others.

① Click here to select the category of movies. We choose **Hollywood Records**.

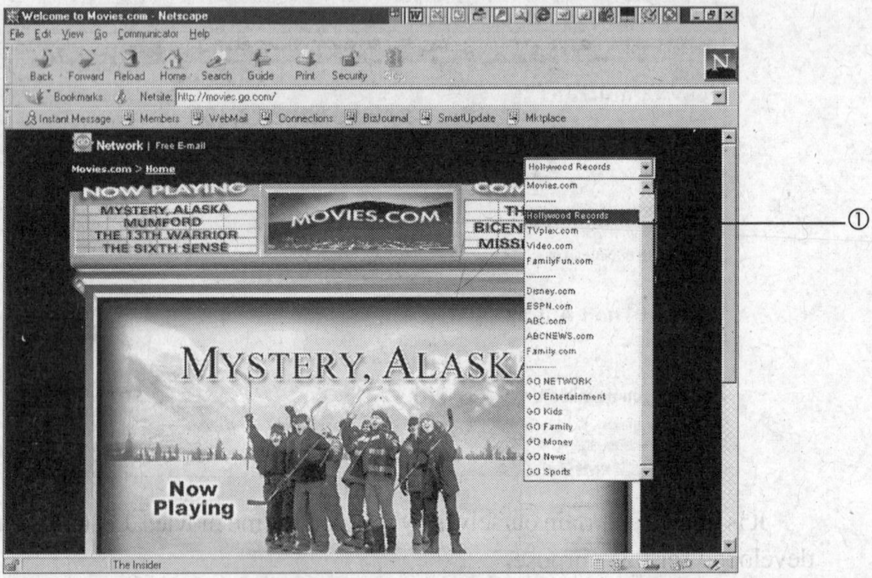

A You could also click here and enter the name of your favourite artist to read inter views etc.

Well folks, it is time to say goodbye to surfing.

B Click here to close your Internet session.

You will have to now disconnect the Internet.

Disconnecting the Internet

Go to the Window status line (one which has the Start button) and you would see the connection icon, right click on this icon and click on the Disconnect button.

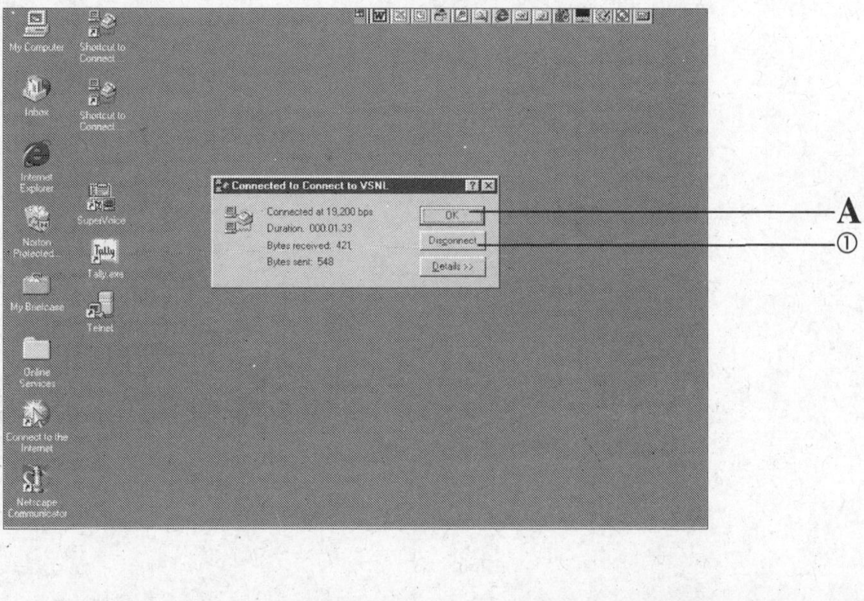

① Click here to disconnect.

② Incase you do not want to get disconnected but you just want to see the displayed information (connected at:, Duration, Bytes received & Bytes sent) then simply click on OK button after seeing the information.

Do not forget this last step, otherwise you may think that since you have closed the browser, you have also disconnected. Unfortunately, this is not the case and unless you disconnect from here, your VSNL's and MTNL's (in case of Delhi) meter is still running.

You have now been disconnected from the net.

By the way don't forget that all this while you have been hooked on to the Net, your VSNL'S hours that you bought, and your telephone bills are running full steam ahead. So take a break and call a friend instead!

REVIEW QUESTIONS

1. **How do you search for a webpage using Internet? Explain the steps involved.**
2. **Visit a website and find out its features.**
3. **Find out the function of the options (e.g. History, Search) available.**
4. **Find out the emoticons that are available. What are they used for?**

10 E-Mails

Sending and receiving e-mails is one of the most popular uses of the Internet. The salient features of e-mail facility are:

- Through Internet you can send and receive messages from anywhere in the world, in a matter of minutes. The only pre requisite is that both the receiver and the sender should have an e-mail connection and, of course, a modem and computer with compatible hardware and software to run the e-mail software.
- Irrespective of where you send or receive the message from, your cost is the same as that of making a local call plus the cost of time slab that you have paid to Internet Service Provider (ISP). This means that whether you send an e-mail to Calcutta or to California you will pay only for a local call! Compared to phone, fax or telex this is certainly the cheapest mode of communication.
- Through e-mail, you can send any type of file – an image file, video clip or a song. Therefore it is very versatile and an open medium.
- Just like mail merge in MS-Word, you can send an e-mail to any number of recipients, thereby saving a lot of time and effort.

A Opening a mail Account.

Double click on Internet Explorer icon on your Desktop.

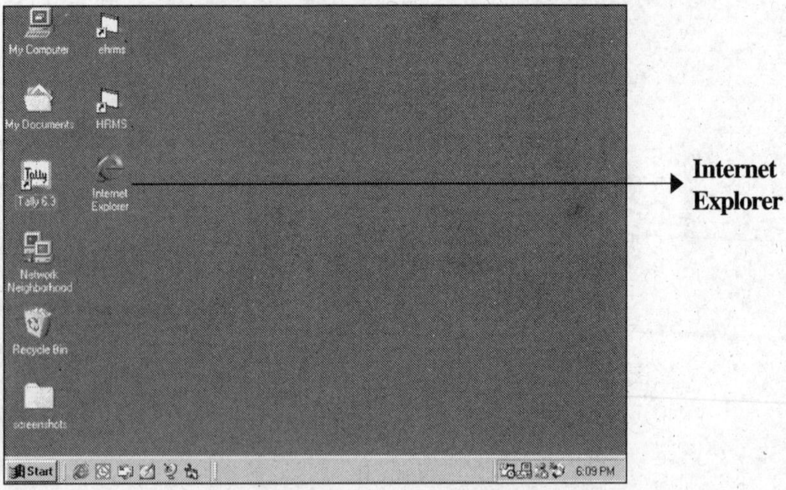

Since we are interested in learning e-mail, we will open "**yahoo.com**", a website that offers free e-mail service. Other sites offering free e-mail service include hotmail.com, indiatimes.com, rediff.com, sify.com, lycos.com and many more.

The homepage of "yahoo.com" will be displayed as shown below. Click on E-mail button.

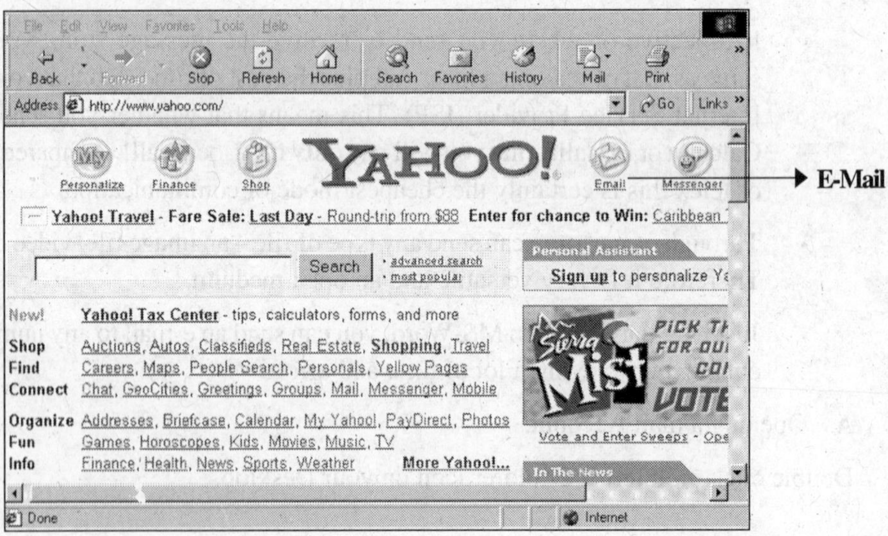

A new webpage would be loaded as shown below.

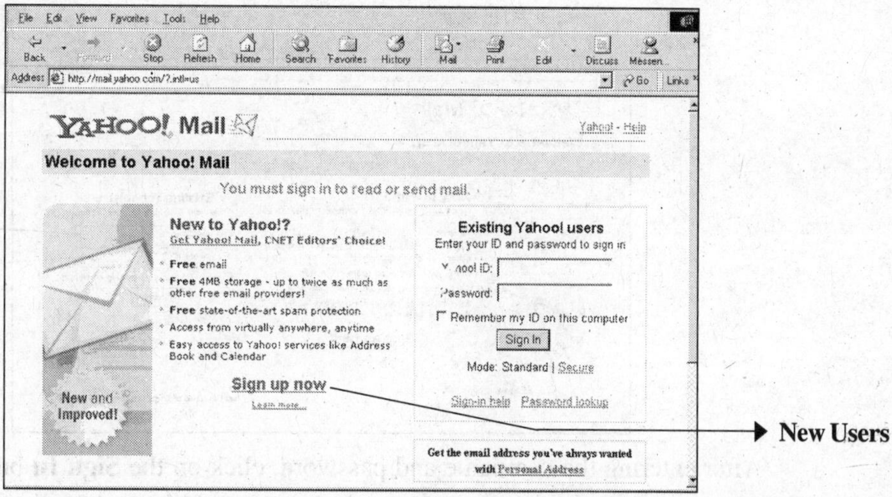

To open an e-mail account with yahoo.com, you will have to fill in a registration form. Once a user is registered he gets an e-mail address. To fill in the registration form click on the "Sign Up Now" button. This would open a new webpage that would display the registration form as shown below:

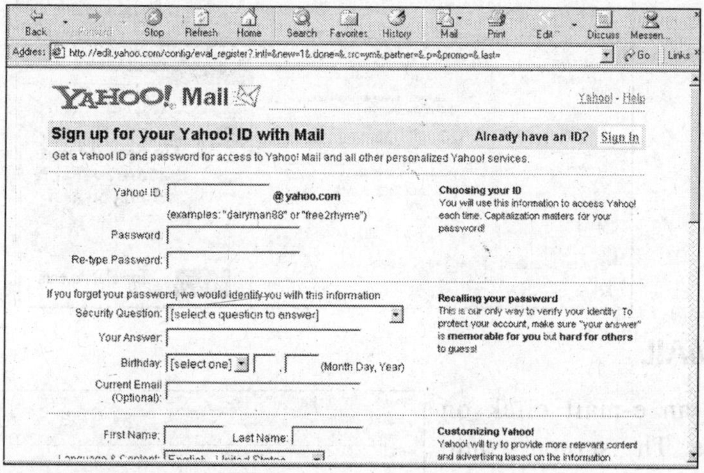

Fill in the registration form. A username and a password have to be entered. This name will later be used for logging into your e-mail account. After you type in all the details click on the submit button. Once you click the submit button, a confirmation message is displayed with your **username**, **password** and **e-mail address**. Once a user registers with a website, he becomes a member and he can simply log into his e-mail account at any time. It is very important to remember the username and password because without this you cannot access your e-mail account.

To log into your e-mail account enter your username and password in the following screen:

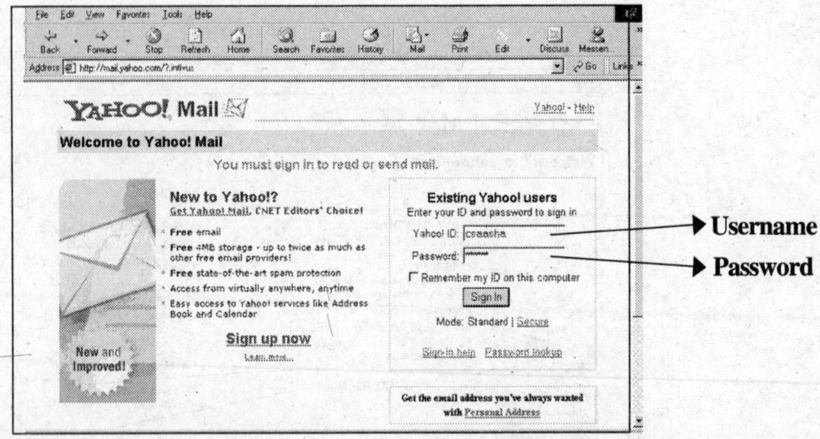

After entering the username and password, click on the **Sign In** button. This would open up your **Inbox**. Inbox is a place where your e-mails are stored.

SENDING E-MAIL

To send an e-mail click on **Compose**. The screen would look as shown:

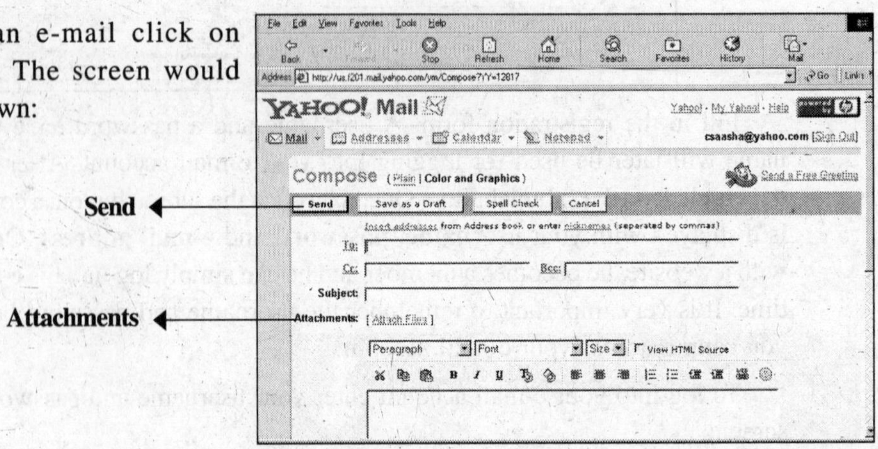

1. In the **To** box, type the name of the recipient. It should take the form **recipient@domain.com**. Make sure you enter the address correctly or the message will return to you.
2. **CC** stands for "Carbon Copy." You can send a message to more than one person by entering multiple addresses. Just put a comma (,) between each address.
3. **BCC** (stands for "Blind Carbon Copy") is used if you want to address an e-mail to a group of people, without them being able to see the names. Now all the recipients mail addresses will remain private. Only YOU will know to whom the mail has been addressed!
4. **Subject** Box is used to specify the subject of the letter.
5. **Message** Box is used to write your message. You can also copy text from a word processing program and paste it into the window.

After typing the letter simply click on the **Send** button. You will get a message informing you that your mail has been sent. Your e-mail address is automatically sent to the recipient. You must keep in mind that sending a mail properly is no proof of it being received properly by the recipient. However, in case you have given a wrong e-mail address, you will get an intimation that your e-mail could not be delivered.

CHECKING E-MAIL

You can check for new e-mail messages by clicking on the **Inbox**. The screen would look as shown below:

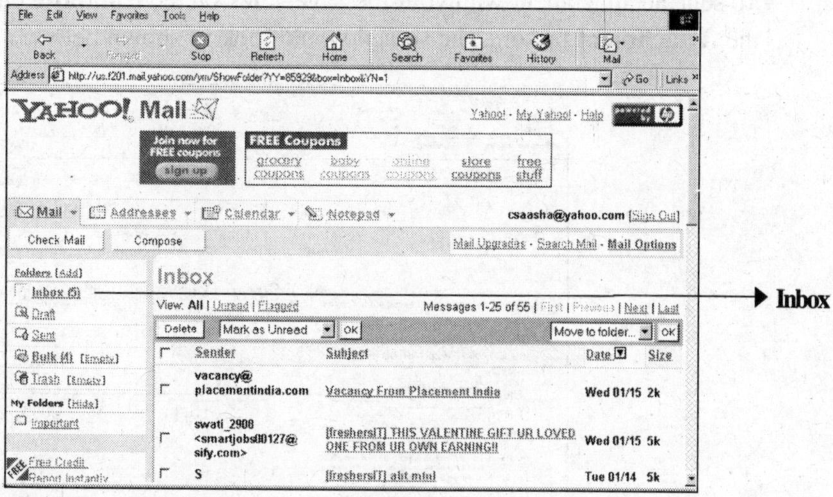

To read an e-mail, simply click on the subject of the e-mail. The screen would look as shown below:

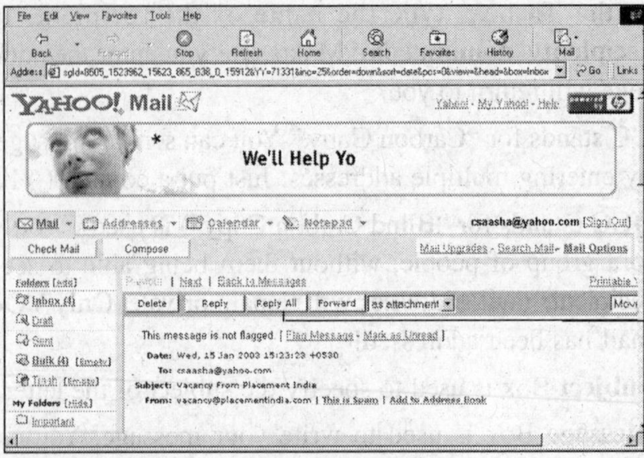

To reply an e-mail, simply click on the **Reply** button. When the Message Box appears, type in the reply and simply click on the send button.

E-MAIL ATTACHMENTS

You can attach formatted documents, images, sound and video files to your e-mail messages. The procedure for attaching files varies depending on the type of e-mail program you use. Most programs allow you to attach multiple files.

Sending Attachments

To send an attachment with your message, click on the **Compose** button and then click on the **Attachment** button. The screen would look as shown below:

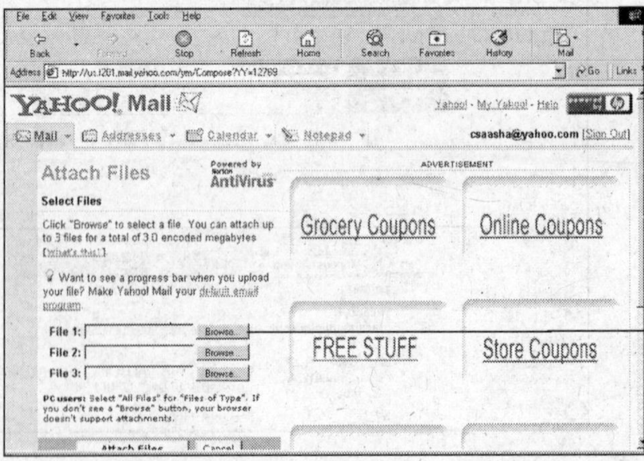

Click on the **Browse** button. This would display a dialog box as shown below:

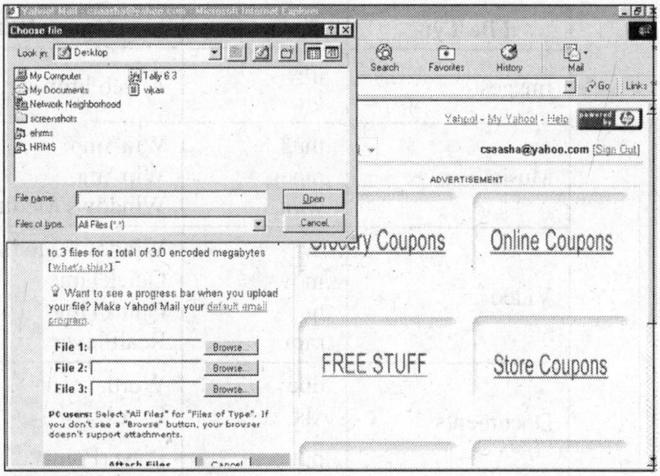

Browse your hard drive or removable disks to locate the file you want to attach. Once you locate it, click on it and then click on **Open** button. Repeat the process if you want to attach multiple files to your message. Then click on **Attach Files** button to attach the files to your message. A message is displayed saying that the files have been attached. Click on the **Done** button to return to the **Compose** window.

Once you click the **Send** button the e-mail along with the attachments will be delivered to the recipient. While attaching files it is always recommended to use a compression software such as **WinZip** to compress your files. This will also help the receiver to download the attachments faster. When you send these zipped files, make sure that the recipient has the software to de-compress these files; if not, send a shareware copy of the software along with the file.

Opening Attachments

One of the most useful features of e-mail is the ability to send files. How do you open an attachment? This depends on the type of file and how your computer is configured.

File Type	Extension	Opens With...
Images	.jpg .gif	A web browser
Music	.mp3 .mpeg .wmf	WinAmp WinAmp Windows Media Player
Video	.avi .mov .qt .ram	Windows Media Player QuickTime QuickTime RealPlayer
Documents	.doc .xls .ppt	Word Excel PowerPoint
Compressed Files	.zip	WinZip

Attachments may be dangerous to your computer. Attachments can conceal viruses and other malicious programs that will destroy your data or cause computer chaos. Unless you know who sent an attachment, **DO NOT OPEN IT**. Even if you do know the source, it is always advisable to scan it with an anti-virus software before you open it. If your computer has an anti-virus program running in the background, it should automatically check for viruses.

Once you make sure that the attachment is safe, you can download it.

Click on the **Download** button. A dialogue box appears as shown below.

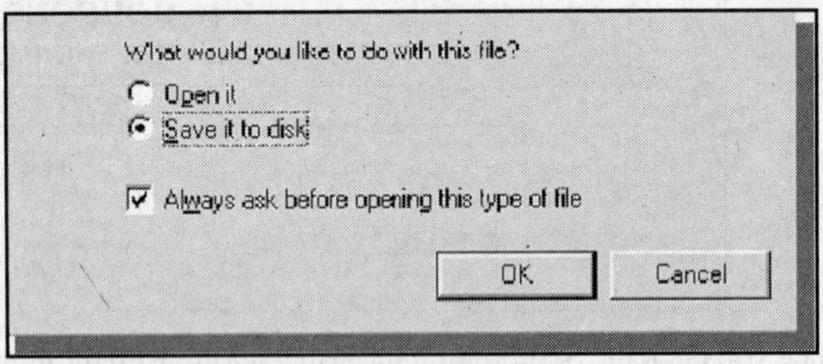

To view the file without saving it, select **Open it** and then click on **OK** button. The application should open, allowing you to view the file.

If you have saved the file, locate the file in the folder you saved it and double-click on it. The appropriate program should open. Alternatively, you can first open the associated application—for instance, MS Word if the you received a ". doc" file—and then locate the file and open it.

TIPS FOR MANAGING E-MAIL

Every day billions of e-mail messages zap across the Internet. If it seems that most of them make their way into your Inbox, you're not alone. "Overwhelming" is how many people feel about this electronic communication. The bad news is that it will only get worse as the volume of e-mail increases. You can avoid drowning in a sea of messages by following some simple steps.

- Periodically scan for new messages and delete the old messages. This would preserve you e-mail account space.
- Create a series of folders to categorize your e-mail, using action items (pending, review etc.) and subjects (travel, newsletters etc.). After you receive messages, file them away for later action and reference. Messages remaining in your Inbox are those requiring immediate action. Reply and then file them too.
- Use brief responses—Everyone is pressed for time these days, so keep your replies brief and to the point. E-mail has developed its own shorthand that doesn't require the formal response of a letter.
- Use meaningful Subject.
- E-mail Filters – You can help avoid clutter in your inbox by setting up filters that will automatically move certain e-mail messages to designated folders.
- Periodically change your account password from protecting your e-mail account from unauthorized users.
- Save a copy of the message in the sent folder. Follow this for any of important mails you send.
- Always zip the attachments if files are very big before sending them.
- Maintain separate e-mail accounts for official work and personal purposes.
- Do not forward junk e-mails or chain letters.
- Do not forget to **log out** before you close your e-mail account.

With this we come to an end of our session on e-mails. I hope that you shall soon be contacting your long lost friends and also benefit professionally from this user-friendly and cost-effective medium.

By now you would agree with me that surfing or browsing the Net or looking for specific information on the Net is a pretty simple thing and does not require you to be a computer wizard.

So best of luck and happy surfing!

Changing your VSNL Password

① Type the address of the website **www.vsnl.com**

② Click here to choose the mode as English.

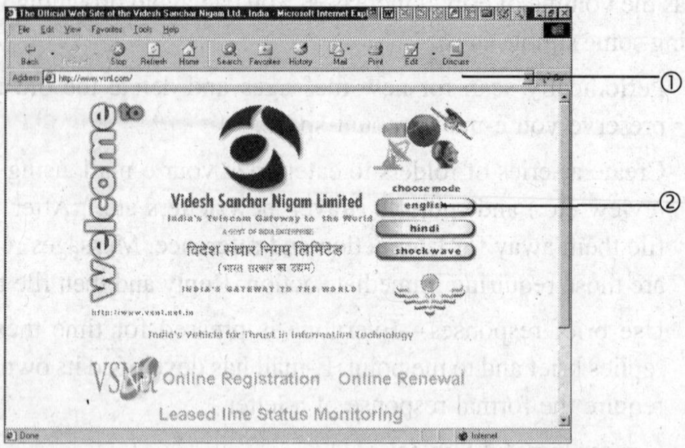

The following screen would be displayed.

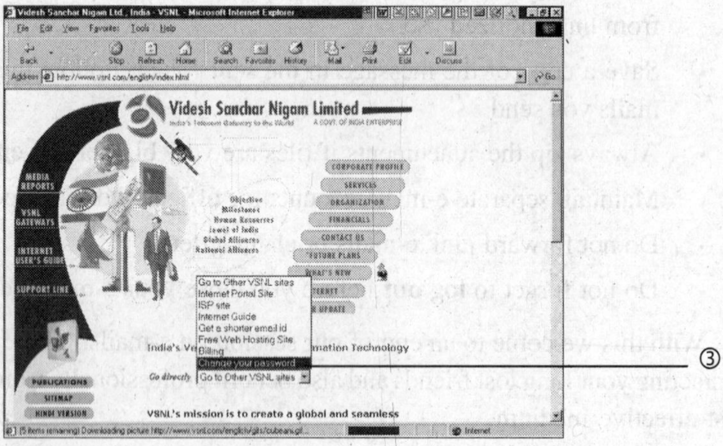

③ Choose '**Change your Password**' option from the drop down menu.

The following screen would be displayed:

④ Click on the option **New Delhi Users** from the list.

The following screen would be displayed:

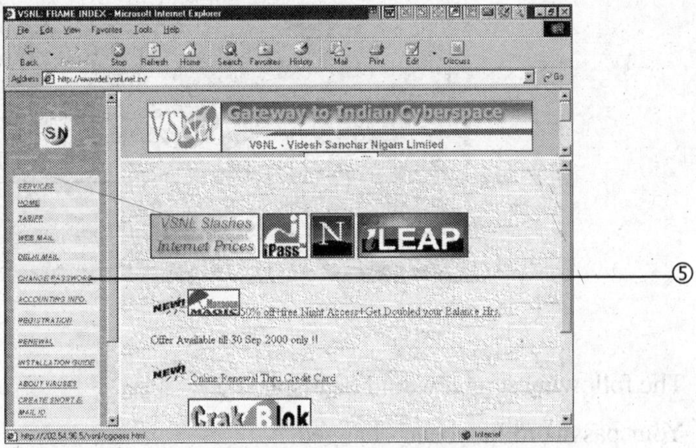

⑤ Click on the **Change Password** option from the menu bar.

The following screen would be displayed:

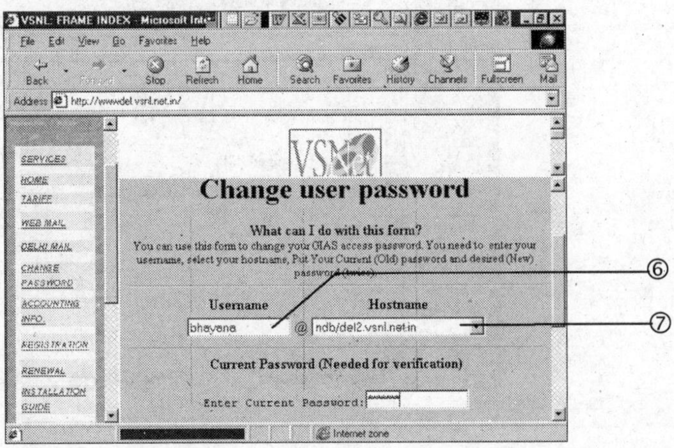

⑥ Type the **Username** here.

⑦ Choose your **server name** from this drop down list.

⑧ Type your **current password** in this box.

⑨ Type your **new password** in this box.

A Retype your new password in this box.

B Click on the **Change My Password** button.

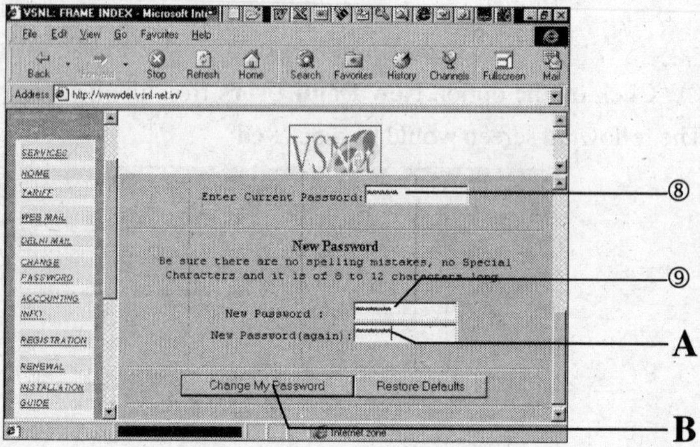

The following screen would be displayed.

Your password has been changed.

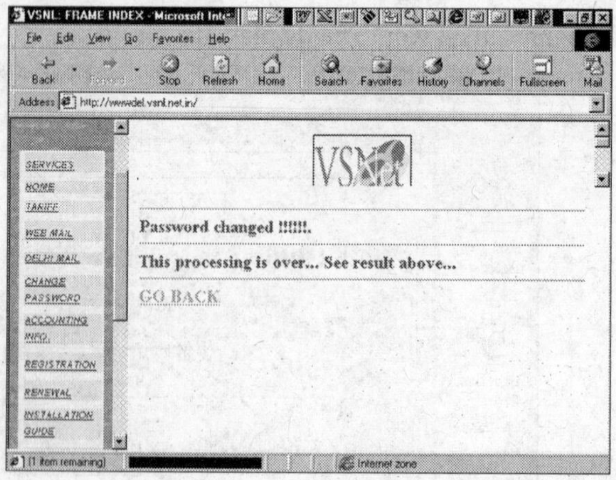

POPULAR INTERNET WEBSITES

E-Mail

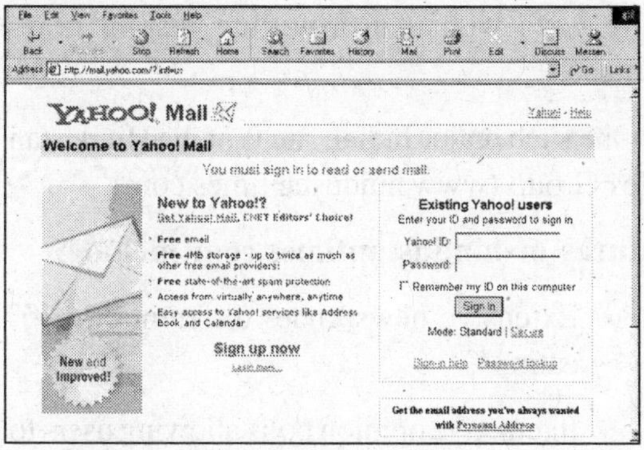

Electronic Mail or E-mail is one of the primary facilities of Internet. It is the fastest and the cheapest form of communication. You can even send greeting cards via e-mail.

One of the most popular website providing free e-mail service is Yahoo Mail (http://mail.yahoo.com).

Features of yahoo.com include:

- Easy to create an e-mail account.
- One of the fastest mail services.
- Provides security.
- Gives the user 6MB Mailbox space.
- Accepts text, images and files as attachment (up to 1.5MB)

E-mail services are also available at the following websites:

HOTMAIL- www.hotmail.com
REDIFFMAIL- www.rediffmail.com
INDIATIMES- mail.indiatimes.com
MAILCITY - www.mailcity.com

Search Engines

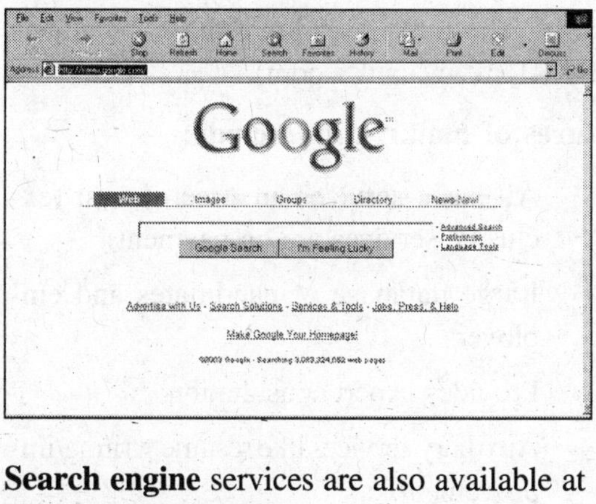

On the Internet you can search for information on any topic/subject. This is possible through websites providing a Search Engine.

One of the most popular search engine is GOOGLE (www.google.com).

Features of google.com include:

- Fastest search results.
- Largest database of web resources.
- Eliminates irrelevant search results.
- Provides search results under classifications like webpages, images, groups, directories and news.
- Provides alternative search options.

Search engine services are also available at the following websites:

YAHOO- www.yahoo.com
ALTAVISTA- www.altavista.com
ASK JEEVES- www.ask.com
KHOJ- www.khoj.com

News

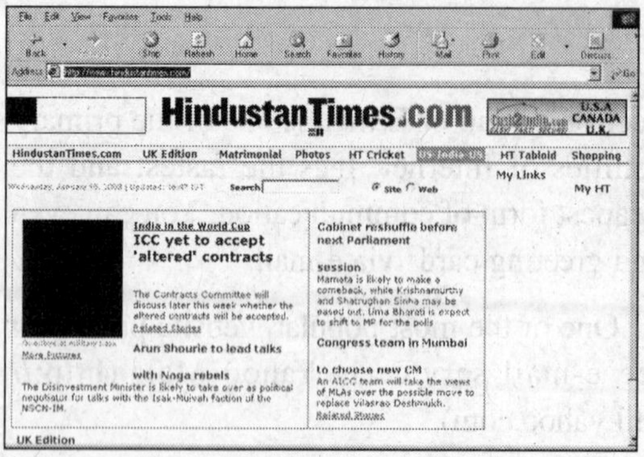

Internet has become one of the major sources of news updates. All the members of the Fourth Estate have websites providing instant news updates.

One such major Indian site is of the Hindustan Times Group (www.hindustantimes.com).

Features of hindustantimes.com include:

- Extensive news under different classifications.
- Interactive opinion polls allowing users to post their views on current issues.

Below are some other popular **News** websites:

TOI- www.indiatimes.com

Aaj Tak- www.aajtak.com

BBC- www.bbc.co.uk

CNN- www.cnn.com

Jobs

One of the major advantages of Internet is searching and applying for jobs. Vacancies of jobs are posted on sites by companies and placement consultants. The most popular Indian job site is NAUKRI (www.naukri.com).

Features of naukri.com include:

- All basic services are free of cost (exclusive services are on payment).
- Large database of candidates and employers.
- Provides expert consultation.
- Auxiliary services like resume writing/improvement.
- Preferred by 152 of the top 200 companies for recruitment.

Below are some other popular **Jobs** websites:

JOBSAHEAD- www.jobsahead.com
MONSTER – www.monster.com
HEADHUNTER- www.headhunter.com
STEPSTONE- www.stepstone.com
CAREERBUILDER-
www.careerbuilder.com

Sports

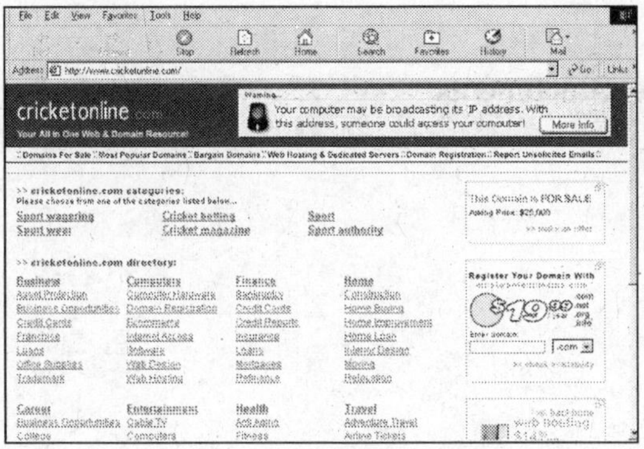

Sports and games are a popular lookout for Internet surfers. One of the popular sites for sports is CRICKET ONLINE (www.cricketonline.com).

Features of cricketonline.com include:

- Wide range of information on cricket.
- Photo gallery on cricket.
- Cricket quiz.
- News on other sports like Golf, Football and Rugby.
- Live coverage

Some other popular **Sports/Games** sites are:

ESPNSTAR- www.espnstar.com
FUNBRAIN – www.funbrain.com
GAMECITY- www.gamecity.com

Downloads

Another advantage of Internet is that you can download a lot of interesting stuff.

A popular website for downloading is ZDNET (www.zdnet.com). Features of zdnet.com include:

- Free downloads.
- Downloads available for different operating systems (e.g. Windows, Apple MAC etc.).
- Wide range of interesting stuff right from Entertainment (songs, games, pictures etc.) to educational (study/reference material, computer software etc.).

Some other dedicated sites for downloading are:

DOWNLOADS- www.downloads.com
CNET – www.cnet.com
FREESTUFF – www.freestuff.com

REVIEW QUESTIONS

1. **Create an e-mail account using yahoo.**
2. **Send an e-mail to your friend with three attachments.**
3. **Give some example for search engines.**

11 Internet Chat

Before Internet became popular, you could communicate with people in other cities, either by making a long distant call (STD or ISD) or by posting letters or by sending a fax which was cumbersome.

Now you can use Internet to communicate with people all over the world. The simplest form is e-mail which is cheap and relatively fast. However e-mail has a serious disadvantage that you cannot communicate in real time. Your e-mail will take at least a couple of minutes to reach the intended person. You may wait indefinitely to get a reply! As you can see, this would be very frustrating for any meaningful discussion.

The fastest medium today is Internet telephony (IPT)—the transportation of telephone calls over the Internet. All you need is a microphone, earphone and special software on your personnel computer to talk to anyone on the Internet. This would make telephonic conversation extremely cheap, but at present, the quality and tariff issues need to be resolved.

Internet Chat provides a compromise solution between e-mail and Internet telephony. Internet Relay Chat (or IRC as it is popularly called) allows you to type your message, and your friend (who could be anywhere in the world, but logged on to the Net at the same time on the same chat site) would receive it almost instantaneously and in the same way he can send his response which will reach you almost instantaneously. Other than the difference of having to type instead of speaking, Chatting is almost as good as speaking to the other person over the phone.

There are many free chat sites on the web through which you can communicate with one or many people from different locations. After you log on to a free chat site, go to the specific chat room where you have agreed to meet the other person.

① Type the site address **www.yahoo.com**

② Click on **Chat** option.

③ Click on **Sign Up for Yahoo Chat** to create a new account.

A If you already have an account with Yahoo you can enter your **Yahoo ID** and **Password** and click on **Sign In** button.

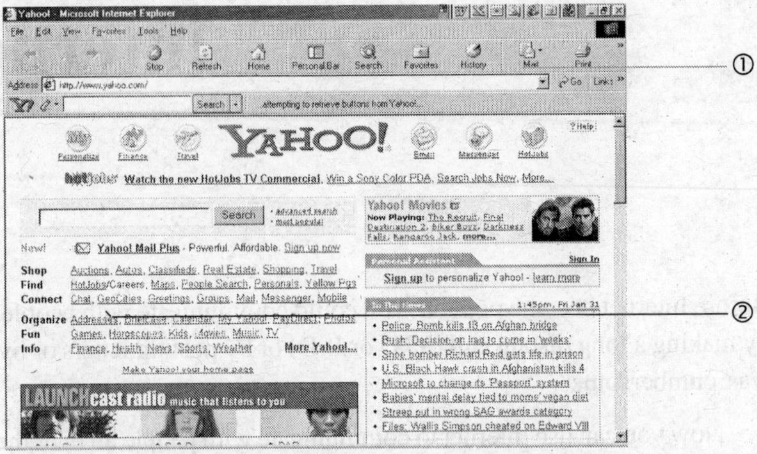

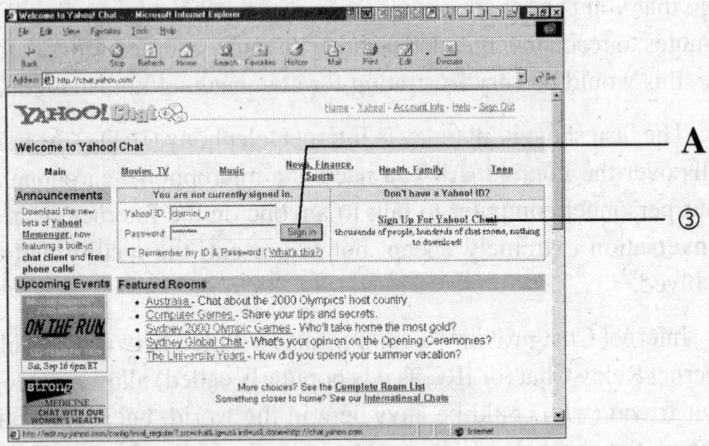

The following screen would be displayed. Fill up the form and click on **Submit** button.

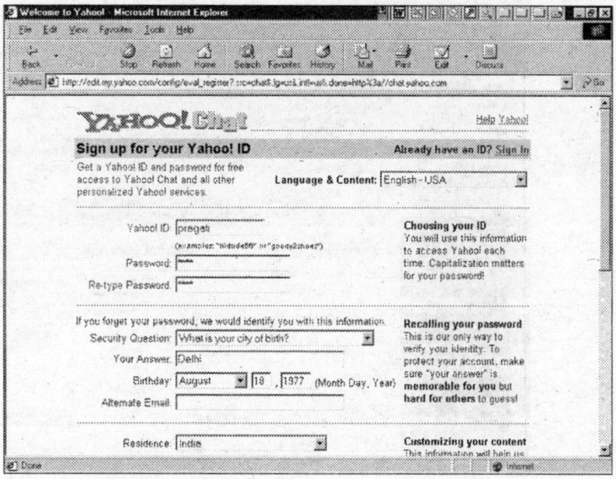

If the ID given by you is already in use you would be notified. In this case you would have to give a different ID. When your Yahoo ID has been created you would be given the following message.

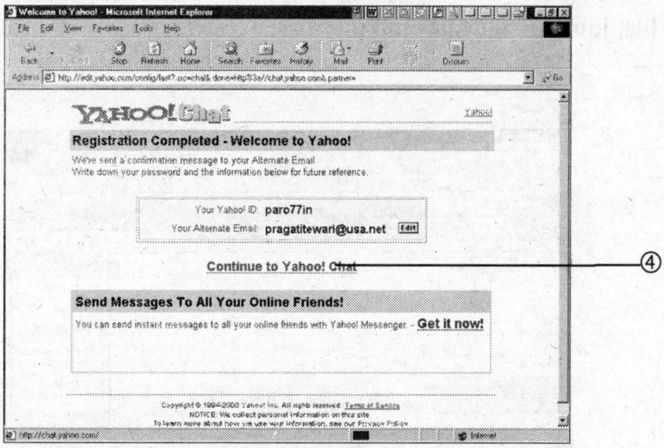

④ Click here to start chatting.

The following screen would be displayed:

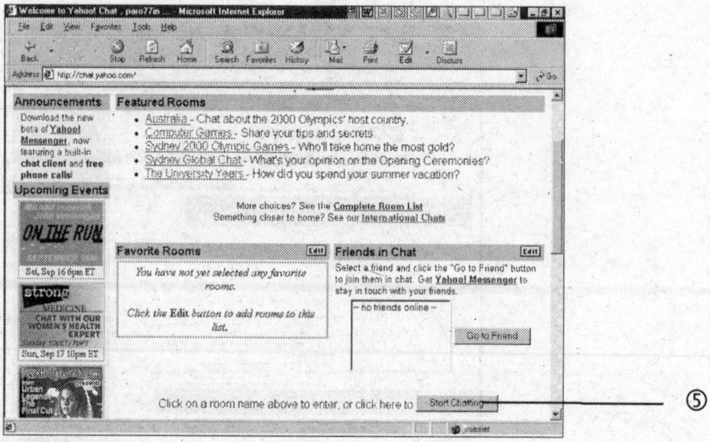

⑤ Click on the **Start Chatting** button. This button takes you into a room called **Chat Central** where you would find many people chatting.

A You can also click on the **Change Room** option to get a list of chat rooms.

The following screen would be displayed. You can see that a discussion is already in progress. Just jump in and start talking.

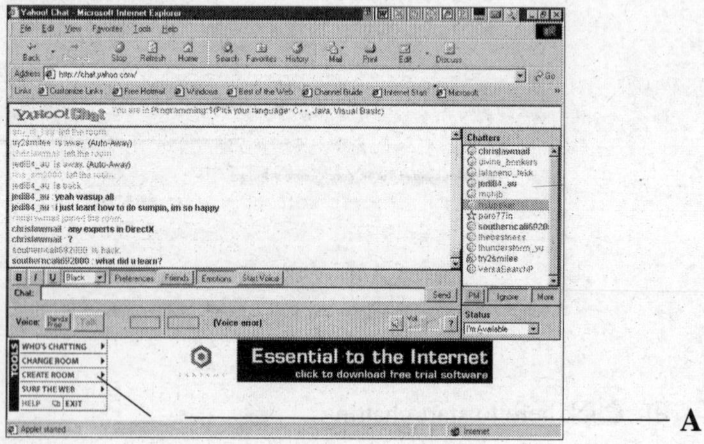

REVIEW QUESTION

1. **Compare e-mail and chat.**

12 Introduction to Web Design

Websites could be basically classified into two categories viz. Static websites and Dynamic websites.

Static Websites

- The word static emphasizes on the fact that the content is not regenerated each time the client (Web Browser) requests the webpage (HTML Page) from the server (Web Server).
- They are the simplest ones to create. These websites usually suit small and medium businesses that do not require regular updates to their site.
- It is used when the site needs only simple features. It does not require any database to store the information.
- HTML can be used to create static webpages. HTML is a versatile language that allows the use of graphics, tables, fonts, colors, hyperlinks, animation and sound in a webpage.
- HTML files are plain text files, so they can be composed and edited on any type of computer... Windows, Mac or UNIX.
- Some other tools that allow the creation of simple webpages include MS Front Page, Dreamweaver, etc.

Dynamic Websites

- The word dynamic emphasizes that the content is regenerated every time a user visits or reloads the site. The content is tailored based on the date, user, country, and many other parameters.

- These websites suit businesses of all sizes that require regular updates. They are used when the sites are very large.
- With a dynamic website, webpages (HTML pages) are created to present information, but all the contents of the site are held in a database (Backend). This means if you want to update the contents of the site, all you need to do is update the database.
- There are a variety of languages available to make dynamic websites. Some examples include CGI (Common Gateway Interface), ASP (Active Server Pages) JSP (Java Server Pages), PHP (Hypertext Preprocessor).
- Dynamic websites also require a backend (database). Examples of the databases include Microsoft SQL Server, Oracle etc.
- Examples of dynamic websites include "Yahoo","Indiatimes","Microsoft","IBM" etc.

TIPS FOR AN EFFECTIVE WEB DESIGN

World Wide Web is an interactive, dynamic, and rapidly changing new communications medium. So issues of accessibility and ease-of-use play a key role. Effective web design is the result of diverse elements. All aspects of page presentation must work together to showcase your site's content in its very best light. You may refer to Section X (MS Front Page) to learn how to develop a Website.

- Short term and long term objectives should be clear. The site content should be Clear, Concise, Unique, Correct and Usable.
- Uniformity—All the webpages of the website should have a recurrent theme. Background colors, font, headers should be consistent throughout. Always try to use default hyperlink colors.
- Websites should be Interactive. Good interactivity engages the user and makes the site memorable.
- User should be provided with aids for Easy Navigation. Links to previous and next pages and links to up and down a hierarchical structure should be provided. Link to the Homepage/Index page should always be provided. Always provide a Site Map.
- Always use paragraphs, headers, and links to break up large blocks of text. Long scrolling screens should be avoided.
- The web page can be made attractive by using graphics and animations. Always avoid using oversized and unoptimized graphics as this would increase the Download Time of the site thereby adding to the frustration of the user. Speed is a very important factor in web surfing. Also do not clutter the page with excessive graphics.

- Ensure that users never lose their work as a result of error on their part or the vagaries of Internet transmission.
- Offer Downloadable Software to play unusual audio and video formats.
- Use Status Mechanisms to keep users aware and informed. We may need to know: whether this is the first time the user has been in the system, where the user is going, where did the user left off in the last session.
- Provide a Search Facility.
- Design for Scalability—Design sites that would work as intended on all platforms and browsers.
- Do not forget to include the Contact Information on your site. Provision must be made to accept user suggestions/feedback.
- Last but not least, your site must be highly Secure. Do not allow unauthorized users play with your customer data.

REVIEW QUESTIONS

1. **What is the need for creating a website?**
2. **What are the differences between static website and dynamic website?**
3. **What are the features of a webpage.**
4. **Create your personal website.**

13 Multimedia

DEFINITION

In simple words, multimedia means multi (many) and media refers to communication/ transfer medium. Multimedia is any combination of text, graphic art, sound, animation and video elements delivered to you by your computer or any other electronic means. A computer's encyclopedia containing images, audio and video effects along with the content is a simple example of a multimedia application. Although the definition of multimedia is fairly simple, making it work can be quite complicated. You would need to understand the importance of each individual element and also have knowledge about the usage of multimedia tools and technologies, to weave the elements of multimedia in a meaningful manner.

Human interactivity forms the core of any multimedia application. This includes response to the commands (clicking on buttons, icons, menu items etc.) dictated by the end user. This type of multimedia–where a user to controls what and when the elements are delivered–is referred to as **Interactive Multimedia**. When users are given navigational control so that they can navigate from one element to another in a non-linear fashion, interactive multimedia becomes **Hypermedia**. The World Wide Web (www) is probably the most successful network information system in history. One of its advantages is certainly the ease of use of its interface. The concept of hypertext and hypermedia has gained familiarity after the introduction of www.

Kiosks and CD-ROM applications are excellent vehicles for presenting information with the dynamics of multimedia. Multimedia equipped PCs are used to host such applications. Such computers come equipped with a CD-ROM drive, a sound card with speakers, microphone and may also include a scanner and a digital camera (Figure 7.1). Multimedia applications also require large amounts of digital memory when stored in the users computer.

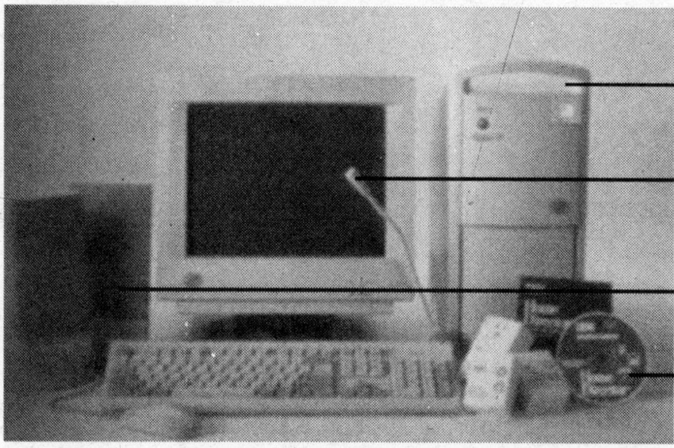

Figure 13.1 *Typical multimedia computer*

Importance of Multimedia

- Multimedia is characterised by an audio-visual interface, which provides an excellent medium for user interactivity.
- It improves information retention. (According to a research conducted by computer technology, people only retain 20% of what they see and 30% of what they hear. But they remember 50% of what they see and hear, and as much as 80% of what they see, hear, and do simultaneously.)
- Computer games are the most common applications of multimedia. Other widely used applications include educational CDs (CBT) and promotional information (new products, marketing schemes etc.).
- Multimedia has also become an integral part of the internet. Webpages can contain animated images, videos and sound effects, in addition to text, to make them more appealing and interactive.

MULTIMEDIA TOOLS

Authoring Tools

The key to successful multimedia production is a seamless integration of multimedia elements for graphic design, content management, production and packaging. The whole process of developing a multimedia package is called **Authoring**. An authoring system is a collection of software tools that help in various aspects of multimedia production. Multimedia elements are woven together using authoring tools. These tools are designed to manage individual multimedia elements and provide user interaction. Multimedia authoring software can be used to make:

- Video productions
- Animations
- Games
- Presentations
- Interactive kiosk applications
- Interactive training
- Simulations, prototypes and technical visualisations

Steps in Multimedia Production

1. ***Media capture:*** Multimedia authoring systems streamline data capture by providing interfaces to a range of image and data capture devices.
2. ***Media conversion:*** Images, audio clips, animation, sequences and video clips exist in a variety of formats. A well-equipped multimedia authoring system will include a set of utilities for converting between many of the commonly used formats.
3. ***Media editing:*** After data has been captured and converted to the native format of the authoring system, it may need some polishing before it is suitable for presentation. For instance, 'noise' can be removed from audio clips, images can be touched up, etc.

Multimedia authoring systems provide media – specific editors for these operations.

4. ***Media composition:*** The core of a multimedia authoring system includes a tool for combining media and specifying their spatial (one image being juxtaposed or placed side-by-side within a second) and temporal (when an audio track is added to a visual sequence) relationships.

ELEMENTS OF MULTIMEDIA

Text

Text, containing words and symbols, is the most common form of communication. It is one of the popularly used mediums of appearance that is used to deliver information accurately and in detail. Usually text provides the core structure to the package. Words are vital elements of multimedia that can appear in the titles, menus, navigation aids and in the content of a multimedia application or project. It is most essential to use words that have the most precise and powerful meanings to express what you need to convey.

A major drawback of using text is that it is not user friendly as compared to the other elements of multimedia. For example: it is harder to read from a screen for long, as it tires the eyes more than reading it in its print version.

Designing with text: From a design perspective, the choice of font size, style and other text attributes needs to be related both to the complexity of the message and to its venue.

Some useful tips for designing the text in your multimedia application:

- use legible fonts that can be easily read.
- vary the font size and style according to the importance of your message.

- indent your paragraphs wherever required.
- explore the effects of different colours and shadows to add depth to your application.
- use menus for easy navigation and meaningful words for menu items.
- use buttons, icons or symbols for user interaction.
- you can also use stylish fonts for displaying attention-grabbing results.

Hyperlinks: Hypertext is the organisation of information units into connected associations that a user can choose to make. An instance of such an association is called a **Hyperlink.** When a user clicks on such a link, more information on the particular topic is displayed. It, therefore, provides the user an option of reading as much information as required. Hyperlinks can contain cross-linking of words not only to words but also to images, videos or sound files. Hyperlinks are used for non-linear navigation, which is not an option available in a sequentially organised book.

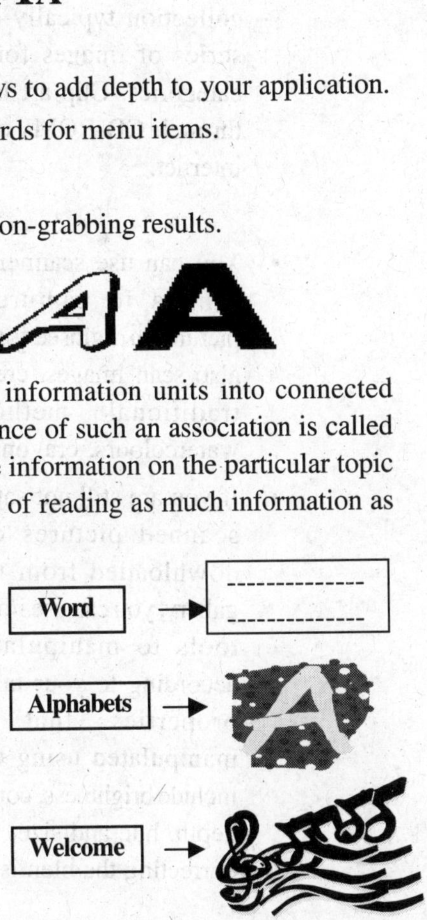

Graphics

Pictures/graphics enhance the overall look of a multimedia package. Pictures express more than normal text and are generally considered as the most important element of a multimedia application.

It is often noticed that a webpage containing numerous images takes longer to download than a simple text based webpage. Image files are therefore compressed to save memory and disk space of your computer. **GIF** (Graphics Interchange Format), **JPEG** (Joint Photographic Experts Group) and **PNG** (Portable Network Graphics) are examples of compressed image file formats.

Pictures can be created using any of the following ways:

- You can use drawing tools like MS paint to create simple pictures. paint allows to create or assemble pictures by drawing straight, wavy or curved lines, using shapes like squares, circles and polygons, or simply by freehand drawing.

- You can insert images from the clipart gallery. A clipart collection typically contains a series of images for different categories. Clip art is available through CD-ROMs or from the internet.

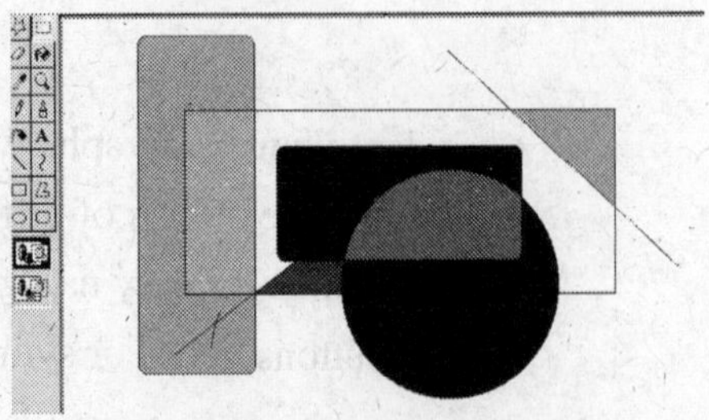

- You can use scanner or digital camera to capture original pictures in digitised form. You can also scan images, created using traditional methods like watercolours, crayons etc.

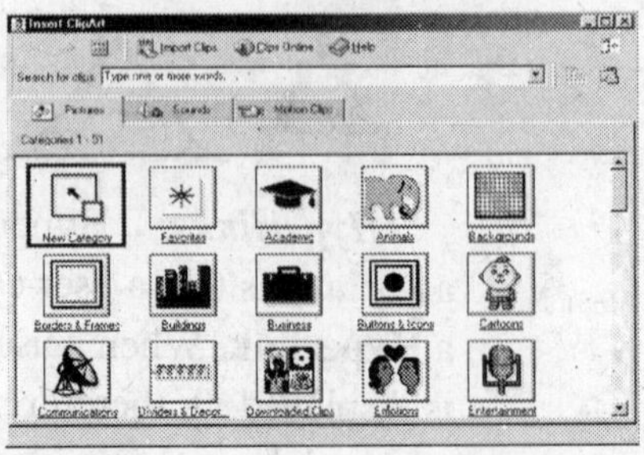

- If you are still not satisfied with scanned pictures or images downloaded from the clipart gallery, you can use image-editing tools to manipulate images according to your taste. Picture properties that can be manipulated using these tools include brightness, contrast, color, depth, hue and size. Apart from correcting the blemishes in your

Digital camera

Scanner

image, you can add additional effects like filters, shadows, patterns, 3D-effects and many more. Image editing tools are indispensable for excellent multimedia production. Adobe Photoshop, Microsoft Photo draw are some examples of image-editing tools.

Some useful tips for adding images in your multimedia application:

- Do not overload your application with too many images. This would not only make your application look clumsy, but it would also consume excessive computer resources.
- Do not include heavy (oversized) graphics.
- Use context – sensitive images.
- To the extent possible, use compressed image file formats. Avoid using unoptimised graphics.
- Pick the right colour or combination of colours for your multimedia application. Colour scheme used for the text should blend well with the images.

Animation

Animation gives visual impact to your multimedia application. In simple terms, it can be defined as an entity moving across the screen. This entity could be a text object or an image. An animation consists of a series of rapidly changing objects, which when blended together gives an illusion of movement. The speed with which each object is replaced by the next one is so rapid that the eye perceives this as motion.

Example: Consider the process of rotating a wheel, the position of the arrow changes so rapidly that it gives an illusion of spinning.

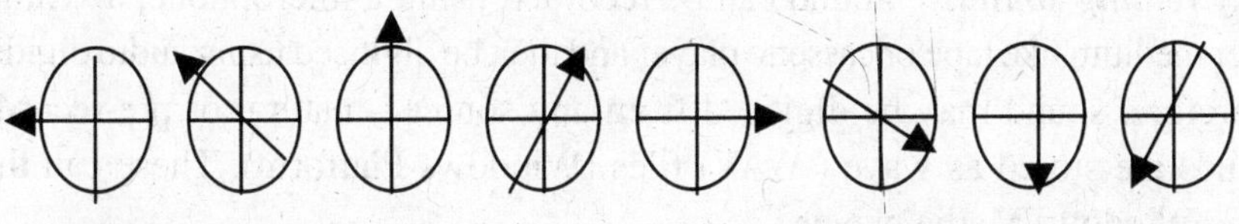

Animation tools: MS powerpoint is a tool used for creating primitive animations. Visual effects like wipes, dissolves, fades and zooms can be added to any object. For example: you can make a text to fly from top or left. Such effects are available with almost all authoring packages. You can create complex animations using tools like Director, 3D Studio Max, CompuServe and Shockwave. Such animations can be ported across platforms and applications by making use of suitable translators.

Some useful tips for adding animations in your multimedia application:

- before you create an animation, organise its execution into a series of logical steps.

First choose the objects in your presentation that you wish to animate, and then decide upon the sequence of animation. In case of complicated presentations, writing a detailed script of the list of activities that will prove useful.

- you can animate one or all objects of an application. As mentioned earlier, applications intended for the web should not contain too many animations as it would affect the download time.
- add user interactivity wherever essential to the application.
- you can combine animations with lively sounds for grabbing the user's attention.

Sound

Sound is used to set the rhythm or a mood in a package. Speech gives an effect of a language (pronunciation) for instance. Proper usage of sound can make all the difference between an ordinary multimedia presentation and a professional one.

Sound types: Musical Instrument Digital Interface (**MIDI**) is a communication standard developed in early 1980's for electronic musical instruments and computers. A MIDI file consists of a list of commands that represent the recordings of musical actions. When these commands are sent to a MIDI Playback device, a sound is produced. The main disadvantage of MIDI data is that it is not digitised. In contrast, **Digital Audio** is a recording that depends on the capabilities of your sound system. Digital audio data are the actual representations of sound data and are stored in the form of thousands of individual numbers known as **Samples**. Digital sound is used for music CDs.

Creating sound: Sound can be recorded using a microphone, a synthesiser, or any other medium like tape or cassette player and then be digitised using audio digitising software. Therefore, sound may be digitised from any source – natural or pre-recorded. Digitised sounds are stored as wave (.WAV) files (Windows Platform). These can then be played using Windows Media player.

Some useful tips for adding sounds to your multimedia application:

- a distorted recording sounds terrible, so before a sound file is added it must be tested for clarity. If required, it must be edited using Audio-Editing tools like Wave Studio Sound or Macromedia's Sound Edit 16-2. It may be worth noting that higher the sound quality, the larger would be the file size.
- decide the kind of sound you need (such as background music, special sound effects or spoken dialogue).
- test the sound, to ensure they are synchronised properly with images and or animations.

Video

If pictures can paint a thousand words, then motion pictures can paint a million. Digital video is the most engaging of multimedia venues and is a powerful tool for bringing users close to the real world.

NTSE (National Television Standards Committee), PAL (Phase Alteration Line), SECAM (Sequential Colour and Memory), HDTV (High Definition Television) are commonly used broadcast and video standards across the globe.

Current television is based on analog technology and fixed international standards for the broadcast and display of images. Computer video, on the other hand is based on digital technology and other standards for displaying images. Digital Video is produced using analog video as a base. The conversion of analog video into its digital equivalent requires a special hardware called **Video Capture Card.**

Video data is also compressed using different compression techniques. MPEG (Motion Pictures Expert Group), JPEG (Joint Photographic Experts Group), P*64, real video are examples of commonly used compressed video formats.

Some useful tips for adding video clips to your multimedia application:

- video clippings which are not appropriately designed can degrade your presentation rather than add value to it. Carefully planned, well-executed clips can make a dramatic difference in a multimedia presentation.
- titles used in video clips should be plain enough to be easily read.
- avoid making busy title screens; use more screen if required.
- again, any multimedia element that is added to an application intended for Web should be compressed to support quick and easy download.

APPLICATIONS OF MULTIMEDIA

Multimedia in Education

As compared to traditional '**Stand and Deliver**' teaching methodology, training imparted using animated, interactive and instructional multimedia applications has proven to be more useful. Apart from making the subject interesting, it increases information retention and learning capacity of the users. The potential for students of all ages to author as part of a creative educational programme that focuses on achievement of goals and competencies rather than time served, will help educators to shift from teacher to facilitator and mentor. Some applications of multimedia in education, are stated below:

- Computer encyclopedias have gained considerable popularity in recent years as they allow the user a non-linear navigation of text; user can quickly access the desired topic.
- The web can be thought of as a global digital multimedia library. The concept of e-learning or online learning using interactive communication tools has grown tremendously with the popularity of www. It is accessible to a large number of people, can be accessed from any where and everywhere and promotes the quality of learning experiences and outcomes.
- Schools are perhaps the most best users for multimedia. Many school reform models propose a shift from a teacher-centered didactic model to a learner-centered model to enable students to learn the subject area faster, and in a much greater depth. Multimedia presentation tools can be used to design, develop, publish, and present course-curriculum concepts to audiences inside and outside the classroom.
- Multimedia based presentations and tutorials provide an easy-to-learn environment for the young generations. Reading and retention skills grow when concepts are explained using animated pictures. It can be a used as a homework helper or serve as a literature guide.
- Multimedia can prove to be tremendously useful in the medical field. It gives an opportunity of indepth, clear and interactive learning of new clinical advancements.
- Multimedia can be used for stimulating different types of environments used for training purposes. For example: flight attendants can be trained to manage terrorism and security by artificially simulating such an environment.
- Libraries, arts and cultural centres, and learner support systems are already using interactive communication tools. Multimedia documents can also be designed to receive information from the reader and subsequently process it to provide individualised solutions. This has added a new dimension to the reading/writing process and the skills involved can be reinforced.

Multimedia in Entertainment

With the arrival of the CD-ROM and the Internet, the entertainment industry made a huge leap into a new era with a winning card–multimedia. Armed with animated images, sounds, full-motion video and interactive capability, multimedia became a dominant factor in today's information age. The fast but steady growth of electronic technology allowed multimedia to gain popularity within a short span of time. Some applications of multimedia in the entertainment field are stated below:

- Games are the first thing that come to mind when we talk about multimedia. Multimedia capabilities are used to develop interactive games with sophisticated animations, 3D and sound effects. These games can be played on the computer, mobile devices or on the Internet. Live internet pay-for-play gaming with multiple players has attained significant popularity.

- Movies and cartoons unleashing full effects of multimedia, which were only available on VHS tapes, are now stored on CD-ROM (VCD) to allow the users to watch on their computer screen. Multi-layered digital versatile disk with more storage capacity and even higher processing speed, is making its way into the market and slowly replacing the CD-ROM. It can be used to view movies and play audio files. Multimedia can be used in voice mail, chatting and video conferencing as well. You can also do real time video conferencing with your colleagues spread across the globe.
- Another common application of multimedia is the advent of animated e-greeting cards for different occasions.
- Wedding albums and family histories can be created on the World Wide Web using the power of multimedia.
- Multimedia has also found its application in hotels, pubs, shopping malls, museums, cinema halls, where stand-alone terminals or kiosks are made available for guiding users. Printers are also usually attached so that users can walk way with a printed copy of the desired information.

Multimedia in Marketing

Advertising has become very prevalent in our daily surroundings, so for a product to stand apart, it is very essential to present it in a dynamic, visually stimulating manner to grab the attention of consumers. The business world is slowly rejecting run of the mill traditional methods (like placing ads in yellow pages, distributing pamphlets, etc.) and adopting solutions from the electronic era. Only companies with a nerve to radically change their marketing strategies for the new millennium will survive and be able to cater to the ever-changing customer's mindset. Applications of multimedia in the marketing field include:

- Presentations–for launching the products of a company. Reaching the target audience with necessary technical services or products requires clear communication, stating the benefits and features, outlining its applications and any other product related details, all presented in a well-designed and interactive manner so that the users familiarise faster. Multimedia presentations are an excellent way to motivate, inform, and captivate a wide range of audiences via PC's, laptops, plasma screens, or kiosks delivered via CD-ROM or the internet.
- Multimedia–to create interactive product catalogues, training tutorials, buyer guides, and information directories with adequate search and navigation facilities to guide the user to easily trace the desired information. A buyer guide can list the nearby dealers,

a comparison of the top brands, maps of the city and other helpful guest services.

- E-mail advertising or placing banner ads on the Internet–an extremely cost effective method of launching a product, promoting an event or selling services. Effective use of multimedia in advertising can make potential clients sit up and make notice.
- Interactive applications–a great way to build brand loyalty and drive inquiries or sales. Sales may be increased by allowing users to view product options real-time. Brand loyalty can be built by giving users a custom application that entertains, informs or assists them.
- Motion, graphical elements, animation, audio and video can be used to more effectively deliver sales, instructional, or marketing messages to differentiate your firm from competitors.

KEY POINTS

- Multimedia is any combination of text, graphic art, sound, animation and video elements delivered to you by your computer or any other electronic means. A computer encyclopaedia containing various images, audio and video effects along with the content is a simple example of a multimedia application.
- The type of multimedia where you allow the user to control what and when the elements are delivered is referred to as interactive multimedia. When users are given navigational control so that they can navigate from one element to another in a non-linear fashion, interactive multimedia becomes hypermedia.
- Kiosks and CD-ROM applications are excellent vehicles for presenting information with the dynamics of multimedia. Multimedia applications require large amounts of digital memory when stored on the computer.
- Multimedia provides excellent audio-visual interface between the user and information. It has also become an integral part of the internet.
- The whole process of developing a multimedia package is called authoring. An authoring system is a collection of software tools that help in various aspects of multimedia production.
- The main steps in multimedia production include media capture, media conversion, media editing and media composition.
- Text, containing words and symbols, is the most common form of communication. It is one of the most popularly used media of appearance, used to deliver information accurately and in detail. From a design perspective, your choice of font size, style and other text attributes should be related both to the complexity of your message and to its venue. A major drawback of using text is that it is not user – friendly compared to the other elements of multimedia. Hypertext is the organisation of information units into connected associations that a user can choose to make. An instance of such an association is called a hyperlink. When a user clicks on such a link, more information on the particular topic is displayed.

- Pictures/graphics enhance the overall look of a multimedia package. Pictures express more than normal text and are generally considered the most important element of a multimedia application. Typically, image files are compressed to save memory and disk space of a computer. GIF, JPEG and PNG are examples of compressed image file formats. Pictures can be created using drawing tools like MS Paint, inserted from the clipart gallery or can be scanned using scanner or any other suitable device. Image-editing tools like Adobe Photoshop, MS Photodraw can be used to manipulate images according to your taste.
- Animation in simple terms can be defined as an entity moving across the screen. This entity could be a text object or an image. It gives visual impact to your multimedia application. An animation consists of a series of rapidly changing objects, which when blended together conveys an illusion of movement. Simple animations can be created using powerpoint; however, you can create complex ones using many of the animation tools available, like Director, 3D Studio Max, CompuServe and Shockwave.
- As compared to traditional 'Stand and Deliver' teaching methodology, training imparted using animated, interactive and instructional multimedia applications can be very useful. Apart from making the subject interesting, it increases information retention and learning capacity of the users. Encyclopedias, schools, libraries, www, learning centers all make use of Multimedia in some form or the other.
- Armed with animated images, sound, full-motion video and interactive capability, multimedia has became a dominant factor in today's information age. Games, Movies, E-greeting cards are some applications of multimedia in the entertainment field.
- Multimedia presentations are an excellent way to motivate, inform, and captivate a wide range of audiences via PC, laptop, plasma screen, or kiosk delivered via CD-ROM or Internet. You can use multimedia to launch/promote your product, advertise, and to create buyer guides, training tutorials, interactive catalogs and many more.
- Sound is used to set the rhythm or a mood in a package. A MIDI file consists of a list of commands that represent the recordings of musical actions and when these commands are sent to a MIDI Playback device, a sound is produced. The main disadvantage of MIDI data is that it is not digitised. In contrast, Digital Audio is a recording that depends on the capabilities of your sound system. Sound can be recorded using a microphone, a synthesiser, or any other medium like tape or cassette player.
- Digital video is the most engaging of multimedia venues, and is a powerful tool for bringing users close to the real world. NTSE (National Television Standards Committee), PAL (Phase Alteration Line), SECAM (Sequential Color and Memory), HDTV (High Definition Television) are commonly used broadcast and video standards across the globe. Current television is based on analog technology and fixed international standards for the broadcast and display of images. Computer video is based on digital technology and other standards for displaying images. The conversion of analog video into its digital equivalent requires a special hardware called **Video Capture Card.** MPEG, JPEG, P*64, Real Video are all examples of commonly used compressed video formats.

REVIEW QUESTIONS

1. **Choose the most appropriate answer:**

   i. Point the odd one out:

   (a) Sound (b) Animation (c) Graphics (d) www

   ii. Which of the following cannot be considered an element of multimedia computer?

   (a) CD ROM (b) Speakers (c) Microphone (d) Network Card

2. **State whether True or False:**

   (a) Multimedia applications require large amounts of digital memory when stored in a user's computer.

   (b) It is not possible to hyperlink words to images or sound files.

   (c) You can manipulate a scanned image using an image-editing tool.

3. **Match the following:**

	X		Y
A.	Vehicle for presenting information with the dynamics of multimedia.	a.	User Interactivity
B.	Combining media and specifying their spatial and temporal relationships.	b.	GIF
C.	Icons, buttons and symbols.	c.	CD-ROM and DVD
D.	Compressed image file format.	d.	MPEG
E.	Compressed video file format.	e.	Media Composition

4. **Fill in the blanks with the appropriate choices listed below:**

   (i) MIDI (ii) Animation (iii) Digital audio (iv) Packaging (v) Hypermedia (vi) Authoring (vii) Hyperlink

   1. In ______________, users are given navigational control so that they can navigate from one element to another in a non-linear fashion.
   2. The whole process of developing a multimedia package is called __________.
   3. When a user clicks on a __________________, more information on the particular topic is displayed.
   4. An __________________ consists of a series of rapidly changing objects, which when blended together gives an illusion of movement.
   5. A __________________ file consists of a list of commands that represent the recordings of musical actions.

5. **Explain in brief the various elements of multimedia.**

6. **Write a short note on applications of multimedia in the field of education.**